U0781491

ALSO SPRACH ZARATHUSTRA

查拉图斯特拉如是说

（经典文库　汉英对照）

［德］尼采⊙著
余杰⊙译

台海出版社

图书在版编目(CIP)数据

查拉图斯特拉如是说：汉英对照 / (德) 尼采著；余杰译. -- 北京：台海出版社，2017.2

ISBN 978-7-5168-1266-2

Ⅰ. ①查… Ⅱ. ①尼… ②余… Ⅲ. ①超人哲学—汉、英 Ⅳ. ① B516.47

中国版本图书馆CIP数据核字(2017)第031047号

查拉图斯特拉如是说：汉英对照

著　　者：(德) 尼采　　译　　者：余　杰

责任编辑：刘　峰　　装帧设计：同人内文化传媒·书装设计

版式设计：同人内文化传媒·书装设计　　责任印制：蔡　旭

出版发行：台海出版社

地　　址：北京市东城区景山东街 20 号　　邮政编码：100009

电　　话：010 － 64041652（发行，邮购）

传　　真：010 － 84045799（总编室）

网　　址：www.taimeng.org.cn/thcbs/default.htm

E－mail：thcbs@126.com

经　　销：全国各地新华书店

印　　刷：北京市燕鑫印刷有限公司

本书如有破损、缺页、装订错误，请与本社联系调换

开　　本：787mm × 1092mm　　1/16

字　　数：609 千字　　印　　张：25.75

版　　次：2017年5月第1版　　印　　次：2017年5月第1次印刷

书　　号：ISBN 978-7-5168-1266-2

定　　价：36.00 元

PART ONE
第一部

PART TWO

第二部

PART THREE
第三部

PART FOUR
第四部

PART ONE

ZARATHUSTRA'S PROLOGUE

1.

WHEN Zarathustra was thirty years old, he left his home and the lake of his home, and went into the mountains. There he enjoyed his spirit and his solitude, and for ten years did not weary of it. But at last his heart changed,- and rising one morning with the rosy dawn, he went before the sun, and spake thus unto it:

Thou great star! What would be thy happiness if thou hadst not those for whom thou shinest!

For ten years hast thou climbed hither unto my cave: thou wouldst have wearied of thy light and of the journey, had it not been for me, mine eagle, and my serpent.

But we awaited thee every morning, took from thee thine overflow, and blessed thee for it.

第一部

查拉图斯特拉的序言

（1）

当查拉图斯特拉三十岁的时候，他离开了自己的家，离开了家中的湖泊，跑去了山里。他在这里尽情地享受着他的精神和孤寂，在十年的时间里，他从未感到厌烦。但是最终，他改变了心意——有一天清晨他在破晓时分就起了床，他来到太阳的面前，然后对太阳说出了以下这些话：

“伟大的星球啊！倘若那些被你照亮的人们都消失了，那么你还会拥有什么快乐啊！”

“在这十年间，你总是来拜访我的山洞；倘若没有我，我的老鹰还有我的蛇，你肯定会对你那耀眼的光芒以及这段旅程感到无聊至极。”

“不过，我们每天清晨都会在这儿等你，我们可以从你那里拿走剩余的东西，并且对你表示深深的祝福。”

Lo! I am weary of my wisdom, like the bee that hath gathered too much honey; I need hands outstretched to take it.

I would fain bestow and distribute, until the wise have once more become joyous in their folly, and the poor happy in their riches.

Therefore must I descend into the deep: as thou doest in the evening, when thou goest behind the sea, and givest light also to the nether-world, thou exuberant star!

Like thee must I go down, as men say, to whom I shall descend.

Bless me, then, thou tranquil eye, that canst behold even the greatest happiness without envy!

Bless the cup that is about to overflow, that the water may flow golden out of it, and carry everywhere the reflection of thy bliss!

Lo! This cup is again going to empty itself, and Zarathustra is again going to be a man.

Thus began Zarathustra's down-going.

2.

Zarathustra went down the mountain alone, no one meeting him. When he entered the forest, however, there suddenly stood before him an old man, who had left his holy cot to seek roots. And thus spake the old man to Zarathustra:

"No stranger to me is this wanderer: many years ago passed he by. Zarathustra he was

“看呀！我对我的智慧感到厌烦，就好比蜜蜂采集了过多的花蜜，我迫切需要人们张开手去拿它。”

“我应该把它传递出去、送出去，直到人群当中的聪明人再一次对他们的愚蠢行为感到无比愉悦，直到穷人会对他们的财富感到幸福快乐。”

“因此，如果我想要获得那样的结果，我就必须下降到深处；如同你在黄昏时分所做的事情一样，你来到了海平面以下，然后把耀眼的光芒也带到了地面以下的世界，啊！你这无比富饶的星球啊！”

“就如同你一样，我也要坚定地往下走——就好像我要下沉的那些人在召唤我去这么做一样。所以我恳请你祝福我有一双静谧的眼睛，能够在不掺杂嫉妒心理的情况下，注视着这个世界，甚至连遇到一个极度快乐的人也是一样！”

“祝福那个即将要溢出水来的杯子，它溢出来的水或许会变成金黄色，而且还能在全世界的范围内承担起你们快乐的反映！”

“看呀！倘若这个杯子想再一次变成空杯子，那么查拉图斯特拉也要再一次变成人类。”

查拉图斯特拉之下山如是开始。

（2）

查拉图斯特拉只身一人下了山，他并没有碰到任何人。不过，正当他走进森林的时候，从茅草屋里出来了一个寻找树根的老者，他突然来到了他的面前。这位老者对查拉图斯特拉说了如下一番话：

called; but he hath altered.

Then thou carriedst thine ashes into the mountains: wilt thou now carry thy fire into the valleys? Fearest thou not the incendiary's doom?

Yea, I recognize Zarathustra. Pure is his eye, and no loathing lurketh about his mouth. Goeth he not along like a dancer?

Altered is Zarathustra; a child hath Zarathustra become; an awakened one is Zarathustra: what wilt thou do in the land of the sleepers?

As in the sea hast thou lived in solitude, and it hath borne thee up. Alas, wilt thou now go ashore? Alas, wilt thou again drag thy body thyself ?"

Zarathustra answered: "I love mankind."

"Why," said the saint, "did I go into the forest and the desert? Was it not because I loved men far too well?

Now I love God: men, I do not love. Man is a thing too imperfect for me. Love to man would be fatal to me."

Zarathustra answered: "What spake I of love! I am bringing gifts unto men."

"Give them nothing," said the saint. "Take rather part of their load, and carry it along with them- that will be most agreeable unto them: if only it be agreeable unto thee!

If, however, thou wilt give unto them, give them no more than an alms, and let them also beg for it!"

"No," replied Zarathustra, "I give no alms. I am not poor enough for that."

“这个四处游荡的流浪者对于我来说，并不陌生，很多年前，他就曾经路过这里。那个时候他被人们称为查拉图斯特拉，但是现在的他变了。”

“当时，你携带着灰烬来到了山里，现在，你会把你的火焰带到山谷里面去吗？难道你就不害怕被人们看做是煽动者而遭受惩罚吗？”

“是的，我能辨别出查拉图斯特拉，他拥有着一双无比清澈的眼睛，他的嘴里也没有掩藏着任何的厌恶。他走起路来的样子是不是特别像一个舞者？”

“查拉图斯特拉的改变可真是巨大啊！查拉图斯特拉已经俨然变成了——一个小孩子、一个有着觉悟的人。现在，你还想对那些正在沉睡的人做些什么呢？”

“你就如同生活在海洋里一样，过着非常孤独的日子，大海让你感觉百无聊赖。唉，你现在是不是想要上岸啊？唉，你是不是想要再一次拖着自己的身体前行呢？”

查拉图斯特拉回答道：“我热爱人类。”

这位圣人说道：“为什么我想要走进森林和荒漠呢？难道这不是因为我过度喜爱人类了吗？ 现在的我喜欢神，我不喜欢人类了。从我的角度来讲，人类是一件拥有很多瑕疵的东西。热爱人类会给我带来致命的影响。”

查拉图斯特拉回答道：“我应该怎么说呢？我愿意把礼物带给人类。”

“不要给他们任何东西。与其这样，还不如直接从他们身上拿走东西以及把沉重的负担强加在他们身上——那样做会让他们感到无比愉快，就如同只有那样做才能让你感到愉悦一样！”

“假如你真的想给他们一些东西的话，那么只给他们一些救济物资就够了，然后让他们恳求！”

The saint laughed at Zarathustra, and spake thus: "Then see to it that they accept thy treasures! They are distrustful of anchorites, and do not believe that we come with gifts.

The fall of our footsteps ringeth too hollow through their streets. And just as at night, when they are in bed and hear a man abroad long before sunrise, so they ask themselves concerning us:

Where goeth the thief ?

Go not to men, but stay in the forest! Go rather to the animals! Why not be like me- a bear amongst bears, a bird amongst birds?"

"And what doeth the saint in the forest?" asked Zarathustra.

The saint answered: "I make hymns and sing them; and in making hymns I laugh and weep and mumble: thus do I praise God.

With singing, weeping, laughing, and mumbling do I praise the God who is my God. But what dost thou bring us as a gift?"

When Zarathustra had heard these words, he bowed to the saint and said: "What should I have to give thee! Let me rather hurry hence lest

I take aught away from thee!"- And thus they parted from one another, the old man and Zarathustra, laughing like schoolboys.

When Zarathustra was alone, however, he said to his heart: "Could it be possible! This old saint in the forest hath not yet heard of it,that God is dead!"

“不可以，”查拉图斯特拉回答道，“我不会只给予他们救济物资，我还没有穷到那个份上。”

这位圣人对着查拉图斯特拉哈哈大笑了起来，他接着说道：“那么，你去看一看，他们究竟会不会接受你的宝物！他们对隐士持有怀疑态度，他们并不会相信我们会带着礼物来这里。”

我们的脚步声在街道上显得异常空洞。到了晚上，他们如果在床上听到有人在还没有天亮的情况下，匆忙地经过这里时，他们或许会问自己：这个小偷到底去什么地方呢？

“不要去寻找人类，留在森林里！去找动物吧！你怎么就一点都不像我呢——成为熊中的王者、鸟中的霸主呢？”

“那么，圣人在森林里，都做些什么呢？”查拉图斯特拉问道。

圣人回答道：“我创作歌曲，并且亲自演唱这些歌曲，当我独自进行乐曲创作的时候，我会大笑、哭泣，甚至喃喃自语，我就是用这样的方式歌颂和赞美神的。”

“我通过唱歌、哭泣、欢笑以及喃喃自语的方式来赞美我心目中的神。可是，你带什么礼物给我们吗？”

当查拉图斯特拉听完这番话以后，他立刻向圣人敬了一个礼，随后他说道：“我能够给你带来什么礼物呢？你不如早点放我走吧！我没准还能从你的身上拿走一些东西呢！”那位老人和查拉图斯特拉就像两个天真无邪的孩子一样露出了笑容，他们就是通过这样的方式进行分别的。

然而，当查拉图斯特拉独自一人的时候，他对自己的心灵说道：“这会成为可能吗！这位身处森林之中的圣人还没有听到，神已经死了！”

3.

When Zarathustra arrived at the nearest town which adjoineth the forest, he found many people assembled in the market-place; for it had been announced that a rope-dancer would give a performance. And Zarathustra spake thus unto the people:

I teach you the Superman. Man is something that is to be surpassed. What have ye done to surpass man?

All beings hitherto have created something beyond themselves: and ye want to be the ebb of that great tide, and would rather go back to the beast than surpass man?

What is the ape to man? A laughing-stock, a thing of shame. And just the same shall man be to the Superman: a laughing-stock, a thing of shame.

Ye have made your way from the worm to man, and much within you is still worm. Once were ye apes, and even yet man is more of an ape than any of the apes.

Even the wisest among you is only a disharmony and hybrid of plant and phantom. But do I bid you become phantoms or plants?

Lo, I teach you the Superman!

The Superman is the meaning of the earth. Let your will say: The Superman shall he the meaning of the earth!

I conjure you, my brethren, remain true to the earth, and believe not those who speak unto you of superearthly hopes! Poisoners are they, whether they know it or not.

（3）

当查拉图斯特拉来到了森林下方最近的小镇上的时候，他发现市集的广场上挤满了人，这是因为有人说一个会在钢丝上行走的人会出现在这里。查拉图斯特拉对这些人说了以下这番话：

“我教给你们关于超人的事情。人类是某种必将被超越的东西。那么，我们究竟要怎么做才能超越人类呢？”

直到今天，任何生物都创造出了某些超越自身的事物：那么，你是想要成为这股伟大海浪当中的退潮，并且重返动物世界，而不是超越人类吗?

对于人类来说，类人猿到底是个什么样的东西呢？他究竟是众人唾弃的笑柄，还是痛苦的耻辱呢？人类对于超人也同样属于这样的情况：一个受到众人唾弃的笑柄，或是痛苦的耻辱。你已经通过某种方式从蠕虫进化为了人类，但是，你体内大部分的物质仍旧是蠕虫的形态。曾经的你是类人猿，但是，甚至是现在的人类都要比类人猿更像猿猴。

甚至是在你们当中最智慧的人，也只不过是一种不和谐、植物和幽灵的混合物而已。但是，我真的会命令你们全都变成鬼魂或是植物吗?

看呀！我教给你们关于超人的事情！

超人就是这片土地的意义所在。让我们大家共同说：“超人将是这片土地的意义所在！”

我恳求你们，我的兄弟，要对这片土地保持真实的自我，并且拒绝相信那些跟你谈论伟大希望的人！他们就是放毒药的人，无论他们自身是不是知晓。

Despisers of life are they, decaying ones and poisoned ones themselves, of whom the earth is weary: so away with them!

Once blasphemy against God was the greatest blasphemy; but God died, and therewith also those blasphemers. To blaspheme the earth is now the dreadfulest sin, and to rate the heart of the unknowable higher than the meaning of the earth!

Once the soul looked contemptuously on the body, and then that contempt was the supreme thing:- the soul wished the body meagre, ghastly, and famished. Thus it thought to escape from the body and the earth.

Oh, that soul was itself meagre, ghastly, and famished; and cruelty was the delight of that soul!

But ye, also, my brethren, tell me: What doth your body say about your soul? Is your soul not poverty and pollution and wretched self-complacency?

Verily, a polluted stream is man. One must be a sea, to receive a polluted stream without becoming impure.

Lo, I teach you the Superman: he is that sea; in him can your great contempt be submerged.

What is the greatest thing ye can experience? It is the hour of great contempt. The hour in which even your happiness becometh loathsome unto you, and so also your reason and virtue.

The hour when ye say: "What good is my happiness! It is poverty and pollution and wretched self-complacency. But my happiness should justify existence itself !"

The hour when ye say: "What good is my reason! Doth it long for knowledge as the lion for

他们就是蔑视生活的人，对令人感到厌倦的土地下毒，让其腐朽：所以我们要远离他们！

曾经亵渎神明就是最大限度的亵渎，可是，神已经死了，所以这些渎神者也都跟着死了。在当下最令人感到畏惧的罪恶就是亵渎大地以及用更加崇高的尊重去对待那些不可知的事件，而不去尊重大地的意义。

曾经，灵魂在肉体上用极其轻蔑的眼光注视着一切，因此，轻蔑是至高无上的东西，——灵魂希望肉体变得贫乏、苍白以及饥饿，它以为通过这样的方式，就能够逃脱肉体和尘世。

噢！灵魂本身才是那个贫乏、苍白以及饥饿的东西；而残忍则是灵魂的快乐所在。

但是，我的兄弟还告诉我：“你的身体都对你的灵魂说了些什么？难道你们的灵魂不贫穷吗？没有污染以及悲惨的沾沾自喜吗？”

的确，人是一条脏污的溪水。他必须成为海洋，才能接受一条脏污的溪水，而不会让自身变得肮脏。

看呀！我教给你们关于超人的事情：他就是那样的海洋，在他的海洋里，能够淹没你们那些伟大的轻蔑。

你们所亲身经历过的最伟大的事情是什么？就是伟大的轻蔑的时刻。在那样的时刻里，甚至你的快乐也会成为令你感到憎恶的事物，同样还有你的理智和道德。

当你说道：“我的幸福快乐有什么好的！它就是贫穷、污染以及一种悲哀的自满。”

当你说道：“我的理性有什么好的！它会像狮子渴求食物一样对知识如饥似渴吗？它就是贫穷、污染以及一种悲哀的自满。”

his food? It is poverty and pollution and wretched self-complacency!"

The hour when ye say: "What good is my virtue! As yet it hath not made me passionate. How weary I am of my good and my bad! It is all poverty and pollution and wretched self-complacency!"

The hour when ye say: "What good is my justice! I do not see that I am fervour and fuel. The just, however, are fervour and fuel!"

The hour when we say: "What good is my pity! Is not pity the cross on which he is nailed who loveth man? But my pity is not crucifixion."

Have ye ever spoken thus? Have ye ever cried thus? Ah! would that I had heard you crying thus!

It is not your sin- it is your self-satisfaction that crieth unto heaven; your very sparingness in sin crieth unto heaven!

Where is the lightning to lick you with its tongue? Where is the frenzy with which ye should be inoculated?

Lo, I teach you the Superman: he is that lightning, he is that frenzy!-

When Zarathustra had thus spoken, one of the people called out:

"We have now heard enough of the rope-dancer; it is time now for us to see him!" And all the people laughed at Zarathustra. But the rope-dancer, who thought the words applied to him, began his performance.

当你说道："我的道德有什么好的！它并没有让我充满热情。我对我的真善美和丑恶是如此的厌倦！它们全都是贫穷、肮脏以及一种悲哀的自满！"

当你说道："我的正义感有什么好的！我并没有发现，我本人是个充满热情、极度活跃的人。然而，正义感却是充满热情，并且极度活跃的！"

当你说道："我的怜悯之心有什么好的！难道那不是对十字架的怜悯吗？那个热爱人类的人却被钉在了十字架上。但是，我的怜悯之心并不一定要把人钉在十字架上。"

你有没有说过这样的话？你有没有这样的哭喊过？啊！我已经听到了你的哭泣声！

那并不是你的罪恶在哭泣——而是你的自我满足感，是你的罪恶当中的吝啬在对蓝天哭泣！

那道用舌头亲吻你的脸庞的闪电到底在哪里？那个清除你的疯狂的它又在什么地方呢？

看呀！我教给你关于超人的事情：他就是那道闪电，他就是那种疯狂！

当查拉图斯特拉说完这番话的时候，人群当中的一个人说道："现在，我们已经听够了那个走钢索的讲话了，是时候让我们见见他了！"

于是，人们开始嘲笑查拉图斯特拉。然而，那个走钢丝的家伙以为这番话是要让他出场，所以他登上了舞台，开始了他的表演。

4.

Zarathustra, however, looked at the people and wondered. Then he spake thus:

Man is a rope stretched between the animal and the Superman- a rope over an abyss.

A dangerous crossing, a dangerous wayfaring, a dangerous looking-back, a dangerous trembling and halting. What is great in man is that he is a bridge and not a goal: what is lovable in man is that he is an over-going and a down-going.

I love those that know not how to live except as down-goers, for they are the over-goers.

I love the great despisers, because they are the great adorers, and arrows of longing for the other shore.

I love those who do not first seek a reason beyond the stars for going down and being sacrifices, but sacrifice themselves to the earth, that the earth of the Superman may hereafter arrive.

I love him who liveth in order to know, and seeketh to know in order that the Superman may hereafter live. Thus seeketh he his own down-going.

I love him who laboureth and inventeth, that he may build the house for the Superman, and prepare for him earth, animal, and plant: for thus seeketh he his own down-going.

I love him who loveth his virtue: for virtue is the will to down-going, and an arrow of longing.

I love him who reserveth no share of spirit for himself, but wanteth to be wholly the spirit of

（4）

然而，查拉图斯特拉看着这群人，之后就沉默了。因此，他说道：

人类就是一条被捆绑在动物和超人之间的绳索——它是一条横跨深渊的绳索。

这是一种非常危险的横越、一种非常危险的徒步旅行、一种非常危险的回眸、一种非常危险的战栗和停顿。

人类的伟大之处就在于，他是一座桥梁，而不是一个目标：人类的可爱之处是跨越，而绝非向下走。

我特别喜欢那些除非他们的生活变成了必须向下走的模式，否则不知道该如何去生活的人们，因为他们就是那些要进行横越的人。

我热爱伟大的轻蔑别人的人，因为他们都是伟人的崇拜者，同时也是渴望登陆其他岸边的箭。

我热爱那些不会去星球以外的地方寻找向下走和做出牺牲的理由，但是他们却是为了大地可以牺牲自己的人，那片土地或许某一天会成为超人的领土。

我热爱那些为了求知欲而活的人，要想知道某一天即将出现的超人究竟是怎样的人。他会因为如此而自愿按照自己的方式向下走。

我热爱那些喜欢发明创造的人，他们会为超人建造房子，并且会为他准备土地、动物以及植物：因为他会自愿按照自己的方式向下走。

我热爱那些喜欢高尚美德的人：因为美德是朝下走的意念力，它是渴求的箭。

我热爱那些不在内心保留任何道德精神，但是又想完全成为他的道德精神的人：因

his virtue: thus walketh he as spirit over the bridge.

I love him who maketh his virtue his inclination and destiny: thus, for the sake of his virtue, he is willing to live on, or live no more.

I love him who desireth not too many virtues. One virtue is more of a virtue than two, because it is more of a knot for one's destiny to cling to.

I love him whose soul is lavish, who wanteth no thanks and doth not give back: for he always bestoweth, and desireth not to keep for himself.

I love him who is ashamed when the dice fall in his favour, and who then asketh: "Am I a dishonest player?"- for he is willing to succumb.

I love him who scattereth golden words in advance of his deeds, and always doeth more than he promiseth: for he seeketh his own down-going.

I love him who justifieth the future ones, and redeemeth the past ones: for he is willing to succumb through the present ones.

I love him who chasteneth his God, because he loveth his God: for he must succumb through the wrath of his God.

I love him whose soul is deep even in the wounding, and may succumb through a small matter: thus goeth he willingly over the bridge.

I love him whose soul is so overfull that he forgetteth himself, and all things are in him: thus all things become his down-going.

I love him who is of a free spirit and a free heart: thus is his head only the bowels of his

此，他就像一种精神一样走过了那座桥梁。

我热爱那些将自己的道德变成个人喜好和使命的人：因此，看在他的道德的份上，他会选择继续生活，或是不再生活下去。

我热爱那些并不渴望拥有过多美德的人。一个美德往往要比两个美德更具有道德意义，因为它更是一个能够让一个人的命运依附于其上的结。

我热爱那些拥有肆意挥霍的灵魂的人，他不会寻求别人的感谢，也不会反过来感谢别人：因为他总是选择把这些赠予给别人，他不希望将这些据为己有。

我热爱那些当骰子按照他的爱好掉落下来的时候，会感到羞耻的人，然后，问道：“我是不是一个不诚实的人？”——因为他选择被毁灭。

我热爱那些证实了未来的人类，并且挽回了过去的人类的人：因为他想要现代的人类毁灭掉自己。

我热爱那些惩罚他的神的人，因为他热爱他的神：因为他必须要被他的神的怒火所毁灭。

我热爱那些即使是灵魂受到了严重伤害，仍能保持极其深沉的人，哪怕是一件非常微小的事件也极有可能将他毁灭：因为只有这样他才会心甘情愿地走过这座桥梁。

我热爱那些灵魂过满的人，他忘记了自己以及关于他的所有的事情：因此，所有的事情都成为了他向下走的诱因。

我热爱那些拥有自由的精神以及自由的心灵的人：他的脑袋里只装着他的心灵；但是他的心灵却造成了让他向下走的结果。

我热爱所有的那些人，他们就如同从人们头顶上的乌云中掉落下来的沉重雨点：他

heart; his heart, however, causeth his down-going.

I love all who are like heavy drops falling one by one out of the dark cloud that lowereth over man: they herald the coming of the lightning, and succumb as heralds.

Lo, I am a herald of the lightning, and a heavy drop out of the cloud: the lightning, however, is the Superman.

5.

When Zarathustra had spoken these words, he again looked at the people, and was silent. "There they stand," said he to his heart;

"there they laugh: they understand me not; I am not the mouth for these ears.

Must one first batter their ears, that they may learn to hear with their eyes? Must one clatter like kettledrums and penitential preachers? Or do they only believe the stammerer?

They have something whereof they are proud. What do they call it, that which maketh them proud? Culture, they call it; it distinguisheth them from the goatherds.

They dislike, therefore, to hear of 'contempt' of themselves. So I will appeal to their pride.

I will speak unto them of the most contemptible thing: that, however, is the last man!"

And thus spake Zarathustra unto the people:

It is time for man to fix his goal. It is time for man to plant the germ of his highest hope.

Still is his soil rich enough for it. But that soil will one day be poor and exhausted, and no

们准确预言了闪电的到来，他们也同样像预言家一样被毁灭。

看呀！我就是预言了闪电到来的预言家，我就是那滴从乌云中掉落下来的沉重雨点：但是，那道闪电却被人们称作是超人。

（5）

当查拉图斯特拉说完上述这番话之后，他再一次看向那群人，之后便保持沉默了。“他们都站在这里，”他对自己的内心说道，“他们在这里嘲笑我，他们无法理解我；我并不是为那些耳朵讲话的嘴巴。”

难道一个人必须要首先打烂他们的耳朵，他们才能学会用眼睛去聆听吗？一个人难道必须要像大鼓和处在斋戒期的说教者一样，发出叮当作响的声音吗？或是难道他们只相信那些说话结巴的人吗？

他们都有一些能够令自己感到无比自豪的东西。他们究竟是如何称呼那些让自己感到骄傲的东西呢？到底是什么东西能够让他们感到无比自豪呢？他们称呼它们为文化；这是能够将他们同牧羊人区别开来的东西。

因此，他们不喜欢听到别人用“轻蔑”之类的话题来谈论他们。所以，我应该对他们的骄傲讲话。

所以我应该跟他们谈论最令人轻视的人，那就是终极之人。

因此，查拉图斯特拉对人们说道：

人们是时候调整自己的目标了。人们已经到了撒下最高希望的种子的时刻了。

lofty tree will any longer be able to grow thereon.

Alas! there cometh the time when man will no longer launch the arrow of his longing beyond man- and the string of his bow will have unlearned to whizz!

I tell you: one must still have chaos in one, to give birth to a dancing star. I tell you: ye have still chaos in you.

Alas! There cometh the time when man will no longer give birth to any star. Alas! There cometh the time of the most despicable man,who can no longer despise himself.

Lo! I show you the last man.

"What is love? What is creation? What is longing? What is a star?"- so asketh the last man and blinketh.

The earth hath then become small, and on it there hoppeth the last man who maketh everything small. His species is ineradicable like that of the ground-flea; the last man liveth longest.

"We have discovered happiness"- say the last men, and blink thereby.

They have left the regions where it is hard to live; for they need warmth. One still loveth one's neighbour and rubbeth against him; for one needeth warmth.

Turning ill and being distrustful, they consider sinful: they walk warily. He is a fool who still stumbleth over stones or men!

A little poison now and then: that maketh pleasant dreams. And much poison at last for a pleasant death.

现在，他的土壤仍旧足够肥沃。但是总有一天，这些土壤会变得贫瘠，消耗殆尽，参天的大树再也没有能力在这里生长。

唉！这个时刻即将到来，人们将再也无法射出渴求超越人类的箭，而他的弓弦也将会忘记该如何进行放箭！

让我来告诉你们：一个人身上必须拥有混乱的状态，才能让一颗翩翩起舞的行星孕育而生。让我来告诉你们：你们的身体里仍旧拥有着混乱的状态。

唉！人们将丧失拥有孕育任何行星的能力的时刻即将到来。

唉！最应该被鄙视的人的时刻即将到来，那样的人再也不会轻蔑他自己。

看呀！我要向你们展示终极之人。

“什么是爱？什么是创造？什么是渴求？什么是一颗繁星？”——终极之人眨巴着眼睛问道。

地球已经变小了，终极之人蹦到了它的上面，让所有的事物都变小了。类似他这样的种族同跳蚤非常相似，无法被根除，终极之人是活的时间最长久的物种。

“我们已经找到了快乐的所在”——终极之人眨巴着眼睛说道。

他们已经离开了非常难以生存的地区；因为他们需要温暖。

一个人仍旧会爱着他的邻居，并且让自己的身体在邻居的身上摩擦；因为他需要温暖。

他们将令人厌恶、不被信任看做是有罪的：他们应该小心翼翼地走路。他仍旧是那个会被石头或是人类绊倒的蠢货！

他们会时不时地投放一点毒药：那样做可以创造出美妙的梦境。最终，他们会利用更多的毒药来获得令人欢喜的死亡。

One still worketh, for work is a pastime. But one is careful lest the pastime should hurt one.

One no longer becometh poor or rich; both are too burdensome. Who still wanteth to rule? Who still wanteth to obey? Both are too burdensome.

No shepherd, and one herd! Everyone wanteth the same; everyone is equal: he who hath other sentiments goeth voluntarily into the madhouse.

"Formerly all the world was insane,"- say the subtlest of them, and blink thereby.

They are clever and know all that hath happened: so there is no end to their raillery. People still fall out, but are soon reconciled- otherwise it spoileth their stomachs.

They have their little pleasures for the day, and their little pleasures for the night, but they have a regard for health.

"We have discovered happiness,"- say the last men, and blink thereby.-

And here ended the first discourse of Zarathustra, which is also called "The Prologue", for at this point the shouting and mirth of the multitude interrupted him. "Give us this last man, O Zarathustra,"- they called out- "make us into these last men! Then will we make thee a present of the Superman!" And all the people exulted and smacked their lips. Zarathustra, however, turned sad, and said to his heart:

"They understand me not: I am not the mouth for these ears.

Too long, perhaps, have I lived in the mountains; too much have I hearkened unto the brooks and trees: now do I speak unto them as unto the goatherds.

一个人仍旧在工作，因为工作对于他来说，就是一种消遣。但是他必须时刻小心，否则这种消遣就会伤害到他。

人们不会再成为穷人或者富人：因为这两者都是沉重的累赘。有谁还想被统治？有谁还想去服从？这两者都是沉重的累赘。

没有牧羊犬，也没有羊群！任何人想要的东西都是相同的；所有的人都是平等的；那些拥有其他情感的人会自愿走进疯人院。

“从前，所有的世界都是疯狂的”——在他们当中最敏感的人眨巴着眼睛说道。

他们非常聪明，并且十分清楚将要发生的事情：所以对于他们来说，逗趣玩笑是不会结束的。人们仍旧会争吵下去，但是很快，他们就会达成和解——否则，会毁坏他们的消化系统。

在白天，他们有着属于自己的小乐趣，到了晚上，他们同样有着属于自己的乐子，但是，他们都把身体健康看得非常重要。

“我们已经找到了快乐所在”——于是，终极之人眨巴着眼睛说道。

查拉图斯特拉的第一次演说到了这里，就告一段落了，我们又把它称作是“查拉图斯特拉的序言”：就在这一刻，人群的尖叫声和欢声笑语打断了他。“快把这个终极之人给我们带来，查拉图斯特拉，”——他们大叫道——“快让我们都变成终极之人！然后，我们就把超人的礼物给你！”这时，所有的人都欣喜若狂地叫了起来。但是，查拉图斯特拉转过身来，脸上露出了悲伤的神情，他用发自肺腑的情感说道：

“他们根本就不了解我；我并不是为这些耳朵讲话的嘴巴。

或许，我在山里住了太久的时间；我听惯了小河的细流声以及树木之间的呼啸声：

Calm is my soul, and clear, like the mountains in the morning. But they think me cold, and a mocker with terrible jests.

And now do they look at me and laugh: and while they laugh they hate me too. There is ice in their laughter."

6.

Then, however, something happened which made every mouth mute and every eye fixed. In the meantime, of course, the rope-dancer had commenced his performance: he had come out at a little door, and was going along the rope which was stretched between two towers, so that it hung above the market-place and the people. When he was just midway across, the little door opened once more, and a gaudily-dressed fellow like a buffoon sprang out, and went rapidly after the first one. "Go on, halt-foot," cried his frightful voice, "go on, lazy-bones, interloper, sallow-face!- lest I tickle thee with my heel! What dost thou here between the towers? In the tower is the place for thee, thou shouldst be locked up; to one better than thyself thou blockest the way!"- And with every word he came nearer and nearer the first one. When, however, he was but a step behind, there happened the frightful thing which made every mouth mute and every eye fixed- he uttered a yell like a devil, and jumped over the other who was in his way. The latter, however, when he thus saw his rival triumph, lost at the same time his head and his footing on the rope; he threw his pole away, and shot downward faster than it, like an eddy

现在，我要像跟牧羊人聊天一样，跟他们进行交谈。

我的灵魂非常平静、非常清澈，就像早晨的山峦。但是他们认为我是一个冷淡的、只会模仿拙劣笑话的人。

现在，他们看着我，嘲笑我：就在他们嘲笑我的同时，还憎恨我。在他们的笑声里掺杂着冰块。”

（6）

然而，就在这个时候，某些事情的发生却让所有人都哑口无言、瞠目结舌。当然，与此同时，那个会在绳索上行走的人开始了他的表演：他从一扇非常小的门里走了出来，并且开始在一个将两个塔连接在一起的绳子上面行走，通过这样做，他能够悬在市场的上方以及人群的头顶。当他刚刚走过绳索的中间部分的时候，那扇小门再一次被打开了，一个穿着俗气，犹如一头水牛的家伙突然从里面冒了出来，并且开始迅速追赶那个表演绳索杂技的人。“快点走，你这个瘸子，”他用令人胆怯的声音大声叫道，“快点走，你这个懒骨头、闯入者、面色枯黄的家伙！——不要让我的后脚跟给你挠痒痒！你都在这个绳索上做了什么？你应该被囚禁在这座塔里面；因为你阻拦了一位本领比你高超的人前行的脚步！”就在他说这些话的同时，他离这位表演绳索杂技的家伙越来越近。然而，就在他距离表演杂技的家伙仅仅一步之遥的时候，发生了一件令所有人哑口无言、瞠目结舌的事情——他就像一个恶魔一样大声喊叫，一个跳步越过了那个阻拦他道路的家伙。但是，当这位杂耍者看到他的对手取得胜利的同时，他的大脑和脚步都在绳索上

of arms and legs, into the depth. The market-place and the people were like the sea when the storm cometh on: they all flew apart and in disorder, especially where the body was about to fall.

Zarathustra, however, remained standing, and just beside him fell the body, badly injured and disfigured, but not yet dead. After a while consciousness returned to the shattered man, and he saw Zarathustra kneeling beside him. "What art thou doing there?" said he at last, "I knew long ago that the devil would trip me up. Now he draggeth me to hell: wilt thou prevent him?"

"On mine honour, my friend," answered Zarathustra, "there is nothing of all that whereof thou speakest: there is no devil and no hell.

Thy soul will be dead even sooner than thy body; fear, therefore, nothing any more!"

The man looked up distrustfully. "If thou speakest the truth," said he, "I lose nothing when I lose my life. I am not much more than an animal which hath been taught to dance by blows and scanty fare."

"Not at all," said Zarathustra, "thou hast made danger thy calling; therein there is nothing contemptible. Now thou perishest by thy calling: therefore will I bury thee with mine own hands."

When Zarathustra had said this the dying one did not reply further; but he moved his hand as if he sought the hand of Zarathustra in gratitude.

失去了平衡，平衡杆也从他的手上滑落了下去，他就像一个由快速旋转的胳膊和腿组成的旋涡一样飞快地向地面坠落，整个市场和广大群众就像风暴来袭的大海一样，立刻乱了手脚，呈现出非常混乱的状态，尤其是表演绳索杂技的人的身体即将要坠落的位置，情况更是如此。

但是，查拉图斯特拉仍旧站在原地，那个表演绳索的人就从他的身边掉了下来，那个人受了非常严重的伤，身体受到了极度的扭曲，但是，他并没有死。过了一会儿，那个身体被摔碎了的家伙恢复了意识，然后他看到了查拉图斯特拉跪在他的身边。“你在这里做什么？”最后他说道，“我在很久以前就知道，恶魔一定会陷害我。现在，他把我拖进了地狱，你能阻止他这样做吗？”

“我的朋友，请以我的荣誉为誓，”查拉图斯特拉答道，“你所说的一切都完全不存在，在我们的世界里，既没有恶魔也没有地狱。你的灵魂的毁灭速度甚至会比你的躯体还要快，因此，你不要再感到恐惧了！”

那个人用充满怀疑的神情注视着他，他说道：“如果你所说的都是事实，那么当我失去自己的生命的时候，我将会一无所有。我不过是一只野兽而已，在人们的棍棒交加以及少量的食物的对待方式下，我学会了在绳索上行走。”

“并不完全是这样的，”查拉图斯特拉说道，“你让危险成为你的专长；那样就不会被其他人鄙视了。现在，你亲手毁灭了自己的专长；因此，我会用自己的双手亲自埋葬你。”

当查拉图斯特拉说完这些话的时候，这位快要死掉的人并没有做进一步的回答。但是，他动了动自己的手，就好像他在寻找查拉图斯特拉的手，以此表达自己的感激之情。

7.

Meanwhile the evening came on, and the market-place veiled itself in gloom. Then the people dispersed, for even curiosity and terror become fatigued. Zarathustra, however, still sat beside the dead man on the ground, absorbed in thought: so he forgot the time. But at last it became night, and a cold wind blew upon the lonely one. Then arose Zarathustra and said to his heart:

Verily, a fine catch of fish hath Zarathustra made to-day! It is not a man he hath caught, but a corpse.

Sombre is human life, and as yet without meaning: a buffoon may be fateful to it.

I want to teach men the sense of their existence, which is the Superman, the lightning out of the dark cloud- man.

But still am I far from them, and my sense speaketh not unto their sense. To men I am still something between a fool and a corpse.

Gloomy is the night, gloomy are the ways of Zarathustra. Come, thou cold and stiff companion! I carry thee to the place where I shall bury thee with mine own hands.

8.

When Zarathustra had said this to his heart, he put the corpse upon his shoulders and set

（7）

与此同时，夜幕就快要降临了，市场被忧郁的气氛所笼罩。接着，聚集在一起的人们开始散去，甚至是人们的好奇心和恐惧的心理也变得厌倦了。但是，查拉图斯特拉仍旧坐在那个死去的表演家的身边，并且陷入了深深的沉思当中：因为他已经忘记了时间。但是，最终天黑了下来，一股寒冷的风吹袭着这里的孤独者。然后，查拉图斯特拉站了起来，用发自肺腑的情感说道：

“说真的，今天，查拉图斯特拉的捕鱼结果收效甚好！他从来都没有抓到过活人，但却抓到了一个尸体。

人生充满了磨难，而且，通常这些磨难都是毫无意义的：一个出演滑稽角色的小丑或许会给它带来毁灭性的打击。

我想用存在的感觉教给人类：那就是超人，从黑暗的人类乌云中迸发出来的闪电。

但是，我离他们非常遥远，而且我的内心并不能诉说他们的内心。在他们的眼中，我的形象就介于一个疯子和一具死尸之间。

夜晚是非常黑暗的，同样黑暗的还有查拉图斯特拉要走的道路。快到这里来，犹如寒冰一样僵硬的同伴！让我背着你去那个我即将用双手亲自埋葬你的地方。”

（8）

当查拉图斯特拉用发自肺腑的情感说完这些话的时候，他把那个尸体扛在了自己的

out on his way. Yet had he not gone a hundred steps, when there stole a man up to him and whispered in his ear- and lo! he that spake was the buffoon from the tower. "Leave this town, O Zarathustra," said he, "there are too many here who hate thee.

The good and just hate thee, and call thee their enemy and despiser; the believers in the orthodox belief hate thee, and call thee a danger to the multitude. It was thy good fortune to be laughed at: and verily thou spakest like a buffoon. It was thy good fortune to associate with the dead dog; by so humiliating thyself thou hast saved thy life to-day. Depart, however, from this town,- or tomorrow I shall jump over thee, a living man over a dead one." And when he had said this, the buffoon vanished; Zarathustra, however, went on through the dark streets.

At the gate of the town the grave-diggers met him: they shone their torch on his face, and, recognising Zarathustra, they sorely derided him. "Zarathustra is carrying away the dead dog: a fine thing that Zarathustra hath turned a grave-digger! For our hands are too cleanly for that roast. Will Zarathustra steal the bite from the devil? Well then, good luck to the repast! If only the devil is not a better thief than Zarathustra!- he will steal them both, he will eat them both!" And they laughed among themselves, and put their heads together.

Zarathustra made no answer thereto, but went on his way. When he had gone on for two hours, past forests and swamps, he had heard too much of the hungry howling of the wolves, and he himself became hungry. So he halted at a lonely house in which a light was burning.

"Hunger attacketh me," said Zarathustra, "like a robber. Among forests and swamps my hunger attacketh me, and late in the night.

肩膀上，然后就上路了。然而，当他还没有走出一百步的时候，一个人趁机溜到了他的身边，并且在他的耳边说起了悄悄话——瞧呀！说话的那个人居然是那个塔里面的小丑。“啊！查拉图斯特拉，你快点离开这个城镇吧，”他说道，“这里有太多痛恨你的人了。善意和公正痛恨你，他们把你看做是他们的敌人以及被轻视的对象；那些尊崇正统观念的信仰者痛恨你，并且称呼你为人们的危险分子。人们嘲笑你，那是你的幸运：你说话的样子真的特别像一个小丑。你把自己和这条死狗联系在一起是你的幸运；通过自取其辱，你今天捡回了一条命。但是，不管怎么样，你都离开这个村子吧！要不然，到了明天，我这个活生生的人就要跨过这个死人了。”当他说完这些话的时候，那个小丑消失了；然而，查拉图斯特拉依旧在黑暗的街道上行走。

在小镇的大门边上，他遇到了一群挖掘坟墓的人；他们用手中的火炬照亮了他的脸，然后，他们认出了那个人就是查拉图斯特拉，他们开始疯狂地嘲笑他。“查拉图斯特拉正在搬运一条死狗；真了不起，查拉图斯特拉要化身为掘坟者了！我们的双手太干净了，没法埋葬这条死狗。查拉图斯特拉会有偷走恶魔的食物的想法吗？去吧，希望你在就餐的时候，能有好运气，只要恶魔不是一个比查拉图斯特拉更加优秀的小偷就行！——他或许会把两个一起偷走，吃掉！”他们并着头，哈哈大笑了起来。

然后，查拉图斯特拉并没有做出任何反应，而是继续朝着他的路前行。当他走了两个小时以后，他穿过了森林以及沼泽，他多次听见饥饿的野狼在嚎叫，但是，他自己也变得饥饿难耐。所以，他在一处孤零零的、里面有亮光的房子前面停了下来。

“饥饿难耐正在袭击我，”查拉图斯特拉说道，“它就像个强盗。在森林和沼泽之中，在幽静的夜晚之中，饥饿在袭击我。”

"Strange humours hath my hunger. Often it cometh to me only after a repast, and all day it hath failed to come: where hath it been?"

And thereupon Zarathustra knocked at the door of the house. An old man appeared, who carried a light, and asked: "Who cometh unto me and my bad sleep?"

"A living man and a dead one," said Zarathustra. "Give me something to eat and drink, I forgot it during the day. He that feedeth the hungry refresheth his own soul, saith wisdom."

The old man withdrew, but came back immediately and offered Zarathustra bread and wine. "A bad country for the hungry," said he; "that is why I live here. Animal and man come unto me, the anchorite. But bid thy companion eat and drink also, he is wearier than thou." Zarathustra answered: "My companion is dead; I shall hardly be able to persuade him to eat." "That doth not concern me," said the old man sullenly; "he that knocketh at my door must take what I offer him. Eat, and fare ye well!"-

Thereafter Zarathustra again went on for two hours, trusting to the path and the light of the stars: for he was an experienced night-walker, and liked to look into the face of all that slept.

When the morning dawned, however, Zarathustra found himself in a thick forest, and no path was any longer visible. He then put the dead man in a hollow tree at his head- for he wanted to protect him from the wolves- and laid himself down on the ground and moss. And immediately he fell asleep, tired in body, but with a tranquil soul.

“在我的饥饿中拥有一些稀奇古怪的幽默。在通常的情况之下，我只有在就餐完毕之后，才会有这样的特征，然而一整天过去了，这样的特征一直都没有出现：那么，它们都到哪里去了呢？”

因此，查拉图斯特拉叩响了这所房子的门。一个老人出现在了查拉图斯特拉的面前，他手里拿着一盏灯，问道：“到底是谁过来拜访我，进入到我的噩梦之中呢？”

“一个活人还有一个死人，”查拉图斯特拉说道，“给我一些吃的东西和水，白天我忘记了要带这些东西。智慧说，喂饱饥饿的人，也同样会安慰自己的灵魂。”

那位老人回屋了，但是他很快就从里面出来了，并且给了查拉图斯特拉一些面包和酒水。“这个地方可不会对饥饿者友善，”他说道，“这就是为什么我会住在这里。无论是动物还是人类都会过来找我这个隐士。但是，你让你的同伴也吃点东西，喝点水吧。他看上去似乎要比你还疲倦。”查拉图斯特拉回答道：“我的同伴死了；我实在没有办法说服他吃东西。”“这跟我一点关系都没有，”那位老人用阴沉的语气说道：“他只要敲了我的门，就必须吃掉我给他提供的东西。吃吧！祝你们一路顺风！”随后，查拉图斯特拉借着星光与路又走了两个小时，他是一位不折不扣的夜间行走爱好者，经验丰富。他喜欢观察一切处于沉睡状态的面孔。然而，当太阳升起的时候，查拉图斯特拉发现他正处在一片茂密的森林之中，在他的面前再也没有任何一条可见的道路了。于是，他把那个尸体放在了和他的脑袋等高的一个中空的树干里——因为他想要保护那个死人免受饿狼的袭击——之后，他便躺在了地上的苔藓里。很快，他就睡着了，他已经精疲力竭了，但是他的灵魂却是如此的宁静。

9.

Long slept Zarathustra; and not only the rosy dawn passed over his head, but also the morning. At last, however, his eyes opened, and amazedly he gazed into the forest and the stillness, amazedly he gazed into himself. Then he arose quickly, like a seafarer who all at once seeth the land; and he shouted for joy: for he saw a new truth. And he spake thus to his heart:

A light hath dawned upon me: I need companions- living ones; not dead companions and corpses, which I carry with me where I will.

But I need living companions, who will follow me because they want to follow themselves- and to the place where I will. A light hath dawned upon me. Not to the people is Zarathustra to speak, but to companions! Zarathustra shall not be the herd's herdsman and hound!

To allure many from the herd- for that purpose have I come. The people and the herd must be angry with me: a robber shall Zarathustra be called by the herdsmen.

Herdsmen, I say, but they call themselves the good and just. Herdsmen, I say, but they call themselves the believers in the orthodox belief.

Behold the good and just! Whom do they hate most? Him who breaketh up their tables of values, the breaker, the lawbreaker:- he, however, is the creator.

Behold the believers of all beliefs! Whom do they hate most? Him who breaketh up their tables of values, the breaker, the law-breaker- he, however, is the creator.

Companions, the creator seeketh, not corpses- and not herds or believers either. Fellow-

（9）

查拉图斯特拉睡了很久，不光是黎明，就连早晨也爬过了他的脑袋。然而，最终他睁开了双眼，他惊讶地注视着无比宁静的森林，也惊讶地注视着他自己。

然后，他飞快地站了起来，就好像是一个历尽千辛万苦找到大陆的海员一样：他快乐地叫了起来，因为他看见了一个崭新的事实。因此，他用发自肺腑的情感说道：

一束光照耀在了我的身上，我需要同伴——活生生的同伴，而不是任由心灵决定何去何从的死去的同伴和尸体。

一束光照耀在了我的身上。查拉图斯特拉不应该跟群众说话，而是应该跟同伴们说话！查拉图斯特拉不应该成为牧羊人和猎犬！从羊群里诱骗更多的小羊——我是为了这个原因才来到这里的。那些群众和牧羊人肯定对我的想法感到颇为恼火；查拉图斯特拉心甘情愿让牧羊人们称自己为强盗。

我说的那些牧羊人，他们称呼自己为有善意和正义感的人。我说的那些牧羊人，他们称呼自己为尊崇正统信仰的使徒。瞧这些善意和正义感！他们最痛恨的人到底是谁？他们最痛恨那些损毁了他们的价值表的人、破坏者以及违法的人——但是，他是创造者。

瞧这些所有信仰的使徒们吧！他们最痛恨的人到底是谁？他们最痛恨那些损毁了他们的价值表的人、破坏者以及违法的人——但是，他是创造者。

创造者寻找的是同伴而不是尸体——同样也不是牧羊人，或是信仰者。创造者所寻找的是共同创造者——那些将全新的价值表写在上面的人们。

创造者寻找的是同伴以及共同收获者；他认为任何事物都已经成熟了，都在等待着

creators the creator seeketh- those who grave new values on new tables.

Companions, the creator seeketh, and fellow-reapers: for everything is ripe for the harvest with him. But he lacketh the hundred sickles: so he plucketh the ears of corn and is vexed.

Companions, the creator seeketh, and such as know how to whet their sickles. Destroyers, will they be called, and despisers of good and evil. But they are the reapers and rejoicers.

Fellow-creators, Zarathustra seeketh; fellow-reapers and fellow-rejoicers, Zarathustra seeketh: what hath he to do with herds and herdsmen and corpses!

And thou, my first companion, rest in peace! Well have I buried thee in thy hollow tree; well have I hid thee from the wolves.

But I part from thee; the time hath arrived. 'Twixt rosy dawn and rosy dawn there came unto me a new truth.

I am not to be a herdsman, I am not to be a grave-digger. Not any more will I discourse unto the people; for the last time have I spoken unto the dead.

With the creators, the reapers, and the rejoicers will I associate: the rainbow will I show them, and all the stairs to the Superman.

To the lone-dwellers will I sing my song, and to the twain-dwellers; and unto him who hath still ears for the unheard, will I make the heart heavy with my happiness.

I make for my goal, I follow my course; over the loitering and tardy will I leap. Thus let my on-going be their down-going!

收获。但是，他缺乏上百把镰刀，所以他用无比愤怒的情绪扒扯着玉米穗。

创造者寻找的是同伴以及懂得该如何把镰刀磨快的人。他们将这些人称呼为毁灭者以及轻视善意和邪恶的人。然而，那些从事收获和庆祝丰收的正是这群人。

查拉图斯特拉寻找的是共同创造者，查拉图斯特拉寻找的是共同收获者以及共同庆祝丰收的人。羊群、牧羊人以及尸体，跟他又有什么关系！

那么，我的第一位同伴，愿你在平和之中安息吧！我会把你安葬在这棵中空的树干里，我要将你藏起来，以此免受恶狼的袭击。

但是，我不得不离开你，离别的时间已经到了。在两个黎明之间，我找到了一个全新的真理的诏示。

我不会成为一名牧羊人，我不会成为一名挖掘坟墓的人。我将不会再给人们讲话。这一次也将是最后一次，我对一个死人讲话。

我会和创造者结交，和那些收获者以及庆祝丰收的人结交；我会向他们展示彩虹以及超人的阶梯。

我会给那些独自一人生活的人以及两个人在一起生活的人献上我的歌声，那有谁的耳朵有不曾听到过的东西，我会让他的内心充满我的快乐。

我会为了我的目标而努力，我会严格遵照我的路途前进，我会越过踌躇者和懒散的人。因此，我的积极前进将成为他们的衰落。

10.

This had Zarathustra said to his heart when the sun stood at noon-tide. Then he looked inquiringly aloft,- for he heard above him the sharp call of a bird. And behold! An eagle swept through the air in wide circles, and on it hung a serpent, not like a prey, but like a friend: for it kept itself coiled round the eagle's neck.

"They are mine animals," said Zarathustra, and rejoiced in his heart.

"The proudest animal under the sun, and the wisest animal under the sun,- they have come out to reconnoitre.

They want to know whether Zarathustra still liveth. Verily, do I still live?

More dangerous have I found it among men than among animals; in dangerous paths goeth Zarathustra. Let mine animals lead me!"

When Zarathustra had said this, he remembered the words of the saint in the forest. Then he sighed and spake thus to his heart:

"Would that I were wiser! Would that I were wise from the very heart, like my serpent!

But I am asking the impossible. Therefore do I ask my pride to go always with my wisdom!

And if my wisdom should some day forsake me:- alas! it loveth to fly away!- may my pride then fly with my folly!"

Thus began Zarathustra's down-going.

（10）

当查拉图斯特拉用发自肺腑的情感说完这些话的时候，太阳已经正午了。然后，他用充满好奇的神情看向高处，因为他听到他的头顶有刺耳的鸟叫声。快看！一只老鹰在空中画了一个大圈子，在那上面悬挂着一条蛇，他看起来不像是猎物，而更像是一位朋友：因为老鹰把这条蛇缠绕在了他的脖子上。

“他们都是我的动物，”查拉图斯特拉说道，他的内心非常欢快。“在太阳之下最值得骄傲的动物以及在太阳之下最聪明的动物——他们都跑出来一探究竟。

他们想知道查拉图斯特拉是否想继续活着。说真的，我还有必要继续活着吗？

我发现人类要比动物们更加具有危险性；查拉图斯特拉在危险的道路上行走。让我的动物们指引我吧！”

当查拉图斯特拉说完这些话的时候，他想起了森林中的圣人所说过的话。然后他叹了口气，用真挚的情感说道：

“我希望让自己变得更加智慧一些！我真切地希望自己可以变得更加聪明一些。就像我的毒蛇一样！

但是，我所希望的是不可能实现的愿望。因此，我请求我的骄傲陪伴着我的智慧！

就好像，我的智慧在某一天会抛弃我——唉！它非常渴望远走高飞！——那么，我愿我的骄傲陪伴着我的愚蠢一起远走高飞！”

因此，查拉图斯特拉开始下山。

ZARATHUSTRA'S SPEECH

1. THE THREE METAMORPHOSES

Three metamorphoses of the spirit do I designate to you: how the spirit becometh a camel, the camel a lion, and the lion at last a child.

Many heavy things are there for the spirit, the strong load-bearing spirit in which reverence dwelleth: for the heavy and the heaviest longeth its strength.

What is heavy? so asketh the load-bearing spirit; then kneeleth it down like the camel, and wanteth to be well laden.

What is the heaviest thing, ye heroes? asketh the load-bearing spirit, that I may take it upon me and rejoice in my strength.

Is it not this: To humiliate oneself in order to mortify one's pride? To exhibit one's folly in order to mock at one's wisdom?

Or is it this: To desert our cause when it celebrateth its triumph? To ascend high mountains to tempt the tempter?

Or is it this: To feed on the acorns and grass of knowledge, and for the sake of truth to suffer hunger of soul?

查拉图斯特拉的演讲

1．三种变形

现在，我来告诉你三种精神变形的方式：精神是如何变成一只骆驼，又从骆驼变成一头狮子，最后再从狮子变成一个小孩。

精神会被给予许多沉重的负担，强壮且能够承载负担的精神崇敬所担负的：精神所要求的沉重的和最为沉重的负担。

什么是沉重的？你可以去问问能够承载负担的精神，然后，像一头骆驼一样跪拜在它的面前，渴望获得沉重的重负。

那么英雄们，什么又是最沉重的呢？去问一问能够承载负担的精神，我会载着它，在我的力量之下尽情庆祝。

事实是不是这样的：为了损害某人的傲慢而当众羞辱他？为了模仿某人的智慧，而展现出他的愚蠢？

又或是这样的情况：当我们庆祝胜利的时候，我们抛弃了这一主张？为了寻找更加具有吸引力的事物，而攀爬高山？

又或是这样的情况：用知识的果实和青草喂养自己，为了顾及真相而忍受灵魂的饥饿？

Or is it this: To be sick and dismiss comforters, and make friends of the deaf, who never hear thy requests?

Or is it this: To go into foul water when it is the water of truth, and not disclaim cold frogs and hot toads?

Or is it this: To love those who despise us, and give one's hand to the phantom when it is going to frighten us?

All these heaviest things the load-bearing spirit taketh upon itself: and like the camel, which, when laden, hasteneth into the wilderness, so hasteneth the spirit into its wilderness.

But in the loneliest wilderness happeneth the second metamorphosis: here the spirit becometh a lion; freedom will it capture, and lordship in its own wilderness.

Its last Lord it here seeketh: hostile will it be to him, and to its last God; for victory will it struggle with the great dragon.

What is the great dragon which the spirit is no longer inclined to call Lord and God? "Thou-shalt," is the great dragon called. But the spirit of the lion saith, "I will."

"Thou-shalt," lieth in its path, sparkling with gold a scale-covered beast; and on every scale glittereth golden, "Thou shalt!"

The values of a thousand years glitter on those scales, and thus speaketh the mightiest of all dragons: "All the values of things glitter on me. All values have already been created, and all created values do I represent. Verily, there shall be no 'I will' any more." Thus speaketh the dragon.

又或是这样的情况：在身体虚弱的时候，拒绝接受安慰者的抚慰，并且结交一些永远听不到你的要求的聋子朋友？

又或是这样的情况：只要那是真相之水，不管它有多么的浑浊，他都会一跃而入，而不厌恶那些冰冷的青蛙和炽热的蛤蟆？

又或是这样的情况：去热爱那些轻视我们的人，当幽灵开始吓唬我们的时候，助它一臂之力？

所有沉重的负担，能够承载负担的精神扛起了重负：它就像那只骆驼一样，急匆匆地向荒野进发。

但是，在最孤寂的荒野上，他遇到了第二种变形：这里的精神变成了一头狮子；他一心想要抓住自由，并且成为这片荒野的统治者。

他在这里寻找他最后的主人：他要成为这里的主人以及最后的上帝的仇人；为了取得胜利，他需要同伟大的巨龙展开激烈的搏斗。

那个精神不再倾向于召唤统治者和上帝的伟大的巨龙究竟是谁？“你应该”是这只伟大的巨龙的名字。但是狮子的精神却说：“我想要。”

“你应该”就躺在路上，浑身散发着金灿灿的光芒，它是一条全身布满鳞片的怪物；他身上的每一处鳞片都闪耀着金色的光芒，“你应该！”

上千年的价值在这些鳞片上闪耀着光芒，因此，在所有的巨龙当中最强大的那只龙说道：“事物的所有价值全都在我的身上散发着光芒。所有已经被创造出来的价值，所有被创造出来的价值——那就是我。说真的，这里再也不会有什么‘我愿意了’。”伟大的巨龙如是说。

My brethren, wherefore is there need of the lion in the spirit? Why sufficeth not the beast of burden, which renounceth and is reverent?

To create new values that, even the lion cannot yet accomplish: but to create itself freedom for new creating that can the might of the lion do.

To create itself freedom, and give a holy Nay even unto duty: for that, my brethren, there is need of the lion.

To assume the right to new values that is the most formidable assumption for a load-bearing and reverent spirit. Verily, unto such a spirit it is preying, and the work of a beast of prey.

As its holiest, it once loved "Thou-shalt": now is it forced to find illusion and arbitrariness even in the holiest things, that it may capture freedom from its love: the lion is needed for this capture.

But tell me, my brethren, what the child can do, which even the lion could not do? Why hath the preying lion still to become a child?

Innocence is the child, and forgetfulness, a new beginning, a game, a self-rolling wheel, a first movement, a holy Yea.

Aye, for the game of creating, my brethren, there is needed a holy Yea unto life: Its own will, willeth now the spirit; his own world winneth the world’s outcast.

Three metamorphoses of the spirit have I designated to you: how the spirit became a camel, the camel a lion, and the lion at last a child.

Thus spake Zarathustra. And at that time he abode in the town which is called The Pied Cow.

我的兄弟们，你们所需要的精神之狮究竟有什么意义啊？那个忍让、崇敬并且可以承担重负的骆驼难道还不够吗？为了创造新的价值—— 甚至狮子也不能完成这样的任务：但是为了新的创造而争取到的自由——这恰恰就是狮子所渴望拥有的力量。

为自身创造自由，并且为对抗义务找出一个神圣的否定理由：我的兄弟们，这就是狮子的工作。

得到新价值的权力——这对于一个能够承担重负、虔诚的精神来说，是最令人感到敬畏的假设。的确，施加在这样的精神之上的是掠夺以及凶残的野兽的行为。

从前，它曾深爱着那个被称为“你应该”的最为神圣的物种，但是，现在它迫不得已要去最崇高的事物中寻找假象，甚至是专横霸道。让它能够以牺牲爱情的代价来掠夺自由：狮子需要这样的掠夺。

但是，我的兄弟们，请告诉我，如果是连狮子都无法办到的事情，你还能指望小孩子做什么？为什么即使是这样，捕食猎物的狮子仍旧想要变成一个孩子？

孩子是天真无邪的、容易忘事的，一个全新的开始、一个游戏、一个自己滚动的轮子、一个原始的动作、一个神圣的肯定。

的确，我的兄弟们，在创造的游戏当中，生活对神圣的肯定的需要是必不可少的：现在，精神成了他的意愿；世界的遗弃者又获得了属于他自己的世界。

我在这里向你们说明了精神的三种变形：精神是如何变成一头骆驼，如何从一头骆驼变成一头狮子，最后又是如何从一头狮子变成一个小孩子的。

查拉图斯特拉如是说。就在那个时候，他抵临了那个被称为“花牛”的小城镇。

2. THE ACADEMIC CHAIRS OF VIRTUE

People commended unto Zarathustra a wise man, as one who could discourse well about sleep and virtue: greatly was he honoured and rewarded for it, and all the youths sat before his chair. To him went Zarathustra, and sat among the youths before his chair. And thus spake the wise man:

Respect and modesty in presence of sleep! That is the first thing! And to go out of the way of all who sleep badly and keep awake at night!

Modest is even the thief in presence of sleep: he always stealeth softly through the night. Immodest, however, is the night-watchman; immodestly he carrieth his horn.

No small art is it to sleep: it is necessary for that purpose to keep awake all day.

Ten times a day must thou overcome thyself: that causeth wholesome weariness, and is poppy to the soul.

Ten times must thou reconcile again with thyself; for overcoming is bitterness, and badly sleep the unreconciled.

Ten truths must thou find during the day; otherwise wilt thou seek truth during the night, and thy soul will have been hungry.

Ten times must thou laugh during the day, and be cheerful; otherwise thy stomach, the father of affliction, will disturb thee in the night.

2. 德行的讲坛

人们都称赞查拉图斯特拉为聪明的人，他尤其善于谈论睡眠和道德：他被赋予伟大的荣誉以及丰厚的奖赏，许多年轻人都会来到他这里聆听讲座。查拉图斯特拉也来到了这位智者的面前，他也同其他的年轻人一样坐在了智者的椅子前面。于是，这位智者开始说道：

让我们用尊重和谦逊的方式对待睡眠吧！这是第一件重要的事情！远离那些睡眠不好以及在夜晚时刻保持清醒状态的人们！

甚至小偷在睡眠面前也是谦逊的：他经常在夜晚悄无声息地偷东西。但是，夜晚的看守人确实不谦虚，并且毫不谦逊地拿起他的号角。

睡眠绝非是一种毫不起眼的艺术：为了达到在夜晚做好梦的意图，在一整天的时间里都保持清醒的状态是必不可少的。

每一天，你必须克制自己十次：这样会让你产生极端的厌倦，这是灵魂的麻醉剂。

每一天，你必须让自己心情顺畅十次，因为克制是痛苦的，心情不舒畅的人就不会睡得好。

每一天，你必须要找到十个事实真相；要不然，你就要在夜晚寻找真相了，那么你的灵魂就会变得饥饿。

每一天，你必须要哈哈大笑十次，保持愉悦的心情；否则，到了晚上，你的胃，这个苦恼之父就会把你吸收掉。

Few people know it, but one must have all the virtues in order to sleep well. Shall I bear false witness? Shall I commit adultery?

Shall I covet my neighbour's maidservant? All that would ill accord with good sleep.

And even if one have all the virtues, there is still one thing needful: to send the virtues themselves to sleep at the right time.

That they may not quarrel with one another, the good females! And about thee, thou unhappy one!

Peace with God and thy neighbour: so desireth good sleep. And peace also with thy neighbour's devil! Otherwise it will haunt thee in the night.

Honour to the government, and obedience, and also to the crooked government! So desireth good sleep. How can I help it, if power like to walk on crooked legs?

He who leadeth his sheep to the greenest pasture, shall always be for me the best shepherd: so doth it accord with good sleep.

Many honours I want not, nor great treasures: they excite the spleen. But it is bad sleeping without a good name and a little treasure.

A small company is more welcome to me than a bad one: but they must come and go at the right time. So doth it accord with good sleep.

Well, also, do the poor in spirit please me: they promote sleep. Blessed are they, especially if one always give in to them.

Thus passeth the day unto the virtuous. When night cometh, then take I good care not to

很少有人知道，但是一个人要想睡得好，就必须拥有所有的美德。我是不是会犯下伪造假目击证人的罪证？我是不是应该承认自己犯下了通奸罪？

我是不是应该垂涎一下我的邻居的女佣？所有的这一切都无法同良好的睡眠保持协调。

而且，即使一个人拥有了所有的美德，他还需要知道一件非常重要的事情：那就是在恰当的时间让这些美德入眠。

他们或许不会跟其他的事物发生争吵，那些受人怜爱的小爱宠啊！不和你发生争执，你这个不幸的家伙！

同上帝和你的邻居和平相处：这就是拥有良好睡眠的条件。同时还要跟你的邻居的恶魔和睦相处！否则，到了晚上，它就会萦绕在你的头顶。

尊敬政府，并且信服他们，即便是跛足的统治者，也是如此！这就是拥有良好睡眠的条件。如果力量要想用瘸腿走路，那么我还能怎么办呢？

他将自己的羊群引导到了最翠绿的牧场，他对于我来说，永远是最出色的牧羊人：只有这样才能同良好的睡眠之间保持协调。

我并不想要过多的荣誉以及伟大的财富：它们只会激发我的坏脾气。但是，人如果没有响当当的名字以及一点小小的财富的话，是不能安稳入睡的。

对于我来说，一个比较狭窄的朋友圈要比一个品性糟糕的朋友圈更能吸引我：但是它们必须在恰当的时间里出现并且离开。只有这样才能同良好的睡眠之间保持协调。

还有，那些精神白痴能够让我愉悦起来：他们有助于促进睡眠。尤其是当人们承认他们有理由的时候，他们是无比幸福的。

summon sleep. It disliketh to be summoned sleep, the lord of the virtues!

But I think of what I have done and thought during the day. Thus ruminating, patient as a cow, I ask myself: What were thy ten overcomings?

And what were the ten reconciliations, and the ten truths, and the ten laughters with which my heart enjoyed itself?

Thus pondering, and cradled by forty thoughts, it overtaketh me all at once sleep, the unsummoned, the lord of the virtues.

Sleep tappeth on mine eye, and it turneth heavy. Sleep toucheth my mouth, and it remaineth open.

Verily, on soft soles doth it come to me, the dearest of thieves, and stealeth from me my thoughts: stupid do I then stand, like this academic chair.

But not much longer do I then stand: I already lie.

When Zarathustra heard the wise man thus speak, he laughed in his heart: for thereby had a light dawned upon him. And thus spake he to his heart:

A fool seemeth this wise man with his forty thoughts: but I believe he knoweth well how to sleep.

Happy even is he who liveth near this wise man! Such sleep is contagious even through a thick wall it is contagious.

A magic resideth even in his academic chair. And not in vain did the youths sit before the preacher of virtue.

就这样，有道德的白天就这么过去了。当夜晚降临的时候，我并不会提醒自己去召唤睡眠。或许睡眠这一道德的统治者，并不喜欢被人们召唤！

但是，我会回想我在这一整天所干的事以及自己的想法。我会开始反复地思考，就像一头奶牛一样有耐心，我会问自己：你那十次的自我克制都是什么？

那十次心情舒畅、十次事实的真相以及十次让我发自内心的捧腹大笑，究竟是些什么呢？

我开始陷入沉思，在这四十个人的思想摇篮里来回晃荡，几乎是在一瞬间，那个未被召唤的、道德的统治者的睡眠将我抓住。

睡眠轻轻地拍打着我的双眼，之后，我的眼睛就变得沉重了起来。睡眠触碰着我的嘴唇，之后，我的嘴唇就张开了。

的确，它用非常轻柔的脚步，悄悄地接近了我，它是最可爱的小偷，它从我这里偷走了我的思想：然后，我就像个傻子一样站在这里，就好比这个书桌一样。

但是，我还没有站立多久之后：我就已经躺下来了。

当查拉图斯特拉听完智者说的这些话的时候，他打心眼里笑了起来：一束光芒照耀在他的身上。他用发自肺腑的情感说道：

这位智者所提出的四十个思想看上去非常愚蠢：但是我相信他知道应该如何安眠。

住在这位智者附近的人会感到无比幸运！类似这样的睡眠是有传染性的——即使是隔着一堵非常厚的墙壁，它仍然是具有传染性的。

他的学术讲座拥有着一种魔力。那些在道德的传教士面前聆听讲座的年轻人并非没有收获。

His wisdom is to keep awake in order to sleep well. And verily, if life had no sense, and had I to choose nonsense, this would be the desirablest nonsense for me also.

Now know I well what people sought formerly above all else when they sought teachers of virtue. Good sleep they sought for themselves, and poppy-head virtues to promote it!

To all those belauded sages of the academic chairs, wisdom was sleep without dreams: they knew no higher significance of life.

Even at present, to be sure, there are some like this preacher of virtue, and not always so honourable: but their time is past. And not much longer do they stand: there they already lie.

Blessed are those drowsy ones: for they shall soon nod to sleep.

Thus spake Zarathustra.

3. BACKWORLDSMEN

Once on a time, Zarathustra also cast his fancy beyond man, like all backworldsmen. The work of a suffering and tortured God, did the world then seem to me.

The dream and diction of a God, did the world then seem to me; coloured vapours before the eyes of a divinely dissatisfied one.

Good and evil, and joy and woe, and I and thou coloured vapours did they seem to me before creative eyes. The creator wished to look away from himself, thereupon he created the world.

他的智慧就是为了能够睡个好觉，要保持清醒的状态。真的，如果生活本就没有意义，我只能被迫选择谬论的时候，那么这或许就是我最想要选择的谬论了。

现在我知道了，当先人们在追求道德的良师的时候，他们究竟在寻找些什么。他们是在为自己寻找良好的睡眠以及麻醉性的道德！

所有受到称赞的学术讲座的智者之智慧，只不过是没有任何梦境的睡眠：他们对于生活重要性的理解并不比我们的高明。

我非常确定，即使是在现在，这个世界上还会存在一些类似这样的道德传教士，他们并不总是受到别人的尊敬：但是，属于他们的时代已经过去了。并且，他们还没有站立多久，就已经倒下去了。

那些昏昏欲睡的人会受到人们的祝福：因为，他们用不了多久就会睡着。

查拉图斯特拉如是说。

3．彼世论者

在很久以前，查拉图斯特拉也跟所有的遁世者一样，将自己的奇思妙想抛到人类的范畴以外去。在那时，我认为整个世界就是一个历经磨难的上帝所创造出来的产物。

那个时候，我认为整个世界就是一个上帝的梦想以及幻想；它是一个毫不满足的神放在眼前的五彩斑斓的烟雾。

善意以及邪恶，快乐和悲痛，我和你——在具有创造性的双眼看来，都是五彩斑斓的烟雾而已。那位创造者不想看到自己——因此，他创造了这个世界。

Intoxicating joy is it for the sufferer to look away from his suffering and forget himself. Intoxicating joy and self-forgetting, did the world once seem to me.

This world, the eternally imperfect, an eternal contradiction's image and imperfect image an intoxicating joy to its imperfect creator: thus did the world once seem to me.

Thus, once on a time, did I also cast my fancy beyond man, like all backworldsmen. Beyond man, forsooth?

Ah, ye brethren, that God whom I created was human work and human madness, like all the Gods!

A man was he, and only a poor fragment of a man and ego. Out of mine own ashes and glow it came unto me, that phantom. And verily, it came not unto me from the beyond!

What happened, my brethren? I surpassed myself, the suffering one; I carried mine own ashes to the mountain; a brighter flame I contrived for myself. And lo! Thereupon the phantom withdrew from me!

To me the convalescent would it now be suffering and torment to believe in such phantoms: suffering would it now be to me, and humiliation. Thus speak I to backworldsmen.

Suffering was it, and impotence that created all backworlds; and the short madness of happiness, which only the greatest sufferer experienceth.

Weariness, which seeketh to get to the ultimate with one leap, with a death-leap; a poor ignorant weariness, unwilling even to will any longer: that created all Gods and backworlds.

Believe me, my brethren! It was the body which despaired of the body it groped with the

历经磨难的人能够可以不看自己所遭受的痛苦，而忘却自己，这实在是一种令人如痴如醉的享受。曾经，这个世界对于我来说就是一个能让我如痴如醉的享受的世界。

这个世界，永远都不会是完美的，它拥有永恒的矛盾形象以及不完美的形象——这对于并非完美的创造者来说是一种令人如痴如醉的享受——曾经，我认为这个世界就是这个样子的。

所以，我也曾经和遁世者一样将我的奇思妙想抛到人类的范畴之外，可是，它真的被抛到人类的范畴之外了吗？

唉！我的兄弟们，我所创造出来的上帝，就如同其他所有的上帝一样，是人类的杰作，是人类的疯狂！

他是一个人，只是一个人和自我意识的可怜的一部分而已。那个鬼魂从灰烬和炽热的火焰中跑了出来，将闪耀的光芒照射在我的身上。真的，他不是天外来客！

我的兄弟们，到底发生了什么事情？我超越了自己，那个饱受磨难的家伙；我带着自己的灰烬去了山里；我为自己创造了更为明亮的火焰。瞧呀！那个鬼魂从我的体内脱离了出来！

在我看来，充分信任类似这样的鬼魂，对于大病初愈的人来说，是极其痛苦的：对于我来说，是磨难和羞辱。因此，我对遁世者说。

痛苦和无能——创造了所有其他的世界；快乐的短暂疯狂，只有那些拥有最为悲痛的经历的人才能感受到。

厌倦要想用一跳，死亡跳跃来达到最后的终结；一个可怜的、无知的厌倦，它甚至都不再想要拥有意志：那个创造了所有诸神和世界的意志。

fingers of the infatuated spirit at the ultimate walls.

Believe me, my brethren! It was the body which despaired of the earth it heard the bowels of existence speaking unto it.

And then it sought to get through the ultimate walls with its head and not with its head only into "the other world."

But that "other world" is well concealed from man, that dehumanised, inhuman world, which is a celestial naught; and the bowels of existence do not speak unto man, except as man.

Verily, it is difficult to prove all being, and hard to make it speak. Tell me, ye brethren, is not the strangest of all things best proved?

Yea, this ego, with its contradiction and perplexity, speaketh most uprightly of its being this creating, willing, evaluing ego, which is the measure and value of things.

And this most upright existence, the ego it speaketh of the body, and still implieth the body, even when it museth and raveth and fluttereth with broken wings.

Always more uprightly learneth it to speak, the ego; and the more it learneth, the more doth it find titles and honours for the body and the earth.

A new pride taught me mine ego, and that teach I unto men: no longer to thrust one's head into the sand of celestial things, but to carry it freely, a terrestrial head, which giveth meaning to the earth!

A new will teach I unto men: to choose that path which man hath followed blindly, and to

我的兄弟们，请相信我！这是肉体对肉体感到了绝望——它用令人着迷的精神的手指在终极的墙壁上摸索着。

我的兄弟们，请相信我！这是肉体对这片土地感到了绝望——它听到了存在的内脏在跟它说话。

然后，它想用自己的头穿过这坚实的终极墙壁——不仅仅是头，它想让自己的整个躯体都进入到“其他的世界”中去。

但是，那个“其他的世界”绝妙地隐藏在人们的视线之外，那个丧失人性、极其残忍的世界，它只不过是天际的空虚；存在的内脏无法跟人们进行沟通，除非它变成人类的形态。

说真的，用证据去证实它的存在，或是让它开口说话，都是极为困难的。

我的兄弟们，请你们告诉我，你们不认为最稀奇古怪的事情就是被证明的最好的事情吗？

是的，这样的我，这个有创造性、有意志和衡量事物价值的我，它的矛盾性以及纷繁复杂的状态，用最正直的方式肯定了它的存在。

这种最为正直的存在，这个“我”——即便是在思考问题时、狂躁时、扑闪着破碎的羽翼飞翔的时候，也会谈及肉体以及需要肉体。

这个“我”随时随地都在学习诚实地讲话；而且它学得越多，就越会找到赞美肉体和大地的诗句。

一个全新的自豪教给了我这个“我”，而我又将这个“我”教给了人类；不要将人的脑袋塞进天际的沙子里面，而是要自由自在地带着这个陆地上的脑袋，这个给予了创

approve of it and no longer to slink aside from it, like the sick and perishing!

The sick and perishing it was they who despised the body and the earth, and invented the heavenly world, and the redeeming blood-drops; but even those sweet and sad poisons they borrowed from the body and the earth!

From their misery they sought escape, and the stars were too remote for them. Then they sighed: "O that there were heavenly paths by which to steal into another existence and into happiness!" Then they contrived for themselves their by-paths and bloody draughts!

Beyond the sphere of their body and this earth they now fancied themselves transported, these ungrateful ones. But to what did they owe the convulsion and rapture of their transport? To their body and this earth.

Gentle is Zarathustra to the sickly. Verily, he is not indignant at their modes of consolation and ingratitude. May they become convalescents and overcomers, and create higher bodies for themselves!

Neither is Zarathustra indignant at a convalescent who looketh tenderly on his delusions, and at midnight stealeth round the grave of his God; but sickness and a sick frame remain even in his tears.

Many sickly ones have there always been among those who muse, and languish for God; violently they hate the discerning ones, and the latest of virtues, which is uprightness.

Backward they always gaze toward dark ages: then, indeed, were delusion and faith something different. Raving of the reason was likeness to God, and doubt was sin.

造大地的意义的脑袋！

我教给了人类一个全新的意志：选择一条人类会盲目跟从的道路，确信这条路是正确的——而不要像生病的人以及即将逝去的人一样，悄无声息地离开它！

那些生病的人以及即将逝去的人——他们蔑视肉体和这片大地，他们发明了神圣的世界和用来赎罪的血滴；但是，这些甜蜜的、令人感到悲伤的毒药，是他们从肉体和大地那里借来的！

他们想从悲痛中逃离出来，行星离他们太过遥远了。然后，他们叹着气说道："真是可悲啊！为什么没有一条天路，能够让我们偷偷地溜到另一个世界和另一个幸福里呢！"于是，他们给自己创造了旁门左道和血腥的饮品。

他们自以为已经摆脱了肉体和这片大地，他们这些忘恩负义的家伙。到底是谁在他们摆脱的时候，给予了他们惊厥和欣喜若狂呢？正是他们的肉体和这片大地。

查拉图斯特拉对待患病的人是非常仁慈的。真的，他并不会对他们自我安慰的方式，或是忘恩负义的态度感到极其愤慨。他们或许会成为逐渐从疾病中痊愈的人，克服重重困难的人，并且为自己创造更加高级的躯体！

查拉图斯特拉对于刚刚痊愈的人也是非常宽厚的，他并不会对那些盯着幻想牢牢不放，半夜起来去他的上帝的坟墓里偷窃的人感到恼羞成怒；但是他为这些痊愈者留下的眼泪，包含着一种身体疾病的状态或是一种病态。

在那些无声祷告、为神而心力交瘁的人群中间，往往夹杂着大量身体有疾病的人；他们极端痛恨有极强的辨别能力的人，憎恨那些最近得道、坦诚的人。

他们经常回顾过去非常黑暗的历史时期：很显然，那时候的假象和信仰都是有所不

Too well do I know those godlike ones: they insist on being believed in, and that doubt is sin. Too well, also, do I know what they themselves most believe in.

Verily, not in backworlds and redeeming blood-drops: but in the body do they also believe most; and their own body is for them the thing-in-itself.

But it is a sickly thing to them, and gladly would they get out of their skin. Therefore hearken they to the preachers of death, and themselves preach backworlds.

Hearken rather, my brethren, to the voice of the healthy body; it is a more upright and pure voice.

More uprightly and purely speaketh the healthy body, perfect and square-built; and it speaketh of the meaning of the earth.

Thus spake Zarathustra.

4. THE DESPISERS OF THE BODY

To the despisers of the body will I speak my word. I wish them neither to learn afresh, nor teach anew, but only to bid farewell to their own bodies, and thus be dumb.

"Body am I, and soul" so saith the child. And why should one not speak like children?

But the awakened one, the knowing one, saith: "Body am I entirely, and nothing more; and soul is only the name of something in the body."

The body is a big sagacity, a plurality with one sense, a war and a peace, a flock and a

同的。理智的混乱与上帝极为相像，对它表示怀疑就是一种罪恶。

我对这些酷似上帝的人颇为了解：他们坚持相信这些观点，并且认为凡是怀疑这些观点的想法都是一种罪恶。与此同时，我心里也非常清楚他们最相信的到底是什么。

说真的，那些不是什么另一个世界，也不是什么用来赎罪的血滴：他们最相信的依旧是他们的肉体；他们把自身的肉体视作是绝无仅有的产物。但是，肉体对于他们来说仍旧是一种非常病态的事物，如果能从自己的肉体之中摆脱出来，他们将会欣喜若狂。因此，他们会去聆听死亡的传教士，而他们自身又在讲演着另一个世界。

我的兄弟们，让我们聆听健康的躯体的声音吧；这是更加正直、更加纯粹的声音。

健康、体格匀称的躯体，说话会显得更加正直、更加纯粹；那是一种能够阐述大地存在的意义的声音。

查拉图斯特拉如是说。

4．肉体的蔑视者

我有一些话，想要说给那些肉体的轻蔑者听。我并不希望他们重新学习，我只是要求他们能够告别自己的肉体——并且因此而成为哑巴。

“我就是肉体和灵魂”——孩子会这么说。为什么我们就不能像小孩子一样说话呢？

但是，觉醒的人以及有觉悟的人说道：“我的全身都是肉体，没有别的东西；灵魂只是我们肉体中某一个物体的名称。”

我们的肉体是一种具有大智慧，单一意义的复杂体，既是战争，也是和平，既是羊

shepherd.

An instrument of thy body is also thy little sagacity, my brother, which thou callest "spirit" a little instrument and plaything of thy big sagacity.

"Ego," sayest thou, and art proud of that word. But the greater thing in which thou art unwilling to believe is thy body with its big sagacity; it saith not "ego," but doeth it.

What the sense feeleth, what the spirit discerneth, hath never its end in itself. But sense and spirit would fain persuade thee that they are the end of all things: so vain are they.

Instruments and playthings are sense and spirit: behind them there is still the Self. The Self seeketh with the eyes of the senses, it hearkeneth also with the ears of the spirit.

Ever hearkeneth the Self, and seeketh; it compareth, mastereth, conquereth, and destroyeth. It ruleth, and is also the ego's ruler.

Behind thy thoughts and feelings, my brother, there is a mighty lord, an unknown sage it is called Self; it dwelleth in thy body, it is thy body.

There is more sagacity in thy body than in thy best wisdom. And who then knoweth why thy body requireth just thy best wisdom?

Thy Self laugheth at thine ego, and its proud prancings. "What are these prancings and flights of thought unto me?" it saith to itself. "A by-way to my purpose. I am the leading-string of the ego, and the prompter of its notions."

The Self saith unto the ego: "Feel pain!" And thereupon it suffereth, and thinketh how it may put an end thereto and for that very purpose it is meant to think.

群，也是牧羊人。

我的兄弟们，我们的肉体当中拥有一个工具，它同样也是一种小小的智慧，你们管这种工具叫“精神”——这是一种小小的工具，但却在你的肉体里扮演着非常聪慧的角色。

你经常会说“我”，并且视这个称呼为自己的骄傲。但是，更加伟大的是——可是你却不愿意去相信——你的肉体以及陪伴着它的大智慧，它不会轻言“我”，而是为“我”付诸行动。

所有感官能感受到的，所有精神能够辨别出来的，从来都没有任何的目的。但是，感官和精神会乐此不疲地说服你相信他们是世间万物的终结：他们是如此的虚荣。

感官和精神就是工具和玩物：在它们的身后，仍旧存在着“自己”，这个存在的“自己”会运用感官的眼睛，同样也会运用精神的耳朵。

“自己”经常进行聆听和寻找，它会去比较、掌握、征服和毁灭。它会被统治，同时它也是“我”的统治者。

我的兄弟们，在你们的思想和感觉背后，存在着一位拥有无比强大的力量的领袖，一位不为人熟知的圣人——那就是“自己”；它就居住在你的肉体里，它就是你的肉体。

隐藏在你的肉体内的理智要多于你的最高智慧当中的理智。谁能够知道为什么你的肉体需要你的最高智慧呢？

你的“自己”在嘲笑你的“我”以及令它引以为傲的跳跃。“对于我来说，这些思想的跳跃和飞翔究竟是些什么东西呢？”我对“自己”说道。“那只是我为了达到目标而走的旁门左道！我是‘我’的极限，也是‘我’的一切观念的敦促者。”

那个“自己”对“我”说道：“感受一点痛苦吧！”因此，“我”开始遭受痛苦的

The Self saith unto the ego: "Feel pleasure!" Thereupon it rejoiceth, and thinketh how it may ofttimes rejoice and for that very purpose it is meant to think.

To the despisers of the body will I speak a word. That they despise is caused by their esteem. What is it that created esteeming and despising and worth and will?

The creating Self created for itself esteeming and despising, it created for itself joy and woe. The creating body created for itself spirit, as a hand to its will.

Even in your folly and despising ye each serve your Self, ye despisers of the body. I tell you, your very Self wanteth to die, and turneth away from life.

No longer can your Self do that which it desireth most: create beyond itself. That is what it desireth most; that is all its fervour.

But it is now too late to do so: so your Self wisheth to succumb, ye despisers of the body.

To succumb so wisheth your Self; and therefore have ye become despisers of the body. For ye can no longer create beyond yourselves.

And therefore are ye now angry with life and with the earth. And unconscious envy is in the sidelong look of your contempt.

I go not your way, ye despisers of the body! Ye are no bridges for me to the Superman!

Thus spake Zarathustra.

洗礼，并且思考究竟应该如何才能摆脱痛苦——它必然会为了这一目的而进行思考。

那个“自己”对“我”说道：“感受一点快乐吧！”因此，“我”开始感受到快乐，并且思考究竟该如何才能经常感受到快乐——它必然会为了这一目的而进行思考。

我想对那些肉体的轻蔑者说一些话。让他们尽情地轻蔑肉体吧！这正是他们出于对自尊心的尊敬。究竟是谁创造了尊敬、轻蔑，价值以及意志呢？

具有创造力的“自己”为自己创造了尊敬和轻蔑，还为自己创造了快乐和悲伤。具有创造力的肉体为自己创造了精神，以此作为它的意志之手。

你们这些肉体的轻蔑者，即便是在你们的癫狂和蔑视之中，你们也是为了“自己”而服务，让我来告诉你们，你们的“自己”要想死亡，了结自己的生命。

你们的“自己”再也不能做出最想做的事情：——创造超出自己的范畴的事物。这就是它最渴求、最诚挚的希望。

不过，现在说什么都已经来不及了：——所以，你们这些肉体的轻蔑者啊！你们的“自己”想要进行自我毁灭。

因为，你们的“自己”想要进行自我毁灭。因此，你们就成为了肉体的轻蔑者。所以，你们再也无法创造出超过自身范畴的事物来了。

因此，你们现在会对生命和这片大地感到非常愤怒。而且一种无意识的嫉妒出现在了你们那充满轻蔑的神情之中。

你们这些肉体的轻蔑者啊！我才不会重走你们的老路！你们并不是为我成为超人而铺设的桥梁！

查拉图斯特拉如是说。

5. JOYS AND PASSIONS

My brother, when thou hast a virtue, and it is thine own virtue, thou hast it in common with no one.

To be sure, thou wouldst call it by name and caress it; thou wouldst pull its ears and amuse thyself with it.

And lo! Then hast thou its name in common with the people, and hast become one of the people and the herd with thy virtue!

Better for thee to say: "Ineffable is it, and nameless, that which is pain and sweetness to my soul, and also the hunger of my bowels."

Let thy virtue be too high for the familiarity of names, and if thou must speak of it, be not ashamed to stammer about it.

Thus speak and stammer: "That is my good, that do I love, thus doth it please me entirely, thus only do I desire the good.

Not as the law of a God do I desire it, not as a human law or a human need do I desire it; it is not to be a guide-post for me to superearths and paradises.

An earthly virtue is it which I love: little prudence is therein, and the least everyday wisdom.

But that bird built its nest beside me: therefore, I love and cherish it now sitteth it beside me on its golden eggs."

Thus shouldst thou stammer, and praise thy virtue.

5. 快乐与热情

我的兄弟们，当你们拥有一种美德的时候，而且它就是你们所特有的美德，你就不能和任何人共同拥有它。

的确，你用名字称呼它，并且爱抚它；你拉扯它的耳朵，同它一起做好玩的游戏。

但是，瞧啊！一旦它拥有了你所称呼它的名字，并且同其他人一起共同拥有它的时候，你就会因为这种道德而成为人群和普通人之中的一员！

你大可以这么说："这种让我的灵魂变得既痛苦又甜蜜的东西是无法用语言来形容的，同时，我的内心的饥饿是无名的。"

让你的道德高贵到无法用亲密的名称来称呼，如果你非要说出那样的名字来，那么就不要感到羞耻，你可以结结巴巴地说。

你可以结结巴巴地说："这是我最重视的善意，它可以最大限度地让我感到快乐，所以，我所渴求的正是这样的善意。

我渴求它，并不是因为它是上帝的法律，也不是因为它是人类的法律，或是人类的需求；它绝对不是通向另一个世界和蓝天的指南。

我热爱它是一种陆地上的道德：它缺乏谨慎，更加缺少智慧。

但是，小鸟在我的身边筑巢：因此，我会热爱它，珍视它——现在，它就坐在金灿灿的蛋上，陪伴在我的身边。"

你应该用这种结结巴巴的口吻说，并且赞美你的道德。

Once hadst thou passions and calledst them evil. But now hast thou only thy virtues: they grew out of thy passions.

Thou implantedst thy highest aim into the heart of those passions: then became they thy virtues and joys.

And though thou wert of the race of the hot-tempered, or of the voluptuous, or of the fanatical, or the vindictive;

All thy passions in the end became virtues, and all thy devils angels.

Once hadst thou wild dogs in thy cellar: but they changed at last into birds and charming songstresses.

Out of thy poisons brewedst thou balsam for thyself; thy cow, affliction, milkedst thou now drinketh thou the sweet milk of her udder.

And nothing evil groweth in thee any longer, unless it be the evil that groweth out of the conflict of thy virtues.

My brother, if thou be fortunate, then wilt thou have one virtue and no more: thus goest thou easier over the bridge.

Illustrious is it to have many virtues, but a hard lot; and many a one hath gone into the wilderness and killed himself, because he was weary of being the battle and battlefield of virtues.

My brother, are war and battle evil? Necessary, however, is the evil; necessary are the envy and the distrust and the back-biting among the virtues.

Lo! how each of thy virtues is covetous of the highest place; it wanteth thy whole spirit to be

曾经，你拥有很多激情，并且你称它们为恶魔。但是，现在你只拥有你的道德：它们正是从你过去的激情里产生出来的。

那么，将你最崇高的目标注入那些激情的内心之中：然后，它们就会成为你的道德和快乐。

尽管你属于脾气暴躁的，或是骄奢淫逸的，或是过分狂热的，又或是报复心重的种族；但是到了最后，你所有的激情都会成为道德，所有的恶魔都会成为天使。

曾经，你的地窖里拥有许多未驯化的野狗：但是，最终它们都变成了小鸟和散发着魅力的女歌手。

你使用毒药为自己制作了止痛药；曾经，你挤出过磨难之牛的乳汁——现在，你饮用着从奶牛的乳头里挤出来的甘甜的奶水。

你的身体之中不会再产生任何的恶魔，除非那是从你的道德的争斗中产生出来的恶魔。

我的兄弟们，如果你是非常幸运的，那么，你只需拥有一种道德就足够了，没必要再拥有其他的道德：因此，你穿过桥梁就会变得更加容易一些。

能够拥有许多道德是非常卓越的事，但是，那也是一种让人难以忍受的命运；许多人因为厌倦了多种道德在战场上进行争斗，而跑到荒野，亲手了结自己的性命。

我的兄弟们，我问问你们，战争和争斗是邪恶的吗？不过，这是必要的邪恶；在道德之中，嫉妒、不信任以及在背后诋毁他人的存在都是必不可少的。

看呀！你的每一种道德最渴求的事情都是些什么？它想让你的整个精神成为它的传令官，它想要你的怒火、仇恨以及爱意当中的全部力量。

its herald, it wanteth thy whole power, in wrath, hatred, and love.

Jealous is every virtue of the others, and a dreadful thing is jealousy. Even virtues may succumb by jealousy.

He whom the flame of jealousy encompasseth, turneth at last, like the scorpion, the poisoned sting against himself.

Ah! my brother, hast thou never seen a virtue backbite and stab itself?

Man is something that hath to be surpassed: and therefore shalt thou love thy virtues, for thou wilt succumb by them.

Thus spake Zarathustra.

6. THE PALE CRIMINAL

Ye do not mean to slay, ye judges and sacrificers, until the animal hath bowed its head? Lo! the pale criminal hath bowed his head: out of his eye speaketh the great contempt.

"Mine ego is something which is to be surpassed: mine ego is to me the great contempt of man": so speaketh it out of that eye.

When he judged himself that was his supreme moment; let not the exalted one relapse again into his low estate!

There is no salvation for him who thus suffereth from himself, unless it be speedy death.

Your slaying, ye judges, shall be pity, and not revenge; and in that ye slay, see to it that ye

任何一种道德都会对其他的道德产生嫉妒的心理，嫉妒是一种非常可怕的事情。甚至道德本身都有可能会被嫉妒所毁灭。

他那包含着嫉妒的烈焰，会像蝎子一样，最终将含有剧毒的毒针转向自己。

噢！我的兄弟们，你们还从来都没有见过一种道德的诽谤和自我伤害吧？

人类是一种应该被超越的物种，因此，你应该相当珍视你的道德——因为，你很有可能会因为它们而被毁灭。

查拉图斯特拉如是说。

6. 苍白的罪犯

你们这些法官和祭司们，在祭品没有低下头，乖乖就范之前，你们肯定不愿意进行杀戮吧？瞧呀！苍白的罪犯低下了他的头：他的眼神中流露出无比轻蔑的神情。

“我的这个‘我’是应该被超越的：我的这个‘我’对于我来说，是人类的最大的蔑视。”：罪犯的眼睛如此说道。

当他评判自己的时候，便是他至高无上的时刻；我们不能让高贵的人再一次下降到他的低下的地位中去！

像他这样因为自己而遭受痛苦的人来说，除了速死之外，没有任何方法可以拯救他。

你们这些法官们，你们的杀戮应该是出于内心的同情，而不是复仇；你们在杀人的时候，还得时刻留意要为生命进行辩护！

你们仅通过和被你们杀戮的人和解是远远不够的。将你们的悲痛转化成对超人的爱

yourselves justify life!

It is not enough that ye should reconcile with him whom ye slay. Let your sorrow be love to the Superman: thus will ye justify your own survival!

"Enemy" shall ye say but not "villain," "invalid" shall ye say but not "wretch," "fool" shall ye say but not "sinner."

And thou, red judge, if thou would say audibly all thou hast done in thought, then would every one cry: "Away with the nastiness and the virulent reptile!"

But one thing is the thought, another thing is the deed, and another thing is the idea of the deed. The wheel of causality doth not roll between them.

An idea made this pale man pale. Adequate was he for his deed when he did it, but the idea of it, he could not endure when it was done.

Evermore did he now see himself as the doer of one deed. Madness, I call this: the exception reversed itself to the rule in him.

The streak of chalk bewitcheth the hen; the stroke he struck bewitched his weak reason. Madness after the deed, I call this.

Hearken, ye judges! There is another madness besides, and it is before the deed. Ah! ye have not gone deep enough into this soul!

Thus speaketh the red judge: "Why did this criminal commit murder? He meant to rob." I tell you, however, that his soul wanted blood, not booty: he thirsted for the happiness of the knife!

But his weak reason understood not this madness, and it persuaded him. "What matter about

意吧：因此，你们就会为你们自己的幸存而辩护！

你们应该称呼他们为“敌人”而不是叫他们“恶棍”；你们应该称呼他们为“残废者”而不是叫他们“流氓”；你们应该称呼他们为“傻子”而不是叫他们“罪人”。

你，这个红色的法官，如果你高调地把你脑子里所想要做的事情，统统说出来的话，那么每一个聆听者都会高呼：“除去这些令人作呕的污秽以及拥有剧毒的毒蛇吧！”

但是，思想和行动本来就是截然不同的两种事，而行动的思想是另一种相异的事情。因果关系之轮并不会在它们之间进行翻滚。一种想法会让这个苍白之人的脸色变得苍白。当他进行犯罪的时候，他就完全具有犯罪的能力，可是，当他完成犯罪之后，他又无法忍受这种犯罪的思想。

从这一刻开始，他会永远将自己视为一个单一行为的实施者。我管这种行为叫做疯狂：特殊的例子会在他的身上转变成原则。

用粉笔描绘出来的线条，可以迷惑母鸡；这无比沉重的一击，迷惑了他那脆弱的理智。我管这种行为叫做事情发生之后的疯狂。

听听吧！你们这些法官们！此外还有另一种疯狂，那就是事情发生之前的疯狂。唉！你们研究这种灵魂的程度还不够深！

因此，红色的法官说道：“为什么这个罪犯会犯下杀人的罪行？他的本意只是抢劫而已啊。”但是，让我来亲自告诉你吧，他的灵魂想要的是鲜血，而不是赃物：他对小刀之幸福是如此的渴望！

但是，他那脆弱的理智并不能理解这种疯狂，而且说服他进行这样的行动。“鲜血有什么价值可言！”它说道，“你为什么不趁着这个大好机会，至少掠夺一点战利品？

blood!" it said; "wishest thou not, at least, to make booty thereby? Or take revenge?"

And he hearkened unto his weak reason: like lead lay its words upon him thereupon he robbed when he murdered. He did not mean to be ashamed of his madness.

And now once more lieth the lead of his guilt upon him, and once more is his weak reason so benumbed, so paralysed, and so dull.

Could he only shake his head, then would his burden roll off; but who shaketh that head?

What is this man? A mass of diseases that reach out into the world through the spirit; there they want to get their prey.

What is this man? A coil of wild serpents that are seldom at peace among themselves so they go forth apart and seek prey in the world.

Look at that poor body! What it suffered and craved, the poor soul interpreted to itself it interpreted it as murderous desire, and eagerness for the happiness of the knife.

Him who now turneth sick, the evil overtaketh which is now the evil: he seeketh to cause pain with that which causeth him pain. But there have been other ages, and another evil and good.

Once was doubt evil, and the will to Self. Then the invalid became a heretic or sorcerer; as heretic or sorcerer he suffered, and sought to cause suffering.

But this will not enter your ears; it hurteth your good people, ye tell me. But what doth it matter to me about your good people!

或是复仇呢？”

他听从了他脆弱的理智的话：他所说过的话就像是铝一样盘旋在他的头顶之上——因此，当他杀了人之后，他就顺便进行了掠夺。他并不愿意因为自己的疯狂而感到羞愧。

现在，他的过失之旅再一次压在了他的肩膀上，他脆弱的理智再一次变得麻木、变得麻痹、变得迟钝。

他唯一能做的就是摇晃着他的脑袋，然后，他就能把压在肩上的负担甩掉；但是，有谁会摇晃他的脑袋呢？

这个人到底是谁？大量的疾病通过精神的力量来到了这个世界；它们来到这里是想要获得它们的猎物。

这个人到底是谁？他是一串互相缠绕、很少和睦相处的野生毒蛇——所以，它们纷纷四散开来，来到这个世界寻找它们的猎物。

快看看这个可怜的肉体吧！它遭受痛苦，并且抱有希望，可怜的灵魂想去了解它们——它们会被理解为具有杀人动机的需求以及对小刀的幸福的渴望。

现在，患有疾病的人会受到当今邪恶因素的打击，他在寻求将给自己造成痛苦的因素转嫁给其他的人，并且给其他的人也带来同样的痛苦的方式。但是，曾经这里也有过其他的时代，拥有过其他的善意和邪恶。

曾经，怀疑以及个人的意志都被看做是邪恶的事物。然后，无能的人就会成为异教徒或是巫师；作为异教徒或是巫师，他会遭受磨难，并且寻求造成磨难的方式。

但是，这样的意志并不会走进你的耳朵里；你告诉我，它会伤害你们那些充满善意的人们。但是，你们那些充满善意的人们到底跟我有什么关系呢！

你们那些所谓的充满善意的人们，拥有许多让我心生怀疑的事情，而且说实话，那

Many things in your good people cause me disgust, and verily, not their evil. I would that they had a madness by which they succumbed, like this pale criminal!

Verily, I would that their madness were called truth, or fidelity, or justice: but they have their virtue in order to live long, and in wretched self-complacency.

I am a railing alongside the torrent; whoever is able to grasp me may grasp me! Your crutch, however, I am not.

Thus spake Zarathustra.

7. READING AND WRITING

Of all that is written, I love only what a person hath written with his blood. Write with blood, and thou wilt find that blood is spirit.

It is no easy task to understand unfamiliar blood; I hate the reading idlers.

He who knoweth the reader, doeth nothing more for the reader. Another century of readers and spirit itself will stink.

Every one being allowed to learn to read, ruineth in the long run not only writing but also thinking.

Once spirit was God, then it became man, and now it even becometh populace.

He that writeth in blood and proverbs doth not want to be read, but learnt by heart.

并不是他们邪恶的一面。我只是希望他们能够拥有一种疯狂，让他们像这位苍白的罪犯一样被毁灭！

说真的，我希望他们的疯狂被称为真相，或是忠诚，又或是正义：但是，他们为了能够活得更加长久，而拥有自己的道德，在悲哀的自鸣得意中成长。

我就是水流旁边的栏杆；只要是有能力抓住我的人，就牢牢地抓住我吧！不过，我不是你们的拐杖。

查拉图斯特拉如是说。

7. 阅读和写作

所有关于写作的东西，我只喜爱那些作者用自己的心血创作出来的东西。用血来写作，你就会发现那种血就是精神。

去理解不为人所熟知的血并不是一项简单的任务；我讨厌所有通过阅读来打发时间的人。

对读者了如指掌的作者，不会给读者创作作品。在另一个世纪里，这样的读者——还有精神会散发出招人厌恶的恶臭。

所有被允许学习阅读的人，在长期的学习过程之中，不仅仅会毁掉写作，同时也会毁掉思考。

曾经，精神就是上帝，然后，它变成了人，现在，它甚至变成了人民群众。

那些作者用自己的心血和箴言写出来的东西，并不想被其他人拿来阅读，而是让人类拿来用心去铭记。

In the mountains the shortest way is from peak to peak, but for that route thou must have long legs. Proverbs should be peaks, and those spoken to should be big and tall.

The atmosphere rare and pure, danger near and the spirit full of a joyful wickedness: thus are things well matched.

I want to have goblins about me, for I am courageous. The courage which scareth away ghosts, createth for itself goblins it wanteth to laugh.

I no longer feel in common with you; the very cloud which I see beneath me, the blackness and heaviness at which I laugh that is your thunder-cloud.

Ye look aloft when ye long for exaltation; and I look downward because I am exalted.

Who among you can at the same time laugh and be exalted?

He who climbeth on the highest mountains, laugheth at all tragic plays and tragic realities.

Courageous, unconcerned, scornful, coercive so wisdom wisheth us; she is a woman, and ever loveth only a warrior.

Ye tell me, "Life is hard to bear." But for what purpose should ye have your pride in the morning and your resignation in the evening?

Life is hard to bear: but do not affect to be so delicate! We are all of us fine sumpter asses and assesses.

What have we in common with the rose-bud, which trembleth because a drop of dew hath formed upon it?

It is true we love life; not because we are wont to live, but because we are wont to love.

山峰和山峰之间最短的距离就是两个山峰顶点之间的距离，但是，如果你想采用这样的路线，你必须拥有足够长的腿。格言应该算是山峰的顶点，而听从这些格言的聆听者们应当是伟大高耸的。

稀有并且纯粹的空气，时刻面临着危险，精神里充满了快乐的邪恶：所有的这一切都是彼此匹配的。

我想让妖怪把我团团围住，因为我是个很有胆量的人。这种胆量可以吓退鬼魂，而且可以为自己创造妖怪——这种胆量需要大笑。

我的感觉不再跟你们的感觉有任何的相同之处；我笑话处于我下方云朵的黑暗和笨重——那就是你的雷雨云。

当你们渴望被高高抬起来的时候，你们仰着脑袋看，但是，我却在朝下看，因为我在高处。

在你们当中，有谁能够做到在大笑的同时，处于高处？

那个攀登上了最高耸的山峰的人，笑看所有悲痛的戏剧和残酷的现实。

用胆量、无忧无虑、轻蔑的、暴虐的——智慧教导我们如是；智慧是一位女士，她只热爱战士。

你们告诉我，“生命是难以承受的重负”。那么究竟是什么原因让你们在清晨骄傲自满，在夜晚卑躬屈膝呢？

生命是难以承受的重负：不要摆出那种撒娇的姿态！我们都是驮着沉重的负担的驮马。我们和那些在一滴露珠的压迫下而震颤的红色花蕾，到底有什么相同之处呢？

我们热爱生命一点也没有错：但是我们热爱它并不是因为我们习惯于生活，而是因

There is always some madness in love. But there is always, also, some method in madness.

And to me also, who appreciate life, the butterflies, and soap-bubbles, and whatever is like them amongst us, seem most to enjoy happiness.

To see these light, foolish, pretty, lively little sprites flit about that moveth Zarathustra to tears and songs.

I should only believe in a God that would know how to dance.

And when I saw my devil, I found him serious, thorough, profound, solemn: he was the spirit of gravity through him all things fall.

Not by wrath, but by laughter, do we slay. Come, let us slay the spirit of gravity!

I learned to walk; since then have I let myself run. I learned to fly; since then I do not need pushing in order to move from a spot.

Now am I light, now do I fly; now do I see myself under myself. Now there danceth a God in me.

Thus spake Zarathustra.

8. THE TREE ON THE HILL

Zarathustra's eye had perceived that a certain youth avoided him. And as he walked alone one evening over the hills surrounding the town called "The Pied Cow," behold, there found he the youth sitting leaning against a tree, and gazing with wearied look into the valley.

为我们习惯于爱。

在爱意中，往往会拥有一些疯狂。但是，在爱意的疯狂当中也时常拥有 些理智。

对于我这个非常热爱生命的人来说，我认为蝴蝶、肥皂泡泡以及所有在人世间同它们拥有相似特征的事物似乎是最能享受幸福的。

当查拉图斯特拉看到这些愚笨、漂亮、生动的小精灵的时候——他被感动的哭泣了起来，并且唱起了歌。

我应该只信仰一个懂得该如何跳舞的上帝。

当我看到我的恶魔的时候，我发现他非常严肃、一丝不苟、深沉、庄重：这是一种具有严重性的精神——在它的渗透下，任何事物都会倒下。

我们去杀戮，并不是因为愤怒的指使，而是因为笑容。快来吧！让我们尽情地杀戮严重的精神吧！

我学会了走路；从那个时候开始，我就让我自己奔跑。我学会了飞翔；从那个时候开始，我不会因为为了更换位置，而事先逼迫自己。

现在我是如此的轻薄，现在我能够自由地翱翔；现在我看到我在自己的上方。现在一个上帝正在我的身上跳舞。

查拉图斯特拉如是说。

8．山上的树

查拉图斯特拉的双眼已经感受到某些年轻人正在尽量地避开他。有一天晚上，他独

Zarathustra thereupon laid hold of the tree beside which the youth sat, and spake thus:

"If I wished to shake this tree with my hands, I should not be able to do so.

But the wind, which we see not, troubleth and bendeth it as it listeth. We are sorest bent and troubled by invisible hands."

Thereupon the youth arose disconcerted, and said: "I hear Zarathustra, and just now was I thinking of him!" Zarathustra answered:

"Why art thou frightened on that account? But it is the same with man as with the tree.

The more he seeketh to rise into the height and light, the more vigorously do his roots struggle earthward, downward, into the dark and deep into the evil."

"Yea, into the evil!" cried the youth. "How is it possible that thou hast discovered my soul?"

Zarathustra smiled, and said: "Many a soul one will never discover, unless one first invent it."

"Yea, into the evil!" cried the youth once more.

"Thou saidst the truth, Zarathustra. I trust myself no longer since I sought to rise into the height, and nobody trusteth me any longer; how doth that happen?

I change too quickly: my to-day refuteth my yesterday. I often overleap the steps when I clamber; for so doing, none of the steps pardons me.

When aloft, I find myself always alone. No one speaketh unto me; the frost of solitude maketh me tremble. What do I seek on the height?

My contempt and my longing increase together; the higher I clamber, the more do I despise

自一人走在一座将被称为“彩色的牛”的村庄包围起来的山峰脚下，他注视着这里，他发现这儿有年轻人倚着一棵树坐了下来，并且用无比疲倦的神情凝视着村庄。因此，查拉图斯特拉将自己的注意力都放在了那颗被年轻人倚靠的树上面，于是，查拉图斯特拉说道：“如果我要用我自己的双手摇晃这棵树的话，我可能摇不动。

但是，我们没法看到风，却能够随心所欲地摇晃它弯曲它。同样的，我们会被无形的手所弯曲所摇晃。”

就在这个时候，年轻人一脸疑惑地站了起来，他说道：“我听到查拉图斯特拉的讲话了，而且就在刚才我还想过他呢！”查拉图斯特拉回答道：“为什么你要如此的担惊受怕？——人和树都是一样的。

它越想寻求变得更高，变得更轻，它的树根就会越向地下、下面生长，潜入漆黑的深处，潜入到恶魔的深处。”

“是啊，潜入到恶魔的深处！”年轻人大叫道，“那么，你是怎么发现我的灵魂的？”

查拉图斯特拉微笑着说道：“许多灵魂除非是在一开始就被创造出来，否则它永远都不会被人发现。”

“是的，潜入到了恶魔的深处！”那个年轻人再一次大叫了起来。

“查拉图斯特拉，你所说的真相。自从我想让自己变得高大的时候，我就不再相信我自己了，并且没有任何人再相信我了；这样的情况是怎么发生的呢？

我的改变太快了：我的今天正在反驳我的昨天。我经常在攀爬的时候，跳过好几个台阶，因为我这样做，没有任何一个台阶会宽恕我。

当我上升的时候，我发现自己是孤独的。没有人能跟我说说话：孤独寂寞的霜冻让

him who clambereth. What doth he seek on the height?

How ashamed I am of my clambering and stumbling! How I mock at my violent panting! How I hate him who flieth! How tired I am on the height!"

Here the youth was silent. And Zarathustra contemplated the tree beside which they stood, and spake thus:

"This tree standeth lonely here on the hills; it hath grown up high above man and beast.

And if it wanted to speak, it would have none who could understand it: so high hath it grown.

Now it waiteth and waiteth, for what doth it wait? It dwelleth too close to the seat of the clouds; it waiteth perhaps for the first lightning?"

When Zarathustra had said this, the youth called out with violent gestures: "Yea, Zarathustra, thou speakest the truth. My destruction I longed for, when I desired to be on the height, and thou art the lightning for which I waited! Lo! what have I been since thou hast appeared amongst us? It is mine envy of thee that hath destroyed me!" Thus spake the youth, and wept bitterly. Zarathustra, however, put his arm about him, and led the youth away with him.

And when they had walked a while together, Zarathustra began to speak thus:

It rendeth my heart. Better than thy words express it, thine eyes tell me all thy danger.

As yet thou art not free; thou still seekest freedom. Too unslept hath thy seeking made thee, and too wakeful.

我疯狂地震颤。我追求这样的高度究竟是为了什么？

我的尝试和我的渴求凝聚在了一起：我攀爬得越高，我就会越看不起那个攀爬的人。他追求那样的高度究竟是为了什么呢？

我对我的攀爬和我的磕磕碰碰感到无比的羞愧！我是如何模仿我那粗重的喘气声的！我是如何痛恨那个飞翔的他的！我是如何在那样的高度之下感到疲惫的！"

这时候，那个年轻人沉默了。查拉图斯特拉静静地注视着这棵在年轻人旁边的树，然后，他说道：

"这棵树孤零零地耸立在这座山上面；它必将成长为非常高耸，能够超越人类和动物的高度的大树。

如果它想说话，那么它所说的话，没有任何人能够听得懂，因为它生长得实在是太高了。

现在，它一直都在等待、等待——那么，它究竟在等待什么呢？它所生活的地方太过于接近天空中的云朵了；它或许在等待天空中的第一道闪电？"

当查拉图斯特拉说完这些话的时候，那个年轻人用非常猛烈的手势说道："是的，查拉图斯特拉，你所说的话都是真相，我之所以寻求那样的高度，就是因为我想要让自己衰落，而你正是我所等待的那所谓的第一道闪电！你可以看看我，自从你来到了我们的中间之后，我都变成了什么？正是我出于对你的嫉妒，将我彻底摧毁了！"——那个少年如是说，并且哭得稀里哗啦的。但是，查拉图斯特拉把他的胳膊放在他身上，将他带走了。

当他们两个人在一起走了一会儿之后，查拉图斯特拉开始对他说：

它撕扯着我的心脏。你的目光所阐述着的你所经历的所有危险要比你用语言表达的清楚得多。

On the open height wouldst thou be; for the stars thirsteth thy soul. But thy bad impulses also thirst for freedom.

Thy wild dogs want liberty; they bark for joy in their cellar when thy spirit endeavoureth to open all prison doors.

Still art thou a prisoner it seemeth to me who deviseth liberty for himself: ah! sharp becometh the soul of such prisoners, but also deceitful and wicked.

To purify himself, is still necessary for the freedman of the spirit. Much of the prison and the mould still remaineth in him: pure hath his eye still to become.

Yea, I know thy danger. But by my love and hope I conjure thee: cast not thy love and hope away!

Noble thou feelest thyself still, and noble others also feel thee still, though they bear thee a grudge and cast evil looks. Know this, that to everybody a noble one standeth in the way.

Also to the good, a noble one standeth in the way: and even when they call him a good man, they want thereby to put him aside.

The new, would the noble man create, and a new virtue. The old, wanteth the good man, and that the old should be conserved.

But it is not the danger of the noble man to turn a good man, but lest he should become a blusterer, a scoffer, or a destroyer.

Ah! I have known noble ones who lost their highest hope. And then they disparaged all high hopes.

你还没有获得自由，你仍旧在寻求自由。长时间的找寻让你如同一个时刻保持清醒不睡觉的人一样。

你想去自由自在的高处，因为天上的繁星渴望你的灵魂。但是你那非常恶劣的本能同样也在渴求自由。

你的野狗也想要自由；当你的精神试图打开所有监狱的房门的时候，它们就会因为高兴而在房间里狂叫。

在我看来，你仍然是一名囚犯——他为自己创造了自由：唉！类似这样的囚犯的灵魂会变得敏捷，同时还会变得阴险狡猾和邪恶。

净化自身，对于精神的自由民来说，仍然是必不可少的步骤。绝大部分的禁锢和污垢仍旧保留在他的体内：他的双眼也会变得清澈。

是的，我了解你的危险。不过，凭借着我的爱和我的希望，我恳求你：不要让你的爱和希望溜掉！

倘若你仍旧感觉自己非常高贵，并且感觉到别人也同样认为你很高贵，尽管他们嫉妒你，还纷纷向你投来邪恶的眼神。你要知道，对于任何一个人来说，一个高贵的人必定会被视为前进道路上的障碍。

同样的，高贵的人也会成为善良之物的障碍，一个高贵的人会成为前进道路上的障碍物：甚至，当高贵的人称他为善良的人的时候，他们也会将他放在一边，置之不理。

高贵的人会创造出全新的事物，和全新的道德。而善良的人们却需要古老的事物，并且要将这些古老的事物保存起来。

不过，高贵之人的危险之处，并不在于他可以将自己变成一个善良的人，而是，他

Then lived they shamelessly in temporary pleasures, and beyond the day had hardly an aim.

"Spirit is also voluptuousness," said they. Then broke the wings of their spirit; and now it creepeth about, and defileth where it gnaweth.

Once they thought of becoming heroes; but sensualists are they now. A trouble and a terror is the hero to them.

But by my love and hope I conjure thee: cast not away the hero in thy soul! Maintain holy thy highest hope!

Thus spake Zarathustra.

9. THE PREACHERS OF DEATH

There are preachers of death: and the earth is full of those to whom desistance from life must be preached.

Full is the earth of the superfluous; marred is life by the many-too-many. May they be decoyed out of this life by the "life eternal"!

"The yellow ones": so are called the preachers of death, or "the black ones." But I will show them unto you in other colours besides.

There are the terrible ones who carry about in themselves the beast of prey, and have no choice except lusts or self-laceration. And even their lusts are self-laceration.

会成为一个大声咆哮的人、嘲笑者，或是一名毁灭者。

唉！我已经知道高贵的人失去了他们最高的希望。并且他们开始污蔑所有的崇高希望。

然后在短暂的快乐当中，他们过起了丝毫不知廉耻、完全没有任何目标计划的生活。

“精神同样也是一种骄奢淫逸的状态。”——他们说道。然后，他们破坏了他们的精神之翼；现在，他们在地上爬行着，弄脏所有啃咬着他们的东西。

曾经，他们认为自己变成了英雄；但是，他们现在却是一群好色之徒。对于他们来说，一个麻烦、一种恐惧也是英雄。

但是，凭借着我的爱和我的希望，我恳求你：不要将你的灵魂驱逐出你的体外！保持你那份神圣的、最崇高的希望！——

查拉图斯特拉如是说。

9．死亡的说教者

有的人是死亡的说教者：同时，在这个世界上存在着许多应该被劝说放弃生命的人。

这个世界上充满了多余的人；生命已经遭受了严重过剩的人口的损害。但愿人们能够被称为“永恒的生命”这一诱饵，引导着离开这个生命！

“穿着黄袍的人”或是“穿着蓝袍的人”：他们就是所谓的死亡的说教者。但是我将要向你们展示他们身上的其他颜色。

这些令人感到胆寒的家伙，拥有着无比野蛮的兽心，他们除了强烈的欲望和自我损害之外，别无选择。甚至，他们强烈的欲望就是自我损害。

They have not yet become men, those terrible ones: may they preach desistance from life, and pass away themselves!

There are the spiritually consumptive ones: hardly are they born when they begin to die, and long for doctrines of lassitude and renunciation.

They would fain be dead, and we should approve of their wish! Let us beware of awakening those dead ones, and of damaging those living coffins!

They meet an invalid, or an old man, or a corpse and immediately they say: "Life is refuted!"

But they only are refuted, and their eye, which seeth only one aspect of existence.

Shrouded in thick melancholy, and eager for the little casualties that bring death: thus do they wait, and clench their teeth.

Or else, they grasp at sweetmeats, and mock at their childishness thereby: they cling to their straw of life, and mock at their still clinging to it.

Their wisdom speaketh thus: "A fool, he who remaineth alive; but so far are we fools! And that is the foolishest thing in life!"

"Life is only suffering": so say others, and lie not. Then see to it that ye cease! See to it that the life ceaseth which is only suffering!

And let this be the teaching of your virtue: "Thou shalt slay thyself! Thou shalt steal away from thyself!"

"Lust is sin," so say some who preach death "let us go apart and beget no children!"

他们还没有变成人类，那些令人感到胆寒的家伙们：但愿他们能够被劝说放弃生命，就此离去吧！

他们就是灵魂的消耗者：当他们刚刚降临到这个世界上的时候，他们就已经开始走向死亡了，并且他们渴求疲倦懒散和放弃权力的教条。

他们会欣然接受自己行将死亡的现实，并且我们应该承认他们的希望！让我们小心提防，阻止死去的家伙被唤醒，或者毁坏这些活生生的棺材！

他们遇见了一个无能的人，或是一位老人，或是一具尸体——他们会立刻说道："生命是被推翻的。"

但是，真正被推翻的是他们自己，还有他们那双只能看到存在的其中一个方面的眼睛。

如果他们在阴沉、忧郁的环境下生活，并且渴求会带来死亡的小小风险，他们就会咬紧牙关，苦苦等待。

或者是，他们会伸手去拿糖果，并且嘲笑自己的孩子气：他们会紧紧抓牢将生命全部悬在上面的稻草，并且嘲笑自己仍然在那个稻草上面。

因此，他们的智慧说道："那些仍旧活在世上的人都是傻子，但是，从目前来看，我们都是傻子！而这是人的生命中最傻的事！"

"生命之中只有痛苦"：别人如是说，这些并不是什么谎言。那么，我恳请你们停止生活吧！当生活只剩下痛苦的时候，我恳请你们停止生活吧！

让这些成为你的道德的教训："你应该杀害自己！你应该将自己偷去！"

"强烈的欲望是一种罪恶，"一些说教的人如是说——"让我们就此离去吧，不要

"Giving birth is troublesome," say others "why still give birth? One beareth only the unfortunate!" And they also are preachers of death.

"Pity is necessary," so saith a third party. "Take what I have! Take what I am! So much less doth life bind me!"

Were they consistently pitiful, then would they make their neighbours sick of life. To be wicked that would be their true goodness.

But they want to be rid of life; what care they if they bind others still faster with their chains and gifts!

And ye also, to whom life is rough labour and disquiet, are ye not very tired of life? Are ye not very ripe for the sermon of death?

All ye to whom rough labour is dear, and the rapid, new, and strange ye put up with yourselves badly; your diligence is flight, and the will to self-forgetfulness.

If ye believed more in life, then would ye devote yourselves less to the momentary. But for waiting, ye have not enough of capacity in you nor even for idling!

Everywhere resoundeth the voices of those who preach death; and the earth is full of those to whom death hath to be preached.

Or "life eternal"; it is all the same to me if only they pass away quickly!

Thus spake Zarathustra.

再生育孩子了！”

“孕育生命是相当麻烦的事，”第二批人说道，“当孕育生命的人注定承担不幸的命运，那么还会有谁去孕育生命！”他们同样也是死亡的说教者。

“拥有怜悯的情感是必要的，”第三批人说道，“拿走关于我的一切物品吧！拿走我自己的身体吧！我和生命之间的联系将会越来越少。”

如果他们能够始终如一地保持怜悯的情感，那么他们就会让周围的邻居们开始厌恶生命。为了恶——将是他们真正的善意。

但是，他们想要摆脱生命，如果他们的锁链和礼物，能够用更快的速度绑紧其他人，他们又该怎么顾及呢?

而对于你们来说，你们的生命是粗重的劳动和永不停歇，你们就没有厌倦生命吗?你们是不是已经足够成熟可以接受死亡的说教了呢?

你们都喜欢充满繁重的体力劳动的生活以及快速、崭新并且奇特的事物——你们对于自己的生活已经忍无可忍；你们的勤奋只不过是想要进行自忘的逃避和意志而已。

如果你对生活抱有更多的信仰，你便不会在那一瞬间奉献你自己。不过，你的自身并没有足够的能力——所以你不能等待，甚至就连消磨时光也不行!

那些传教死亡的人的声音在四周回荡着；而这个世界上充满了应该被劝说放弃生命的人。

或是“永恒的生命”：这些对于我来说都是一样的——只要他们能够快点离开这里！

查拉图斯特拉如是说。

10. WAR AND WARRIORS

By our best enemies we do not want to be spared, nor by those either whom we love from the very heart. So let me tell you the truth!

My brethren in war! I love you from the very heart. I am, and was ever, your counterpart. And I am also your best enemy. So let me tell you the truth!

I know the hatred and envy of your hearts. Ye are not great enough not to know of hatred and envy. Then be great enough not to be ashamed of them!

And if ye cannot be saints of knowledge, then, I pray you, be at least its warriors. They are the companions and forerunners of such saintship.

I see many soldiers; could I but see many warriors! "Uniform" one calleth what they wear; may it not be uniform what they therewith hide!

Ye shall be those whose eyes ever seek for an enemy for your enemy. And with some of you there is hatred at first sight.

Your enemy shall ye seek; your war shall ye wage, and for the sake of your thoughts! And if your thoughts succumb, your uprightness shall still shout triumph thereby!

Ye shall love peace as a means to new wars and the short peace more than the long.

You I advise not to work, but to fight. You I advise not to peace, but to victory. Let your work be a fight, let your peace be a victory!

One can only be silent and sit peacefully when one hath arrow and bow; otherwise one

10. 战争与战士

我们绝不希望我们最好的敌人宽恕我们，也不愿意让我们心中的挚爱宽恕我们。所以让我来告诉你们事实的真相！

我的那些正在作战的兄弟们！我发自内心地爱着你们。我曾经一度是你们的伙伴。与此同时，我也是你们最好的敌人。所以让我来告诉你们事实的真相吧！

我非常了解你们内心当中的仇恨和嫉妒。你们还没有优秀到能够理解仇恨和嫉妒的程度。那么，你们也就没有足够优秀，会为它们感到无比羞耻！

如果你不能成为知识的圣人，那么，我恳求你，至少成为知识的战士吧！他们会是这些圣人的伴侣和先驱。我看见过许多战士；让我看到许多战士吧！他们身上穿的衣服被人们称为“军装”；而隐藏在他们里面的，就不是军装而已了！

你们应该是那些永远用目光去寻找一名敌人的人——属于你们的敌人。你们当中的某些人，在看到第一眼的时候，心中应该会充满仇恨。

你们应该寻找敌人，你们应该发动战争，为了你们的思想而殊死拼搏！如果你们的思想被毁灭了，那么，你们的忠诚仍然要高呼胜利！

你们应该热爱和平，因为它是未来战争的一种手段——你们应该投入更多的精力去热爱短暂的和平而不是长久的和平。

我不会给你们的工作提出建议，但是我会给你们的战斗提出建议。我不会给你们的和平提出建议，但是我会给你们的胜利提出建议。让你们的工作成为一种战斗，让你们

prateth and quarrelleth. Let your peace be a victory!

Ye say it is the good cause which halloweth even war? I say unto you: it is the good war which halloweth every cause.

War and courage have done more great things than charity. Not your sympathy, but your bravery hath hitherto saved the victims.

"What is good?" ye ask. To be brave is good. Let the little girls say: "To be good is what is pretty, and at the same time touching."

They call you heartless: but your heart is true, and I love the bashfulness of your goodwill. Ye are ashamed of your flow, and others are ashamed of their ebb.

Ye are ugly? Well then, my brethren, take the sublime about you, the mantle of the ugly!

And when your soul becometh great, then doth it become haughty, and in your sublimity there is wickedness. I know you.

In wickedness the haughty man and the weakling meet. But they misunderstand one another. I know you.

Ye shall only have enemies to be hated, but not enemies to be despised. Ye must be proud of your enemies; then, the successes of your enemies are also your successes.

Resistance that is the distinction of the slave. Let your distinction be obedience. Let your commanding itself be obeying!

To the good warrior soundeth "thou shalt" pleasanter than "I will." And all that is dear unto you, ye shall first have it commanded unto you.

的和平成为一场胜利！

你们说，好的主张甚至能够将战争神圣化？让我来告诉你们：是伟大的战争能够将任何的主张神圣化。

战争和勇气所做的伟大的事迹要比慈善做的还要多。不是你们的同情心，而是你们的勇敢拯救了许多牺牲者。

“什么才是好的呢？”你们问道。勇敢就是好的。小女孩们说：

“美丽动人，并且能够感人至深就是好的。”

他们都抱怨你们没有勇气：但是你们的内心是真实的，我热爱你们善意的腼腆。你们为自己的缺点而感到羞愧，而其他人会为他们的衰落感到惭愧。

你们是丑陋的吗？那么，我的兄弟们，将崇高的丑陋斗篷披在你们的身上吧！

当你们的灵魂变得伟大，变得骄傲自满，在你们的崇高当中，拥有着邪恶。我了解你们。

在邪恶之中，骄傲自满的人会碰上心理软弱的人。但是，他们会彼此误解对方。我了解你们。

你们应该只拥有被仇恨的敌人，而不能拥有被轻视的敌人。你们必须为你们的敌人感到骄傲；并且，要将你们敌人的胜利看做是自己的胜利。

抵抗——这就是和奴役的差别所在。让你们的抵抗成为服从。让你们的命令也成为服从吧！

一个伟大的战士更加喜欢听“你们应该”而不是“我想要”。所有你们所钟爱的事物，你们应该首先让别人下达命令，再给你们。

Let your love to life be love to your highest hope; and let your highest hope be the highest thought of life!

Your highest thought, however, ye shall have it commanded unto you by me and it is this: man is something that is to be surpassed.

So live your life of obedience and of war! What matter about long life! What warrior wisheth to be spared!

I spare you not, I love you from my very heart, my brethren in war!

Thus spake Zarathustra.

11. THE NEW IDOL

Somewhere there are still peoples and herds, but not with us, my brethren: here there are states.

A state? What is that? Well! open now your ears unto me, for now will I say unto you my word concerning the death of peoples.

A state, is called the coldest of all cold monsters. Coldly lieth it also; and this lie creepeth from its mouth: "I, the state, am the people."

It is a lie! Creators were they who created peoples, and hung a faith and a love over them: thus they served life.

Destroyers, are they who lay snares for many, and call it the state: they hang a sword and a

让你们对生活的热爱变成对你们最崇高的希望的热爱；让你们最崇高的希望成为你们生活当中最崇高的思想！

但是，你们最崇高的思想，应该是在我的命令下统治你们——就是这样：人类就是一种注定要被超越的事物。

所以，你们过着服从和战争的生活吧！活得长久有什么意义吗！哪个战士想要得到宽恕呢！

我不会宽恕你们，我发自内心地爱着你们，我的那些浴血沙场的兄弟们！

查拉图斯特拉如是说。

11．新偶像

我的兄弟们，有些地方直到现在都还拥有民族和种群，但那些地方绝不是我们这里，我们这里只拥有国家。

一个国家？国家是什么东西？好吧！现在，打开你的耳朵好好听我说，从现在开始，我将会跟你说一些关于民族的衰亡的事例。

一个国家，被人们称为是所有冷酷的怪兽之中最为冷酷无情的。他还会冷酷地说谎；这就是从他的嘴里爬出来的谎话：“我，国家，就是民族。”

这就是一个谎言！他们创造了民族，并且为他们高高地悬挂了一种信仰和一种爱，他们是创造者，他们为生命服务。

毁灭者会给许多人放下陷阱，并且管这些陷阱叫做国家：他们会在他们的头上悬挂

hundred cravings over them.

Where there is still a people, there the state is not understood, but hated as the evil eye, and as sin against laws and customs.

This sign I give unto you: every people speaketh its language of good and evil: this its neighbour understandeth not. Its language hath it devised for itself in laws and customs.

But the state lieth in all languages of good and evil; and whatever it saith it lieth; and whatever it hath it hath stolen.

False is everything in it; with stolen teeth it biteth, the biting one. False are even its bowels.

Confusion of language of good and evil; this sign I give unto you as the sign of the state. Verily, the will to death, indicateth this sign! Verily, it beckoneth unto the preachers of death!

Many too many are born: for the superfluous ones was the state devised!

See just how it enticeth them to it, the many-too-many! How it swalloweth and cheweth and recheweth them!

"On earth there is nothing greater than I: it is I who am the regulating finger of God" thus roareth the monster. And not only the long-eared and short-sighted fall upon their knees!

Ah! even in your ears, ye great souls, it whispereth its gloomy lies! Ah! it findeth out the rich hearts which willingly lavish themselves!

Yea, it findeth you out too, ye conquerors of the old God! Weary ye became of the conflict, and now your weariness serveth the new idol!

Heroes and honourable ones, it would fain set up around it, the new idol! Gladly it basketh

一把剑和一百种欲望。

只要是这个地方仍旧存在着民族，那么国家在这里就是不被人所理解的，他们会痛恨它，视它为邪恶的眼睛以及抵抗法律和传统的罪恶。

我将这些标志统统给你：每一个民族都拥有属于自己的包含善与恶的语言：这样的语言即使是他们的邻居也是没有办法理解的。任何一个民族都是在它们的法律和传统的习俗中发明了这样的语言。

但是，国家会利用一切善与恶的语言说谎；它们说的任何话都是谎言，它们所拥有的一切都是偷来的。

任何事物都有虚假的一面；我将这些被看做是一种状态的标志给你。说真的，这样的标志表明了一心求死的意志！真的，它能吸引死亡的说教者！

数不胜数的人来到了这个世界：国家就是为了这些多余的人而被创造出来的！让我们来看看，它是如何来诱使这些多余的人口的！看看它是如何吞噬他们、啃咬他们以及消化他们的！

噢！在这个世界上，没有任何事物要比我还要伟大：我就是那个控制上帝的手指的人——这些怪物咆哮着，跪了下来，不仅仅是长耳朵、眼光短浅的人！

唉！对于你们这些耳朵和伟大的灵魂啊！它们在轻声向你们诉说着阴暗的谎言！唉！它们发现了这些心甘情愿浪费的富有的心灵！

是的，它们也发现了你，你们是古老的上帝的征服者！你们厌倦成为矛盾的冲突对象，现在，你们的厌倦心理要为新的偶像服务！

它心甘情愿受到英雄们和那些备受人们崇敬的人们的统领，新的偶像！它非常乐意

in the sunshine of good consciences, the cold monster!

Everything will it give you, if ye worship it, the new idol: thus it purchaseth the lustre of your virtue, and the glance of your proud eyes.

It seeketh to allure by means of you, the many-too-many! Yea, a hellish artifice hath here been devised, a death-horse jingling with the trappings of divine honours!

Yea, a dying for many hath here been devised, which glorifieth itself as life: verily, a hearty service unto all preachers of death!

The state, I call it, where all are poison-drinkers, the good and the bad: the state, where all lose themselves, the good and the bad: the state, where the slow suicide of all is called "life."

Just see these superfluous ones! They steal the works of the inventors and the treasures of the wise. Culture, they call their theft and everything becometh sickness and trouble unto them!

Just see these superfluous ones! Sick are they always; they vomit their bile and call it a newspaper. They devour one another, and cannot even digest themselves.

Just see these superfluous ones! Wealth they acquire and become poorer thereby. Power they seek for, and above all, the lever of power, much money these impotent ones!

See them clamber, these nimble apes! They clamber over one another, and thus scuffle into the mud and the abyss.

Towards the throne they all strive: it is their madness as if happiness sat on the throne!

将自己沐浴在伟大的良心的日光之中——这个冷酷的怪兽！

如果你们愿意去崇拜它的话，它就会把所有的事物都给你们，这个新的偶像：它会购买你那充满了光亮的道德光泽以及骄傲的眼神凝视。

它想通过你的方式引诱那些多余的应该被劝说放弃生命的人！是的，它发明了一种地狱般的阴谋诡计，一匹死掉的骏马，配着拥有神圣荣誉的，叮当作响的马鞍！

是的，它决定了很多人的死亡，它自身就像生命一样熠熠生辉的死亡：说真的，它对于死亡的说教者来说，是一种非常伟大的功绩。

我管它叫国家，所有喝毒药的人，无论是好人还是坏人：这个国家里面的所有人全都迷失了自己，无论是好人还是坏人：这个国家，是广大人民群众的慢性自杀——它被称为“生命”。

让我们快来看看这些多余的人群！他们偷走了创造者的作品以及聪明的人留下来的宝藏。文化，他们管这些叫偷窃——并且对于他们来说，任何的事物都会变成脆弱和麻烦！

让我们快来看看这些多余的人群！他们往往非常虚弱；他们大口地吐着胃液，然后管这个叫做报纸。他们彼此之间互相吞噬，他们甚至不能消化掉对方。

让我们快来看看这些多余的人群！他们越是富有，最后就会变得越是贫穷。他们寻找的是力量，一种凌驾于所有力量之上的力量以及数不清的金钱——这些都是非常重要的东西！

快看看他们攀爬，他们这些手脚灵活的猴子们！他们彼此之间互相攀爬，并且互相扭打着掉进了泥浆和深渊里。

他们所有人都想无限接近梦寐以求的权位：这就是他们的疯狂——在他们眼里，就

Ofttimes sitteth filth on the throne. and ofttimes also the throne on filth.

Madmen they all seem to me, and clambering apes, and too eager. Badly smelleth their idol to me, the cold monster: badly they all smell to me, these idolaters.

My brethren, will ye suffocate in the fumes of their maws and appetites! Better break the windows and jump into the open air!

Do go out of the way of the bad odour! Withdraw from the idolatry of the superfluous!

Do go out of the way of the bad odour! Withdraw from the steam of these human sacrifices!

Open still remaineth the earth for great souls. Empty are still many sites for lone ones and twain ones, around which floateth the odour of tranquil seas.

Open still remaineth a free life for great souls. Verily, he who possesseth little is so much the less possessed: blessed be moderate poverty!

There, where the state ceaseth there only commenceth the man who is not superfluous: there commenceth the song of the necessary ones, the single and irreplaceable melody.

There, where the state ceaseth pray look thither, my brethren! Do ye not see it, the rainbow and the bridges of the Superman?

Thus spake Zarathustra.

好像幸福就坐在那个权位之上！然而，坐在权位上面的往往只是泥土而已。——皇帝的座位往往也在泥土里面。

在我看来，他们全都是疯狂的人，攀爬的猴子以及热情过度的人。他们不过就是散发着恶臭的偶像，这些冷酷的怪兽：对于我来说，他们的身上散发着非常恶心的腐臭味。

我的兄弟们，你们愿意在他们用嘴呼出的香气和食欲中窒息而死吗？

我奉劝你们最好打破窗户，跳进户外的空气之中！

最好离那些令人感到作呕的气味远一点！快点逃离这些多余的偶像吧！

最好离那些令人感到作呕的气味远一点！快点逃离这些人类牺牲的雾气吧！

伟大的灵魂仍旧可以在这片大地上自由自在的生活。现在仍旧有许多地方，那些热爱隐居的人士，可以独自一人或是成群结伴地隐藏在这里，在这样的地方，到处漂浮着宁静的海洋的香气。

伟大的灵魂仍然可以享受自由自在的生活。说真的，一个人如果占有的东西越少，那么他被占有的东西也就越少：适度的贫穷是会受到祝福的！

这里，就是国家灭亡的地方——这里只有不多余的人才能存在下来：必要之人的歌声，那独一无二、无法替换的悠扬旋律才会开始。

这里，就是国家灭亡的地方——我的兄弟们！抬起头看吧！你们没有看到彩虹和超人之桥吗？

查拉图斯特拉如是说。

12. THE FLIES IN THE MARKET-PLACE

Flee, my friend, into thy solitude! I see thee deafened with the noise of the great men, and stung all over with the stings of the little ones.

Admirably do forest and rock know how to be silent with thee. Resemble again the tree which thou lovest, the broad-branched one silently and attentively it o'erhangeth the sea.

Where solitude endeth, there beginneth the market-place; and where the market-place beginneth, there beginneth also the noise of the great actors, and the buzzing of the poison-flies.

In the world even the best things are worthless without those who represent them: those representers, the people call great men.

Little do the people understand what is great that is to say, the creating agency. But they have a taste for all representers and actors of great things.

Around the devisers of new values revolveth the world: invisibly it revolveth. But around the actors revolve the people and the glory: such is the course of things.

Spirit, hath the actor, but little conscience of the spirit. He believeth always in that wherewith he maketh believe most strongly in himself!

Tomorrow he hath a new belief, and the day after, one still newer. Sharp perceptions hath he, like the people, and changeable humours.

12. 市场之蝇

我的朋友，快快逃到你的孤独中去吧！我看到你因为伟大人物发出的喧嚣而感到颇为苦恼，并且被小人物的钉刺螫伤了。

森林和岩石清楚地知道应该如何庄严地寂静地陪伴在你的身边。再一次，模仿你最钟爱的那棵树吧！那棵拥有宽大树枝的大树——它寂静地、专心致志的在海上聆听。

当一个地方的孤独停止了，那么这里就会出现市场；而且当这个地方出现市场之后，这里就会出现伟大的表演者的噪声以及毒蝇的嗡嗡声。

在这个世界上，即使是最完美的事物，如果没有表演者把它呈现出来，那么它也是毫无价值的。那些将事物呈现出来的人，被群众称为伟大的人。

人们并不知道什么才是伟大——也就是说，他们根本不清楚什么是创造。但是他们都能细细地品味所有呈现大事情的表演者。

这个世界围绕着创造了新价值的人们旋转——用无形的方式进行旋转。而人民群众和光辉会围绕着这些表演者旋转：整个世界就是这样运行的。

表演者也有精神，但是他们的精神缺乏知觉。他总是信任能够让他获得好结果的一切，并且让别人充分相信他的一切！

明天，他就会拥有一种新的信仰，在明天之后，他又会拥有一种更加崭新的信仰。他就跟群众一样，拥有敏锐的感觉以及不稳定的性情。

为了混淆视听，这就是他想去证明的。令人抓狂——这就是他想让人信服的。并且，

To upset that meaneth with him to prove. To drive mad that meaneth with him to convince. And blood is counted by him as the best of all arguments.

A truth which only glideth into fine ears, he calleth falsehood and trumpery. Verily, he believeth only in Gods that make a great noise in the world!

Full of clattering buffoons is the market-place, and the people glory in their great men! These are for them the masters of the hour.

But the hour presseth them; so they press thee. And also from thee they want Yea or Nay. Alas! thou wouldst set thy chair betwixt For and Against?

On account of those absolute and impatient ones, be not jealous, thou lover of truth! Never yet did truth cling to the arm of an absolute one.

On account of those abrupt ones, return into thy security: only in the market-place is one assailed by Yea? or Nay?

Slow is the experience of all deep fountains: long have they to wait until they know what hath fallen into their depths.

Away from the market-place and from fame taketh place all that is great: away from the market-Place and from fame have ever dwelt the devisers of new values.

Flee, my friend, into thy solitude: I see thee stung all over by the poisonous flies. Flee thither, where a rough, strong breeze bloweth!

Flee into thy solitude! Thou hast lived too closely to the small and the pitiable. Flee from their invisible vengeance! Towards thee they have nothing but vengeance.

鲜血对于他来说可以算作是所有论证中最好的论据。一个真相，如果只能悄然进入聪慧的耳朵，那么他会认为那是虚假和华而不实的东西。说真的，他只相信那些能够在这个世界上制造伟大的噪音的上帝！

市场上充满了发出喧闹声的丑角，而群众则以这些伟大的人为荣！将他们看做是当今世界的主人。

但是，当今的世界向他们施压，所以他们就会向你们施加压力。并且他们会让你道出“是”或是“不是”。唉！你会把你的凳子摆放在服从以及抵抗之间吗？

啊！你们这些热爱真理的人们，不要嫉妒那些绝对并且毫无耐心的人啊！真相从来就没有挽过一个绝对之人的臂膀。

快快远离那些鲁莽无礼的人，回到你的现实的世界中去吧：一个人只有在市场的环境下才会受到“是”或是“不是”的猛烈攻击？

缓慢是所有幽深的喷泉的经验之谈：它们会苦苦地等待，直到它们知道了掉入到下面的东西是什么。

一切伟大的事物，都是在远离市场，并且远离荣耀的情况下才会发生的：全新的价值的创造者只有在远离市场和荣耀的情况之下才会孕育而生。

我的朋友们，快点逃到你们的孤独中去吧：我看到你们被拥有剧毒的苍蝇蜇遍全身。快点逃到猛烈的暴风肆虐的地方去吧！

快点逃到你们的孤独中去吧！你们所过的生活距离小东西和可怜虫实在是太近了。快点逃离它们看不见的复仇吧！它们接近你的目的只有一个，那就是复仇。

不要再抬起一只胳膊反抗它们了！它们的数量实在是太多了，而你的命运最多也不

Raise no longer an arm against them! Innumerable are they, and it is not thy lot to be a fly-flap.

Innumerable are the small and pitiable ones; and of many a proud structure, rain-drops and weeds have been the ruin.

Thou art not stone; but already hast thou become hollow by the numerous drops. Thou wilt yet break and burst by the numerous drops.

Exhausted I see thee, by poisonous flies; bleeding I see thee, and torn at a hundred spots; and thy pride will not even upbraid.

Blood they would have from thee in all innocence; blood their bloodless souls crave for and they sting, therefore, in all innocence.

But thou, profound one, thou sufferest too profoundly even from small wounds; and ere thou hadst recovered, the same poison-worm crawled over thy hand.

Too proud art thou to kill these sweet-tooths. But take care lest it be thy fate to suffer all their poisonous injustice!

They buzz around thee also with their praise: obtrusiveness, is their praise. They want to be close to thy skin and thy blood.

They flatter thee, as one flattereth a God or devil; they whimper before thee, as before a God or devil. What doth it come to! Flatterers are they, and whimperers, and nothing more.

Often, also, do they show themselves to thee as amiable ones. But that hath ever been the prudence of the cowardly. Yea! the cowardly are wise!

过是个苍蝇拍而已。

这些小东西和可怜虫的数量非常之多；许多拥有令人为之自豪的大楼，会被从天而降的雨滴和地里的杂草毁掉。

你并不是石头；但是，数不胜数的雨滴已经将你击空了。在这些雨点的击打下，你会破碎，并且爆炸。

我看到，你在毒蝇的骚扰下，已经精疲力竭；我看到你的身上出现了一百个小红点，那些红点正在流血；你的傲慢甚至让你完全不在乎被责骂。

它们在完全不顾及任何后果的情况下，吸食你的鲜血；鲜血正是它们无血的灵魂所渴求的东西——因此，它们会义无反顾地叮咬。

但是，深沉的你，即使是比较小的伤口，也会让你遭受到非常巨大的伤痛；并且在你还没有完全恢复正常的情况下，那些拥有剧毒的动物们就又会爬上了你的手。

我知道你太过于骄傲自满，不会亲手杀害这些贪吃的动物。但是你要时刻注意，别让自己的命运遭受到它们拥有剧毒的不公正！

它们嗡嗡地盘旋在你的周围，对你夸夸其谈：给你带来巨大的困扰就是它们的赞美。它们想接近你的皮肤和你的鲜血。

它们在你的面前阿谀奉承，就像它们在一个上帝或是恶魔的面前阿谀奉承一样：它们在你的面前哭泣，就像它们在一个上帝或是恶魔的面前哭泣一样。这实在是太没有意思了！它们就是一些会阿谀奉承和哭诉的家伙，除此之外它们什么也不是。

它们还经常在你的面前展现出自己和蔼可亲的一面。但是，这是胆小鬼的审慎。是的！胆小鬼们都是聪明的人！他们用他们受到限制的灵魂，思考着你，你总是受到他们的怀疑，

They think much about thee with their circumscribed souls thou art always suspected by them! Whatever is much thought about is at last thought suspicious.

They punish thee for all thy virtues. They pardon thee in their inmost hearts only for thine errors.

Because thou art gentle and of upright character, thou sayest: "Blameless are they for their small existence." But their circumscribed souls think: "Blamable is all great existence."

Even when thou art gentle towards them, they still feel themselves despised by thee; and they repay thy beneficence with secret maleficence.

Thy silent pride is always counter to their taste; they rejoice if once thou be humble enough to be frivolous.

What we recognise in a man, we also irritate in him. Therefore be on your guard against the small ones!

In thy presence they feel themselves small, and their baseness gleameth and gloweth against thee in invisible vengeance.

Sawest thou not how often they became dumb when thou approachedst them, and how their energy left them like the smoke of an extinguishing fire?

Yea, my friend, the bad conscience art thou of thy neighbours; for they are unworthy of thee. Therefore they hate thee, and would fain suck thy blood.

Thy neighbours will always be poisonous flies; what is great in thee that itself must make them more poisonous, and always more fly-like.

任何让人多想的事物，到最后都会遭到人们的质疑。

他们因为你所有的道德而惩罚你。他们在他们的内心里宽恕——你所有的过错。

你那温和的以及正直的个性让你说道：“它们因为自身渺小的存在，而不应该受到责备。”但是，他们那受到限制的灵魂则在思考：“所有伟大的存在都是应该受到责备的。”

甚至，当你对它们表示友善的时候，它们仍旧感觉到自己被你轻视了；它们就会用秘密的罪行偿还你的仁慈。你那安静的傲慢总是和它们的品位相对立；如果有一天你能够卑微到足以变得轻浮，那么它们就会喜笑颜开。

我们从一个人的身上发现了什么，我们就同样能让那个东西激怒那个人。因此，你最好提高警惕，时刻提防那些小人吧！

在你的面前，它们感觉到自己非常渺小，它们的卑微会站起来反抗你，并且燃烧成不可见的复仇。

难道你不知道当你悄然接近它们的时候，它们就会变得闷不作声，它们的能量是如何像一个即将消逝的火焰所产生的烟雾一样离开它们呢？是的，我的朋友们，你让你的邻居们感到良心需要自责，因为它们跟你实在是毫不相称。因此，它们痛恨你，并且心甘情愿地吮吸你的鲜血。

你的邻居们往往都是拥有剧毒的苍蝇；你具有的伟大——会让它们变得更加有毒，更加像一只苍蝇。

我的朋友们，你们快逃到你们的孤独中去吧！快点逃到猛烈的暴风肆虐的地方去吧！你的命运最多也不过是个苍蝇拍而已。

Flee, my friend, into thy solitude and thither, where a rough strong breeze bloweth. It is not thy lot to be a fly-flap.

Thus spake Zarathustra.

13. CHASTITY

I love the forest. It is bad to live in cities: there, there are too many of the lustful.

Is it not better to fall into the hands of a murderer, than into the dreams of a lustful woman?

And just look at these men: their eye saith it they know nothing better on earth than to lie with a woman.

Filth is at the bottom of their souls; and alas! if their filth hath still spirit in it!

Would that ye were perfect at least as animals! But to animals belongeth innocence.

Do I counsel you to slay your instincts? I counsel you to innocence in your instincts.

Do I counsel you to chastity? Chastity is a virtue with some, but with many almost a vice.

These are continent, to be sure: but doggish lust looketh enviously out of all that they do.

Even into the heights of their virtue and into their cold spirit doth this creature follow them, with its discord.

And how nicely can doggish lust beg for a piece of spirit, when a piece of flesh is denied it!

查拉图斯特拉如是说。

13．贞洁

我非常热爱森林，在城市里生活的感觉实在是太糟糕了；这里有太多太多绿意葱葱的景色了。

如果落入一个杀人犯的手里,而不是落入一个贪图欲望的女人的梦境里岂不是更好？

让我们来好好看看这些人：他们的眼睛告诉我们——他们还不知道，在这个世界上还有比跟女人躺在一起更加美妙的事。

他们的灵魂底部满是污秽；唉！真是悲哀！他们的污秽里还拥有精神呢！

你们应当是完美的——至少要像动物们一样完美！但是，就算是动物们也有纯真。

我有没有建议过你们去杀戮自身的本能意识？我只是建议你们保留你们本能意识中的纯真。

我有没有建议过你们去禁欲？禁欲对于某些人来说是一种美德，但是，对于大多数人来说，禁欲基本等同于一种罪恶。

一点也不假，后面的这种人是有自制力的，但是犹如狗一般的欲望肆无忌惮的从他们的所作所为中反映了出来。

即便是在他们的道德顶点和冰冷的灵魂里，这样的怪物也会跟随着他们，令他们感到不安。

当这条充满欲望的狗得不到一块新鲜的肉时，它究竟会如何用善意的态度恳求一块

Ye love tragedies and all that breaketh the heart? But I am distrustful of your doggish lust.

Ye have too cruel eyes, and ye look wantonly towards the sufferers. Hath not your lust just disguised itself and taken the name of fellow-suffering?

And also this parable give I unto you: Not a few who meant to cast out their devil, went thereby into the swine themselves.

To whom chastity is difficult, it is to be dissuaded: lest it become the road to hell to filth and lust of soul.

Do I speak of filthy things? That is not the worst thing for me to do.

Not when the truth is filthy, but when it is shallow, doth the discerning one go unwillingly into its waters.

Verily, there are chaste ones from their very nature; they are gentler of heart, and laugh better and oftener than you.

They laugh also at chastity, and ask: "What is chastity?

Is chastity not folly? But the folly came unto us, and not we unto it.

We offered that guest harbour and heart: now it dwelleth with us let it stay as long as it will!"

Thus spake Zarathustra.

精神呢？

你们喜欢悲剧和一切令人悲痛万分的事物？但是，我对你们这种犹如狗一般的欲望持怀疑态度。

你们拥有过度残忍的双眼，你们会用嬉戏放纵的神情看着那些遭受磨难的人们。难道你们的欲望没有将自己伪装起来，然后称呼自己是应受到怜悯的对象吗？

现在，我将这个比喻告诉给你们：要想驱逐恶魔，而让自己变成卑贱的人，并不在少数。

人们认为如果禁欲的实现是非常困难的话，那么它就应该被人们放弃：否则的话，它就会成为通往地狱的道路——换句话来讲，就是灵魂的污秽和欲望。

我有说过什么污秽、不干净的事情吗？对于我来说，这样的作为并不是最糟糕的。求知欲极强的人之所以不愿意跳入到水里面，不是因为真相的污秽，而是因为真相的空虚。

说真的，有很多人，他们的本质就是禁欲的；他们拥有非常温和的心灵，并且他们的笑容要比你们的更加绽放，笑的频率也比你们的更加频繁。

同样，他们也会嘲笑禁欲，并且问道："什么叫做禁欲？"

难道禁欲不是一种荒唐的想法吗？但是，这种荒唐是来找的我们，而不是我们去找的它。

我们将心和房奉献给了客人，现在他就住在我们这里，让他想在这里待多久，就待多久吧！

查拉图斯特拉如是说。

14. THE FRIEND

"One, is always too many about me" thinketh the anchorite. "Always once one that maketh two in the long run!"

I and me are always too earnestly in conversation: how could it be endured, if there were not a friend?

The friend of the anchorite is always the third one: the third one is the cork which preventeth the conversation of the two sinking into the depth.

Ah! there are too many depths for all anchorites. Therefore, do they long so much for a friend, and for his elevation.

Our faith in others betrayeth wherein we would fain have faith in ourselves. Our longing for a friend is our betrayer.

And often with our love we want merely to overleap envy. And often we attack and make ourselves enemies, to conceal that we are vulnerable.

"Be at least mine enemy!" thus speaketh the true reverence, which doth not venture to solicit friendship.

If one would have a friend, then must one also be willing to wage war for him: and in order to wage war, one must be capable of being an enemy.

One ought still to honour the enemy in one’s friend. Canst thou go nigh unto thy friend, and not go over to him?

14．朋友

“在我的身边，总是有那么一个人非常的多余，”隐士这么想到。“总是有那么一个人——到了最后，他一定会变成两个人！”

我和我自己经常会无比诚挚地进行谈话：如果我连一个朋友都没有的话，那么这样的境遇我又怎么能忍受得了呢?

隐士的朋友，往往都是第三者：第三者就是那个能够阻止两个人的谈话陷入更加幽深的深处的浮木。

唉！对于隐士来说，他们的深处实在是太多了。因此，他们非常需要一个朋友，能够时不时地拉自己一把。

我们信任别人的地方，恰恰表现出我们相信自信并且无法做到的地方，我们对拥有一个朋友的渴望就是我们的背叛者。

在通常的情况之下，我们希望用爱来超越嫉妒。并且我们经常攻击，给自己树敌，隐藏我们自身最容易受到伤害的地方。

“你至少应该成为我的敌人吧！”——真正的崇敬如是说道，它不愿意冒着风险恳求友谊。

如果一个人需要一个朋友，那么，他同样还要愿意跟那个人之间引发战争：并且为了引发战争，那个人必须具备成为一名敌人的能力。

我们应当尊敬我们的朋友当中的敌人。你能不能在接近你的朋友的情况下，还能不

In one's friend one shall have one's best enemy. Thou shalt be closest unto him with thy heart when thou withstandest him.

Thou wouldst wear no raiment before thy friend? It is in honour of thy friend that thou showest thyself to him as thou art? But he wisheth thee to the devil on that account!

He who maketh no secret of himself shocketh: so much reason have ye to fear nakedness! Aye, if ye were Gods, ye could then be ashamed of clothing!

Thou canst not adorn thyself fine enough for thy friend; for thou shalt be unto him an arrow and a longing for the Superman.

Sawest thou ever thy friend asleep to know how he looketh? What is usually the countenance of thy friend? It is thine own countenance, in a coarse and imperfect mirror.

Sawest thou ever thy friend asleep? Wert thou not dismayed at thy friend looking so? O my friend, man is something that hath to be surpassed.

In divining and keeping silence shall the friend be a master: not everything must thou wish to see. Thy dream shall disclose unto thee what thy friend doeth when awake.

Let thy pity be a divining: to know first if thy friend wanteth pity. Perhaps he loveth in thee the unmoved eye, and the look of eternity.

Let thy pity for thy friend be hid under a hard shell; thou shalt bite out a tooth upon it. Thus will it have delicacy and sweetness.

Art thou pure air and solitude and bread and medicine to thy friend? Many a one cannot loosen his own fetters, but is nevertheless his friend's emancipator.

伤害到他？

你的朋友应该是你最好的敌人。当你抵抗他的时候，你应该是最接近他的内心的时候。

你是不是不想在你的朋友面前穿上衣服？如果你将真实的自己完全展示给你的朋友，那么这样算不算是对他的尊重？这样看来，他想要诅咒你去地狱也就不足为奇了！

那个不隐藏任何秘密的人，会让其他人倍感愤怒：你们有很多的理由去畏惧赤身裸体！唉！如果你们是神仙的话，那么，你们就会为身上穿着的衣服感到羞耻！你们不能为了你们的朋友，将自己装点得异常华美；你们应该是他射向超人的一把希望的弓箭。

你有没有观察你那正在睡梦中的朋友——来了解他睡觉时的相貌如何？通常，你的朋友的相貌是什么样子的？那是映射在粗糙、不完美的镜子里，你真实的相貌。

你有没有观察你那正在睡梦中的朋友？你会不会因为他们的相貌而感到大失所望呢？噢！我的朋友们，人类是某种注定要被超越的物种。朋友应该是那种审时度势，善于维持寂静的大师：你不必看你想要看到的任何一件事。你的梦应该将你的朋友在不睡觉的情况下所做的事对你和盘托出。

让你的怜悯之心成为一个忖度吧：这样你才能首先知道你的朋友是否需要怜悯。或许，他喜欢你那不为所动的眼睛以及永恒的眼神。

让你为朋友着想的怜悯之心隐藏在可以压断牙齿的坚硬的硬壳之下吧。这样你才能拥有敏锐和甜蜜。

你会给予你的朋友们纯净的空气、孤独、面包以及药物吗？有太多的人不能解除自己的锁链，然而，他们的朋友却是解救他们的人。

Art thou a slave? Then thou canst not be a friend. Art thou a tyrant? Then thou canst not have friends.

Far too long hath there been a slave and a tyrant concealed in woman. On that account woman is not yet capable of friendship: she knoweth only love.

In woman's love there is injustice and blindness to all she doth not love. And even in woman's conscious love, there is still always surprise and lightning and night, along with the light.

As yet woman is not capable of friendship: women are still cats, and birds. Or at the best, cows.

As yet woman is not capable of friendship. But tell me, ye men, who of you are capable of friendship?

Oh! your poverty, ye men, and your sordidness of soul! As much as ye give to your friend, will I give even to my foe, and will not have become poorer thereby.

There is comradeship: may there be friendship!

Thus spake Zarathustra.

15. THE THOUSAND AND ONE GOALS

Many lands saw Zarathustra, and many peoples: thus he discovered the good and bad of many peoples. No greater power did Zarathustra find on earth than good and bad.

No people could live without first valuing; if a people will maintain itself, however, it must

你是奴隶吗？那么，你就不能做朋友。你是暴君吗？那么，你就不能拥有朋友。

在相当长的一段时间里，女人的身上隐藏着奴隶和暴君。那样的女人还不能够完全了解友谊：她唯一知道的就是爱情。在女人的爱情里，她经常对一切她所不爱的事物，持有偏激和盲目的态度。

甚至在女人有意识的爱情当中，也往往有突变、电闪雷鸣和黑夜陪伴着光明。

然而，女人还不能够完全了解友谊：女人们仍旧是猫、小鸟。或者，用最好的方式描述就是奶牛。

然而，女人还不能够完全了解友谊。但是，请告诉我，你们男人们，到底又有谁能够完全了解友谊呢？

噢！你们这些悲惨的男人们！我诅咒你们灵魂当中的贫穷和污秽！你们给予朋友们的，就是我给予我的敌人们的，而且我并不会因为这样而变得贫穷。

拥有了伙伴关系：也就拥有了友情！

查拉图斯特拉如是说。

15. 千个与一个目标

查拉图斯特拉曾经到过很多地方，见到过很多民族：因此，他发现了许多拥有善意的民族和拥有恶意的民族。查拉图斯特拉发现，在这个世界上，没有任何一种力量要比善与恶更加强大。

任何一个民族如若不事先进行评估的话，都是不可能存在的；倘若一个民族想要维

not value as its neighbour valueth.

Much that passed for good with one people was regarded with scorn and contempt by another: thus I found it. Much found I here called bad, which was there decked with purple honours.

Never did the one neighbour understand the other: ever did his soul marvel at his neighbour's delusion and wickedness.

A table of excellencies hangeth over every people. Lo! it is the table of their triumphs; lo! it is the voice of their Will to Power.

It is laudable, what they think hard; what is indispensable and hard they call good; and what relieveth in the direst distress, the unique and hardest of all, they extol as holy.

Whatever maketh them rule and conquer and shine, to the dismay and envy of their neighbours, they regard as the high and foremost thing, the test and the meaning of all else.

Verily, my brother, if thou knewest but a people's need, its land, its sky, and its neighbour, then wouldst thou divine the law of its surmountings, and why it climbeth up that ladder to its hope.

"Always shalt thou be the foremost and prominent above others: no one shall thy jealous soul love, except a friend" that made the soul of a Greek thrill: thereby went he his way to greatness.

"To speak truth, and be skilful with bow and arrow" so seemed it alike pleasing and hard to the people from whom cometh my name the name which is alike pleasing and hard to me.

持自己的话，那么，它的价值就不能跟它的邻居的价值相一致。

我发现，许多被一个民族视作是善的事物会受到其他人的轻蔑和鄙视。我还发现在这里被人们称为恶的，在那里却穿着象征荣誉的紫色袍子。

一个人根本就不可能了解他的邻居：他的灵魂往往会因为他的邻居的假象和邪恶而感到震惊。

每一个民族的头顶上都悬着一种价值。看呀！那是他们获得胜利的标志；瞧呀！那是他们权力意志的声音。

他们认为一切难以成功的事情都是值得人们称赞的；他们把那些必不可少的和困难的看做是善；那些独特的、极其费力的事物，能够挽救深陷巨大压力的——都会被称赞是神圣的。

那些能够让他们统治、征服和闪耀的，能够让他们的邻居们绝望和嫉妒的，它们认为这事物是世界上最高级的领先者，它是世界万物的检验和意义所在。

说真的，我的兄弟们，如果你们已经了解了一个民族的需求、它的领地、它的天空、它的邻居，那么你就能够猜测到它获得胜利的真理，那么，你也就能够了解它为什么要在通向希望的梯子上攀爬。

“你应该常常处于最前沿、最突出的位置，凌驾于别人之上：除了你的朋友之外，你那嫉妒的灵魂将不会再爱任何一个人”——这让一个希腊人的灵魂因为激动而震颤：因此，他走上了自己那条通往伟大的道路。

“说真话，并且熟练运用弓和箭”——这句话是出自我的名字的民族认为非常振奋人心和难能可贵的——这句话对于我来说，也意味着愉悦和任重。

"To honour father and mother, and from the root of the soul to do their will" this table of surmounting hung another people over them, and became powerful and permanent thereby.

"To have fidelity, and for the sake of fidelity to risk honour and blood, even in evil and dangerous courses" teaching itself so, another people mastered itself, and thus mastering itself, became pregnant and heavy with great hopes.

Verily, men have given unto themselves all their good and bad. Verily, they took it not, they found it not, it came not unto them as a voice from heaven.

Values did man only assign to things in order to maintain himself he created only the significance of things, a human significance! Therefore, calleth he himself "man," that is, the valuator.

Valuing is creating: hear it, ye creating ones! Valuation itself is the treasure and jewel of the valued things.

Through valuation only is there value; and without valuation the nut of existence would be hollow. Hear it, ye creating ones!

Change of values that is, change of the creating ones. Always doth he destroy who hath to be a creator.

Creating ones were first of all peoples, and only in late times individuals; verily, the individual himself is still the latest creation.

Peoples once hung over them tables of the good. Love which would rule and love which

“尊敬父亲和母亲，从灵魂的深处，遵从他们的意愿。”——其他的民族高悬着这句话，而从此变得强大、经久不衰。

“保持忠诚，为了忠诚而冒着荣誉和鲜血的风险，甚至做出邪恶、危险的事，都会在所不惜”——另外一个民族则记住了这个教训，它彻底了解了它，并且拥有了富有重大意义的伟大希望。

说真的，善与恶完全是依靠人类进行自制的。真的，它们并不是随意获得的，也不是被发现的，也不是从蓝天传来的声音。

人类只有在为了维持自身存在的情况下，才会给予万物价值——他创造了世间万物的意义，一个人类的意义！因此，他称自己为“人”，换句话来讲，就是评估者。

进行评估就是创造：你们这些创造者们，都给我好好听着吧！评估本身就是拥有价值的事物的宝藏和珠宝。

通过评估，便会产生价值；如果没有评估，存在之结果就只能是一具空壳。你们这些创造者们，给我好好听着吧！

价值的改变——换句话来讲，就是创造者的改变。创造者经常进行破坏。

起初，创造者们是整个民族，只是到了后来，他们才成为独立的个人；说真的，这些独立的个人仍旧是最初的创造品。

曾经，民族将善之美高悬于头顶。寻求统治之爱和服从之爱共同为他们创造了这样的美。

人群中的愉悦要早于“我”的愉悦：只要当良知还是对于人群而言，“我”就只能说是感到内心愧疚了。

would obey, created for themselves such tables.

Older is the pleasure in the herd than the pleasure in the ego: and as long as the good conscience is for the herd, the bad conscience only saith: ego.

Verily, the crafty ego, the loveless one, that seeketh its advantage in the advantage of many it is not the origin of the herd, but its ruin.

Loving ones, was it always, and creating ones, that created good and bad. Fire of love gloweth in the names of all the virtues, and fire of wrath.

Many lands saw Zarathustra, and many peoples: no greater power did Zarathustra find on earth than the creations of the loving ones "good" and "bad" are they called.

Verily, a prodigy is this power of praising and blaming. Tell me, ye brethren, who will master it for me? Who will put a fetter upon the thousand necks of this animal?

A thousand goals have there been hitherto, for a thousand peoples have there been. Only the fetter for the thousand necks is still lacking; there is lacking the one goal. As yet humanity hath not a goal.

But pray tell me, my brethren, if the goal of humanity be still lacking, is there not also still lacking humanity itself?

Thus spake Zarathustra.

说真的，阴险狡诈、没有爱的“我”，在绝大多数人的利益里，找寻自己的利益——这并不是人群的起源，而是人群的毁灭。

热爱者和创造者，他们往往会创造出善与恶。爱情的烈焰和愤怒在所有道德的名义下闪耀着光芒。查拉图斯特拉到过很多地方，他见到过很多民族：但是，查拉图斯特拉发现，在这个世界上没有任何一种力量要比热爱者的创造力更强大的力量——他们将那些称为“善”和“恶”。

说真的，这种赞美和责备的力量就是个奇才。我的兄弟们，快告诉我，究竟有谁能帮我制服它呢？究竟有谁能在这头怪兽的上千个脖子上套上锁链呢？

时至今日，我们已经拥有了一千个目标，同样我们还拥有着一千个民族。我们唯一缺少的仍旧是套住上千个脖子的锁链，我们还缺少一个目标。然而，人类还没有任何目标呢。

但是，我的兄弟们，快快告诉我，如果人类仍旧缺乏目标，那么，这个世界上也就不存在人类了吧？

查拉图斯特拉如是说。

16. NEIGHBOUR-LOVE

Ye crowd around your neighbour, and have fine words for it. But I say unto you: your neighbour-love is your bad love of yourselves.

Ye flee unto your neighbour from yourselves, and would fain make a virtue thereof: but I fathom your "unselfishness."

The thou is older than the I; the thou hath been consecrated, but not yet the I: so man presseth nigh unto his neighbour.

Do I advise you to neighbour-love? Rather do I advise you to neighbour-flight and to furthest love!

Higher than love to your neighbour is love to the furthest and future ones; higher still than love to men, is love to things and phantoms.

The phantom that runneth on before thee, my brother, is fairer than thou; why dost thou not give unto it thy flesh and thy bones? But thou fearest, and runnest unto thy neighbour.

Ye cannot endure it with yourselves, and do not love yourselves sufficiently: so ye seek to mislead your neighbour into love, and would fain gild yourselves with his error.

Would that ye could not endure it with any kind of near ones, or their neighbours; then would ye have to create your friend and his overflowing heart out of yourselves.

Ye call in a witness when ye want to speak well of yourselves; and when ye have misled him

16. 邻人之爱

你们全都聚集在你们的邻居身边，并且利用美好的语言博得他们的共鸣。但是，我要在这里对你们说：你们的邻居——只是你们糟糕的自我怜爱。

你们脱离自己的身体，逃到你们的邻居那里，并且心甘情愿把你们的邻居视为一种道德：但是我彻底看穿了你们的“无私利他主义”。

你要比你自己年长；你已经被神圣化了，但是我却没有：因此，一个人向他的邻居示好。

我有建议过你们去热爱你们的邻居吗？我宁肯建议你们远离你们的邻居，并且将爱意带向远方！

热爱远方的人，热爱未来的人，要远远高于热爱你们的邻居；对于我而言，我认为热爱事物和鬼魂，仍旧要比热爱人类更加高尚。

我的兄弟们，在你们面前游荡的鬼魂们，要比你优美得多，你为什么不把你自身的肉体和骨头给它呢？但是，你出于害怕，便逃到了你的邻居那里去了。

你们无法忍受自己，你们也无法足够的热爱自己：所以你们想用爱误导你们的邻居，并且心甘情愿用他的错误掩饰你们自己。

我希望你们无法忍受任何处于你们附近的人，或是他们的邻居；然后，到了那个时候，你们就只能被迫创造你们的朋友以及他快要溢出来的心灵。

当你想要夸耀自己的时候，你们可以叫来一个见证人。当你们诱惑他，让他打心底里赞美你们，那么，你们同样会在心底里赞美你们自己。

to think well of you, ye also think well of yourselves.

Not only doth he lie, who speaketh contrary to his knowledge, but more so, he who speaketh contrary to his ignorance. And thus speak ye of yourselves in your intercourse, and belie your neighbour with yourselves.

Thus saith the fool: "Association with men spoileth the character, especially when one hath none."

The one goeth to his neighbour because he seeketh himself, and the other because he would fain lose himself. Your bad love to yourselves maketh solitude a prison to you.

The furthest ones are they who pay for your love to the near ones; and when there are but five of you together, a sixth must always die.

I love not your festivals either: too many actors found I there, and even the spectators often behaved like actors.

Not the neighbour do I teach you, but the friend. Let the friend be the festival of the earth to you, and a foretaste of the Superman.

I teach you the friend and his overflowing heart. But one must know how to be a sponge, if one would be loved by overflowing hearts.

I teach you the friend in whom the world standeth complete, a capsule of the good, the creating friend, who hath always a complete world to bestow.

And as the world unrolled itself for him, so rolleth it together again for him in rings, as the growth of good through evil, as the growth of purpose out of chance.

诳语者不仅仅是说谎话的人，说着与自己的知识相对立的话，而且还坦言与他的纯真相对立的话。因此，你们在这样的交流的场合下，叙说着自己，并且利用你们自己欺骗你们的邻居。

因此，愚蠢的人说道："同人打交道会毁坏一个人的性格，尤其是对于一个毫无性格的人而言，情况更是如此。"

这个人之所以要去奔赴他的邻居家，是因为他要去那里找寻他自己，而另一个人去他的邻居家，是因为他要想在那里彻底忘记他自己。你们那失败的自我怜爱让孤独成为了你们的监狱。

远方的人会因为你们这种热爱临近的人的情感而付出惨痛的代价，当你们是五个人聚集在一起的时候，往往，第六个人是必须要死的。

我并不喜欢你们那些节日庆典：我发现这里有太多的表演者，甚至这里的观众也经常表现得像个演员。

我并不会教你们热爱邻居，而是教你们如何交朋友。让你们的朋友们成为你们的世界上的节日庆典以及一种超人的预感。

我把朋友和他快要溢出的心灵教给你们。但是，如果你们想要受到快要溢出的心灵的热爱，你们就必须知道该如何成为一块海绵。

我用隐藏着完整的世界以及善意的躯壳的朋友教你们——具有创造性的朋友，往往会馈赠一个完整的世界。

这个世界为他揭示自己，然后又再一次为了他卷了起来，就好比恶成长为了善，就好比偶然演变成了目的一样。

Let the future and the furthest be the motive of thy to-day; in thy friend shalt thou love the Superman as thy motive.

My brethren, I advise you not to neighbour-love I advise you to furthest love!

Thus spake Zarathustra.

17. THE WAY OF THE CREATING ONE

Wouldst thou go into isolation, my brother? Wouldst thou seek the way unto thyself? Tarry yet a little and hearken unto me.

"He who seeketh may easily get lost himself. All isolation is wrong": so say the herd. And long didst thou belong to the herd.

The voice of the herd will still echo in thee. And when thou sayest, "I have no longer a conscience in common with you," then will it be a plaint and a pain.

Lo, that pain itself did the same conscience produce; and the last gleam of that conscience still gloweth on thine affliction.

But thou wouldst go the way of thine affliction, which is the way unto thyself? Then show me thine authority and thy strength to do so!

Art thou a new strength and a new authority? A first motion? A self-rolling wheel? Canst thou also compel stars to revolve around thee?

Alas! there is so much lusting for loftiness! There are so many convulsions of the ambitions!

让遥远的将来和最远的未来成为你今天的动机；你应该热爱你朋友身上的超人，并且以此作为自己存在的理由。

我的兄弟们，我建议你们不要热爱你们的邻居——我建议你们热爱远方的人们！

查拉图斯特拉如是说。

17．创世者之路

我的兄弟，你会进入被孤立的状态吗？你会寻求进入你自己身体的方式吗？静候片刻，并且仔细聆听。

“那个寻求这样的方式的人很容易就会迷失自己。所有的孤立状态都是错误的”：人群如是说。而且，你在很长一段时间里都将属于人群。

人群的声音仍旧在你的脑海里回荡。而且当你说道：“我的良知将不再跟你有任何相似之处，”然后，它就会成为一种悲叹，一种痛苦。

看呀！痛苦所做的事情跟良知所产生的事情是一样的；而且良知最后的微弱光芒仍旧照耀在你的苦难之上。

但是，你会选择遭受苦难的方式，降临在你身上的会是哪种方式？那么，向我展示一下你的权威以及你的力量吧！

你是否拥有全新的力量？新的权威？最初的动作？一个自我滚动的轮子？你能不能迫使天上的繁星围绕着你旋转？

唉！追求崇高的欲望太过于强烈了！这里有许多因为雄心壮志而引发的骚动！快快

Show me that thou art not a lusting and ambitious one!

Alas! there are so many great thoughts that do nothing more than the bellows: they inflate, and make emptier than ever.

Free, dost thou call thyself? Thy ruling thought would I hear of, and not that thou hast escaped from a yoke.

Art thou one entitled to escape from a yoke? Many a one hath cast away his final worth when he hath cast away his servitude.

Free from what? What doth that matter to Zarathustra! Clearly, however, shall thine eye show unto me: free for what?

Canst thou give unto thyself thy bad and thy good, and set up thy will as a law over thee? Canst thou be judge for thyself, and avenger of thy law?

Terrible is aloneness with the judge and avenger of one's own law. Thus is a star projected into desert space, and into the icy breath of aloneness.

To-day sufferest thou still from the multitude, thou individual; to-day hast thou still thy courage unabated, and thy hopes.

But one day will the solitude weary thee; one day will thy pride yield, and thy courage quail. Thou wilt one day cry: "I am alone!"

One day wilt thou see no longer thy loftiness, and see too closely thy lowliness; thy sublimity itself will frighten thee as a phantom. Thou wilt one day cry: "All is false!"

There are feelings which seek to slay the lonesome one; if they do not succeed, then must

向我展示一下你不是那种拥有强烈欲望和雄心壮志的人！

唉！这里有太多的伟大想法，但是，它们唯一能做的就是大声地嘶吼；它们变得膨胀，并且变得比以往的任何时候都更加空虚。

你是不是称呼自己是自由自在的人？我能够听到在你的脑中占据支配地位的思想，而不是你逃离了一个束缚。

你是否具有逃离一个束缚的资格？当他抛弃自己被奴役的状态的时候，许多人就会抛弃他最后的价值。

从哪里摆脱，获得自由？这些对于查拉图斯特拉来说是否重要！但是，很显然，你的眼睛在向我表述：究竟从哪里摆脱并且获得自由？

你能不能把自己的善与恶给予自己，并且将你的意志转换成控制你言行举止的法律？你能不能成为自己的评价者，并且成为你的法律的复仇者？

孤独就是可怕的评判者和一个为人自己制定的法律的复仇者。因此，一颗行星被投射到荒凉孤寂的太空，被投射到孤独那冰冷的呼吸里。

今天，你们这些独立的个人仍旧遭受到来自广大人群的迫害；今天，你们的勇气和你们的希望仍旧没有任何减弱的趋势。

但是，总有一天，你们会厌倦孤独，总有一天你们会释放出你们的傲慢，还有你们那令人胆寒的勇气。总有一天，你们会大叫道："我太孤独了！"

总有一天，你们将会看到自己不再处于高耸的位置，你们会看到自己是如此的接近卑微下贱的地位；你们的崇高气质将会向一个幽灵一样出来惊吓你们。总有一天，你们会大叫道："所有的一切都是虚假的！"

they themselves die! But art thou capable of it to be a murderer?

Hast thou ever known, my brother, the word "disdain"? And the anguish of thy justice in being just to those that disdain thee?

Thou forcest many to think differently about thee; that, charge they heavily to thine account. Thou camest nigh unto them, and yet wentest past: for that they never forgive thee.

Thou goest beyond them: but the higher thou risest, the smaller doth the eye of envy see thee. Most of all, however, is the flying one hated.

"How could ye be just unto me!" must thou say "I choose your injustice as my allotted portion."

Injustice and filth cast they at the lonesome one: but, my brother, if thou wouldst be a star, thou must shine for them none the less on that account!

And be on thy guard against the good and just! They would fain crucify those who devise their own virtue they hate the lonesome ones.

Be on thy guard, also, against holy simplicity! All is unholy to it that is not simple; fain, likewise, would it play with the fire of the fagot and stake.

And be on thy guard, also, against the assaults of thy love! Too readily doth the recluse reach his hand to any one who meeteth him.

To many a one mayest thou not give thy hand, but only thy paw; and I wish thy paw also to have claws.

But the worst enemy thou canst meet, wilt thou thyself always be; thou waylayest thyself in caverns and forests.

在这个世界上存在想屠杀孤独寂寞的人的感受；如果他们不能成功的话，那么，他们就必须死！但是，你是否具备了——成为一名屠杀者所应具备的能力？

我的兄弟们，你们是否已经知道“蔑视”这个词语？可是遭受过你们那正义的折磨，对于那些蔑视你们的人，你们能否平等对待呢？

你们迫使许多人认为你们是与众不同的；他们把这些都看做是你的冷酷。你悄然的接近他们，然后又离开了他们：他们会因为这件事永远也不原谅你。

你越过了他们：但是，你上升得越高，嫉妒的眼睛就会看你越渺小。但是，最被人所痛恨的是飞行者。

“你们怎么会心甘情愿对我公平看待呢！”你必须说——“我替我自己选择你们的不公正作为我应该获得的份额。”

他们将不公正和污秽抛给了那些孤独寂寞的人们：但是，我的兄弟，如果你想成为一颗繁星的话，那么你就不能因此而减少照耀他们的次数！

你要时刻提防那些正人君子！他们非常乐意迫害那些发明了自己的道德的人——他们非常痛恨孤独寂寞的人们。

同样，你还要时刻提防神圣的愚笨头脑！所有不简单的事情都会被看做是不神圣的；同样地，他们也特别喜欢玩火——摆弄那些曾经烧死过异教徒的柴火堆。

与此同时，你还要时刻提防你的爱的突袭！孤独寂寞的人会过快的把他们的手伸向他们刚刚碰到的陌生人。

但是有太多的人，你不能向他们伸出双手，而只能伸出你的爪子；并且我希望你的爪子能够带有锋利的钩子。

Thou lonesome one, thou goest the way to thyself! And past thyself and thy seven devils leadeth thy way!

A heretic wilt thou be to thyself, and a wizard and a sooth-sayer, and a fool, and a doubter, and a reprobate, and a villain.

Ready must thou be to burn thyself in thine own flame; how couldst thou become new if thou have not first become ashes!

Thou lonesome one, thou goest the way of the creating one: a God wilt thou create for thyself out of thy seven devils!

Thou lonesome one, thou goest the way of the loving one: thou lovest thyself, and on that account despisest thou thyself, as only the loving ones despise.

To create, desireth the loving one, because he despiseth! What knoweth he of love who hath not been obliged to despise just what he loved!

With thy love, go into thine isolation, my brother, and with thy creating; and late only will justice limp after thee.

With my tears, go into thine isolation, my brother. I love him who seeketh to create beyond himself, and thus succumbeth.

Thus spake Zarathustra.

18. OLD AND YOUNG WOMEN

"Why stealest thou along so furtively in the twilight, Zarathustra? And what hidest thou so

但是，你们所能遇到的最糟糕的敌人，永远都是你们自己；你在山洞和森林里伏击你自己。

孤独寂寞的人，你们正走在通向自己的大道！你的道路在沿着你自己以及你的七个恶魔向前延伸！

对于你本人来讲，你将是异教徒、女巫、预言者、傻瓜、怀疑者、不圣洁者、恶棍。

你已经准备好在自己创造的火焰中，烧死自己；如果你不首先成为一堆灰烬的话，你又怎么能成为焕然一新的人呢！

孤独寂寞的人，你正走在创造者的道路上：你要把你的七个恶魔创造成一个伟大的上帝！

孤独寂寞的人，你正走在拥有爱意的人的道路上：你非常热爱你自己，也正是因为这样，你非常看不起自己，就好比只有拥有爱意的人才会蔑视！

拥有爱意的人渴望创造，因为他会蔑视别人！如果一个人不是刚好被迫蔑视自己喜爱的东西的话，那么这样的人知道什么是爱吗！

带着你的爱和你的创造步入你的孤独中去吧！我的兄弟。我热爱那些为了超越自己而进行创造并且就这样行之毁灭的人。

查拉图斯特拉如是说。

18．老妇人和年轻的妇人

“查拉图斯特拉，你为什么要在黎明偷偷摸摸地行走呢？究竟是什么小心翼翼地隐

carefully under thy mantle?

Is it a treasure that hath been given thee? Or a child that hath been born thee? Or goest thou thyself on a thief's errand, thou friend of the evil?"

Verily, my brother, said Zarathustra, it is a treasure that hath been given me: it is a little truth which I carry.

But it is naughty, like a young child; and if I hold not its mouth, it screameth too loudly.

As I went on my way alone to-day, at the hour when the sun declineth, there met me an old woman, and she spake thus unto my soul:

"Much hath Zarathustra spoken also to us women, but never spake he unto us concerning woman."

And I answered her: "Concerning woman, one should only talk unto men."

"Talk also unto me of woman," said she; "I am old enough to forget it presently."

And I obliged the old woman and spake thus unto her:

Everything in woman is a riddle, and everything in woman hath one solution it is called pregnancy.

Man is for woman a means: the purpose is always the child. But what is woman for man?

Two different things wanteth the true man: danger and diversion. Therefore wanteth he woman, as the most dangerous plaything.

藏在你的斗篷里面呢?

那会是赐予你的宝藏吗?或是属于你的、已经降临人世的小孩?或是你在给一个小偷跑腿，你那恶魔的朋友?”

说真的，我的兄弟，查拉图斯特拉说道，那是一件给予我的宝藏，那是我随时放在身上的一点小小的真相。

但是，它就像一个年轻的小孩子一样顽皮、淘气；如果我不能够捂住他的嘴，他就会大声地尖叫。

今天，当我独自一人走在我的道路上的时候，太阳开始落山了，就在这时，我碰到了一个老妇人，然后，她对我的灵魂说道：

“查拉图斯特拉也跟我们女性说过很多话，但是他从来都没有跟我们说过任何涉及有关女性的话。”

然后我回答：“有关于女性的话题，人们只能谈论有关男性的话题。”

“那可以跟我聊一聊有关于女性的话题，”她说道，“我的岁数太大了，过不了多久，我就会忘了咱们之前谈话的内容。”

在这位老妇人的强迫之下，我对她说道：

“有关于女性的任何事情都是一个谜，有关于女性的任何事物都只有一个解决办法——它被人们称为怀孕。”

男人寻找女人只有一个目的：那个目的往往是关于生育孩子的。但是，女人寻求男人什么呢?

真正的男人想要两种东西：危险和消遣。因此，男人会想要女人，作为他最具危险

Man shall be trained for war, and woman for the recreation of the warrior: all else is folly.

Too sweet fruits these the warrior liketh not. Therefore liketh he woman; bitter is even the sweetest woman.

Better than man doth woman understand children, but man is more childish than woman.

In the true man there is a child hidden: it wanteth to play. Up then, ye women, and discover the child in man!

A plaything let woman be, pure and fine like the precious stone, illumined with the virtues of a world not yet come.

Let the beam of a star shine in your love! Let your hope say: "May I bear the Superman!"

In your love let there be valour! With your love shall ye assail him who inspireth you with fear!

In your love be your honour! Little doth woman understand otherwise about honour. But let this be your honour: always to love more than ye are loved, and never be the second.

Let man fear woman when she loveth: then maketh she every sacrifice, and everything else she regardeth as worthless.

Let man fear woman when she hateth: for man in his innermost soul is merely evil; woman, however, is mean.

Whom hateth woman most? Thus spake the iron to the loadstone: "I hate thee most, because

性的玩物。

男人应该接受残酷的训练，从而为上战场做好充分的准备，而女人则要为勇士的重生做好准备：任何的事物都是愚蠢的。

太过于甘甜的水果——这些是勇士们不喜欢的东西。因为，他喜欢女人；即使是最甜美的女人也是充满苦涩的。

女人要比男人更加理解孩子们，但是，男人要比女人表现得更像个孩子。

在每一个真正的男人的心里面，都藏着一个小孩子：他想要玩耍。然后，你们女人，发现了隐藏在男人内心里面的小孩子！

让女人成为一个玩物吧！就像珍贵的石头一样纯粹和漂亮，并且被一个还没有到来的世界的道德所照亮。

让一颗行星的光芒在你的爱意中闪耀吧！让你的希望说：“我可以容忍超人！”

让你的爱意成为你的勇猛吧！带着你的爱意，你就可以突袭那个用恐惧启发你的人！

让你的爱意成为你的荣誉吧！女人对荣誉的概念知之甚少。但是，让它成为你的荣誉吧：要永远付出比自己所得到的还要多的爱，永远也不要成为第二个人。

当她付出爱的时候，让男人害怕女人：让她做出种种的牺牲以及所有在她看来都是毫无价值的东西。

当她仇恨的时候，让男人害怕女人：因为男人的灵魂的最内在的部分就是恶魔；然而，女人的灵魂的最内在的部分是刻薄。

在这个世界上，有哪种人最痛恨女人？——铁对天然磁石说道：“我最讨厌的是你，因为你是那么有吸引力，但是，你太过虚弱，就连自己都无法吸引。”

thou attractest, but art too weak to draw unto thee."

The happiness of man is, "I will." The happiness of woman is, "He will."

"Lo! now hath the world become perfect!" thus thinketh every woman when she obeyeth with all her love.

Obey, must the woman, and find a depth for her surface. Surface, is woman's soul, a mobile, stormy film on shallow water.

Man's soul, however, is deep, its current gusheth in subterranean caverns: woman surmiseth its force, but comprehendeth it not.

Then answered me the old woman: "Many fine things hath Zarathustra said, especially for those who are young enough for them.

Strange! Zarathustra knoweth little about woman, and yet he is right about them! Doth this happen, because with women nothing is impossible?

And now accept a little truth by way of thanks! I am old enough for it!

Swaddle it up and hold its mouth: otherwise it will scream too loudly, the little truth."

"Give me, woman, thy little truth!" said I. And thus spake the old woman:

"Thou goest to women? Do not forget thy whip!"

Thus spake Zarathustra.

男人的幸福快乐就是“我会”。女人的幸福快乐就是“他会”。

“瞧呀！现在，这个世界变得完美了！”——当女人服从于她所有的爱，任何一个女人都会这么想。

任何一个女人都必须服从，并且为她的外表找到一种深度。外表是女人的灵魂，就像是浅层的水面上移动的、猛烈的薄膜。

然而，男人的灵魂是深沉的，他的水流会从地下的洞穴中喷涌而出：女人会推测它的力量，但是，她不能完全理解那种力量。

因此，我对那个老妇人说道：“查拉图斯特拉说过许多非常美好的事物，尤其是对于那些足够年轻的人来说。”

真是太奇怪了！查拉图斯特拉竟然不了解女人，然而，他所说的关于女性的东西又都是完全正确的！这样的情况之所以能够发生，是因为如果没有女人，任何事情都会成为不可能？

现在，通过感谢的方式，我已经能够接受真相了，我的年龄已经足够大到可以接受它们了。

束缚住它，并且管住它的嘴：否则，它定会大声地尖叫，小小的真相。

“把它给我，女人，你们的小小的真相，”我说道。于是，那个老妇人回答道：“你想要去找女人了？别忘了拿着你的鞭子。”

查拉图斯特拉如是说。

19. THE BITE OF THE ADDER

One day had Zarathustra fallen asleep under a fig-tree, owing to the heat, with his arms over his face. And there came an adder and bit him in the neck, so that Zarathustra screamed with pain. When he had taken his arm from his face he looked at the serpent; and then did it recognise the eyes of Zarathustra, wriggled awkwardly, and tried to get away.

"Not at all," said Zarathustra, "as yet hast thou not received my thanks! Thou hast awakened me in time; my journey is yet long." "Thy journey is short," said the adder sadly; "my poison is fatal." Zarathustra smiled. "When did ever a dragon die of a serpent's poison?" said he. "But take thy poison back! Thou art not rich enough to present it to me." Then fell the adder again on his neck, and licked his wound.

When Zarathustra once told this to his disciples they asked him: "And what, O Zarathustra, is the moral of thy story?" And Zarathustra answered them thus:

The destroyer of morality, the good and just call me: my story is immoral.

When, however, ye have an enemy, then return him not good for evil: for that would abash him. But prove that he hath done something good to you.

And rather be angry than abash any one! And when ye are cursed, it pleaseth me not that ye should then desire to bless. Rather curse a little also!

And should a great injustice befall you, then do quickly five small ones besides. Hideous to

19. 毒蛇之咬

有一天，查拉图斯特拉在一棵无花果树下睡觉，出于天气炎热的关系，查拉图斯特拉把胳膊放在了自己的脸上。然而，就在这个时候，一条蝰蛇爬了过来，它一下就咬了查拉图斯特拉的脖子，于是，疼痛难忍的查拉图斯特拉尖叫了起来。当他把胳膊从脸上拿开的时候，他看到了那条毒蛇；那条蛇通过那双眼睛认出了那人就是查拉图斯特拉，所以它笨拙地扭动着尾巴，试图逃离这里。

“你还不能走，”查拉图斯特拉说道，“因为，你还没有接受我的感谢呢！正是你及时地把我从睡眠中唤醒，我的旅途才会变得长久。”“不，你的旅途会变得很短，”那条蝰蛇悲哀地说道，“我的毒液是致命的。”查拉图斯特拉笑了起来。“从什么时候开始，一条龙会被一条毒蛇的毒液毒死？”查拉图斯特拉说道，“快把你的毒液带回去吧！你还没有富裕到可以把它呈现给我。”于是，那条毒蛇再一次爬上了他的脖子，开始吮吸他的伤口。

有那么一次，当查拉图斯特拉把这件事告诉他的学徒们之后，他们问他：“那么，查拉图斯特拉，你这个故事的寓意到底是什么呢？”查拉图斯特拉回答道：

道德的毁灭者以及善意和公正在召唤我：我的故事是不道德的。但是，当你拥有一个敌人的时候，那么，他就会以德报怨：因为，这会让他感到局促不安。他要证明他确实给你做过一些好事。他宁可生气也不会让任何人感到惶恐不安！我可不想让你们渴求受到祝福。我宁可让你们也受到点诅咒！

behold is he on whom injustice presseth alone.

Did ye ever know this? Shared injustice is half justice. And he who can bear it, shall take the injustice upon himself!

A small revenge is humaner than no revenge at all. And if the punishment be not also a right and an honour to the transgressor, I do not like your punishing.

Nobler is it to own oneself in the wrong than to establish one's right, especially if one be in the right. Only, one must be rich enough to do so.

I do not like your cold justice; out of the eye of your judges there always glanceth the executioner and his cold steel.

Tell me: where find we justice, which is love with seeing eyes?

Devise me, then, the love which not only beareth all punishment, but also all guilt!

Devise me, then, the justice which acquitteth every one except the judge!

And would ye hear this likewise? To him who seeketh to be just from the heart, even the lie becometh philanthropy.

But how could I be just from the heart! How can I give every one his own! Let this be enough for me: I give unto every one mine own.

Finally, my brethren, guard against doing wrong to any anchorite. How could an anchorite forget! How could he requite!

Like a deep well is an anchorite. Easy is it to throw in a stone: if it should sink to the bottom, however, tell me, who will bring it out again?

一个伟大的不公正降临在了你的身上，然后，还有五个小的不公正也很快来到你的旁边。他用无比丑陋的眼神注视着受到不公正的压迫的人们。

你是否了解这些？能够共享的非正义就是一半的正义。他如果能够承受，那么他就应该将这种不公正扛在自己的身上！

一个小小的复仇要比完全不复仇更加有人性。如果惩罚不仅仅是一种权力，而且还是对罪人的一种尊敬的话，那么我就不喜欢你的惩罚。

在错误的道路上摆正自己，要比建立自己的公平正义更加高尚，尤其是如果他本身就是正确的。但是，一个人只有在足够富有的情况之下，才可以这么做。

我并不喜欢你那种冰冷的正义；你那审判之眼总是在注视着执行者和他那冰冷的刀剑。

告诉我：从哪里能够找到我们的正义？什么才是用眼睛能够看到的爱？

那么，请设计我吧！那种爱不仅仅会承受所有的惩罚，同时还会惩罚所有的罪恶！

那么，请设计我吧！那种正义将任何有罪的人都无罪释放了，除了法官！你是否也听到了这样的事情？对于那个打心底里寻求公平正义的人来说，甚至是谎言也会成为慈善。

但是，我应该如何从内心深处拥有正义感呢！我要怎样做才能让所有人拥有他们本来就拥有的一切！

这些对于我来说已经足够了：我要将我自身的全部赋予所有人。

最终，我的兄弟们，时刻警惕不对任何的隐士做错误的事情。对于一个隐士来说，他怎么能够忘记！他又怎么去答谢！

一个隐士就像是一口深水井。向里面扔一个石头非常的简单：但是，请告诉我，如果这个石头沉到了这口深水井的井底，谁能够把那块石头重新给我捞上来？时刻提防不

Guard against injuring the anchorite! If ye have done so, however, well then, kill him also!

Thus spake Zarathustra.

20. CHILD AND MARRIAGE

I have a question for thee alone, my brother: like a sounding-lead, cast I this question into thy soul, that I may know its depth.

Thou art young, and desirest child and marriage. But I ask thee: Art thou a man entitled to desire a child?

Art thou the victorious one, the self-conqueror, the ruler of thy passions, the master of thy virtues? Thus do I ask thee.

Or doth the animal speak in thy wish, and necessity? Or isolation? Or discord in thee?

I would have thy victory and freedom long for a child. Living monuments shalt thou build to thy victory and emancipation.

Beyond thyself shalt thou build. But first of all must thou be built thyself, rectangular in body and soul.

Not only onward shalt thou propagate thyself, but upward! For that purpose may the garden of marriage help thee!

A higher body shalt thou create, a first movement, a spontaneously rolling wheel a creating one shalt thou create.

要伤害隐士！但是，一旦你这么做了，那么，你就要杀掉他！

查拉图斯特拉如是说。

20．孩子与婚姻

我的兄弟们，我有一个问题想问问你们：我将这个问题扔进了你们的灵魂里面，它就像一个测深锤一样，我能够利用它知道里面的深度。

你非常年轻，你渴望拥有孩子和婚姻。但是，我要问问你：你是否有满足拥有一个孩子的渴望的权力？

你是凯旋的勇士？征服自我的人？你的激情的统治者？你的道德的主人？我想问问你。

动物们是否在你的意愿、必要性下进行交谈？或是隔离的状态？或是你内心中的不和谐因素？

我会让你的胜利和自由渴求有一个孩子。你应该给你的胜利和解放建立活生生的丰碑。

你应该建立超越你自己的丰碑。但是，首先你必须要建立你自己，呈直角形的身体和灵魂。

你不应该向前面宣传你自己，而是应该向上宣传你自己！因为这样做，婚姻的花园才可以帮助你！

你应该创造一个更加高耸的身体，一个初始的运动，一个不由自主进行翻滚的轮子——你应该创造一个具有创造性的东西。

Marriage: so call I the will of the twain to create the one that is more than those who created it. The reverence for one another, as those exercising such a will, call I marriage.

Let this be the significance and the truth of thy marriage. But that which the many-too-many call marriage, those superfluous ones ah, what shall I call it?

Ah, the poverty of soul in the twain! Ah, the filth of soul in the twain! Ah, the pitiable self-complacency in the twain!

Marriage they call it all; and they say their marriages are made in heaven.

Well, I do not like it, that heaven of the superfluous! No, I do not like them, those animals tangled in the heavenly toils!

Far from me also be the God who limpeth thither to bless what he hath not matched!

Laugh not at such marriages! What child hath not had reason to weep over its parents?

Worthy did this man seem, and ripe for the meaning of the earth: but when I saw his wife, the earth seemed to me a home for madcaps.

Yea, I would that the earth shook with convulsions when a saint and a goose mate with one another.

This one went forth in quest of truth as a hero, and at last got for himself a small decked-up lie: his marriage he calleth it.

That one was reserved in intercourse and chose choicely. But one time he spoilt his company for all time: his marriage he calleth it.

Another sought a handmaid with the virtues of an angel. But all at once he became the

婚姻：所以，我让两个人创造了一个超越了他们所创造出来的事物。对于其他人的尊敬，当那些人行事类似这样的意愿的时候，我就管这个叫婚姻。

让它成为你的婚姻的重要意义和真相。但是有太多的事物叫做婚姻了，那些多余的事物——噢，我应该管它们叫什么呢？

噢，灵魂的贫穷！噢，灵魂的污秽！噢，可怜的自鸣得意！

他们管这些都叫做婚姻；并且，他们说他们的婚姻是在蓝天被创造出来的。那么，我并不喜欢这样，拥有多余事物的蓝天！不，我并不喜欢他们，那些动物们都被困在蓝天里做苦工！

上帝在距离我很远的地方，一瘸一拐地走向那一边，去祝福与他不相匹配的事物！

我们不能笑话这样的婚姻！究竟有什么样的孩子在没有任何理由的情况下，冲他们的父母哭泣呢？

看起来，这个男人是有价值的，并且足够成熟能够理解这片土地的意义：但是当我看到他的妻子的时候，这片土地在我看来就像是一个鲁莽之人的家。

是的，当一个圣人和一只鹅进行配对之后，我就会让这片土地在震颤之下开始摇晃。

他以一个英雄的身份追查事情的真相，最终他所得到的却是一个小小的谎言：他管这叫做他的婚姻。

这桩婚姻保存在交流和精挑细选的选择中。但是有一次，他把他的公司的一切全都毁坏了：他管这叫做他的婚姻。

还有一天，他寻找一个拥有天使般美德的女佣人。但是，突然之间，他成为了一个女人的女佣人，而到了现在，他同样希望自己能够成为一名天使。

handmaid of a woman, and now would he need also to become an angel.

Careful, have I found all buyers, and all of them have astute eyes. But even the astutest of them buyeth his wife in a sack.

Many short follies that is called love by you. And your marriage putteth an end to many short follies, with one long stupidity.

Your love to woman, and woman's love to man ah, would that it were sympathy for suffering and veiled deities! But generally two animals alight on one another.

But even your best love is only an enraptured simile and a painful ardour. It is a torch to light you to loftier paths.

Beyond yourselves shall ye love some day! Then learn first of all to love. And on that account ye had to drink the bitter cup of your love.

Bitterness is in the cup even of the best love: thus doth it cause longing for the Superman; thus doth it cause thirst in thee, the creating one!

Thirst in the creating one, arrow and longing for the Superman: tell me, my brother, is this thy will to marriage?

Holy call I such a will, and such a marriage.

Thus spake Zarathustra.

21. VOLUNTARY DEATH

Many die too late, and some die too early. Yet strange soundeth the precept: "Die at the right

我小心翼翼地找到了所有的买家，并且我发现他们每一个人都拥有一双狡猾、诡计多端的眼睛。但是，即使是在他们中间最诡计多端的人也会用一个大麻袋来买他的妻子。

许多小小的愚蠢，都被你称为爱。并且你的婚姻用一个长久的愚蠢给这些小小的愚蠢画上了句号。

你热爱女人，女人热爱男人——噢，那么遭受磨难以及给神灵蒙上神秘的面纱，算不算是一种同情呢！但是，通常来讲，两种动物会彼此照亮对方。

但是，即使是你的挚爱也只是一个兴奋异常的笑容，和充满痛苦的热情。那是一把为你照亮通向更高处的道路的火炬。

总有一天，你会喜欢上这种超越自我的感觉！但是，首先你要先学会如何去爱。并且为了达到目的，你必须喝掉一杯苦涩的爱意之水。

即便那杯子里装的是挚爱，那里面也是苦涩的：他这么做是因为他渴望超人；他这么做是因为你们非常饥渴，拥有创造力的产物！

拥有创造力的产物的饥渴，弓箭以及对超人的渴望：快点告诉我，我的兄弟们，这就是你们想要结婚的意愿吗?

我会称这些为神圣的意志和神圣的婚姻。

查拉图斯特拉如是说。

21. 自由的死亡

有许多人死得太晚了，而有些人则死得太早了。有的格言听起来非常古怪：要在适

time!

Die at the right time: so teacheth Zarathustra.

To be sure, he who never liveth at the right time, how could he ever die at the right time? Would that he might never be born! Thus do I advise the superfluous ones.

But even the superfluous ones make much ado about their death, and even the hollowest nut wanteth to be cracked.

Every one regardeth dying as a great matter: but as yet death is not a festival. Not yet have people learned to inaugurate the finest festivals.

The consummating death I show unto you, which becometh a stimulus and promise to the living.

His death, dieth the consummating one triumphantly, surrounded by hoping and promising ones.

Thus should one learn to die; and there should be no festival at which such a dying one doth not consecrate the oaths of the living!

Thus to die is best; the next best, however, is to die in battle, and sacrifice a great soul.

But to the fighter equally hateful as to the victor, is your grinning death which stealeth nigh like a thief, and yet cometh as master.

My death, praise I unto you, the voluntary death, which cometh unto me because I want it.

And when shall I want it? He that hath a goal and an heir, wanteth death at the right time for the goal and the heir.

当的时候死去！

在适当的时候死去：查拉图斯特拉所受的就是这样的教育。

我们很确定，他从来都没有生活在恰当的时期，那么他又怎么能在恰当的时候死去呢？与其是这样的结果，他还不如不出生呢！——因此，我向那些多余的人们提出建议。

但是，即使是那些多余的人们也会给他们的死亡带来很多忙乱，甚至是中空的坚果也想要被砸裂。

任何人都会把死亡看做是一件非常重要的事情：但是，死亡并不是一种节日的庆祝活动。并且还没有人学会如何举办最完美的节日庆祝活动。

我将要向你展示的完整死亡，会成为一种刺激因素以及对于生活的承诺。

他的死亡，得意扬扬地完整地死去，身旁被充满希望和有前途的人们团团围住。

一个人应该学会如何死亡；并且在这个世界上并不应该存在将即将死去的人供奉给活着的人的誓言的仪式！

死亡是最好的方式，那么仅次于死亡的最好的方式就是在战斗中死去，并且牺牲一个伟大的灵魂。

但是，斗士和胜利者一样，都是令人感到憎恨的，你那露齿而笑的死亡就如同一个小偷一样偷走了你——并且像一个主人一样来到这里。

我的死亡，我赞美你，自愿的死亡，它会降临在我的身上，因为，这正是我想要的。

那么，我应该什么时候需要它呢？——他拥有一个目标以及一个继承人，为了他的目标以及他的继承人，他想在适当的时候死去。

And out of reverence for the goal and the heir, he will hang up no more withered wreaths in the sanctuary of life.

Verily, not the rope-makers will I resemble: they lengthen out their cord, and thereby go ever backward.

Many a one, also, waxeth too old for his truths and triumphs; a toothless mouth hath no longer the right to every truth.

And whoever wanteth to have fame, must take leave of honour betimes, and practise the difficult art of going at the right time.

One must discontinue being feasted upon when one tasteth best: that is known by those who want to be long loved.

Sour apples are there, no doubt, whose lot is to wait until the last day of autumn: and at the same time they become ripe, yellow, and shrivelled.

In some ageth the heart first, and in others the spirit. And some are hoary in youth, but the late young keep long young.

To many men life is a failure; a poison-worm gnaweth at their heart. Then let them see to it that their dying is all the more a success.

Many never become sweet; they rot even in the summer. It is cowardice that holdeth them fast to their branches.

Far too many live, and far too long hang they on their branches. Would that a storm came and shook all this rottenness and worm-eatenness from the tree!

除了他对他的目标和他的继承人的尊重之外，他不会在生命的避难所之中悬挂更多衰弱的怒火。

说真的，我并不像绳索的制造者：他们延长他们的绳索，因此，他们就可以向后走。

同样，很多人因为太过于年长，而无法接受他的真相和胜利；一个没有牙齿的嘴巴是不可能再有接受任何事实真相的权力的。

无论是谁想要拥有名誉，他都必须及时离开荣誉，并且要克服种种困难，练习如何在适当的时刻前行。

当一个人品尝到最美味的东西的时候，他必须停止享用美餐：这是只有那些想要长期得到爱的人们才懂得的道理。

毫无疑问，这个世界上存在酸苹果，它们都在等待直到秋天最后一天的到来：就在与此同时，它们变得成熟、散发出金黄色，然后变得干瘪。

在某些时代里，心灵是第一位的，而在其他的时代里，则是精神被摆在第一的位置。有些人在年轻的时候，就已经白发苍苍，而有些人虽然已经过了年轻的时代，却仍旧保持着年轻的状态。

在这个世界上，有许许多多的人的生活都是非常失败的；一个拥有剧毒的虫子在啃咬他们的心灵。接着，让他们看一看，他们奄奄一息的状态会愈发像是一种成功。

许多人永远也不会变得甘甜，他们甚至在夏天就开始腐烂了。将它们快速固定在它们的树枝上，是一种胆怯的行为。

有太多的生命，有太多的事物悬挂在它们的树枝之上。会有一场暴风将所有早已腐烂的以及被有毒的虫子咬烂的果实从树上摇晃下来！

Would that there came preachers of speedy death! Those would be the appropriate storms and agitators of the trees of life! But I hear only slow death preached, and patience with all that is "earthly."

Ah! ye preach patience with what is earthly? This earthly is it that hath too much patience with you, ye blasphemers!

Verily, too early died that Hebrew whom the preachers of slow death honour: and to many hath it proved a calamity that he died too early.

As yet had he known only tears, and the melancholy of the Hebrews, together with the hatred of the good and just the Hebrew Jesus: then was he seized with the longing for death.

Had he but remained in the wilderness, and far from the good and just! Then, perhaps, would he have learned to live, and love the earth and laughter also!

Believe it, my brethren! He died too early; he himself would have disavowed his doctrine had he attained to my age! Noble enough was he to disavow!

But he was still immature. Immaturely loveth the youth, and immaturely also hateth he man and earth. Confined and awkward are still his soul and the wings of his spirit.

But in man there is more of the child than in the youth, and less of melancholy: better understandeth he about life and death.

Free for death, and free in death; a holy Naysayer, when there is no longer time for Yea: thus understandeth he about death and life.

That your dying may not be a reproach to man and the earth, my friends: that do I solicit

快速死亡的说教者正在向这里走来！他们将会成为生命之树上的适当的风暴和挑拨离间者！但是我只能听见缓慢的死亡在进行大肆地说教，耐心就“人间”。

唉！你用人间来说教耐心？这种尘世容忍你的已经够多的了，你这个亵渎神灵的人！

说真的，希伯来人消失得太早了，他是受人尊敬的慢性死亡的说教者：许多人都证明他是在一场重大的灾难中，过早死亡的。

然而，他所能够知道的只有哭泣以及希伯来人的忧郁和悲哀，在善意和正义的憎恶下，团结在一起——希伯来耶稣：然后他抓住了渴望已久的死亡。

但是，他却停留在那片荒野之上，远离善意和公平！然后，他或许会学会应该如何生活下去，并且热爱这片土地——以及这里的欢声笑语！

我的兄弟们，请相信吧！他去世得太早了；他自己会否认他在我这个年纪所获得的教条！他还没有高贵到可以否认这些教条的程度！但是，他仍旧是非常不成熟的。不成熟的他会去热爱年轻人，不成熟的他同样也会憎恨人们以及这片土地。他的灵魂以及他的精神的翅膀仍旧处于令人感到尴尬的受限制状态。

但是，在成年人的心目中拥有的小孩要比年轻人的多，并且他们拥有更少的忧郁状态：能够更好地理解他的生活和死亡。

自由自在的死亡；一个神圣的反对者，当我们不再拥有说是的时间：就要去理解他的死亡和生活。

奄奄一息的你对于人们和这片土地来说，或许不是一种责备，我的朋友们：我在恳求你的灵魂之蜜。

from the honey of your soul.

In your dying shall your spirit and your virtue still shine like an evening after-glow around the earth: otherwise your dying hath been unsatisfactory.

Thus will I die myself, that ye friends may love the earth more for my sake; and earth will I again become, to have rest in her that bore me.

Verily, a goal had Zarathustra; he threw his ball. Now be ye friends the heirs of my goal; to you throw I the golden ball.

Best of all, do I see you, my friends, throw the golden ball! And so tarry I still a little while on the earth pardon me for it!

Thus spake Zarathustra.

22. THE BESTOWING VIRTUE

1.

When Zarathustra had taken leave of the town to which his heart was attached, the name of which is "The Pied Cow," there followed him many people who called themselves his disciples, and kept him company. Thus came they to a crossroad. Then Zarathustra told them that he now wanted to go alone; for he was fond of going alone. His disciples, however, presented him at his departure with a staff, on the golden handle of which a serpent twined round the sun.

你的精神和你的道德将会在奄奄一息的你的身体内散发出闪耀的光芒，就像在夜晚照耀着这片土地的夕阳余晖；要不然，你的死亡将是不能够让人感到满意的。

因此，我会死去，你们这些朋友们会因为我的缘故而更加热爱这片土地；并且我会再一次成为在她的身上安息的土壤。

说真的，查拉图斯特拉有一个目标；他扔掉了他的球。现在，让你的朋友们成为我的目标的继承人吧；我会把金灿灿的球抛给你。

我的朋友们，我能看到你们，当然是最好的，扔出金灿灿的球吧！所以，我还要在这片土地上逗留一小段时间——请你们可以谅解我！

查拉图斯特拉如是说。

22．赠予的德行

（1）

当查拉图斯特拉离开这个小镇，前往令他的内心魂牵梦绕的地方的时候，那个被人们称为“花牛”的镇子，在他的身后跟随着许许多多的人，他们都说自己是查拉图斯特拉的门徒，并且随时陪伴在查拉图斯特拉的身旁。然后，他们这群人来到了一个十字路口。于是，查拉图斯特拉告诉他们，他现在想一个人走；因为他特别喜欢独自一个人前行。但是，他的门徒们在他将要离去的地方，向他展示了一个权杖，那个权杖的金色的手柄上，有一条环绕着太阳的毒蛇。查拉图斯特拉看到这个权杖之后，非常的开心，他

Zarathustra rejoiced on account of the staff, and supported himself thereon; then spake he thus to his disciples:

Tell me, pray: how came gold to the highest value? Because it is uncommon, and unprofiting, and beaming, and soft in lustre; it always bestoweth itself.

Only as image of the highest virtue came gold to the highest value. Goldlike, beameth the glance of the bestower. Gold-lustre maketh peace between moon and sun.

Uncommon is the highest virtue, and unprofiting, beaming is it, and soft of lustre: a bestowing virtue is the highest virtue.

Verily, I divine you well, my disciples: ye strive like me for the bestowing virtue. What should ye have in common with cats and wolves?

It is your thirst to become sacrifices and gifts yourselves: and therefore have ye the thirst to accumulate all riches in your soul.

Insatiably striveth your soul for treasures and jewels, because your virtue is insatiable in desiring to bestow.

Ye constrain all things to flow towards you and into you, so that they shall flow back again out of your fountain as the gifts of your love.

Verily, an appropriator of all values must such bestowing love become; but healthy and holy, call I this selfishness.

Another selfishness is there, an all-too-poor and hungry kind, which would always steal the selfishness of the sick, the sickly selfishness.

打算从今以后都用这个来当他的拐杖；然后，他对他的门徒们说道：

告诉我，祈祷：为什么金子会拥有最贵重的价值？因为金子是非常不同寻常的、利润极高的、闪闪发光，并且散发着柔软的光泽；它总是给自己赋予价值。

只有当最崇高的道德的形象被赋予金子的时候，它才能拥有最昂贵的价值。犹如金子一般，闪耀着赋予者的目光，金子的光泽在月亮和太阳之间，创造了和平。

最昂贵的道德是非常不同寻常的、利润极高的、闪闪发光，并且散发着柔软的光泽；一种被赋予的道德就是最昂贵的道德。

说真的，我非常了解你们，我的门徒们，你们和我一样，都在努力寻找被赋予的道德。你们应该和小猫和狼有什么共同点吗？

你们非常渴望让自己成为牺牲品以及礼物：因此，你们非常渴望在你们的灵魂之中积聚所有的财富。

你那贪得无厌的灵魂在奋力寻找宝藏和珠宝，因为你那渴望得到被赋予的灵魂是永远也不会感到满足的。

你阻挡任何事物流向你的方向，并且进入你的身体，这样它们就会像你的爱的礼物一样，再一次离开你的喷泉。

说真的，你们那赋予的爱必须成为种种价值的掠夺者，但是，我称这种自私自利为健康和神圣。

这里还有另一种自私自利，一个极度贫穷、极度饥饿的人，他总是想偷窃——虚弱的自私自利，处在虚弱状态下的自私自利。

偷窃者会把目光放在任何闪耀着光芒的东西之上；在饥饿的渴望之下，他能够知道

With the eye of the thief it looketh upon all that is lustrous; with the craving of hunger it measureth him who hath abundance; and ever doth it prowl round the tables of bestowers.

Sickness speaketh in such craving, and invisible degeneration; of a sickly body, speaketh the larcenous craving of this selfishness.

Tell me, my brother, what do we think bad, and worst of all? Is it not degeneration? And we always suspect degeneration when the bestowing soul is lacking.

Upward goeth our course from genera on to super-genera. But a horror to us is the degenerating sense, which saith: "All for myself."

Upward soareth our sense: thus is it a simile of our body, a simile of an elevation. Such similes of elevations are the names of the virtues.

Thus goeth the body through history, a becomer and fighter. And the spirit what is it to the body? Its fights' and victories' herald, its companion and echo.

Similes, are all names of good and evil; they do not speak out, they only hint. A fool who seeketh knowledge from them!

Give heed, my brethren, to every hour when your spirit would speak in similes: there is the origin of your virtue.

Elevated is then your body, and raised up; with its delight, enraptureth it the spirit; so that it becometh creator, and valuer, and lover, and everything's benefactor.

When your heart overfloweth broad and full like the river, a blessing and a danger to the lowlanders: there is the origin of your virtue.

谁拥有巨额的财富；并且始终徘徊在赋予者的桌子旁。

虚弱述说着强烈的渴望和不可见的退化；一个患有疾病的身体，在述说着这种自私自利所拥有的盗窃意图的强烈渴求。

我的兄弟们，请告诉我，我们所认为的坏事情是什么？最糟糕的事情是什么？难道它不是退化吗？——当馈赠的灵魂严重缺乏的时候，我们总是倾向于怀疑退化。

我们的进程会从普通的种类跃升到超凡脱俗的种类。但是令我们感到害怕的是不断退化的感觉，它好像在说："这些全都是我的。"

我们的意识在向上飞升：那是我们身体的明喻，那是一种提升的明喻。类似这样的提升的明喻就是道德的代名词。当身体经历了历史的变迁之后，它就会变成一个斗士。还有精神——它对于身体来说，究竟是什么东西呢？它是战斗和胜利的先驱者，它是陪在身边的同伴和反复出现的回声。

明喻，是所有善意和邪恶的代名词；它们并不会脱口而出，它们只能暗示。一个愚笨的人会从它们那里寻求知识！

我的兄弟们，当你们的精神开始在明喻中说话的时候，我恳请你们留意每时每刻：这里会有你们的道德的起源。

然后，你们的躯体就会得到升华，并且被抬高；内心充满喜悦，并且对它的精神感到着迷；于是，它成为了创造者、评估者、恋人以及任何事情的施恩者。

当你们的心灵向四周泛滥，并且向河流一样充实的时候，来自低地的人们就会得到祝福和危险：这就是你们的道德的起源。

当人们对你们的称赞已经超越了赞美和批判的时候，你们的意志就会命令所有的事

When ye are exalted above praise and blame, and your will would command all things, as a loving one's will: there is the origin of your virtue.

When ye despise pleasant things, and the effeminate couch, and cannot couch far enough from the effeminate: there is the origin of your virtue.

When ye are willers of one will, and when that change of every need is needful to you: there is the origin of your virtue.

Verily, a new good and evil is it! Verily, a new deep murmuring, and the voice of a new fountain!

Power is it, this new virtue; a ruling thought is it, and around it a subtle soul: a golden sun, with the serpent of knowledge around it.

2.

Here paused Zarathustra awhile, and looked lovingly on his disciples.

Then he continued to speak thus and his voice had changed:

Remain true to the earth, my brethren, with the power of your virtue! Let your bestowing love and your knowledge be devoted to be the meaning of the earth! Thus do I pray and conjure you.

Let it not fly away from the earthly and beat against eternal walls with its wings! Ah, there hath always been so much flown-away virtue!

Lead, like me, the flown-away virtue back to the earth yea, back to body and life: that it may

情，就好比一个充满爱的意志：这就是你们的道德的起源。

当你们蔑视令人感到愉快的事情，柔软舒适的长沙发，但是它又远没有达到柔软的程度：这就是你们的道德的起源。

但你们对某一种意志充满信任的时候，当任何需要的改变对于你们来说，都是势在必行的时候：这就是你们的道德的起源。

说真的，这是一种全新的善与恶！说真的，这是一种崭新的、深沉的喃喃自语声，它是一个新的喷泉的声音！

这种全新的道德拥有强大的力量；这是一种具有统治力的想法，并且围绕着一个微不足道的灵魂：一个金灿灿的太阳，并且知道毒蛇就缠绕在它的周围。

（2）

查拉图斯特拉在这里停留了一会儿，并且用非常深情的眼神看着他的门徒们。然后，他继续说道——他改变了他的嗓音：

我的兄弟们，要利用你们道德的力量对这片土地保持真实！让你们馈赠的爱和知识成为这片土地的意义所在！因此，我在这里恳求你们。

不要让它飞离这片尘世，不要让它用自己的翅膀拍击永恒的墙壁！噢，在这个世界上，总是有许许多多逃掉的道德吧！

那个领头的，就像我一样，飞离这里的道德的领头人重新回到了这片土地之上——是的，它回到了肉体和生活之中：它或许会给地球赋予它自身的含义，一个人类的含义！

give to the earth its meaning, a human meaning!

A hundred times hitherto hath spirit as well as virtue flown away and blundered. Alas! in our body dwelleth still all this delusion and blundering: body and will hath it there become.

A hundred times hitherto hath spirit as well as virtue attempted and erred. Yea, an attempt hath man been. Alas, much ignorance and error hath become embodied in us!

Not only the rationality of millenniums also their madness, breaketh out in us. Dangerous is it to be an heir.

Still fight we step by step with the giant Chance, and over all mankind hath hitherto ruled nonsense, the lack-of-sense.

Let your spirit and your virtue be devoted to the sense of the earth, my brethren: let the value of everything be determined anew by you! Therefore shall ye be fighters! Therefore shall ye be creators!

Intelligently doth the body purify itself; attempting with intelligence it exalteth itself; to the discerners all impulses sanctify themselves; to the exalted the soul becometh joyful.

Physician, heal thyself: then wilt thou also heal thy patient. Let it be his best cure to see with his eyes him who maketh himself whole.

A thousand paths are there which have never yet been trodden; a thousand salubrities and hidden islands of life. Unexhausted and undiscovered is still man and man's world.

Awake and hearken, ye lonesome ones! From the future come winds with stealthy pinions, and to fine ears good tidings are proclaimed.

直到今天，飞离这里的精神和道德，所犯下的错误已经超过了一百次。唉！所有这些假象和笨拙的状态仍旧存在于我们的体内：随后，它们就成为了躯体和意志。

直到今天，精神和道德已经尝试了上百次，也失败了上百次。是的，这是人类的尝试。唉，自此，我们的身体里包含了越来越多的无知和错误！

不单单是千禧年的合理性行动——同样还有它们的疯狂，在我们的体内爆发了。所以，成为一名继任者是一件非常危险的事情。

在巨大的机遇面前，我们仍旧一步接着一步的进行战斗，在所有人之上，裁决谬论，缺乏意识的事物。

我的兄弟们，将你们的精神和你们的道德投入到对土地的感知之上：让你们再重新评判一下世间万物的价值所在！因此，你们应该成为战士！因此，你们应该成为创造者！

躯体非常明智的净化着自己；用赞扬自己的智慧去尝试；让所有的冲动将具有洞察力的人神圣化；并且让高尚的灵魂变得欢快愉悦。

内科医生可以治愈你们：那么，同样的，你们能够治愈好你们的病人。让它成为他最好的解药，并且用他的眼睛去观察究竟是谁创造了完整的他。

这里有一千条尚未被人们踩踏的道路；上千个有益身心健康的地方以及隐藏的生命之岛。人类和人类的世界仍旧是没有用尽的，没有被观察透彻的。

你们这些孤单的人们，你们都醒一醒，好好用耳朵听着！带有隐秘的小翅膀的风从遥远的未来来到这里，而漂亮的耳朵则在宣布美好的佳音。

今天，你们这些孤独的人们，你们这些脱离尘世的人们，终有一天，你们会成为

Ye lonesome ones of to-day, ye seceding ones, ye shall one day be a people: out of you who have chosen yourselves, shall a chosen people arise: and out of it the Superman.

Verily, a place of healing shall the earth become! And already is a new odour diffused around it, a salvation-bringing odour and a new hope!

3.

When Zarathustra had spoken these words, he paused, like one who had not said his last word; and long did he balance the staff doubtfully in his hand. At last he spake thus and his voice had changed:

I now go alone, my disciples! Ye also now go away, and alone! So will I have it.

Verily, I advise you: depart from me, and guard yourselves against Zarathustra! And better still: be ashamed of him! Perhaps he hath deceived you.

The man of knowledge must be able not only to love his enemies, but also to hate his friends.

One requiteth a teacher badly if one remain merely a scholar. And why will ye not pluck at my wreath?

Ye venerate me; but what if your veneration should some day collapse? Take heed lest a statue crush you!

Ye say, ye believe in Zarathustra? But of what account is Zarathustra! Ye are my believers:

一个民族：在选择了你们的那个群体里，定会产生一个被人们所选择的民族——那就是超人。

说真的，这片土地应该会成为一个具有治愈效果的地方！它是一种已经在四周弥漫开来的全新的香气，这是一种能够带来救赎的气味——这是全新的希望！

（3）

当查拉图斯特拉说完这些话的时候，他停顿了，就像一个还没有说完最后一句话的人；他长时间用双手摆弄着那个权杖，心中充满了怀疑。最后，他说道——他改变了他的嗓音：

我的门徒们，我现在要一个人前行了！你们现在也可以动身了，独自一人！就像我一样。

说真的，我建议你们：离开我，并且提醒自己要时刻提防查拉图斯特拉！而且最好要替他感到羞耻！或许他会欺骗你。

一个拥有丰富学识的人不仅要热爱他的敌人们，同时也要痛恨他的朋友们。

如果一个人只能是一名学者的话，他就会用非常恶劣的方式报答他的老师。那么，为什么你不拉扯我的花环呢？

你们尊敬我；但是，如果有一天你们的尊敬分崩离析了呢？要时刻提防，不要让雕像压在你们的身上！

你们说，你们相信查拉图斯特拉？但是你们从哪些方面相信查拉图斯特拉！

but of what account are all believers!

Ye had not yet sought yourselves: then did ye find me. So do all believers; therefore all belief is of so little account.

Now do I bid you lose me and find yourselves; and only when ye have all denied me, will I return unto you.

Verily, with other eyes, my brethren, shall I then seek my lost ones; with another love shall I then love you.

And once again shall ye have become friends unto me, and children of one hope: then will I be with you for the third time, to celebrate the great noontide with you.

And it is the great noontide, when man is in the middle of his course between animal and Superman, and celebrateth his advance to the evening as his highest hope: for it is the advance to a new morning.

At such time will the down-goer bless himself, that he should be an over-goer; and the sun of his knowledge will be at noontide.

"Dead are all the gods: Now do we desire the superman to live." Let this be our final will at the great noontide!

" and only when ye have all denied me, will I return unto you.

Verily, with other eyes, my brethren, shall I then seek my lost ones; with another love shall I then love you." Zarathustra, I., "The Bestowing Virtue."

你们是我的信徒们：但是你们从哪些方面认定自己是信徒！

你们还没有寻找你们自己：可是你们找到了我。所有的信徒们都找到了我；因此，任何的信仰都是毫无价值的。

现在我命令你们都离开我的视线，找寻你们自己；只有当你们所有人全都否认我的时候，我才会回到你们的身边。

说真的，我的兄弟们，我会用另一双眼睛找寻我失去的人们；我会用另一种爱去关爱你们。

并且，你们会再一次成为我的朋友，拥有同一个希望的孩子们：这样的话，我就会第三次和你们在一起，共同庆祝这一伟大的时刻。

当人们处在动物和超人之间，把庆祝他的发展直到夜晚作为他最崇高的希望：这就是伟大的时刻，这就是一个崭新的清晨的提前到来。

“所有的神灵都死了：现在，我们要渴望像超人一样去生活。”——让这句话成为我们在伟大的时刻之中的最后意愿吧！

查拉图斯特拉如是说。

23. THE CHILD WITH THE MIRROR

After this Zarathustra returned again into the mountains to the solitude of his cave, and withdrew himself from men, waiting like a sower who hath scattered his seed. His soul, however, became impatient and full of longing for those whom he loved: because he had still much to give them. For this is hardest of all: to close the open hand out of love, and keep modest as a giver.

Thus passed with the lonesome one months and years; his wisdom meanwhile increased, and caused him pain by its abundance.

One morning, however, he awoke ere the rosy dawn, and having meditated long on his couch, at last spake thus to his heart: Why did I startle in my dream, so that I awoke? Did not a child come to me, carrying a mirror?

"O Zarathustra" said the child unto me "look at thyself in the mirror!"

But when I looked into the mirror, I shrieked, and my heart throbbed: for not myself did I

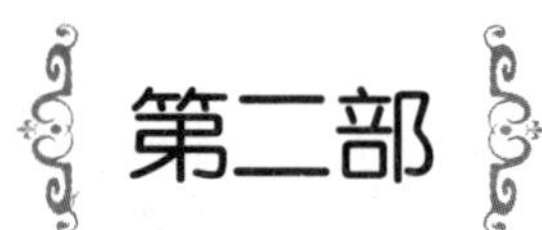

23．持着镜子的小孩

查拉图斯特拉再一次回到了深山里，他来到了那个偏僻荒凉的洞穴，他离开了那些人，就像一个播撒种子的播种者一样苦苦等待。但是，他的灵魂开始变得不耐烦，并且时刻不停地渴望能够见到那些他爱着的人们：因为，他仍旧会把太多的东西给予他们。这是万事中最困难的：在爱中合上张开的手掌，并且始终让谦逊作为一个给予者。

于是，就这样，孤独寂寞的一个月过去了，一年过去了；与此同时，他的智慧也在与日俱增，并且这种丰富的智慧会令他感到非常痛苦。

然而，有一天早晨，他在朝霞到来之前起床了，然后，他在沙发上静静地沉思了很长的时间，最终他对自己的内心说道：为什么我要在自己的梦境中感到惊慌失措，以致于让我从梦中惊醒？难道没有一个小孩子向我走过来吗？手里还拿着一面镜子？

“噢，查拉图斯特拉，——”那个小孩子对我说道，“好好看看镜子里的你吧！”

但是，当我看向镜子里的时候，我尖叫了起来，我的心开始剧烈地颤动起来：因为我从镜子里看到的根本就不是我自己，那里面呈现的是一个魔鬼的诡异笑容和嘲笑。

see therein, but a devil's grimace and derision.

Verily, all too well do I understand the dream's portent and monition: my doctrine is in danger; tares want to be called wheat!

Mine enemies have grown powerful and have disfigured the likeness of my doctrine, so that my dearest ones have to blush for the gifts that I gave them.

Lost are my friends; the hour hath come for me to seek my lost ones!

With these words Zarathustra started up, not however like a person in anguish seeking relief, but rather like a seer and a singer whom the spirit inspireth. With amazement did his eagle and serpent gaze upon him: for a coming bliss overspread his countenance like the rosy dawn.

What hath happened unto me, mine animals? said Zarathustra. Am I not transformed? Hath not bliss come unto me like a whirlwind?

Foolish is my happiness, and foolish things will it speak: it is still too young so have patience with it!

Wounded am I by my happiness: all sufferers shall be physicians unto me!

To my friends can I again go down, and also to mine enemies! Zarathustra can again speak and bestow, and show his best love to his loved ones!

My impatient love overfloweth in streams, down towards sunrise and sunset. Out of silent mountains and storms of affliction, rusheth my soul into the valleys.

Too long have I longed and looked into the distance. Too long hath solitude possessed me: thus have I unlearned to keep silence.

说真的，我非常了解梦想的前兆和忠告：我的教条已经处在危险之中了；野豌豆籽想被人们称为小麦！

我的敌人们已经成长的非常强大，并且它损毁了我的教条的相似性，以致于，我最挚爱的人们会红着脸接受我送给他们的礼物。

我的朋友们全都消失了；现在是时候让我去寻找那些我失去的朋友们了！在说完这些话之后，查拉图斯特拉站了起来，然而，他看上去并不像是一位饱受痛苦，想要找到解脱的人，而是像一位精神得到鼓舞的探寻者、歌手。他的鹰和毒蛇用非常惊异的眼神凝视着他：因为一个即将到来的祝福撒播在他的面容之上，看上去就像早上的朝一样。

我的身上究竟发生了什么事？还有我的动物们呢？——查拉图斯特拉说道。我没有被变形吧？祝福没有像龙卷风一样席卷我的全身吧？

我的快乐是愚蠢的，并且那些愚蠢的事物会说：它毕竟还是太小了——所以我们对它要有十足的耐心！

我被自己的快乐弄得遍体鳞伤：所有遭遇磨难的人都将是降临在我身上的内科医生！为了我的朋友，我还可以再一次平静下来，同样还有我的敌人们！查拉图斯特拉再一次说道，并且向他所爱的人展示了他的爱！

我那迫不及待的爱在溪流里充溢着，那条溪流朝着日升日落的地方顺流而下。离开寂静的深山和苦难的暴风，将我的灵魂冲刷进山谷。

在很长的一段时间里，我用渴望的眼神注视着远方。在很长的一段时间里，孤独寂寞占据着我的身体：因此，我忘记了该如何保持寂静。

Utterance have I become altogether, and the brawling of a brook from high rocks: downward into the valleys will I hurl my speech.

And let the stream of my love sweep into unfrequented channels! How should a stream not finally find its way to the sea!

Forsooth, there is a lake in me, sequestered and self-sufficing; but the stream of my love beareth this along with it, down to the sea!

New paths do I tread, a new speech cometh unto me; tired have I become like all creators of the old tongues. No longer will my spirit walk on worn-out soles.

Too slowly runneth all speaking for me: into thy chariot, O storm, do I leap! And even thee will I whip with my spite!

Like a cry and an huzza will I traverse wide seas, till I find the Happy Isles where my friends sojourn;

And mine enemies amongst them! How I now love every one unto whom I may but speak! Even mine enemies pertain to my bliss.

And when I want to mount my wildest horse, then doth my spear always help me up best: it is my foot's ever ready servant:

The spear which I hurl at mine enemies! How grateful am I to mine enemies that I may at last hurl it!

Too great hath been the tension of my cloud: 'twixt laughters of lightnings will I cast hail-showers into the depths.

总而言之，我开始变得说话吞吞吐吐，从高耸的岩石里流下来的小河的哗哗声：在它流进山谷的时候，我会慷慨激昂地进行我的演讲。

并且让我的爱意之流横扫人迹罕至的水道！你见过哪条溪流最终找不到并入大海的水道！

坦白地讲，我的内心里有一个湖泊，它非常幽静，并且过度自信；但是，我的爱意之流将它一并带在身上，顺流直下——最终并入到了大海之中！

我踏在了崭新的道路之上，一个全新的声音来到了我的面前；我开始变得厌倦——就像所有的创造者那样——操持着古老的语言。我的精神将不会再走在被磨坏的鞋底上了。

它们缓慢地跑过来跟我说：——走入你的二轮战车，噢，是暴风，我能跳过去的！即使是你，也免不了遭受我那怨恨的鞭打！

我会像喊着口号，呼喊着万岁一样穿过宽阔的海洋，直到我发现我的朋友们在此逗留的快乐小岛；而且，我的敌人们也在他们其中！现在，我会热爱所有那些我能够与他们进行交谈的人！即使是我的敌人们也属于我的快乐世界。

但是，当我要骑上我那匹最狂野的骏马的时候，我的长矛总是能够助我一臂之力爬上马背：它就是随时准备为我的脚服务的仆人：

这就是我向我的敌人们抛掷的长矛！我对他们是如此的感恩戴德，以致我会在最后的时刻才把我的那个长矛投掷出去！

我的云朵的拉伸力实在是太大了：我会在闪电的笑声之间，把冰雹投向深处。

我的内心会喘起粗气，然后，将它扔出去；它会狂暴地将暴风吹向深山里：因此，

Violently will my breast then heave; violently will it blow its storm over the mountains: thus cometh its assuagement.

Verily, like a storm cometh my happiness, and my freedom! But mine enemies shall think that the evil one roareth over their heads.

Yea, ye also, my friends, will be alarmed by my wild wisdom; and perhaps ye will flee therefrom, along with mine enemies.

Ah, that I knew how to lure you back with shepherds' flutes! Ah, that my lioness wisdom would learn to roar softly! And much have we already learned with one another!

My wild wisdom became pregnant on the lonesome mountains; on the rough stones did she bear the youngest of her young.

Now runneth she foolishly in the arid wilderness, and seeketh and seeketh the soft sward mine old, wild wisdom!

On the soft sward of your hearts, my friends! on your love, would she fain couch her dearest one!

Thus spake Zarathustra.

24. IN THE HAPPY ISLES

The figs fall from the trees, they are good and sweet; and in falling the red skins of them break. A north wind am I to ripe figs.

寂静就到来了。

说真的，我的快乐就像是一阵暴风一样来到了我的身边，还有我的自由！但是我的敌人们会认为那些邪恶的家伙们在他们的头顶上肆意的咆哮。

是的，还有我的朋友们，你们也会被我狂野的智慧吓到；或许，你们会因此而逃掉，连同我的敌人们一起逃掉。

噢，我知道应该如何用牧羊人的长笛诱惑你回心转意！噢，我那犹如猛狮一般的智慧定能学会如何用轻柔的方式吼叫！并且，我们已经跟另一个人学到了很多东西！

对于那些孤零零的山峰来说，我的狂野的智慧会变得富有意义；她在粗糙的石头上，承担着她的年轻中最小的那部分。

现在，她用非常愚笨的脚步奔向干燥荒芜的荒野，并且开始寻找柔软的草皮——我的古老的、狂野的智慧！

我的朋友们！在你们内心的柔软的草地之上——在你们的爱之上，她会欣然地让她最挚爱的人坐在那上面！

查拉图斯特拉如是说。

24．在快乐的岛屿上

无花果从树上掉了下来，它们是非常甘甜、非常优质的水果；当它们在下落的过程之中，它们表面的红色外皮破裂了。是一阵北风催熟了这些无花果。

这些教条就像那些无花果一样，掉落在了你们的身上。我的朋友们：现在，吸收它

Thus, like figs, do these doctrines fall for you, my friends: imbibe now their juice and their sweet substance! It is autumn all around, and clear sky, and afternoon.

Lo, what fullness is around us! And out of the midst of superabundance, it is delightful to look out upon distant seas.

Once did people say God, when they looked out upon distant seas; now, however, have I taught you to say, Superman.

God is a conjecture: but I do not wish your conjecturing to reach beyond your creating will.

Could ye create a God? Then, I pray you, be silent about all Gods! But ye could well create the Superman.

Not perhaps ye yourselves, my brethren! But into fathers and forefathers of the Superman could ye transform yourselves: and let that be your best creating!

God is a conjecture: but I should like your conjecturing restricted to the conceivable.

Could ye conceive a God? But let this mean Will to Truth unto you, that everything be transformed into the humanly conceivable, the humanly visible, the humanly sensible! Your own discernment shall ye follow out to the end!

And what ye have called the world shall but be created by you: your reason, your likeness, your will, your love, shall it itself become! And verily, for your bliss, ye discerning ones!

And how would ye endure life without that hope, ye discerning ones? Neither in the inconceivable could ye have been born, nor in the irrational.

But that I may reveal my heart entirely unto you, my friends: If there were gods, how could

们的果汁和它们甘甜的果肉！现在已经是秋天了，下午的天空晴空万里。

瞧呀！我们的四周充满了绿意盎然！并且在这种超级富足的物质之外，抬头看向远方的海洋也会让你们感到心旷神怡。

人们曾经在他们抬起头看向遥远的海洋的时候，呼唤上帝；但是现在，我会告诉你们，应该呼唤超人。

上帝只是人们的一种主观臆想：但是，我不想让你们去臆想超越你们那具有创造性的意志的东西。

你们能不能创造出一个上帝？——之后，我会向你们祈祷，对所有的神灵都保持默不作声的状态！但是，你们可以创造出超人。

或许不是你们，我的兄弟们！而是超人的父亲和先父能够改变你们，并且让它成为你们的最好的创造物！

上帝只是人们的一种主观臆想：但是，我应该希望你们能够在只局限于你们可以感知到的东西的范围内，臆想事物。

你们能感知上帝吗？让这种意义把事实真相告诉你，任何事物都会转变成人类可以感知的事物，转变成人们用肉眼能够看到的事物，转变成人类能够感觉到的事物！你们自身的辨别力将会陪伴你们直到最后！

并且，那个被你们称作是世界的东西就是由你们创造出来的：它会成为你们的理性、你们的相似性、你们的意志以及你们的爱！说真的，对于你们这些具有洞察力的人们来说，它会成为你们的快乐世界！

你们这些具有洞察力的人们是如何在没有任何希望的情况下，忍受生活的艰辛呢？

I endure it to be no God! Therefore there are no Gods.

Yea, I have drawn the conclusion; now, however, doth it draw me.

God is a conjecture: but who could drink all the bitterness of this conjecture without dying? Shall his faith be taken from the creating one, and from the eagle his flights into eagle-heights?

God is a thought it maketh all the straight crooked, and all that standeth reel. What? Time would be gone, and all the perishable would be but a lie?

To think this is giddiness and vertigo to human limbs, and even vomiting to the stomach: verily, the reeling sickness do I call it, to conjecture such a thing.

Evil do I call it and misanthropic: all that teaching about the one, and the plenum, and the unmoved, and the sufficient, and the imperishable!

All the imperishable that's but a simile, and the poets lie too much.

But of time and of becoming shall the best similes speak: a praise shall they be, and a justification of all perishableness!

Creating that is the great salvation from suffering, and life's alleviation. But for the creator to appear, suffering itself is needed, and much transformation.

Yea, much bitter dying must there be in your life, ye creators! Thus are ye advocates and justifiers of all perishableness.

For the creator himself to be the new-born child, he must also be willing to be the child-bearer, and endure the pangs of the child-bearer.

你们既不是在让人难以想象的情况下，也不是在毫无理性的情况下出生的。但是，我还会向你们完全地显露我的内心世界，我的朋友们：如果这个世界上存在神灵的话，那么，我应该怎样忍受在没有神灵的世界里生活呢！所以，这个世界上不存在神灵。

是的，我已经做出了最终的结论；但是现在，这个结论吸引了我。

上帝只是人们的一个主观臆想：但是，有谁能够在不死掉的情况下，喝掉所有的臆想的苦涩之水呢？具有创造性的人们是否应该剥夺他的信仰，并且从老鹰的翱翔转变成老鹰的顶点？

上帝是一种思想——它能够让所有的直线变得弯曲，让所有的挺拔变得站立不稳。这是为什么？时间终究会流逝，但是所有会消逝的事物就都是谎言吗？让我们把这种轻率和头晕目眩比作是人类的四肢，它甚至会在胃里面呕吐：说真的，我会把臆想这类事情的情况称作是晕眩的疾病。

我会称它为恶魔以及愤世嫉俗：它们会教导充满物质的空间、不为所动、富足以及流芳百世！任何事物都是不朽的——这就是一种明喻，诗人们对此说了太多的谎言。

但是在时间和变化的过程当中，最优美的明喻会说：它们应该得到赞美，而所有终将逝去的事物都会得到赦免！

创造性——它就是摆脱苦难和生活的缓和剂的伟大救星。但是对于任何创造者来说，苦难本身以及转变是必不可少的。

是的，在你们的生活当中，必定会有更加痛苦的垂死挣扎，你们这些创造者们！所以，你们就是所有终将逝去的事物的拥护者和辩护者。

因为，创造者本身就是新出生的孩子，那么同样，他必须甘愿成为养育子女的人，

Verily, through a hundred souls went I my way, and through a hundred cradles and birth-throes. Many a farewell have I taken; I know the heart-breaking last hours.

But so willeth it my creating Will, my fate. Or, to tell you it more candidly: just such a fate willeth my Will.

All feeling suffereth in me, and is in prison: but my willing ever cometh to me as mine emancipator and comforter.

Willing emancipateth: that is the true doctrine of will and emancipation so teacheth you Zarathustra.

No longer willing, and no longer valuing, and no longer creating! Ah, that that great debility may ever be far from me!

And also in discerning do I feel only my will's procreating and evolving delight; and if there be innocence in my knowledge, it is because there is will to procreation in it.

Away from God and Gods did this will allure me; what would there be to create if there were Gods!

But to man doth it ever impel me anew, my fervent creative will; thus impelleth it the hammer to the stone.

Ah, ye men, within the stone slumbereth an image for me, the image of my visions! Ah, that it should slumber in the hardest, ugliest stone!

Now rageth my hammer ruthlessly against its prison. From the stone fly the fragments: what's that to me?

并且还要忍受养育子女的人在肉体上承受到的痛苦。

说真的，当我走在自己的道路上的时候，我穿过了上百个灵魂、上百个摇篮以及分娩的剧痛。我已经经历了无数次再会；我知道最后的那几个小时是非常让人心痛的。

但是我那具有创造性的意志和我的命运是如此的坚定。或是用更加坦率、诚恳的语气跟你说：这就是命运——我的意愿。

所有的感觉都在我的体内遭受着苦难，它们都被囚禁在了监狱里：但是，我的意愿会像我的解放者和安慰者一样，回到我的身边。

要想被解放：这就是意愿和解放的真正的教条——查拉图斯特拉就是这么教育你们的。

不会再有意愿，不会再有评估，也不会再有创造性！噢，这样伟大的虚弱或许会永远离我远去！

同样，在辨别的过程当中，我只能感觉到我的意愿那种生育和进化的快感；如果你说我的知识里拥有无知、天真的成分，那是因为那里面有想要生儿育女的意愿。

这种意愿在诱惑我远离上帝和众神；如果这里有众神的话，那么，这里会有什么东西会被创造出来呢！

但是，人类在驱使我那热烈的、具有创造性的意愿；驱使铁锤撞击石头。

噢，人类，在这些石头里藏着一个正在熟睡的我的形象，那是我的视觉的形象！噢，它应该沉睡在最坚硬、最丑陋的石头里！

现在，我拿起我的铁锤无情地猛击那个监狱。一些小碎片从石头上被溅了起来：那是我的什么？

我会完成它的：因为一个阴影降临在了我的身上——所有最平静、最明亮的东西全

I will complete it: for a shadow came unto me the stillest and lightest of all things once came unto me!

The beauty of the Superman came unto me as a shadow. Ah, my brethren! Of what account now are the Gods to me!

Thus spake Zarathustra.

25. THE PITIFUL

My friends, there hath arisen a satire on your friend: "Behold Zarathustra! Walketh he not amongst us as if amongst animals?"

But it is better said in this wise: "The discerning one walketh amongst men as amongst animals."

Man himself is to the discerning one: the animal with red cheeks.

How hath that happened unto him? Is it not because he hath had to be ashamed too oft?

O my friends! Thus speaketh the discerning one: shame, shame, shame that is the history of man!

And on that account doth the noble one enjoin upon himself not to abash: bashfulness doth he enjoin on himself in presence of all sufferers.

Verily, I like them not, the merciful ones, whose bliss is in their pity: too destitute are they of bashfulness.

都降临到了我的身上！

超人的美感犹如一个影子一样来到了我的身上。我的兄弟们！现在，它对于我来说，就是众神！

查拉图斯特拉如是说。

25．怜悯者

我的朋友们，一个讽刺从你们的朋友们当中产生了：“快看查拉图斯特拉！他不在我们的中间行走，就好像他在动物的中间行走一样？”

但是这句话应该用更好的方式说出来：“拥有辨别力的人在我们的中间行走，就好像在动物的中间行走一样。”

人本身就是具有辨别力的生物：拥有红色面颊的动物。

这样的事情是如何发生在他的身上？是不是因为他平时感到羞愧的次数太多了？

噢，我的朋友们！具有辨别力的人说道：羞耻、羞耻、羞耻——这就是人类的历史！

考虑到这个原因，高尚的人命令他不要再感到羞愧：他在所有遭受苦难的人的面前，命令他不要再感到羞愧。

说真的，我并不喜欢他们，那些宽大仁慈的人们，他们的幸福快乐都在他们的怜悯之中：他们十分缺乏羞愧。

如果我必须要变得怜悯，我讨厌那个称呼；如果我真成了怜悯者，那么，我宁愿站在远处。

If I must be pitiful, I dislike to be called so; and if I be so, it is preferably at a distance.

Preferably also do I shroud my head, and flee, before being recognised: and thus do I bid you do, my friends!

May my destiny ever lead unafflicted ones like you across my path, and those with whom I may have hope and repast and honey in common!

Verily, I have done this and that for the afflicted: but something better did I always seem to do when I had learned to enjoy myself better.

Since humanity came into being, man hath enjoyed himself too little: that alone, my brethren, is our original sin!

And when we learn better to enjoy ourselves, then do we unlearn best to give pain unto others, and to contrive pain.

Therefore do I wash the hand that hath helped the sufferer; therefore do I wipe also my soul.

For in seeing the sufferer suffering thereof was I ashamed on account of his shame; and in helping him, sorely did I wound his pride.

Great obligations do not make grateful, but revengeful; and when a small kindness is not forgotten, it becometh a gnawing worm.

"Be shy in accepting! Distinguish by accepting!" thus do I advise those who have naught to bestow.

I, however, am a bestower: willingly do I bestow as friend to friends. Strangers, however, and the poor, may pluck for themselves the fruit from my tree: thus doth it cause less shame.

同样的，我宁愿把自己的头包裹起来，然后在被别人认出来之前跑掉：这就是我对你下达的命令，我的朋友们！

但愿我的命运能够带领所有像你一样未受到折磨的人以及那些在希望、就餐和令人愉快的事物上跟我非常相似的人安然通过我的道路！

说真的，我已经带领那些受到过磨难的人们通过了我的道路：但是，看起来，当我学会如何更好地让自己享受的时候，我就会做一些更加具有善意的事情。

自从人性成为了生命的存在，人类就很少让自己得到享受：我的兄弟们，这就是我们最初的罪恶！

并且，当我们懂得该如何更好地让我们自己得到享受的时候，那么，我们就会忘记该如何更好地把痛苦带给别人，并且设法创造痛苦。

因此，我会冲刷那双帮助过遭受苦难的人的手；同样，我还会擦拭我的灵魂。

因为我亲眼见证了受害者在遭受苦难——因此，我更加对他的羞耻感到惭愧，帮助他的话，只能是让他的傲慢受到伤害和痛苦。

伟大的义务并不会创造出感激，而是复仇；并且当很小的善意与仁慈并没有被人们淡忘的话，那么它们就会成为令人痛苦的虫子。

“要羞于接受！要在接受中加以区分和辨别！”——这就是我给那些没有资格得到赠予的人们的建议。

但是，我自己也是个赠予者：我非常乐意用朋友的身份将东西赠予给我的朋友们。但是，那些陌生人和贫穷的人会从我的树上偷偷地摘下果实：这样做会产生更少的羞愧感。

Beggars, however, one should entirely do away with! Verily, it annoyeth one to give unto them, and it annoyeth one not to give unto them.

And likewise sinners and bad consciences! Believe me, my friends: the sting of conscience teacheth one to sting.

The worst things, however, are the petty thoughts. Verily, better to have done evilly than to have thought pettily!

To be sure, ye say: "The delight in petty evils spareth one many a great evil deed." But here one should not wish to be sparing.

Like a boil is the evil deed: it itcheth and irritateth and breaketh forth it speaketh honourably.

"Behold, I am disease," saith the evil deed: that is its honourableness.

But like infection is the petty thought: it creepeth and hideth, and wanteth to be nowhere until the whole body is decayed and withered by the petty infection.

To him however, who is possessed of a devil, I would whisper this word in the ear: "Better for thee to rear up thy devil! Even for thee there is still a path to greatness!"

Ah, my brethren! One knoweth a little too much about every one! And many a one becometh transparent to us, but still we can by no means penetrate him.

It is difficult to live among men because silence is so difficult.

And not to him who is offensive to us are we most unfair, but to him who doth not concern us at all.

If, however, thou hast a suffering friend, then be a resting-place for his suffering; like a hard

但是，乞讨者就必须完全避开这样的事！说真的，将东西施舍给他们，会让人感到烦恼，但是，不将东西施舍给他们，同样会让人们感到烦恼。

同样的，还有罪人和糟糕的道德心！相信我，我的朋友们：道德心的刺激教会了人们去叮咬。

但是，最糟糕的事情是那些琐碎、微不足道的想法。说真的，我们宁可做些邪恶的事情，也不会拥有一些琐碎的想法！

当然，你说道："微不足道的恶魔中的快乐会宽恕许多伟大的恶魔的行为。"但是，这里的人并不希望被宽恕。

邪恶的行为就像煮沸的开水：它会感到愤怒、感到不愉快，并且突然喷发——它体面地说道。

"快看呀！我是疾病，"邪恶的行为说道：这就是它值得被人们尊敬的品质。

但是，琐碎的想法就像传染：它会悄悄地爬行，将自己隐藏起来，它想让自己无所不在——直到它的整个身体都开始变得腐朽，并且在微不足道的传染的作用下枯萎。

但是，对于他这个内心被一个恶魔占据的人来说，我会在他的耳边轻声地说："你最好应该抬起你的恶魔！即使是这样，对于你来说，这里仍旧有一条通向伟大的道路！"

噢，我的兄弟们！他对于任何人的了解都太深入了！并且太多的人向我们保持透明的状态，但是，我们仍然不能洞察他。

在人类当中生存是一件非常困难的事情，因为保持寂静特别难。

对于我们来说，那个经常冒犯我们的家伙并不是最不公平的，真正最不公平的是他从来就没有关心过我们。

bed, however, a camp-bed: thus wilt thou serve him best.

And if a friend doeth thee wrong, then say: "I forgive thee what thou hast done unto me; that thou hast done it unto thyself, however how could I forgive that!"

Thus speaketh all great love: it surpasseth even forgiveness and pity.

One should hold fast one's heart; for when one letteth it go, how quickly doth one's head run away!

Ah, where in the world have there been greater follies than with the pitiful? And what in the world hath caused more suffering than the follies of the pitiful?

Woe unto all loving ones who have not an elevation which is above their pity!

Thus spake the devil unto me, once on a time: "Even God hath his hell: it is his love for man."

And lately, did I hear him say these words: "God is dead: of his pity for man hath God died."

So be ye warned against pity: From thence there yet cometh unto men a heavy cloud! Verily, I understand weather-signs!

But attend also to this word: All great love is above all its pity: for it seeketh to create what is loved!

"Myself do I offer unto my love, and my neighbour as myself" such is the language of all creators.

All creators, however, are hard.

但是，如果你有一个正在遭受磨难的朋友，然后你为那个遭受苦难的朋友找了一个可以安静休息的地方，比如一张硬床，帆布床：因此，你能用最好的方式服侍他。

如果你的一个朋友有负于你，然后你说道："我原谅你对我所做的一切；但是，你对自己也做出了这样的事，我又怎么能谅解你呢！"

因此，所有伟大的爱说道：它甚至超越了原谅和怜悯。

一个人应该快速地、牢牢地抓住他的心；因为，他一旦失去它，理智就会快速地逝去！

噢，在这个世界上，究竟哪里的愚蠢要比怜悯还要伟大？在这个世界上，究竟哪里产生的磨难要比怜悯的愚蠢还要多？

悲痛降临到了所有拥有爱的人身上，他们的爱还没有达到超过他们的怜悯的程度！

因此，有那么一次，恶魔对我说："即使是上帝，也有属于自己的地狱：那就是他对于人类的爱。"

最近，我听到他说了这样的话："上帝已经死了，将自己的怜悯施加给人类的上帝已经死了。"

所以，你们大家要小心提防怜悯：从那以后，有一朵厚重的云彩来到了人世间！说真的，我理解那些天气迹象带来的含义！

但是，我同样还要说：所有伟大的爱都会高于它自身的怜悯：因为它在寻找——创造什么是爱的理念！

"我会把我的爱奉献给我自己，还有我的邻居们"——这就是所有的创造者都会说的话。

但是，所有的创造者们，都是非常冷酷无情的。

Thus spake Zarathustra.

26. THE PRIESTS

And one day Zarathustra made a sign to his disciples, and spake these words unto them:

"Here are priests: but although they are mine enemies, pass them quietly and with sleeping swords!

Even among them there are heroes; many of them have suffered too much : so they want to make others suffer.

Bad enemies are they: nothing is more revengeful than their meekness. And readily doth he soil himself who toucheth them.

But my blood is related to theirs; and I want withal to see my blood honoured in theirs."

And when they had passed, a pain attacked Zarathustra; but not long had he struggled with the pain, when he began to speak thus:

It moveth my heart for those priests. They also go against my taste; but that is the smallest matter unto me, since I am among men.

But I suffer and have suffered with them: prisoners are they unto me, and stigmatised ones. He whom they call Saviour put them in fetters:

In fetters of false values and fatuous words! Oh, that some one would save them from their Saviour!

查拉图斯特拉如是说。

26．教士们

有一天，查拉图斯特拉给他的门徒们做出了一个手势，然后对他们说了如下一番话：

“这些是我的牧师们：但是，他们同样也是我的敌人，带着剑悄然地从他们身边经过。

即使是在这些人中，也有很多英雄；他们当中的大多数都遭受过很多磨难：所以，他们想让其他人也遭受他们曾经遭受过的磨难。

他们都是很恶劣的敌人：他们的温顺要比任何事物都更加充满仇恨。很显然，他要染脏任何接触过他们的人。

但是，我和他们是有血缘关系的；尽管这样，我还是想观察被他们敬重的，有关于我的血缘。”

当他们相继去世的时候，一种悲痛的感觉突袭了查拉图斯特拉，但是，他还没和那种悲痛斗争多久，就说了一下这番话：

那些牧师深深地触动了我的心灵。同样，他们还跟我的品味作对，不过，自从我成为人类当中的一员之后，这些对于我来说都是最无关紧要的小事。

但是，我遭受到了苦难，并且同他们一起经历磨难：他们把罪犯和蒙上污名的人都交给了我。那个被人们称为救世主的人，给这些人戴上了锁链：

伪造的价值和愚蠢的话语的锁链！噢，那就是将他们从他们的救世主那里拯救出来的人啊！

On an isle they once thought they had landed, when the sea tossed them about; but behold, it was a slumbering monster!

False values and fatuous words: these are the worst monsters for mortals long slumbereth and waiteth the fate that is in them.

But at last it cometh and awaketh and devoureth and engulfeth whatever hath built tabernacles upon it.

Oh, just look at those tabernacles which those priests have built themselves! Churches, they call their sweet-smelling caves!

Oh, that falsified light, that mustified air! Where the soul may not fly aloft to its height!

But so enjoineth their belief: "On your knees, up the stair, ye sinners!"

Verily, rather would I see a shameless one than the distorted eyes of their shame and devotion!

Who created for themselves such caves and penitence-stairs? Was it not those who sought to conceal themselves, and were ashamed under the clear sky?

And only when the clear sky looketh again through ruined roofs, and down upon grass and red poppies on ruined walls will I again turn my heart to the seats of this God.

They called God that which opposed and afflicted them: and verily, there was much hero-spirit in their worship!

And they knew not how to love their God otherwise than by nailing men to the cross!

As corpses they thought to live; in black draped they their corpses; even in their talk do I

他们曾经在一个小岛上，认为他们已经着陆了，当海水将他们抛起来的时候，他们睁眼看到，原来它是一个正在沉睡的大怪物！

伪造的价值和愚蠢的话语：对于凡人们来说，可以称得上是最恐怖的怪物——他们一直在沉睡，静静地等待着他们的命运的到来。

但是最后，他们会走过来，在清醒的状态下，吞噬掉任何建立在住棚之上的东西。

噢，你们快来看看，那些由牧师们自己搭建起来的住棚啊！教堂，他们管这些带有甜蜜气息的洞穴叫做教堂！

噢，那个根本不存在的光芒和必须存在的空气！在这里，灵魂或许不能飞升到它想要达到的高度！

但是，他们的信仰命令道："你们都跪下来，爬上台阶，你们这些罪人！"

说真的，与其见到他们的羞愧和虔诚的被扭曲的眼睛，我宁可见到一个厚颜无耻的人！

究竟是谁给他们建造了这样的洞穴和用来赎罪的台阶？为什么不是那些寻求隐藏自己，在晴朗的天空下感到羞愧的人们呢？

并且，只有当晴朗的天空再一次看向被毁坏的房顶以及被毁坏的房顶上的青草和红色的罂粟花的时候——我才会重新将我的内心朝向这个上帝的位置之上。

他们称那些反对并且折磨他们的神灵为上帝：说真的，他们的崇拜中拥有太多的英雄主义精神！

而且，他们除了把人钉在十字架上之外，不知道该如何爱他们的上帝！

他们认为应该像死人一样生活；他们将自己的尸体覆盖在黑色的斗篷里；甚至在跟

still feel the evil flavour of charnel-houses.

And he who liveth nigh unto them liveth nigh unto black pools, wherein the toad singeth his song with sweet gravity.

Better songs would they have to sing, for me to believe in their Saviour: more like saved ones would his disciples have to appear unto me!

Naked, would I like to see them: for beauty alone should preach penitence. But whom would that disguised affliction convince!

Verily, their Saviours themselves came not from freedom and freedom's seventh heaven! Verily, they themselves never trod the carpets of knowledge!

Of defects did the spirit of those Saviours consist; but into every defect had they put their illusion, their stop-gap, which they called God.

In their pity was their spirit drowned; and when they swelled and o'erswelled with pity, there always floated to the surface a great folly.

Eagerly and with shouts drove they their flock over their foot-bridge; as if there were but one foot-bridge to the future! Verily, those shepherds also were still of the flock!

Small spirits and spacious souls had those shepherds: but, my brethren, what small domains have even the most spacious souls hitherto been!

Characters of blood did they write on the way they went, and their folly taught that truth is proved by blood.

But blood is the very worst witness to truth; blood tainteth the purest teaching, and turneth it

他们说话的时候，我仍旧能够感受到荡涤古旧的尸屋的邪恶气息。

他和那些人紧密地生活在一起，生活在黑色的池水里，在那里面，蟾蜍唱着带有甜美的吸引力的歌曲。

他们会唱更加优美的歌曲，让我去相信他们的救世主：他的门徒们会更像被拯救的人一样，出现在我的面前！

我喜欢看他们赤裸着身体：因为，单靠貌美就可以说教赎罪。但是，他们会伪装被痛苦说服！

说真的，他们的救世主本身并不是来自自由和自由的第七蓝天！说真的，他们自身从来都没有踩踏过知识的地毯！

那些救世主的精神是由种种的缺陷构成的；但是，他们会把他们的假象以及被他们称为上帝的临时替代人放到所有的缺陷当中。

他们的精神被淹没在了他们的怜悯之中；当他们的内心充满了怜悯，那么一个伟大的愚蠢往往会浮出水面。在渴望和尖叫的驱使下，人们一齐涌向人行天桥；就好像通向未来的人行天桥只有这一个而已！说真的，那些牧羊人同样也是成群聚集的！

那些牧羊人拥有微不足道的精神和广阔无边的灵魂：但是，我的兄弟们，即使是最无边无际的灵魂也会被禁锢在狭小的领域之内！他们会在所到之处写下自己的血缘特征，而且他们的愚蠢教给他们，真理是被鲜血证明的。

但是，鲜血是真理的最糟糕的见证者；鲜血污染了最纯净的教义，并且把它变成了欺骗和发自内心的仇恨。

当一个人为了自己的教义而穿过火海——就足够证明这一点！

into delusion and hatred of heart.

And when a person goeth through fire for his teaching what doth that prove! It is more, verily, when out of one's own burning cometh one's own teaching!

Sultry heart and cold head; where these meet, there ariseth the blusterer, the "Saviour."

Greater ones, verily, have there been, and higher-born ones, than those whom the people call Saviours, those rapturous blusterers!

And by still greater ones than any of the Saviours must ye be saved, my brethren, if ye would find the way to freedom!

Never yet hath there been a Superman. Naked have I seen both of them, the greatest man and the smallest man:

All-too-similar are they still to each other. Verily, even the greatest found I all-too-human!

Thus spake Zarathustra.

27. THE VIRTUOUS

With thunder and heavenly fireworks must one speak to indolent and somnolent senses.

But beauty's voice speaketh gently: it appealeth only to the most awakened souls.

Gently vibrated and laughed unto me to-day my buckler; it was beauty's holy laughing and thrilling.

At you, ye virtuous ones, laughed my beauty to-day. And thus came its voice unto me:

说真的，当一个人自己的教义从他自身的烈火中产生，情况就更是如此！

炽热的内心和冰冷的头脑；在这两者相遇的地方，肯定会出现怒吼咆哮之人，也就是人们所说的“救世主”。

说真的，这个世界上存在过伟大的人以及拥有更加高尚的身世的人，而不是人们所说的救世主，还有那些兴高采烈的怒吼咆哮之人！

我的兄弟们，如果你们能够发现通往自由的方法！你们就不应该去拯救那些救世主，而应该拯救比他们更加伟大的人们。

在这个世界上还从未出现过超人。最高大的人和最矮小的人，我曾经见过他们两个赤身裸体的模样。

从各个方面来讲，他们彼此之间都太过于相似了。说真的，甚至是最高大的人也会发现自己太过于像人了。

查拉图斯特拉如是说。

27. 有德之人

在电闪雷鸣和犹如天国般壮美的烟花之下，一个人谈及了懒惰和昏昏欲睡的感觉。

但是，美貌用温柔的声音说道：很显然，这只是针对最清醒的灵魂来说。

今天，我的小圆盾轻柔地颤动着，并且向我微笑；那是美貌神圣的笑容和令人激动的颤动。

今天，你们，你们这些有德之人，向我的美貌微笑。随后，一个声音对我说道：“他

"They want to be paid besides!"

Ye want to be paid besides, ye virtuous ones! Ye want reward for virtue, and heaven for earth, and eternity for your to-day?

And now ye upbraid me for teaching that there is no reward-giver, nor paymaster? And verily, I do not even teach that virtue is its own reward.

Ah! this is my sorrow: into the basis of things have reward and punishment been insinuated and now even into the basis of your souls, ye virtuous ones!

But like the snout of the boar shall my word grub up the basis of your souls; a ploughshare will I be called by you.

All the secrets of your heart shall be brought to light; and when ye lie in the sun, grubbed up and broken, then will also your falsehood be separated from your truth.

For this is your truth: ye are too pure for the filth of the words: vengeance, punishment, recompense, retribution.

Ye love your virtue as a mother loveth her child; but when did one hear of a mother wanting to be paid for her love?

It is your dearest Self, your virtue. The ring's thirst is in you: to reach itself again struggleth every ring, and turneth itself.

And like the star that goeth out, so is every work of your virtue: ever is its light on its way and travelling and when will it cease to be on its way?

Thus is the light of your virtue still on its way, even when its work is done. Be it forgotten

们也想得到回报！”

你们要得到回报，你们这些有德之人！你们想要道德、蓝天以及永恒作为你们今天的报酬吗？

现在，你们训斥我，就是因为我教导你们，这里根本没有什么给予回报之人和分发报酬的人？说真的，我甚至都没有教导过你们道德是它自身的报酬。唉！这就是我的悲哀：深入到回报和被暗示惩罚的事物的核心——现在，我甚至要深入到你们的灵魂的核心，你们这些有德之人！但是，我的话语肯定会像野猪的鼻子一样掘出你们的灵魂的核心；你们会称我为犁头。

所有隐藏在你们内心当中的秘密都会被一一揭开；当你们躺在太阳下，被人们挖出来，支离破碎，你们的谎言也会脱离你们的真相。

这就是你们的真相：对于污秽的语言来说，你们太过于纯洁了：复仇、惩罚、酬谢以及报应。

你们热爱你们的道德，就好比一个母亲热爱她的孩子一样：但是，你们什么时候听说过一个母亲想让她付出的母爱得到回报？

它是你们的挚爱，你们的道德。钟声的渴望就隐藏在你们的体内：它挣扎着要再一次接近其他的钟声，并且改变自己。

就像天上的行星会有熄灭的时候一样，你们的道德所作出的每一个杰作也会面临同样的境遇：它的光芒是否会照射在它的道路和旅途中——它什么时候会停止在它的道路上闪耀光芒？

你们的道德之光仍旧照耀在它的道路之上，即使是它的任务已经完成。虽然它们会

and dead, still its ray of light liveth and travelleth.

That your virtue is your Self, and not an outward thing, a skin, or a cloak: that is the truth from the basis of your souls, ye virtuous ones!

But sure enough there are those to whom virtue meaneth writhing under the lash: and ye have hearkened too much unto their crying!

And others are there who call virtue the slothfulness of their vices; and when once their hatred and jealousy relax the limbs, their "justice" becometh lively and rubbeth its sleepy eyes.

And others are there who are drawn downwards: their devils draw them. But the more they sink, the more ardently gloweth their eye, and the longing for their God.

Ah! their crying also hath reached your ears, ye virtuous ones: "What I am not, that, that is God to me, and virtue!"

And others are there who go along heavily and creakingly, like carts taking stones downhill: they talk much of dignity and virtue their drag they call virtue!

And others are there who are like eight-day clocks when wound up; they tick, and want people to call ticking virtue.

Verily, in those have I mine amusement: wherever I find such clocks I shall wind them up with my mockery, and they shall even whirr thereby!

And others are proud of their modicum of righteousness, and for the sake of it do violence to all things: so that the world is drowned in their unrighteousness.

Ah! how ineptly cometh the word "virtue" out of their mouth! And when they say: "I am

被人们所遗忘，并且灰飞烟灭，但是它们的光芒仍旧活着，并且在这个世界上传播。

你们的道德就是你们自身的写照，它并不是一种外在的事物，一种皮肤，或是一件斗篷：它是来源于你们的灵魂根基的真理，你们这些有德之人！

但是，毫无疑问，这个世界上存在道德在皮鞭的挥打下来回翻滚的人：你们已经听到了他们太多的哀嚎声！

在这个世界上，有些人，他们管道德叫做他们的恶习的懒惰、怠慢；而且，一旦当他们的仇恨和嫉妒让他们全身心放松了下来的话，他们的“正义”就会变得充满活力，并且开始擦拭它困倦的双眼。

还有一种人，他们会被拖着往下走：他们的恶魔会拖着他们往下走。但是，他们陷得越深，他们的眼睛闪耀的光芒就会越刺眼，他们就越会渴望见到他们的上帝。

唉！他们的呐喊声同样也传到了你们的耳朵里，你们这些有德之人：“那个上帝不是我的，还有那个道德也不是！”

还有的人，他们迈着沉重的步伐，脚下发出咯吱咯吱的声音，就好像将装满石头的运货马车推下山一样：他们谈论得最多的就是尊严和道德——他们缓慢，并且吃力地前行，他们呼唤道德！

有些人，当他们因为兴奋而紧张的时候，他们就像是八天的时钟：他们会发出嘀嗒的声音，并且希望人们称它们为滴答作响的道德。

说真的，在那里我能找到属于我的乐趣：无论我从哪里找到类似这样的时钟，我都会用我那笨拙可笑的模仿给它们上紧发条，因此，它们就会开始疯狂地打转！

还有些人，他们会对自己的仅有的那一点正义感感到无比骄傲，由于它会对所有的

just," it always soundeth like: "I am just revenged!"

With their virtues they want to scratch out the eyes of their enemies; and they elevate themselves only that they may lower others.

And again there are those who sit in their swamp, and speak thus from among the bulrushes: "Virtue that is to sit quietly in the swamp.

We bite no one, and go out of the way of him who would bite; and in all matters we have the opinion that is given us."

And again there are those who love attitudes, and think that virtue is a sort of attitude.

Their knees continually adore, and their hands are eulogies of virtue, but their heart knoweth naught thereof.

And again there are those who regard it as virtue to say: "Virtue is necessary"; but after all they believe only that policemen are necessary.

And many a one who cannot see men's loftiness, calleth it virtue to see their baseness far too well: thus calleth he his evil eye virtue.

And some want to be edified and raised up, and call it virtue: and others want to be cast down, and likewise call it virtue.

And thus do almost all think that they participate in virtue; and at least every one claimeth to be an authority on "good" and "evil."

But Zarathustra came not to say unto all those liars and fools: "What do ye know of virtue! What could ye know of virtue!"

事物做出亵渎的行为：所以，整个世界都会陷入他们的邪恶和非正义当中。

唉！从他们的嘴巴里说出“道德”这样的字眼是多么的愚蠢和荒谬！当他们说：“我是公平正义的，”这句话往往更像是：“我是公平——报仇雪恨的！”

在他们的道德的帮助下，他们想挖掉他们的敌人的双眼；他们要提升自己，他们这样做的唯一目的就是可以降低别人的地位。

在这个世界上，还存在有这么一种人，他们会坐在深陷的沼泽之中，然后从芦苇丛中说道：“道德——就是安静地坐在沼泽里。

我们不会叮咬任何人，同时能够远离那些肆意叮咬别人的人；并且在所有的问题上，我们都拥有它给予我们的想法。”

有些人，他们非常热爱态度和看法，而且他们认为道德就是一种态度。

他们的膝盖继续崇拜，他们的双手就是道德的颂词，但是，他们的内心却对此一无所知。

有的人，他们会把这些看做是道德，并且说道：“道德是一种必不可少的事物。”但是，他们终究只相信警察是必不可少的。

有许多人都看不到人类的崇高品质，他们用道德把自身的卑微看得太过于美好，因此，他称他的眼睛为邪恶的双眼道德。

有些人想受到熏陶和启发，并且被举高，他们管这个叫道德，有些人要往下走，同样地，他们也管这个叫道德。

几乎所有的人都认为自己已经参与到了道德的活动当中，并且至少，他们任何一个人都宣称自己是“善”与“恶”的权威。

但是，查拉图斯特拉来到这里，并不是要对所有的骗子和愚蠢之人说：“你们究竟

But that ye, my friends, might become weary of the old words which ye have learned from the fools and liars:

That ye might become weary of the words "reward," "retribution," "punishment," "righteous vengeance."

That ye might become weary of saying: "That an action is good is because it is unselfish."

Ah! my friends! That your very Self be in your action, as the mother is in the child: let that be your formula of virtue!

Verily, I have taken from you a hundred formulae and your virtue's favourite playthings; and now ye upbraid me, as children upbraid.

They played by the sea then came there a wave and swept their playthings into the deep: and now do they cry.

But the same wave shall bring them new playthings, and spread before them new speckled shells!

Thus will they be comforted; and like them shall ye also, my friends, have your comforting and new speckled shells!

Thus spake Zarathustra.

28. THE RABBLE

Life is a well of delight; but where the rabble also drink, there all fountains are poisoned.

懂不懂什么是道德！你们对于道德都了解多少！”

而是说：“我的朋友们，你们已经听腻了那些骗子和愚蠢之人所说的陈腔滥调。”

你们或许已经厌倦了那些听过无数遍的词语：“报酬”、“报应”、“惩罚”以及“公平正义的复仇”。

你们已经厌倦了这样说：“这样的行为是好的，因为它是大公无私的。”

唉！我的朋友们！你们自身的缩影就隐藏在你们的所作所为之中，就好比母亲的母爱隐藏在她的孩子当中一样，让它成为你们的道德的准则吧！

说真的，我从你们那里拿走了一百个准则和惯例以及你们的道德最钟爱的玩物，现在，你们开始斥责我，就像训斥小孩一样训斥我。

他们在海边玩耍——然后，一股海浪横扫了过来，把他们的玩具都卷到了海洋的深处：现在，他们只能大声叫喊。

但是，与之前完全相同的海浪还会给他们带来全新的玩具，并且把崭新的、带有斑点的贝壳呈现在他们的面前！

因此，他们得到了安慰；同样的，我的朋友们，你们也会像他们一样得到安慰——还有崭新的、带有斑点的贝壳！

查拉图斯特拉如是说。

28. 贱民

生活就是快乐的源泉；但是那些贱民们同样会来这里饮用水源，所有的泉水都被人

To everything cleanly am I well disposed; but I hate to see the grinning mouths and the thirst of the unclean.

They cast their eye down into the fountain: and now glanceth up to me their odious smile out of the fountain.

The holy water have they poisoned with their lustfulness; and when they called their filthy dreams delight, then poisoned they also the words.

Indignant becometh the flame when they put their damp hearts to the fire; the spirit itself bubbleth and smoketh when the rabble approach the fire.

Mawkish and over-mellow becometh the fruit in their hands: unsteady, and withered at the top, doth their look make the fruit-tree.

And many a one who hath turned away from life, hath only turned away from the rabble: he hated to share with them fountain, flame, and fruit.

And many a one who hath gone into the wilderness and suffered thirst with beasts of prey, disliked only to sit at the cistern with filthy camel-drivers.

And many a one who hath come along as a destroyer, and as a hailstorm to all cornfields, wanted merely to put his foot into the jaws of the rabble, and thus stop their throat.

And it is not the mouthful which hath most choked me, to know that life itself requireth enmity and death and torture-crosses:

But I asked once, and suffocated almost with my question: What? is the rabble also necessary for life?

下了毒。

我非常乐意看到任何干净、清洁的事物，但是我讨厌看到咧开的嘴巴以及对不纯洁的事物的渴望。

他们将自己的目光投向了泉水的底部：现在，他们抬起头注视着我，并且露出了令人作呕的微笑。

他们用自己贪婪的欲望污染了神圣的泉水；并且当他们说他们那肮脏的梦想令人感到愉快的时候，他们还污染了美好的词语。当他们将自身沉闷、沮丧的心灵扔向火焰的时候；愤愤不平的情绪就会变成炽热的烈焰；当贱民靠近火焰的时候，他们的精神本身就会开始沸腾，并且冒出烟雾。他们手上的水果就会变得淡而无味、过度成熟：变幻无常、枯萎的顶部，看他们的样子是要创造水果树。

许多人都对生活感到厌倦，其实他们只是对那些贱民感到厌倦而已：他不愿意同他们共享泉水、火焰和水果。

许多人都走进了荒僻的荒野，并且和捕食的野兽一样遭受饥饿难耐的痛苦，他们只是不喜欢跟肮脏的骆驼骑行者一同坐在水池旁边。

许多人都是作为破坏者出现的，他们对于所有的玉米田来说，就是冰雹暴风，他们想要做的仅仅是把他的脚放进贱民的下巴里，然后堵塞他们的喉咙。

并不是要用一口呛死我的方式去了解生活本身也需要憎恨、死亡以及折磨的十字架：

但是，有一次，我差点被自己提出的问题搞得喘不过气来：对于贱民来说，什么是他们生活所必需的东西？

在生命的粮堂中，有毒的泉水、臭气冲天的火焰、污秽的梦想以及驱虫是必不可少

Are poisoned fountains necessary, and stinking fires, and filthy dreams, and maggots in the bread of life?

Not my hatred, but my loathing, gnawed hungrily at my life! Ah, ofttimes became I weary of spirit, when I found even the rabble spiritual!

And on the rulers turned I my back, when I saw what they now call ruling: to traffic and bargain for power with the rabble!

Amongst peoples of a strange language did I dwell, with stopped ears: so that the language of their trafficking might remain strange unto me, and their bargaining for power.

And holding my nose, I went morosely through all yesterdays and to-days: verily, badly smell all yesterdays and to-days of the scribbling rabble!

Like a cripple become deaf, and blind, and dumb thus have I lived long; that I might not live with the power-rabble, the scribe-rabble, and the pleasure-rabble.

Toilsomely did my spirit mount stairs, and cautiously; alms of delight were its refreshment; on the staff did life creep along with the blind one.

What hath happened unto me? How have I freed myself from loathing? Who hath rejuvenated mine eye? How have I flown to the height where no rabble any longer sit at the wells?

Did my loathing itself create for me wings and fountain-divining powers? Verily, to the loftiest height had I to fly, to find again the well of delight!

Oh, I have found it, my brethren! Here on the loftiest height bubbleth up for me the well of delight! And there is a life at whose waters none of the rabble drink with me!

的东西吗？

不是我的仇恨，而是我的厌恶在饥饿的啃咬我的生活！唉，我经常对精神感到非常厌倦，尤其是当我发现甚至连贱民也是具有精神的时候！

现在，当我看到他们管什么叫统治支配的时候，我将身子转向了统治者：我们要和贱民交换和交易权力！

我生活在说着对于我来说完全陌生的语言的人群当中，我将自己的耳朵堵起来：这样的话，他们那些非法交易的对话以及他们对权力的交易，对于我来说仍旧是非常陌生的。

然后，我捏住自己的鼻子，愁眉苦脸地穿过了所有的过去和今天：说真的，所有过去和今天的贱民都散发着令人作呕的气味！就像是跛子变得耳聋、眼花和哑巴一样——我生活了很长的时间，或许我没有和有权力的贱民、会写字的贱民以及令人愉悦的贱民生活在一起。

我的精神在吃力地、小心翼翼地攀爬台阶；快乐的救济物就是它恢复精神和体力的物品；在强力的支撑下，生活和盲目的人一起匍匐前行。

我的身上究竟发生了什么事？我要怎样才能将自己从厌恶中解脱出来？到底是谁让我的双眼恢复了活力？我要怎么样才能飞到一个再也没有贱民坐在水井旁边的高地？

我自身的厌恶能不能给我创造翅膀和神圣的源泉的力量呢？

说真的，我要飞到最高耸的高度，再一次去发现快乐的水井！

噢，我发现它了，我的兄弟们！这里有一种生活，在那其中，我不用再跟任何贱民共同分享神圣的泉水！

Almost too violently dost thou flow for me, thou fountain of delight! And often emptiest thou the goblet again, in wanting to fill it!

And yet must I learn to approach thee more modestly: far too violently doth my heart still flow towards thee:

My heart on which my summer burneth, my short, hot, melancholy, over-happy summer: how my summer heart longeth for thy coolness!

Past, the lingering distress of my spring! Past, the wickedness of my snowflakes in June! Summer have I become entirely, and summer-noontide!

A summer on the loftiest height, with cold fountains and blissful stillness: oh, come, my friends, that the stillness may become more blissful!

For this is our height and our home: too high and steep do we here dwell for all uncleanly ones and their thirst.

Cast but your pure eyes into the well of my delight, my friends! How could it become turbid thereby! It shall laugh back to you with its purity.

On the tree of the future build we our nest; eagles shall bring us lone ones food in their beaks!

Verily, no food of which the impure could be fellow-partakers! Fire, would they think they devoured, and burn their mouths!

Verily, no abodes do we here keep ready for the impure! An ice-cave to their bodies would our happiness be, and to their spirits!

And as strong winds will we live above them, neighbours to the eagles, neighbours to the

你近乎狂暴地向我喷涌而来，你这快乐的源泉！经常处于干涸状态的你，再一次成为了要被灌满的高脚杯！

我必须学会用更加谦卑的方式向你接近：但是，我的内心依旧用过于猛烈的方式向你涌去：

我的内心在我的夏日里尽情地燃烧，我那短暂的、炎热的、令人忧郁的，过度快乐的夏日：我的内心是多么的渴望你的冰爽！

我的春天依旧残留的苦恼都已成了往事！我的六月雪花的恶毒都已经成了往事！我已经完完全全变成了夏天，夏天的正午时分！

在最高耸的高地的夏日，拥有凉爽的泉水和令人欣喜若狂的宁静：噢，快来吧！我的朋友们，这样的宁静或许会变得比以前更加令人感到无忧无虑！

因为这是属于我们的高地，属于我们的家园：我们生活的这个地方对于所有不干净的事物和他们的渴求来说，都太高耸了、太陡峭了，根本没法生存。

现在，将你们清澈的双眼投向我的快乐的水井，我的朋友们！它怎么会因此而变得浑浊呢！它应该会嘲笑来回击你们的清纯。

我们将自己的安乐窝建在未来之树上；老鹰会把放在它们喙里的食物带给我们！

说真的，没有食物的不纯净之人可以成为伙伴的参与者！他们认为自己吞噬掉，并且灼烧了他们嘴唇的是火焰！

说真的，在我们这里没有任何住所可以提供给那些道德败坏的人！我们会很乐意给他们的躯体和他们的精神准备一个冰冻的洞穴！

我们会像强烈的暴风一样，生活在他们之上，与老鹰为邻，与大雪为邻，与太阳为

snow, neighbours to the sun: thus live the strong winds.

And like a wind will I one day blow amongst them, and with my spirit, take the breath from their spirit: thus willeth my future.

Verily, a strong wind is Zarathustra to all low places; and this counsel counselleth he to his enemies, and to whatever spitteth and speweth: "Take care not to spit against the wind!"

Thus spake Zarathustra.

29. THE TARANTULAS

Lo, this is the tarantula's den! Wouldst thou see the tarantula itself? Here hangeth its web: touch this, so that it may tremble.

There cometh the tarantula willingly: Welcome, tarantula! Black on thy back is thy triangle and symbol; and I know also what is in thy soul.

Revenge is in thy soul: wherever thou bitest, there ariseth black scab; with revenge, thy poison maketh the soul giddy!

Thus do I speak unto you in parable, ye who make the soul giddy, ye preachers of equality! Tarantulas are ye unto me, and secretly revengeful ones!

But I will soon bring your hiding-places to the light: therefore do I laugh in your face my laughter of the height.

Therefore do I tear at your web, that your rage may lure you out of your den of lies, and that

邻：所以，要像强烈的暴风一样生活。

总有一天，我会像一阵风一样在他们中间尽情地吹拂，并且用我的精神，夺走他们的精神的气息：所以，这就是我未来的意志。

说真的，查拉图斯特拉对于所有的低地来说，就是一阵强风；并且他将这个忠告提议给了他的敌人们，并且说道："千万小心，不要和狂风作对！"

查拉图斯特拉如是说。

29．毒蜘蛛

快瞧呀！这就是毒蜘蛛的巢穴！你能从这个巢穴里看到毒蜘蛛吗？毒蜘蛛编织的网就悬在上面：你碰一碰它，它没准会瑟瑟发抖。

那只毒蜘蛛非常满意地朝这边爬了过来：欢迎光临，毒蜘蛛！你后背上的黑色是你的三角形和象征；而且我同样还知道你的灵魂中都藏有些什么。

你的灵魂里藏有复仇：无论你在什么地方进行叮咬，被你叮咬过的地方都会产生黑色的疤痕；在复仇的鼓动下，你的毒液会让灵魂头晕眼花！

因此，我给你讲述寓言故事，你让灵魂眼花缭乱，你们这些鼓吹平等的传教士！你们就是我们身上的毒蜘蛛，秘密进行复仇的毒蜘蛛！

但是，我很快就会将你们的藏匿地点公之于众：因此，我会当着面嘲笑你们，那是我的笑容的高度。

所以，我会撕扯你们编织的蜘蛛网，你们的怒火或许会诱惑你们脱离你们的藏匿巢

your revenge may leap forth from behind your word "justice."

Because, for man to be redeemed from revenge that is for me the bridge to the highest hope, and a rainbow after long storms.

Otherwise, however, would the tarantulas have it. "Let it be very justice for the world to become full of the storms of our vengeance" thus do they talk to one another.

"Vengeance will we use, and insult, against all who are not like us" thus do the tarantula-hearts pledge themselves.

"And 'Will to Equality' that itself shall henceforth be the name of virtue; and against all that hath power will we raise an outcry!"

Ye preachers of equality, the tyrant-frenzy of impotence crieth thus in you for "equality": your most secret tyrant-longings disguise themselves thus in virtue-words!

Fretted conceit and suppressed envy perhaps your fathers' conceit and envy: in you break they forth as flame and frenzy of vengeance.

What the father hath hid cometh out in the son; and oft have I found in the son the father's revealed secret.

Inspired ones they resemble: but it is not the heart that inspireth them but vengeance. And when they become subtle and cold, it is not spirit, but envy, that maketh them so.

Their jealousy leadeth them also into thinkers' paths; and this is the sign of their jealousy they always go too far: so that their fatigue hath at last to go to sleep on the snow.

In all their lamentations soundeth vengeance, in all their eulogies is maleficence; and being

穴，那么，你们的复仇就会从你们的词语“正义”背后跳出来。

因此，对于人类来说，它们应该从复仇中得到救赎——而它对于我来说，就是通向最崇高的希望的桥梁，它就是漫长的暴风之后的彩虹。

否则的话，它就会被毒蜘蛛们所占有。“让这个充斥着我们复仇的风暴的世界变得公平正义吧！”——毒蜘蛛的内心向它们保证道。

“还有‘想要平等的意愿’——自此之后，它就会成为道德的代名词；并且它会对抗任何令我们揭竿而起、疯狂抗议的力量！”

你们这些鼓吹平等的传教士，无能的暴政狂热在你们寻求平等的过程中疯狂呐喊：你们最神秘的暴政渴望用道德的话语将它们自身伪装了起来！

焦躁的狂妄自大以及受到镇压的嫉妒——或许你们的先父们狂妄自大并且拥有嫉妒的心理：在你们休息的间歇，它们就像狂热的复仇烈焰一样向前挺进。

先父们究竟在他们的孩子里面隐藏了些什么呢，而且我经常在孩子的内心里发现父亲想要揭露的秘密。

它们跟受到启发的人们非常相似：但是，它们并没有受到心灵的启发——而是受到了复仇的启发。当它们变得狡猾、心狠手辣，那并不是受到它们的精神，而是受到了它们的嫉妒的驱使。

它们的嫉妒心理还带领它们进入了思想者的道路当中；这就是它们的嫉妒心理的典型标志——它们总是走得非常遥远：只有这样，到最后，它们的疲倦才会让它们睡在冰冷的雪地里。

它们所有的哀歌中都含有报复的意味，在它们所有的颂歌当中都含有恶毒的罪行；

judge seemeth to them bliss.

But thus do I counsel you, my friends: distrust all in whom the impulse to punish is powerful!

They are people of bad race and lineage; out of their countenances peer the hangman and the sleuth-hound.

Distrust all those who talk much of their justice! Verily, in their souls not only honey is lacking.

And when they call themselves "the good and just," forget not, that for them to be Pharisees, nothing is lacking but power!

My friends, I will not be mixed up and confounded with others.

There are those who preach my doctrine of life, and are at the same time preachers of equality, and tarantulas.

That they speak in favour of life, though they sit in their den, these poison-spiders, and withdrawn from life is because they would thereby do injury.

To those would they thereby do injury who have power at present: for with those the preaching of death is still most at home.

Were it otherwise, then would the tarantulas teach otherwise: and they themselves were formerly the best world-maligners and heretic-burners.

With these preachers of equality will I not be mixed up and confounded. For thus speaketh justice unto me: "Men are not equal."

对于它们来说，被人们评判是天赐的福分。

但是，我因此想要忠告你们，我的朋友们：永远也不要相信那些惩罚的冲动非常强大的人！

它们是拥有恶劣的种族和血统；从它们的相貌不难看出，它们可以等同于刽子手以及侦探猎犬。

不要相信任何过多谈论它们的正义感的人们！说真的，它们的灵魂里缺乏的不只是令人愉悦的东西。

并且，当它们称呼自己为“善良和正义”的时候，不要忘记，倘若它们要想成为从形式上遵守教义的法利赛人，它们唯一缺乏的就是——力量！

我的朋友们，我永远不会跟其他人混杂在一起。

这里有鼓吹我的人生教条的说教者，与此同时，它们还是鼓吹平等和毒蜘蛛的说教者。

它们说它们会支持生命，尽管它们坐在它们的巢穴之中，它们都是有剧毒的蜘蛛，它们脱离了生命——因为，如果它们不这么做的话，它们就会做出伤害别人的事情。

它们选择伤害的目标全都是在当下拥有权力和力量的人：因为那些说教死亡的人绝大多数都在国内。

要不然的话，毒蜘蛛们就会开始说：它们曾经是这个世界上最棒的诽谤者以及火烧异教徒的家伙。

我绝不会跟这些鼓吹平等的说教者混杂在一起。因此正义会对我说道：“人与人之间是不平等的。”

And neither shall they become so! What would be my love to the Superman, if I spake otherwise?

On a thousand bridges and piers shall they throng to the future, and always shall there be more war and inequality among them: thus doth my great love make me speak!

Inventors of figures and phantoms shall they be in their hostilities; and with those figures and phantoms shall they yet fight with each other the supreme fight!

Good and evil, and rich and poor, and high and low, and all names of values: weapons shall they be, and sounding signs, that life must again and again surpass itself!

Aloft will it build itself with columns and stairs life itself: into remote distances would it gaze, and out towards blissful beauties therefore doth it require elevation!

And because it requireth elevation, therefore doth it require steps, and variance of steps and climbers! To rise striveth life, and in rising to surpass itself.

And just behold, my friends! Here where the tarantula's den is, riseth aloft an ancient temple's ruins just behold it with enlightened eyes!

Verily, he who here towered aloft his thoughts in stone, knew as well as the wisest ones about the secret of life!

That there is struggle and inequality even in beauty, and war for power and supremacy: that doth he here teach us in the plainest parable.

How divinely do vault and arch here contrast in the struggle: how with light and shade they strive against each other, the divinely striving ones.

它们不会做出任何改变！如果我说了其他什么话，那么我对超人的热爱会变成什么呢？

它们会聚集在一千个桥梁和桥墩之上，共同奔向未来，在它们当中往往会有比别的群体更多的战争和不平等：这是我伟大的爱驱使我这样说的！

它们会成为对抗中幻象和幽灵的创造者；在那些幻象和幽灵的帮助下，它们会同彼此进行至高无上的战斗！

善意和邪恶、富有和贫穷、高大和低矮以及所有道德的代名词：它们会成为武器以及生命必须一次又一次超越自己的令人印象深刻的标志！

它会用圆柱和阶梯将自己建造在高耸的地方——生命本身，会驻足凝视遥远的远方，并且看向无比幸福的美好事物——所以，它需要提升自己！

而且，因为它需要提升自己，所以，它需要台阶，它需要不同的阶梯和攀登者！站起来为了生活而奋斗，站起来将自己超越。

快看呀！我的朋友们！这里就是毒蜘蛛的巢穴，它从一个古老的寺庙遗址中浮现了出来——快用你们开明的双眼注视着它吧！

说真的，它将自己的思想耸立在石头之上，它对于生命的秘密的了解程度丝毫不亚于这个世界上最聪慧的人们！

在这个世界上，甚至在美丽的事物当中也会存在斗争和不平等以及为了争夺权力和至高无上的地位而引发的战争：这就是它在最普通的寓言故事中要传达给我们的东西。

拱顶和拱门如此巧妙地在斗争中形成了鲜明的对比：它们是如何利用光亮和阴影来同彼此进行对抗的，为了目标而不懈奋斗的家伙们。

Thus, steadfast and beautiful, let us also be enemies, my friends! Divinely will we strive against one another!

Alas! There hath the tarantula bit me myself, mine old enemy! Divinely steadfast and beautiful, it hath bit me on the finger!

"Punishment must there be, and justice" so thinketh it: "not gratuitously shall he here sing songs in honour of enmity!"

Yea, it hath revenged itself! And alas! now will it make my soul also dizzy with revenge!

That I may not turn dizzy, however, bind me fast, my friends, to this pillar! Rather will I be a pillar-saint than a whirl of vengeance!

Verily, no cyclone or whirlwind is Zarathustra: and if he be a dancer, he is not at all a tarantula-dancer!

Thus spake Zarathustra.

30. THE FAMOUS WISE ONES

The people have ye served and the people's superstition not the truth! all ye famous wise ones! And just on that account did they pay you reverence.

And on that account also did they tolerate your unbelief, because it was a pleasantry and a by-path for the people. Thus doth the master give free scope to his slaves, and even enjoyeth their presumptuousness.

因此，让我们也成为坚定不变和美丽出众的敌人们吧！我的朋友们！我们也会不懈奋斗，巧妙地对抗彼此！

唉！毒蜘蛛一定是咬到我了，我那古老的敌人！那个坚定不变、美丽出众的毒蜘蛛咬了我的手指头！

“我一定要惩罚它，伸张正义”——我这么想着：“它绝不会无缘无故地出现在这里歌唱向仇恨致敬的歌曲！”

是的，它为自己报仇了雪恨！唉！现在它同样也会让我的灵魂因为要复仇而变得头晕目眩！

但是，我是不会变得头晕目眩的，我的朋友们快点把我绑在这块石柱之上吧！我要成为一名石柱的圣人，而不是充满复仇情绪的龙卷风！

说真的，查拉图斯特拉并不是什么旋风或者龙卷风：如果他是一名舞者的话，那么，他也不会是一名毒蜘蛛舞者！

查拉图斯特拉如是说。

30. 著名的智者

一切著名的智者啊！你们所提供的服务全都是为了人民和人民的迷信——而不是为了事实的真相！正是因为这个原因，他们特别敬重你。

而且，也正是这个原因，他们能够容忍你们的不信仰，因为这种不信仰不过是人们的小幽默和旁门左道罢了。就好比奴隶的主人让奴隶们获得自由，他们甚至会以专横放

But he who is hated by the people, as the wolf by the dogs is the free spirit, the enemy of fetters, the non-adorer, the dweller in the woods.

To hunt him out of his lair that was always called "sense of right" by the people: on him do they still hound their sharpest-toothed dogs.

"For there the truth is, where the people are! Woe, woe to the seeking ones!" thus hath it echoed through all time.

Your people would ye justify in their reverence: that called ye "Will to Truth," ye famous wise ones!

And your heart hath always said to itself: "From the people have I come: from thence came to me also the voice of God."

Stiff-necked and artful, like the ass, have ye always been, as the advocates of the people.

And many a powerful one who wanted to run well with the people, hath harnessed in front of his horses a donkey, a famous wise man.

And now, ye famous wise ones, I would have you finally throw off entirely the skin of the lion!

The skin of the beast of prey, the speckled skin, and the dishevelled locks of the investigator, the searcher, and the conqueror!

Ah! for me to learn to believe in your "conscientiousness," ye would first have to break your venerating will.

Conscientious so call I him who goeth into God-forsaken wildernesses, and hath broken his

肆为乐。

但是，被人们所深恶痛绝的，就如同被狗痛恨的狼一样，是自由的思想者，是被禁锢的敌人，从不盲目崇拜，居住在树林之中的人。

把他从他的藏匿地里搜寻出来——这就是人们常常所说的“正义的意义”：他们还常常惹怒拥有最锋利的牙齿的恶犬来咬他。

“有真相的地方，就会有人民！唉！寻找真相的人是会遭受到痛苦的！”——类似这样的话语总是在人们的耳边回荡。

唉！著名的智者啊！你们曾经让人民的崇拜变得合理：你们管这个叫“真理的意志”。

并且，你们的内心常常对自己说道：“我是从人民大众中走出来的，从那里走出来的还有上帝的声音。”

你们总是那么顽固、狡猾，就像驴子一样，你们是人民的辩护者。

许多非常有权力的人为了能够讨好人民大众，会在他们的马的前面带上一头驴，还有一位聪明的智者。

著名的智者啊！我现在终于能够完全脱去披在你们身上的狮子皮了！

这是有斑点的、凶残的捕食者的皮肤，它是调查者、研究者以及征服者！

唉！对于我来说，要想让我相信你们是求真的，那么，你们应该首先粉碎掉你们的崇敬的意志。然后前往被上帝遗弃的荒野的人——才是真正的求真者。

毋庸置疑，在被太阳灼烧的黄色的沙子里，他也渴望拥有丰富的泉水，生命在树荫下休息的小岛。

venerating heart.

In the yellow sands and burnt by the sun, he doubtless peereth thirstily at the isles rich in fountains, where life reposeth under shady trees.

But his thirst doth not persuade him to become like those comfortable ones: for where there are oases, there are also idols.

Hungry, fierce, lonesome, God-forsaken: so doth the lion-will wish itself.

Free from the happiness of slaves, redeemed from Deities and adorations, fearless and fear-inspiring, grand and lonesome: so is the will of the conscientious.

In the wilderness have ever dwelt the conscientious, the free spirits, as lords of the wilderness; but in the cities dwell the well-foddered, famous wise ones the draught-beasts.

For, always, do they draw, as asses the people's carts!

Not that I on that account upbraid them: but serving ones do they remain, and harnessed ones, even though they glitter in golden harness.

And often have they been good servants and worthy of their hire. For thus saith virtue: "If thou must be a servant, seek him unto whom thy service is most useful!

The spirit and virtue of thy master shall advance by thou being his servant: thus wilt thou thyself advance with his spirit and virtue!"

And verily, ye famous wise ones, ye servants of the people! Ye yourselves have advanced with the people's spirit and virtue and the people by you! To your honour do I say it!

But the people ye remain for me, even with your virtues, the people with purblind eyes the

但是，他的渴望并不会说服他成为那些尽情享受的安逸者之一：因为有绿洲的地方，同样也会有偶像。

饥饿的、残暴的、孤独的、被上帝所遗弃的：狮子的意志希望如此。

脱离奴隶的快乐，从上帝和所有的崇拜中获得救赎，无所畏惧而让人感到生畏，伟大而孤独，这就是求真者的意志。

求真者以及自由的思想者，他们往往是荒野的主人，他们就像荒野的领主一样，生活在这里；而在城市里，居住着著名的智者和饥饿的肉食者。

因为它们总是跟驴子一样，推拉着——人民之车！

我肯定不会因为这个原因而去责备他们：尽管他们的车具闪耀着金灿灿的光芒，他们仍旧是为人们服务，走在人民之车前面的野兽。

他们常常是优秀的，值得赚取薪俸的公仆。因此，道德如是说：“如果你必须要当一名仆人的话，那么就去寻找那个能够让你的服务得到最大的发挥的人吧！”

你的主人的精神和道德，会因为你为他提供的服务而有所提升：那么，你也会随着他的精神和道德一起得到提升！

说真的，一切著名的智者啊！一切人民的奴仆啊！你们随着人民的精神和道德一起得到了提升——人民也会因为你而得到提升！在我看来，这是你们的荣誉！

但是，尽管拥有你们自己的道德，你们仍旧是人民，拥有盲目的双眼的人民——对什么是精神根本一无所知的人民！

精神就是生命对自己进行切割：生命会因为自己所遭受到的磨难而增长知识——你们在之前不是已经了解了吗？

people who know not what spirit is!

Spirit is life which itself cutteth into life: by its own torture doth it increase its own knowledge, did ye know that before?

And the spirit's happiness is this: to be anointed and consecrated with tears as a sacrificial victim, did ye know that before?

And the blindness of the blind one, and his seeking and groping, shall yet testify to the power of the sun into which he hath gazed, did ye know that before?

And with mountains shall the discerning one learn to build! It is a small thing for the spirit to remove mountains, did ye know that before?

Ye know only the sparks of the spirit: but ye do not see the anvil which it is, and the cruelty of its hammer!

Verily, ye know not the spirit's pride! But still less could ye endure the spirit's humility, should it ever want to speak!

And never yet could ye cast your spirit into a pit of snow: ye are not hot enough for that! Thus are ye unaware, also, of the delight of its coldness.

In all respects, however, ye make too familiar with the spirit; and out of wisdom have ye often made an almshouse and a hospital for bad poets.

Ye are not eagles: thus have ye never experienced the happiness of the alarm of the spirit. And he who is not a bird should not camp above abysses.

Ye seem to me lukewarm ones: but coldly floweth all deep knowledge. Ice-cold are the

精神的幸福就是被泪水所涂抹，并且被神圣化为供奉的牺牲者——你们不是已经知道这些了吗？

盲目之人的盲目以及他的寻找和摸索，恰恰证实了他所看到的太阳的权力——你们不是已经知道这些了吗？

拥有求知欲的人应该和山峰一起学习建筑！对于精神来说，移除群山是一件轻而易举的事——你们不是已经知道这些了吗？

你们只能看到精神的火花：但是，你们不知道精神是怎样的一块铁砧以及它的铁锤的残忍！

说真的，你们并不知道精神的傲慢！但是，如果精神的谦卑想开口说话，你们肯定更加无法容忍！

你们还从来没有把你们的精神扔到积满雪的深坑里的经历：因为你们还没有足够热！你们同样也不会意识到它的凉爽带给人的快乐。

但是，在我看来，无论从任何的角度来看，你们都让自己和精神之间保持太过于亲密的关系；你们还经常把智慧作为邪恶诗人的诊所和医院。

你们并不是老鹰：因此你们永远也不会体验到精神恐慌所带给你的快乐。不属于鸟类的人，不应该在深渊之上安营扎寨。

在我看来，你们都是不温不火的：但是，所有深奥的知识，都在冰冷地流动着。精神之水井的最深处是极其冰冷的：但是对于炽热的双手和劳动者来说，却非常舒服、提神。

一切著名的智者啊！你们笔直地站在我的面前，令人肃然起敬——你们不会被任何

innermost wells of the spirit: a refreshment to hot hands and handlers.

Respectable do ye there stand, and stiff, and with straight backs, ye famous wise ones! no strong wind or will impelleth you.

Have ye ne'er seen a sail crossing the sea, rounded and inflated, and trembling with the violence of the wind?

Like the sail trembling with the violence of the spirit, doth my wisdom cross the sea my wild wisdom!

But ye servants of the people, ye famous wise ones how could ye go with me!

Thus spake Zarathustra.

31. THE NIGHT-SONG

'Tis night: now do all gushing fountains speak louder. And my soul also is a gushing fountain.

'Tis night: now only do all songs of the loving ones awake. And my soul also is the song of a loving one.

Something unappeased, unappeasable, is within me; it longeth to find expression. A craving for love is within me, which speaketh itself the language of love.

Light am I: ah, that I were night! But it is my lonesomeness to be begirt with light!

Ah, that I were dark and nightly! How would I suck at the breasts of light!

And you yourselves would I bless, ye twinkling starlets and glow-worms aloft! and would

强大的暴风或者意志所驱使。

你们还从来都没有见到过一艘被狂风暴雨吹得肿胀的帆船颤抖着横越海洋吧?

我的智慧就像被精神的狂暴所震颤的帆船一样，横越海洋——我的充满狂野的智慧!

但是，一切著名的智者啊！你们都是人民的仆人——你们又怎么能够跟我一同前往呢!

查拉图斯特拉如是说。

31．夜之歌

黑夜已经到来：所有喷泉的喷涌声越来越响亮。同样的，我的灵魂也是响亮的喷泉。

黑夜已经到来：现在，所有歌颂爱人的歌曲都已经被唤醒了。同样的，我的灵魂也是一首歌颂爱人的歌曲。

我的身上有着一种从未被安抚过，从未得到平息的东西；它想要放声表达出来。我的身上有一种对爱的渴望，它正在诉说着爱情的话语。

我就是光芒：唉！我还真希望自己是黑夜！但是，被光芒包围就是我的孤独啊!

唉，我真希望我是黑暗和黑夜！我会怎样吮吸光芒的乳房，以此来满足我的饥渴!

闪闪发亮的小星星和在天上散发着光芒的小虫子啊，我会祝福你们，并且被你们的光芒的礼物所祝福!

但是，我生活在自己的光芒之中，我重新吮吸从我的身上爆发出来的火焰。

rejoice in the gifts of your light.

But I live in mine own light, I drink again into myself the flames that break forth from me.

I know not the happiness of the receiver; and oft have I dreamt that stealing must be more blessed than receiving.

It is my poverty that my hand never ceaseth bestowing; it is mine envy that I see waiting eyes and the brightened nights of longing.

Oh, the misery of all bestowers! Oh, the darkening of my sun! Oh, the craving to crave! Oh, the violent hunger in satiety!

They take from me: but do I yet touch their soul? There is a gap 'twixt giving and receiving; and the smallest gap hath finally to be bridged over.

A hunger ariseth out of my beauty: I should like to injure those I illumine; I should like to rob those I have gifted: thus do I hunger for wickedness.

Withdrawing my hand when another hand already stretcheth out to it; hesitating like the cascade, which hesitateth even in its leap: thus do I hunger for wickedness!

Such revenge doth mine abundance think of: such mischief welleth out of my lonesomeness.

My happiness in bestowing died in bestowing; my virtue became weary of itself by its abundance!

He who ever bestoweth is in danger of losing his shame; to him who ever dispenseth, the hand and heart become callous by very dispensing.

Mine eye no longer overfloweth for the shame of suppliants; my hand hath become too hard

我并不懂得接受者的快乐；而且，我经常梦想着：偷窃应该比接受更加幸福。

我的贫穷就是我的双手从来都没有停止过给予；我的嫉妒让我看到充满期待的眼睛以及渴望的光明之夜。

啊，所有给予者的不幸啊！啊，我的太阳的偏食啊！啊，寻求渴望的渴望啊！啊，藏在满足中的狂暴的饥饿啊！

他们从我这里得到了给予：但是，我有没有触碰过他们的灵魂呢？在给予和接受之间存在着一个鸿沟；而最终，即使是最小的鸿沟也会被架上桥梁。

一种饥饿出现在了我的美感之中：我应该去伤害那些被我的光芒所照耀的人们；我应该去偷窃那些被我所给予礼物的人们：——我是如此如饥似渴地想要做些坏事。

当其他人想伸出手来握住我的手的时候，我会把自己的手缩回去；我开始犹豫不决，就像倾泻而下的瀑布一样犹豫不决：——我是如此如饥似渴地想做些坏事！

我的丰富思维思考着这样的报复：我的孤独产生了这样的邪念。

我给予时的幸福会因为给予而消亡；我的道德已经厌倦了它自身的这种丰盈的状态！

时常给予的人会处于失去他自身名誉的危险当中；因为长期给予的人的双手和心灵，终究会因为经常给予而生出粗糙的茧子。

我的双眼不会再为恳求者的羞耻而热泪盈眶；我的双手变得非常坚硬，不能再感受到来自施舍之人的双手的颤抖。

我的眼泪和我的柔软的内心究竟去了什么地方了呢？啊，所有给予者的孤独啊！啊，所有散发光芒之人的沉静啊！

for the trembling of filled hands.

Whence have gone the tears of mine eye, and the down of my heart? Oh, the lonesomeness of all bestowers! Oh, the silence of all shining ones!

Many suns circle in desert space: to all that is dark do they speak with their light but to me they are silent.

Oh, this is the hostility of light to the shining one: unpityingly doth it pursue its course.

Unfair to the shining one in its innermost heart, cold to the suns: thus travelleth every sun.

Like a storm do the suns pursue their courses: that is their travelling. Their inexorable will do they follow: that is their coldness.

Oh, ye only is it, ye dark, nightly ones, that extract warmth from the shining ones! Oh, ye only drink milk and refreshment from the light's udders!

Ah, there is ice around me; my hand burneth with the iciness! Ah, there is thirst in me; it panteth after your thirst!

'Tis night: alas, that I have to be light! And thirst for the nightly! And lonesomeness!

'Tis night: now doth my longing break forth in me as a fountain, for speech do I long.

'Tis night: now do all gushing fountains speak louder. And my soul also is a gushing fountain.

'Tis night: now do all songs of loving ones awake. And my soul also is the song of a loving one.

Thus sang Zarathustra.

许多类似太阳的恒星会在荒凉的太空中旋转：它们会用自己的光芒同所有黑暗的事物对话——但是对于我来讲，它们都是非常沉静的。

啊，这是光芒对于其他发光的一切的敌意：它会毫无怜悯地继续追寻它的道路。

如果用内心的最深处去感受的话，任何太阳对于其他发光的一切，都是极其不公平的，对于其他的太阳来说是无比冷酷的——它依然如此地继续追寻它前进的道路。

太阳就像一阵风暴一样追寻着它们的道路：这就是它们的旅行。它们遵循着它们不可阻挡的意志：这就是它们的冷酷无情。

啊，只有你们，黑暗和黑夜的你们，从闪耀着光芒的事物中汲取温暖！啊，只有你们会在光芒的乳房前吮吸安慰提神的乳汁！

啊，我的四周全是冰；我的双手因为极度的寒冷而开始灼烧！啊，我的内心充满了渴望；而我的这种渴望是渴求你们的渴望！

黑夜已经到来了：唉，到头来，我还是要成为光芒啊！对黑夜的渴求呢！对孤独的渴求呢！

黑夜已经到来了：现在，我的渴望之泉正在我的体内喷涌着——因为它要放声高呼！

黑夜已经到来了：现在，所有的泉水的喷涌之声愈发的强烈了。而且我的灵魂本身也是一个喷涌的泉水。

黑夜已经到来了：现在，所有歌颂爱人的歌曲都被唤醒了。而且我的灵魂本身也是一首歌颂爱人的歌曲。

查拉图斯特拉如是说。

32. THE DANCE-SONG

One evening went Zarathustra and his disciples through the forest; and when he sought for a well, lo, he lighted upon a green meadow peacefully surrounded with trees and bushes, where maidens were dancing together. As soon as the maidens recognised Zarathustra, they ceased dancing; Zarathustra, however, approached them with friendly mien and spake these words:

Cease not your dancing, ye lovely maidens! No game-spoiler hath come to you with evil eye, no enemy of maidens.

God's advocate am I with the devil: he, however, is the spirit of gravity. How could I, ye light-footed ones, be hostile to divine dances? Or to maidens' feet with fine ankles?

To be sure, I am a forest, and a night of dark trees: but he who is not afraid of my darkness, will find banks full of roses under my cypresses.

And even the little God may he find, who is dearest to maidens: beside the well lieth he quietly, with closed eyes.

Verily, in broad daylight did he fall asleep, the sluggard! Had he perhaps chased butterflies too much?

Upbraid me not, ye beautiful dancers, when I chasten the little God somewhat! He will cry, certainly, and weep but he is laughable even when weeping!

And with tears in his eyes shall he ask you for a dance; and I myself will sing a song to his

32．跳舞之歌

一天晚上，查拉图斯特拉同他的门徒们一起穿越了森林；当他寻找一口水井的时候，他点亮了被树丛和灌木包围起来的绿色的草地，年轻的姑娘们都聚集在这里尽情地跳舞。很快，这些年轻的姑娘们就认出了查拉图斯特拉，她们全都停止了舞蹈；但是，查拉图斯特拉用非常友好的姿态来到了她们的面前，并且对她们说了以下这番话：

你们不要停止舞蹈，你们这些惹人喜爱的年轻姑娘们！凡是来到这里的人，都不是败坏兴致和氛围的人，也绝不是少女的敌人。

我是站在恶魔的面前，为上帝辩护的人：但是那个恶魔是严重的精神。脚步轻盈的少女们啊！我怎么会是神圣的舞蹈，或是少女漂亮的脚踝的仇人呢？

确切地说，我是介于森林和黑夜之间的黑暗之树：但是那些并不畏惧我的黑暗的人，能够在我的柏树下找到满是玫瑰花的幽深小径。他甚至能够找到那些年轻的少女们最喜爱的小神仙：他安静地躺在水井的旁边，闭上了双眼。

说真的，这个大懒鬼竟然在明亮无比的光芒下睡着了！他或许是因为曾经想要追逐太多的蝴蝶吗？

你们这些漂亮的舞者们，如果我要稍稍惩罚一下这个小神仙的话，请你们不要为此而责备我！毋庸置疑，他会大喊，还会放声哭泣——但是即使是他在哭泣的时候，他的脸上也会露出笑容！

他会在眼睛里闪烁着泪珠的时候，邀请你跟他一起跳舞；而我本人则会为他的舞蹈

dance:

A dance-song and satire on the spirit of gravity my supremest, powerfulest devil, who is said to be "lord of the world."

And this is the song that Zarathustra sang when Cupid and the maidens danced together:

Of late did I gaze into thine eye, O Life! And into the unfathomable did I there seem to sink.

But thou pulledst me out with a golden angle; derisively didst thou laugh when I called thee unfathomable.

"Such is the language of all fish," saidst thou; "what they do not fathom is unfathomable.

But changeable am I only, and wild, and altogether a woman, and no virtuous one:

Though I be called by you men the 'profound one,' or the 'faithful one,' 'the eternal one,' 'the mysterious one.'

But ye men endow us always with your own virtues alas, ye virtuous ones!"

Thus did she laugh, the unbelievable one; but never do I believe her and her laughter, when she speaketh evil of herself.

And when I talked face to face with my wild Wisdom, she said to me angrily: "Thou willest, thou cravest, thou lovest; on that account alone dost thou praise Life!"

Then had I almost answered indignantly and told the truth to the angry one; and one cannot answer more indignantly than when one "telleth the truth" to one's Wisdom.

For thus do things stand with us three. In my heart do I love only Life and verily, most when I hate her!

献上一首歌曲：

这是一首专为舞蹈定制的歌曲，并且给那个对于我来说最高大、最强有力的恶魔，被人们称之为“世界的领主”的严重的精神唱出了深深的讽刺——

这就是丘比特和年轻貌美的少女们共舞的时候，查拉图斯特拉献上的歌曲：噢，生命！最近我一直都在凝视着你的双眼，而且我好像跌入了深不可测的深处。

但是，你用一把黄金的钩子把我拉了上来；当我说你深不可测的时候，你就会嘲笑我。

“所有的鱼类都是这么说的，”你说道，“它们自身无法预知的深度，就是深不可测的。”

但是，我这个人的特点就是多变和狂野，总而言之，我就是个妇女，我就是一个毫无道德的妇人：

尽管，你们这些男人会称我为“深沉的人”，或是“非常忠诚的人”、“永恒之人”、“充满神秘感的人”。

但是，你们男人经常把你们自身的道德赋予我们——“唉，你们这些有道德的人啊！”

她曾经嘲笑过，这简直是让人难以相信的；但是当它自谤时，我是永远也不会相信她以及她的笑声的。

当我和我那狂野的智慧进行面对面的交谈的时候，她非常气愤地对我说：“你要生命，渴望生命，你爱生命；综上所述，你要赞美生命！”

我给了她一个几乎恼羞成怒的回答，并且我把事实的真相告诉给了这个气愤的人，当我们把事实的真相告诉给自己的智慧的时候，那就是恼羞成怒的答复。

对于我们来说，一切的事物都是这样对立着的，从我的内心来看，我只热爱生命——

But that I am fond of Wisdom, and often too fond, is because she remindeth me very strongly of Life!

She hath her eye, her laugh, and even her golden angle-rod: am I responsible for it that both are so alike?

And when once Life asked me: "Who is she then, this Wisdom?" then said I eagerly: "Ah, yes! Wisdom!

One thirsteth for her and is not satisfied, one looketh through veils, one graspeth through nets.

Is she beautiful? What do I know! But the oldest carps are still lured by her.

Changeable is she, and wayward; often have I seen her bite her lip, and pass the comb against the grain of her hair.

Perhaps she is wicked and false, and altogether a woman; but when she speaketh ill of herself, just then doth she seduce most."

When I had said this unto Life, then laughed she maliciously, and shut her eyes. "Of whom dost thou speak?" said she. "Perhaps of me?

And if thou wert right is it proper to say that in such wise to my face! But now, pray, speak also of thy Wisdom!"

Ah, and now hast thou again opened thine eyes, O beloved Life! And into the unfathomable have I again seemed to sink.

Thus sang Zarathustra. But when the dance was over and the maidens had departed, he

说真的，当我恨她的时候，恰恰是我最爱她的时候！

但是，倘若我热爱智慧，或者太过于热爱智慧，那是因为它让我对生命保持着强烈的渴望！

她拥有生命的眼睛以及生命的笑容，甚至还有生命的金钩：它们两个是如此相像，难道我要对此负责吗？

当生命有一次问我："这个智慧，她到底是谁？"——于是，我充满渴望地答道："唉！是的！智慧！"

人们渴望能够追求她，但是却得不到满足，人们只能隔着面纱注视着她，他们只能伸出手指穿过网孔才能抓住她。

她是不是很漂亮呢？我又怎么会知道呢！但是，即使是经验最老到的鲤鱼也免不了咬住她的诱饵。

她是易变的、固执的；我经常能够看到她在啃咬自己的嘴唇，并且用梳子捋顺她那头长发。

或许，它是邪恶，并且虚伪的，它也许是彻头彻尾的女人；但是当它自谤时，刚好是它最有诱惑力的时候。

当我说完这番话的时候，生命用充满恶意的姿态笑了起来，并且闭上了双眼。"你说的那个人到底是谁？"它说道，"没准说的是我吧？"

即使你说的都是对的——但是，你怎么胆敢在当着我的面的情况下，说出这样的话呢！但是现在，我恳求你说一说你的智慧吧！

唉，亲爱的生命啊！你又再一次睁开了双眼！我好像陷入了深不可测的深度。

became sad.

"The sun hath been long set," said he at last, "the meadow is damp, and from the forest cometh coolness.

An unknown presence is about me, and gazeth thoughtfully. What! Thou livest still, Zarathustra?

Why? Wherefore? Whereby? Whither? Where? How? Is it not folly still to live?

Ah, my friends; the evening is it which thus interrogateth in me. Forgive me my sadness!

Evening hath come on: forgive me that evening hath come on!"

Thus sang Zarathustra.

33. THE GRAVE-SONG

"Yonder is the grave-island, the silent isle; yonder also are the graves of my youth. Thither will I carry an evergreen wreath of life."

Resolving thus in my heart, did I sail o'er the sea.

Oh, ye sights and scenes of my youth! Oh, all ye gleams of love, ye divine fleeting gleams! How could ye perish so soon for me! I think of you to-day as my dead ones.

From you, my dearest dead ones, cometh unto me a sweet savour, heart-opening and melting. Verily, it convulseth and openeth the heart of the lone seafarer.

于是，查拉图斯特拉如是歌唱。但是，当舞蹈结束的时候，那些年轻漂亮的姑娘们都离开了这里，他开始伤感了起来。

“太阳早就已经日落西山了，”最后，他说道，“青草地已经变得潮湿了，并且从森林里吹来了一股凉气。”

一个不为人所知的东西站在我的旁边，沉思地注视着我。什么！你还活着，查拉图斯特拉？

为什么要生存下来呢？你能从此获得什么好处吗？靠什么生活呢？方向在哪里呢？究竟应该如何生活呢？依旧选择生活下去，难道不是非常愚蠢的做法吗？

唉，我的朋友们；这是夕阳在对我进行严刑拷打。请原谅我的悲伤！

傍晚已经来临了：请原谅我吧！傍晚已经来临了！

查拉图斯特拉如是说。

33．坟茔之歌

“那里是坟茔之岛，那是个非常寂静的地方；在那里，同样也有属于我的青春的坟茔。我经常会带着一个四季常绿的生命花圈去那里。”

因此，我在心中下了决心，我要漂洋过海来到坟茔之岛。

噢，属于我的青春的景象和幻想啊！噢，生命的微光啊，那神圣的、稍纵即逝的微光啊！你们怎么能这么快就消逝呢！现在，我正思念着你们，就如同我在思念那些逝去的人一样。

我的最挚爱的死去的人啊，一种甜蜜的、让人敞开心扉，并且融化心灵的香气向我

Still am I the richest and most to be envied I, the lonesomest one! For I have possessed you, and ye possess me still. Tell me: to whom hath there ever fallen such rosy apples from the tree as have fallen unto me?

Still am I your love's heir and heritage, blooming to your memory with many-hued, wild-growing virtues, O ye dearest ones!

Ah, we were made to remain nigh unto each other, ye kindly strange marvels; and not like timid birds did ye come to me and my longing nay, but as trusting ones to a trusting one!

Yea, made for faithfulness, like me, and for fond eternities, must I now name you by your faithlessness, ye divine glances and fleeting gleams: no other name have I yet learnt.

Verily, too early did ye die for me, ye fugitives. Yet did ye not flee from me, nor did I flee from you: innocent are we to each other in our faithlessness.

To kill me, did they strangle you, ye singing birds of my hopes! Yea, at you, ye dearest ones, did malice ever shoot its arrows to hit my heart!

And they hit it! Because ye were always my dearest, my possession and my possessedness: On that account had ye to die young, and far too early!

At my most vulnerable point did they shoot the arrow namely, at you, whose skin is like down or more like the smile that dieth at a glance!

But this word will I say unto mine enemies: What is all manslaughter in comparison with what ye have done unto me!

飘了过来。说真的，它让孤独的远航者惊颤和释怀。

我依旧是那个最富有的，最受到别人嫉妒的——我这个无比孤独的人啊！因为，我曾经占有过你们，你们也依旧占有着我。那么请告诉我：这树上的金色苹果，是否像为我倾倒一样，为别人倾倒过呢？

我仍旧是你们的爱的继承者和遗产，噢，我最挚爱的，我会让你的记忆里盛开色彩鲜艳、野生的道德！

唉，那些珍奇和古怪的奇物啊！我们生来就应该彼此紧靠在一起，当你们靠近我和我的渴望的时候，并不像是胆小的小鸟——而是像拥有信仰的人走向能够被相信的人一样！

是的，就像我一样，你们同样也是由忠诚和爱的永恒制造而成的，难不成我现在要为你们的背信弃义而另外给你们取新的名字吗？神圣的闪光和稍纵即逝的微弱之光啊：我还从来都没有学过其他的名字呢。

说真的，你们这些逃亡者啊，你们死得太快了。但是，你们从来都没有逃避过我，我也从来都没有逃避过你们：存在于我们之间的背信弃义是非常无辜的。

鸣唱着歌曲的，我的希望之鸟啊！他们为了杀害我，不惜将你们勒死！是的，恶意与怨恨总是将弓箭瞄向我最挚爱的你们——用来打击我的心脏！

而且，它们打中了！因为，你们永远都是我最挚爱的，我的占有物和被占有物：所以从这些方面来讲，你们不得过早地死亡！

它们将手中的箭射向了我最容易受到伤害的地方——向你们这些娇嫩并且稍纵即逝的微笑，射出了它们的弓箭！

但是，我会对我的敌人们说出这句话：将杀人罪同你们对我所做的一切相比较的话，又算得上是什么大事呢！

Worse evil did ye do unto me than all manslaughter; the irretrievable did ye take from me: thus do I speak unto you, mine enemies!

Slew ye not my youth's visions and dearest marvels! My playmates took ye from me, the blessed spirits! To their memory do I deposit this wreath and this curse.

This curse upon you, mine enemies! Have ye not made mine eternal short, as a tone dieth away in a cold night! Scarcely, as the twinkle of divine eyes, did it come to me as a fleeting gleam!

Thus spake once in a happy hour my purity: "Divine shall everything be unto me."

Then did ye haunt me with foul phantoms; ah, whither hath that happy hour now fled!

"All days shall be holy unto me" so spake once the wisdom of my youth: verily, the language of a joyous wisdom!

But then did ye enemies steal my nights, and sold them to sleepless torture: ah, whither hath that joyous wisdom now fled?

Once did I long for happy auspices: then did ye lead an owl-monster across my path, an adverse sign. Ah, whither did my tender longing then flee?

All loathing did I once vow to renounce: then did ye change my nigh ones and nearest ones into ulcerations. Ah, whither did my noblest vow then flee?

As a blind one did I once walk in blessed ways: then did ye cast filth on the blind one's course: and now is he disgusted with the old footpath.

And when I performed my hardest task, and celebrated the triumph of my victories, then did

你们对我所做的一切邪恶的事情，胜于所有的杀人罪行：你们从我这里夺去的是无法弥补的：——因此，我要对你们说，我的敌人们！

杀掉你们并不是我的青春的幻想和最挚爱的奇迹！我的玩伴将你们从我的身边带走，受到祝福的精神！为了纪念他们的记忆，我将这个花环和这个诅咒保存了起来。

对你们使用的诅咒，我的敌人们！你们就像让一块石头在冰冷的黑夜里消失一样，让我的永恒变得短暂！闪耀着光芒的神圣的眼睛，向我走来几乎是不可能发生的——这就好像是一个稍纵即逝的微弱光芒！

我的纯净曾经在充满了快乐的一个小时里说道：“一切的神圣都将归我所有。”

然后，你们跟污秽的幽灵一起萦绕在我的头顶；唉，曾经的快乐时光，现在早已经逃之夭夭了！

“每时每刻，神圣都归我所有，”曾经，我的青春的智慧如此说道。说真的，这就是令人愉悦的智慧的语言！

但是，你们这些敌人们盗走了我的黑夜，并且将它们卖给了彻夜不眠的苦难：唉，曾经的快乐智慧，现在也已经逃之夭夭了吗？

曾经，我非常渴望快乐的支持：然后，你们指引一个驯养猫头鹰的人穿越我的道路，这是一个非常对立的标志。唉，无论何时，我都要进行脆弱的憧憬，然后再逃之夭夭吗？
我曾经发誓放弃所有令人厌恶的事物：然后，你们将我的身边以及离我最近的事物都变成了腐烂的污秽。唉，难道我要做出最高贵的许愿，然后再逃之夭夭吗？

曾经有那么一次，我就像一个盲人一样，走在被祝福的道路之上：然后，你们在盲人行进的道路上扔了很多污秽之物：现在，他对过去的道路感到非常的厌恶。

ye make those who loved me call out that I then grieved them most.

Verily, it was always your doing: ye embittered to me my best honey, and the diligence of my best bees.

To my charity have ye ever sent the most impudent beggars; around my sympathy have ye ever crowded the incurably shameless. Thus have ye wounded the faith of my virtue.

And when I offered my holiest as a sacrifice, immediately did your "piety" put its fatter gifts beside it: so that my holiest suffocated in the fumes of your fat.

And once did I want to dance as I had never yet danced: beyond all heavens did I want to dance. Then did ye seduce my favourite minstrel.

And now hath he struck up an awful, melancholy air; alas, he tooted as a mournful horn to mine ear!

Murderous minstrel, instrument of evil, most innocent instrument! Already did I stand prepared for the best dance: then didst thou slay my rapture with thy tones!

Only in the dance do I know how to speak the parable of the highest things: and now hath my grandest parable remained unspoken in my limbs!

Unspoken and unrealised hath my highest hope remained! And there have perished for me all the visions and consolations of my youth!

How did I ever bear it? How did I survive and surmount such wounds? How did my soul rise again out of those sepulchres?

Yea, something invulnerable, unburiable is with me, something that would rend rocks

当我完成了最艰巨的任务，并且开始庆祝我的胜利的时候，你们让那些爱我的人们大声叫喊，我是最令他们感到悲痛的人。

说真的，这些从来都是你们的所作所为：你们让我最好的蜂蜜变得更加甘苦，这极大地伤害了我的最出色的蜜蜂的辛勤工作。

你们总是把最厚颜无耻的乞讨者送到我的慈善中心；你们让最无可救药的无耻之徒将我的怜悯之心团团围住。然后，你们伤害了我的道德信仰。

当我把我的最神圣当做一种牺牲拿出来的时候，你们的“虔诚”立刻就将它的奢华的礼物放在了它的边上：这样一来，我的最神圣就会在你们那浓厚的烟雾中被呛到喘不过气来。

曾经，我特别想跳舞，因为我从来就没有跳过舞：我想在所有的蓝天之上跳舞。然后，你们就会引诱我最喜爱的吟游诗人。

而现在，他留着一头糟糕的、充满忧郁气息的头发；唉，他就像在我耳边忧伤的喇叭一样，发出嘟嘟的声音！

凶残的歌手，恶魔的工具，最无辜的你啊！我已经准备好跳最华美的舞步了：然而，你的音调扼杀了我的狂热！

我只有在跳舞的时候，才懂得最高尚之物的寓言：——现在，最重要的寓言依旧保存在我的四肢内，只字未提！

我的最高希望仍旧保持着未被说出、未被发现的状态！关于我的青春的所有形象和所有安慰全都消失了！

我要如何承受这些呢？我要如何在这样的伤口之下幸存并且克服它呢？我的灵魂究

asunder: it is called my will. Silently doth it proceed, and unchanged throughout the years.

Its course will it go upon my feet, mine old Will; hard of heart is its nature and invulnerable.

Invulnerable am I only in my heel. Ever livest thou there, and art like thyself, thou most patient one! Ever hast thou burst all shackles of the tomb!

In thee still liveth also the unrealisedness of my youth; and as life and youth sittest thou here hopeful on the yellow ruins of graves.

Yea, thou art still for me the demolisher of all graves: Hail to thee, my Will! And only where there are graves are there resurrections.

Thus sang Zarathustra.

34. SELF-SURPASSING

"Will to Truth" do ye call it, ye wisest ones, that which impelleth you and maketh you ardent?

Will for the thinkableness of all being: thus do I call your will!

All being would ye make thinkable: for ye doubt with good reason whether it be already thinkable.

But it shall accommodate and bend itself to you! So willeth your will. Smooth shall it become and subject to the spirit, as its mirror and reflection.

竟要怎么做才能再一次从坟茔里屹立而起呢？

是的，对于我来说有些事情是无懈可击的，它是无法被掩盖的，可以将岩石撕成碎片的事物：它就是所谓的我的意志。它一直沉默寡言的、一成不变的度过了很多年。

我那古老的意志，它依靠我的腿走在我的道路之上；它的本性是冷酷无情的，不会受到伤害的。

我的全身只有脚后跟是最有可能受到伤害的地方。你，我的忍耐的意志啊，你一成不变地存在着！你已经从所有的坟茔里找到出路了！

在你的内心中还存在着我尚未实现的青春；你就像生命和青春一样充满了希望，坐在墓地黄色的废墟之上。

是的，你一直都是我的所有坟茔的破坏者：我的意志，我向你致敬！只要是坟茔存在的地方，就会有复活。

查拉图斯特拉如是歌唱。

34. 自我克服

你们这些最聪明的智者们，你们称激励你们、燃烧你们的激情是“寻求事实真相的意志”吗？

但是我却要称你们的意志为能够理解世间万物的意志！

你们想让在世间存在的万物都能够被理解：因为你们有着很好的理由去怀疑：世间的万物早就可以被理解了。

但是，世间的万物都会屈服于你们！你们的意志要如是。

That is your entire will, ye wisest ones, as a Will to Power; and even when ye speak of good and evil, and of estimates of value.

Ye would still create a world before which ye can bow the knee: such is your ultimate hope and ecstasy.

The ignorant, to be sure, the people they are like a river on which a boat floateth along: and in the boat sit the estimates of value, solemn and disguised.

Your will and your valuations have ye put on the river of becoming; it betrayeth unto me an old Will to Power, what is believed by the people as good and evil.

It was ye, ye wisest ones, who put such guests in this boat, and gave them pomp and proud names ye and your ruling Will!

Onward the river now carrieth your boat: it must carry it. A small matter if the rough wave foameth and angrily resisteth its keel!

It is not the river that is your danger and the end of your good and evil, ye wisest ones: but that Will itself, the Will to Power the unexhausted, procreating life-will.

But that ye may understand my gospel of good and evil, for that purpose will I tell you my gospel of life, and of the nature of all living things.

The living thing did I follow; I walked in the broadest and narrowest paths to learn its nature.

With a hundred-faced mirror did I catch its glance when its mouth was shut, so that its eye might speak unto me. And its eye spake unto me.

它应该变得毕恭毕敬，并且服从于精神，就像精神的镜子和形象一样。

这就是你们整个的意志，你们这些智者们，你们的权力意志；即便是你们谈及善与恶以及价值的评定的时候也是如此。

你们依旧可以创造一个你们可以对其屈膝下跪的世界：这就是你们的终极的希望和最后的心醉神迷。

毋庸置疑，愚昧无知的人、人民群众——他们就像是在一条河上漂浮的小船：在那条小船上，庄严肃穆的价值评估将自己伪装了起来，坐在那上面。

你们曾经把你们的意志和你们的评估置于演变的小河之上；被人民群众给予肯定评价的善与恶的事物，在我看来，就是一个古老的意志。

啊，你们这些聪明的智者啊！你们将这样的客人放在这条船上，并且用奢华的装饰品和令人引以为豪的名字对他们进行乔装打扮——你们和你们的统治意志！

现在，这条河正在推着你们的小船向前进发：这条河必须承载着它。就算是大浪吐着泡沫，愤怒地撞击着小船的龙骨，那又算得了什么呢！

你们这些聪明的智者们，对于你们来说，真正危险的并不是河流以及你们的善与恶的终结，而是意志本身，权力的意志——永不知疲倦、具有创造性的生命意志！

但是，我想让你们了解我的善与恶的说教，为了能够达到这一目的，我会将关于我的生命之教义以及所有生命形式的本性的教义告诉你们。

我曾经跟踪考察过生命形式的本性；我在宽宽窄窄的道路上前行，跟随它们，了解它们的本性。

我在有一百个面孔的镜子里，抓住了生命的注视，当它把自己的嘴巴闭上的时候，它的眼睛就会开始跟我说话。而且，它的眼睛曾经跟我说过话。

But wherever I found living things, there heard I also the language of obedience. All living things are obeying things.

And this heard I secondly: Whatever cannot obey itself, is commanded. Such is the nature of living things.

This, however, is the third thing which I heard namely, that commanding is more difficult than obeying. And not only because the commander beareth the burden of all obeyers, and because this burden readily crusheth him:

An attempt and a risk seemed all commanding unto me; and whenever it commandeth, the living thing risketh itself thereby.

Yea, even when it commandeth itself, then also must it atone for its commanding. Of its own law must it become the judge and avenger and victim.

How doth this happen! so did I ask myself. What persuadeth the living thing to obey, and command, and even be obedient in commanding?

Hearken now unto my word, ye wisest ones! Test it seriously, whether I have crept into the heart of life itself, and into the roots of its heart!

Wherever I found a living thing, there found I Will to Power; and even in the will of the servant found I the will to be master.

That to the stronger the weaker shall serve thereto persuadeth he his will who would be master over a still weaker one. That delight alone he is unwilling to forego.

And as the lesser surrendereth himself to the greater that he may have delight and power over

但是，无论我在哪里发现了生物，我总是能够听到关于服从的话语。所有的生命形式都必须服从。

这是我听到的第二件事：倘若不想服从于自己，那就要听候别人的命令。这就是所有生命形式的本性。

然而，我听到的第三件事——就是命令要比服从困难得多。而且，产生这样的情况的原因，并不是因为命令别人要承担所有服从者的负担，而是因为这种负担或许会把他压垮。

而且，对于我来说，所有的命令都是一种尝试以及一种风险；当生物做出命令的时候，他就要冒着生命之风险。

是的，即使当他命令自己的时候，他也必须为这样的命令而付出相应的代价。他一定会成为自己的法律的法官、报仇者和受害者。

为什么会发生这样的事！我曾经问过自己。究竟是什么说服生物去服从、去命令，甚至服从命令的呢？

伟大的智者们啊！请聆听我的话吧！认真地考察，我是否已经深入到了生命本身的核心部分，并且到了核心的根基！

无论我在何地发现生物，我都能在那里找到权力的意志；我甚至在服从者的意志当中，发现了要想成为主人的意志。

弱者的意志说服了弱者自身，让他为强者服务，与此同时，这种弱者的意志还想要成为比他更加弱小的意志的主人。这是他不愿意放弃的唯一的快乐。

弱者向强者投降，以此获得统治更弱者带来的快乐，同样的，弱者顺从于他的权力

the least of all, so doth even the greatest surrender himself, and staketh life, for the sake of power.

It is the surrender of the greatest to run risk and danger, and play dice for death.

And where there is sacrifice and service and love-glances, there also is the will to be master. By by-ways doth the weaker then slink into the fortress, and into the heart of the mightier one and there stealeth power.

And this secret spake Life herself unto me. "Behold," said she, "I am that which must ever surpass itself.

To be sure, ye call it will to procreation, or impulse towards a goal, towards the higher, remoter, more manifold: but all that is one and the same secret.

Rather would I succumb than disown this one thing; and verily, where there is succumbing and leaf-falling, lo, there doth Life sacrifice itself for power!

That I have to be struggle, and becoming, and purpose, and cross-purpose ah, he who divineth my will, divineth well also on what crooked paths it hath to tread!

Whatever I create, and however much I love it, soon must I be adverse to it, and to my love: so willeth my will.

And even thou, discerning one, art only a path and footstep of my will: verily, my Will to Power walketh even on the feet of thy Will to Truth!

He certainly did not hit the truth who shot at it the formula: 'Will to existence': that will doth not exist!

For what is not, cannot will; that, however, which is in existence how could it still strive for

意志，并且为了权力不惜付出生命的代价。

冒着风险和拿死亡当赌注就是强者的屈服。

只要有牺牲、服务和爱的凝视的地方，就会有要想成为主人的意志。弱者会通过旁门左道悄悄地进入强者的堡垒以及心里——并且偷走力量。

这是生命曾经跟我说过的一个小秘密。“看啊，”他说道，“我必须要经常超越自己。”

毋庸置疑，你们管这个叫具有创造性的意志，或是追求一个更高、更远、更加复杂多样的目标的冲动：不过这些都只是一件事，相同的秘密。

我宁肯选择死，也不会跟这样的事物脱离关系，说真的，有屈服和树叶飘落的地方，就会有为了权力而牺牲自己的生命！

我一定要努力成为争斗、变化的目的，和目的的对立面——唉，谁能够猜出我的意志，那么他一定也可以猜出它遵循着的崎岖的道路！

无论我创造出了什么东西，我会如何去爱它——很快，我就会成为它的对手以及我的爱的对手：我的意志要我如是。

你们这些求知者，不过就是我的意志的一条道路和足迹：说真的，我的权力的意志也会跟随在你们的真相意志的后面！

那些说着“存在的意志”的人，是不可能发现真理的，那样的意志根本就是不存在的！

因为不存在的事物是不能拥有意志的；但是，那些本来已经存在的事物，为何还要努力追求存在呢！

existence!

Only where there is life, is there also will: not, however, Will to Life, but so teach I thee Will to Power!

Much is reckoned higher than life itself by the living one; but out of the very reckoning speaketh the Will to Power!"

Thus did Life once teach me: and thereby, ye wisest ones, do I solve you the riddle of your hearts.

Verily, I say unto you: good and evil which would be everlasting it doth not exist! Of its own accord must it ever surpass itself anew.

With your values and formulae of good and evil, ye exercise power, ye valuing ones: and that is your secret love, and the sparkling, trembling, and overflowing of your souls.

But a stronger power groweth out of your values, and a new surpassing: by it breaketh egg and egg-shell.

And he who hath to be a creator in good and evil verily, he hath first to be a destroyer, and break values in pieces.

Thus doth the greatest evil pertain to the greatest good: that, however, is the creating good.

Let us speak thereof, ye wisest ones, even though it be bad. To be silent is worse; all suppressed truths become poisonous.

And let everything break up which can break up by our truths! Many a house is still to be built!

Thus spake Zarathustra.

只有存在生命的地方，才会存在意志：但是，这种意志不是生命的意志，而是——让我告诉你们——那是权力的意志！

许多事物都被生物看做是比生命更加高级的存在；这种辨别就是权力的意志发挥了作用！

曾经有一天，生命教育了我：啊，聪明的智者们啊！我要用生命教育我的方式解决你们心中的谜题。

说真的，我要对你们说：处于永恒不朽的善与恶——那是不存在的！凭借善与恶自身的意愿，他们一定要时常超越自己。

你们这些利用善与恶的价值和惯例施展你们的权力的评价者们：这是你们秘密的爱以及你们的灵魂的光芒、震颤和泛滥。

但是，从你们的价值里，会出现一个更加强大的权力，一个全新的自我超越：它会破壳而出。

说真的，那个创造了善与恶的人，必将要首先成为一名破坏者，将价值打得粉碎。

所以，最强大的恶也是最大的善的一个组成部分：但是，这就是具有创造性的善。

让我们好好谈谈吧，聪明的智者们，尽管谈话是一件不好的事情，但是保持安静要比谈话更加糟糕；所有被隐藏的真相都会成为毒药。

让我们的真理将一切能够被打碎的东西都打碎吧！还有很多房子等待着被建设呢！

查拉图斯特拉如是说。

35. THE SUBLIME ONES

Calm is the bottom of my sea: who would guess that it hideth droll monsters!

Unmoved is my depth: but it sparkleth with swimming enigmas and laughters.

A sublime one saw I to-day, a solemn one, a penitent of the spirit: Oh, how my soul laughed at his ugliness!

With upraised breast, and like those who draw in their breath: thus did he stand, the sublime one, and in silence:

O'erhung with ugly truths, the spoil of his hunting, and rich in torn raiment; many thorns also hung on him but I saw no rose.

Not yet had he learned laughing and beauty. Gloomy did this hunter return from the forest of knowledge.

From the fight with wild beasts returned he home: but even yet a wild beast gazeth out of his seriousness an unconquered wild beast!

As a tiger doth he ever stand, on the point of springing; but I do not like those strained souls; ungracious is my taste towards all those self-engrossed ones.

And ye tell me, friends, that there is to be no dispute about taste and tasting? But all life is a dispute about taste and tasting!

Taste: that is weight at the same time, and scales and weigher; and alas for every living thing that would live without dispute about weight and scales and weigher!

Should he become weary of his sublimeness, this sublime one, then only will his beauty

35. 崇高者

我的海底非常平静，有谁会知道，在它的下面藏有滑稽可笑的怪兽！

我的深度是不可动摇的，但是在水中畅游的谜团和笑声却在散发着光彩。我今天看到了一位崇高并且严肃的人，他是精神的忏悔者：噢，我的灵魂在嘲笑他的丑陋呢！

他挺起了胸膛，就好像在大口地呼吸一样：这个高尚的人，就这么安静地站着。

在他的身上悬着很多丑陋的真相，那都是他捕猎获得的战利品，他穿着破破烂烂的衣服，上面还有很多刺——可是我没有看到玫瑰花。

他还没有学到微笑和美貌。这位捕猎者忧郁地从知识的森林里走了出来。

在和凶猛的野兽进行搏斗之后，他回到了家：但是，在他的严肃里还存在着另一个狂野的野兽——那是一个从没有被征服过的野兽！

他就像一头随时准备跳跃的老虎一样站在那里；但是，我并不喜欢那些令人紧张的灵魂；而且我还讨厌他们一切以自我为中心的态度。

朋友们，我恳请你们告诉我，品味的谈论是不存在争端的吧？但是，整个的生命就是品味的争论！

品味：与此同时，也是重量、天平以及掌权者；任何生命要想生存，而不是为了重量、天平以及掌权者而争论是非常悲哀的！

他应该会对他的高尚感到厌倦，这位高尚的人，只有到了那个时候，他的美貌

begin and then only will I taste him and find him savoury.

And only when he turneth away from himself will he o'erleap his own shadow and verily! into his sun.

Far too long did he sit in the shade; the cheeks of the penitent of the spirit became pale; he almost starved on his expectations.

Contempt is still in his eye, and loathing hideth in his mouth. To be sure, he now resteth, but he hath not yet taken rest in the sunshine.

As the ox ought he to do; and his happiness should smell of the earth, and not of contempt for the earth.

As a white ox would I like to see him, which, snorting and lowing, walketh before the plough-share: and his lowing should also laud all that is earthly!

Dark is still his countenance; the shadow of his hand danceth upon it. O'ershadowed is still the sense of his eye.

His deed itself is still the shadow upon him: his doing obscureth the doer. Not yet hath he overcome his deed.

To be sure, I love in him the shoulders of the ox: but now do I want to see also the eye of the angel.

Also his hero-will hath he still to unlearn: an exalted one shall he be, and not only a sublime one: the ether itself should raise him, the will-less one!

He hath subdued monsters, he hath solved enigmas. But he should also redeem his monsters

才会真正开始——只有到了那个时候，我才会喜爱他，并且开始认为他能够迎合我的口味。

只有当他背叛自己的时候，他才能跳过属于他自己的阴影——真的，跳进他的太阳里。

他在树荫下坐了太长的时间；精神的忏悔者的脸颊开始变得苍白；他几乎在他的期待中被活活饿死。

他的眼睛中仍旧带有轻蔑的眼神，他的嘴唇里隐藏着厌恶。毋庸置疑，他现在正在休息，但是，他还是没有在太阳光的下面休息。

他应该像一头牛一样，他的幸福快乐应该有泥地的味道，而不是轻蔑泥土的味道。

我特别喜欢看见他像一头白色的牛一样，在犁前低着头，发出哼哼的声音：而它的喘气声同样也应该是赞美大地的一切！

他的面容仍然是黑色的；他的双手在那上面尽情地舞蹈。他的眼神的含义仍旧隐藏在阴影之中。

他自己的所作所为仍旧是将他掩盖起来的影子：他的行为掩盖了行为人。但是，他还未曾克服他自身的行为。

毋庸置疑，我喜欢类似牛的肩膀，但是我现在，同样想看到天使的眼睛。

同样地，他应该忘却他的英雄般的意志：他应该不仅仅成为一名品德高尚的人，而且还是一名被高抬高举的人：——以太应该可以抬高他，这个没有意志的人！

他曾经驯服过野兽，曾经解决过难题。但是，他同样应该救赎他驯服过的野兽和解决过的谜题；并且将它们改造成天使一般的孩子。

and enigmas; into heavenly children should he transform them.

As yet hath his knowledge not learned to smile, and to be without jealousy; as yet hath his gushing passion not become calm in beauty.

Verily, not in satiety shall his longing cease and disappear, but in beauty! Gracefulness belongeth to the munificence of the magnanimous.

His arm across his head: thus should the hero repose; thus should he also surmount his repose.

But precisely to the hero is beauty the hardest thing of all. Unattainable is beauty by all ardent wills.

A little more, a little less: precisely this is much here, it is the most here.

To stand with relaxed muscles and with unharnessed will: that is the hardest for all of you, ye sublime ones!

When power becometh gracious and descendeth into the visible I call such condescension, beauty.

And from no one do I want beauty so much as from thee, thou powerful one: let thy goodness be thy last self-conquest.

All evil do I accredit to thee: therefore do I desire of thee the good.

Verily, I have often laughed at the weaklings, who think themselves good because they have crippled paws!

The virtue of the pillar shalt thou strive after: more beautiful doth it ever become, and more graceful but internally harder and more sustaining the higher it riseth.

然而，他的知识还没有学会该如何微笑，也没有学会该如何嫉妒：他的激情之流还没有在美貌中平静过。

说真的，他的渴求不应该在满足中停止以及消失，而应该在美里。怜悯属于慷慨之人的宽宏大量。

他将自己的手交叉放在头上：英雄应该休息；同样，他应该克服他的休息。

但是准确地说，对于英雄而言，美是世界上最难的事。任何满腔热血的意志都无法得到它。

或多，或少：在这里已算过分了，在这里已算是超级厉害了。

高尚的人啊！同进行放松，休息的肌肉和未被利用的意志站在一起：这对于你们来说，是最难的事。

当力量变得高尚，并且下降到人们可以看见的程度——我会将这种屈尊的态度称为美。

我会向你们这些权力者无比热情的要求美：让你们的善意成为你们最后的自我战胜吧。

我相信你会做任何邪恶的事情：因此，我强烈渴望你是善者。

说真的，我经常耻笑那些因为脚瘸了就称呼自己是善良的弱者！

你应当努力学习柱子的美德：但是，强大——它升得越高，越漂亮和优雅——它的内在的抵抗力就会越来越强大。

是的，这些高尚的人啊！有一天，你们也会变得漂亮，并且举起镜子，照着自己的美貌。

Yea, thou sublime one, one day shalt thou also be beautiful, and hold up the mirror to thine own beauty.

Then will thy soul thrill with divine desires; and there will be adoration even in thy vanity!

For this is the secret of the soul: when the hero hath abandoned it, then only approacheth it in dreams the superhero.

Thus spake Zarathustra.

36. THE LAND OF CULTURE

Too far did I fly into the future: a horror seized upon me.

And when I looked around me, lo! there time was my sole contemporary.

Then did I fly backwards, homewards and always faster. Thus did I come unto you, ye present-day men, and into the land of culture.

For the first time brought I an eye to see you, and good desire: verily, with longing in my heart did I come.

But how did it turn out with me? Although so alarmed I had yet to laugh! Never did mine eye see anything so motley-coloured!

I laughed and laughed, while my foot still trembled, and my heart as well. "Here forsooth, is the home of all the paintpots," said I.

With fifty patches painted on faces and limbs so sat ye there to mine astonishment, ye present-day men!

然后，你的灵魂就会因为神圣的渴望而变得蠢蠢欲动；在你的浮夸当中甚至还存在有崇拜！

这就是灵魂的秘密：当英雄将灵魂抛弃之后，只有超级英雄会在梦里，悄然接近他。

查拉图斯特拉如是说。

36. 文化之邦

我在文化的世界里飞得太远了：一种莫名的恐惧抓住了我。

当我环顾四周的时候，看呀！时间才是我独一无二的同代者。

然后，我开始向后飞，朝着家的方向飞——我加快了飞翔的速度。今天的人们啊！我来到了你们的身边，我来到了文化之邦。

这是我有生以来第一次用温和的眼睛以及诚挚的渴望来看望你们：说真的，我是带着无比渴望的内心来到这里的。

但是，在这之后怎么样了呢？尽管我非常恐惧——我实在控制不住自己笑了出来：我的眼睛还从来都没有看到过如此这般被颜色点缀的事物！

我一直在哈哈大笑，而与此同时，我的双脚和我的内心仍旧在颤抖着。“这里竟然是所有带颜料的瓦罐的故乡！”——我说道。

今天的人们啊！你们的面孔和四肢都被涂抹成了各式各样的色彩——我无比惊讶地看着你们坐在那里！

And with fifty mirrors around you, which flattered your play of colours, and repeated it!

Verily, ye could wear no better masks, ye present-day men, than your own faces! Who could recognise you!

Written all over with the characters of the past, and these characters also pencilled over with new characters thus have ye concealed yourselves well from all decipherers!

And though one be a trier of the reins, who still believeth that ye have reins! Out of colours ye seem to be baked, and out of glued scraps.

All times and peoples gaze divers-coloured out of your veils; all customs and beliefs speak divers-coloured out of your gestures.

He who would strip you of veils and wrappers, and paints and gestures, would just have enough left to scare the crows.

Verily, I myself am the scared crow that once saw you naked, and without paint; and I flew away when the skeleton ogled at me.

Rather would I be a day-labourer in the nether-world, and among the shades of the by-gone! Fatter and fuller than ye, are forsooth the nether-worldlings!

This, yea this, is bitterness to my bowels, that I can neither endure you naked nor clothed, ye present-day men!

All that is unhomelike in the future, and whatever maketh strayed birds shiver, is verily more homelike and familiar than your "reality."

For thus speak ye: "Real are we wholly, and without faith and superstition": thus do ye plume yourselves alas! even without plumes!

在你们的四周有五十面镜子，它们在奉承并且反复地呈现你们的颜色之戏剧！

说真的，再好的面具也无法胜过你们的面孔，有谁能够认出你来吗！

在你们的身上都记录着来自过去的记号，而这些记号又被新的记号覆盖了——因此，你们能够很好地躲过任何破解密码之人的调查！

尽管有人会去调查内脏，但是，你们能够让谁相信你们还拥有内脏呢！

你们看起来好像是被颜料和胶合碎片烘烤而成的。

每个时代的人民都是在你们那夹杂着各种各样颜色的面纱中偷偷地注视着的；所有的习俗和信念都在你们的手势里交谈着。

那个摘掉你们的面纱、裹布、颜料和手势的人，必定会在他的面前发现能够吓跑乌鸦的东西。

说真的，我就是那个所谓能够吓跑乌鸦的东西，我曾经看见过你们的赤身裸体，身上毫无色彩；当这具骸骨在冲我眉目传情的时候，我赶紧跑掉了。

我宁愿在一个地下的世界里以及早已逝去的灵魂中当劳工！因为生活在那里的人们的内容要比你们更加丰富！

今天的人们啊，我的内心的悲痛就是：我既无法容忍你们赤身裸体，也无法容忍你们穿上衣服！

说真的，未来的令人不安的焦虑以及让迷路的鸟儿战栗的事物，都要比你们所谓的“实在”让人心安和熟悉的多。

因为你们如是说：“我们就是彻彻底底的实在，我们没有信仰也没有迷信。”你们

Indeed, how would ye be able to believe, ye divers-coloured ones! ye who are pictures of all that hath ever been believed!

Perambulating réfutations are ye, of belief itself, and a dislocation of all thought. UNTRUSTWORTHY ones: thus do I call you, ye real ones!

All periods prate against one another in your spirits; and the dreams and pratings of all periods were even realer than your awakeness!

Unfruitful are ye: Therefore do ye lack belief. But he who had to create, had always his presaging dreams and astral premonitions and believed in believing!

Half-open doors are ye, at which grave-diggers wait. And this is your reality: "Everything deserveth to perish."

Alas, how ye stand there before me, ye unfruitful ones; how lean your ribs! And many of you surely have had knowledge thereof.

Many a one hath said: "There hath surely a God filched something from me secretly whilst I slept? Verily, enough to make a girl for himself therefrom!"

"Amazing is the poverty of my ribs!" thus hath spoken many a present-day man.

Yea, ye are laughable unto me, ye present-day men! And especially when ye marvel at yourselves!

And woe unto me if I could not laugh at your marvelling, and had to swallow all that is repugnant in your platters!

As it is, however, I will make lighter of you, since I have to carry what is heavy; and what

就这样塞满了自己的嘴巴，但是没有吞咽的咽喉！

的确，你们这些涂抹颜色的人，你们怎么能够相信呢！——你们是所有信仰的图画！

你们是信仰的反证以及所有思想的混乱错位。你们这些真实的人，我要称呼你们为不可信者！

任何的时代都会在你们的精神当中互相谩骂；即使是任何时代的梦想和谩骂也要比你们苏醒着的理智更加真实！

你们是无法生孩子的：因此，你们缺乏信仰。被创造出来的人总是有预感的梦想以及灵魂世界的征兆——并且他对信仰深信不疑！

你们就是半开着的大门，而挖掘墓穴的人们就等候在外面。这就是你们的实在："任何事物都值得被毁灭。"

唉，无法生育的人啊，枯瘦的骸骨啊！你们就站在我的面前，在你们当中想必一定有自知之明的人吧！

他说："我很确定，一个上帝在趁我睡觉的时候，偷走了属于我的东西？说真的，他偷走的那些东西都足以制作一个女孩了！"

"我的骸骨的枯瘦真是令人惊讶啊！"很多今天的人们说道。

是的，今天的人们啊！你们让我发笑！特别是当你们自己都觉得惊讶的时候！

如果我不能笑话你们的自我惊讶，并且不得以吞掉你们的盘子里的令人作呕的液体的话，那我就太悲哀了！

但是，我会轻轻地承载着你，因为，我承担着沉重的负担；如果蜜蜂和小虫子同样降落在我的肩膀上，那又算得了什么呢！

matter if beetles and May-bugs also alight on my load!

Verily, it shall not on that account become heavier to me! And not from you, ye present-day men, shall my great weariness arise.

Ah, whither shall I now ascend with my longing! From all mountains do I look out for fatherlands and motherlands.

But a home have I found nowhere: unsettled am I in all cities, and decamping at all gates.

Alien to me, and a mockery, are the present-day men, to whom of late my heart impelled me; and exiled am I from fatherlands and motherlands.

Thus do I love only my children's land, the undiscovered in the remotest sea: for it do I bid my sails search and search.

Unto my children will I make amends for being the child of my fathers: and unto all the future for this present-day!

Thus spake Zarathustra.

37. IMMACULATE PERCEPTION

When yester-eve the moon arose, then did I fancy it about to bear a sun: so broad and teeming did it lie on the horizon.

But it was a liar with its pregnancy; and sooner will I believe in the man in the moon than in the woman.

说真的，我的肩膀并不会因为这样而变得更加沉重！今天的人们啊！你们并没有给我带来最大的疲倦。

唉，我现在还要和我的渴望一起攀爬呢！我会从所有的山峰上寻找我的故乡。

但是，无论我身处何地，都无法找到我的故乡：所有的城市都是我旅途中的一部分，所有的大门都是我旅行的起始点。

就在刚才，我的内心将我自己抛给了现在的人们，现在，他们只是一些能够逗我发笑的陌生人而已；我被我的故乡驱逐出来了。

因此，我只爱我的孩子们的故乡以及在最遥远的海洋里未被人们探索到的地方：我命令我的帆永远在海上探索。

身为我的祖先们的子民，我要向他们赎罪，并且，我要用所有的未来，赎回所有的现在！

查拉图斯特拉如是说。

37．无瑕的知识

当昨天夜晚的月亮出来的时候，它在地平线上是显得那么的宽广，那么的富饶，我猜测，它好像要诞生一个太阳一样。

但是，其实它是在用它的怀孕说谎话；很快，我开始相信月亮上的男人而不是女人。

毋庸置疑，这种胆小的夜晚狂欢者丝毫没有一点男子气概。说真的，他带着一种极其糟糕的心态经过屋顶。

To be sure, little of a man is he also, that timid night-reveller. Verily, with a bad conscience doth he stalk over the roofs.

For he is covetous and jealous, the monk in the moon; covetous of the earth, and all the joys of lovers.

Nay, I like him not, that tom-cat on the roofs! Hateful unto me are all that slink around half-closed windows!

Piously and silently doth he stalk along on the star-carpets: but I like no light-treading human feet, on which not even a spur jingleth.

Every honest one's step speaketh; the cat however, stealeth along over the ground. Lo! cat-like doth the moon come along, and dishonestly.

This parable speak I unto you sentimental dissemblers, unto you, the "pure discerners!" You do I call covetous ones!

Also ye love the earth, and the earthly: I have divined you well! but shame is in your love, and a bad conscience ye are like the moon!

To despise the earthly hath your spirit been persuaded, but not your bowels: these, however, are the strongest in you!

And now is your spirit ashamed to be at the service of your bowels, and goeth by-ways and lying ways to escape its own shame.

"That would be the highest thing for me" so saith your lying spirit unto itself "to gaze upon life without desire", and not like the dog, with hanging-out tongue:

To be happy in gazing: with dead will, free from the grip and greed of selfishness cold and

因为这个在月中的修道士非常贪婪并且嫉妒心很强；他贪图得到大地和爱人的所有快乐。

不，我并不爱他，那只屋檐上的猫！我非常讨厌那些在半开的窗户外偷看的家伙！

它会虔诚地、静悄悄地走过由星星组成的地毯：但是，我讨厌那些走路不留痕迹，也不使用叮当作响的马刺的人们。

每一个诚实的人的步伐都有声音；但是，猫却用偷偷潜入的方式走在地面上。瞧呀！月亮就像那只猫一样，不正直的前行着。

多愁善感的伪善者，“找寻纯真的求知者！”我将这个比喻给予你们。我称你们为贪婪的肉欲者！

你们同样也热爱着大地和大地的一切：我曾经预言过你们！——但是，你们的爱当中存在羞耻以及糟糕的心境——你们就像是月亮一样！

人们劝说你们，让你们的精神轻视大地的一切，但是，他们无法说服你们的内脏：然而，这些内脏正是你们体内最强大的东西！

现在，你们的精神会因为你们的内脏服务而感到耻辱，它一定会利用旁门左道逃离它自身的耻辱。

“这对于我来说是最为高尚的事情”——你们的说谎的精神对你们如是说道——用没有期待的目光，而不是像将舌头伸在外面的狗一样注视着生活：

在注视的过程中享受快乐：只有死亡才能摆脱束缚以及自私的贪婪——冷淡和灰色覆盖全身，那令人如痴如醉的月亮的眼睛！

ashy-grey all over, but with intoxicated moon-eyes!

That would be the dearest thing to me" thus doth the seduced one seduce himself ",to love the earth as the moon loveth it, and with the eye only to feel its beauty.

And this do I call immaculate perception of all things: "to want nothing else from them, but to be allowed to lie before them as a mirror with a hundred facets."

Oh, ye sentimental dissemblers, ye covetous ones! Ye lack innocence in your desire: and now do ye defame desiring on that account!

Verily, not as creators, as procreators, or as jubilators do ye love the earth!

Where is innocence? Where there is will to procreation. And he who seeketh to create beyond himself, hath for me the purest will.

Where is beauty? Where I must will with my whole Will; where I will love and perish, that an image may not remain merely an image.

Loving and perishing: these have rhymed from eternity. Will to love: that is to be ready also for death. Thus do I speak unto you cowards!

But now doth your emasculated ogling profess to be "contemplation!" And that which can be examined with cowardly eyes is to be christened "beautiful!" Oh, ye violators of noble names!

But it shall be your curse, ye immaculate ones, ye pure discerners, that ye shall never bring forth, even though ye lie broad and teeming on the horizon!

Verily, ye fill your mouth with noble words: and we are to believe that your heart overfloweth, ye cozeners?

“这对于我来说是最为挚爱的事情”——因此，勾引别人的人会勾引他自己——就像月亮喜爱大地一样热爱它，它的眼睛只能感受到它的美。

我会把这个叫做所有事情的无瑕的感知：不想从他们那里获得任何东西，只好躺在它们的旁边，就像拥有一百个刻面的镜子一样。

噢，你们这些敏感的伪善者！你们这些贪婪的人们！你们的渴望中缺乏纯真：现在，你们因为这样的情况诽谤自己的渴望！

说真的，你们对于大地的热爱还不及喜欢创造的创造者和生育者！

纯真何在？纯真就是对生育的渴望的地方。对于我来说，谁能够创造出高于自己的生命存在，那么他就拥有最纯真的意志。

美何在？美是一个我必须要用自己的全部意志去“意志”的地方；在那个我愿意爱和消亡，一个形象将不仅仅只是一个形象的地方。

爱和消亡：它们自始至终都是合辙押韵的。寻求爱的意志：就是随时准备接受死亡的意志。懦夫们，我向你们如是说！

但是，你们认为你们那柔弱的目光是“沉思”！而所有受到懦弱者目光的检查的都被称作是“美”！噢，你们是高贵的名字的玷污者！

无瑕的学者啊！纯粹的求知者啊！永远无法生育后代就是你们得到的诅咒，尽管你们厚重地、饱满地躺在水平线上！

说真的，你们满嘴都是高尚的语言：并且你们迫使我们相信，你们的心灵在泛滥着，你们这些诳语者啊！

But my words are poor, contemptible, stammering words: gladly do I pick up what falleth from the table at your repasts.

Yet still can I say therewith the truth to dissemblers! Yea, my fish-bones, shells, and prickly leaves shall tickle the noses of dissemblers!

Bad air is always about you and your repasts: your lascivious thoughts, your lies, and secrets are indeed in the air!

Dare only to believe in yourselves in yourselves and in your inward parts! He who doth not believe in himself always lieth.

A God's mask have ye hung in front of you, ye "pure ones": into a God's mask hath your execrable coiling snake crawled.

Verily ye deceive, ye "contemplative ones!" Even Zarathustra was once the dupe of your godlike exterior; he did not divine the serpent's coil with which it was stuffed.

A God's soul, I once thought I saw playing in your games, ye pure discerners! No better arts did I once dream of than your arts!

Serpents' filth and evil odour, the distance concealed from me: and that a lizard's craft prowled thereabouts lasciviously.

But I came nigh unto you: then came to me the day, and now cometh it to you, at an end is the moon's love affair!

See there! Surprised and pale doth it stand before the rosy dawn!

For already she cometh, the glowing one, her love to the earth cometh! Innocence and

但是，我的语言是粗糙的、不值一顾的、结结巴巴的语言：我非常喜欢捡起从你们的盛宴的桌子上掉落的食物。

我仍旧可以用这个把真相告诉给伪善者！是的，我的鱼骨头、贝壳以及冬青叶，都应该让你们的鼻子感到奇痒无比，伪善者啊！

围绕在你们和你们的盛宴周围的空气总是非常浑浊的：你们贪图肉欲的思想、你们的谎言以及你们的秘密全都隐藏在这浑浊的空气当中！

你要首先敢于相信你们自己——你们自己和你们的内部器官吧！那些不相信自己的人永远都是诳者。

你们这些“纯洁的”人们啊：你们将一个上帝的面具悬挂在你们的面前，而你们那令人憎恶的蛇就在上帝的面具里盘旋着爬行。

说真的，沉思者们，你们还真是很擅长欺骗啊！甚至是查拉图斯特拉，曾经也被你们那神似上帝的外表所蒙蔽；他并没有猜到究竟是什么样的蛇被塞到了这个上帝的面具里。

纯粹的求知者啊！我曾经在跟你们玩游戏的时候看见了一个上帝的灵魂，我从没有见过比你们的伪造更加出众的艺术！

我们之间的距离为我隐藏了毒蛇的污秽以及恶魔的气味，隐藏了潜伏在那里的一个蜥蜴之肉欲的阴谋诡计。

但是，我走近你：紧接着，白天为我到来了，——而现在，它也为你们到来了，月亮的爱情往事终究是要有结局的！

看看这里吧！它站在红灿灿的黎明面前，震惊的脸色苍白！

因为闪耀着光芒的夏日已经来了，它对于地球的爱也已经到来了！

creative desire, is all solar love!

See there, how she cometh impatiently over the sea! Do ye not feel the thirst and the hot breath of her love?

At the sea would she suck, and drink its depths to her height: now riseth the desire of the sea with its thousand breasts.

Kissed and sucked would it be by the thirst of the sun; vapour would it become, and height, and path of light, and light itself!

Verily, like the sun do I love life, and all deep seas.

And this meaneth to me knowledge: all that is deep shall ascend to my height!

Thus spake Zarathustra.

38. SCHOLARS

When I lay asleep, then did a sheep eat at the ivy-wreath on my head, it ate, and said thereby: "Zarathustra is no longer a scholar."

It said this, and went away clumsily and proudly. A child told it to me.

I like to lie here where the children play, beside the ruined wall, among thistles and red poppies.

A scholar am I still to the children, and also to the thistles and red poppies. Innocent are they, even in their wickedness.

太阳所有的爱就是纯真和具有创造性的渴望！

看看这里吧！黎明是多么迫不及待地跨越海洋！你们难道没有感觉到它的爱的渴望以及炽热的喘气吗？

它想要吮吸海水，并且将海水的深度转变成它的高度：与此同时，海洋的渴望创造了数以千计的乳房。

因为大海愿意被太阳的渴望亲吻和吮吸；它想要成为空气、高度以及光明的路线，甚至变成光明！

说真的，我就像太阳那样，热爱生命以及所有幽深的海洋。

而我称这个为知识：所有的深度都会抬升到我的高度！

查拉图斯特拉如是说。

38．学者

当我昏昏欲睡的时候，一只山羊开始吃戴在我头上的常春藤之花冠——它边吃边说："查拉图斯特拉已经不再是一名学者了。"

那只山羊说完这些之后，便用笨拙和骄傲的步伐扬长而去。这些都是一个小朋友告诉给我的。

我非常喜欢躺在这里，小朋友们在残破的墙壁旁边的蓟草与红罂粟里嬉戏玩耍的地方。

对于小朋友们和蓟草、红罂粟来说，我仍然是一名学者，即使是他们在做坏事的时候，他们依旧是纯真的。

But to the sheep I am no longer a scholar: so willeth my lot blessings upon it!

For this is the truth: I have departed from the house of the scholars, and the door have I also slammed behind me.

Too long did my soul sit hungry at their table: not like them have I got the knack of investigating, as the knack of nut-cracking.

Freedom do I love, and the air over fresh soil; rather would I sleep on ox-skins than on their honours and dignities.

I am too hot and scorched with mine own thought: often is it ready to take away my breath. Then have I to go into the open air, and away from all dusty rooms.

But they sit cool in the cool shade: they want in everything to be merely spectators, and they avoid sitting where the sun burneth on the steps.

Like those who stand in the street and gape at the passers-by: thus do they also wait, and gape at the thoughts which others have thought.

Should one lay hold of them, then do they raise a dust like flour-sacks, and involuntarily: but who would divine that their dust came from corn, and from the yellow delight of the summer fields?

When they give themselves out as wise, then do their petty sayings and truths chill me: in their wisdom there is often an odour as if it came from the swamp; and verily, I have even heard the frog croak in it!

Clever are they they have dexterous fingers: what doth my simplicity pretend to beside their

但是对于山羊来说，我已经不再是一名学者了：我的命运要我如是。——那么，就让这个命运被祝福吧！

因为这就是真相：我已经离开了学者的家，而且，我狠狠地关掉了我背后的大门。

我那饥饿的灵魂已经在他们的餐桌边坐了太久了：我对于调查研究的态度跟压碎坚果的态度并不一样。而他们却正如是。

我非常热爱自由以及新鲜土壤上方的空气；我宁愿酣睡在牛皮之上，而不是在他们的荣耀和尊严之上。

我因为自身思想的缘故，灼烧了自己：它们经常夺走我的呼吸。然后，我就会跑到开放的空气当中，远离所有落满灰尘的房间。

但是，他们表情冷漠地坐在凉爽的树荫下：无论他们来到什么地方，他们都只想当一名看客，而避免坐在被太阳光照射的石阶上面。

他们就像那些站在街道上，张着嘴看着过往的行人的人们：他们就这么等候着，张大了嘴巴看着别人的思想。

谁用手触碰他们的话，他们就会像装着面粉的袋子一样，不自觉地扬起一片灰尘：但是有谁能够猜到他们的灰尘到底是来自谷物里，还是来自于夏日菜地的金灿灿的快乐呢？

当他们自认为非常聪明的时候，他们那些琐碎的话语和真相就会让我汗毛直立：在他们的智慧当中往往会有一种来自泥沼的气息；说真的，我甚至从他们的智慧里听到了青蛙呱呱叫的声音！

他们非常聪明——他们拥有非常灵巧的手指：我的单纯质朴和他们的复杂多变之间存在着什么关系呢！他们的手指懂得抽线、编结，与纺织：因此，他们能够编织出精神

multiplicity! All threading and knitting and weaving do their fingers understand: thus do they make the hose of the spirit!

Good clockworks are they: only be careful to wind them up properly! Then do they indicate the hour without mistake, and make a modest noise thereby.

Like millstones do they work, and like pestles: throw only seed-corn unto them! they know well how to grind corn small, and make white dust out of it.

They keep a sharp eye on one another, and do not trust each other the best. Ingenious in little artifices, they wait for those whose knowledge walketh on lame feet, like spiders do they wait.

I saw them always prepare their poison with precaution; and always did they put glass gloves on their fingers in doing so.

They also know how to play with false dice; and so eagerly did I find them playing, that they perspired thereby.

We are alien to each other, and their virtues are even more repugnant to my taste than their falsehoods and false dice.

And when I lived with them, then did I live above them. Therefore did they take a dislike to me.

They want to hear nothing of any one walking above their heads; and so they put wood and earth and rubbish betwixt me and their heads.

Thus did they deafen the sound of my tread: and least have I hitherto been heard by the most learned.

的长筒袜！

他们都是非常出色的钟表：如果有人可以适当地帮它们拧紧发条！那么，他们会丝毫不差地指示出时间，并且会发出谦卑的滴答声。

他们就像磨盘和碾槌一样工作着：向他们的身上抛洒玉蜀黍的种子！——他们非常了解该如何磨碎小的谷物，并且让它们变成白色的粉末。

他们非常擅长观察彼此的手指，并且彼此之间不存在任何的信任。他们设计了一些很小的阴谋诡计，他们的知识全靠跛脚行走——他们就像是蜘蛛一样在此静候着。

我看到他们总是小心翼翼地准备着他们的毒药；并且用玻璃质地的手套保护着他们的双手。

他们还知道该如何玩假的骰子；我经常能够看到他们饶有兴致地玩着，并且他们会因此而汗如雨下。

我和他们之间并不认识，而且他们的道德让我感受到的厌恶更甚于我对他们的虚伪和虚假的骰子的厌恶。

当我跟他们在一起生活的时候，我居住在他们的上面。因此，他们都非常讨厌我。

他们不希望听到任何人在他们的头顶上走动；所以，他们在我和他们的头顶之间摆放了一些木头、土壤和垃圾。

的确，他们把我走路发出的声响全都隔绝了：到现在为止，最著名的学者还未曾听说过我的名字。

他们在我和他们之间，摆放了所有人类的错误和弱点——他们把这个称之为他们房子的“虚假的天花板”。

All mankind's faults and weaknesses did they put betwixt themselves and me: they call it "false ceiling" in their houses.

But nevertheless I walk with my thoughts above their heads; and even should I walk on mine own errors, still would I be above them and their heads.

For men are not equal: so speaketh justice. And what I will, they may not will!

Thus spake Zarathustra.

39. Poets

"SINCE I have known the body better"- said Zarathustra to one of his disciples- "the spirit has only been to me symbolically spirit; and all the 'imperishable'- that is also but a parable."

"So have I heard you say once before," answered the disciple, "and then you added: 'But the poets lie too much.' Why did you say that the poets lie too much?"

"Why?" said Zarathustra. "You ask why? I do not belong to those who may be asked after their Why.

Is my experience but of yesterday? It is long ago that I experienced the reasons for my opinions.

Should I not have to be a cask of memory, if I also wanted to have my reasons with me?

It is already too much for me even to retain my opinions; and many a bird flies away.

And sometimes, also, do I find a fugitive creature in my dovecote, which is alien to me, and

但是，不管怎么样，我用我的思想走在他们的头顶之上；我甚至应该用我自身的错误走在他们的头顶之上，那仍旧是在他们的头顶之上。

因为人与人之间是不平等的：正义如是说。而我所想要做的事，他们没有支配的权力！

查拉图斯特拉如是说。

39. 诗人

“自从我更加全面的了解了人类的身体之后”——查拉图斯特拉跟他的一个徒弟说道——“精神对于我来说，就只是某种象征意义上的精神；而所有的不朽——也仅仅是一个明喻。”

“我在之前曾经听你们说过，”查拉图斯特拉的徒弟回答道，“随后，你添加道：‘但是，诗人们太善于说谎话了。’为什么你要说诗人们太善于说谎话了？”

“为什么？”查拉图斯特拉说道，“你问我为什么？我并不是那种随便被人们问为什么的人。”

难道我的经验都只是来自昨天的吗？在很长的时间里，我已经用我自己的想法验证过我的理论了。

难道我必须得是一个记忆之桶，以便为自己留下很多的理由吗？

对于我来说，我无法为自己留住想法和论据；很多鸟儿都展翅高飞了。

有些时候，我会在我的鸽房里发现一只迷路的小鸟，由于它根本就不认识我，所以，

trembles when I lay my hand upon it.

But what did Zarathustra once say to you? That the poets lie too much?- But Zarathustra also is a poet.

Believe you that he there spoke the truth? Why do you believe it?"

The disciple answered: "I believe in Zarathustra." But Zarathustra shook his head and smiled.-

Belief does not sanctify me, said he, least of all the belief in myself.

But granting that some one did say in all seriousness that the poets lie too much: he was right- we do lie too much.

We also know too little, and are bad learners: so we are obliged to lie.

And which of us poets has not adulterated his wine? Many a poisonous hotchpotch has evolved in our cellars: many an indescribable thing has there been done.

And because we know little, therefore are we pleased from the heart with the poor in spirit, especially when they are young women!

And even of those things are we desirous, which old women tell one another in the evening. This do we call the eternally feminine in us.

And as if there were a special secret access to knowledge, which chokes up for those who learn anything, so do we believe in the people and in their "wisdom."

This, however, do all poets believe: that whoever pricks up his ears when lying in the grass or on lonely slopes, learns something of the things that are between heaven and earth.

当我把手放在它的身上的时候，它会全身发颤。

但是，查拉图斯特拉曾经跟我们说过什么吗？诗人们太善于说谎话了？——但是，查拉图斯特拉本人也是一位诗人。

你是否相信他说的这些是真实的？为什么你要相信这些呢？

查拉图斯特拉的徒弟回答道：“我相信查拉图斯特拉。”但是，查拉图斯特拉微笑着摇了摇头。

他说道：“信仰并不能将我神圣化，至少是那些对于我而言的信仰。”

但是，假设有人非常严肃地说道诗人们非常善于说谎：那么他说的是真的，——我们确实太善于说谎了。

我们知道的太少，我们都是愚笨的学习者：所以，我们不得不说谎。

在我们这些诗人当中，有哪位没有伪造过他的红酒？许许多多的毒液都存储在我们的地窖里：很多无法用语言来形容的事情也都是在这里完成的。

因为我们知道的太少，因此，我们发自内心的喜爱那些疯癫的人，尤其是那些疯癫的年轻女人们！

我们迫切地想要知道老妇女们在晚上彼此讲述的故事，我们管这个叫做我们身上永恒的女性气质。

我们好像知道有一条特殊的通向知识的秘密通路，而这条道路不会让任何拥有学识的人通过，所以，我们要相信民众和他们的“智慧”。

但是，所有的诗人们都相信：无论是谁竖起耳朵躺在草地上或是荒凉的斜坡之上，

And if there come to them tender emotions, then do the poets always think that nature herself is in love with them:

And that she steals to their ear to whisper secrets into it, and amorous flatteries: of this do they plume and pride themselves, before all mortals!

Ah, there are so many things between heaven and earth of which only the poets have dreamed!

And especially above the heavens: for all gods are poet-symbolisations, poet-sophistications!

Ever are we drawn aloft- that is, to the realm of the clouds: on these do we set our gaudy puppets, and then call them gods and supermen:-

Are not they light enough for those chairs!- all these gods and supermen?-

Ah, how I am weary of all the inadequate that is insisted on as actual! Ah, how I am weary of the poets!

When Zarathustra so spoke, his disciple resented it, but was silent. And Zarathustra also was silent; and his eye directed itself inwardly, as if it gazed into the far distance. At last he sighed and drew breath.-

I am of today and heretofore, said he then; but something is in me that is of the morrow, and the day following, and the hereafter.

I became weary of the poets, of the old and of the new: superficial are they all to me, and shallow seas.

They did not think sufficiently into the depth; therefore their feeling did not reach to the bottom.

都能或多或少学到一点蓝天和大地之间的事情。

如果他们能够得到温柔的情感的话，那么，他们往往会相信大自然也在爱着他们：

他们会相信大自然会悄然来到他们的耳边，低声地道出秘密和情话：他们在所有的凡人面前引以为豪，引以为荣！

啊，蓝天和大地之间有着这么多的事情，而它们只有诗人们才梦想过！

而且，特别是天上的事情：因为所有的神仙都是诗人的象征和造作！

说真的，我们总是被带向高处——换句话讲，就是云朵的国度：

在那里，我们能够摆放艳丽的木偶，并且管它们叫做神灵和超人。

他们都足够轻，能够坐在这样的位子上！——这些神灵和超人们！

唉，我应该如何厌倦所有不充分的内容，并且被坚持成为真实的东西！

唉，我应该如何厌倦那些诗人们呢！

当查拉图斯特拉说完这些话的时候，他的徒弟对此表示非常不满，但是他还是保持默不作声的状态。而查拉图斯特拉同样也保持一言不发；他将他的目光移向内部，就好像目视着远方一样。最终，他叹息着吸了口气。

“我属于今天和过去”，他随后说道，“但是我的身上拥有着属于明天、后天以及未来的事物。

我已经变得厌倦老的和新的诗人了：对于我而言，他们都太过于肤浅了，全都是没有深度的海洋。”

他们并没有深入地思考过；因此，他们的感觉并没有达到最深处。

一点点淫乐，一点点沉闷：这些就是他们最好的沉思。

Some sensation of voluptuousness and some sensation of tedium: these have as yet been their best contemplation.

Ghost-breathing and ghost-whisking, seems to me all the jingle-jangling of their harps; what have they known hitherto of the fervor of tones!-

They are also not pure enough for me: they all muddle their water that it may seem deep.

And rather would they thereby prove themselves reconcilers: but mediaries and mixers are they to me, and half-and-half, and impure!-

Ah, I cast indeed my net into their sea, and meant to catch good fish; but always did I draw up the head of some ancient God.

Thus did the sea give a stone to the hungry one. And they themselves may well originate from the sea.

Certainly, one finds pearls in them: thereby they are the more like hard molluscs. And instead of a soul, I have often found in them salt slime.

They have learned from the sea also its vanity: is not the sea the peacock of peacocks?

Even before the ugliest of all buffaloes does it spread out its tail; never does it tire of its lace-fan of silver and silk.

Disdainfully does the buffalo glance thereat, nigh to the sand with its soul, closer still to the thicket, nighest, however, to the swamp.

What is beauty and sea and peacock-splendour to it! This parable I speak to the poets.

Their spirit itself is the peacock of peacocks, and a sea of vanity!

对于我来说，他们的竖琴的声音只不过是鬼魂的喘息以及飞奔；直到现在，他们还能从声音的狂热中了解些什么呢！

他们对于我来说，并不是足够纯洁：他们会搅混他们的水，以此让它看上去更加幽深。

他们心甘情愿被人们认为是矛盾调解人：但是我认为他们是依违两可者、搅局者以及不纯洁的人！

啊，我的确在他们的海洋里撒下了我的网，我的本意是要在他们的海洋里抓到大鱼；但是，我总是抓到一些古老的神灵的头颅。

因此，大海把一块石头赠予了饥饿之人。就好像他们自己也是来自于这片大海。

人们能从那里面发现珍珠，这一点也不假：所以，这让他们看上去更像是质地坚硬的贝类软体动物。我经常发现，在他们的身上，咸的软泥已经被灵魂所替代。

同样地，他们还从海洋那里学到了虚荣：难道海洋不是所有的孔雀当中最虚荣的吗？

即便是在最丑陋的水牛面前，它也会伸展开它的尾巴；它绝不会对展开它的银丝的花边扇感到厌烦。

水牛用充满蔑视的眼光注视着，它的灵魂靠近了沙子，更加靠近丛林，最靠近的是沼泽。

这是何等的美丽、海洋和孔雀之屏啊！这就是我讲述给诗人的寓言故事。

说真的，他们的精神本身就是所有孔雀之中最虚荣的，它是虚荣之海！

诗人的精神需要观看者，他们就是水牛！

Spectators seeks the spirit of the poet- should they even be buffaloes!-

But of this spirit became I weary; and I see the time coming when it will become weary of itself.

Yes, changed have I seen the poets, and their glance turned towards themselves.

Penitents of the spirit have I seen appearing; they grew out of the poets.-

Thus spoke Zarathustra.

40. Great Events

THERE is an isle in the sea- not far from the Blessed isles of Zarathustra- on which a volcano ever smokes; of which isle the people, and especially the old women amongst them, say that it is placed as a rock before the gate of the under-world; but that through the volcano itself the narrow way leads downwards which conducts to this gate.

Now about the time that Zarathustra sojourned on the Blessed isles, it happened that a ship anchored at the isle on which stands the smoking mountain, and the crew went ashore to shoot rabbits. About the noontide hour, however, when the captain and his men were together again, they saw suddenly a man coming towards them through the air, and a voice said distinctly: "It is time! It is the highest time!" But when the figure was nearest to them (it flew past quickly, however, like a shadow, in the direction of the volcano), then did they recognize with the greatest surprise that it was Zarathustra; for they had all seen him before except the captain himself, and they loved him as the people love: in such wise that love and awe were combined

但是我开始对这种精神感到厌倦了；我感觉他们对自己感到厌倦的时候也已经到来了。

是的，我曾经看到过诗人发生了改变，诗人们将目光转向了自己。

我已经看到诗人的忏悔者出现了；他们就是从诗人们中产生的。

查拉图斯特拉如是说。

40．大事件

在海洋中有一座岛屿，它距离查拉图斯特拉的祝福之岛并不遥远，在那个小岛上面有一个总是冒着烟雾的火山，据那个小岛上面的人，尤其是他们当中的老妇人说，它被当做是一块岩石安放在地下世界的大门口；而通过这座火山的狭窄道路能够直接引导到地下世界的门口。

查拉图斯特拉在这个祝福之岛上逗留的时候，碰巧看到一艘船在这个冒着烟雾的火山旁边停泊，而船上的船员纷纷下船带着猎枪猎杀兔子去了。然而，到了正午时分，当船长和他的船员们再一次聚集在一起的时候，他们突然看到一个人穿过空地，并且朝他们这里走过来，他用无比清晰的声音说道："现在是时候了，现在已经到了最合适的时候了！"但是，当他走到离他们近的不能再近的地方的时候（他就像一个影子一样，快速地朝火山的方向飞奔而去），在这之后，他们才充满惊讶地认出那人就是查拉图斯特拉；因为在他们当中，除了船长以外，其他人曾经都见过查拉图斯特拉本人，他们热爱查拉图斯特拉就像广大人民热爱他一样：等量的爱和敬畏被这样的智慧地混合在了一起。

in equal degree.

"Behold!" said the old helmsman, "there goes Zarathustra to hell!"

About the same time that these sailors landed on the fire-isle, there was a rumor that Zarathustra had disappeared; and when his friends were asked about it, they said that he had gone on board a ship by night, without saying where he was going.

Thus there arose some uneasiness. After three days, however, there came the story of the ship's crew in addition to this uneasiness- and then did all the people say that the devil had taken Zarathustra. His disciples laughed, sure enough, at this talk; and one of them said even: "Sooner would I believe that Zarathustra has taken the devil." But at the bottom of their hearts they were all full of anxiety and longing: so their joy was great when on the fifth day Zarathustra appeared amongst them.

And this is the account of Zarathustra's interview with the fire-dog:

The earth, said he, has a skin; and this skin has diseases. One of these diseases, for example, is called "man."

And another of these diseases is called "the fire-dog": concerning him men have greatly deceived themselves, and let themselves be deceived.

To fathom this mystery did I go o'er the sea; and I have seen the truth naked, verily! barefooted up to the neck.

Now do I know how it is concerning the fire-dog; and likewise concerning all the spouting and subversive devils, of which not only old women are afraid.

"Up with you, fire-dog, out of your depth!" cried I, "and confess how deep that depth is!

“快看呀！”一个老舵手说道，“查拉图斯特拉这是要往地狱的方向去啊！”

几乎是在同一时间，这些水手们登陆了这座烈焰之岛，这座岛上有谣言说，查拉图斯特拉消失了；当他的朋友们被别人询问的时候，他们说他在夜晚上了一艘船走了，他并没有说出他要去的目的地。

所以，某种不安的忧虑开始出现。然而，三天以后，除了这种不安的焦虑以外，又有了水手们的阐述，紧接着，所有的人都说，是恶魔把查拉图斯特拉抓走了。查拉图斯特拉的门徒们对此只是笑笑，他们当中的一个人说道：“与其这样，我更相信是查拉图斯特拉抓走了恶魔。”但是，在他们的内心深处，他们充满了焦虑和渴求：所以，到了第五天，当他们看到查拉图斯特拉出现在他们当中的时候，他们非常高兴。

而这是查拉图斯特拉和火焰猎犬进行谈话的内容：

他说，地球有一层皮肤；而且这层皮肤拥有疾病。我举个例子，在这些疾病当中有一个就是所谓的“人类”。

而另一个疾病则是被称为“火焰猎犬”的家伙：关于这条猎犬，人类在彼此之间已经说了很多的谎语。

为了深入了解这一谜团，我横越海洋，我已经看到了赤裸裸的真理，说真的，从脚踝一直到脖子的真理。

现在，我已经知道了有关于火焰猎犬的真理，也由此知道了那些不仅仅是老妇人畏惧的，推翻以及破坏性极强的恶魔的真理。

“火焰猎犬，你从你的深度中出来吧！”我大喊道，“道出你的深度到底有多深！

Whence comes that which you snort up?

You drink copiously at the sea: that does your embittered eloquence betray! In sooth, for a dog of the depth, you take your nourishment too much from the surface!

At the most, I regard you as the ventriloquist of the earth: and ever, when I have heard subversive and spouting devils speak, I have found them like you: embittered, mendacious, and shallow.

You understand how to roar and obscure with ashes! You are the best braggarts, and have sufficiently learned the art of making dregs boil.

Where you are, there must always be dregs at hand, and much that is spongy, hollow, and compressed: it wants to have freedom.

'Freedom' you all roar most eagerly: but I have unlearned the belief in 'great events,' when there is much roaring and smoke about them.

And believe me, friend Hullabaloo! The greatest events- are not our noisiest, but our still hours.

Not around the inventors of new noise, but around the inventors of new values, does the world revolve; inaudibly it revolves.

And just own to it! Little had ever taken place when your noise and smoke passed away. What, if a city did become a mummy, and a statue lay in the mud!

And this do I say also to the o'erthrowers of statues: It is certainly the greatest folly to throw salt into the sea, and statues into the mud.

In the mud of your contempt lay the statue: but it is just its law, that out of contempt, its life

你究竟是从何处获得的呕吐物？”

你大口大口地喝着海水：你的雄辩的苦涩向我诉说着！说真的，你这来自深处的火焰猎犬，你从大地的表面拿走了太多的营养物！

我最多将你们视为大地的腹语术者；当我听到破坏和推翻的恶魔说话的时候，我发现他们特别像你，充满苦涩的、虚假的，并且肤浅的。

你们知道应该如何嘶吼以及用灰烬蒙蔽天空，你们是最出色的吹牛者，你们充分地了解了让污垢沸腾的艺术。

无论你们身在哪里，你们都必将让污垢和腐烂、空洞并且被压的物体跟随着你们，它们想要拥有自由。

“自由”是你们呼喊的最热切的口号：不过，当“大事变”被过多的咆哮和烟雾笼罩的时候，我便对它们失去了应有的信仰。

我的朋友，亲爱的地狱之闹事者啊！请相信我吧！最伟大的事变——并不是我们最喧闹的，而是我们最宁静的时候。

世界并不会绕着新噪音的发明者，而是围绕着新价值的创造者旋转，它就这么悄无声息地旋转着。

所以就招了吧！当你的噪音和烟雾消失殆尽的时候，产生的效果是微乎其微的。倘若一个城市变成了一个木乃伊，那么一个瘫倒在泥浆里的雕像又算得了什么呢！

雕像就瘫倒在你们的轻蔑的泥土里：但是这正是它得以存在的道理，它的生活和活生生的美感再一次从轻蔑之中产生了出来！

and living beauty grow again!

With diviner features does it now arise, seducing by its suffering; and verily! it will yet thank you for o'erthrowing it, you subverters!

This counsel, however, do I counsel to kings and churches, and to all that is weak with age or virtue- let yourselves be o'erthrown! That you may again come to life, and that virtue- may come to you!-"

Thus spoke I before the fire-dog: then did he interrupt me sullenly, and asked: "Church? What is that?"

"Church?" answered I, "that is a kind of state, and indeed the most mendacious. But remain quiet, you dissembling dog! you surely know your own species best!

Like yourself the state is a dissembling dog; like you does it like to speak with smoke and roaring- to make believe, like you, that it speaks out of the heart of things.

For it seeks by all means to be the most important creature on earth, the state; and people think it so."

When I had said this, the fire-dog acted as if mad with envy. "What!" cried he, "the most important creature on earth? And people think it so?" And so much vapor and terrible voices came out of his throat, that I thought he would choke with vexation and envy.

At last he became calmer and his panting subsided; as soon, however, as he was quiet, I said laughingly:

"You are angry, fire-dog: so I am in the right about you!

And that I may also maintain the right, hear the story of another fire-dog; he speaks actually

它现在用更加神圣的身形矗立在你们的面前，那个身形遭受到的磨难让它自身拥有了更大的诱惑力；说真的，你们这些破坏者啊！它还要感谢你们曾经颠覆过它们呢！

但是，我会把这个忠告给予国王和教堂以及所有年龄的或是道德的虚弱者——让你们被颠覆！你们或许会再一次获得新生，而道德也会因此而来到你们的身边！

我在火焰猎犬的面前如是说：随后，它愤愤地打断了我的讲话，并且问道："教堂，教堂是什么东西？"

"教堂是什么东西？"我回答道，"教堂是一种国家，它是最虚假的那一种。但是，要保持安静啊！你这伪善的猎犬！你们当然最了解你们自己的同类！

那个国家就像你们一样，是一条伪善的猎犬；为了让人们相信它说的话是发自肺腑的，它会像你一样，灵巧地利用烟雾和咆哮发言。

因为国家会用尽一切办法争做地球上最重要的生物，而人民也会这么认为。"

当我说这些话的时候，那条火焰猎犬因为无比嫉妒而像发了疯似的狂叫。"什么！"它大吼道，"地球上最重要的生物？而且人们也会这么认为？"大量的蒸汽和可怕的声音从它的喉咙里喷涌而出，这让我认为它会因为苦恼和嫉妒而窒息。

最终，它变得更加平静，它的喘气声也随之减弱了，但是它刚默不作声，我就笑着说道：

"你这条火焰猎犬，你生气了，所以，我说过的关于你的话是正确的！

为了捍卫我自己的判断，让我来给你讲述一个关于另一只火焰猎犬的故事吧！他确实是在用大地的心声来讲述。

out of the heart of the earth.

Gold does his breath exhale, and golden rain: so does his heart desire. What are ashes and smoke and hot dregs to him!

Laughter flits from him like a variegated cloud; adverse is he to your gargling and spewing and grips in the bowels!

The gold, however, and the laughter- these does he take out of the heart of the earth: for, that you mayst know it,- the heart of the earth is of gold."

When the fire-dog heard this, he could no longer endure to listen to me. Abashed did he draw in his tail, said "bow-wow!" in a cowed voice, and crept down into his cave.-

Thus told Zarathustra. His disciples, however, hardly listened to him: so great was their eagerness to tell him about the sailors, the rabbits, and the flying man.

"What am I to think of it!" said Zarathustra. "Am I indeed a ghost?

But it may have been my shadow. You have surely heard something of the Wanderer and his Shadow?

One thing, however, is certain: I must keep a tighter hold of it; otherwise it will spoil my reputation."

And once more Zarathustra shook his head and wondered. "What am I to think of it!" said he once more.

"Why did the ghost cry: 'It is time! It is the highest time!'

For what is it then- the highest time?"-

它呼出的气体就是金子和金灿灿的雨水：它的内心要它如是。那么，灰屑、烟雾与炽热的污垢，对于它来说，又有何用处呢！

笑容就像一片五彩斑斓的云朵一样从它的身边飞过；它仇视你的逆气、呕吐以及腹部的剧痛！

然而，金子和笑声——它是从大地的内心中取出来的；因为你们或许会知道，大地的内心就是由金子构成的。”

当火焰猎犬听完这些话的时候，它实在无法忍受继续听我慢慢道来了。

它不安地摇晃着它的尾巴，用一种恐吓的声音说道：“哇哇！”然后，它就爬进了它的洞穴。

查拉图斯特拉如是说，但是，他的徒弟们却几乎没有倾听过他的话；他们是无比迫切地想跟他谈谈船上的水手们、兔子们以及会飞奔的人。

“我究竟应该如何解释这些呢！”查拉图斯特拉说道。“难道我真的是一个鬼魂吗？”

但是，它或许是我的影子。我敢肯定，你们一定听说过一些有关旅行者与他的影子的故事吧！

不过，有一件事情我是肯定的：我必须要更严厉地抓住它，要不然的话，它就会毁掉我的名誉。

而查拉图斯特拉再一次惊讶地摇了摇他的脑袋。“我究竟应该如何解释这些呢！”查拉图斯特拉再一次说道。

“为什么那个灵魂会尖叫：‘现在是时候了，现在是最合适的时候了！’

那么对于什么样的事情来说——现在是最合适的时候了呢？”

Thus spake Zarathustra.

41. The Soothsayer

"-AND I saw a great sadness come over mankind. The best turned weary of their works.

A doctrine appeared, a faith ran beside it: 'All is empty, all is alike, all hath been!'

And from all hills there re-echoed: 'All is empty, all is alike, all hath been!'

To be sure we have harvested: but why have all our fruits become rotten and brown? What was it fell last night from the evil moon?

In vain was all our labor, poison has our wine become, the evil eye hath singed yellow our fields and hearts.

Arid have we all become; and fire falling upon us, then do we turn dust like ashes:- yea, the fire itself have we made aweary.

All our fountains have dried up, even the sea has receded. All the ground tries to gape, but the depth will not swallow!

'Alas! where is there still a sea in which one could be drowned?' so soundeth our plaint- across shallow swamps. Even for dying have we become too weary; now do we keep awake and live on- in sepulchres."

Thus did Zarathustra hear a soothsayer speak; and the foreboding touched his heart and transformed him. Sorrowfully did he go about and wearily; and he became like to those of

查拉图斯特拉如是说。

41．预言家

“当我看到一个极大的悲哀降临到了人间。即便是最优秀的人也会对自己的工作感到厌倦。

一个教条出现了，一个信仰在它的旁边陪伴着它：‘一切皆空，一切都是相同的，一切都已经完了！’

任何一个山丘都回荡着这样的声音:‘一切皆空,一切都是相同的,一切都已经完了！’

毋庸置疑，我们曾经收获过：但是，为什么我们所有的水果都已经腐烂，并且变成了棕色呢？昨天晚上的邪恶的月亮到底掉落到哪里去了呢？

我们所做的任何工作都是徒劳的，我们的酒水变成了毒药，散播厄运的眼睛让我们的田地和我们的内心变得焦黄。

我们所有人都变得无比贫瘠；倘若烈焰降临在我们的身上，那么我们就会像灰烬一样变成尘土，是的，我们也让火焰变得疲倦了。

我们所有的泉水都变得干涸了，即使是海洋也退潮了。整个大地都裂开了，但是深渊并不愿意将我们吞噬！

哎！能够将我们淹死的海水究竟在什么地方？我们的抱怨如是说，但是这样的抱怨只是在浅的沼泽里来回横越。我们甚至会对死亡感到过于厌倦；现在我们仍旧保持着清醒的状态，并且继续在死穴里生活。”

whom the soothsayer had spoken.-

Said he to his disciples, a little while, and there comes the long twilight. Alas, how shall I preserve my light through it!

That it may not smother in this sorrowfulness! To remoter worlds shall it be a light, and also to remotest nights!

Thus did Zarathustra go about grieved in his heart, and for three days he did not take any meat or drink: he had no rest, and lost his speech. At last it came to pass that he fell into a deep sleep. His disciples, however, sat around him in long night-watches, and waited anxiously to see if he would awake, and speak again, and recover from his affliction.

And this is what Zarathustra said when he awoke; his voice, however, came to his disciples as from afar:

Hear, I pray you, the dream that I dreamed, my friends, and help me to divine its meaning!

A riddle is it still to me, this dream; the meaning is hidden in it and encaged, and do not yet fly above it on free pinions.

All life had I renounced, so I dreamed. Night-watchman and grave-guardian had I become, aloft, in the lone mountain-fortress of Death.

There did I guard his coffins: full stood the musty vaults of those trophies of victory. Out of glass coffins did vanquished life gaze upon me.

The odour of dust-covered eternities did I breathe: sultry and dust-covered lay my soul. And who could have aired his soul there!

查拉图斯特拉听到一个卜者如是说；而故事的预言深深地触动了查拉图斯特拉的内心，并且改变了他。他悲伤地、疲倦地走着；他成为了卜者所说过的人们之一。

他对他的徒弟们说道，过不了多久，这里就会迎来漫长的黎明。哎，在这漫长的黎明里，我应该如何保存我的光亮呢！

我该如何让它不在这样的悲痛中窒息！它还要成为遥远的世界和夜晚的光亮呢！

心情无比悲痛的查拉图斯特拉就这样在这里走着，在接下来的三天时间里，他既没有吃饭也没有喝水：他没有休息，也从不说话。最终，他陷入了深深的沉睡当中。然而，他的门徒们，围着他坐成一圈，整天整夜地守护着他，他们充满焦虑地等待着，看看他是否会醒过来，然后开始再次说话，并且从他遭受到的磨难中彻底康复。

这就是查拉图斯特拉从睡梦中醒来之后，对他的门徒们进行的说教；但是，他的门徒们觉得他的声音似乎来自远方。

我的朋友们，请倾听我所做的梦吧！我恳请你们帮助我猜测这些梦境的含义！

这个梦对于我来说，仍旧是一个谜团；它的含义就隐藏在那里面，而且不能够用自由的翅膀在那上面飞翔。

我做梦梦见我将我的全部人生彻底抛弃了。我在死亡堡垒的孤独的群山里成为了守夜者和守坟者。

我就在这里看守着死神的棺材：黑暗的墓穴里充满了胜利的战利品。消失的生命透过玻璃棺材注视着我。

我呼吸着永恒的夹杂着灰尘的香气：我的狂躁的夹杂着尘土的灵魂被重压着。有谁能够在这个地方减弱他的灵魂呢！

Brightness of midnight was ever around me; lonesomeness cowered beside her; and as a third, death-rattle stillness, the worst of my female friends.

Keys did I carry, the rustiest of all keys; and I knew how to open with them the most creaking of all gates.

Like a bitterly angry croaking ran the sound through the long corridors when the leaves of the gate opened: ungraciously did this bird cry, unwillingly was it awakened.

But more frightful even, and more heart-strangling was it, when it again became silent and still all around, and I alone sat in that malignant silence.

Thus did time pass with me, and slip by, if time there still was: what do I know thereof! But at last there happened that which awoke me.

Thrice did there peal peals at the gate like thunders, thrice did the vaults resound and howl again: then did I go to the sate.

Alpa! cried I, who carries his ashes to the mountain? Alpa! Alpa! who carries his ashes to the mountain?

And I pressed the key, and pulled at the gate, and exerted myself. But not a finger's-breadth was it yet open:

Then did a roaring wind tear the folds apart: whistling, whizzing, and piercing, it threw to me a black coffin.

And in the roaring and whistling and whizzing, the coffin burst open, and spouted out a thousand peals of laughter.

午夜的光亮总是围绕在我的身边；孤独也坐在她的身边；第三个是时断时续的喘着粗气的死神的沉默，她是我的异性朋友当中最坏的一个。

我随身带着钥匙，它是所有钥匙当中最锈迹斑斑的一个；我知道该如何用它们打开最吱吱作响的大门。

当两扇门的门叶被打开的时候，它的声音就像悲痛的蛙鸣一样，传遍了整个悠长的走廊：这只夜鸟愤愤地鸣叫着，它是多么不愿意被叫醒。

但是，当四周的一切都开始变得宁静，而我独自一人坐在这充满恶意的寂静当中的时候，这种反复的宁静会显得更加恐怖，让我的内心更加悲苦。

时间就这样悄然逝去，倘若还有时间的话：我又怎么会知道呢！但是让我幡然醒悟的事情最后还是发生了。

大门被敲响了三次，就像是闪电雷鸣一样，黑暗的墓穴的回声也出现了三次，于是，我来到了大门口。

吓！我大喊道，究竟是谁把他的灰烬带到山上来了？吓！吓！究竟是谁把他的灰烬带到山上来了？

我转动着手中的钥匙，推着大门，我拼尽全力地推着，而疲惫不堪。但是那扇门没有丝毫被推开的迹象：

就在这时候，一股咆哮的风暴推开了两扇门的门叶：它疯狂地呼啸着、嘶吼着，并且扔给我一个黑色的棺材。

在疯狂地呼啸、嘶吼中，棺材被打开了，上千个笑声从那里面喷涌而出。

上千个孩子的、天使的、猫头鹰的、愚蠢之人的以及孩子般大小的蝴蝶的丑陋之脸

And a thousand caricatures of children, angels, owls, fools, and child-sized butterflies laughed and mocked, and roared at me.

Fearfully was I terrified thereby: it prostrated me. And I cried with horror as I ne'er cried before.

But my own crying awoke me:- and I came to myself.-

Thus did Zarathustra relate his dream, and then was silent: for as yet he knew not the interpretation thereof. But the disciple whom he loved most arose quickly, seized Zarathustra's hand, and said:

"Your life itself interprets to us this dream, O Zarathustra!"

Are you not yourself the wind with shrill whistling, which bursts open the gates of the fortress of Death?

Are you not yourself the coffin full of many-hued malices and angel-caricatures of life?

Like a thousand peals of children's laughter comes Zarathustra into all sepulchres, laughing at those night-watchmen and grave-guardians, and whoever else rattles with sinister keys.

With your laughter will you frighten and prostrate them: fainting and recovering will you demonstrate your power over them.

And when the long twilight comes and the mortal weariness, even then will you not disappear from our firmament, you advocate of life!

New stars have you made us see, and new nocturnal glories: verily, laughter itself have you spread out over us like a many-hued canopy.

冲着我边笑边骂。

因此，我非常害怕，我被推倒在地。我被吓得号啕大哭，就好像我以前从来都没有哭过似的。

但是我被我自己的哭声叫醒了——我终于恢复了意识。

查拉图斯特拉讲述完了他做的梦，然后，他开始默不作声：因为他根本就不知道应该如何解释这个梦。但是，在众多的门徒当中，最被查拉图斯特拉看中的那个门徒很快就站了起来，他一把抓住了查拉图斯特拉的手，然后说道：

你的人生已经向我们解释了你的梦境，噢，查拉图斯特拉！

难道你不是打开死神堡垒之门的疯狂呼啸的风暴吗？

难道你不是装满了五彩斑斓的恶意，以及天使丑陋面孔的那个黑色棺材吗？

说真的，查拉图斯特拉就像一千个孩子的欢声笑语一样，走到每一个逝去的人的房间里，去笑看那些守夜者和守坟者以及掌管着罪恶的钥匙的管理员。

通过你的笑声，你可以让他们感到恐惧，从而推倒他们：头晕目眩和幡然醒悟能够向他们展示凌驾于他们之上的力量。

当漫长的黎明和致命的疲倦到来的时候，你不会从我们的苍穹中消失，你这个生命的倡导者！

你让我们看到了新的行星以及夜间新的光辉：说真的，你就像五颜六色的幕帐一样，把你的欢声笑语撒播在我们的头上。

现在，孩子们的笑容会从棺材里传出来；现在，一股强猛的风暴朝这里袭来，它克服了所有的致命的疲倦：你自己就是它的保证者和卜者！

Now will children's laughter ever from coffins flow; now will a strong wind ever come victoriously to all mortal weariness: of this you are yourself the pledge and the prophet!

They themselves did you dream, your enemies: that was your sorest dream.

But as you awoke from them and came to yourself, so shall they awaken from themselves-and come to you!

Thus spoke the disciple; and all the others then thronged around Zarathustra, grasped him by the hands, and tried to persuade him to leave his bed and his sadness, and return to them. Zarathustra, however, sat upright on his couch, with an absent look. Like one returning from long foreign sojourn did he look on his disciples, and examined their features; but still he knew them not. When, however, they raised him, and set him upon his feet, behold, all on a sudden his eye changed; he understood everything that had happened, stroked his beard, and said with a strong voice:

"Well! this has just its time; but see to it, my disciples, that we have a good repast; and without delay! Thus do I mean to make amends for bad dreams!

The soothsayer, however, shall eat and drink at my side: and verily, I will yet show him a sea in which he can drown himself!"-

Thus spoke Zarathustra. Then did he gaze long into the face of the disciple who had been the dream-interpreter, and shook his head.-

毋庸置疑，他们在你的梦境中出现了，你的敌人：这是最令你感到痛苦的梦境。

但是，既然你已经从他们那里醒了过来，并且恢复了意识，那么，他们自己也应该醒过来——并且来找你！

查拉图斯特拉的门徒们如是说；其他的门徒们随后也来到了查拉图斯特拉的身边，他们纷纷用手牢牢地抓住他，并且试图劝说他离开他的床以及他悲伤的情绪，让他回到他们当中来。但是，查拉图斯特拉笔直地坐在他的床上，脸上一副心不在焉的样子。他就像是一个久未重逢的人一样，意味深长地看着他的门徒们，然后仔细查看他们的面部表情；他还是没有认出他们。一直到他们把他从床上扶起来，让他站定之后，他的眼睛突然发生了变化，他弄明白了刚才发生的所有事情，他捋着胡须，用非常洪亮的声音说道：

“好吧！所有的一切都来得太恰到好处了：我的朋友们，请留心好好地给我们做一顿丰盛的美餐吧！请不要耽搁！我想通过这样的方式，为我的噩梦赎罪！

但是，那位卜者应该坐在我的身边陪我共享美餐，说真的，我会向他展示一个可以将他自己淹死的海洋！”

查拉图斯特拉如是说。然后，他久久地凝视着那个解释梦境的门徒的面孔，随后摇了摇头。

42. Redemption

WHEN Zarathustra went one day over the great bridge, then did the cripples and beggars surround him, and a hunchback spoke thus to him:

"Behold, Zarathustra! Even the people learn from you, and acquire faith in your teaching: but for them to believe fully in you, one thing is still needful- you must first of all convince us cripples! Here have you now a fine selection, and verily, an opportunity with more than one forelock! The blind can you heal, and make the lame run; and from him who has too much behind, could you well, also, take away a little;- that, I think, would be the right method to make the cripples believe in Zarathustra!"

Zarathustra, however, answered thus to him who so spoke: When one takes his hump from the hunchback, then does one take from him his spirit- so do the people teach. And when one gives the blind man eyes, then does he see too many bad things on the earth: so that he curses him who healed him. He, however, who makes the lame man run, inflicts upon him the greatest injury; for hardly can he run, when his vices run away with him- so do the people teach concerning cripples. And why should not Zarathustra also learn from the people, when the people learn from Zarathustra?

It is, however, the small thing to me since I have been amongst men, to see one person lacking an eye, another an ear, and a third a leg, and that others have lost the tongue, or the

42. 赎救

有一天，当查拉图斯特拉途径一座大桥的时候，许多瘸子和乞丐们纷纷上前将查拉图斯特拉围住，其中一个驼背的人对他说道：

“快看啊！那人是查拉图斯特拉！一般的人们都从你这里学习知识，从你的说教中获得信仰：但是，如果想让他们完全信任你的话，有一件事情是必不可少的——首先，你必须要说服我们这些残疾人！现在，你拥有一个非常不错的选择，说真的，这是一个可以通过多方面把握住的好机会！你能够让盲人重见光明，你能够让瘸子重新奔跑起来；你能够帮助肩负沉重负担的人减轻负担：——在我看来，我认为这是查拉图斯特拉能够让这些残疾人们相信他的好办法！”

不过，查拉图斯特拉对这位讲话的人如是回答道：当一个人拿走了驼背者身上的驼背，那么，他就会同样拿走驼背者身上的精神——一般的人民大众都是这样说的。当一个人给予盲人能够看清世界的双眼，那么，那个盲人同样也会看清这个世界上许许多多肮脏的事情：所以，他会诅咒那个将他的眼睛治好的人。然而，那个将瘸子的腿治好，让他重新奔跑的人，却给瘸子带来了莫大的伤害；因为，每一次当他开始奔跑的时候，隐藏在他身上的邪恶就会跑出来——这些都是一般的人民大众对于残疾人的一些看法。当一般的人民大众从查拉图斯特拉的身上学习东西的时候，为什么查拉图斯特拉就不能从一般的人民大众那里也学习一些东西呢？

自从我和人民群众生活在一起的时候，我就发现了：有的人缺少一只眼睛，有的人

nose, or the head.

I see and have seen worse things, and divers things so hideous, that I should neither like to speak of all matters, nor even keep silent about some of them: namely, men who lack everything, except that they have too much of one thing- men who are nothing more than a big eye, or a big mouth, or a big belly, or something else big,- reversed cripples, I call such men.

And when I came out of my solitude, and for the first time passed over this bridge, then I could not trust my eyes, but looked again and again, and said at last: "That is an ear! An ear as big as a man!" I looked still more attentively- and actually there did move under the ear something that was pitiably small and poor and slim. And in truth this immense ear was perched on a small thin stalk- the stalk, however, was a man! A person putting a glass to his eyes, could even recognize further a small envious countenance, and also that a bloated little soul dangled at the stalk. The people told me, however, that the big ear was not only a man, but a great man, a genius. But I never believed in the people when they spoke of great men- and I hold to my belief that it was a reversed cripple, who had too little of everything, and too much of one thing.

When Zarathustra had spoken thus to the hunchback, and to those of whom the hunchback was the mouthpiece and advocate, then did he turn to his disciples in profound dejection, and said:

My friends, I walk amongst men as amongst the fragments and limbs of human beings!

This is the terrible thing to my eye, that I find man broken up, and scattered about, as on a

缺少一只耳朵，第三个人缺少一条腿，而其他的人要么没有舌头，要么没有鼻子，有的甚至失去了脑袋。不过，在我看来，这些都只是比较小的恶。

我看见并且曾经看见过比这更加糟糕的事情，更加丑陋和恐怖的事情，我并不愿意将它们和盘托出，但是又不想一直对此守口如瓶：有的人缺少一切，但是一件东西对于他们来说已经算多了，有的人只有一只大眼睛、一张大嘴、一个大肚皮，或是其他什么特别大的东西——我会管类似这样的人叫反面的残疾人。

当我从自身的孤独当中走出来，并且在人生中第一次走过这座大桥的时候，我都不敢相信自己的双眼，我看了再看，然后我说道："这是一个耳朵啊！这是一个跟人一样大的耳朵啊！"但是，我更加迫不及待地去查看，没错，一个既可怜又衰弱的小东西在这个巨大的耳朵后面缓慢地移动着。说真的，这个巨大的耳朵就坐落在一个非常瘦小的茎上——但是，这个瘦小的茎竟然是一个人！在眼睛上戴上眼镜的人，能够辨别出具有嫉妒心的面孔，而且还有一个傲慢的小灵魂在茎上摇晃着、悬挂着。然而，一般的人告诉我，那个巨大的耳朵不仅仅是一个人，它还是一个非常伟大的人，一个非常有天赋的人。但是，当他们谈及伟大的人的时候，我是完全不会相信他们的——我依旧坚持自己的信念，这就是一个"什么东西都缺少，一件东西又太多"的反面的残疾人。

当查拉图斯特拉跟那个发表了言论的驼背者和驼背者所代表、所辩护的人说完这些话的时候，他非常沮丧地转向他的门徒们，然后说道：

说真的，我的朋友们，我在人群之中行走的时候，就好像走在人类的碎片和四肢当中！

我发现人类是支离破碎的、四肢被抛撒，就好像在战场和屠宰场里面一样，这些场

battle- and butcher-ground.

And when my eye flees from the present to the bygone, it finds ever the same: fragments and limbs and fearful chances- but no men!

The present and the bygone upon earth- ah! my friends- that is my most unbearable trouble; and I should not know how to live, if I were not a seer of what is to come.

A seer, a purposer, a creator, a future itself, and a bridge to the future- and alas! also as it were a cripple on this bridge: all that is Zarathustra.

And you also asked yourselves often: "Who is Zarathustra to us? What shall he be called by us?" And like me, did you give yourselves questions for answers.

Is he a promiser? Or a fulfiller? A conqueror? Or an inheritor? A harvest? Or a ploughshare? A physician? Or a healed one?

Is he a poet? Or a genuine one? An emancipator? Or a subjugator? A good one? Or an evil one?

I walk amongst men as the fragments of the future: that future which I contemplate.

And it is all my poetisation and aspiration to compose and collect into unity what is fragment and riddle and fearful chance.

And how could I endure to be a man, if man were not also the composer, and riddle-reader, and redeemer of chance!

To redeem what is past, and to transform every "It was" into "Thus would I have it!"- that only do I call redemption!

Will- so is the emancipator and joy-bringer called: thus have I taught you, my friends! But

景对于我的双眼来说，是非常恐怖的事情。

当我的双眼从当前逃离到过去的时候，就会发现事实都是一样的：破碎的断片、四肢和恐怖的机遇——但是，没有人类！

大地的现在和过去啊！——哎！我的朋友们！——这就是最令我难以容忍的困难；而且如果我不能提前看到即将到来的东西，那么我就不会知道应该如何生活下去。

预知者、意志者、创造者以及未来本身和能够通往未来的大桥——哎！从某种意义上来说，站在这座大桥上的残疾人：全部都是查拉图斯特拉。

你们经常自问:“对于我们来说,查拉图斯特拉是什么呢？我们应该如何称呼他呢？”你们会不会像我一样把问题作为自己的答案。

他是一个爱承诺的人吗？或是一个履行诺言的人？一个征服者？或是一个继承者？一个收获者？或是犁刃吗？一个医生？或是大病初愈的人吗？

他是一位诗人？或是一个真诚的人？他是一个解放者？还是一个征服者？他是好人吗？还是坏人？

我走在人群当中，就好像走在未来的碎片之中：那个未来是我能够看到的未来。

我所有的想象和渴望是组成断片、谜团以及恐怖的机遇的统一体。

假如人类不是诗人、不是猜谜者以及机遇的救赎者，那么，我又怎么能忍受成为人类呢！

去拯救过去的人们，将“已如是”改变为“我曾要它如是”——这就是我所说的赎救！

意志——这就是解放者和传播幸福快乐者的名字：朋友们，我曾经如是教过你们！

now learn this likewise: the Will itself is still a prisoner.

Willing emancipates: but what is that called which still puts the emancipator in chains?

"It was": thus is the Will's teeth-gnashing and most lonesome tribulation called. Impotent towards what has been done- it is a malicious spectator of all that is past.

Not backward can the Will will; that it cannot break time and time's desire- that is the Will's most lonesome tribulation.

Willing emancipates: what does Willing itself create in order to get free from its tribulation and mock at its prison?

Ah, a fool becomes every prisoner! Foolishly delivers itself also the imprisoned Will.

That time does not run backward- that is its animosity: "That which was": so is the stone which it cannot roll called.

And thus does it roll stones out of animosity and ill-humor, and takes revenge on whatever does not, like it, feel rage and ill-humor.

Thus did the Will, the emancipator, become a torturer; and on all that is capable of suffering it takes revenge, because it cannot go backward.

This, yes, this alone is revenge itself: the Will's antipathy to time, and its "It was."

A great folly dwells in our Will; and it became a curse to all humanity, that this folly acquired spirit!

The spirit of revenge: my friends, that has hitherto been man's best contemplation; and where there was suffering, it was claimed there was always penalty.

但是，现在你们也要好好学学这个啊！意志本身仍旧是一名囚犯。

意志能够解放一切：但是，如果解放者仍旧被禁锢在锁链之中，那么我们应该怎么称呼这样的行为呢？

“已如是”：意志的咬牙切齿和最孤独的苦难如是称道。对于所有的既定事实，它根本无力改变，所以，对于过去的一切来说，它就是一个充满恶意的观察者。

意志不能改变过去,它没有办法击败时间和时间的渴求——这就是意志最孤独的苦难。

意志能够解放一切：但是，它究竟要怎么做才能从苦难中得到自救，并且嘲笑它的监狱呢？

哎，所有的囚犯都变成了疯子！被囚禁的意志也开始进行疯狂地自我救赎。

那段时光是无法倒退的——这就是它的愤怒：“已如是者”——就是那块意志不能一脚踢开的石头。

因此，意志因为无比的愤怒和恶劣的情绪踢走了很多石头，它在找寻那些能够感受到愤怒和坏脾气的人，并且伺机实施报仇。

因此，意志这个解放者成为了一个歹毒之人，它对于任何能够忍受痛苦的事物都实施报复，因为，它自身不能回到过去。

是的，这就是报复，这就是意志对于时间以及时间的“已如是”的憎恶。

说真的，我们的意志里存在着一个伟大的疯狂：这是种获得了精神的疯狂，它成为了所有人类的诅咒。

我的朋友们，报复的精神，那是人类直到现在最优秀的思考和沉思：

只要是苦难存在的地方，就必定存在相应的惩罚。

"Penalty," so calls itself revenge. With a lying word it feigns a good conscience.

And because in the willer himself there is suffering, because he cannot will backwards- thus was Willing itself, and all life, claimed- to be penalty!

And then did cloud after cloud roll over the spirit, until at last madness preached: "Everything perishes, therefore everything deserves to perish!"

"And this itself is justice, the law of time- that he must devour his children:" thus did madness preach.

"Morally are things ordered according to justice and penalty. Oh, where is there deliverance from the flux of things and from the 'existence' of penalty?" Thus did madness preach.

"Can there be deliverance when there is eternal justice? Alas, unrollable is the stone, 'It was': eternal must also be all penalties!" Thus did madness preach.

"No deed can be annihilated: how could it be undone by the penalty! This, this is what is eternal in the 'existence' of penalty, that existence also must be eternally recurring deed and guilt!

Unless the Will should at last deliver itself, and Willing become non-Willing-:" but you know, my brothers, this fabulous song of madness!

Away from those fabulous songs did I lead you when I taught you: "The Will is a creator."

All "It was" is a fragment, a riddle, a fearful chance- until the creating Will says thereto: "But thus would I have it."-

Until the creating Will says thereto: "But thus do I will it! Thus shall I will it!"

“惩罚”，这是报复的自我称谓：它用谎言掩盖善意的良心。

因为，意志者不能向后运用意志而感到无比苦恼，所以意志和生命应该被看做是惩罚。

现在，一朵又一朵的云彩积压在精神之上：直到疯狂开始说教起来：

“世间万物都是会消亡的，因此，世间万物都拥有消亡的权力！”

“这个时间的定律：时间必须吞噬掉它的孩子们，这却是所谓的正义”：疯狂如是说教道。

“世间万物都是按照正义和惩罚而道德地进行安排的。啊，究竟哪里才是万物之潮和生存惩罚之潮里面的救赎呢？”疯狂如是说教道。

“假如永恒的正义真的存在，那么，拯救是否有可能呢？哎，‘已如是’这块石头是无法被推开的：一切的惩罚也必须是永恒的！”疯狂如是说教道。

“任何的行为都不能被摧毁：它又怎么能够被惩罚解除呢！‘生存’惩罚里面的永恒——必须也要永恒的再现行为和罪过！”

除非意志本身能够在最后关头实现自救，并且让意志成为不意志。但是，我的朋友们，你们都知道这个疯狂的寓言故事！

当我告诉你们：“意志是一个创造者”的时候，我曾经引领你们远离这些疯狂的寓言故事。

所有的“已如是”就是一个残缺的碎片、一个谜题以及恐怖的机遇——直到具有创造性的意志说道：“但是我曾要它如是！”

直到具有创造性的意志说道：“但是我要它如是！我将要它如是！”

But did it ever speak thus? And when does this take place? has the Will been unharnessed from its own folly?

Has the Will become its own deliverer and joy-bringer? has it unlearned the spirit of revenge and all teeth-gnashing?

And who has taught it reconciliation with time, and something higher than all reconciliation?

Something higher than all reconciliation must the Will will which is the Will to Power-: but how does that take place? Who has taught it also to will backwards?

-But at this point it chanced that Zarathustra suddenly paused, and looked like a person in the greatest alarm. With terror in his eyes did he gaze on his disciples; his glances pierced as with arrows their thoughts and arrear-thoughts. But after a brief space he again laughed, and said soothedly:

"It is difficult to live amongst men, because silence is so difficult- especially for a babbler."-

Thus spoke Zarathustra. The hunchback, however, had listened to the conversation and had covered his face during the time; but when he heard Zarathustra laugh, he looked up with curiosity, and said slowly:

"But why does Zarathustra speak otherwise to us than to his disciples?"

Zarathustra answered: "What is there to be wondered at! With hunchbacks one May well speak in a hunchbacked way!"

"Very good," said the hunchback; "and with pupils one may well tell tales out of school.

它不是已经如是说过了吗？这样的如是说究竟是在什么时候发生的呢？意志已经从它自身的疯狂之中得到自我救赎了吗？

意志成为了让自己得到救赎，并且带来欢声笑语的人吗？它是否已经忘记了复仇的精神和所有的咬牙切齿呢？

究竟是谁在教他同时间进行和谈，究竟是谁把比和谈还要高尚的事物教给了他呢？

这种权力意志必定会追求比所有的和谈还要高尚的东西：但是，它如何成为可能呢？是谁教它向后运用意志的呢？

但是，当查拉图斯特拉说到这里的时候，他突然变成了一个看似受到了非常大的惊吓的人，令他停止了说教，他凝视着他的门徒们，眼睛里带着恐惧；他的目光就像弓箭一样刺穿了他们的想法以及思想之后的想法。但是，过了一段时间之后，他再一次笑了起来，并且异常平静地说道：

“在人类当中生活是非常困难的事情，因为保持寂静是非常困难的——尤其是对于一个特别喜欢说话的人来说。”

查拉图斯特拉如是说道。然而，那个驼背的长者时不时地捂着脸倾听着他的讲话；当他听到查拉图斯特拉开始哈哈大笑的时候，他充满好奇地抬起了头，并且缓慢地说道：

“为什么，当查拉图斯特拉跟我们说话的时候，讲话的内容和他跟他的门徒们所说的有所不同呢？”

查拉图斯特拉回答道：“这有什么好奇怪的呢！我们本来就应该用驼背的方式跟驼背的人说话啊！”

“回答的非常好，”驼背的人说道，“我们也应该向学生们传授学校里讲的内容。”

But why does Zarathustra speak otherwise to his pupils- than to himself?"-

43. Manly Prudence

NOT the height, it is the declivity that is terrible!

The declivity, where the gaze shoots downwards, and the hand grasps upwards. There does the heart become giddy through its double will.

Ah, friends, do you divine also my heart's double will?

This, this is my declivity and my danger, that my gaze shoots towards the summit, and my hand would rather clutch and lean- on the depth!

To man clings my will; with chains do I bind myself to man, because I am pulled upwards to the Superman: for there does my other will tend.

And therefore do I live blindly among men, as if I knew them not: that my hand may not entirely lose belief in firmness.

I know not you men: this gloom and consolation is often spread around me.

I sit at the gateway for every rogue, and ask: Who wishes to deceive me?

This is my first manly prudence, that I allow myself to be deceived, so as not to be on my guard against deceivers.

Ah, if I were on my guard against man, how could man be an anchor to my ball! Too easily would I be pulled upwards and away!

但是，为什么查拉图斯特拉跟他的学生们谈话的内容，和跟自己说话的内容不一样呢？

43. 人类的智慧

高处其实并不可怕，真正让人感到害怕的是斜坡！

当你站在斜坡上，而两眼向下张望的时候，此时，你的双手却在向上攀爬。这样的双重意志会让人头晕目眩、眼花缭乱。

哎，我的朋友们，你们是否也能猜测到我的内心的双重意志呢？

我的斜坡和危险就是向上张望顶峰，我的双手却要抓住并且倾斜在——深处之上！

我的意志依附于人类；我用锁链将自己捆绑在人类的身上，因为我是被吸引寻找超人的：因此，我的其他意志也会去往那里。

所以，我会盲目地生活在人类当中，就好像我根本就不了解他们一样：我这样做的目的就是不想让自己的双手失去对于坚硬物体的信仰。

我并不了解你们这些人：这样的黑暗和慰藉经常围绕在我的身边。

我为了每一个流氓，坐在门廊边，然后我问道："你们当中有谁想要欺骗我？"

这是我人生中第一个人间的智慧，我允许自己受到他人的欺骗，而不是让自己时刻提防着欺骗者。

哎，如果我为了对抗众人，而进行自我防卫的话，那么，人们还怎么做我的皮球的铁锚啊！我将会很容易被他人夺去或者被吸引到高处！

This providence is over my fate, that I have to be without foresight.

And he who would not languish amongst men, must learn to drink out of all glasses; and he who would keep clean amongst men, must know how to wash himself even with dirty water.

And thus spoke I often to myself for consolation: "Courage! Cheer up! old heart! An unhappiness has failed to befall you: enjoy that as thy- happiness!"

This, however, is my other manly prudence: I am more forbearing to the vain than to the proud.

Is not wounded vanity the mother of all tragedies? Where, however, pride is wounded, there there grows up something better than pride.

That life may be fair to behold, its game must be well played; for that purpose, however, it needs good actors.

Good actors have I found all the vain ones: they play, and wish people to be fond of beholding them- all their spirit is in this wish.

They represent themselves, they invent themselves; in their neighborhood I like to look upon life- it cures of melancholy.

Therefore am I forbearing to the vain, because they are the physicians of my melancholy, and keep me attached to man as to a drama.

And further, who conceives the full depth of the modesty of the vain man! I am favorable to him, and sympathetic on account of his modesty.

From you would he learn his belief in himself; he feeds upon your glances, he eates praise

这种天意在控制着我的命运，我不能拥有先见之明。

那个不愿意在人群中因为口渴而憔悴的人一定能学会饮用所有杯子当中的水；那个想在众人当中保持干净的人，一定会去学该如何用污水清洁自己。

我经常会说一些安慰自己的话语："鼓起勇气来！振作起来！老当益壮的内心！苦恼和忧愁不会降临在你的身上：享受你的快乐吧！"

但是，这是我第二个人间的智慧：我容忍爱慕虚荣之人更甚于骄傲自负之人。

难道满是伤口的虚荣不是所有悲剧的母亲吗？但是，在傲慢受到伤害的地方，必定会长出比傲慢更加高级的事物。

如果生活要成为一出精彩绝伦的好戏，那么，它就必须拥有好的表演；但是，要想达到这样的目的，它还需要非常好的演员。

我发现所有爱慕虚荣的人们都是非常伟大的演员：他们进行表演，并且他们希望其他人喜欢看他们的表演——他们的整个精神全都存在于这样的意志里。

他们互相表演，互相创造；我就喜欢待在他们的旁边，注视着生命——它能够治愈悲伤的情绪。

因此，我要容忍虚荣，因为，他们都是我的忧郁的内科医生，他们把我和人类维系在一起，就像把我和戏剧维系在一起一样。

究竟有谁能够猜测出虚荣之人的谦逊态度的整个深度呢！我非常喜欢他，并且对他的谦逊感到同情。

他可以从你们这里学到信仰，他用你们的目光进行滋养，他从你们的手心里采集可以食用的赞美。

out of your hands.

Your lies does he even believe when you lie favorably about him: for in its depths sighs his heart: "What am I?"

And if that be the true virtue which is unconscious of itself- well, the vain man is unconscious of his modesty!-

This is, however, my third manly prudence: I am not put out of conceit with the wicked by your timorousness.

I am happy to see the marvels the warm sun hatches: tigers and palms and rattlesnakes.

Also amongst men there is a beautiful brood of the warm sun, and much that is marvellous in the wicked.

In truth, as your wisest did not seem to me so very wise, so found I also human wickedness below the fame of it.

And oft did I ask with a shake of the head: Why still rattle, you rattlesnakes?

There is still a future even for evil! And the warmest south is still undiscovered by man.

How many things are now called the worst wickedness, which are only twelve feet broad and three months long! Some day, however, will greater dragons come into the world.

For that the Superman may not lack his dragon, the super-dragon that is worthy of him, there must still much warm sun glow on moist virgin forests!

Out of your wild cats must tigers have evolved, and out of your poison-toads, crocodiles: for the good hunter shall have a good hunt!

只要你们说一些夸赞他的谎言，他就会相信你们的谎言：因为他的内心在深处叹息道：“我究竟是个什么呢？”

倘若真正的道德是没有意识的——那么，爱慕虚荣的人就不会发觉他身上的谦逊！

这是我第三个人间的智慧：不会让你们的担惊受怕令我对于恶人的表演感到厌倦。

我非常乐意看到温暖的太阳在孕育着奇迹：老虎、棕榈树和响尾蛇。

在茫茫的人群当中，温暖的阳光也会有很好的孕育，在邪恶之人当中也拥有很多不可思议的事物。

事实是，对于我来说，在你们当中最聪明的人，并不是真正的聪明，而且，我也觉得在人群中的智者，也没有他的名誉那般令人感到惊异。

我经常摇晃着脑袋问自己：响尾蛇，为什么你们仍旧要摇响你们的尾巴呢？

就算是恶魔也有属于自己的未来！即便是人类也有尚未找到的最温暖的南方。

现在，很多已经被称为最糟糕的邪恶之物也不过只有十二英尺宽，三个月之久而已！然而，更加庞大的巨龙光临这个世界的一天终究会到来。

为了使超人也有属于自己的巨龙，而超巨龙不足以称之为超人：许多温暖的阳光就必须在潮湿的远古森林中散发出光芒！

你们这些狂野的野猫必须要进化成老虎，你们这些充满剧毒的蟾蜍必须要进化成鳄鱼：因为好的猎人必须要有好的猎物！

说真的，善良者和正直者啊！在你们的身上有太多可以被嘲笑的东西了，尤其是你们对于所谓的“恶魔”的恐惧！

你们的灵魂对于伟大的事物太过于陌生了，因此，你们会认为即使是善意里的超人

And verily, you good and just! In you there is much to be laughed at, and especially your fear of what has hitherto been called "the devil!"

So alien are you in your souls to what is great, that to you the Superman would be frightful in his goodness!

And you wise and knowing ones, you would flee from the solar-glow of the wisdom in which the Superman joyfully baths his nakedness!

You highest men who have come within my ken! this is my doubt of you, and my secret laughter: I suspect you would call my Superman- a devil!

Ah, I became tired of those highest and best ones: from their "height" did I long to be up, out, and away to the Superman!

A horror came over me when I saw those best ones naked: then there grew for me the pinions to soar away into distant futures.

Into more distant futures, into more southern souths than ever artist dreamed of: there, where gods are ashamed of all clothes!

But disguised do I want to see you, you neighbors and fellowmen, and well-attired and vain and estimable, as "the good and just;"-

And disguised will I myself sit amongst you- that I may mistake you and myself: for that is my last manly prudence.-

Thus spoke Zarathustra.

也是非常吓人的。

你们这些智者和有学识的人啊！你们将会逃离智慧的炙热光芒，而超人则光着身子在那里面快乐的享受日光浴！

你们是我所见过的最高等的人！这是我对于你们的怀疑和我的神秘的微笑：我猜想到你们仍会管我的超人称做是恶魔吧！

哎，我已经开始对那些高等的人和最出色的人感到厌倦了：我非常期望能从他们的“高度”爬升得更高、更远，一直上升到超人那里去！

当我看到那些最出色的人全都赤身裸体的时候，一股恐惧感向我袭来：于是，我的翅膀带着我直插云霄，飞向了遥远的未来。

飞向更加遥远的未来，飞向对于艺术家来说从未幻想过的更南的南方去：在那个地方，神灵们会因为穿上衣服而蒙羞！

啊，我的邻居们啊，我的同胞们啊，我希望看到你们能够伪装起来，虚荣的、令人尊敬的，就像那些善良者和正直者一样。

我也要将自己伪装起来，坐在你们中间——让我无法认出你们或是自己：而这是我最后一个人间的智慧。

查拉图斯特拉如是说。

44. The Stillest Hour

WHAT has happened to me, my friends? You see me troubled, driven forth, unwillingly obedient, ready to go- alas, to go away from you!

Yes, once more must Zarathustra retire to his solitude: but unjoyously this time does the bear go back to his cave!

What has happened to me? Who orders this?- Ah, my angry mistress wishes it so; she spoke to me. Have I ever named her name to you?

Yesterday towards evening there spoke to me my still hour: that is the name of my terrible mistress.

And thus did it happen- for everything must I tell you, that your heart may not harden against the suddenly departing one!

Do you know the terror of him who falls asleep?-

To the very toes he is terrified, because the ground gives way under him, and the dream begins.

This do I speak to you in parable. Yesterday at the still hour did the ground give way under me: the dream began.

The hour-hand moved on, the timepiece of my life drew breath- never did I hear such stillness around me, so that my heart was terrified.

Then was there spoken to me without voice: "You know it, Zarathustra?"-

And I cried in terror at this whispering, and the blood left my face: but I was silent.

44．最寂静的时刻

我的朋友们，在我的身上究竟发生了什么事？你们看到我被烦恼困扰，被驱使着向前进发，极不情愿地服从着，并且随时准备离开——哎，从你们的身边离开！

是的，查拉图斯特拉必须重新回到他的寂静中去：但是，这一次重返洞穴的灰熊却并不高兴！

我的身上究竟发生了什么事？到底是谁命令着我呢？——哎，我那怒不可遏的情妇要我如是：她跟我说，我曾经把她的名字告诉过你们吗？

就在昨天的夜晚，我的沉默的时刻跟我说道：这就是我那令人毛骨悚然的情妇的真实姓名。

事情就是这样发生的——我必须要把事情的经过全都告诉你们，好让你们这些人对于突然离开的人们不至于太心狠手辣！

你是否了解睡着的人们的恐惧呢？

睡着的人从头到脚都感到害怕，因为大地在他的脚下塌陷，他的梦境开始了。

这就是我给你们讲的寓言故事。昨天，在沉默的时刻，夜落了，梦境开始了。

时针在前行着，我的生命之钟在大口地呼吸——我从来没有在我的周围听到过类似这样的沉默，所以，我的内心开始害怕了。

随后，一个无声的声音跟我说道：“查拉图斯特拉，你知道那个吗？”

当我听到这个在我耳边的轻声细语的时候，我出于恐惧而尖叫了起来，鲜血离开了我的面庞，而我却默不作声。

Then was there once more spoken to me without voice: "You know it, Zarathustra, but you do not speak it!"-

And at last I answered, like one defiant: "Yes, I know it, but I will not speak it!"

Then was there again spoken to me without voice: "You will not, Zarathustra? Is this true? Conceal yourself not behind your defiance!"-

And I wept and trembled like a child, and said: "Ah, I would indeed, but how can I do it! Exempt me only from this! It is beyond my power!"

Then was there again spoken to me without voice: "What matter about yourself, Zarathustra! Speak your word, and perish!"

And I answered: "Ah, is it my word? Who am I? I await the worthier one; I am not worthy even to perish by it."

Then was there again spoken to me without voice: "What matter about yourself? you are not yet humble enough for me. Humility has the hardest skin."-

And I answered: "What has not the skin of my humility endured! At the foot of my height do I dwell: how high are my summits, no one has yet told me. But well do I know my valleys."

Then was there again spoken to me without voice: "O Zarathustra, he who has to remove mountains removes also valleys and plains."-

And I answered: "As yet has my word not removed mountains, and what I have spoken has not reached man. I went, indeed, to men, but not yet have I attained to them."

紧接着，那个无声的声音再一次在我的耳边说道：“查拉图斯特拉，你知道那个的，你只是不说罢了！”

最终，我用目中无人的轻蔑态度回答道：“是的，我知道那个，但是我就是不想说出来！”

然后，那个无声的声音又一次对我说道：“查拉图斯特拉，你不想说出来吗？这是真的吗？请你不要把你自己隐藏在你这种蔑视的态度背后吧！”

我就像一个小孩子一样，哭泣着、颤抖着，然后我说道：“哎，是的，我的确很愿意，但是我应该怎么做呢！请将我从这里免除吧！它已经超过了我的力量！”

那个无声的声音又说了：“查拉图斯特拉，你自己有什么关系呢！说出你内心的话语，然后就消逝吧！”

然后，我回答道：“哎，那是我说的话吗？我究竟是谁？我在等候一个比我更加具有价值的人，我的价值还不足以因为它而去死呢。”

随后，那个无声的声音又开始说了：“你自己有什么关系呢？在我看来，你不足够卑微，谦卑可是最坚硬的皮肤。”

然后，我回答道：“我的谦卑之皮肤还真是什么都无法忍受啊！我就居住在我的高度的脚下：我的峰顶究竟有多高呢？还没有人告诉过我。但是，我对我的深谷非常了解。”

那个无声的声音再一次说道：“噢，查拉图斯特拉，那个移动山峰的人，同样也会移动山谷和平原吧！”

然后，我回答道：“但是，我的说教还没有移动过山峰，我的说教还从未触及过人类。的确，我曾经去找过人类，但是，我还从未达到人群。”

Then was there again spoken to me without voice: "What know you thereof! The dew falls on the grass when the night is most silent."-

And I answered: "They mocked me when I found and walked in my own path; and certainly did my feet then tremble.

And thus did they speak to me: you forgot the path before, now do you also forget how to walk!"

Then was there again spoken to me without voice: "What matter about their mockery! you are one who have unlearned to obey: now shall you command!

Know you not who is most needed by all? He who commands great things.

To execute great things is difficult: but the more difficult task is to command great things.

This is your most unpardonable obstinacy: you have the power, and you will not rule."-

And I answered: "I lack the lion's voice for all commanding."

Then was there again spoken to me as a whispering: "It is the still words which bring the storm. Thoughts that come with doves' footsteps guide the world.

O Zarathustra, you shall go as a shadow of that which is to come: thus will you command, and in commanding go foremost."-

And I answered: "I am ashamed."

Then was there again spoken to me without voice: "You must yet become a child, and be without shame.

The pride of youth is still upon you; late have you become young: but he who would become

随后，那个无声的声音又开始对我说道："你都知道些什么呢？当夜晚到了最沉默的时刻，露珠就会降落在青草地上。"

我回答道："当我找到了，并且走在我自己的道路上的时候，他们开始嘲笑我；那么我的双脚必然会颤抖。

因此，他们跟我说：之前，你忘记了道路，现在你还忘记了该如何走路！"

随后，那个无声的声音再一次对我说道："他们对你的嘲笑又有什么关系呢！你们是那些忘记了服从的人：现在，该是你们进行发号施令的时候了！

难道你不清楚究竟谁才是最被需要的人吗？那就是能够统领伟大事业的人。

执行伟大的事业是非常困难的：但是，比这更加困难的任务是统领这些伟大的事业。

这就是你们最不可饶恕的固执：你们拥有力量，但是你们却不愿意去统治。"

然后，我回答道："要想发号施令，我缺乏的是狮吼。"

那个无声的声音又一次在我的耳边轻声说道："沉默的语言能够带来大风暴。被鸽子的脚步带过来的想法可以引导世界。

噢，查拉图斯特拉，你应该像到来之物的影子一样前行：你将会发号施令，在你命令的时候，你将成为先驱者。"

然后，我回答道："我很是羞愧。"

之后，那个无声的声音又对我说道："你必须要成为一个孩子，而且不能感受到惭愧之感。"

你的身上仍旧有着青春的傲慢；你的青春会迟来，想要成为孩子的人，必将克服他的青春。

a child must overcome even his youth."-

And I considered a long while, and trembled. At last, however, did I say what I had said at first. "I will not."

Then did a laughing take place all around me. Alas, how that laughing lacerated my bowels and cut into my heart!

And there was spoken to me for the last time: "O Zarathustra, your fruits are ripe, but you are not ripe for your fruits!

So must you go again into solitude: for you shall yet become mellow."-

And again was there a laughing, and it fled: then did it become still around me, as with a double stillness. I lay, however, on the ground, and the sweat flowed from my limbs.

-Now have you heard all, and why I have to return into my solitude. Nothing have I kept hidden from you, my friends.

But even this have you heard from me, who is still the most reserved of men- and will be so!

Ah, my friends! I should have something more to say to you! I should have something more to give to you! Why do I not give it? Am I then a niggard?-

When, however, Zarathustra had spoken these words, the violence of his pain, and a sense of the nearness of his departure from his friends came over him, so that he wept aloud; and no one knew how to console him. In the night, however, he went away alone and left his friends.

我考虑了良久，浑身震颤着。不过，最终我还是说了我最初就说过的话。“我不乐意。”

随后，在我的周围爆发出了一阵笑声。哎，那阵笑声是如何地撕裂我的内脏，并且刺穿我的心脏啊！

那个无声的声音最后一次对我说道：“噢，查拉图斯特拉，你的果实已经成熟了，但是，对于那些果实来说，你还不够成熟！

所以，你必须再一次进入到你的孤独当中：让你变得甘甜而成熟。”

笑声又一次出现了，随后，它又逃走了：于是，我的四周变得安静了下来，这就像是一种双重的安静。但是，我躺在地面上，汗液开始从我的四肢上不断地流下来。

——现在，你们已经听到了一切，你们知道了我为什么要回到我的孤独中去。我没有向你们隐藏任何的秘密。我的朋友们。

我已经把这些全部都告诉给你们了，我这最缄默的人，愿意永远保持缄默的人！

哎，我的朋友们！我还有一些话想跟你们说！我还有些东西想给你们！但是，我为什么不把它给你们呢？难道我是吝啬的小气鬼吗？

但是，当查拉图斯特拉说完这些话的时候，他浑身剧烈的疼痛以及想到即将从他的朋友身边离去的紧密感向他袭来，于是，他开始号啕大哭起来；没有人知道应该如何安慰他。但是，在夜晚的时候，他仍旧会离开他的朋友们，独自一人走掉。

45. The Wanderer

THEN, when it was about midnight, Zarathustra went his way over the ridge of the isle, that he might arrive early in the morning at the other coast; because there he meant to embark. For there was a good roadstead there, in which foreign ships also liked to anchor: those ships took many people with them, who wished to cross over from the Blessed isles. So when Zarathustra thus ascended the mountain, he thought on the way of his many solitary wanderings from youth onwards, and how many mountains and ridges and summits he had already climbed.

I am a wanderer and mountain-climber, said he to his heart. I love not the plains, and it seems I cannot long sit still.

And whatever may still overtake me as fate and experience- a wandering will be therein, and a mountain-climbing: in the end one experiences only oneself.

The time is now past when accidents could befall me; and what could now fall to my lot which would not already be my own!

45．漫游者

当时间已经到了午夜的时候，查拉图斯特拉来到了小岛的山脊处，以便他能够在第二天的早上到达另一个海岸，因为，他想在那里登船。这里有一个非常理想的停泊处，即便是来自海外的船只也喜欢在这里停泊：那些船只载着很多人，他们都是想离开幸福之岛，出去渡海的人。所以，当查拉图斯特拉攀登山峰的时候，他回想起了很多从年轻时代到现在的孤独旅行以及许许多多曾经攀登过的山峰、山脊和峰顶。

他发自肺腑地说，我是一个热爱旅行的人，也是喜欢攀爬山峰的人。我不喜欢平原，看起来，我好像并不太适应长时间坐着。

不管我会碰上什么样的命运和经历——旅游和攀登山峰都是不可缺少的因素，因为，到最后，一个人的经历只是他自己的。

降临在我身上的机遇早已过去了；究竟有什么事情能够降临在我的身上，而且不曾属于过我呢！

我的那个“我”——它仅仅是向我走来，它和它的四处漂泊，散播在万物和机遇里

It returns only, it comes home to me at last- my own Self, and such of it as has been long abroad, and scattered among things and accidents.

And one thing more do I know: I stand now before my last summit, and before that which has been longest reserved for me. Ah, my hardest path must I ascend! Ah, I have begun my most lonesome wandering!

Yet he who is of my nature does not avoid such an hour: the hour that says to him: Now only do you go the way to your greatness! Summit and abyss- these are now comprised together!

You go the way to your greatness: now has it become your last refuge, what was hitherto your last danger!

You go the way to your greatness: it must now be your best courage that there is no longer any path behind you!

You go the way to your greatness: here shall no one steal after you! your foot itself has effaced the path behind you, and over it stands written: Impossibility.

And if all ladders henceforth fail you, then must you learn to mount upon your own head: how could you mount upward otherwise?

Upon your own head, and beyond your own heart! Now must the gentlest in you become the hardest.

He who has always much-indulged himself, sickens at last by his much-indulgence. Praises on what makes hardy! I do not praise the land where butter and honey- flow!

To learn to look away from oneself, is necessary in order to see many things.- this hardiness

的各个部分，终于回家了！

此外，我还知道一件事情：我现在就站在我最后的峰顶之上，面对着一直为我保留着的事物。哎，我一定要走上最困难的道路！哎，我已经开始了我最孤独的旅程！

然而，跟我拥有同样个性的人并不会躲避这样的时刻：这个时刻在对他说：现在，你已经无路可走，只好走在通往伟大的道路之上！峰顶和深渊，现在已经组合到一起了！

你走在通往伟大的道路之上：它曾经是你最后的危险，现在，它成为了你最后的避难所。

你走在通往伟大的道路之上：它必须要成为你最大的勇气，因为在你的身后已经无路可走了！

你走在通往伟大的道路之上：在这里，没有人会悄悄地跟在你的背后！你自己的脚步会抹去你身后的道路上铭记着的字样：不可能。

如果所有的梯子想让你失败，那么你必须要学会在你的头顶上进行攀登：要不然，你怎么才能向上爬呢？

在你的头顶上，在你的内心里学习攀登吧！现在，你内心当中的最温和已经变成了最坚强。

那些总是对自己过度骄纵的人，到了最后，必定会因他的过度骄纵而得病。赞美那些能够让人坚强的一切吧！我不会去赞扬流淌着奶油和蜂蜜的国度！

学会从远处观看，是了解周围事物的必不可少的环节。这是每一个攀爬山峰的人必须具备的坚强的特质。

is needed by every mountain-climber.

Yet he who is obtrusive with his eyes as a discerner, how can he ever see more of anything than its foreground!

But you, O Zarathustra, would view the ground of everything, and its background: thus must you mount even above yourself- up, upwards, until you have even your stars under you!

Yes! To look down upon myself, and even upon my stars: that only would I call my summit, that has remained for me as my last summit!-

Thus spoke Zarathustra to himself while ascending, comforting his heart with harsh maxims: for he was sore at heart as he had never been before. And when he had reached the top of the mountain-ridge, behold, there lay the other sea spread out before him; and he stood still and was long silent. The night, however, was cold at this height, and clear and starry.

I recognize my destiny, said he at last, sadly. Well! I am ready. Now has my last lonesomeness begun.

Ah, this sombre, sad sea, below me! Ah, this sombre nocturnal vexation! Ah, fate and sea! To you must I now go down!

Before my highest mountain do I stand, and before my longest wandering: therefore must I first go deeper down than I ever ascended:

-Deeper down into pain than I ever ascended, even into its darkest flood! So wills my fate. Well! I am ready.

Whence come the highest mountains? so did I once ask. Then did I learn that they come out

那些求知欲强和瞪着大眼睛的人，除了表面显著的东西以外，还能看到什么吗？

噢，查拉图斯特拉啊！你能够观察到任何事物的显著特征和背景：所以，你必须攀登到你的头顶之上——一直向上、向上，直到你发现你的星星都在你的脚下！

是的！向下注视着你自己，甚至是注视着你的星星：只有那被我称为自己的峰顶，为我保留到最后的峰顶！

查拉图斯特拉一边攀登着，一边说着，并且用严酷的格言抚慰着自己的内心：因为他心中的剧痛是他在以前从未感受过的。当他爬到了山峰的顶端，向四周张望的时候，他就会看到另一个海洋就在他的眼前伸展了开来；然后，他就安静地站在那里，默不作声。但是，到了夜晚，站在这个高度是非常寒冷的，这里天空清澈、星云密布。

我看出了我的命运，他最后伤心地说道，好吧！我已经准备好了。现在，属于我的最后的孤独终于要开始了。

哎，这片忧郁的、悲伤的海洋就在我的脚下！哎，这阴沉的、夜间的苦恼！哎，命运啊！哎，海洋啊！现在，我必须要向着你们下降！

我站在我的最高耸的山峰面前，我面对着我最遥远的旅途：所以，我必须首先下降到比之前还要深的地方去：

我要下降到更深的痛苦中去，甚至下降到最黑暗的深渊之中！我的命运要我如是。好吧！我已经准备好了。

那些最为高耸的山峰都是从哪里过来的？我曾经这么问道。然后，我才知道，它们是从海洋那里过来的。

of the sea.

That testimony is inscribed on their stones, and on the walls of their summits. Out of the deepest must the highest come to its height.-

Thus spoke Zarathustra on the ridge of the mountain where it was cold: when, however, he came into the vicinity of the sea, and at last stood alone amongst the cliffs, then had he become weary on his way, and eagerer than ever before.

Everything as yet sleeps, said he; even the sea sleeps. Drowsily and strangely does its eye gaze upon me.

But it breaths warmly- I feel it. And I feel also that it dreams. It tosses about dreamily on hard pillows.

Hark! Hark! How it groans with evil recollections! Or evil expectations?

Ah, I am sad along with you, you dusky monster, and angry with myself even for your sake.

Ah, that my hand has not strength enough! Gladly, indeed, would I free you from evil dreams!-

And while Zarathustra thus spoke, he laughed at himself with melancholy and bitterness. What! Zarathustra, said he, will you even sing consolation to the sea?

Ah, you amiable fool, Zarathustra, you too-blindly confiding one! But thus have you ever been: ever have you approached confidently all that is terrible.

Every monster would you caress. A whiff of warm breath, a little soft tuft on its paw:- and immediately were you ready to love and lure it.

这样的证词都铭刻在了它们的石头之上以及它们的峰顶的石壁上。最高耸要想达到这样的高度，必须要从最深处开始。

查拉图斯特拉在冰冷的山峰上如是说：但是，当他来到海洋附近，并且终于独自一人站在悬崖峭壁之中的时候，他才开始对他的旅途感到疲倦，而更加渴望的情绪充斥着他的内心。

世间万物都已经睡着了，他说道；即使是海洋也进入了梦乡。它那双睡眼惺忪的眼神，充满好奇地看着我。

但是，我可以感受得到，它的呼吸是温暖的。而且我还同样感受到了它的梦境。在睡梦之中，它在枕头上来回翻滚着。

聆听吧！聆听吧！它是如何独自抱怨种种不幸的回忆啊！或是不幸的预期？

哎，你这个暗淡的怪物，我为你感到悲痛，我甚至因为你的原因而怨恨自己。

哎，我的双手根本就没有足够的力气！说真的，能够把你从不幸的梦境之中解救出来，我感到非常高兴！

查拉图斯特拉一边说着这些话，一边忧郁地、苦涩地笑着自己。怎么样！查拉图斯特拉，他说道，你会向着大海歌唱抚慰人心的曲子吗？

哎，你这个友善的白痴，查拉图斯特拉，你真是过度盲目，轻易相信他人的人啊！但是，你向来如此：你经常会充满自信地接近任何可怕的事物。

你会去抚摸所有的怪物。一点点温暖的呼吸，一点点柔软的爪子毛：——而你马上就准备开始爱它，诱惑它。

爱，只要是热爱一切事物的爱，都是最孤单者的危险，说真的，我的爱里的疯狂和

Love is the danger of the most lonesome one, love to anything, if it only live! Laughable, verily, is my folly and my modesty in love!-

Thus spoke Zarathustra, and laughed thereby a second time. Then, however, he thought of his abandoned friends- and as if he had done them a wrong with his thoughts, he upbraided himself because of his thoughts. And forthwith it came to pass that the laugher wept- with anger and longing wept Zarathustra bitterly.

46. The Vision and the Riddle

1.

WHEN it got abroad among the sailors that Zarathustra was on board the ship- for a man who came from the Blessed isles had gone on board along with him,- there was great curiosity and expectation. But Zarathustra kept silent for two days, and was cold and deaf with sadness; so that he neither answered looks nor questions. On the evening of the second day, however, he again opened his ears, though he still kept silent: for there were many curious and dangerous things to be heard on board the ship, which came from afar, and was to go still further. Zarathustra, however, was fond of all those who make distant voyages, and dislike to live without danger. And behold! when listening, his own tongue was at last loosened, and the ice of his heart broke. Then did he begin to speak thus:

谦卑真是让人捧腹大笑！

查拉图斯特拉如是说，他第二次笑了起来。但是，在那个时候，他想到了他那些被抛弃的朋友们——就好像，他在他的思想中对他的朋友们做出了不好的事情，他因为自己的思念而责骂自己。但是，当他正在微笑的时候，他却突然开始啜泣了起来——查拉图斯特拉因为生气和渴求而伤心地哭泣。

46．幻觉与谜题

（1）

当查拉图斯特拉登上船的消息被船员们知道，并且他们得知还有一个来自幸福之岛的人跟着他一同登上船之后，这些船员便产生了极强的好奇心和期望。但是，查拉图斯特拉一连两天都没有开口说话，并且，他因为悲痛而浑身冰凉，耳朵也听不见声音。他既不会反映其他人的目光，也不会回答船员们提出的任何问题。但是，到了第二天的晚上，他开始张开他的耳朵，尽管他仍旧保持着沉默的状态：因为在这艘从远方而来，并且朝更远的方向驶去的船上，能听到许许多多令人感到好奇和充满危险的故事。然而，查拉图斯特拉特别喜欢那些进行遥远的海上航行的人，他不喜欢充满平淡的生活。快看啊！当他正在聆听的时候，他的嘴巴终于松弛了下来，他那冰冷的内心终于被打破了。然后，他开始如是说道：

你们这些无所畏惧的冒险者和探险者啊！你们这些在令人闻风丧胆的海洋上和狡猾

To you, the daring venturers and adventurers, and whoever has embarked with cunning sails upon frightful seas,-

To you the enigma-intoxicated, the twilight-enjoyers, whose souls are allured by flutes to every treacherous gulf:

-For you dislike to grope at a thread with cowardly hand; and where you can divine, there do you hate to calculate-

To you only do I tell the enigma that I saw- the vision of the most lonesome one.-

Gloomily walked I lately in corpse-colored twilight- gloomily and sternly, with compressed lips. Not only one sun had set for me.

A path which ascended daringly among boulders, an evil, lonesome path, which neither herb nor shrub any longer cheered, a mountain-path, crunched under the daring of my foot.

Mutely marching over the scornful clinking of pebbles, trampling the stone that let it slip: thus did my foot force its way upwards.

Upwards:- in spite of the spirit that drew it downwards, towards the abyss, the spirit of gravity, my devil and archenemy.

Upwards:- although it sat upon me, half-dwarf, half-mole; paralysed, paralysing; dripping lead in my ear, and thoughts like drops of lead into my brain.

"O Zarathustra," it whispered scornfully, syllable by syllable, "you stone of wisdom! you threw yourself high, but every thrown stone must- fall!

O Zarathustra, you stone of wisdom, you sling-stone, you star-destroyer! Yourself threw you

的船帆共同出海的人们啊！

你们这些沉醉于谜题和乐于享受黄昏的人们啊！你们这些被充满魔力的笛声吸引到叛逆的海湾的人们啊！

你们讨厌用胆怯的双手抓住一根绳子而进行摸索；因为，你们但凡可以进行猜测，都绝不会去归纳测算。

只有当我面对你们的时候，我才会说出我亲眼所见的谜团——最孤独者的幻象。

最近，我紧咬着嘴唇，面色忧郁地走在灰色的黎明之中。很多太阳都为我西匿了。

我的道路顽固地在被腐蚀的泥土中向上升着，那是一条充满恶意的、无比孤独的、没有小草和灌木的道路，那是一条山间小路，它在我勇敢的脚下发出嘎吱嘎吱的刺耳声。

我的脚不声不响地在发出轻蔑的声响的石头上走着，踩踏那些让它溜滑的小石头：所以，我的脚迫使自己向上升。

向上升——强行向下拉动的精神，奔向深渊的精神，严重的精神，我的恶魔和敌人。

向上升——尽管严重的精神就那样瘫坐在我的旁边，既像小矮人，又像鼹鼠；它的瘫坐让我的四肢也感到无力，它把铅滴注入到了我的耳朵里面，类似铅滴的思想进入到了我的大脑之中。

“啊，查拉图斯特拉，”他一字一句充满讽刺地低声说道，“你这智慧之石！你把自己高高地抛了起来，但是，每一个被抛向空中的石头，都一定会掉落下来！

啊，查拉图斯特拉，你这智慧之石，被抛起来的石头，星星的毁灭者！你将自己高高地抛了起来，但是，每一个被抛向空中的石头，都一定会掉落下来！

so high,- but every thrown stone- must fall!

Condemned of yourself, and to your own stoning: O Zarathustra, far indeed threw you your stone- but upon yourself will it recoil!"

Then was the dwarf silent; and it lasted long. The silence, however, oppressed me; and to be thus in pairs, one is verily lonesomer than when alone!

I ascended, I ascended, I dreamt, I thought,- but everything oppressed me. A sick one did I resemble, whom bad torture wearies, and a worse dream reawakens out of his first sleep.-

But there is something in me which I call courage: it has hitherto slain for me every dejection. This courage at last bade me stand still and say: "Dwarf! Thou! Or I!"-

For courage is the best killer,- courage which attacks: for in every attack there is sound of triumph. Man, however, is the most courageous animal: thereby has he overcome every animal. With sound of triumph has he overcome every pain; human pain, however, is the sorest pain.

Courage kills also giddiness at abysses: and where does man not stand at abysses! Is not seeing itself- seeing abysses?

Courage is the best killer: courage kills also fellow-suffering. Fellow-suffering, however, is the deepest abyss: as deeply as man looks into life, so deeply also does he look into suffering.

Courage, however, is the best killer, courage which attacks: it kills even death itself; for it says: "Was that life? Well! Once more!"

In such speech, however, there is much sound of triumph. He who has ears to hear, let him hear.-

啊，查拉图斯特拉，你被认定是被自己的石头置于死地，你把石头高高地抛了起来——但是它必定会降落在你的头顶之上！”

所以，小矮人安静了下来，它沉默了很久。但是，这种安静的氛围压迫着我，说真的，虽然我跟他是两个人，但是当独自一人的时候，他比我还要孤单！

我不断地攀登着，不断地攀登着，我梦想着，我思考着——但是所有的一切都在压迫着我。我就像一个生了病的人，刚刚因为它的罪恶的折磨而疲倦地入睡，却又被一个更加恶劣的梦境重新唤醒。

但是，我的身上还有一些东西，我管它叫勇敢：一直以来，它都是所有的失望的杀戮者。最终，这种勇敢命令我安静地站在原地，然后它说道：“小矮人！你或是我！”

因为勇敢，在发动进攻的时候的勇敢是最好的杀戮者：因为在任何的战斗之中，都会有取得胜利的战歌。但是，人类是最有胆量的动物：人类已经征服了所有的动物。在战歌的音乐背景下，他克服了所有的伤痛；但是，人类的伤痛是所有疼痛当中最痛苦的。

勇敢同样也会在深渊的旁边杀戮晕眩：人类不都站在深渊之上吗！难道他不是四处张望一下，就能看到深渊的吗？

勇敢是最出色的杀戮者：它同样也会杀戮怜悯之心。但是，怜悯是最深的深渊：它的深度就跟人类看向生活的深度一样，它看向磨难同样的幽深。

但是，勇敢，在发动攻击的时候的勇敢是最出色的杀戮者：它甚至会去杀戮死亡；因为它说道：“这就是曾经的生命吗？好吧！那就再来一次吧！”

在这样的演说当中，存在着许许多多的胜利战歌。那些能够用耳朵倾听的人，就让他们尽情地聆听吧！

2.

"Halt, dwarf!" said I. "Either I- or you! I, however, am the stronger of the two:- you knowest not my abysmal thought! It- could you not endure!"

Then happened that which made me lighter: for the dwarf sprang from my shoulder, the prying sprite! And it squatted on a stone in front of me. There was however a gateway just where we halted.

"Look at this gateway! Dwarf!" I continued, "it has two faces. Two roads come together here: these has no one yet gone to the end of.

This long lane backwards: it continues for an eternity. And that long lane forward- that is another eternity.

They are antithetical to one another, these roads; they directly abut on one another:- and it is here, at this gateway that they come together. The name of the gateway is inscribed above: 'This Moment.'

But should one follow them further- and ever further and further on, think you, dwarf, that these roads would be eternally antithetical?"-

"Everything straight lies," murmured the dwarf, contemptuously. "All truth is crooked; time itself is a circle."

"You spirit of gravity!" said I wrathfully, "do not take it too lightly! Or I shall let you squat where you squat, Haltfoot,- and I carried you high!"

（2）

“停下来，小矮人！”我说道，“是我还是你，我是我们当中最强大的，你并不了解我犹如深渊般幽深的想法！你是无法容忍它的！”

紧接着，出现了一下子让我身上的负担减轻的事情：那个小矮人从我的肩膀上跳了下来，这个疏忽大意的小家伙！然后，它蹲坐在我面前的一块石头上。但是，就在我们两个站着的地方，恰好有一扇大门。

“快看看这扇大门啊！小矮人！”我继续说道，“这扇大门有两个门面。两条道路在此处汇集到一起：但是，还没有人曾经走到它们的尽头。

那条向后的长长的通路，延伸至永恒。而那条向前的长长的通路，则延伸至另一个永恒。

这两条通路是彼此对立的，并且彼此紧密地靠在一起，而这里的大门就是它们交汇的地方。这扇大门的名字被刻在了上面：‘刹那’。

但是，倘若有人沿着这两条通路的其中一条向前走——并且一直走，永远地走着，小矮人，你仔细想一想，这两条通路最终会产生冲突吗？”

“任何的事物都是笔直向前的，”小矮人轻蔑地喃喃自语道，“所有的真相都是虚假的，时间本身就是一个圆圈。”

“你，严重的精神，”我恼羞成怒地说道：“不要如此草率地答复我！要不然，我就会把你这个小瘸子扔到你应该坐的地方去，——记住，我可是把你带到高处的那个人！”

"Observe," continued I, "This Moment! From the gateway, This Moment, there runs a long eternal lane backwards: behind us lies an eternity.

Must not whatever can run its course of all things, have already run along that lane? Must not whatever can happen of all things have already happened, resulted, and gone by?

And if everything has already existed, what think you, dwarf, of This Moment? Must not this gateway also- have already existed?

And are not all things closely bound together in such wise that This Moment draws all coming things after it? Consequently- itself also?

For whatever can run its course of all things, also in this long lane outward- must it once more run!-

And this slow spider which creeps in the moonlight, and this moonlight itself, and you and I in this gateway whispering together, whispering of eternal things- must we not all have already existed?

-And must we not return and run in that other lane out before us, that long weird lane- must we not eternally return?"-

Thus did I speak, and always more softly: for I was afraid of my own thoughts, and arrear-thoughts. Then, suddenly did I hear a dog howl near me.

Had I ever heard a dog howl thus? My thoughts ran back. Yes! When I was a child, in my most distant childhood:

-Then did I hear a dog howl thus. And saw it also, with hair bristling, its head upwards,

"好好观察观察这个'刹那'吧！"我继续说道，"从这一刹那的大门起，一条长长的、永恒的通路开始向后延展：一个永恒就矗立在我们的背后。"

在世间万物之中，能够奔跑的人，不是应该都已经跑完了那条通路了吗？在世间万物之中，能够达到的人，不是应该都已经达到了完成，并且过去了吗？

倘若世间万物都已经存在过了，那么，小矮人，你又对这样的"刹那"作何解释呢？这扇大门不是应该也已经存在过了吗？

世间万物难道不是紧密地连在一起，为了让这刹那拖拉着未来的一切吗？并且也因此决定了它自己吗？

所以，世间万物之中能够奔跑的人，它们必须再一次遵循前面这条长长的通路！

这只在夜光下缓慢爬动的蜘蛛，明媚的月光本身以及在这扇大门旁轻声诉说永恒的事物的你和我——我们不是应该也早已存在过了吗？

我们不应该重新回来，跑完摆在我们面前的那条道路，那条伴有古怪事物的长路——我们不应该永恒地再次归来吗？

我用非常轻柔的声音如是说：因为，我非常惧怕我的思想和思考之后的思想。突然之间，我听到一只狗在靠近我的地方吠叫。

我曾经听到过一只狗在我的身边吠叫吗？我的思想开始往回跑了。是的！当我还是个孩子的时候，在我最遥远的童年时期。

在那个时候，我确实听到了一只狗在吼叫。我同时还看到它的毛发和竖起的头部在震颤着，在安静的午夜，就算是狗也会相信鬼魂。

所以，这只狗激起了我的怜悯之心。就在那个时候，一轮满月悄无声息地爬上了屋

trembling in the still midnight, when even dogs believe in ghosts:

-So that it excited my commiseration. For just then went the full moon, silent as death, over the house; just then did it stand still, a glowing globe- at rest on the flat roof, as if on some one's property:-

Thereby had the dog been terrified: for dogs believe in thieves and ghosts. And when I again heard such howling, then did it excite my commiseration once more.

Where was now the dwarf? And the gateway? And the spider? And all the whispering? Had I dreamt? Had I awakened? 'Twixt rugged rocks did I suddenly stand alone, dreary in the dreariest moonlight.

But there lay a man! And there! The dog leaping, bristling, whining- now did it see me coming- then did it howl again, then did it cry:- had I ever heard a dog cry so for help?

And verily, what I saw, the like had I never seen. A young shepherd did I see, writhing, choking, quivering, with distorted countenance, and with a heavy black serpent hanging out of his mouth.

Had I ever seen so much loathing and pale horror on one countenance? He had perhaps gone to sleep? Then had the serpent crawled into his throat- there had it bitten itself fast.

My hand pulled at the serpent, and pulled:- in vain! I failed to pull the serpent out of his throat. Then there cried out of me: "Bite! Bite!"

"Its head off! Bite!"- so cried it out of me; my horror, my my hatred, my loathing, my pity, all my good and my bad cried with one voice out of me.-

顶；它就那么一动不动地站着，犹如一个闪闪发亮的球体——安静地停留在屋顶之上，就好像它是某人的私有财产。

所以，这让狗开始担惊受怕了起来：因为，狗相信这个世界上存在小偷和鬼魂。当我再一次听到类似这样的吼叫的时候，我的怜悯之心再一次被激发了出来。

那个小矮人现在到哪里去了？那扇大门现在到哪里去了？还有那只蜘蛛呢？所有的耳边细语？我的梦境？我真的醒过来了吗？我突然发现自己正独自站在粗糙的岩石中间，在这最忧郁的月光之下。

但是，这里躺着一个人！就在这里！那只竖起毛发的狗跳着、嘶吼着——现在，它看见我正朝它这边走来，它开始再一次吼叫了起来，我曾经听到过一只狗为了寻求帮助而这样的吼叫吗？

说真的，我所看见的东西都是我在以前从未见到过的。我看到了一个年轻的牧羊人，他喘着气，面部因为痉挛而扭曲的表情，一条黑色的毒蛇就悬在他的嘴边。

我曾经见到过一个面孔上拥有如此之多的悲痛和苍白的恐惧吗？或许，他曾经睡着了，然后，那条黑色的毒蛇爬进了他的喉咙，然后迅速地咬住了他。

我用自己的双手使劲拽那条蛇，使劲拽：但这一切都是白费力气！我并没能把那条黑色的毒蛇从他的喉咙里拽出来。一股叫喊从我的嘴巴里跑了出来：“咬他！咬他！咬掉他的头！咬他！”

我的恐惧、我的仇恨、我的痛恨、我的可怜如是喊道，我的所有善与恶不约而同地从我的嘴里喊了出来。

勇敢的追寻者围在了我的身边！探险者啊！你们这些在令人胆寒的海洋上和狡猾的帆

You daring ones around me! You venturers and adventurers, and whoever of you have embarked with cunning sails on unexplored seas! You enigma-enjoyers!

Solve to me the enigma that I then beheld, interpret to me the vision of the most lonesome one!

For it was a vision and a foresight:- what did I then behold in parable? And who is it that must come some day?

Who is the shepherd into whose throat the serpent thus crawled? Who is the man into whose throat all the heaviest and blackest will thus crawl?

-The shepherd however bit as my cry had admonished him; he bit with a strong bite! Far away did he spit the head of the serpent:- and sprang up.-

No longer shepherd, no longer man- a transfigured being, a light-surrounded being, that laughed! Never on earth laughed a man as he laughed!

O my brothers, I heard a laughter which was no human laughter,- and now gnaws a thirst at me, a longing that is never allayed.

My longing for that laughter gnaws at me: oh, how can I still endure to live! And how could I endure to die at present!-

Thus spoke Zarathustra.

47. Involuntary Bliss

WITH such enigmas and bitterness in his heart did Zarathustra sail o'er the sea. When,

一同探索尚未被发现的海洋的探险者啊！你们这些谜一样的探险者们！

快快解决掉我亲眼所见的谜团吧，快快解释一下最孤独者的幻象吧！

因为这就是一种幻象，是一种预见：那么，我在这些寓言之中都能看到些什么东西呢？究竟谁是那个终究会在某一天到来的人？

谁是那个悬在蛇口之外的牧羊人呢？那个能够容忍最沉重、最黑暗的事物的人是谁？

不过，那个牧羊人还是像我告诫他的叫喊那样咬了，他使劲咬了下去！他将蛇头扔到了很远的地方，然后，自己跳了起来。

他不再是一个牧羊人，他不再是一个人——他是一个已经改变了外形的物体，笼罩在亮光之中的物体，他笑了起来！在这片大地之上，还从来都没有一个人像他那样笑过！

噢，我的兄弟们，我听到了一股笑声，那不是人类的笑声，而现在，一种饥渴、一种从未缓和过的渴望正在吞噬着我。

我对于那股笑声的渴求正在吞噬着我：噢，我怎么能继续容忍着生活下去呢！我怎么能忍受着现在而去死呢！

查拉图斯特拉如是说。

47．违愿的幸福

查拉图斯特拉的内心隐藏着这样的谜团和苦难，漂洋过海，但是，当查拉图斯特拉离开幸福之岛和他的朋友们的第四天的时候，他已经克服了自己身上种种的痛苦：他那

however, he was four day-journeys from the Blessed isles and from his friends, then had he overcame all his pain:- triumphantly and with firm foot did he again accept his fate. And then talked Zarathustra in this wise to his exulting conscience:

Alone am I again, and like to be so, alone with the pure heaven, and the open sea; and again is the afternoon around me.

On an afternoon did I find my friends for the first time; on an afternoon, also, did I find them a second time:- at the hour when all light becomes stiller.

For whatever happiness is still on its way 'twixt heaven and earth, now seeks for lodging a luminous soul: with happiness has all light now become stiller.

O afternoon of my life! Once did my happiness also descend to the valley that it might seek a lodging: then did it find those open hospitable souls.

O afternoon of my life! What did I not surrender that I might have one thing: this living plantation of my thoughts, and this dawn of my highest hope!

Companions did the creator once seek, and children of his hope: and lo, it turned out that he could not find them, except he himself should first create them.

Thus am I in the midst of my work, to my children going, and from them returning: for the sake of his children must Zarathustra perfect himself.

For in one's heart one loves only one's child and one's work; and where there is great love to oneself, then is it the sign of pregnancy: so have I found it.

Still are my children verdant in their first spring, standing nigh one another, and shaken in

坚定的、胜利的脚掌再一次站在了他的命运之上。所以，查拉图斯特拉对他的欣喜若狂的善意说：

我又一次孤独一人，我心甘情愿如此，独自一人和纯粹的蓝天以及自由的大海在一起：而下午再一次围绕在了我的身边。

有一天下午，我第一次找到了我的朋友们；同样也是一天的下午，我第二次找到了他们：——当所有的光亮都变得无比宁静的时候。

因为任何幸福都在蓝天和大地之间进行旅行，它们在寻求一个闪闪发亮的灵魂：作为它的住所，幸福会让所有的光亮变得更加宁静。

啊，我的生命之下午啊！我的幸福也曾经下降到山谷里找寻住所：然后，它发现了那些自由的、环境舒适的灵魂。

啊，我的生命之下午啊！我放弃了所有，就为了能够有机会得到那个唯一的东西：我的思想的生动的花园和我的最高希望的黎明啊！

有那么一次，创造者找寻同伴和他的希望的孩子们：但是后来他才明白，如果不首先创造他们的话，他就没法找到他们。

因此，我在工作的中途，向我的那些孩子们走去，并且回到他们中间：为了这些孩子们着想，查拉图斯特拉必须保护他自己。

因为一个人的内心当中只会深爱自己的孩子和自己的工作，伟大的自爱所在的地方，就是孕育生命的征兆：所以，我发现了这些。

我的孩子们在微风的吹拂下，彼此紧挨着站在一起，在他们的第一个春天里显出无比翠绿的颜色，这就是我的花园和我最肥沃的土壤里的树木。说真的，这种树密集生长

common by the winds, the trees of my garden and of my best soil.

And verily, where such trees stand beside one another, there are Blessed isles!

But one day will I take them up, and put each by itself alone: that it may learn solitude and defiance and prudence.

Gnarled and crooked and with flexible hardness shall it then stand by the sea, a living lighthouse of unconquerable life.

Yonder where the storms rush down into the sea, and the snout of the mountain drinks water, shall each on a time have his day and night watches, for his testing and recognition.

Recognized and tested shall each be, to see if he be of my type and lineage:- if he be master of a long will, silent even when he speaks, and giving in such wise that he takes in giving:-

-So that he may one day become my companion, a fellow-creator and fellow-enjoyer with Zarathustra:- such a one as writes my will on my law-tablets, for the fuller perfection of all things.

And for his sake and for those like him, must I perfect myself: therefore do I now avoid my happiness, and present myself to every misfortune- for my final testing and recognition.

And verily, it were time that I went away; and the wanderer's shadow and the longest tedium and the still hour- have all said to me: "It is the highest time!"

The word blew to me through the keyhole and said "Come!" The door sprang subtly open to me, and said "Go!"

But I lay enchained to my love for my children: desire spread this snare for me- the desire

的地方就是幸福之岛！

但是，总有一天我会将它们从土壤里连根拔起，并且分别栽种它们：以便让它们都能够学到孤独、傲慢和谨慎。

我要它们长出多节的树枝，弯曲着，刚柔并济地矗立在海洋之上，一个无法征服的生命的生动的灯塔。

就在那大风暴奔泻到海洋的地方，在那山峰的长鼻痛饮海水的地方，每一个树木都会拥有值白班和夜班的时候，以便让它被测试，被认知。

它必定会被测试，被认知，让人们知道它是否是我的族类和后代：让人们知道它是一个长久意志的主人，即使是它说话的时候，也是无比安静的，给予的时候就像如不得已而取得一样：

因此，总有一天他会成为我的同伴，一个同查拉图斯特拉在一起的共同创造者的同伴：他是一个能够将我的意志，让世间万物得到进一步完善的意志，写在我的桌子上。

为了它和它的同类着想，我必须好好保护自己：所以，我现在要躲开我的幸福，并且将自己呈现在所有的灾祸面前——来作为我最终的测试和认知。

说真的，我到了该离开的时间了；旅途者的影子、最长久的居住和最沉闷的时刻异口同声地告诉我：“现在是最佳的时刻了！”

话语像风一样穿过钥匙孔向我袭来，它说道：“快来吧！”大门被巧妙地开启了，并且说道：“快走吧！”

但是，我被我对自己的孩子的怜爱所禁锢，渴望、对于爱的渴望为我布置了这个陷

for love- that I should become the prey of my children, and lose myself in them.

Desiring- that is now for me to have lost myself. I possess you, my children! In this possessing shall everything be assurance and nothing desire.

But brooding lay the sun of my love upon me, in his own juice stewed Zarathustra,- then did shadows and doubts fly past me.

For frost and winter I now longed: "Oh, that frost and winter would again make me crack and crunch!" sighed I:- then arose icy mist out of me.

My past burst its tomb, many pains buried alike woke up:- fully slept had they merely, concealed in corpse-clothes.

So called everything to me in signs: "It is time!" But I- heard not, until at last my abyss moved, and my thought bit me.

Ah, abysmal thought, which are my thought! When shall I find strength to hear you burrowing, and no longer tremble?

To my very throat throbs my heart when I hear them burrowing! your muteness even is like to strangle me, you abysmal mute one!

As yet have I never ventured to call you up; it has been enough that I- have carried you about with me! As yet have I not been strong enough for my final lion-wantonness and playfulness.

Sufficiently formidable to me has your weight ever been: but one day shall I yet find the strength and the lion's voice which will call you up!

阱——我应该成为我的孩子们的牺牲者，并且因为他们而失去自己。

渴望——对于我而言，就是迷失自我。我占有着你们，我的孩子们！在这样的占有当中，任何的事物都是安全并且没有任何渴望的。

但是，我的爱之太阳就在我的头顶上徘徊，不肯离去，查拉图斯特拉在自己的汁液中饱受煎熬——就在那个时候，阴影和怀疑从我的身边飞过。

我现在开始渴望寒冷和冬季的到来：“噢，那寒冷和冬季会再一次让我瑟瑟发抖，浑身打战吧！”我叹了口气说道：——那时候，冰冷的迷雾从我的身上油然而生。

我的过去打破了它的坟茔，许多被埋葬的痛苦苏醒了过来：它们隐藏在尸体的裹布里，足足地睡上了一觉。

所以，一切的事物都用信号向我说道：“现在是时候了！”但是我并没有听到这股声音，直到最后，我的深渊开始动荡，我的思想开始啃咬我。

噢，我的思想啊，我那犹如深渊般的思想啊！我什么时候能够具备听到你们的挖掘和不再颤抖的声音的能力呢?

当我听到他们在挖掘的时候，我的喉咙在猛烈地颤动我的心脏！你那犹如深渊般的无言，你那想令我窒息的无言！

我还从来都没有勇气呼唤你到上面来；我已经受够了将你藏匿起来，我还不够强大，没有狮子的最终的放纵和勇敢。

你的重量足够让我感到敬畏，但是，我总有一天会找到勇气，并且用狮子的声音呼唤你！

倘若我能够在这些方面征服自己的话，那么，我同样可以在更加伟大的事情中征服

When I shall have overcame myself therein, then will I overcome myself also in that which is greater; and a victory shall be the seal of my perfection!-

Meanwhile do I sail along on uncertain seas; chance flatters me, smooth-tongued chance; forward and backward do I gaze-, still see I no end.

As yet has the hour of my final struggle not come to me- or does it come to me perhaps just now? with insidious beauty do sea and life gaze upon me round about:

O afternoon of my life! O happiness before eventide! O haven upon high seas! O peace in uncertainty! How I distrust all of you!

Distrustful am I of your insidious beauty! Like the lover am I, who distrusts too sleek smiling.

As he pushes the best-beloved before him- tender even in severity, the jealous one-, so do I push this blissful hour before me.

Away with you, you blissful hour! With you has there come to me an involuntary bliss! Ready for my severest pain do I here stand:- at the wrong time have you come!

Away with you, you blissful hour! Rather harbor there- with my children! Hasten! and bless them before eventide with my happiness!

There, already approaches eventide: the sun sinks. Away- my happiness!-

Thus spoke Zarathustra. And he waited for his misfortune the whole night; but he waited in vain. The night remained clear and calm, and happiness itself came closer and closer to him. Towards morning, however, Zarathustra laughed to his heart, and said mockingly: "Happiness runs after me. That is because I do not run after women. Happiness, however, is a woman."

自己，而一场轰轰烈烈的胜利就是我的完美的印记！

与此同时，我会航行在充满未知和变数的海洋之上，机遇和甜言蜜语在讨好我，我开始瞻前顾后的张望，可是，我仍旧看不到终点。

我的最后的决斗时刻还没有到来——又或许它现在正在往这里赶来呢？真的，海洋和生命在用阴险狡猾的美凝视着我。

啊，我的生命之下午啊！啊，黄昏之前的下午啊！啊，大海之中的停泊处啊！啊，不确定之中的平静啊！我是如何地不信任你们啊！

我对你们这种阴险狡猾的美持不信任的态度！我就像一个情人一样，不信任一个太过于圆滑的微笑！

我就像这位嫉妒者温柔地、认真地推开他的挚爱一样，推开了幸福的时刻。

幸福的时刻啊！请你们离开我吧！你们出人意料地给我带来了幸福，而我现在却要准备好接受最痛苦的疼痛，你们来得实在太不是时候了！

幸福的时刻啊！请你们离开我吧！你带着孩子们去那里找寻住所吧！快点啊！用我的幸福在黄昏之前祝福他们吧！

夜晚已经悄然临近了：太阳正在下落。快点离开我吧——我的幸福！

查拉图斯特拉如是说。他一整夜都在等待他的不幸的到来；但是，他的等待都是徒劳的。夜晚仍旧是清晰的、宁静地，而幸福则离他越来越近。但是，黎明将至的时候，查拉图斯特拉发自内心地笑了起来，他嘲笑地说道：“幸福在追赶着我。那是因为我不追逐妇人的缘故。但是，幸福就是一个妇人。”

48. Before Sunrise

O HEAVEN above me, you pure, you deep heaven! you abyss of light! Gazing on you, I tremble with divine desires.

Up to your height to toss myself- that is my depth! In your purity to hide myself- that is my innocence!

The God veils his beauty: thus hide you your stars. You speak not: thus proclaim you your wisdom to me.

Mute o'er the raging sea have you risen for me to-day; your love and your modesty make a revelation to my raging soul.

In that you came to me beautiful, veiled in your beauty, in that you spoke to me mutely, obvious in your wisdom:

Oh, how could I fail to divine all the modesty of your soul! Before the sun did you come to me- the most lonesome one.

We have been friends from the beginning: to us are grief, gruesomeness, and ground common; even the sun is common to us.

We do not speak to each other, because we know too much-: we keep silent to each other, we smile our knowledge to each other.

Are you not the light of my fire? have you not the sister-soul of my insight?

48. 日出之前

啊，在我头顶之上的天啊，纯粹并且深沉的天啊！光亮的深渊啊！当我注视着你的时候，我因为神圣的渴望而瑟瑟发抖。

跳上你的高度——这才是我的深度！我将自己隐藏在你的纯净之中——这就是我的天真无邪！

上帝被他的美貌所掩盖了：同样地，你也掩盖了你的星星。你不说话：你向我宣告了你的智慧。

今天，你一言不发地在惊涛骇浪之中向我走来，你的爱和谦逊在向我的愤怒的灵魂昭示真相。

你优雅地向我走来，隐藏在你的美貌之下，你用沉默的话语跟我谈话，用你的智慧展示着自己。

啊，我怎么能猜不透你的灵魂的谦逊呢！在太阳的面前，你向我走来——向这里最孤独的人走来。

我们从一开始就是好朋友：我们有着共同的悲痛、恐惧和深度；甚至太阳也共同属于我们。

我们彼此之间根本就不说话，因为我们都太了解对方了：我们彼此之间保持沉默，并且用微笑同对方交换知识。

难道你不是我的火焰之光吗？难道你不是我的见解的姊妹灵魂吗？

Together did we learn everything; together did we learn to ascend beyond ourselves to ourselves, and to smile uncloudedly:-

-Uncloudedly to smile down out of luminous eyes and out of miles of distance, when under us constraint and purpose and guilt stream like rain.

And wandered I alone, for what did my soul hunger by night and in labyrinthine paths? And climbed I mountains, whom did I ever seek, if not you, upon mountains?

And all my wandering and mountain-climbing: a necessity was it merely, and a makeshift of the unhandy one:- to fly only, wants my entire will, to fly into you!

And what have I hated more than passing clouds, and whatever taints you? And my own hatred have I even hated, because it tainted you!

The passing clouds I detest- those stealthy cats of prey: they take from you and me what is common to us- the vast unbounded Yes- and Amen- saying.

These mediators and mixers we detest- the passing clouds: those half-and-half ones, that have neither learned to bless nor to curse from the heart.

Rather will I sit in a tub under a closed heaven, rather will I sit in the abyss without heaven, than see you, you luminous heaven, tainted with passing clouds!

And oft have I longed to pin them fast with the jagged gold-wires of lightning, that I might, like the thunder, beat the drum upon their kettle-bellies:-

-An angry drummer, because they rob me of your Yes and Amen!- you heaven above me, you pure, you luminous heaven! you abyss of light!- because they rob you of my Yes and

曾经，我们两个在一起学习了一切；并且学习到应该如何超越自我，升华自己和不加怀疑的微笑：

从远处用散发着光芒的眼睛向下微笑着，抑制、意图和错误在我们的下面像雨水一样冒着蒸汽。

当我独自一个人散步的时候，在夜晚，在错综复杂的小路上，我的灵魂到底需要什么来填饱饥饿呢？当我在攀登山峰的时候，如果我不是在寻找你的话，那么我是在山峰上寻找谁呢？

我的所有的散步和所有攀爬的山峰：那仅仅是笨拙的人的必要和权宜之计而已：我整个的意志要独自飞翔，它要向你的方向飞翔！

究竟是什么东西要比那些从身边飞过的云朵以及玷污你的一切都更加让你感到痛恨呢？我甚至会痛恨自己的仇恨，因为它也同样玷污了你！

我厌恶那些从身边飞过的云朵，我厌恶那些悄悄爬过的野猫：它们夺走了我们共有的东西——一个不受限制、无限的肯定和祝福。

我们都痛恨这些中间介入者和好事者——从身边飞过的云朵：它们是不彻底的事物，它们既没有从心底里学会祝福，也没有学会诅咒。

我宁愿坐在一个安放在蓝天底下的浴盆里，我宁愿坐在没有蓝天的深渊里，也不会去看你，你这个散发着光芒的蓝天，被飞过的云朵玷污的蓝天！

我经常设想用金黄色的闪电之金属线快速地将它们系在一起，而我或许会像一道闪电一样，在他们瓦罐似的肚子上击鼓：

一个恼羞成怒的鼓手，因为他们从我这里偷走了你们的肯定和祝福！那个在我的头

Amen.

For rather will I have noise and thunders and tempest-blasts, than this discreet, doubting cat-repose; and also amongst men do I hate most of all the soft-treaders, and half-and-half ones, and the doubting, hesitating, passing clouds.

And "he who cannot bless shall learn to curse!"- this clear teaching dropt to me from the clear heaven; this star stands in my heaven even in dark nights.

I, however, am a blesser and a Yes-sayer, if you be but around me, you pure, you luminous heaven! you abyss of light!- into all abysses do I then carry my beneficent Yes-saying.

A blesser have I become and a Yes-sayer: and therefore strove I long and was a striver, that I might one day get my hands free for blessing.

This, however, is my blessing: to stand above everything as its own heaven, its round roof, its azure bell and eternal security: and blessed is he who thus blesses!

For all things are baptized at the font of eternity, and beyond good and evil; good and evil themselves, however, are but fugitive shadows and damp afflictions and passing clouds.

It is a blessing and not a blasphemy when I teach that "above all things there stands the heaven of chance, the heaven of innocence, the heaven of hazard, the heaven of wantonness."

"Of Hazard"- that is the oldest nobility in the world; that gave I back to all things; I emancipated them from bondage under purpose.

This freedom and celestial serenity did I put like an azure bell above all things, when I taught that over them and through them, no "eternal Will"- wills.

顶之上的蓝天啊！那个纯粹的、散发着光芒的蓝天啊！纯粹的光之深渊啊！因为他们从我这里偷走了你们的肯定和祝福！

我喜欢噪音、雷电和肆虐的暴风雨，而不喜欢这种谨慎的、充满疑虑的猫的安息，同样地，在人群当中，我最讨厌所有的悄悄走路的人，不彻底的人，充满疑虑、犹豫地飞过之云。

“如果他不会祝福，那就去学诅咒！”这个清晰的教育从蓝天降临到了我的头上，这个行星即便是在黑暗的深夜也会在我的蓝天里闪闪发亮。

但是，我是一个祝福者，一个肯定者，倘若是你，纯粹的、散发着光亮的蓝天的你围绕在我的身边！你这光之深渊啊！我将会把我的祝福和肯定一并送到所有的深渊里面去。

我成为了一名祝福者，一名肯定者：而且，我曾经为此奋斗过，我曾经是一名奋斗者，让我终于拥有一个自由自在的手去祝福。

然而，这就是我的祝福：站在世间万物之上，就好像那是它的蓝天、它的圆屋顶、湛蓝的钟和永恒的安全似的：而祝福者也会受到祝福的！

世间万物都会在永恒的洗礼盘里接受洗礼，超越善与恶；但是，善与恶本身不过就是逃亡的影子、潮湿的苦难和飞过的云朵而已。

说真的，当我说道：“在世间万物之上矗立着机遇的天、天真无邪的天、偶然的天以及放肆的天。”这不是一种亵渎神明的行为，而是一种祝福。

“偶然地”——这是世界上最古老的贵族的称号；我将它归还给了世间万物；我将它们从目的的奴役中解放了出来。

当我说：“无论是在世间万物之上，还是在世间万物本身之中，都不存在‘永恒的

This wantonness and folly did I put in place of that Will, when I taught that "In everything there is one thing impossible- rationality!"

A little reason, to be sure, a germ of wisdom scattered from star to star- this leaven is mixed in all things: for the sake of folly, wisdom is mixed in all things!

A little wisdom is indeed possible; but this blessed security have I found in all things, that they prefer- to dance on the feet of chance.

O heaven above me! you pure, you lofty heaven! This is now your purity to me, that there is no eternal reason-spider and reason-cobweb:- -That you are to me a dancing-floor for divine chances, that you are to me a table of the Gods, for divine dice and dice-players!-

But you blush? Have I spoken unspeakable things? Have I abused, when I meant to bless you?

Or is it the shame of being two of us that makes you blush!- do you bid me go and be silent, because now- day comes?

The world is deep:- and deeper than e'er the day could read. Not everything may be uttered in presence of day. But day comes: so let us part!

O heaven above me, you modest one! you glowing one! O you, my happiness before sunrise! The day comes: so let us part!-

Thus spoke Zarathustra.

意志’。”我把这个犹如蔚蓝色的钟一样的自由和天空的宁静放在了世间万物之上。

当我说：“世间万物之中有一件事是永远也不可能的——合乎理性。”我把这种放肆和疯狂放在了这个“永恒的意志”的位置之上。

毋庸置疑，一点点的理智，一个智慧的萌芽，从这个星球撒播到另一个星球之上，这种酵母被混在了世间万物之中：为了疯狂着想，智慧也被混在了世间万物之中！

的确，一点小小的智慧是很有可能的；但是在世间万物中，我发现了受到祝福的安全，也让它们宁肯选择在机遇的脚上跳舞。

啊，我头顶之上的蓝天啊！你这纯粹的、高耸的蓝天啊！现在，对于我来说，你是纯净的，这里没有永恒的理智之蜘蛛，也没有理智之网：——因为，你对于我来说就是一个为神圣的机遇准备的跳舞场；因为你对于我来说就是为神圣的骰子和玩骰子的人准备的神桌！

但是你脸红了吗？难道我说了不该说的东西了吗？当我打算祝福你的时候，我难道亵渎你了吗？

或者是因为我们两个人的缘故让你感到羞愧而脸红吗！——是你命令我离去，并且保持安静，就是因为白昼就要来临了吗？

这个世界是深邃的：——它远比白昼所能想象的深邃。并不是所有的事物都能在白昼的面前说出来的。但是，这一天终究会到来：所以，就让我们在此分别吧！

啊，我头顶之上的蓝天啊！谦逊并且闪闪发光的蓝天啊！啊，你，我的日出之前的幸福啊！这一天终究会到来的：就让我们在此分别吧！

查拉图斯特拉如是说。

49. Virtue That Diminishes

1.

WHEN Zarathustra was again on the continent, he did not go straightway to his mountains and his cave, but made many wanderings and questionings, and ascertained this and that; so that he said of himself jestingly: "Lo, a river that flows back to its source in many windings!" For he wanted to learn what had taken place among men during the interval: whether they had become greater or smaller. And once, when he saw a row of new houses, he marvelled, and said:

"What do these houses mean? no great soul put them up as its simile!

Did perhaps a silly child take them out of its toy-box? Would that another child put them again into the box!

And these rooms and chambers- can men go out and in there? They seem to be made for silk dolls; or for dainty-eaters, who perhaps let others eat with them."

And Zarathustra stood still and meditated. At last he said sorrowfully: "There has everything become smaller!

Everywhere do I see lower doorways: he who is of my type can still go therethrough, but- he must stoop!

49. 萎缩的德行

（1）

当查拉图斯特拉再一次来到大陆上的时候，他并没有径直走向他攀爬的山峰和他的洞穴，而是到处游走、漫步，并且经常问一些这样或者那样的问题，他自我嘲讽道："看啊！这是一条拥有很多曲线，回流到源头的小河！"因为他想知道，在他不在的这段时间里，在人们中间到底都发生了些什么事情：人类究竟是变大了呢？还是变小了呢？当他再一次看到一排崭新的房屋的时候，他无比震惊地说道：

"这些房子是干什么用的？说真的，任何伟大的灵魂都不会将自己当做是一种象征而建造起来！

或许是一个愚蠢的小孩子将它们从他的玩具盒子里拿了出来？如果是那样的话，那么另一个小孩子肯定会把它们再一次放回到玩具盒子里面去！

还有这些房间和大厅——人们真的能在那里面来去自如吗？它们看起来像是丝绸制作的娃娃；或是为了贪吃的猫准备的。"

而查拉图斯特拉安静地站在那里，他在沉思。最后，他悲伤地说道："这里的任何事物都变小了！

无论我走到任何地方，我都能看到非常矮小的门：和我有同样身高的人还能过去，但是——他必须得弯着腰过去！

啊，究竟要到什么时候我才能再一次回到我的家乡，再也不用弯着腰穿过去了——

Oh, when shall I arrive again at my home, where I shall no longer have to stoop- shall no longer have to stoop before the small ones!"- And Zarathustra sighed, and gazed into the distance.-

The same day, however, he spoke on the virtue that makes small.

2.

I pass through this people and keep my eyes open: they do not forgive me for not envying their virtues.

They bite at me, because I say to them that for small people, small virtues are necessary- and because it is hard for me to understand that small people are necessary!

Here am I still like a cock in a strange farm-yard, at which even the hens peck: but on that account I am not unfriendly to the hens.

I am courteous towards them, as towards all small annoyances; to be prickly towards what is small, seems to me wisdom for hedgehogs.

They all speak of me when they sit around their fire in the evening- they speak of me, but no one thinks- of me!

This is the new stillness which I have experienced: their noise around me spreads a mantle over my thoughts.

They shout to one another: "What is this gloomy cloud about to do to us? Let us see that it

回到再也不用对侏儒弯着腰的家乡！”——查拉图斯特拉叹了口气，随后，他开始眺望远方。

但是，就在同一天，他讲了侏儒的道德。

（2）

我从这个人的身边走过，我一直让我的眼睛张开着：因为我没有嫉妒他们的道德，所以，他们是不会原谅我的。

他们啃咬我，因为我对他们说，侏儒必须拥有属于侏儒的道德——我始终都很难理解侏儒存在的必要性！

我仍旧像一个古怪农场里面的雄鸡，即使是母鸡也会啄咬我，但是，这并不能说明我对母鸡们是不友好的。

我对待它们非常有礼貌，就如同对待一个小小的麻烦一样，我认为对于渺小的事物竖起尖刺，那是刺猬的智慧。

到了夜晚，当他们围坐在篝火面前的时候，他们都在谈论我——他们都在反复谈论着我，但是，在他们当中没有一个思索着我！

这是我刚刚经历过的全新的宁静：他们的喧闹在我的周围为我的思想披上了一个斗篷。

他们彼此叫喊着：“这充满忧郁的云朵到底想向我们索要什么呢？我们要小心提防别让它给我们带来一种传染病吧！”

does not bring a plague upon us!"

And recently did a woman seize upon her child that was coming to me: "Take the children away," cried she, "such eyes scorch children's souls."

They cough when I speak: they think coughing an objection to strong winds- they divine nothing of the boisterousness of my happiness!

"We have not yet time for Zarathustra"- so they object; but what matter about a time that "has no time" for Zarathustra?

And if they should altogether praise me, how could I go to sleep on their praise? A girdle of spines is their praise to me: it scratches me even when I take it off.

And this also did I learn among them: the praiser does as if he gave back; in truth, however, he wants more to be given him!

Ask my foot if their lauding and luring strains please it! to such measure and ticktack, it likes neither to dance nor to stand still.

To small virtues would they rather lure and laud me; to the ticktack of small happiness would they rather persuade my foot.

I pass through this people and keep my eyes open; they have become smaller, and ever become smaller:- the reason thereof is their doctrine of happiness and virtue.

For they are moderate also in virtue,- because they want comfort. With comfort, however, moderate virtue only is compatible.

To be sure, they also learn in their way to stride on and stride forward: that, I call their

最近，一个女人抓住了她的孩子，让他不要向我靠近，“快让孩子们都避开吧！”她大喊道，“这样的眼睛会烧毁孩子们的灵魂。”

当我说话的时候，他们开始咳嗽：他们认为咳嗽是对猛烈的风暴的抵抗，他们根本无法猜测到我的幸福的欢悦！

“我们没有多余的时间留给查拉图斯特拉了。”——他们开始如是反对着，不过，一个“没有时间”留给查拉图斯特拉的时间，又能具有什么价值呢？

即便是他们聚在一起夸奖我，那么，在他们的夸奖之下，我又怎么能睡得着觉呢？对于我来说，他们的夸奖就是一条腰带：即使我将它拿掉，它还是在用刺扎我。

而这些也是我从人们当中学到的：称赞者假装想得到回报的样子，但是，事实上他想要的回报比假装索要的更多！

你可以问问我的脚，看看它们是否喜欢他们的赞美和充满诱惑的音乐！说真的，它并不愿意在那样的滴答节拍下跳舞，或者安静地站在原地。

他们会向我赞美他们自己的小道德，并且诱惑我；他们喜欢用小幸福的滴答节拍说服我的脚。

我从这个人身边走过，并且让我的眼睛张开着；他们已经变得越来越小，而且还将继续变得越来越小——他们变得越来越小的原因是由于他们的幸福的教条和道德。

因为在道德中，他们同样保持谦虚——因为他们要寻求舒适安逸。但是，只有谦逊的道德，才能跟舒适安逸和睦共处，协调一致。

毋庸置疑，他们也在用他们自己的方式学着前进的脚步：我管这叫跛行。因此，他们变成了所有匆忙的人们的障碍物。

hobbling.- Thereby they become a hindrance to all who are in haste.

And many of them go forward, and look backwards thereby, with stiffened necks: those do I like to run up against.

Foot and eye shall not lie, nor give the lie to each other. But there is much lying among small people.

Some of them will, but most of them are willed. Some of them are genuine, but most of them are bad actors.

There are actors without knowing it amongst them, and actors without intending it-, the genuine ones are always rare, especially the genuine actors.

Of man there is little here: therefore do their women masculinize themselves. For only he who is man enough, will- save the woman in woman.

And this hypocrisy found I worst amongst them, that even those who command feign the virtues of those who serve.

"I serve, you serve, we serve"- so chants here even the hypocrisy of the rulers- and alas! if the first lord be only the first servant!

Ah, even upon their hypocrisy did my eyes' curiosity alight; and well did I divine all their fly- happiness, and their buzzing around sunny window-panes.

So much kindness, so much weakness do I see. So much justice and pity, so much weakness.

Round, fair, and considerate are they to one another, as grains of sand are round, fair, and considerate to grains of sand.

他们当中的许多人在向前走的时候，还会挺着僵硬的脖子回头看：我非常愿意碰见这样的人。

脚和眼睛是不会说谎的，也不会互相拆穿谎话。但是，在侏儒当中却有相当多的谎言。

他们当中的有些人是有意志的，不过，他们当中的绝大多数人是“被意志”的。他们当中的有些人是诚实正直的，但是，他们当中的绝大多数人是恶劣的表演者。

在他们当中有一些非自觉的，不是出于本意的表演者，那些诚实正直的人永远都是稀缺的，特别是诚实正直的表演者。

他们很少具有男性的特点：因此，妇人们会将自己男性化。只有男人味十足的人，才能够拯救妇人。

而这是我在他们中间发现的最糟糕的伪善，即使是命令者也会假装服务者的道德。

“我服务，你服务，我们大家都服务”——统治者的伪善也如是歌唱着，倘若最高的领主仅仅是最高的奴仆，那该有多么的不幸啊！

哎，我那冒着好奇之光的眼睛能够看见他们的伪善，我很好地猜到了他们的蝇的幸福和面向阳光的玻璃窗。

在充满仁慈和善意的地方，我同样看到了同等的软弱。在充满争议和怜悯的地方，我同样看到了同等的软弱。

他们会用圆滑的、公平公正的、慎重的态度对待彼此，有如圆滑、公平和慎重的沙粒一样。

谦逊地拥抱小小的幸福——这就是他们所谓的“安命”！并且与此同时，他们早已

Modestly to embrace a small happiness- that do they call "submission"! and at the same time they peer modestly after a new small happiness.

In their hearts they want simply one thing most of all: that no one hurt them. Thus do they anticipate every one's wishes and do well to every one.

That, however, is cowardice, though it be called "virtue."-

And when they chance to speak harshly, those small people, then do I hear therein only their hoarseness- every draught of air makes them hoarse.

Shrewd indeed are they, their virtues have shrewd fingers. But they lack fists: their fingers do not know how to creep behind fists.

Virtue for them is what makes modest and tame: therewith have they made the wolf a dog, and man himself man's best domestic animal.

"We set our chair in the midst"- so says their smirking to me- "and as far from dying gladiators as from satisfied swine."

That, however, is- mediocrity, though it be called moderation.-

3.

I pass through this people and let fall many words: but they know neither how to take nor how to retain them.

They wonder why I came not to revile venery and vice; and verily, I came not to warn

谦逊地偷偷观察到了新的小小的幸福。

在他们的内心当中，他们非常渴望一件事：那就是不能让任何人伤害他们。因此，他们对所有人都非常体贴，并且擅长随机应变。

但是，这就是懦弱的行为，尽管这被人们称为“道德”。

而当他们偶然严厉的说话的时候，我唯一能听到的只有他们的刺耳的叫声——因为每一阵风都会让他们感觉到喉咙嘶哑。

的确，他们是无比狡猾的，他们的道德拥有灵巧的手指。但是，他们没有拳头：他们的手指不知道该如何弯曲形成一个拳头。

在他们看来，道德能够让世间万物谦逊而驯服：就这样，他们把狼变成了狗，将人变成了最好的家畜。

“我们将椅子放在了正中间”——他们傻笑着对我说道——“快要死去的角斗士和欢喜的猪豚的距离是相等的。”

但是，这就是平庸，尽管人们称它为“节制”。

（3）

我从这个人身边走过，并且抛掷了很多话语：但是，他们并不懂得该如何获取，也不懂得该如何保留它们。

他们在好奇为什么我会来这里，而不咒骂纵欲和恶意；说真的，我来到这里也不是为了警醒别人时刻提防扒手！

against pickpockets either!

They wonder why I am not ready to abet and whet their wisdom: as if they had not yet enough of wiseacres, whose voices grate on my ear like slate-pencils!

And when I call out: "Curse all the cowardly devils in you, that would rather whimper and fold the hands and adore"- then do they shout: "Zarathustra is godless."

And especially do their teachers of submission shout this;- but precisely in their ears do I love to cry: "Yes! I am Zarathustra, the godless!"

Those teachers of submission! Wherever there is anything puny, or sickly, or scabby, there do they creep like lice; and only my disgust prevents me from cracking them.

Well! This is my sermon for their ears: I am Zarathustra the godless, who says: "Who is more godless than I, that I may enjoy his teaching?"

I am Zarathustra the godless: where do I find my equal? And all those are my equals who give to themselves their Will, and divest themselves of all submission.

I am Zarathustra the godless! I cook every chance in my pot. And only when it has been quite cooked do I welcome it as my food.

And verily, many a chance came imperiously to me: but still more imperiously did my Will speak to it,- then did it lie imploringly upon its knees-

-Imploring that it might find home and heart with me, and saying flatteringly: "See, O Zarathustra, how friend only comes to friend!"-

But why talk I, when no one has my ears! And so will I shout it out to all the winds:

他们在好奇为什么我没有准备好教唆和刺激他们的智慧：就好像他们中间还没有足够多的自作聪明的人，但是，那些自作聪明的人的声音就像石笔一样在我的耳朵上响着！

当我大声吼道："我诅咒在你们身上所有懦弱的恶魔，它们钟爱呜咽，双手交叉着崇拜"——然后他们开始叫喊道："查拉图斯特拉是无神的。"

他们的安命之教师叫喊得尤其响亮——；但是，我非常喜欢对着他们的耳朵叫喊："是的！我就是查拉图斯特拉，我就是无神的！"

那些安命之教师啊！凡是拥有卑鄙癖疥与病疾的地方，他们就会像虱子一样爬行；并且只有我的厌恶才会阻止我去压碎他们。

好吧！这就是我对他们的耳朵进行的说教：我是无神的查拉图斯特拉，他说道："有谁能够比我还要无神，让我尽情享受他的说教？"

我就是无神的查拉图斯特拉：我的同胞们都在什么地方？我的同胞们是将他们的意志给予自己，并且被剥夺了对所谓安命的知情权。

我就是无神的查拉图斯特拉！我把所有的机遇都放在我的铁锅里烹煮。等到那些机遇被烹煮完毕后，我才会欢迎它们成为我的养料。

说真的，许多机遇都会傲慢地向我走来：但是，我的意志会用更加傲慢的姿态对他们说话，——然后，他们立刻会跪倒在我的面前。

他们恳求我能够在这里找到住所和热切的心，他们讨好地对我说道："看啊！查拉图斯特拉，只有朋友才会前来拜访朋友啊！"

但是，当所有人都不聆听我的讲话的时候，那么我何必要说话，所以，我对所有的风喊叫道：

You ever become smaller, you small people! You crumble away, you comfortable ones! You will yet perish-

-By your many small virtues, by your many small omissions, and by your many small submissions!

Too tender, too yielding: so is your soil! But for a tree to become great, it seeks to twine hard roots around hard rocks!

Also what you omit weaves at the web of all the human future; even your naught is a cobweb, and a spider that lives on the blood of the future.

And when you take, then is it like stealing, you small virtuous ones; but even among knaves honor says that "one shall only steal when one cannot rob."

"It gives itself"- that is also a doctrine of submission. But I say to you, you comfortable ones, that it takes to itself, and will ever take more and more from you!

Ah, that you would renounce all half-willing, and would decide for idleness as you decide for action!

Ah, that you understood my word: "Do ever what you will- but first be such as can will.

Love ever your neighbor as yourselves- but first be such as love themselves-

-Such as love with great love, such as love with great contempt!" Thus speaks Zarathustra the godless.-

But why talk I, when no one has my ears! It is still an hour too early for me here.

My own forerunner am I among this people, my own cockcrow in dark lanes.

你们这些侏儒们，你们会永远变小，你们这些贪图舒适安逸的家伙们，你们会被剥落的干干净净，你们的意志会因为你们许多小小的道德、小小的省略以及小小的安命而消逝！

你们太过于脆弱，太过于屈服了：这里本来是你们出生的土地，但是如果一棵树要想长高，它就必须用强韧的树根紧紧抱住坚硬的岩石！

你们所遗漏的东西正在给所有的人类的未来编织着蜘蛛网；即使你们的无能也是一个蜘蛛网以及一个生活在未来的血液之上的蜘蛛。

小小的有德之人啊！当你们获取的时候，就好像偷窃一样；但是，即便是对于偷窃者来说，荣誉也有权力说话：“只有在不能抢劫的地方，才允许偷窃。”

“这是给予的”——这同时也是安命的教条。但是，我要告诉你们，你们这些贪图舒适安逸的家伙们，这些都是拿来的，它还将会在你们的身上拿走越来越多的东西！

啊，你们为何不丢弃所有的“半意识”呢，你们为什么不决定将懒惰作为你们的抉择的行动呢！

啊，你们理解我的话语的含义：“去做你们想做的事情吧！——但是，你们首先要做一个有意志的人。

热爱你们的邻居就像热爱你们自己一样——但是，你们首先要成为能够自我怜爱的人。——成为用伟大的热爱和伟大的轻蔑怜爱自己的人！”无神的查拉图斯特拉如是说道。

但是，当没有人聆听我的话语的时候，我为何要开口说话！这个时刻对于我来说，实在是太早了。

在这个人民当中，我是自己的先驱者，在黑暗的道路之上，我是黑夜里的破晓。

But their hour comes! And there comes also mine! Hourly do they become smaller, poorer, unfruitfuller,- poor herbs! poor earth!

And soon shall they stand before me like dry grass and prairie, and verily, weary of themselves- and panting for fire, more than for water!

O blessed hour of the lightning! O mystery before noontide!- Running fires will I one day make of them, and heralds with flaming tongues:-

-Herald shall they one day with flaming tongues: It comes, it is nigh, the great noontide!

Thus spoke Zarathustra.

50. The Mount of Olives

WINTER, a bad guest, sits with me at home; blue are my hands with his friendly hand-shaking.

I honor him, that bad guest, but gladly leave him alone. Gladly do I run away from him; and when one runs well, then one escapes him!

With warm feet and warm thoughts do I run where the wind is calm- to the sunny corner of my olive-mount.

There do I laugh at my stern guest, and am still fond of him; because he clears my house of flies, and quiets many little noises.

但是，属于他们的时刻到来了！同样地，属于我的时刻也来到了！时间一分一秒地过去，他们变得越来越小，越来越落魄，越来越无法繁殖——可怜的盆草和可怜的土地啊！

很快，他们就会像干燥的草地和大草原一样站在我的面前，说真的，他们对于自己也产生了厌倦——他们更加需要的是火而不是水！

啊，受到祝福的闪电之时刻啊！啊，矗立在正午之前的谜团啊！——终有一天，我会让他们成为奔跑的烈焰，成为舌头冒火的预言家：

——终有一天，他们会成为舌头冒火的预言家：那伟大的正午就要来了，它离这里越来越近。

查拉图斯特拉如是说。

50．在橄榄山上

冬天，一个邪恶的客人，跟我一起坐在家里；我的双手因为他那友好的握手而变得毫无血色。

我尊敬他，那个邪恶的客人，但是我喜欢他独自坐在一个地方。我特别喜欢从他的身边跑开；当你跑得足够快的时候，你就能离开他！

我用温暖的双脚和温暖的思想跑到了风平浪静的地方——跑到了我的橄榄山之上被太阳照射的角落。

在那里，我嘲笑着我的严肃的客人，我仍旧非常喜欢他；因为他帮忙清理掉了我的房子里的苍蝇，并且帮我平息了许许多多的小噪音。

一两个苍蝇的嗡嗡声并不会让他感到遭受到了苦难，他让所有的道路变得孤独寂寞，

For he suffers it not if a gnat wants to buzz, or even two of them; also the lanes makes he lonesome, so that the moonlight is afraid there at night.

A hard guest is he,- but I honor him, and do not worship, like the tenderlings, the pot-bellied fire-idol.

Better even a little teeth-chattering than idol-adoration!- so wills my nature. And especially have I a grudge against all ardent, steaming, steamy fire-idols.

Him whom I love, I love better in winter than in summer; better do I now mock at my enemies, and more heartily, when winter sits in my house.

Heartily, verily, even when I creep into bed-: there, still laughs and wantons my hidden happiness; even my deceptive dream laughs.

I, a- creeper? Never in my life did I creep before the powerful; and if ever I lied, then did I lie out of love. Therefore am I glad even in my winter-bed.

A poor bed warms me more than a rich one, for I am jealous of my poverty. And in winter she is most faithful to me.

With a wickedness do I begin every day: I mock at the winter with a cold bath: on that account grumbles my stern house-mate.

Also do I like to tickle him with a wax-taper, that he may finally let the heavens emerge from ashy-grey twilight.

For especially wicked am I in the morning: at the early hour when the pail rattles at the well,

因此，在那里，夜晚的月光也会感到害怕。

他是一个非常强硬的客人，但是我尊敬他，并不是像虚弱者之对于大肚腩的火神那样崇拜他。

即使是小小的唇枪舌剑也要比崇拜偶像什么的强得多！——我的天性让我如是。特别是我非常讨厌所有热情的、蒸汽的火神。

那个我所挚爱的，我在冬季要比在夏季更加热爱的他，我现在嘲笑了我的敌人们，而且当冬天在我的房子里坐下的时候，我的嘲笑要比之前更加剧烈。

真的，要更加剧烈一些，甚至是当我爬上床之后：——甚至于我的隐藏的幸福仍旧在嘲笑和嬉戏打闹；即使是我的具有欺骗性的梦境也会嘲笑。

我，难道是一个爬行者吗？在我的人生当中，我还从来都没有在力量的面前爬行过；而且如果我躺下来的话，那么，我是为了爱情而选择躺下来。因此，当我在冬天躺在床上的时候，我还是非常高兴的。

一个破旧的床要比奢华的床更能温暖我。因为我总是嫉妒我的贫穷。在冬季，她是对我最忠诚的。

每一天的开始，我都会做一件非常邪恶的事情：我用冰冷的淋浴嘲笑冬季：为此，我的严肃的客人曾经抱怨和怨恨过。

同样地，我还喜欢用一个细蜡烛哄他开心，所以，到了最后，他让蓝天从灰色的曙光之中展现了出来。

特别是在早晨的时候，我会做坏事，在清晨的时候，提桶在井里面发出声响，而马匹则在灰色的道路上喘着炽热的粗气：

我开始烦躁的等待，直到最后清澈的蓝天出现在我的面前，雪之胡须的冬季天空，

and horses neigh warmly in grey lanes:-

Impatiently do I then wait, that the clear sky may finally dawn for me, the snow-bearded winter-sky, the hoary one, the white-head,-

-The winter-sky, the silent winter-sky, which often stifles even its sun!

Did I perhaps learn from it the long clear silence? Or did it learn it from me? Or has each of us created it himself?

Of all good things the origin is a thousandfold,- all good roguish things spring into existence for joy: how could they always do so- for once only!

A good roguish thing is also the long silence, and to look, like the winter-sky, out of a clear, round-eyed countenance:-

-Like it to stifle one's sun, and one's inflexible solar will: verily, this art and this winter-roguishness have I learned well!

My best-loved wickedness and art is it, that my silence has learned not to betray itself by silence.

Clattering with diction and dice, I outwit the solemn assistants: all those stern watchers, shall my will and purpose elude.

That no one might see down into my depth and into my ultimate will- for that purpose did I create the long clear silence.

Many a shrewd one did I find: he veiled his countenance and made his water muddy, that no one might see therethrough and thereunder.

But precisely to him came the shrewder distrusters and nut-crackers: precisely from him did

默不作声的冬季天空，

它甚至经常憋闷于冬天的太阳里的冬季天空！

我或许可以从中学习长久、清澈的沉默？又或是让它从我这里学习吗？又或是我们都各自发明？

任何事物都有着上千种来源——所有的恶作剧都会为了快乐而存在，他们又何止仅仅做一次呢！

一个好的善事和恶作剧同样也是长久的沉默，正如冬天里的天空一样，在散发着光亮的圆圆的眼睛里窥视着：

——犹如冬季的天空一样，憋闷了自己的太阳，憋闷了自己不屈挠的太阳的意志：说真的，我已经将这种技艺和这种冬天的恶作剧学习得很透彻了！

那是我最钟爱的恶作剧和技艺，我的寂静已经学会了不因沉默而暴露自己。

用措辞和骰子的喋喋不休，我以机智战胜了庄严的助手：我的意志和目的会躲避所有那些严肃的观看者们。

没有任何人能够窥探到我的内心深处，窥探到我的终极的意志——正是出于这个目的，我为自己创造了长久、清澈的寂静。

我发现了很多精明的人：他蒙住了自己的面孔，并且让他的水变得浑浊，让人们无法从那里看到下面。

但是那些更加精明的不信任的人以及敲碎坚果的人们，在向他走来：他们正要从他那里钓上最隐秘的大鱼！

they fish his best-concealed fish!

But the clear, the honest, the transparent- these are for me the wisest silent ones: in them, so profound is the depth that even the clearest water does not- betray it.-

You snow-bearded, silent, winter-sky, you round-eyed whitehead above me! Oh, you heavenly parable of my soul and its wantonness!

And must I not conceal myself like one who has swallowed gold- lest my soul should be ripped up?

Must I not wear stilts, that they may overlook my long legs- all those enviers and injurers around me?

Those dingy, fire-warmed, used-up, green-tinted, ill-natured souls- how could their envy endure my happiness!

Thus do I show them only the ice and winter of my peaks- and not that my mountain winds all the solar girdles around it!

They hear only the whistling of my winter-storms: and know not that I also travel over warm seas, like longing, heavy, hot south-winds.

They commiserate also my accidents and chances:- but my word says: "Suffer the chance to come to me: innocent is it as a little child!"

How could they endure my happiness, if I did not put around it accidents, and winter-privations, and bear-skin caps, and enmantling snowflakes!

-If I did not myself commiserate their pity, the pity of those enviers and injurers!

-If I did not myself sigh before them, and chatter with cold, and patiently let myself be

不过，在我看来，最聪明的寂静者们就是那些清澈的、诚实的以及坦率的人们：在他们的内心深处是那么的深沉，即便是最清澈的水也不能将它暴露出来。

啊，雪之胡须的冬季天空，默不作声的冬季天空，拥有圆圆的眼睛的沉默者啊！啊，你就是我的灵魂和快乐的神圣预言啊！

我不得不将自己隐藏起来，就像吞噬金子的人一样——唯恐我的灵魂被他们撕碎吗？

我不得不踩着高跷走路，让我周围的那些嫉妒者和受伤者不去注视着我的长长的腿吗？

那些肮脏的、烟熏的、疲惫不堪的、发霉的、恶意的灵魂——他们的嫉妒又怎能忍受我的幸福呢！

我只愿意向他们展示我的峰顶之上的冰雪和寒冬——而不愿意向他们展示我的太阳围绕着的山峰！

他们只能听到我的寒冬风暴的呼啸声：但是他们并不知道我同样还会穿越温暖的海洋，就像充满渴望的、沉重的、炙热的南部之风一样。

他们同样会同情我的不幸和机遇：——但是我说道：“让机遇来到我的身边吧！它就像一个小孩子一样天真无邪！”

倘若我不散播不幸和机遇、寒冬的苦难、熊皮的帽子以及包裹在它周围的雪花之外套，他们又怎么能够忍受我的幸福呢！

倘若我不同情这些嫉妒者和受伤者的慈悲！

倘若我不在他们的面前叹息，与寒冷交谈，并且耐心地让自己被他们的慈悲所包围！

swathed in their pity!

This is the wise waggish-will and good-will of my soul, that it conceals not its winters and glacial storms; it conceals not its chilblains either.

To one man, solitude is the flight of the sick one; to another, it is the flight from the sick ones.

Let them hear me chattering and sighing with winter-cold, all those poor squinting knaves around me! With such sighing and chattering do I flee from their heated rooms.

Let them sympathise with me and sigh with me on account of my chilblains: "At the ice of knowledge will he yet freeze to death!"- so they mourn.

Meanwhile do I run with warm feet here and there on my olive-mount: in the sunny corner of my olive-mount do I sing, and mock at all pity.-

Thus sang Zarathustra.

51. Passing By

THUS slowly wandering through many peoples and divers cities, did Zarathustra return by round-about roads to his mountains and his cave. And behold, thereby came he unawares also to the gate of the great city. Here, however, a foaming fool, with extended hands, sprang forward to him and stood in his way. It was the same fool whom the people called "the ape of Zarathustra:" for he had learned from him something of the expression and modulation of language, and perhaps liked also to borrow from the store of his wisdom. And the fool talked

这就是我的灵魂明智的意志和善意的意志，它并不会隐藏自己的寒冬和冰川风暴；它同样也不会隐藏自己的冻疮。

对于一个人来说，孤独是身体虚弱者的避难所，而另外一种孤独则是远离疾病的安全住所。

所有那些贫穷的围在我身边的斜眼的无赖们，让他们聆听我和冬天的寒冷的谈话以及叹息吧！在这样的叹息和交谈之中，我逃离了他们那炎热的房间。

让他们同情我的冻疮，并且为我感到叹息吧："我们将会看着他冻死在知识的冰窖里！"——他们如是悲叹道。

与此同时，我用温暖的脚掌在我的橄榄山上到处奔跑：我会在我的橄榄山上被太阳照射的角落里歌唱，并且嘲笑所有的慈悲。

查拉图斯特拉如是唱着。

51. 路过

查拉图斯特拉缓慢地游历了许多民族和各种各样的城市，然后他采取绕道的方式回到了他的山峰和他的洞穴。不过，快看啊！在查拉图斯特拉行走的时候，他不知不觉来到了伟大城市的大门口。然而，这里有一个满嘴吐着泡沫的傻子，将两只手伸开，朝他跑来，阻挡住了查拉图斯特拉的去路。这个傻子和被人们成为"查拉图斯特拉之猿"的傻子是同一个人。因为他曾经从查拉图斯特拉那里学过一些语言的表达和腔调的调整，

thus to Zarathustra:

O Zarathustra, here is the great city: here have you nothing to seek and everything to lose.

Why would you wade through this mire? Have pity upon your foot! Spit rather on the gate of the city, and- turn back!

Here is the hell for hermits' thoughts: here are great thoughts seethed alive and boiled small.

Here do all great sentiments decay: here may only rattle-boned sensations rattle!

Smell you not already the shambles and cookshops of the spirit? Steams not this city with the fumes of slaughtered spirit?

See you not the souls hanging like limp dirty rags?- And they make newspapers also out of these rags!

Hear you not how spirit has here become a verbal game? Loathsome verbal swill does it vomit forth!- And they make newspapers also out of this verbal swill.

They hound one another, and know not where! They inflame one another, and know not why! They tinkle with their pinchbeck, they jingle with their gold.

They are cold, and seek warmth from distilled waters: they are inflamed, and seek coolness from frozen spirits; they are all sick and sore through public opinion.

All lusts and vices are here at home; but here there are also the virtuous; there is much appointable appointed virtue:-

Much appointable virtue with scribe-fingers, and hardy sitting-flesh and waiting-flesh, blessed with small breast-stars, and padded, haunchless daughters.

他还借用了查拉图斯特拉的智慧的宝藏。那个傻子对查拉图斯特拉如是说：

啊，查拉图斯特拉，这里就是伟大之城：在这里你将会一无所有，同时也会一无所失。

为什么你会涉过泥沼？请爱惜你的脚掌吧！宁肯唾弃伟大之城的大门，并且转身离去！

这里是所有隐士的思想的地狱：这里所有的思想都会被活生生地煮沸。

在这里，所有伟大的情感都会腐朽：在这里只有骨头的哀嚎！

你有没有闻到精神的庖房和肉食店的腐臭味呢？这个城市里不是蒸腾着杀戮的精神的香气吗？

难道你看不到那些像干瘪和肮脏的破布一样悬挂起来的灵魂吗？——并且他们会在这样的破布中制造出新闻！

难道你听不到吗？在这里，精神是如何成为一个口头的游戏？精神吐出了令人厌恶的言语的污秽，——同样，他们会从这样的言语的污秽中制造出新闻！

他们彼此互相追逐，却不知自己身在何处！他们彼此互相激怒，却不知原因何在！他们敲击着他们的金色黄铜，他们把他们的黄金敲得叮当响。

他们是冰冷的，他们从蒸馏水中寻找温暖，他们浑身炙热，却在冰冷的精神当中寻找清凉，在大众言论的影响下，他们会生病和受伤。

这里是所有的欲望和所有的罪恶的家园；但是这里同时也是道德的家园；这里拥有很多实用的、有用的道德：

很多有用的道德都拥有抄写员一样的手指，强壮的文坐和期待之臀，以装饰女郎的乳房和腰肢引以为豪。

There is here also much piety, and much faithful spittle-licking and spittle-backing, before the God of Hosts.

"From on high," drips the star, and the gracious spittle; for the high, longs every starless bosom.

The moon has its court, and the court has its moon-calves: to all, however, that comes from the court do the mendicant people pray, and all appointable mendicant virtues.

"I serve, you serve, we serve"- so prays all appointable virtue to the prince: that the merited star may at last stick on the slender breast!

But the moon still revolves around all that is earthly: so revolves also the prince around what is earthliest of all- that, however, is the gold of the shopman.

The God of the Hosts of war is not the God of the golden bar; the prince proposes, but the shopman- disposes!

By all that is luminous and strong and good in you, O Zarathustra! Spit on this city of shopmen and return back!

Here flows all blood putridly and tepidly and frothily through all veins: spit on the great city, which is the great slum where all the scum froths together!

Spit on the city of compressed souls and slender breasts, of pointed eyes and sticky fingers-

-On the city of the obtrusive, the brazen-faced, the pen-demagogues and tongue-demagogues, the overheated ambitious:-

Where everything maimed, ill-famed, lustful, untrustful, over-mellow, sickly-yellow and seditious, festers perniciously:-

这里，在军队之上帝的面前，拥有很多虔诚、很多正教，实行谄媚。

勋章和优雅的唾沫从高处掉落下来，因此，那些没有勋章的人们都会抬起头仰望着天空。

月亮有属于它自己的朝堂，而朝堂也拥有它自己的月牙儿，所以，那些乞讨食物的人们，怀着行乞的道德的人们，祈祷着所有从朝堂里掉落下来的东西。

“我服务，你服务，我们大家都服务”——所有实用的道德对王子乞讨：最终，这个应得的勋章就会簪在细长的胸膛之上！

但是，月亮始终围绕着所有世俗的东西旋转：王子也会围绕着所有的世俗的东西旋转——那就是小商贩的金子。

战争军队之神并不是金块之神；王子在有所酝酿着，但是小商贩在处理着！

啊，查拉图斯特拉啊！你身上的一切都是那么的灿烂、强壮和善良！唾弃这座伟大之城的小商贩们，然后转身离去吧！

这里所有的血液在血管里流淌着，它腐烂、微温，并且轻薄；唾弃这座伟大之城，这里就是所有的废弃之物汇聚在一起的巨大的贫民窟！

唾弃这被压缩的灵魂和细长的胸脯之城，这拥有尖尖的眼睛和黏黏的手指的城市。

唾弃这流氓的城市，这个厚面皮，笔之煽动者和舌头之煽动者，这太过于激动的野心勃勃者：

这里的一切都是残缺、畸形、贪欲、不被信任、烂熟、黄病、脓溃而有毒的：

唾弃这座伟大的城市，然后转身离开吧！

-Spit on the great city and turn back!-

Here, however, did Zarathustra interrupt the foaming fool, and shut his mouth.-

Stop this at once! called out Zarathustra, long have your speech and your species disgusted me!

Why did you live so long by the swamp, that you yourself had to become a frog and a toad?

Flows there not a tainted, frothy, swamp-blood in your own veins, when you have thus learned to croak and revile?

Why went you not into the forest? Or why did you not till the ground? Is the sea not full of green islands?

I despise your contempt; and when you warned me- why did you not warn yourself?

Out of love alone shall my contempt and my warning bird take wing; but not out of the swamp!-

They call you my ape, you foaming fool: but I call you my grunting-pig,- by your grunting, you spoil even my praise of folly.

What was it that first made you grunt? Because no one sufficiently flattered you:- therefore did you seat yourself beside this filth, that you might have cause for much grunting,-

-That you might have cause for much vengeance! For vengeance, you vain fool, is all your foaming; I have divined you well!

But your fools'-word injures me, even when you are right! And even if Zarathustra's word were a hundred times justified, you would ever- do wrong with my word!

Thus spoke Zarathustra. Then did he look on the great city and sighed, and was long silent.

然而，就在这个时候，查拉图斯特拉打断了那个口吐泡沫的傻子的讲话，并且让那个傻子闭上嘴巴。

快点停下来吧！查拉图斯特拉大喊道，你的讲话和你的同类，在很长一段时间内都让我感到非常恶心！

为什么你要在沼泽里住这么长的时间，直到你自己都变成了一只青蛙和一只蛤蟆呢？

你自己的血管里不是流淌着污染的、轻薄的、沼泽之血吗？所以，你才学会了咯咯咯地鸣叫和辱骂吗？

为什么你不去森林里呢？或是为什么你不耕种土地呢？难道大海当中不是充满了绿意葱葱的岛屿吗？

我鄙视你们的轻蔑，当你们在警告我的时候——你们为什么不警告你们自己呢？

仅仅是因为爱，我的轻蔑和我的警告之鸟才会展开翅膀翱翔；而不是在沼泽里翱翔！

人们都说你是我的猿类，你这个口吐泡沫的傻子：但是，我要将你称作是我的爱发牢骚的猪——由于你的爱发牢骚，甚至破坏了我对于傻子的赞扬。

最早能够让你发牢骚的是什么呢？因为所有人都不足以讨好你：——因此，你坐在了污水的旁边，你还会有更多的发牢骚的理由，

那样的话，你也就有了更多报复的理由！你这个怠慢的傻子啊！你的报复就是你的所有的嗔怒；我已经彻底猜透了你！

但是，你那种傻子的话语伤害了我，即便你说的话是对的！而且，即使查拉图斯特拉的话语的真实性被检验了上百遍，可你还是错用了我的话语！

At last he spoke thus:

I loathe also this great city, and not only this fool. Here and there- there is nothing to better, nothing to worsen.

Woe to this great city!- And I would that I already saw the pillar of fire in which it will be consumed!

For such pillars of fire must precede the great noontide. But this has its time and its own fate.-

This precept, however, give I to you, in parting, you fool: Where one can no longer love, there should one- pass by!-

Thus spoke Zarathustra, and passed by the fool and the great city.

52. The Apostates

1.

AH, LIES everything already withered and grey which but lately stood green and many-hued on this meadow! And how much honey of hope did I carry hence into my beehives!

Those young hearts have already all become old- and not old even! only weary, ordinary, comfortable:- they declare it: "We have again become pious."

Of late did I see them run forth at early morn with valorous steps: but the feet of their

查拉图斯特拉如是说道。然后，他抬起头看着这座伟大的城市，叹了口气，并且在很长的时间里一言不发。最后，他如是说道：

我不仅仅是讨厌这个口吐泡沫的傻子，我还讨厌这座伟大之城。无论是在何处，都无所可善，也无所可恶。

我真替这座伟大之城感到悲哀！——但愿，我能够看到被烈火吞噬的石柱啊！

即便是这样的石柱也必须要在伟大的正午之前来到这里。但是，它有一定的时间以及一定的命运。

傻子啊！在分手道别的时候，我对你进行了这样的说教：自己不能再爱的地方，自己应该离开！

查拉图斯特拉如是说，然后他离开了那个傻子和那座伟大之城。

52．叛教者

（1）

唷！在这片最近还绿意葱葱的青草地上，如今已经变得枯萎而凋零了！我从这里将多少的蜂蜜之希望带回到我的蜂房里了啊！

那些年轻的心灵都已经开始变老了——甚至都没有变老！只是变得厌倦、变得平庸、变得舒适安逸：——他们宣称：“我们再一次开始变得虔诚。”

近来，我看到他们在清晨用勇猛的脚步奔跑：但是，他们的知识之脚开始变得疲倦，

knowledge became weary, and now do they malign even their morning valor!

Many of them once lifted their legs like the dancer; to them winked the laughter of my wisdom:- then did they bethink themselves. Just now have I seen them bent down- to crawl before the cross.

Around light and liberty did they once flutter like gnats and young poets. A little older, a little colder: and already are they mystifiers, and mumblers and mollycoddles.

Did perhaps their hearts despond, because solitude had swallowed me like a whale? Did their ear perhaps hearken yearningly-long for me in vain, and for my trumpet-notes and herald-calls?

-Ah! Ever are there but few of those whose hearts have persistent courage and exuberance; and in such remains also the spirit patient. The rest, however, are cowardly.

The rest: these are always the great majority, the common-place, the superfluous, the all-too-many- those all are cowardly!-

Him who is of my type, will also the experiences of my type meet on the way: so that his first companions must be corpses and fools.

His second companions, however- they will call themselves his believers,- will be a living host, with much love, much folly, much unbearded veneration.

To those believers shall he who is of my type among men not bind his heart; in those spring-times and many-hued meadows shall he not believe, who knows the fickly faint-hearted human species!

现在，他们甚至开始诽谤他们的晨间的勇猛！

说真的，他们中的大多数人都曾经像舞蹈者那样举起他们的腿；我的智慧的笑声向他们眨着眼睛示意：——然后，他们便会开始思考自己。现在，我甚至于都能看到他们弯下身子，向十字架的前方爬去！

他们曾经围绕着光亮和自由，扑闪着翅膀就像是蚊蚋和年轻的诗人一样。但却渐渐变老而渐渐变冷：现在，他们已然成为了神秘者、含糊其辞的人以及懦夫。

或许，他们的内心会让他们丧失勇气，因为孤独寂寞就像一头鲸鱼一样吞噬了我？或许，他们的耳朵已经渴望已久，但却没有聆听于我以及我的喇叭的鸣奏和我的先驱者的呐喊？

啊！在这里只有极少数的人拥有坚忍不拔的勇气和神清气爽的快活；在这些极少数的人的精神当中同样也拥有十足的耐心。但是，剩下的人都是胆小的懦夫。

其余的人：他们永远都是占大多数的人，他们是平庸的、多余的，严重过剩的人——他们全部都是懦夫！

跟我是同类的人，也同样会遇到我的同类的经验：所以，他的第一个同伴必定是尸体和傻子。

但是，他的第二个同伴，是自称为他的信徒的人们，是带着很多的爱，很多的傻气，很多健壮，受人尊敬的富有生气的大众。

我在人类当中的同伴，绝对不能让他的心灵依附于那些所谓的信徒们的身上；无论是任何人知道了浮躁而胆怯的人类种族之后，他们都不会相信这样的春季时光和五颜六色的草地！

Could they do otherwise, then would they also will otherwise. The half-and-half spoil every whole. That leaves become withered,- what is there to lament about that!

Let them go and fall away, O Zarathustra, and do not lament! Better even to blow amongst them with rustling winds,-

-Blow amongst those leaves, O Zarathustra, that everything withered may run away from you the faster!-

2.

"We have again become pious"- so do those apostates confess; and some of them are still too pusillanimous thus to confess. To them I look into the eye,- before them I say it to their face and to the blush on their cheeks: You are those who again pray!

It is shameful to pray! Not for all, but for you, and me, and whoever has his conscience in his head. For you it is shameful to pray!

You know it well: the faint-hearted devil in you, which would rather fold its arms, and place its hands in its bosom, and take it easier:- this faint-hearted devil persuades you that "there is a God!"

Thereby, however, do you belong to the light-dreading type, to whom light never permits repose: now must you daily thrust your head deeper into obscurity and vapor!

And verily, you choose the hour well: for just now do the nocturnal birds again fly abroad.

他们可以做别的事情，那么就让他们做别的事情吧。一样一半毁坏了一个整体。叶子开始变得枯萎，——为什么要悲叹那个呢！

啊，查拉图斯特拉啊，让他们死掉并且消亡吧！不要感到悲叹！最好要用沙沙作响的风猛吹它。

啊，查拉图斯特拉啊，猛吹那些树叶吧，让世间万物凋零的东西飞快地离开你！

（2）

“我们再一次变得虔诚”——那些叛教者这样坦白道；他们当中的某些人甚至还会胆怯于这样的坦白。我看着他们的眼睛，我当着他们的面和他们红红的面颊说道：“你们是再一次祈祷的人们！”

但是祈祷是非常可耻的！不是对于所有人来说都是可耻的，而是对于你，对于我以及脑海里存留着良知的人们来说。对于你来说，祈祷就是非常可耻的！

你很清楚：胆小、懦弱的恶魔就隐藏在你的体内，他宁愿将自己的胳膊折起来，然后随意地将双手放在胸前——这个胆小、懦弱的恶魔在说服你，“在这个世界上存在上帝！”

但是，你是属于那种非常害怕光亮的人，属于在光亮下永远也无法休息的人：现在，你每天都必须将自己的头插到更深的阴暗和蒸汽之中！

说真的，你选择的时刻非常恰当：因为就在现在，在夜里出没的鸟儿们开始再一次在外面翱翔了。所有惧怕光亮的人们的时刻就要来临了，黄昏的时刻和休闲的时刻就要

The hour has come for all light-dreading people, the vesper hour and leisure hour, when they do not- "take leisure."

I hear it and smell it: it has come- their hour for hunt and procession, not indeed for a wild hunt, but for a tame, lame, snuffling, soft-treaders', soft-prayers' hunt,-

-For a hunt after susceptible simpletons: all mouse-traps for the heart have again been set! And whenever I lift a curtain, a night-moth rushes out of it.

Did it perhaps squat there along with another night-moth? For everywhere do I smell small concealed communities; and wherever there are closets there are new devotees therein, and the atmosphere of devotees.

They sit for long evenings beside one another, and say: "Let us again become like little children and say, 'good God!'"- ruined in mouths and stomachs by the pious confectioners.

Or they look for long evenings at a crafty, lurking cross-spider, that preaches prudence to the spiders themselves, and teaches that "under crosses it is good for web-spinning!"

Or they sit all day at swamps with angle-rods, and on that account think themselves profound; but whoever fishes where there are no fish, I do not even call him superficial!

Or they learn in godly-gay style to play the harp with a hymn-poet, who would rather harp himself into the heart of young girls:- for he has tired of old girls and their praises.

Or they learn to shudder with a learned semi-madcap, who waits in darkened rooms for spirits to come to him- and the spirit runs away entirely!

Or they listen to an old roving howl- and growl-piper, who has learned from the sad winds

来临了，但是他们并没有休闲的时光。

我听到，并且闻到了：这个时刻马上就要来了——他们捕猎和列队行进的时刻来了，那并不是追捕野兽的捕猎，而是对于驯服的、跛足的、抽着鼻子的以及轻声祈祷者的捕猎。

一种追逐灵魂的伪善者之猎手：所有打击要害的捕鼠陷阱都已经安置好了！无论我从哪里拉起一扇窗帘，总会有夜间的飞蛾突然从里面飞出来。

难道它跟另一只夜间的飞蛾蹲守在这里？因为，我在任何地方都能够嗅到小小的隐秘的公社，只要是有密室的地方，就必定会有新的皈依者的到来以及皈依者的气味。

在慢慢的长夜里，他们彼此挨着坐在一起，然后说道："让我们再一次成为小孩子，并且嘟囔着 '亲爱的上帝！' "——虔诚的制造糖果的人，毁掉了嘴和胃。

或是，他们在慢慢的长夜中注视着一只灵巧的、潜伏的十字架之蜘蛛，这只蜘蛛会对它的同伴们进行审慎的说教，并且教育着"在十字架的下面是最适合编织蛛网的地方"！

又或是，他们一整天都拿着吊杆，坐在沼泽边，他们因此而认为自己非常深厚；但是，无论是谁在没有鱼出没的地方钓上来大鱼，我甚至会称他为肤浅的人！

或是他们欢快地、虔诚地在圣歌的诗人那里学习如何弹奏竖琴，那个圣歌的诗人最喜欢吹奏他的竖琴以此俘获年轻少女的芳心：——因为他已经厌倦了老女孩以及她们的赞美。

或是，他们从博学多才的鲁莽之人那里学会该如何发抖，这个鲁莽之人在黑暗的房间里等待着幽灵来到他的身边——然而，幽灵却完全跑掉了！

或是他们聆听年老浪游和咆哮的风笛手，模仿了悲伤的微风和悲伤之声的风笛手；

the sadness of sounds; now pips he as the wind, and preaches sadness in sad strains.

And some of them have even become night-watchmen: they know now how to blow horns, and go about at night and awaken old things which have long fallen asleep.

Five words about old things did I hear last night at the garden-wall: they came from such old, sorrowful, arid night-watchmen.

"For a father he cares not sufficiently for his children: human fathers do this better!"-

"He is too old! He now cares no more for his children,"- answered the other night-watchman.

"Has he then children? No one can prove it unless he himself prove it! I have long wished that he would for once prove it thoroughly."

"Prove? As if he had ever proved anything! Proving is difficult to him; he lays great stress on one's believing him."

"Ay! Ay! Belief saves him; belief in him. That is the way with old people! So it is with us also!"-

-Thus spoke to each other the two old night-watchmen and light-scarers, and tooted then sorrowfully on their horns: so did it happen last night at the garden-wall.

To me, however, did the heart writhe with laughter, and was like to break; it knew not where to go, and sunk into the midriff.

It will be my death yet- to choke with laughter when I see asses drunken, and hear night-watchmen thus doubt about God.

现在，他如同微风一样在风中咆哮，在忧伤的格调中说教着悲伤。

他们之中的一些人甚至成为了夜间的看守人：他们现在知道该如何吹奏号角了，并且知道在夜间的巡游中，唤醒了所有已经沉睡了很久的老东西了。

昨天晚上我在花园的围墙那里，听到了关于老东西的五句话：这些话甚至是从年迈的、悲伤的、沉闷的夜间看守人的嘴里说出来的。

“作为一个父亲来说，他并没有很好地照顾他的孩子们：人类的父亲在照顾孩子这方面要比他强得多！”

“他实在是太老了！他现在已经不再照顾他的孩子们了”——另一个夜间的看守人回答道。

“那么，他有孩子吗？但是，除非他自己证明，其他人都没法证明！很久以来，我一直期盼着他能够彻彻底底地证明一下自己。”

“证明？就好像他已经证明了所有的事情一样！证明对于他来说是非常困难的；他讨厌证明，他只是在强迫别人相信他而已。”

“哎！信仰拯救了他，他的心中有信仰。那就是老人的道路，也同样是我们的道路！”

——这两个年迈的夜间看守人和光之恐怖者在如是交谈着，然后他们忧伤地吹奏了号角：以上就是昨天晚上在花园的围墙边发生的事情。

但是，对于我来说，我的内心因为笑容而感到绞痛；我的心好像要碎掉一样；它早已迷失了方向，并且沉到了横隔膜里。

说真的，那几乎要了我的小命——因此，当我看到驴子喝得伶仃大醉的时候，我忍住了笑，而且，我听到了夜间的看守人如是地怀疑上帝。

Has the time not long since passed for all such doubts? Who may nowadays awaken such old slumbering, light-shunning things!

With the old Deities has it long since come to an end:- and verily, a good joyful Deity-end had they!

They did not "twilight" themselves to death- that do people fabricate! On the contrary, they- laughed themselves to death once on a time!

That took place when the ungodliest utterance came from a God himself- the utterance: "There is but one God! you shall have no other gods before me!"-

-An old grim-beard of a God, a jealous one, forgot himself in such wise:-

And all the gods then laughed, and shook upon their thrones, and exclaimed: "Is it not just divinity that there are gods, but no God?"

He that has an ear let him hear.-

Thus talked Zarathustra in the city he loved, which is surnamed "The Pied Cow." For from here he had but two days to travel to reach once more his cave and his animals; his soul, however, rejoiced unceasingly on account of the nighness of his return home.

53. The Return Home

O SOLITUDE! My home, solitude! Too long have I lived wildly in wild remoteness, to return to you without tears!

一切所谓的怀疑不是都已经过去了很长的时间了吗？现在，还会有谁胆敢在白天吵醒这样的古老的沉睡和避光的东西呢！

所有的诸神早就已经结束了：——说真的，他们拥有了一种善良和欢快的神圣的结束！

他们并没有像“缠绵的黎明”那样死去——尽管人们说了谎话！与之正好相反，他们却因为大笑死掉了！

最不信奉神灵的言论出自上帝——他说道：“在这个世界上只存在一个上帝！除了我之外，你们不应该有其他的上帝！”

一个有着胡子，面目狰狞的老上帝，一个嫉妒之人，他如是遗忘了自己：

于是，所有的上帝都笑了起来，他们在他们的宝座上摇晃着，并且大声地叫喊道：“难道那不正是神圣的吗？拥有诸神，但却没有上帝？”

让所有拥有耳朵的都仔细聆听吧。

查拉图斯特拉在他热爱的被人们称为“心爱的班牛”镇里如是说道。要想从这里走到他的洞穴和他的动物们那里去，需要至少两天的时间；他的灵魂因为重返家园的日子越来越近，而不间断地欢呼庆祝。

53．归乡

啊，孤独！孤独啊！我的家园！我在陌生而遥远的地方生活了太久，以至于我重返家园的时候，一滴眼泪也没有流出来！

Now threaten me with the finger as mothers threaten; now smile upon me as mothers smile; now say just: "Who was it that like a whirlwind once rushed away from me?-

-Who when departing called out: 'Too long have I sat with solitude; there have I unlearned silence!' That have you learned now- surely?

O Zarathustra, everything do I know; and that you were more forsaken amongst the many, you unique one, than you ever were with me!

One thing is forsakenness, another matter is solitude: that have you now learned! And that amongst men you will ever be wild and strange:

-Wild and strange even when they love you: for above all they want to be treated indulgently!

Here, however, are you at home and house with yourself; here can you utter everything, and unbosom all motives; nothing is here ashamed of concealed, congealed feelings.

Here do all things come caressingly to your talk and flatter you: for they want to ride upon your back. On every simile do you here ride to every truth.

Honestly and openly may you here talk to all things: and verily, it sounds as praise in their ears, for one to talk to all things- directly!

Another matter, however, is forsakenness. For, do you remember, O Zarathustra? When your bird screamed overhead, when you stood in the forest, irresolute, ignorant where to go, beside a corpse:-

-When you spoke: 'Let my animals lead me! More dangerous have I found it among men

现在，你就像母亲一样，用手指轻柔地抚摸着我；现在，你就像母亲一样，冲着我微笑；现在，你刚好说道："曾经就像一阵龙卷风一样从我的身边离开的人到底是谁啊？"

他在离别的时候大叫道："我和孤独在一起坐了太长的时间；所以，我都已经忘记了沉默！"那么，现在你已经学会了沉默了吧？

啊，查拉图斯特拉啊！这个世界上的所有事情我都知道；你这独特的人，我知道你在人群之中的时候，要比跟我在一起的时候，更加孤独！

现在，你已经学会了吧！寂寞是一回事，而孤独是另外一回事！你在人群当中永远都是狂野的、陌生的：

——甚至当他们爱你的时候，你仍旧是狂野和陌生的：总而言之，他们要被纵容对待！

但是，在这里，你在你的房子和你的家里；你在这里可以想说什么就说什么，释放所有的动机；在这里，任何隐藏的、凝固的情感都不是可耻的事情。

在这里，任何的事物都会轻柔地来到你的身边，跟你谈话并且讨好你：因为他们要骑在你的背上驰骋。而你也在这里骑着所有的寓言和所有的真相。

在这里，你可以诚实地、公开地对任何的事物谈话：说真的，当一个人能够直接跟任何的事物进行交流，听起来就像是他们耳中的赞美！

要不然的话，那就是寂寞了。啊！查拉图斯特拉，你还记得吗？当你的鸟儿在头顶上尖叫的时候，当你站在森林里，站在死尸的旁边，为了该向何处走而犹豫不定、恼羞成怒的时候：

你说道："让我的动物们给我指路吧！我发现，身处在人群之中，要比身处在动物

than among animals:'- That was forsakenness!

And do you remember, O Zarathustra? When you sat in your isle, a well of wine giving and granting amongst empty buckets, giving and distributing amongst the thirsty:

-Until at last you alone sat thirsty amongst the drunken ones, and wailed nightly: 'Is taking not more blessed than giving? And stealing yet more blessed than taking?'- That was forsakenness!

And do you remember, O Zarathustra? When your still hour came and drove you forth from yourself, when with wicked whispering it said: 'Speak and perish!'-

-When it disgusted you with all your waiting and silence, and discouraged your humble courage: That was forsakenness!"-

O solitude! My home, solitude! How blessedly and tenderly speaks your voice to me!

We do not question each other, we do not complain to each other; we go together openly through open doors.

For all is open with you and clear; and even the hours run here on lighter feet. For in the dark, time weighs heavier upon one than in the light.

Here fly open to me all beings' words and word-cabinets: here all being wants to become words, here all becoming wants to learn of me how to talk.

Down there, however- all talking is in vain! There, forgetting and passing-by are the best wisdom: that have I learned now!

He who would understand everything in man must handle everything. But for that I have too

们当中危险得多，”——这就是寂寞！

啊！查拉图斯特拉，你还记得吗？当你坐在你的岛屿之上，就好像在空空的水桶里给予和准予的酒水之源泉，在饥渴的人群中进行给予和分发：

——直到最后，口渴的你独自一人坐在痛饮而大醉的人们的中间，并且在夜晚号啕大哭：“获取不是要比给予更加幸福吗？偷盗不是要比获取更加幸福吗？”——这就是寂寞。

啊！查拉图斯特拉，你还记得吗？当你在宁静的时刻来到这里，并且激励自己前行的时候，它会用邪恶的低声细语说道：“说话并且毁灭！”

这时，它就会让你对你所有的等待和沉默感到恶心，并且挫败你卑微的勇气：“这就是寂寞！”

啊！孤独！孤独啊！我的家园！你跟我说话的声音是如此的甜美和柔和啊！

我们并不会彼此质疑，我们也同样不会彼此抱怨，我们会真诚地对待彼此。

你的一切都是那么开朗，那么清澈，在这里，即便是时光也会用更加轻薄的步伐奔跑。因为，时光在黑夜里要比在光明中承担更加沉重的负担。

在这里，所有的言语和言语的宝藏，全都突然向我飞来：在这里，任何的事物都想成为言语，在这里，任何的事物都想从我这里学习说话的本领。

不过，在山的下面，所有的谈话都是毫无用处的！在这里，遗忘和离开才是最好的智慧：这是我现在已经明白了的道理！

能够理解人类心中所有的事物的人，必须能够驾驭一切。但是，我的双手又不屑于驾驭一切。

clean hands.

I do not like even to inhale their breath; alas! that I have lived so long among their noise and bad breaths!

O blessed stillness around me! O pure odours around me! How from a deep breast this stillness fetches pure breath! How it hearkens, this blessed stillness!

But down there- there speaks everything, there is everything misheard. If one announce one's wisdom with bells, the shopmen in the market-place will out-jingle it with pennies!

Everything among them talks; no one knows any longer how to understand. Everything falls into the water; nothing falls any longer into deep wells.

Everything among them talks, nothing succeeds any longer and accomplishes itself. Everything cackles, but who will still sit quietly on the nest and hatch eggs?

Everything among them talks, everything is out-talked. And that which yesterday was still too hard for time itself and its tooth, hangs today, outchamped and outchewed, from the mouths of the men of today.

Everything among them talks, everything is betrayed. And what was once called the secret and secrecy of profound souls, belongs to-day to the street-trumpeters and other butterflies.

O human hubbub, you wonderful thing! you noise in dark streets! Now are you again behind me:- my greatest danger lies behind me!

In indulging and pitying lay ever my greatest danger; and all human hubbub wishes to be indulged and tolerated.

With suppressed truths, with fool's hand and befooled heart, and rich in petty lies of pity:-

我甚至不喜欢呼吸他们的呼吸；哎！我在他们的噪音和恶劣的呼吸当中生活了太久了！

啊，幸福的宁静围绕在我的身边！啊，纯粹的香气围绕在我的身边！这宁静是如何从深深的胸膛里呼吸着纯净的空气啊！这幸福的宁静是如何进行聆听的啊！

但是在山的下面——那里在讲述着一切，那里的一切都会被误解。那里的人们用钟声来宣称他们的智慧，市场里的小商贩们会用铜钱的叮当响声来扰乱它！

在他们当中，一切都说话；但是没有人知道该如何去理解。

那里的一切都掉入了水中；但是没有任何事物掉落到了幽深的泉水里。

在他们当中，一切都说话，但是没有任何事物可以取得成功和成就。一切都会发生咯咯的声音，但是，安静地坐在巢中，孵出小鸡的是谁呢？

在他们当中，一切都说话，一切都没完没了的说话。就在昨天，时间和时间的牙齿还是坚硬的，而到了今天，它们已被嚼碎，到了今天，它们已经被人们含在了嘴里。

在他们当中，一切都说话，一切都被揭露了。曾经所有被称作秘密，被称为深奥的灵魂的秘密，到了今天，全都属于大街上的喇叭吹奏者和其他的小飞虫。

啊，令人感到惊奇的人类啊！你那黑色街道里的噪音！现在，你又一次来到了我的后面：——我最伟大的危险就隐藏在我的身后！

在纵容和怜悯之中，永远隐藏着我最伟大的危险，所有人类的喧嚣都希望能够被纵容和容忍。

拥抱着被抑制的真相，傻子的双手和愚笨的心灵，富有怜悯之心的小谎言：——因此，我如是生活在人类当中。

thus have I ever lived among men.

Disguised did I sit amongst them, ready to misjudge myself that I might endure them, and willingly saying to myself: "You fool, you do not know men!"

One unlearns men when one lives amongst them: there is too much foreground in all men- what can far-seeing, far-longing eyes do there!

And, fool that I was, when they misjudged me, I indulged them on that account more than myself, being habitually hard on myself, and often even taking revenge on myself for the indulgence.

Stung all over by poisonous flies, and hollowed like the stone by many drops of wickedness: thus did I sit among them, and still said to myself: "Innocent is everything petty of its pettiness!"

Especially did I find those who call themselves "the good," the most poisonous flies; they sting in all innocence, they lie in all innocence; how could they- be just towards me!

He who lives amongst the good- pity teaches him to lie. Pity makes stifling air for all free souls. For the stupidity of the good is unfathomable.

To conceal myself and my riches- that did I learn down there: for every one did I still find poor in spirit. It was the lie of my pity, that I knew in every one.

That I saw and scented in every one, what was enough of spirit for him, and what was too much!

Their stiff wise men: I call them wise, not stiff- thus did I learn to slur over words.

The grave-diggers dig for themselves diseases. Under old rubbish rest bad vapors. One should not stir up the marsh. One should live on mountains.

我曾经将自己伪装起来，坐在他们的中间，随时准备反抗自己而容忍了他们，并且心甘情愿地说服自己："你这个傻子，你根本就不了解人类！"

当他生活在人们中间，他不认识别人，在人类当中拥有太多的背景——那些可以高瞻远瞩的眼睛又有什么用处呢！

曾经我也是个傻子，当他们错认了我的时候，我纵容了他们，多过纵容我自己，我经常为了这种纵容而替自己报仇。

从头到脚全都被有毒的蝇子蛰了，并且就像许多邪恶之滴蚀空了的石头一样：因此，我坐在了他们的中间，并且对我自己说道："一切微不足道的东西都是无辜的！"

特别是那些将自己称为充满善意的人，我发现是拥有最致命的毒液的蝇子；他们会叮咬所有无辜的人，他们会玷污一切的纯洁；他们怎么能够公平公正地对待我呢！

生活在善意和怜悯之中的人，——慈悲教会他如何撒谎。慈悲会为所有自由自在的灵魂带去令人无法呼吸的空气。因为善意的愚蠢是深不可测的。

我曾经在这里学会了如何隐藏我自己和我的富有：我发现所有的人都是心灵比较匮乏的人，那是我的慈悲之谎言，我了解了所有的人。

我看到并且闻了每一个人，那是具有充足的精神的，拥有非常多的精神！

他们的拘谨的聪明之人：我叫他们为聪明之人，而不是拘谨——所以我已经学会了轻描淡写的语言。

挖掘坟墓的人，我叫他们为研究者和实验家，所以我就学会了用语言作游戏。

那些挖掘坟墓的人为自己挖出了疾病。隐藏在古老的垃圾之下的是恶劣、糟糕的蒸

With blessed nostrils do I again breathe mountain-freedom. Freed at last is my nose from the smell of all human hubbub!

With sharp breezes tickled, as with sparkling wine, sneezes my soul- sneezes, and shouts self-congratulatingly: "Health to you!"

Thus spoke Zarathustra.

54. The Three Evils

1.

IN MY dream, in my last morning-dream, I stood today on a promontory- beyond the world; I held a pair of scales, and weighed the world.

Alas, that the rosy dawn came too early to me: she glowed me awake, the jealous one! Jealous is she always of the glows of my morning-dream.

Measurable by him who has time, weighable by a good weigher, attainable by strong pinions, divinable by divine nutcrackers: thus did my dream find the world:-

My dream, a bold sailor, half-ship, half-hurricane, silent as the butterfly, impatient as the falcon: how had it the patience and leisure to-day for world-weighing!

Did my wisdom perhaps speak secretly to it, my laughing, wide-awake day-wisdom, which mocks at all "infinite worlds"? For it says: "Where force is, there becomes number the master:

汽。他们不应该搅动沼泽。他们不应该生活在山上。

我用受到祝福的鼻孔呼吸着山峰——自由。最终，我的鼻子从所有人类的喧嚣当中获得了自由！

剧烈的风就如同酿的酒一样，我的灵魂打了喷嚏，打了喷嚏，并且在自我的祝贺之中大声叫道：“愿你健康！”

查拉图斯特拉如是说。

54．三件恶

（1）

在我的梦境之中，在我的最后的清晨之梦中，我站在一座岛屿之上——置身于世界之外；我手里拿着一具天平，称量着这个世界。

哎，紫色的黎明曙光到来的实在是太快了：她用明亮的光芒把我唤醒，这嫉妒的人！她总是嫉妒我清晨之梦的光辉。

我的梦境觉得世界就是如此：它可以被拥有时间的人测算，可以被精确的仪器称量，可以被坚硬的羽毛触碰到，可以被神圣的猜谜者猜透：因此，我的梦境发现了世界：

我的梦想就是一个大胆的水手，一半是船，一半是龙卷风，犹如蝴蝶一样安静，犹如猎鹰一样急躁：今天的他是如何有着耐心和慵懒从而称量世界的呢！

那个嘲笑着“无限的世界”的我的智慧，我的微笑的、白天的智慧偷偷地跟他说道：

it has more force."

How confidently did my dream contemplate this finite world, not new-fangledly, not old-fangledly, not timidly, not entreatingly:-

-As if a big round apple presented itself to my hand, a ripe golden apple, with a coolly-soft, velvety skin:- thus did the world present itself to me:-

-As if a tree nodded to me, a broad-branched, strong-willed tree, curved as a recline and a foot-stool for weary travellers: thus did the world stand on my promontory:-

-As if delicate hands carried a casket towards me- a casket open for the delectation of modest adoring eyes: thus did the world present itself before me today:-

-Not riddle enough to scare human love from it, not solution enough to put to sleep human wisdom:- a humanly good thing was the world to me to-day, of which such bad things are said!

How I thank my morning-dream that I thus at today's dawn, weighed the world! As a humanly good thing did it come to me, this dream and heart-comforter!

And that I may do the like by day, and imitate and copy its best, now will I put the three worst things on the scales, and weigh them humanly well.-

He who taught to bless taught also to curse: what are the three best cursed things in the world? These will I put on the scales.

Voluptuousness, passion for power, and selfishness: these three things have hitherto been best cursed, and have been in worst and falsest repute- these three things will I weigh humanly well.

“凡是力量所在的地方，必将有统治者，因为她拥有更加强大的力量。”

我的梦境不喜新厌旧、不胆怯、不哀求，它是如何自信地沉思这个有限的世界的呢：

——就好像一个巨大的圆苹果将自己呈现在我的手上，一个熟透了的、金灿灿的苹果，它有着柔软而醇和的果皮：世界如是将自己呈现在我的面前。

——就好像一棵树冲我点头，那是一颗拥有宽大树枝，意志坚强的树，将自己弯曲起来，为疲倦的旅途者们提供弯椅和足凳：世界如是将自己呈现在我的岛屿面前。

——就好像一对纤细的双手将一个珠宝箱带到了我的身边——让谦逊、崇拜的眼光愉悦的珠宝箱：今天，世界如是将自己呈现在我的面前。

——它并不是一种足以将人们给予它的爱吓走的谜团，它不是一种解决方案，足以让人们的智慧休眠，今天对于我来说，世界上被人们称为恶事的其实就是善事，人间的善事！

我是如何在今天的破晓时分，感谢我的清晨之梦境，并且称量世界的！这个梦境和安抚心灵的东西就像人间的善意的事情一样来到我的身边！

在白天我可以做到同样的事情，并且模仿和复制它的优点！现在我要将三种最恶的事物放在天平之上，我会用极其人道的方式对它们进行称量的。

说教祝福的人同样也会说教诅咒：那么，世界上最好的三大诅咒之物究竟都是什么呢？我要把它们全都放在天平之上。

纵欲、追求权力的热情以及自私：从古至今，这三种事物就是最被诅咒的，拥有最糟糕和最虚假的名誉——我将会用非常人道的方式对它们进行称量。

好吧！这里就是我的岛屿，这里就是海洋——它无比欢乐愉悦地向我翻滚而来，这

Well! Here is my promontory, and there is the sea- it rolls here to me, shaggily and fawningly, the old, faithful, hundred-headed dog-monster that I love!-

Well! Here will I hold the scales over the weltering sea: and also a witness do I choose to look on- you, the hermit-tree, you, the strong-odoured, broad-arched tree that I love!-

On what bridge goes the now to the hereafter? By what constraint do the high stoop to the low? And what enjoins even the highest still- to grow upwards?-

Now stand the scales poised and at rest: three heavy questions have I thrown in; three heavy answers carries the other scale.

2.

Voluptuousness: to all hair-shirted despisers of the body, a sting and stake; and, cursed as "the world," by all the afterworldly: for it mocks and befools all erring, misinferring teachers.

Voluptuousness: to the rabble, the slow fire at which it is burnt; to all wormy wood, to all stinking rags, the prepared heat and stew furnace.

Voluptuousness: to free hearts, a thing innocent and free, the garden-happiness of the earth, all the future's thanks-overflow to the present.

Voluptuousness: only to the withered a sweet poison; to the lion-willed, however, the great cordial, and the reverently saved wine of wines.

Voluptuousness: the great symbolic happiness of a higher happiness and highest hope. For to

个我爱的年迈而且忠诚的千头怪兽!

好吧！我将在翻滚的海洋之上抱着那个天平：并且我会挑选一个目击者注视着你，你，你这海上的孤树，我所热爱的浓香四溢的枝叶繁盛的树!

现在，要怎样从桥上去往未来的世界呢？究竟是什么压迫着居高者屈服于卑微者？究竟是什么命令着最高者继续上升？

现在这个天平稳定且安静：我在一端掷下了三个非常沉重的问题，在另一端我则放下了三个沉重的答案。

（2）

纵欲：对于那些所有穿着忏悔服的肉躯之身的鄙视者是一种毒刺，一种标桩；并且被所有的遁世者诅咒为“这个世界”，因为纵欲嘲笑并且愚弄了所有的迷途和诡伪的说教者。

纵欲：对于乌合之众来说，就是煎烤的温火；对于腐朽的木头和散发着臭气的破布，就是炽热的熔炉。

纵欲：对于自由的心灵来说，就是天真无邪、自由自在，是地上的快乐花园，是未来对于现在源源不断的感谢。

纵欲：仅仅对于憔悴者是一种甜蜜的毒药；但是对于拥有狮子意志的人来说，则是一种伟大的慰藉，是小心谨慎的保存着的美酒。

纵欲：一个更高的幸福和最高的希望的伟大的幸福的标志。因为对于许多人来说，

many is marriage promised, and more than marriage,-

-To many that are more unknown to each other than man and woman:- and who has fully understood how unknown to each other are man and woman!

Voluptuousness:- but I will have hedges around my thoughts, and even around my words, lest swine and libertine should break into my gardens!-

Passion for power: the glowing scourge of the hardest of the heart-hard; the cruel torture reserved for the cruel themselves; the gloomy flame of living pyres.

Passion for power: the wicked gadfly which is mounted on the vainest peoples; the scorner of all uncertain virtue; which rides on every horse and on every pride.

Passion for power: the earthquake which breaks and upbreaks all that is rotten and hollow; the rolling, rumbling, punitive demolisher of whited sepulchres; the flashing interrogative-sign beside premature answers.

Passion for power: before whose glance man creeps and crouches and drudges, and becomes lower than the serpent and the swine:- until at last great contempt cries out of him-,

Passion for power: the terrible teacher of great contempt, which preaches to their face to cities and empires: "Away with you!"- until a voice cries out of themselves: "Away with me!"

Passion for power: which, however, mounts alluringly even to the pure and lonesome, and up to self-satisfied elevations, glowing like a love that paints purple felicities alluringly on earthly heavens.

Passion for power: but who would call it passion, when the height longs to stoop for power!

结婚和超于结婚都是可以被人接受的。

——对于许多人要比对于男人和女人们更加无知——没有人能够彻底明白男人和女人之间的彼此互不相知！

纵欲：——但是我要用藩篱保卫我的思想，甚至保卫我的话语，以防止卑鄙者和浪人闯进我的花园！

追求权力的热情：这就是铁心肠的人的炽热的皮鞭：最为冷血的人为残酷者保存着的苦难：这就是焚尸场的阴暗的烈火。

追求权力的热情：在最繁重的民族身上积聚的令人憎恶的牛蝇：所有不坚定的道德的谩骂者：它驾驭在所有的马匹和所有的自豪之上。

追求权力的热情：这毁坏并且粉碎了所有腐朽和空洞的地震：这纯白棺椁的毁灭者；这抗击不成熟的答案的散发着光芒的疑问。

追求权力的热情：在它炯炯有神的眼睛之前，人类在地上爬行、屈辱并且受到奴役，他们甚至变得比猪和蛇还要地位低下：——直到最后他的心里叫喊出了神圣的轻蔑。

追求权力的热情：神圣轻蔑的恐怖的说教者，它在所有的城池和国王的面前演讲：“给我滚远点！”——直到一种回声从他们的嘴里叫喊出来：“给我滚远点！”

追求权力的热情：它的甘甜甚至上升到了纯洁、孤独以及自我满足的高度，如同伟大的爱一样炽热地在地面上涂绘紫色的幸福天堂。

追求权力的热情：但是当最高的统治者想要屈服于伟大的权力之下，谁还能称它为狂热呢？说真的，在类似这样的渴望和屈辱之中，不会存在身体的虚弱和疾病！

孤独的高度并不会总是保持着孤独和自给自足；山峰可以来到山谷，高度之风可以

nothing sick or diseased is there in such longing and descending!

That the lonesome height may not forever remain lonesome and self-sufficing; that the mountains may come to the valleys and the winds of the heights to the plains:-

Oh, who could find the right prenomen and honoring name for such longing! "Giving virtue"- thus did Zarathustra. Once name the unnamable.

And then it happened also,- and verily, it happened for the first time!- that his word blessed selfishness, the wholesome, healthy selfishness, that springs from the powerful soul:-

-From the powerful soul, to which the high body appertains, the handsome, triumphing, refreshing body, around which everything becomes a mirror:

-The pliant, persuasive body, the dancer, whose symbol and epitome is the self-enjoying soul. Of such bodies and souls the self-enjoyment calls itself "virtue."

With its words of good and bad does such self-enjoyment shelter itself as with sacred groves; with the names of its happiness does it banish from itself everything contemptible.

Away from itself does it banish everything cowardly; it says: "Bad- that is cowardly!" Contemptible seem to it the ever-solicitous, the sighing, the complaining, and whoever pick up the most trifling advantage.

It despises also all bitter-sweet wisdom: for verily, there is also wisdom that blooms in the dark, a night-shade wisdom, which ever sighs: "All is vain!"

Shy distrust is regarded by it as base, and every one who wants oaths instead of looks and hands: also all over-distrustful wisdom,- for such is the mode of cowardly souls.

Baser still it regards the obsequious, doggish one, who immediately lies on his back, the

来到平原：——

啊，究竟有谁能够知道这种渴望的恰当的名称和称号呢！查拉图斯特拉曾经称这个没有名字的渴望为——“给予的道德”。

随后就发生了这件事，说真的，类似这样的事还是第一次发生！——他将自私称作是可被祝福的，那个从强大的灵魂之中流出来的干净并且健康的自私：——

从强有力的、美丽的、胜利的，创造了肉身所附属的强大的灵魂，在它的四周，任何事物都成为了一面透明的镜子。

这种轻柔动人的肉身，这跳舞之人，它的标本和特征就是自己享受快乐的灵魂。这样的肉身之躯和这样的自我享受快乐的灵魂称自己为“道德”。

这样的自我享受利用善恶之言论隐藏自己，就像神圣的丛林一样；用自己的幸福之名义从自身放逐了所有可被蔑视的事物。

也从自身放逐了所有胆怯的事物；它说：胆怯——那就是一种邪恶！对于它来说，那永恒的悲痛者，叹息之人，遭受不幸之人，贪图小利之人都是可被蔑视的。

它同样也蔑视了任何在不幸之中注视着的智慧：说真的，也有在黑暗的夜晚盛开出智慧的花朵，那是一种黑色的智慧，它经常叹息道：“一切皆虚空”！

它以令人感到羞愧的怀疑为可鄙，它以那些承认誓言不承认人类的人为可鄙：它也以过分地怀疑智慧为可鄙，因为这就是胆怯的灵魂的通路。

它以阿谀奉承、狗样的、降服的、顺从的人为卑下；也以有着降服的、狗样的、虔诚的，以及阿谀奉承的、顺从的智慧为卑下。

submissive one; and there is also wisdom that is submissive, and doggish, and pious, and obsequious.

Hateful to it altogether, and a loathing, is he who will never defend himself, he who swallows down poisonous spittle and bad looks, the all-too-patient one, the all-endurer, the all-satisfied one: for that is the mode of slaves. Whether they be servile before gods and divine spurnings, or before men and stupid human opinions: at all kinds of slaves does it spit, this blessed selfishness!

Bad: thus does it call all that is spirit-broken, and sordidly-servile- constrained, blinking eyes, depressed hearts, and the false submissive style, which kisses with broad cowardly lips.

And spurious wisdom: so does it call all the wit that slaves, and hoary-headed and weary ones affect; and especially all the cunning, spurious-witted, curious-witted foolishness of priests!

The spurious wise, however, all the priests, the world-weary, and those whose souls are of feminine and servile nature- oh, how has their game all along abused selfishness!

And precisely that was to be virtue and was to be called virtue- to abuse selfishness! And "selfless"- so did they wish themselves with good reason, all those world-weary cowards and cross-spiders!

But to all those comes now the day, the change, the sword of judgment, the great noontide: then shall many things be revealed!

And he who proclaims the ego wholesome and sacred, and selfishness blessed, verily, he, the prognosticator, speaks also what he knows: "Behold, it comes, it is night, the great noontide!"

Thus spoke Zarathustra.

它嫉妒、憎恶并且痛恨那些永远不进行自我保护的人，那些吞噬了剧毒的唾液和仇视的人，那些太过于容忍的人，那些长期受到苦难折磨，太过于柔顺之人：

因为，这就是奴隶的态度。

这可被祝福的自私，它唾弃所有种类的奴隶：不管他们是在诸神、在神圣的步武之前卑躬屈膝，还是在人类、在并不聪慧的人类的言论之前卑躬屈膝！

任何屈辱的，任何卑躬屈膝的，受到束缚的、遭受压缩的，眨着眼睛的，沮丧的内心的，那些虚伪的、粗从的种类，那以庞大并且胆怯的嘴唇亲吻的，它都称为作恶。

所有的奴隶和年迈并且疲倦的人们的智慧：特别是说教者全部恶劣的、狂妄自大的、太过于狡猾的聪敏都称之为虚假的智慧！

但是这样的虚假之哲人，这样的说教者，这样的愤世嫉俗之人以及天性阴柔、奴性的人们——哎，他们究竟是如何错误地使用了自私啊！

他们甚至把滥用自私称作是道德！并且名为道德——所以，所有的愤世嫉俗者、胆怯者以及十字架之上的蜘蛛们，他们会用充分的理由如是愿望着“大公无私”！

不过，对于那些人来说，现在，那样的时刻已经来到了，这个巨大的变革，这个裁判之刃，这伟大的正午：往往在这个时候，很多的事情会被昭示出来！

说真的，那些宣称我是健康的、神圣的，并且对自私的人带去祝福，这预言家，他也同样演说着他所知道的东西：“快瞧啊！那个时刻已经到来了，它已经在逼近了，这伟大的正午！”

查拉图斯特拉如是说。

55. The Spirit of Gravity

1.

MY MOUTHPIECE- is of the people: too coarsely and cordially do I talk for Angora rabbits. And still stranger sounds my word to all ink-fish and pen-foxes.

My hand- is a fool's hand: woe to all tables and walls, and whatever has room for fool's sketching, fool's scrawling!

My foot- is a horse-foot; therewith do I trample and trot over stick and stone, in the fields up and down, and am bedevilled with delight in all fast racing.

My stomach- is surely an eagle's stomach? For it preferrs lamb's flesh. Certainly it is a bird's stomach.

Nourished with innocent things, and with few, ready and impatient to fly, to fly away- that is now my nature: why should there not be something of bird-nature therein!

And especially that I am hostile to the spirit of gravity, that is bird-nature:- verily, deadly hostile, supremely hostile, originally hostile! Oh, where has my hostility not flown and misflown!

Thereof could I sing a song- - and will sing it: though I be alone in an empty house, and must sing it to my own ears.

Other singers are there, to be sure, to whom only the full house makes the voice soft, the

55. 重力之精灵

（1）

我的舌头——就是人民大众的舌头：我粗糙地、诚挚地跟安哥拉的兔子们进行谈话。但是对于所有的墨水之鱼以及钢笔之狐来说，我的话语仍旧显得格外奇怪。

我的双手——就是一个傻子的双手：悲哀啊！所有的桌子和墙壁，为傻子提供绘画以及涂鸦的地方！

我的双脚——就是一匹马的双脚；所以，我能够在木棍和石头之上践踏和慢跑，在田地里上下游荡，我是一个极度热爱飞速行走的魔鬼。

我的胃——毋庸置疑，就是一只老鹰的胃！因为它倾向于啃食羊羔的肉身，说真的，它的确是一只老鹰的胃。

我受到天真无邪的东西的滋养，并且迫不及待随时准备飞走，找寻一切，这就是我的天性：难道在这样的本质当中，不存在老鹰的本质吗！

特别是我是重力之精灵的敌人，那就是老鹰的本质：说真的，这是致命的敌人、崇高的敌人、先天的敌人！啊，我的敌意不是已经飞遍了所有可到之处了吗！

因此，我能够唱一首歌——我会唱一首歌：尽管我孤身一人在一栋非常空虚的房子里，我必须要为了我自己的耳朵献唱。

说真的，这里还有其他的歌手，只有在屋子里面全都是人的时候，他们的嗓音会变得轻柔，手指具有说服力，眼睛富有表情，心脏苏醒：但是，我和那些人并不是同类。

hand eloquent, the eye expressive, the heart wakeful:- those do I not resemble.-

2.

He who one day teaches men to fly will have shifted all landmarks; to him will all landmarks themselves fly into the air; the earth will he christen anew- as "the light body."

The ostrich runs faster than the fastest horse, but it also thrusts its head heavily into the heavy earth: thus is it with the man who cannot yet fly.

Heavy to him are earth and life, and so wills the spirit of gravity! But he who would become light, and be a bird, must love himself:- thus do I teach.

Not, to be sure, with the love of the side and infected, for with them stinks even self-love!

One must learn to love oneself- thus do I teach- with a wholesome and healthy love: that one may endure to be with oneself, and not go roving about.

Such roving about christens itself "brotherly love"; with these words has there hitherto been the best lying and dissembling, and especially by those who have been burdensome to every one.

And verily, it is no commandment for today and tomorrow to learn to love oneself. Rather is it of all arts the finest, subtlest, last and patientest.

For to its possessor is all possession well concealed, and of all treasure-pits one's own is last excavated- so causes the spirit of gravity.

Almost in the cradle are we apportioned with heavy words and worths: "good" and "evil"-

（2）

终有一天，那个教会人类飞翔的家伙，会转移所有的地标；所有的地标将因为他的关系而飞向天空；他会给它们命名为“轻灵者”。

鸵鸟奔跑的速度要比最快的野马的奔跑速度还要快，但是，它同样会把自己的脑袋深深地插进大地里面，不能自由翱翔的人类同样如此。

重力之精灵如是意愿，对于他来说，大地和生活是沉重的，我如是教导，但凡能够成为轻灵者的人，都必须懂得自爱。

说真的，不能让生病的人和受到感染的爱同在，如若与他们同在的话，甚至连自爱也会散发出臭气！

一个人必须热爱自己，用全身心的、健健康康的爱去热爱自己，我如是教导：只有这样人们才会懂得容忍，而不会神魂颠倒。

这样的神魂颠倒称自己为“兄弟般的爱”；从古至今，类似这样的话语一直都是最好的谎言和欺诈，尤其是在那些觉得世界是无比繁重的人们中间。

说真的，懂得学习自爱，这并不是今天和明天的戒律。它是所有的艺术当中最精巧、最巧妙的、最新以及最坚韧者。

这就是重力之精灵所要做的工作：将财产占有者所有的财宝妥善隐藏起来，并且在所有的金银窖中最后挖掘自己的财宝。

几乎是在摇篮里的时候，他们就已经将沉重的话语和评价施加在了我们的身上，他们将这样的礼物称为“善”和“恶”。正因为它的缘故，我们的生命被饶恕了。

so calls itself this dowry. For the sake of it we are forgiven for living.

And therefore suffers one little children to come to one, to forbid them betimes to love themselves- so causes the spirit of gravity.

And we- we bear loyally what is apportioned to us, on hard shoulders, over rugged mountains! And when we sweat, then do people say to us: "Yes, life is hard to bear!"

But man himself only is hard to bear! The reason thereof is that he carries too many extraneous things on his shoulders. Like the camel kneels he down, and lets himself be well laden.

Especially the strong load-bearing man in whom reverence resides. Too many extraneous heavy words and worths loads he upon himself- then seems life to him a desert!

And verily! Many a thing also that is our own is hard to bear! And many internal things in man are like the oyster- repulsive and slippery and hard to grasp;-

So that an elegant shell, with elegant adornment, must plead for them. But this art also must one learn: to have a shell, and a fine appearance, and sagacious blindness!

Again, it deceives about many things in man, that many a shell is poor and pitiable, and too much of a shell. Much concealed goodness and power is never dreamt of; the choicest dainties find no tasters!

Women know that, the choicest of them: a little fatter a little leaner- oh, how much fate is in so little!

Man is difficult to discover, and to himself most difficult of all; often lies the spirit concerning the soul. So causes the spirit of gravity.

这就是重力之精灵所要做的工作：把小孩子们聚在一起，禁止他们自爱！

我们——我们忠贞不渝地站在苦难的肩膀之上，走过崎岖的山峰！当我们汗流浃背的时候，人们会跟我们说道：“是的，生活是让人难以承受的！”

但是，只有人类本身才是难以承受的！这样说的原因就在于在自己的肩膀之上，他肩负了许多彼此没有关联的事物和评价，他就像骆驼一样跪了下来，并且让自己好好地驮上重载。

特别是能够肩负重载的性格最刚毅的人，他的脑中满是尊严。他将太多的彼此不相干的话语和评价肩负在自己的肩膀之上：现在，生命对于他来说，就是一片沙漠！

说真的，甚至于许多属于我们的事物也是难以承受的，人类内心当中的很多事物都跟牡蛎一样，令人反感，滑腻，并且非常难以捕捉。

因此，必须要有带有珠光宝气的贝壳为他们进行辩护。甚至于这种艺术也必须去学习：拥有一个贝壳，一种惹人怜爱的外表以及聪慧的盲目！

其次，在人们的心中存在着很多的欺诈，许多贝壳都是微不足道、不中用的，这样的贝壳太多了。很多被隐藏起来的善意和权力永远也不会被人们梦到；最精美的美味佳肴难道还找不到赏味者吗！

唯独女人当中的卓绝者知道这些：一丁点儿的肥以及一丁点儿的瘦——啊，在这一丁点儿之上究竟悬挂着多少命运啊！

这就是重力之精灵所要做的工作：让人类很难被发现，让人类之中的自己尤为难以发现；精神往往会欺骗灵魂。

但是，但凡发现了自己的人会说：这就是我的善与恶：所以，他让谈论“一切皆善，

He, however, has discovered himself who says: This is my good and evil: therewith has he silenced the mole and the dwarf, who say: "Good for all, evil for all."

Neither do I like those who call everything good, and this world the best of all. Those do I call the all-satisfied.

All-satisfiedness, which knows how to taste everything,- that is not the best taste! I honor the refractory, fastidious tongues and stomachs, which have learned to say "I" and "Yes" and "No."

To chew and digest everything, however- that is the genuine swine-nature! Ever to say you-A- that has only the ass learned, and those like it!-

Deep yellow and hot red- so wants my taste- it mixes blood with all colors. Yet he who whitewashes his house, betrays to me a whitewashed soul.

With mummies, some fall in love; others with phantoms: both alike hostile to all flesh and blood- oh, how repugnant are both to my taste! For I love blood.

And there will I not reside and abide where every one spits and spews: that is now my taste,- rather would I live amongst thieves and perjurers. Nobody carries gold in his mouth.

Still more repugnant to me, however, are all lick-spittles; and the most repugnant animal of man that I found, did I christen "parasite": it would not love, and would yet live by love.

Unhappy do I call all those who have only one choice: either to become evil beasts, or evil beast-tamers. Amongst such would I not build my tabernacle.

Unhappy do I also call those who have ever to wait,- they are repugnant to my taste- all the toll-gatherers and traders, and kings, and other landkeepers and shopkeepers.

一切皆恶”的鼹鼠和侏儒们沉默不语。

说真的，我讨厌称世间万物为至善，称这个世界为至善的人们。

我称他们为“一切之满足者”。

“一切之满足”，他们知道该如何赏识世间万物——这并不是最好的赏识，我的敬重曾经学会说：“我”和“是与否”的那些倔强的、挑三拣四的舌头和胃。

咀嚼并且消化所有的事物，但是，这就是真正的猪的本质！也只有驴子以及跟驴子同属一个种类的生物永远懂得说：“是呀！”

我的品位如是要求：深黄色和热红色——它混合了血液和所有的颜色。然而，粉刷了房屋的人，必定会向我显露被粉刷过的灵魂。

有些人喜欢僵尸，有些人喜欢鬼魂：这两者都是肉身和血液的敌人——啊，这两者是如何地违背了我的品位！因为我非常热爱鲜血。

我不喜欢居住在被人们唾弃、令人作呕的地方：这就是我现在的品位，我宁愿居住在小偷和伪证者中间。没有人会在他的嘴巴里衔着黄金。

但是，所有的吮痰者更是让我感到厌恶：我找到了人类当中最令人厌恶的东西，我给它起名为“寄生虫”：它不愿意拥有爱，但却愿意寄生于爱。

我会称那些只有一种选择的人为不快乐：他们要么成为邪恶的野兽，要么成为邪恶的野兽的驯服者。我可不愿意在他们之中建立我自己的神龛。

我同样也会称那些需要永远等待的人们为不快乐：他们全都违背了我的品位——所有的税吏、小商贩、国王以及所有的地主和店主们。

同样地，我也学会了期待，彻底地期待，但是我只会期待我自己。同时我也学会了

I learned waiting also, and thoroughly so,- but only waiting for myself. And above all did I learn standing and walking and running and leaping and climbing and dancing.

This however is my teaching: he who wishes one day to fly, must first learn standing and walking and running and climbing and dancing:- one does not fly into flying!

With rope-ladders learned I to reach many a window, with nimble legs did I climb high masts: to sit on high masts of perception seemed to me no small bliss;-

-To flicker like small flames on high masts: a small light, certainly, but a great comfort to cast-away sailors and ship-wrecked ones!

By divers ways and wendings did I arrive at my truth; not by one ladder did I mount to the height where my eye roves into my remoteness.

And unwillingly only did I ask my way- that was always counter to my taste! Rather did I question and test the ways themselves.

A testing and a questioning has been all my travelling:- and verily, one must also learn to answer such questioning! That, however,- is my taste:

-Neither a good nor a bad taste, but my taste, of which I have no longer either shame or secrecy.

"This- is now my way,- where is yours?" Thus did I answer those who asked me "the way." For the way- it does not exist!

Thus spoke Zarathustra.

在一切之上站立、行走、奔跑、跳跃、攀爬以及跳舞。

这就是我的教导：要想有一天在天空翱翔的人，必须首先学会如何站立、行走、奔跑、攀爬以及跳舞：因为人们不能根据飞翔学会飞翔！

我学会了踩着绳索梯，来到许多的窗户面前，并且通过敏捷的双腿攀爬到了高耸的桅杆之上：坐在高耸的知识的桅杆上，对于我来说似乎不是小小的祝福。

如同小小的火焰一样在高耸的桅杆上闪烁：说真的，这只是小小的光亮，但是它对于那些遭遇苦难的船员和因船只失事落水的人们来说，却是莫大的安慰！

通过不同的方式和途径我来到了我的真理的面前；我不是仅仅通过一个阶梯攀登上我的目光可以眺望远方的高处。

我不愿意跟别人请教我的道路——因为，那总是违背我的品位！我宁愿提问并且检验道路本身。

一种试炼、一种质疑就是我的旅行的全部：——说真的，一个人必须要学会回答类似这样的问题！这就是我的品位：

不是善意的品位也不是邪恶的品位，而是我自己的品位，在那里面，我不再拥有羞愧或是秘密。

“这里，现在这里就是我的道路——那么，你的道路在哪里呢？”我如是地回答了那些提问“这条道路”的人们，因为这条道路，根本就不存在！

查拉图斯特拉如是说。

56. Old and New Tablets

1.

HERE do I sit and wait, old broken law-tablets around me and also new half-written law-tablets. When comes my hour?

-The hour of my descent, of my down-going: for once more will I go to men.

For that hour do I now wait: for first must the signs come to me that it is my hour- namely, the laughing lion with the flock of doves.

Meanwhile do I talk to myself as one who has time. No one tells me anything new, so I tell myself my own story.

2.

When I came to men, then found I them resting on an old infatuation: all of them thought they had long known what was good and bad for men.

An old wearisome business seemed to them all talk of virtue; and he who wished to sleep well spoke of "good" and "bad" before retiring to rest.

This somnolence did I disturb when I taught that no one yet knows what is good and bad:-unless it be the creator!

56. 旧榜与新榜

（1）

我坐在这里静静地等待，老旧的、破损的旧榜以及写完一半的新榜围绕在我的身边，我的时刻究竟何时才能到来呢？

我的下降的时刻，我的毁灭的时刻：我乐意再一次走向人间。

因为，我现在正在等待着那个时刻的到来：一开始一定是我的时刻的迹象的到来——换句话说就是，这个迹象就是跟鸽子群一起欢声笑语的狮子。

与此同时，我就像悠闲懒散的人一样自言自语。没有人给我讲新鲜事，所以，我只好对自己说起自己。

（2）

当我来到人群当中的时候，我发现他们全都居住在古老的痴心迷醉之上：他们所有人都想着他们很久之前就已知道什么才是人类的善与恶。

对于他们来说，所有有关道德的谈论都好像是一种古老的令人感觉乏味的事情；要想安心睡觉的人，在休息之前先谈谈有关善与恶的事情吧！

我搅乱了这种困倦，当我教导人的时候说没有人知道什么才是善与恶：——除非它是创造者。

-It is he, however, who creates man's goal, and gives to the earth its meaning and its future: he only effects it that anything is good or bad.

And I bade them upset their old academic chairs, and wherever that old infatuation had sat; I bade them laugh at their great moralists, their saints, their poets, and their saviours.

At their gloomy sages did I bid them laugh, and whoever had sat admonishing as a black scarecrow on the tree of life.

On their great grave-highway did I seat myself, and even beside the carrion and vultures-and I laughed at all their bygone and its mellow decaying glory.

Like penitential preachers and fools did I cry wrath and shame on all their greatness and smallness. Oh, that their best is so very small! Oh, that their worst is so very small! Thus did I laugh.

Thus did my wise longing, born in the mountains, cry and laugh in me; a wild wisdom, verily!- my great pinion-rustling longing.

And oft did it carry me off and up and away and in the midst of laughter; then flew I quivering like an arrow with sun-intoxicated rapture:

-Out into distant futures, which no dream has yet seen, into warmer souths than ever sculptor conceived,- where gods in their dancing are ashamed of all clothes:

(That I may speak in parables and halt and stammer like the poets: and verily I am ashamed that I have still to be a poet!)

Where all becoming seemed to me dancing of gods, and wantoning of gods, and the world

然而，创造者就是创造人类的目标，并且给予大地含义和未来的人：只有他才能行之有效地创造善与恶。

我命令他们掀翻他们古老的学术之椅，所有古老的傲慢所坐过的地方；我命令他们嘲笑他们的伟大的道德家、伟大的圣人、诗人们以及他们的救世主。

我命令他们嘲笑他们的忧郁的哲人，嘲笑那些犹如黑色的稻草人一样坐着的人，让他们远离生命之树。

我坐在了他们伟大的坟墓的道路之上，甚至于坐在死尸和鹫鸟的旁边——我嘲笑他们所有的过去以及过去腐烂衰败的光辉。

说真的，我就像忏悔的说教者以及傻子一样，我恼羞成怒，并且毁坏了他们所有的伟大和渺小！他们的善意也是如此的渺小！啊，他们的极恶也是如此的渺小！所以，我哈哈大笑了起来。

因此，我那诞生于群山之上的聪慧的渴求，对我连哭带笑了起来；说真的，这是一种非常粗犷的聪慧——这是一种猛冲的伟大之翅膀的渴望。

她总是带着我向天上翱翔，在欢声笑语的中间！因此，我就像一支对太阳之欣喜感到如痴如醉的弓箭一样，摇晃着飞翔！

我飞到了就连梦想都触及不到的未来，飞到了就连艺术家都无法想象的更加炽热的南方：在那里，所有的诸神全都光着身子跳舞，他们以所有的衣服为耻辱。

——我如是说着寓言，就像诗人一样木讷、结巴：说真的，我以我仍旧是一位诗人而感到羞耻！——

对于我来说，那里的一切都成为了跳舞的诸神，成为了诸神的嬉戏打闹，世界变得

unloosed and unbridled and fleeing back to itself:-

-As an eternal self-fleeing and re-seeking of one another of many gods, as the blessed self-contradicting, recommuning, and refraternising with one another of many gods:-

Where all time seemed to me a blessed mockery of moments, where necessity was freedom itself, which played happily with the goad of freedom:-

Where I also found again my old devil and arch-enemy, the spirit of gravity, and all that it created: constraint, law, necessity and consequence and purpose and will and good and evil:-

For must there not be that which is danced over, danced beyond? Must there not, for the sake of the nimble, the nimblest,- be moles and clumsy dwarfs?-

3.

There was it also where I picked up from the path the word "Superman," and that man is something that must be overcome.

-That man is a bridge and not a goal- rejoicing over his noontides and evenings, as advances to new rosy dawns:

-The Zarathustra word of the great noontide, and whatever else I have hung up over men like purple evening-afterglows.

Also new stars did I make them see, along with new nights; and over cloud and day and night, did I spread out laughter like a gay-colored canopy.

自由并且不受限制，所有的一切全都返璞归真；——

那里的一切就像是无量神祇的一种永恒的自我逃脱以及自己的返璞归真；好像是无量神祇的一种能够被祝福的自我的冲突、自我的和解、自我的重新创造；——

对于我来说，那里的一切的时间，就像是能够被祝福的瞬间之嘲弄，在那里，自由是必需品，幸福快乐地跟自由的毒螫一起嬉戏打闹；——

在那里，我再一次发现了我的古代的恶魔和大敌，重力之精灵以及他的创造品：约束和戒律、必需品和后果、意图和意愿以及善与恶；

在那里，跳舞之人能够在它的上面翩翩起舞，凌驾于它所能触及的地方，难道这不是理所当然的吗？在那里，为了敏捷和美丽的缘故，鼹鼠和愚笨的侏儒难道不是必不可少的吗？

（3）

同样地，我还在那里的大道之上捡起了“超人”这两个大字，同时我也看出了人类是必须要超越的一种东西。

人类是一座桥梁，而不是一个目标——那些喜欢他的正午时分和夜晚的人，把它当做是通向崭新的、炽热的黎明的通路：

喜欢伟大的正午时分的查拉图斯特拉之名言，喜欢我如同紫色的夕阳余晖般高悬在人们的头顶之上。

说真的，我能够让他们看到崭新的星星以及陪伴着它们的崭新的黑夜；在白天和夜

I taught them all my poetisation and aspiration: to compose and collect into unity what is fragment in man, and riddle and fearful chance;-

-As composer, riddle-reader, and redeemer of chance, did I teach them to create the future, and all that has been- to redeem by creating.

The past of man to redeem, and every "It was" to transform, until the Will says: "But so did I will it! So shall I will it-"

-This did I call redemption; this alone taught I them to call redemption.- -

Now do I await my redemption- that I may go to them for the last time.

For once more will I go to men: amongst them will my sun set; in dying will I give them my choicest gift!

From the sun did I learn this, when it goes down, the exuberant one: gold does it then pour into the sea, out of inexhaustible riches,-

-So that the poorest fisherman rows even with golden oars! For this did I once see, and did not tire of weeping in beholding it.- -

Like the sun will also Zarathustra go down: now sits he here and waits, old broken law-tablets around him, and also new law-tablets- half-written.

4.

Behold, here is a new table; but where are my brothers who will carry it with me to the

晚以及云朵之上，我开怀大笑就如同色彩斑斓的苍穹一样。

我将我所有的梦想以及我所有的渴望全都教给了它们：将人们心灵当中的碎片、谜题以及令人畏惧的巧合组合在一起，形成一个整体。

就好像一个诗人、一个解决谜题的人、一个巧遇的救世主，我教导他们创造未来，我教导他们在这样的创造之中救赎过去，救赎人类的过去，改变所有的“过去是如此”，一直到意志开口说道：“但我愿意它如是！我将愿它如是！”

我管这个叫做救赎；我教他们只能管这个叫做救赎。

现在，我所期待的是属于我自己的救赎——那样，我就可以最后一次向人们当中走去。

我要再一次向人群中间走去：我的太阳会在他们中间沉落和消亡，我要给他们我最珍贵的礼物！

我要从沉落的太阳当中学习这些，那充实渊博的太阳啊！就在它沉落的时候，它将自己数不尽的金银财宝统统倾泻到了大海之中：——

所以，最贫穷的渔民，现在都摇晃着金灿灿的船桨划着水：我曾经看到过这样的情形，我不知疲倦地啜泣了起来。

查拉图斯特拉也跟那个太阳一样开始沉落：现在，他就坐在这里，静静地期待着，在那破碎的旧榜和半写的新榜中间。

（4）

快看啊！这里就是一张新榜；但是，跟我一起将它带到山谷和肉身的腹地，兄弟们

valley and into hearts of flesh?-

Thus demands my great love to the remotest ones: be not considerate of your neighbor! Man is something that must be overcome.

There are many divers ways and modes of overcoming: see you thereto! But only a fool thinks: "man can also be overleapt."

Overcome yourself even in your neighbor: and a right which you can seize upon, shall you not allow to be given you!

What you do can no one do to you again. Lo, there is no requital.

He who cannot command himself shall obey. And many a one can command himself, but still sorely lacks self-obedience!

5.

Thus wishes the type of noble souls: they desire to have nothing gratuitously, least of all, life.

He who is of the rabble wishes to live gratuitously; we others, however, to whom life has given itself- we are ever considering what we can best give in return!

And verily, it is a noble dictum which says: "What life promises us, that promise will we keep- to life!"

One should not wish to enjoy where one does not contribute to the enjoyment. And one

都是谁呢？

所以，我对于距离遥远的人们的深厚的爱如是要求：“千万不要对你们的邻居留有情面！人类是必须要被超越的一种东西。”

所以你看：在这个世界上存在着许许多多、各不相同的征服的道路和模式！但是，只有一个傻子才会想到：“人类同样也会被越过”。

超越你自己，即使是在你的邻居当中：拥有力量夺取的你绝不能容忍被给予，这就是你的权力！

你对别人所做的事情，其他人是无法对你做到的。看呀，这里并没有报答和酬谢。

无法命令自己的人就应当服从。在这个世界上有很多人能够命令自己，但是，他们仍旧缺乏自我服从！

（5）

高贵的灵魂的族类如是愿望：他们希望带着感恩的心去接受一切事物，至少是生命。

只有恶棍才会想要得来全不费工夫的生命：但是，对于我们来说，生命是需要自给的——我们能够想到的总是我们能够给予的最高的回报！

说真的，那是一句高尚的人生格言：“生命给我们带来的允诺，我们愿意对于生命维持着那份允诺！”

一个人不应该在不能够为享乐做出贡献的地方渴望着享乐！一个人不应当渴望着享乐！

所以，享乐和天真无邪是最无耻的事情，这两者都不愿意被人们追求。

should not wish to enjoy!

For enjoyment and innocence are the most bashful things. Neither like to be sought for. One should have them,- but one should rather seek for guilt and pain!-

6.

O my brothers, he who is a firstling is ever sacrificed. Now, however, are we firstlings!

We all bleed on secret sacrificial altars, we all burn and broil in honor of ancient idols.

Our best is still young: this excites old palates. Our flesh is tender, our skin is only lambs' skin:- how could we not excite old idol-priests!

In ourselves dwells he still, the old idol-priest, who broils our best for his banquet. Ah, my brothers, how could firstlings fail to be sacrifices!

But so wishes our type; and I love those who do not wish to preserve themselves, the down-going ones do I love with my entire love: for they go beyond.-

7.

To be true- that can few be! And he who can, will not! Least of all, however, can the good be true.

Oh, those good ones! Good men never speak the truth. For the spirit, thus to be good, is a

自己可以拥有它——但是自己宁肯选择寻求罪恶和痛苦！

（6）

啊，我的兄弟们，头一胎出生的儿子往往是被牺牲的。但是，现在我们就是那头一胎出生的儿子！

我们在秘密的、献祭的神坛上流淌着鲜血，我们都被焚烧去祭奠古代的偶像。

我们的最出色者仍旧非常年轻：这也激起了年迈者的味觉。我们的肉身是柔软的，我们的皮肤是犹如羊羔般的皮肤：——我们又怎么能不激起古老的偶像之崇拜者的馋涎呢！

这古老的偶像之崇拜者，仍旧居住在我们自己的心目当中，他烘烤了我们当中最出色的人，以此来作为他的盛宴。啊，我的兄弟们啊！头一胎的儿子是如何不被牺牲的啊！

但是，我们的同类们如是意愿：而且我热爱着那些不想将自己保存下来的人，我会用我全部的爱去热爱那些下沉并且毁灭的人们：因为，他们走向了超越。

（7）

要想真实，很少有人能够做到这一点！而且那些能够做到这一点的人，也不会愿意显露真实！但是，至少拥有善意的人是能够做到真实的。

啊，那些拥有善意的人们啊！拥有善意的人们永远也不会说出真相。因为如是修善就是一种精神的疾病。

malady.

They yield, those good ones, they submit themselves; their heart repeats, their soul obeys: yet he who obeys, does not listen to himself!

All that is called evil by the good, must come together in order that one truth may be born. O my brothers, are you also evil enough for this truth?

The daring venture, the prolonged distrust, the cruel No, the tedium, the cutting-into-the-quick- how seldom do these come together! Out of such seed, however- is truth produced!

Beside the bad conscience has hitherto grown all knowledge! Break up, break up, you discerning ones, the old law-tablets!

8.

When the water has planks, when gangways and railings o'erspan the stream, verily, he is not believed who then says: "All is in flux."

But even the simpletons contradict him. "What?" say the simpletons, "all in flux? Planks and railings are still over the stream!

"Over the stream all is stable, all the values of things, the bridges and bearings, all 'good' and 'evil': these are all stable!"-

Comes, however, the hard winter, the stream-tamer, then learn even the wittiest distrust, and verily, not only the simpletons then say: "Should not everything- stand still?"

那些拥有善意的人们，他们退让，他们屈服于自己；他们的内心在重复说着之前所说过的话，他们内心深处的灵魂在服从：然而，服从的人，却并未听从于他自己！

拥有善意的人所谓的一切的罪恶都必须有秩序的聚集在一起，从一个真相中诞生。啊，我的兄弟们啊！你们的罪恶也足以产生类似这样的真相吗?

无所畏惧的冒险、长期的不信任、残忍的否定、憎恶、当机立断，所有的这些全都没有聚集在一起！但是，真理的的确确是从这样的种子之中培养出来的！

迄今为止，所有的知识都是从邪恶的良心的旁边产生出来的！你们这些求知者啊！打碎、打碎这陈旧的榜！

（8）

说真的，当水面上铺上了木板，当溪流上搭起了漂浮的桥，这个时候，说着“任何事物都是在流动的”的人，是不会被人们所相信的。

甚至于傻子也会反驳他的理论。“你说什么？”傻子说道，“任何事物都是在流动的吗?

木板和漂浮的桥正在静静地躺在溪流的上面呢！”

“在溪流的上面，所有的事物都是固定的，所有有价值的东西，漂浮的桥梁、概念，所有的‘善’与‘恶’：这些东西都是固定的！”

然而，寒风刺骨的冬天来到了，溪流被冻住了，在这个时候，就算是最聪慧的人也会产生怀疑。在这个时候，说出“任何事物难道不会静静地停下来吗？”的人，可就不

"Fundamentally stands everything still"- that is an appropriate winter doctrine, good cheer for an unproductive period, a great comfort for winter-sleepers and fireside-loungers.

"Fundamentally stands everything still"-: but contrary thereto, preaches the thawing wind!

The thawing wind, a bullock, which is no ploughing bullock- a furious bullock, a destroyer, which with angry horns breaks the ice! The ice however- - breaks gangways!

O my brothers, is not everything at present in flux? Have not all railings and gangways fallen into the water? Who would still hold on to "good" and "evil"?

"Woe to us! Hail to us! The thawing wind blows!"- Thus preach, my brothers, through all the streets!

9.

There is an old illusion- it is called good and evil. Around soothsayers and astrologers has hitherto revolved the orbit of this illusion.

Once did one believe in soothsayers and astrologers; and therefore did one believe, "Everything is fate: you shall, for you must!"

Then again did one distrust all soothsayers and astrologers; and therefore did one believe, "Everything is freedom: you can, for you will!"

O my brothers, concerning the stars and the future there has hitherto been only illusion, and not knowledge; and therefore concerning good and evil there has hitherto been only illusion

只是傻子而已了。

“任何事物根本就不会静静地停下来”——这是一个非常适宜的冬天的教条，一种非生产性的时代的善，对冬天安眠的人以及在炉火旁边的懒人的伟大的安慰。

“任何事物根本就不会静静地停下来”：——但是，自古以来的春风，反对了这样的冬天的教条。

融冰之风就是一头公牛，一头不懂得耕犁的公牛——一头凶悍无比的公牛，一个破坏者，它用它的愤怒的牛角粉碎了冰块！但是这冰块又破坏了漂浮的桥！

啊，我的兄弟们啊！从现在来看，任何的事物难道不是处于流动的状态之下吗？所有的木板不是全都掉落到水里去了吗？

究竟是谁仍旧固守着“善”与“恶”呢？“悲哉我们！快哉我们！融冰之风在猛烈地吹拂！”——我的兄弟们啊，如是说教贯穿所有的大街小巷啊！

（9）

在这个世界上有一种古老的幻觉——那就是被人们称作是善与恶的东西。从古至今，这个幻象之轨道就一直围绕着预言家和占星家旋转。所以，人们会相信“世间万物都是命中注定的，你能够，因为你如是意欲！”

然后，人们开始再一次怀疑所有的预言家和占星家，因此，人们开始相信，“世间万物都是自由自在的。你可以，因为你意欲”！

啊，我的兄弟们啊！自古以来，有关于繁星和未来，只有幻象而没有真知，所以，

and not knowledge!

10.

"You shall not rob! you shall not kill!"- such precepts were once called sacred; before them did one bow the knee and the head, and take off one's shoes.

But I ask you: Where have there ever been better robbers and killers in the world than such sacred precepts?

Is there not even in all life- robbing and killing? And for such precepts to be called sacred, was not truth itself thereby- slain?

-Or was it a sermon of death that called sacred what contradicted and dissuaded from life?- O my brothers, break up, break up for me the old law-tablets!

11.

It is my sympathy with all the past that I see it is abandoned,-

-Abandoned to the favor, the spirit and the madness of every generation that comes, and reinterprets all that has been as its bridge!

A great potentate might arise, an artful prodigy, who with approval and disapproval could strain and constrain all the past, until it became for him a bridge, a harbinger, a herald, and a

有关于善与恶，也只有幻象而没有真知！

（10）

“你不应该偷窃！你不应该杀戮！”——曾经，类似这样的诫命被人们称为是神圣的；人们在这样的诫命面前会跪拜在地，低下头颅，并且脱掉自己的鞋子。

但是，我要问问你们：“在这个世界上，哪里还有比神圣的诫命还要凶狠的偷窃者和杀戮者吗？

在所有的生命之中，就不存在偷窃者和杀戮者吗？而且，如果他们称这些是神圣的，那么，他们自己不也是——杀戮了真相吗？”

那么，对抗并且劝止了生命，从而被称为神圣的，难道不是一种死之教条吗？啊，我的兄弟们啊！粉碎，为了我粉碎这古老的旧榜吧！

（11）

这就是我对于所有过去的同情，我看到它被抛弃了：——

——被抛弃于每一个新世代之怜恤、之精神、之疯狂，新时代会重新诠释一切已存在的作为自己的桥梁。

一个伟大的统治者会继而崛起，一个狡猾的奇才，他能够利用赞同和非难拉紧和束缚所有的过去，直到它能够成为他的一座桥梁、一种前期的征兆，以及传令官和雄鸡在

cock-crowing.

This however is the other danger, and my other sympathy:- he who is of the rabble, his thoughts go back to his grandfather,- with his grandfather, however, does time cease.

Thus is all the past abandoned: for it might some day happen for the rabble to become master, and drown all time in shallow waters.

Therefore, O my brothers, a new nobility is needed, which shall be the adversary of all rabble and potentate rule, and shall inscribe anew the word "noble" on new law-tablets.

For many noble ones are needed, and many kinds of noble ones, for a new nobility! Or, as I once said in parable: "That is just divinity, that there are gods, but no God!"

12.

O my brothers, I consecrate you and point you to a new nobility: you shall become procreators and cultivators and sowers of the future;-

-not to a nobility which you could purchase like traders with traders' gold; for little worth is all that has its price.

Let it not be your honor henceforth whence you come, but where you go! Your Will and your feet which seek to overcome you- let these be your new honor!

Not that you have served a prince- of what account are princes now!- nor that you have become a bulwark to that which stands, that it may stand more firmly.

清晨的鸣叫。

但是，还有其他的危险以及其他的同情：——但凡是贱民，他的思想都会追溯到他的祖先，但是，时间早已跟他的祖先中断了联系。

所有的过去已经如是被抛弃了：因为那些恶棍们终究有一天会成为主人，并且将所有的时间全都淹没在浅水里面。

因此，我的兄弟们啊！我们迫切需要一种全新的高贵，它应该成为所有的恶棍以及暴君的敌人，并且在新榜上题写“高贵”这两个大字。

许多高贵的人们都想拥有一种全新的高贵，因为，那些高贵的人们需要这种高贵；又或是说，像我曾经说的那样：“这就是神性，这里有诸神，但是没有上帝！”

（12）

啊，我的兄弟们啊！我将你们神圣化，并且为你们指向一种新的高贵：你们应该成为未来的创造者、栽培者以及播种者。——

说真的，你们不能像商人那样，通过交易黄金的方式购买高贵；但凡是拥有价格的东西，都没有什么价值。

你们身上的荣耀并不是你们从何处而来，而是你们要去往何处！你们的意志以及你们的脚步想要超越你们，让它成为你们的新的荣耀吧！

说真的，你们并不是在伺候王子——现在的王子又算得了什么呢！——也并不是你们成为王子的屏障，就能够让他的地位变得更加坚固。

Not that your family have become courtly at courts, and that you have learned- gay-colored, like the flamingo- to stand long hours in shallow pools:

(For ability-to-stand is a merit in courtiers; and all courtiers believe that to blessedness after death pertains- permission-to-sit!)

Nor even that a Spirit called Holy, led your forefathers into promised lands, which I do not praise: for where the worst of all trees grew- the cross,- in that land there is nothing to praise!-

-And verily, wherever this "Holy Spirit" led its knights, always in such campaigns did- goats and geese, and wry-heads and guy-heads run foremost!-

O my brothers, not backward shall your nobility gaze, but outward! Exiles shall you be from all fatherlands and forefather-lands!

Your children's land shall you love: let this love be your new nobility,- the undiscovered in the remotest seas! For it do I bid your sails search and search!

To your children shall you make amends for being the children of your fathers: all the past shall you thus redeem! This new table do I place over you!

13.

"Why should one live? All is vain! To live- that is to thresh straw; to live- that is to burn oneself and yet not get warm.-

说真的，并不是你们在宫廷里面成为了非常有礼貌的族群，也不是你们已经了解了奢华的装扮，就像艳丽的火烈鸟一样，长时间地站立在浅沼之中！（因为在一般的宫廷侍臣当中，拥有站立的能力是一种恩惠；并且所有的宫廷侍臣都相信坐着的许可是只有当他们死去之后才能够拥有的祝福！）

也不是被称为神圣的一种精灵，领导着你们的先祖来到那个我不会去赞美的充满希望的大陆！因为在那里面拥有着恶木——十字架——的地方，这是一片没有东西可赞美的地方！

说真的，不管是在什么地方，这个“神圣的小精灵”总是如临大敌一样，领导着他的骑士——山羊和鹅，而思想扭曲的人以及拥有偏见的人往往会走在队伍的最前面！

啊，我的兄弟们啊！你们的高贵不应该朝后方凝视，而是应该向外面凝视！你们应当从所有的父母之邦以及先辈的领土被放逐！

你们应当热爱着你们的孩子们的国土：让这种热爱成为你们的全新的高贵——在最遥远的海洋之上，从未被发现过的国土！我命令你们扬帆起航，去搜寻它！

为了你们的孩子，你们应该纠正你们是你们先辈们的孩子的错误认识：你们应当如是救赎所有的过去！我将这种新榜高高地悬于你们的头颅之上！

（13）

为什么人类需要生活呢？所有的一切都是非常空虚的！为了生活——就是要鞭打稻草；为了生活——就是自己燃烧自己，而无法获得暖意。

Such ancient babbling still passes for "wisdom"; because it is old, however, and smells mustily, therefore is it the more honored. Even mould ennobles.-

Children might thus speak: they shun the fire because it has burnt them! There is much childishness in the old books of wisdom.

And he who ever "threshes straw," why should he be allowed to rail at threshing! Such a fool one would have to muzzle!

Such persons sit down to the table and bring nothing with them, not even good hunger:- and then do they rail: "All is vain!"

But to eat and drink well, my brothers, is verily no vain art! Break up, break up for me the law-tablets of the never-joyous ones!

14.

"To the clean are all things clean"- thus say the people. I, however, say to you: To the swine all things become swinish!

Therefore preach the visionaries and bowed-heads (whose hearts are also bowed down): "The world itself is a filthy monster."

For these are all unclean spirits; especially those, however, who have no peace or rest, unless they see the world from the backside- the afterworldly!

To those do I say it to the face, although it sound unpleasantly: the world resembles man, in

类似这样的古老的胡言乱语，仍旧被人们当做是“智慧”而流传了下来；但是，因为它非常古老，并且散发着迂腐的味道，所以，它更加受到了人们的尊重。所以，发霉成为了高贵。

孩子们会这样说道：因为，烈火烧到了他们，所以，他们要躲开烈火！在古老的智慧之书中，你能找到很多非常幼稚、孩子气的地方。

那些总是用鞭子抽打稻草的人，他凭什么咒骂他们！快快堵住这个傻子的嘴巴吧！

这样的人坐在桌子的旁边，他们全都空着手，什么都没有拿，甚至于连饥饿都没有带来：——所以他们开始咒骂：“所有的一切都是非常空虚的！”

但是，我的兄弟们啊，很好地吃喝确实是名副其实的艺术啊！粉碎，为了我粉碎永远也不快乐的人们的榜！

（14）

“对于那些干净的人来说，世间万物都是洁净的”——人们如是说道。但是，我要对你们说：对于那些猪来说，世间万物都有猪的味道！

所以，空虚主义者，低头的人们（他们的内心也垂了下来）宣称：“这个世界本身就是一只非常污秽的怪物。”

因为他们所有人全都是非常不干净的精神，尤其是那些内心无法平静的遁世者，除非他们能够从事物的背面观看这个世界——这是非常真实的！

我当着他们所有人的面说，尽管这些话听起来会让人感到非常不舒服：但是这个世

that it has a backside,- so much is true!

There is in the world much filth: so much is true! But the world itself is not therefore a filthy monster!

There is wisdom in the fact that much in the world smells badly: loathing itself creates wings, and fountain-divining powers!

In the best there is still something to loathe; and the best is still something that must be overcome!-

O my brothers, there is much wisdom in the fact that much filth is in the world!-

15.

Such sayings did I hear pious afterworldly speak to their consciences, and verily without wickedness or guile,- although there is nothing more guileful in the world, or more wicked.

"Let the world be as it is! Raise not a finger against it!"

"Let whoever will choke and stab and skin and scrape the people: raise not a finger against it! Thereby will they learn to renounce the world."

"And your own reason- this shall you yourself stifle and choke; for it is a reason of this world,- thereby will you learn yourself to renounce the world."-

-Shatter, shatter, O my brothers, those old law-tablets of the pious! Tatter the maxims of the

界就跟人类一样，它也有属于自己的背面——这是非常真实的！

在这个世界上，存在着许许多多的污秽：这是非常真实的！但是，这个世界本身并不会因此而成为一只非常污秽的怪物！

在这个世界上存在着许许多多的智慧：这是非常真实的！即便，这个世界有着很多的腐臭的气味：但是即便是憎恶本身也能创造出翅膀以及天马行空之想象力的力量！

在最出色的人们当中，仍旧会存在着一些让人感到憎恶的东西；在最出色的人们当中，仍旧会存在着一些必须被超越的东西！

啊，我的兄弟们啊！事实上，即便是在那样的话语里同样存在着很多的智慧，那就是在这个世界上有着许许多多的污秽！

（15）

我能够听到那些虔诚的遁世者们对于他们的良知不停地重复着这样的话语，说真的，他们并没有过错或是没有犯罪——尽管在这个世界上再也没有比这个还要恶劣或者更加罪恶的事情了。

“就让这个世界成为它一直以来那个样子的世界吧！不要伸出手指去反抗它！”

“那些想要阻塞、想要刺戳、想要祸害以及剥削人民的人们，就随他们去吧：不要伸出手指去反抗他们！他们因此会愿意学习放弃整个世界。”

“你自己的理由——你应该让它将自己阻塞并且封闭起来，为了这个世界的理由——你会因此而愿意学习放弃整个世界。”

world-maligners!-

16.

"He who learns much unlearns all violent cravings"- that do people now whisper to one another in all the dark lanes.

"Wisdom wearies, nothing is worth while; you shall not crave!"- this new table found I hanging even in the public markets.

Break up for me, O my brothers, break up also that new table! The weary-o'-the-world put it up, and the preachers of death and the jailer: for lo, it is also a sermon for slavery:-

Because they learned badly and not the best, and everything too early and everything too fast; because they ate badly: from thence has resulted their ruined stomach;-

-For a ruined stomach, is their spirit: it persuades to death! For verily, my brothers, the spirit is a stomach!

Life is a well of delight, but to him in whom the ruined stomach speaks, the father of affliction, all fountains are poisoned.

To discern: that is delight to the lion-willed! But he who has become weary, is himself merely "willed"; with him play all the waves.

And such is always the nature of weak men: they lose themselves on their way. And at last asks their weariness: "Why did we ever go on the way? All is indifferent!"

啊，我的兄弟们啊！粉碎，粉碎了那些虔诚者们的破旧的榜！扯碎这些愤世嫉俗的人们的格言。

（16）

现在，人们在所有的黑暗的道路上低声细语道：“博学多才的人已经遗忘了所有强烈的渴望。”

我甚至看到这新榜高高地悬于市场之上：“智慧可以让人感到厌倦，任何事物都是毫无价值可言的，你不应该有渴求！”

啊，我的兄弟们啊，为了我粉碎，为了我粉碎这新榜！厌倦世界的人、死亡之说教者以及监狱看守：因为，你们看啊！它也是一种对于奴役的说教。

因为他们学到的是坏东西，而不是好东西，学习任何的事物都太早，太过于快速了；因为他们吃了糟糕的东西：因此，那些东西损害了他们的胃。

他们的精神就是一种受到了伤害的胃：它劝说着死亡！说真的，我的兄弟们啊！他们的精神就是一种胃！

生活就是快乐的源泉，但是，对于受到了伤害的胃来说，那个苦难之父，在他们的内心说话的人，所有的泉水全都是有剧毒的。

求知：拥有着狮子意志的人，就是一种快乐！但是，对于自己只不过是被意欲的人来说，则变得厌倦，所有的波浪都在玩弄他。

通常，这就是弱者的本性：他们在他们的道路上迷失了自己。最终，他们的厌倦就

To them sounds it pleasant to have preached in their ears: "Nothing is worth while! You shall not will!" That, however, is a sermon for slavery.

O my brothers, a fresh blustering wind comes Zarathustra to all way-weary ones; many noses will he yet make sneeze!

Even through walls blows my free breath, and into prisons and imprisoned spirits!

Willing emancipates: for willing is creating: so do I teach. And only for creating shall you learn!

And also the learning shall you learn only from me, the learning well!- He who has ears let him hear!

17.

There stands the boat- there goes it over, perhaps into vast nothingness- but who wills to enter into this "Perhaps"?

None of you want to enter into the death-boat! How should you then be world-weary ones!

World-weary ones! And have not even withdrawn from the earth! Eager did I ever find you for the earth, amorous still of your own earth-weariness!

Not in vain does your lip hang down:- a small worldly wish still sits on it! And in your eye-floats there not a little cloud of unforgotten earthly bliss?

会发问："我们这是要往哪里进发呢？一切的一切都是那么的不同！"

人们会在他们的耳边如此说教，他们喜欢："任何事物都是毫无价值的！你们不应该意欲！"然而，这是一种对于奴役的说教。

啊，我的兄弟们啊，查拉图斯特拉犹如一阵清新凉爽的风一样来到了所有疲倦者的道路之上：他将会让很多的鼻子打喷嚏！

我那自由自在的呼吸甚至能够穿透墙壁，来到牢狱和被囚禁的精神之中！

意欲的解放者：因为意欲就意味着创造：所以，我如是教育人们。你们唯一应该学习的就是：创造！

你们从我这里最一开始学习的应该也只是学习的方法，优秀的学习方法。——就让那些有耳朵的人们聆听吧！

（17）

这里停泊着一条船——它要航行到那里去，或是，航行到无边无际的虚无空间——但是，有谁会愿意心甘情愿地进入到这个所谓的"或许"之中去呢？

在你们这些人当中，没有一个人会愿意乘上这条死亡之船！那么，你们如何会对这个世界感到厌倦呢！

对这个世界感到厌倦的人们啊！你们甚至都没有从这片大地上撤离！从我来看，我认为你们更加渴望大地，更加热爱着属于你们自己的大地之疲倦！

你们那向下悬着的嘴唇是不是很徒劳：——在那其中，依旧有着一种小小的、尘世

There are on the earth many good inventions, some useful, some pleasant: for their sake is the earth to be loved.

And many such good inventions are there, that they are like woman's breasts: useful at the same time, and pleasant.

You world-weary ones, however! You earth-idlers! You, shall one beat with stripes! With stripes shall one again make you sprightly limbs.

For if you be not invalids, or decrepit creatures, of whom the earth is weary, then are you sly sloths, or dainty, sneaking pleasure-cats. And if you will not again run gaily, then shall you-pass away!

To the incurable shall one not seek to be a physician: thus teaches Zarathustra:- so shall you pass away!

But more courage is needed to make an end than to make a new verse: that do all physicians and poets know well.-

18.

O my brothers, there are law-tablets which weariness framed, and law-tablets which slothfulness framed, corrupt slothfulness: although they speak similarly, they want to be heard differently.-

See this languishing one! Only a span-breadth is he from his goal; but from weariness has he

的愿望！在你们的眼睛里——难道不是漂浮着无法被忘却的世俗的祝福之云团吗？

在这片大地之上，有着许许多多的伟大发明，在这些发明当中，有些是非常有用处的，有些是能够给人们带来快乐的：从这些方面来看，这片大地是非常可爱的。

在这片大地之上，有着许许多多的伟大发明，它们就像是女人们的乳房：在非常有用处的同时，还能够给人们带来快乐。

但是，你们这些对世界感到厌倦的人们！你们这些大地之懒惰者们！应该有人拿着鞭子抽打你们以示激励！应该有人拿着鞭子抽打你们，让你们的双腿焕发青春和活力。

倘若你们并不是为了大地所摒弃的残废而衰老不幸之人，那么你们就是狡猾的懒惰者或是贪吃者，夜行的、灵巧之巡游者。倘若你们不能再一次欢乐地奔跑，那么你们就应该走向死亡！

查拉图斯特拉如是教育人们：人们不应该为不能够治愈疾病的人寻找医生，所以，你们就应该走向死亡！

但是，创造一个结束，要比创造一个新的篇章需要更多的勇气和胆量：这些是所有的医生和诗人们都非常清楚的。

（18）

啊，我的兄弟们啊！这里的榜是以厌倦作为框架建立起来的，是以怠慢、腐败的怠慢为框架建立起来的：尽管，他们所说的话是基本一致的，但是，他们却要被人们听出不同的区别来。

lain down obstinately in the dust, this brave one!

From weariness yawns he at the path, at the earth, at the goal, and at himself: not a step further will he go,- this brave one!

Now glows the sun upon him, and the dogs lick at his sweat: but he lies there in his obstinacy and preferrs to languish:-

-A span-breadth from his goal, to languish! you will have to drag him into his heaven by the hair of his head- this hero!

Better still that you let him lie where he has lain down, that sleep may come to him, the comforter, with cooling patter-rain.

Let him lie, until of his own accord he awakens,- until of his own accord he repudiates all weariness, and what weariness has taught through him!

Only, my brothers, see that you scare the dogs away from him, the idle skulkers, and all the swarming vermin:-

-All the swarming vermin of the "cultured," that- feast on the sweat of every hero!-

19.

I form circles around me and sacred boundaries; ever fewer ascend with me ever higher mountains: I build a mountain-range out of ever holier mountains.-

But wherever you would ascend with me, O my brothers, take care lest a parasite ascend

快看啊！这个在这里坐以待毙的人！他距离他的目标仅仅只有一步之遥；但是怠倦的他顽固地躺在灰尘之中，这个英勇无比的人！

他因为厌倦而在道路、大地、目标以及他自己的身上打起了哈欠，他绝对不会再往前走一步了，这个英勇无比的人！

现在，太阳就在他的头顶之上燃烧着，而小狗们则用舌头舔舐他身上的汗：但是，他非常顽固地躺在这里，他宁愿选择忍受被渴死的折磨：——

他距离他的目标仅仅只有咫尺之遥，他心甘情愿被渴死！你们必须要拖拽着他脑袋上的头发，将他拉到他的天堂里面去——这位英勇无比的英雄！

但是，你们最好还是应该让他躺在他应该躺下来的地方，睡眠是个安慰者，它能够让冰冷的、淅淅沥沥的雨点滴落在他的身上。

让他就这么躺着吧！直到他自己从睡梦中醒过来，——直到他自己拒绝所有的厌倦，直到他自己的厌倦彻底地教训了他一番！

我的兄弟们，你们只是将那些小狗们从他的身边吓跑了，百无聊赖的狐群以及所有群居的毒蛇：

——所有接受过“文化教育”的群居的毒蛇，他们饱餐着一切的英雄烈士们的血汗！

（19）

我在我的周围划出了一个圆圈以及神圣的边界线；我攀爬的山峰越高耸，跟随着我的人就会越少：我建立了一条由永久神圣的群山构成的山脉。

with you!

A parasite: that is a reptile, a creeping, cringing reptile, that tries to fatten on your infirm and sore places.

And this is its art: it divines where ascending souls are weary, in your trouble and dejection, in your sensitive modesty, does it build its loathsome nest.

Where the strong are weak, where the noble are all-too-gentle- there builds it its loathsome nest; the parasite lives where the great have small sore-places.

What is the highest of all species of being, and what is the lowest? The parasite is the lowest species; yet he who is of the highest species feeds most parasites.

For the soul which has the longest ladder, and can go deepest down: how could there fail to be most parasites upon it?-

-The most comprehensive soul, which can run and stray and rove furthest in itself; the most necessary soul, which out of joy flings itself into chance:-

-The soul in Being, which plunges into Becoming; the possessing soul, which seeks to attain desire and longing:-

-The soul fleeing from itself, which overtakes itself in the widest circuit; the wisest soul, to which folly speaks most sweetly:-

-The soul most self-loving, in which all things have their current and counter-current, their ebb and their flow:- oh, how could the loftiest soul fail to have the worst parasites?

啊，我的兄弟们啊，无论你们在何处跟我一起攀爬高处，都一定要好好照顾自己，以免让那些寄生虫依附在你的身上，一同攀爬到了高处！

一种寄生虫：那是一种爬行类的蛀虫，那是一种将自己蜷缩起来，在地面上爬行的蛀虫，它会拼尽全力吸食你们身上脆弱以及疼痛的地方，以此来给自己提供养分。

而这就是它的狡猾多端：他猜测到了在哪里攀升的灵魂会感到厌倦，在你的麻烦以及沮丧里，在你的极其敏感的谦卑里，它建造了属于它自己的令人憎恶的巢穴。

在那个力量强大者虚弱，高雅之人极其绅士的地方——它建造了属于它自己的令人憎恶的巢穴；那种寄生虫通常依附在伟大之人身上疼痛并且隐秘的地方。

在这个世界上所有的种群当中，哪个种群是最高级的，而哪个种群是最低级的？那种爬行类的蛀虫就是所有种群中最低级的；然而，在所有种群中最高级的种群却供养着数量最多的寄生虫。

因为拥有最悠长的梯子的灵魂，能够下沉到最深处：他究竟要怎么做才能避免遭到寄生虫的依附呢？

——最富足的灵魂，能够在自身当中尽情地向前奔跑和游荡；最必不可少的灵魂，则会为了快乐而将自己投掷到机遇当中：

——存在的灵魂会陷入生存之中；而占有之灵魂会寻求获得渴望和期望的办法：

——灵魂正在逃离自己，但是，在更加广阔的环路之中，它又在追赶着自己；而对于最聪慧的灵魂来说，它们最容易受到愚蠢的诱惑：

——在最自我怜爱的灵魂的心灵当中，所有的事物都有属于自己的顺流和逆流，有着属于自己的潮汐和潮落：——噢，最高耸的灵魂究竟是如何避免被寄生虫依附的呢？

20.

O my brothers, am I then cruel? But I say: What falls, that shall one also push!

Everything of today- it falls, it decays; who would preserve it! But I- I wish also to push it!

Know you the delight which rolls stones into precipitous depths?- Those men of today, see just how they roll into my depths!

A prelude am I to better players, O my brothers! An example! Do according to my example!

And him whom you do not teach to fly, teach I pray you- to fall faster!-

21.

I love the brave: but it is not enough to be a swordsman,- one must also know whereon to use swordsmanship!

And often is it greater bravery to keep quiet and pass by, that thereby one may reserve oneself for a worthier foe!

You shall only have foes to be hated; but not foes to be despised: you must be proud of your foes. Thus have I already taught.

For the worthier foe, O my brothers, shall you reserve yourselves: therefore must you pass

（20）

啊，我的兄弟们啊，我真的非常残忍吗？但是我要说的是：本就已经倒下来的东西，就应该把它推落！

现如今，所有的事物一旦倒了下来，就会腐朽；有谁会愿意保留它们呢！但是，我同样非常赞同应该把它推落！

我想你们都知道将石头滚进陡峭的深处所带来的快乐吧？——看看今天的人类吧！他们是如何地滚落到自己的深处！

啊，我的兄弟们啊，我是更加出色的表演者的一首开场曲！举一个例子！那么，也就按照我举的例子做吧！

那个你们不愿意教他飞行的人，我在这里恳请你们教他——让他用更快的速度坠落！

（21）

我喜欢英勇无比的人：但是仅靠这些还不足以成为一名剑士——人们还必须需要知道应该在何处使用剑术！

然而，保持安静并且离开，则是更加伟大的勇敢，因此，人们应当为了更有价值的敌人而保护自己！

你们应该只拥有能够被仇恨的敌人，而不能拥有能够被鄙视的敌人：你们必须要为了你们的敌人而感到骄傲和自豪。我曾经如是教导过你们。

by many a one,-

-Especially many of the rabble, who din your ears with noise about people and peoples.

Keep your eye clear of their For and Against! There is there much right, much wrong: he who looks on becomes wroth.

Therein viewing, therein hewing- they are the same thing: therefore depart into the forests and lay your sword to sleep!

Go your ways! and let the people and peoples go theirs!- gloomy ways, verily, on which not a single hope glints any more!

Let there the trader rule, where all that still glitters is- traders' gold. It is the time of kings no longer: that which now calls itself the people is unworthy of kings.

See how these peoples themselves now do just like the traders: they pick up the small advantage out of all kinds of rubbish!

They lay lures for one another, they lure things out of one another,- that they call "good neighborliness." O blessed remote period when a people said to itself: "I will be- master over peoples!"

For, my brothers, the best shall rule, the best also wills to rule! And where the teaching is different, there- the best is lacking.

啊，我的兄弟们啊，你们应该为了更加具有价值的敌人而保护好自己：因此，你们必须从很多的事情旁边经过，——

——尤其是从许多的恶棍身边经过，他们会用有关于人民和民族的喧嚣声在你的耳边喋喋不休。

擦亮你们的眼睛好好看看他们的“肯定”和“否定”吧！在那里越是正确的地方，就越是错误：无论是谁看了都会变得暴怒。

观看以及拔出刀子劈砍——其实这两者都是一码事：所以，赶快动身向森林进发，并且将你们的刀剑收起来吧！

走你们自己的路吧！让人民和民族走属于他们的道路吧！——说真的，黑暗、忧郁的道路，丝毫没有一丝的希望之光亮！

就让那些商人们统治那里吧，在那里，商人们的金银财宝仍旧在散发着晶莹剔透的光亮。现在，那里再也不是国王的统治时代了：现在，它将自己称为人民，而不应当出现国王。

你们好好看看这些人民吧！看看他们现在的所作所为是如何恰似商人们的作为：他们从所有的垃圾之中捡起了蝇头小利！

他们彼此互相诱惑，互相欺骗——他们将此称之为“美好的邻人之谊”。啊，遥远的古代是能够受到祝福的，在那个时候，人们对自己说道：“我会成为凌驾于人民之上的主人！”

所以，我的兄弟们啊，只有最优秀的人才能统治，最优秀的人也能够利用意欲进行统治！在教育方式方法不同的地方，必然会缺乏最优秀的人。

22.

If they had- bread for nothing, alas! for what would they cry! Their maintainment- that is their true entertainment; and they shall have it hard!

Beasts of prey, are they: in their "working"- there is even plundering, in their "earning"- there is even over-reaching! Therefore shall they have it hard!

Better beasts of prey shall they thus become, subtler, cleverer, more man-like: for man is the best beast of prey.

All the animals has man already robbed of their virtues: that is why of all animals it has been hardest for man.

Only the birds are still beyond him. And if man should yet learn to fly, alas! to what height- would his rapacity fly!

23.

Thus would I have man and woman: fit for war, the one; fit for maternity, the other; both, however, fit for dancing with head and legs.

And lost be the day to us in which a measure has not been danced. And false be every truth which has not had laughter along with it!

（22）

倘若他们的面包分文不值的话，哎！他们到底在哭诉着什么！他们对于生命的维持——才是他们真正的消遣，他们的生活将是异常艰辛和困苦的！

他们是捕猎的怪兽：在他们所谓的“工作”之中——有着抢劫、掠夺，在他们的“收获”之中——有着欺骗！因此，他们的生活将是异常艰辛、困苦的！

所以，他们会成为更加优秀、更加敏锐、更加聪明的捕猎之野兽，他们更像是人类：因为人类就是最优秀的捕猎之野兽。

人类曾经抢夺了所有动物的道德：也正是因为这样，在所有动物当中，人类拥有最艰辛苦难的生命。

在这些动物当中只有天上的鸟儿能够凌驾于人类之上。倘若人类学会了在天空中翱翔，哎，他们的强取豪夺之心究竟能飞到什么高度呢！

（23）

但是，我希望男人和女人们都能如此：男人非常适合战争，而女人们则更加适合传宗接代，而这两者都适合用脑袋和腿跳舞。

在此期间，没有舞蹈可跳的日子着实是一种缺失。任何不能够带来欢声笑语的真理全都是虚假的！

24.

Your marriage-arranging: see that it be not a bad arranging! You have arranged too hastily: so there follows therefrom- marriage-breaking!

And better marriage-breaking than marriage-bending, marriage-lying!- Thus spoke a woman to me: "Indeed, I broke the marriage, but first did the marriage break- me!

The badly paired found I ever the most revengeful: they make every one suffer for it that they no longer run singly.

On that account want I the honest ones to say to one another: "We love each other: let us see to it that we maintain our love! Or shall our pledging be blundering?"

-"Give us a set term and a small marriage, that we may see if we are fit for the great marriage! It is a great matter always to be twain."

Thus do I counsel all honest ones; and what would be my love to the Superman, and to all that is to come, if I should counsel and speak otherwise!

Not only to propagate yourselves onwards but upwards- thereto, O my brothers, may the garden of marriage help you!

25.

He who has grown wise concerning old origins, lo, he will at last seek after the fountains of

（24）

请多留心你们的婚约：注意别让它是糟糕的婚约！你们的婚约定的太过于仓促了：因此，接下来所发生的后果就是婚约的破裂！

但是，婚约的破裂要比婚约的妥协以及婚约的谎言好得多！——一个女人如是对我说道："的确，我打破了婚约，但是，那是因为婚姻首先打破了我！"

我发现恶劣的怨对是复仇之心最重的：他们让整个世界遭受苦难，这个世界上的每一个人都再也不能只身一人前行。

正是出于那样的原因，我希望诚实正直的人们可以互相转告："我们彼此相爱：让我们多多留心我们是如何维持我们的爱意的！或是我们的誓言是一种错误吗？"

——"请给我们一个条件以及一个小小的婚姻，这样的话，我们就可以看看我们到底适不适合结婚！成双成对向来都是一件重大的事情。"

所以，我要给所有诚实正直的人们提出忠告；倘若让我提出忠告并且说些别的什么东西的话，那么，我对于超人以及一切来自未来的爱还能算是什么！

啊，我的兄弟们啊，不仅仅是激励你们向前进，并且激励着你们向上进发——所以，婚姻的花园或许能够帮助你们！

（25）

那些在古老的种群当中成长起来的智者，快看啊！最终，他一定会去寻找未来的泉

the future and new origins.-

O my brothers, not long will it be until new peoples shall arise and new fountains shall rush down into new depths.

For the earthquake- it chokes up many wells, it causes much languishing: but it brings also to light inner powers and secrets.

The earthquake discloses new fountains. In the earthquake of old peoples new fountains burst forth.

And whoever calls out: "Lo, here is a well for many thirsty ones, one heart for many longing ones, one will for many instruments":- around him collects a people, that is to say, many attempting ones.

Who can command, who must obey- that is there attempted! Ah, with what long seeking and solving and failing and learning and re-attempting!

Human society: it is an attempt- so I teach- a long seeking: it seeks however the ruler!-

-An attempt, my brothers! And no "contract"! Destroy, I pray you, destroy that word of the soft-hearted and half-and-half!

26.

O my brothers! With whom lies the greatest danger to the whole human future? Is it not with the good and just?-

水以及寻找新的族群。

啊，我的兄弟们啊，要不了多长时间，新的族群就会崛起，而且新的泉水会冲刷进新的深度。

地震堵塞了很多泉水，它直接导致了巨大的对于泉水的渴望：但是与此同时，它也点燃了内在的力量和秘密。

地震揭示了新的泉水。在古老的族群的大动荡之中，全新的泉水也随即喷涌而出。

不管是谁大声叫道："快看啊！这里是为许多口渴的人准备的泉水，是为许多拥有渴求的人准备的心灵，有为许多工具提供发明的意志"——在他的周围，聚集起了很多人，也就是说，很多跃跃欲试、充满渴望的人。

能够发号施令的人，同样也必须服从——这是一种试验！哎，那么漫长的寻找、那么漫长的猜详、那么漫长的失败、那么漫长的学习以及那么漫长的重复试验！

我如是教育人们，人类的社会：就是一种试验，一种漫长的寻找：然而，它寻找的是一位统治者！

我的兄弟们啊，一种试验，没有任何所谓的"契约"！我恳请你们摧毁，摧毁那些拥有温柔的心灵的人们以及骑墙派的言论！

（26）

啊，我的兄弟们啊，究竟是在什么样的人当中会藏有全人类的未来最重大的危险呢？难道不是在那些正人君子和公平正义的人们的身上吗？

-As those who say and feel in their hearts: "We already know what is good and just, we possess it also; woe to those who still seek thereafter!

And whatever harm the wicked may do, the harm of the good is the harmfulest harm!

And whatever harm the world-maligners may do, the harm of the good is the harmfulest harm!

O my brothers, into the hearts of the good and just looked some one once on a time, who said: "They are the Pharisees." But people did not understand him.

The good and just themselves were not free to understand him; their spirit was imprisoned in their good conscience. The stupidity of the good is unfathomably wise.

It is the truth, however, that the good must be Pharisees- they have no choice!

The good must crucify him who creates his own virtue! That is the truth!

The second one, however, who discovered their country- the country, heart and soil of the good and just,- it was he who asked: "Whom do they hate most?"

The creator, hate they most, him who breaks the law-tablets and old values, the breaker,- him they call the law-breaker.

For the good- they cannot create; they are always the beginning of the end:-

-They crucify him who writes new values on new law-tablets, they sacrifice to themselves the future- they crucify the whole human future!

The good- they have always been the beginning of the end.-

因为那些人的心理感受到并且说出："我们已经知道了什么是善意和正义，我们也已经拥有了善意和正义；悲哉！那些仍旧在寻找善意以及正义的人们！"

但凡是邪恶的人就能够做出伤害的事，然而，充满善意的人做出的伤害却最具有致命性的伤害！

但凡是恶意诽谤这个世界的人就能够做出伤害的事，然而，充满善意的人做出的伤害却最具有致命性的伤害！

啊，我的兄弟们啊，曾经有些人看透了拥有善意的人以及正义之人的心灵，他们说道："他们是法利赛人。"但是，人们并不能理解他们。

充满善意的人以及正义之人也不能理解他们，因为他们的精神全都被禁锢在了他们的良心之中。充满善意之人的愚笨是深不可测的聪慧。

但是，这就是真理，充满善意的人一定就是法利赛人——他们别无选择！

充满善意之人必须要迫害那个创造了自我道德的人！这就是真理！

但是，第二个人发现了他们的国家——发现了充满善意之人以及正义之人的国家和心灵——他问道："哪些人是他们最痛恨的？"

他们最痛恨的是那些创造者，那些创造者毁坏了古老的评价和评价之榜，这个毁灭者，那个法律的破坏者——人们称他为罪人。

但是他们无法创造拥有善意的人；他们始终都是终结的开端：他们将在新榜上编写新的评价的人钉死在十字架上；他们为了自己从而牺牲了未来——他们将整个人类的未来全都钉死了！

充满善意的人——他们始终都是终结的开端。

27.

O my brothers, have you also understood this word? And what I once said of the "last man"?- -

With whom lies the greatest danger to the whole human future? Is it not with the good and just?

Break up, break up, I pray you, the good and just!- O my brothers, have you understood also this word?

28.

You flee from me? You are frightened? You tremble at this word?

O my brothers, when I enjoined you to break up the good, and the law-tablets of the good, then only did I embark man on his high seas.

And now only comes to him the great terror, the great outlook, the great sickness, the great nausea, the great seasickness.

False shores and false securities did the good teach you; in the lies of the good were you born and bred. Everything has been radically contorted and distorted by the good.

But he who discovered the country of "man," discovered also the country of "man's future." Now shall you be sailors for me, brave, patient!

（27）

啊，我的兄弟们啊，你们也全都理解了这些话了吗？理解了我曾经谈及过的有关于“末后人”的话题了吗？

究竟在什么样的人身上藏有整个人类未来的最重大的危险？它们难道不就藏身于那些充满善意的人以及正义之人的身上吗？

粉碎吧！粉碎吧！我恳请你们粉碎那些充满善意的人以及那些正义之人吧！——啊，我的兄弟们啊，你们也全都理解了这些话了吗？

（28）

你们想要从我的身边逃走吗？你们难道害怕了吗？你们听到了这些话语之后颤抖了吗？

啊，我的兄弟们啊，我命令你们粉碎了那些充满善意的人以及正义之人的新榜，只有在这样的时刻，我才能够让人类在崇高的大海之上漂泊。

到了现在，那些伟大的恐怖、广阔的景色、严重的恶心和晕眩以及晕船全都降临到了他的身上。

充满善意的人教会了你们虚假的海岸以及虚假的安全；你们诞生并且孕育于善意之人的谎言之中。世间万物全都遭到了充满善意之人彻底地歪曲和曲解。

但是发现了“人类”的国家的人，同样也发现了“人类的未来”的国家。现在，你

Keep yourselves up betimes, my brothers, learn to keep yourselves up! The sea storms: many seek to raise themselves again by you.

The sea storms: all is in the sea. Well! Cheer up! You old seaman-hearts!

What of fatherland! There strives our helm where our children's land is! Therewards, stormier than the sea, storms our great longing!-

29.

"Why so hard!"- said to the diamond one day the charcoal; "are we then not near relatives?"-

Why so soft? O my brothers; thus do I ask you: are you then not- my brothers?

Why so soft, so submissive and yielding? Why is there so much negation and abnegation in your hearts? Why is there so little fate in your looks?

And if you will not be fates and inexorable ones, how can you one day- conquer with me?

And if your hardness will not glance and cut and chip to pieces, how can you one day- create with me?

For the creators are hard. And blessed must it seem to you to press your hand upon millenniums as upon wax,-

们应该成为我的水手，勇敢并且充满耐心吧！

我的兄弟们千万不要错失良机啊，你们要学着不要错失良机啊！海上的大风暴：许多人都在寻找着你，以求你能够救助他们！

大海之上刮起了风暴：大海之中包含了世间万物。好的！前进吧！你们这些无比英勇的海上冒险者们！

让我们推动舵柄，朝着我们的孩子们的国度进发吧！那里的风暴要比大海里的更凶猛，我们伟大的充满渴求的风暴！

（29）

“为什么要如此的坚硬！”——有一天，黑炭对钻石说道，“难不成，我们之间是近亲的关系？”

为什么要如此的坚硬？啊，我的兄弟们啊，我如是问问你们：你们难道不是我的兄弟们吗？

为什么要如此的柔软、如此的顺从、如此的屈服呢？为什么在你们的心灵当中，会有如此之多的否定和拒绝呢？为什么在你们的面孔之中拥有如此之少的绝不屈服于命运的色彩呢？

倘若你们并不想成为宿命论主义者并且不屈不挠的话，那么在将来，你们依靠什么来征服我？

倘若你们的坚硬并不能爆炸并且碎裂，粉碎成碎片，那么在将来，你们要怎么才能跟我一起创造呢？

-Blessed to write upon the will of millenniums as upon brass,- harder than brass, nobler than brass. Entirely hard is only the noblest.

This new table, O my brothers, put I up over you: Become hard!-

30.

O you, my Will! you change of every need, my needfulness! Preserve me from all small victories!

You fatedness of my soul, which I call fate! you In-me! Over-me! Preserve and spare me for one great fate!

And your last greatness, my Will, spare it for your last- that you may be inexorable in your victory! Ah, who has not perished to his victory!

Ah, whose eye has not bedimmed in this intoxicated twilight! Ah, whose foot has not faltered and forgotten in victory- how to stand!-

-That I may one day be ready and ripe in the great noon-tide: ready and ripe like the glowing ore, the lightning-bearing cloud, and the swelling milk-udder:-

-Ready for myself and for my most hidden Will: a bow eager for its arrow, an arrow eager for its star:-

-A star, ready and ripe in its noontide, glowing, pierced, blessed, by annihilating sun-

因为创造者是坚强的。而且你一定要以那作为你的幸福，你将自己的手按压在千载重荷之上，就好像按压在蜂蜡之上一样。

必须要以那为幸福，在千载重荷的意志之上进行书写，就好像在铜板上进行书写一样，——不过它们要比铜板更加坚硬，比铜板更加高贵，只有最高贵者才是完全坚硬的。

啊，我的兄弟们啊，我要将这一新榜挂于你们之上："成为坚强的人吧！"

（30）

啊，你，我的意志！你，你是所有需求的枢纽，你是我迫切需要的人啊！快将我保存起来以避免所有的小型的胜利吧！

你，就是我所谓的命中注定的，我的灵魂之命运啊！你就在我的体内啊！为了一种伟大的命运，请你好好保护我啊！

我的意志啊！为了你的最后，真爱着你的最后的伟大——能够让你在你的胜利之中不屈不挠！哎，不是为了自己的胜利而去征服了的又是谁呢！

哎，在迷醉的破晓时分，有谁的眼睛没有变得模糊和昏暗呢！哎，在取得胜利的时候，有谁的双脚没有蹒跚、踉跄着行走——无法站立！

——终有一天我能够在伟大的正午时分完备而成熟：就像闪耀着耀眼的光芒的矿石、就像电闪雷鸣的乌云，就像膨胀的乳房一样完备而成熟：——

——为了我自己以及我的最为隐秘的意志而做好准备：一张弓无比渴望地看着它的弓箭，而一只弓箭则无比渴望地看着它的星星：——

——一颗行星在正午时分能够达到完备和成熟，被毁灭的太阳之弓箭灼烧、被射穿

arrows:-

-A sun itself, and an inexorable sun-will, ready for annihilation in victory!

O Will, you change of every need, my needfulness! Spare me for one great victory!- -

Thus spoke Zarathustra.

57. The Convalescent

1.

ONE morning, not long after his return to his cave, Zarathustra sprang up from his couch like a madman, crying with a frightful voice, and acting as if some one still lay on the couch who did not wish to rise. Zarathustra's voice also resounded in such a manner that his animals came to him frightened, and out of all the neighboring caves and lurking-places all the creatures slipped away- flying, fluttering, creeping or leaping, according to their variety of foot or wing. Zarathustra, however, spoke these words:

Up, abysmal thought out of my depth! I am your cock and morning dawn, you overslept reptile: Up! Up! My voice shall soon crow you awake!

Unbind the fetters of your ears: listen! For I wish to hear you! Up! Up! There is thunder enough to make the very graves listen!

And rub the sleep and all the dimness and blindness out of your eyes! Hear me also with

并且受到祝福：——

——一个太阳，一种不屈不挠的太阳之意志，已经准备好在胜利的时候毁灭！

啊，意志啊，你就是所有的需要的枢纽，你是我迫切需要的人啊！为了一种伟大的命运，请你好好保护我啊！

查拉图斯特拉如是说。

57．新愈者

（1）

就在查拉图斯特拉重新回到他的洞穴不久之后的一天清晨，查拉图斯特拉就像一个疯子一样从他的沙发上蹿跳了起来，他用令人胆寒的声音大喊了起来，就好像一个仍旧躺在沙发上，丝毫没有起来的打算的人一样。查拉图斯特拉仍旧继续地叫喊着，因此，他的老鹰和蛇全都无比惊恐地看着他，在他周围的洞穴和比较隐秘的地方里面的动物们——飞的飞、走的走、爬的爬或是跳的跳，全都溜走了，但是，查拉图斯特拉如是说道：

快起来，我的深不可测的思想啊！从深处起来啊！你这个贪睡的大爬虫啊！我就是你的雄鸡以及清晨的曙光：起来！起来！要不了多久，我的叫喊声就能把你吵醒！

解开束缚着你的耳朵的锁链：仔细倾听吧！因为我想让你听到！起来！起来！这里拥有足以让所有的墓穴倾听的惊雷！

擦拭掉你们眼睛里的睡意以及所有的昏暗和盲目！也用你们的眼睛倾听我：甚至对

your eyes: my voice is a medicine even for those born blind.

And once you are awake, then shall you ever remain awake. It is not my custom to awake great-grandmothers out of their sleep that I may bid them- sleep on!

You stir, stretch yourself, wheeze? Up! Up! Not wheeze, shall you,- but speak to me! Zarathustra calls you, Zarathustra the godless!

I, Zarathustra, the advocate of living, the advocate of suffering, the advocate of the circuit- you do I call, my most abysmal thought!

Joy to me! you come,- I hear you! My abyss speaks, my lowest depth have I turned over into the light!

Joy to me! Come here! Give me your hand- - ha! let be! aha!- - Disgust, disgust, disgust- - - alas to me!

2.

Hardly, however, had Zarathustra spoken these words, when he fell down as one dead, and remained long as one dead. When however he again came to himself, then was he pale and trembling, and remained lying; and for long he would neither eat nor drink. This condition continued for seven days; his animals, however, did not leave him day nor night, except that the eagle flew forth to fetch food. And what it fetched and foraged, it laid on Zarathustra's couch: so that Zarathustra at last lay among yellow and red berries, grapes, rosy apples, sweet-

于那些生来就盲目地人来说，我的声音也是可以带来光明的药物。

一旦你醒过来，你应该永久地保持着清醒的状态。叫醒还在熟睡的我的老祖母们，然后再吩咐她们接着睡觉，并不是我的习惯！

你自己搅动、伸展四肢，并且喘息了吗？起来！起来！你不应该喘息的——你应该只对我说话！查拉图斯特拉在叫你，查拉图斯特拉这个无神者！

我，查拉图斯特拉，我是生命的辩护者、苦难的辩护者、循环的辩护者——我呼唤着你，我这最深不可测的想法啊！

快乐啊！你来了啊！——我听到你的声音了！我的深渊在说话，我把我最深的深渊转移到了光明之中！

快乐啊！快来我这里吧！把你的双手给我！——哈，啊哈哈！——哈哈，憎恶，憎恶！哎！——悲哀啊！

（2）

但是，就在查拉图斯特拉刚说完这些话的时候，他就像一个死去的人一样一头栽倒在地，他就像死了一样，在地上躺了好久好久。然而，当他再一次恢复意识之后，他的脸色苍白，浑身颤抖，并且仍旧保持躺着的状态，在很长的一段时间之内，他既不吃饭也不喝水。类似这样的情况一连持续了七天；但是他的动物们无论白天还是夜晚全都寸步不离地守候在他的身边，除了老鹰会时不时地飞走寻找食物。并且它会把它抓到的和掠夺的食物放在他的床榻之上：就这样，到了最后，查拉图斯特拉躺在了黄色以及红色的浆果、

smelling herbage, and pine-cones. At his feet, however, two lambs were stretched, which the eagle had with difficulty carried off from their shepherds.

At last, after seven days, Zarathustra raised himself upon his couch, took a rosy apple in his hand, smelt it and found its smell pleasant. Then did his animals think the time had come to speak to him.

"O Zarathustra," said they, "now have you lain thus for seven days with heavy eyes: will you not set yourself again upon your feet?

Step out of your cave: the world waits for you as a garden. The wind plays with heavy fragrance which seeks for you; and all brooks would like to run after you.

All things long for you, since you have remained alone for seven days- step forth out of your cave! All things want to be your physicians!

Did perhaps a new knowledge come to you, a bitter, grievous knowledge? Like leavened dough lay you, your soul arose and swelled beyond all its bounds.-"

-O my animals, answered Zarathustra, talk on thus and let me listen! It refreshes me so to hear your talk: where there is talk, there is the world as a garden to me.

How charming it is that there are words and tones; are not words and tones rainbows and seeming bridges 'twixt the eternally separated?

To each soul belongs another world; to each soul is every other soul a back-world.

Among the most alike does semblance deceive most delightfully: for the small gap is most

葡萄、红红的苹果、散发着甜美芳香的牧草以及松球的中间。就在他的脚边，放置着两只小羊羔，这两只小羊羔是那只老鹰费了很大的力气从他们的牧羊人那里抢过来的。

最终，到了七天之后，查拉图斯特拉从他的床榻上起来了，他用手拿起了一个红红的苹果，放在鼻子边闻了闻，查拉图斯特拉发现这个苹果散发着令人愉悦的芳香。紧接着，他的动物们开始认为他们是时候跟查拉图斯特拉聊聊天了。

“啊，查拉图斯特拉，”他们说道，“你已经紧闭双眼在这里躺了七天七夜了；难道，你自己不再打算重新站起来了吗？

从你的洞穴中出来：这个世界就像是一个花园一样等候着你的到来。散发着浓郁的芳香的风在寻找着你；所有的小溪全都喜欢跟随在你的身后。

自从你在这里连续躺了七天七夜之后，世间万物全都期盼着你——快从你的洞穴中走出来吧！世间万物都想要成为你的医生呢！

或许你已经有了一种全新的自知，一种苦涩的、痛苦的自知？你就像被发酵过的面团一样躺着，你的灵魂被唤起，并且膨胀到超出了自身的范围。”

——啊，我的动物们啊，查拉图斯特拉回答道，你们如是说下去，让我好好听一听！听你们说话真是让我感到神清气爽：对于我来说，只要是有谈话的地方，就会有如同一个花园一样的世界。

这些话语和这些腔调是多么的充满魅力啊；难道这些话语和腔调不是两个永远被隔离的事物的彩虹和桥梁吗？

不同的灵魂归属于不同的世界；任何一个灵魂都是其他灵魂的另一个世界。

在彼此最相似的事物当中，错觉诉说着最欢快的谎言：因为最小的鸿沟是最难跨越的。

对于我来说——我的身体之外怎么能够存在另一个我呢？这里根本就不存在我的身

difficult to bridge over.

For me- how could there be an outside-of-me? There is no outside! But this we forget on hearing tones; how delightful it is that we forget!

Have not names and tones been given to things that man may refresh himself with them? It is a beautiful folly, speaking; therewith dances man over everything.

How lovely is all speech and all falsehoods of tones! With tones dances our love on variegated rainbows.-

-"O Zarathustra," said then his animals, "to those who think like us, things all dance themselves: they come and hold out the hand and laugh and flee- and return.

Everything goes, everything returns; eternally rolls the wheel of existence. Everything dies, everything blossoms forth again; eternally runs on the year of existence.

Everything breaks, everything is integrated anew; eternally builds itself the same house of existence. All things separate, all things again greet one another; eternally true to itself remains the ring of existence.

Every moment begins existence, around every 'Here' rolls the ball 'There.' The middle is everywhere. Crooked is the path of eternity."-

-O you wags and barrel-organs! answered Zarathustra, and smiled once more, how well do you know what had to be fulfilled in seven days:-

-And how that monster crept into my throat and choked me! But I bit off its head and spat it

体之外的地方！当我们听着音乐的时候，我们全然忘记了这些；这是多么令人感到欣喜的遗忘啊！

人类可以在其中恢复精神的万物，不是都被给予了名称和腔调了吗？说话就是一种非常漂亮的愚蠢；所以，人类能够在世间万物之上舞蹈。

所有的谈话以及所有的虚假的腔调是多么的可爱啊！我们的爱意在音调的伴奏之下，开始在五彩缤纷的彩虹之上翩翩起舞。

“啊，查拉图斯特拉，”他的动物们说道，“对于那些像我们一样进行思考的人而言，世间万物都在跳舞：它们走出来、伸出手、欢声笑语，奔跑——并且如此循环。”

“世间万物消亡了，世间万物又重获新生了：存在之车轮，在永恒地轮回着。世间万物凋零了，世间万物又再一次重获新生；存在之时间，永恒地奔走着。”

“世间万物都会破碎，世间万物又会重获新生；存在之本身会永恒地建造相同的存在之房屋。世间万物都会彼此分开，世间万物还会再一次重逢，存在之轮回对于自身来说永恒地保持着真实。”

“存在每时每刻都在开始，星球在‘这里’永恒地围绕着所有的‘那里’旋转，任何的地方都是宇宙的中心。永恒的道路是扭曲不平的。”

啊，你们这些喋喋不休的人和手风琴！查拉图斯特拉回答道，并且他再一次微笑了起来，你们怎么会知道那些必将会在七天之内完成的事情呢：

——你们怎么会知道那头怪兽会悄然爬进我的喉咙里，并且让我窒息的呢！但是我把那头怪兽的头咬了下来，并且将它从我的嘴巴里吐了出去。

你们——你们已经以他创作出了一首抒情诗了吗？但是，现在我就躺在这里，仍然被那些撕咬和唾弃弄得疲惫不堪，仍然为了我自身的救赎而患上疾病。

away from me.

And you- you have made a lyre-lay out of it? Now, however, do I lie here, still exhausted with that biting and spitting-away, still sick with my own salvation.

And you looked on at it all? O my animals, are you also cruel? Did you like to look at my great pain as men do? For man is the cruel animal.

At tragedies, bull-fights, and crucifixions has he hitherto been happiest on earth; and when he invented his hell, behold, that was his heaven on earth.

When the great man cries-: immediately runs the little man there, and his tongue hangs out of his mouth for very lusting. Yet he calls it his "pity."

The little man, especially the poet- how passionately does he accuse life in words! Hearken to him, but do not fail to hear the delight which is in all accusation!

Such accusers of life- them life overcomes with a glance of the eye. "You love me?" says the insolent one; "wait a little, as yet have I no time for you."

Towards himself man is the cruel animal; and in all who call themselves "sinners" and "bearers of the cross" and "penitents," do not overlook the voluptuousness in their plaints and accusations!

And I myself- do, I thereby want to be man's accuser? Ah, my animals, this only have I learned hitherto, that for man his evil is necessary for his best,-

-That all that is evil is the best power, and the hardest stone for the highest creator; and that man must become better and more evil:-

你们难道已经彻底地观察这些了吗？啊，我的动物们啊，难道你们也这么残酷和冷血吗？你们喜欢注视着我遭受到的巨大的痛苦，就像是人类做的那样吗？因为人类就是残忍的动物。

从古至今，人类把观察悲剧、决斗以及酷刑看作是这个世界上最幸福的事情，看啊，当他发明了地狱的时候，那就是人类在这片大地之上的天堂。

当伟大之人开始叫喊：那些渺小的人就会立即跑到那里去，并且从他的嘴巴里面伸出最具贪婪之欲望的舌头。但是，他称它为“怜悯”。

那渺小之人，尤其是诗人——他是如何充满激情地用话语来控诉自己的生命！好好听一听他说的话吧！但是千万不要遗漏他的所有的控诉之中的贪婪之欲望！

生命仅仅用注视的双眼就征服了这些控诉生命的人们。“你爱我吗？”这个傲慢无礼之人说道，“稍等一会儿吧，我目前还没有时间回答你。”

人类对于自己来说就是残忍冷血的动物；在所有称自己为“罪人”、“肩负十字架之人”以及“忏悔者”的心目当中，千万不能忽略他们在诉苦和控诉当中所流露出来的贪婪之欲望！

我，我自己——所以，我想要成为人类的控诉者？哎，我的动物们啊，自古以来，我只知道人类心中的邪恶对于他们内心当中的善意来说，是必不可少的，——

——所有的邪恶就是他们最强有力的力量，那是最高等的创造者的最坚硬的石头；因此，人类必须变得更好，但也更坏：——

不是因为我被捆绑在了这个苦难的火刑之柱上，我才知道人类是最邪恶的——而是我叫喊着，叫喊着人类从未叫喊过的声音：

Not to this torture-stake was I tied, that I know man is bad,- but I cried, as no one has yet cried:

"Ah, that his evil is so very small! Ah, that his best is so very small!"

The great disgust at man- it strangled me and had crept into my throat: and what the soothsayer had presaged: "All is alike, nothing is worth while, knowledge strangles."

A long twilight limped on before me, a fatally weary, fatally intoxicated sadness, which spoke with yawning mouth.

"Eternally he returns, the man of whom you are weary, the small man"- so yawned my sadness, and dragged its foot and could not go to sleep.

A cavern, became the human earth to me; its breast caved in; everything living became to me human dust and bones and mouldering past.

My sighing sat on all human graves, and could no longer arise: my sighing and questioning croaked and choked, and gnawed and nagged day and night:

-"Ah, man returns eternally! The small man returns eternally!"

Naked had I once seen both of them, the greatest man and the small man: all too like one another- all too human, even the greatest man!

All too small, even the greatest man!- that was my disgust at man! And the eternal return also of the small man!- that was my disgust at all existence!

Ah, Disgust! Disgust! Disgust!- - Thus spoke Zarathustra, and sighed and shuddered; for he remembered his sickness. Then did his animals prevent him from speaking further.

“哎，人类的邪恶实在是太微不足道了！哎，人类的善意也同样非常渺小！”

对于人类的伟大憎恶——它将我紧紧地勒住，爬进了我的喉咙：预言家所预示过的：“世间万物都是相似的，任何事物都是毫无价值的，知识能够让人窒息。”

在漫长的黑夜当中，一种致命的厌倦，致命并且迷醉的悲哀迈着踉跄的脚步来到了我的面前，它用打着哈欠的嘴巴说起了话。

“你所厌倦的渺小之人的永恒之回归”——我的悲哀如是说道，它拖拽着自己的脚，已经不能安心沉睡。

对于我来说，人类的大地已经成为一处坟墓；它的胸部在下沉，对于我来说，任何存在着的事物都成为了人类的尘埃、骨头，成为一种腐朽的过去。

我的悲伤之叹息坐在了所有人类的坟墓之上，并且它再也无法站起来了：我的悲伤之哀叹以及我的质疑没日没夜发着牢骚，哽咽着、啃咬着以及抱怨着：

——“哎，人类永久地回归了！渺小之人永久地回归了！”

我曾经看到过这两者的赤身裸体的状态，最伟大之人以及最渺小之人；这两者都太过于相似了，太像人类了——甚至于最伟大之人也太像人类了！

这两者都太过于渺小了，甚至于最渺小之人也太过于渺小了！——这就是我对于人类的憎恶！即便是最渺小之人也同样是永久地循环！——这就是我对于所有的存在的憎恶！

哎，憎恶！憎恶！憎恶！——查拉图斯特拉如是说，然后他叹了口气，并且颤抖了起来，因为他想起了他的疾病。因此，他的动物们开始阻止查拉图斯特拉，不让他再继续说下去。

"Do not speak further, you convalescent!"- so answered his animals, "but go out where the world waits for you like a garden.

Go out to the roses, the bees, and the flocks of doves! Especially, however, to the singing-birds, to learn singing from them!

For singing is for the convalescent; the sound ones may talk. And when the sound also want songs, then want they other songs than the convalescent."

-"O you wags and barrel-organs, do be silent!" answered Zarathustra, and smiled at his animals. "How well you know what consolation I created for myself in seven days!

That I have to sing once more- that consolation did I create for myself, and this convalescence: would you also make another lyre-lay thereof?"

-"Do not talk further," answered his animals once more; "rather, you convalescent, prepare for yourself first a lyre, a new lyre! For behold, O Zarathustra! For your new lays there are needed new lyres.

Sing and bubble over, O Zarathustra, heal your soul with new lays: that you may bear your great fate, which has not yet been any one's fate!

For your animals know it well, O Zarathustra, who you are and must become: behold, you are the teacher of the eternal return,- that is now your fate!

That you must be the first to teach this teaching- how could this great fate not be your greatest danger and infirmity!

“你不要再继续说下去了，你这个还处于恢复期的病人！”——他的动物们如是回答道，快点出去吧，那个犹如花园一般的世界正在等待着你。

快快去玫瑰花丛、蜜蜂之群以及鸽子之群里去吧！特别是到能够歌唱的鸟儿那里去吧，从它们那里学习唱歌的本领！

因为唱歌对于还处于恢复期的病人来说是非常合适的；只有身心健康的人才可以说话，当身心健康的人也想要唱歌的时候，他会比还处于恢复期的病人更加有唱别的歌曲的欲望。

“啊，你们这喋喋不休之人和手风琴，你们要保持安静！”查拉图斯特拉回答道，然后他开始冲着他的动物们微笑。“你们是如何知道我在这七天七夜里，我为我自己所创造的安慰呢！

我还要再一次歌唱——我为我自己创造的安慰以及一种大病渐愈：所以，你们愿意创作一首抒情诗吗？”

——“你不要再说话了，”他的动物们再一次回答道，“你这个还未恢复的病人啊！你自己最好预先准备一把竖琴！”啊，查拉图斯特拉，因为你的全新的诗歌需要新的竖琴进行伴奏。

啊，查拉图斯特拉啊，纵情高歌，用新的诗歌治愈你的灵魂：可以让你承担起所有人都没有的属于你的伟大的命运！

啊，查拉图斯特拉啊，你的动物们对你非常了解，他们知道你是什么样的人，知道你必将成为什么样的人：快看啊！你就是那永恒的循环的说教者——现在，这就是你的命运！

你必定是说教这一理论的第一人——这一伟大的命运怎么能不成为你的最伟大的危

Behold, we know what you teach: that all things eternally return, and ourselves with them, and that we have already existed times without number, and all things with us.

You teach that there is a great year of Becoming, a prodigy of a great year; it must, like a sand-glass, ever turn up anew, that it may anew run down and run out:-

-So that all those years are like one another in the greatest and also in the small, so that we ourselves, in every great year, are like ourselves in the greatest and also in the small.

And if you would now die, O Zarathustra, behold, we know also how you would then speak to yourself:- but your animals beseech you not to die yet!

You would speak, and without trembling, buoyant rather with bliss, for a great weight and worry would be taken from you, you patientest one!-

'Now do I die and disappear,' would you say, 'and in a moment I am nothing. Souls are as mortal as bodies.

But the plexus of causes returns in which I am intertwined,- it will again create me! I myself pertain to the causes of the eternal return.

I come again with this sun, with this earth, with this eagle, with this serpent- not to a new life, or a better life, or a similar life:

-I come again eternally to this identical and selfsame life, in its greatest and its small, to teach again the eternal return of all things,-

-To speak again the word of the great noontide of earth and man, to announce again to man

险和疾病呢！

快看啊！我们都知道你在说教什么：世间万物都在永恒的循环，我们和世间万物是一样的，我们存在的次数已经不能用数字来计算了，我们和世间万物是合为一体的。

你教育人，在这个世界上有一种“生成之大年”，存在着一种伟大的年当中的奇观，它必定会像一个沙漏一样永久地翻新，永久地运转和流转：

——因此，所有那些岁月在最伟大之处类似，同样也在最渺小之处类似，所以，我们自己在所有的伟大之年中的最伟大之处类似，同样也在最渺小之处类似。

啊，查拉图斯特拉啊，倘若你现在就死去了，快看啊，到了那个时候，我们仍然知道你是如何跟你自己进行对话的——但是，你的动物们恳求你现在还不能死去！

希望你开口说话，无所畏惧且自满，因为一种巨大的重量和担忧都想从你的身上脱离出来，你这最能够容忍的人！

现在，我会死去，并且消失，你会说，而且过不了多久，我就会变成虚无。灵魂就像人类的躯体一样终有一死。

但是，我所缠绕的因果关系之结节如是循环着——它会再一次创造我！我自己属于永恒之循环的因果关系。

我同这里的太阳、这片大地、这里的老鹰、这里的毒蛇一起，重头来过——但是这并不是什么新的生命，不是什么更美好的生命，也不是什么相同的生命：

我再一次重新成为这一相同且同一的生命，在最伟大和最渺小的事物当中，重新教育人们世间万物的永恒之循环，

——再一次谈及这片大地的伟大正午以及人类，并且重新向人类宣讲超人。

我已经说过了我的说教。我被我自己的说教击倒了：我的永恒的命运如是意欲——

the Superman.

I have spoken my word. I break down by my word: so wills my eternal fate- as announcer do I perish!

The hour has now come for the down-goer to bless himself. Thus- ends Zarathustra's down-going.'"- -

When the animals had spoken these words they were silent and waited, so that Zarathustra might say something to them; but Zarathustra did not hear that they were silent. On the contrary, he lay quietly with closed eyes like a person sleeping, although he did not sleep; for he communed just then with his soul. The serpent, however, and the eagle, when they found him silent in such wise, respected the great stillness around him, and prudently retired.

58. The Great Longing

O MY soul, I have taught you to say "today" as "once on a time" and "formerly," and to dance your measure over every Here and There and Yonder.

O my soul, I delivered you from all by-places, I brushed down from you dust and spiders and twilight.

O my soul, I washed the petty shame and the by-place virtue from you, and persuaded you to stand naked before the eyes of the sun.

With the storm that is called "spirit" did I blow over your surging sea; all clouds did I blow

我就像宣讲者一样，就此死亡！

现在已经到了下沉之人为自己祝福的时候了。因此，查拉图斯特拉的下沉如是结束了。

当他的动物们说完这些话的时候，他们全都默不作声，静静地等待着，他们心里想着查拉图斯特拉或许会跟他们说些什么话；但是查拉图斯特拉并没有意识到他的动物们全都默不作声。而是正好相反，查拉图斯特拉闭上了双眼，安静地躺了下来，就像是一个正在沉睡的人，尽管他并没有睡觉；因为在这个时刻，他的灵魂正在思考。但是，当毒蛇、老鹰发现查拉图斯特拉是如此安静的时候，为了对他周围的伟大的宁静致以崇高的尊敬，他们全都小心翼翼地离开了。

58. 伟大的渴望

啊，我的灵魂啊，我已经跟你说过了“今天”就是“曾经的过去”以及“以前”，估量所有的这里、那里以及遥远的天边，和你一起共舞。

啊，我的灵魂啊，我带你离开了你那偏僻的地方，我将你从你的尘土、蜘蛛以及黎明里拍打了下来。

啊，我的灵魂啊，我从你的身上冲刷掉了微不足道的羞耻以及偏僻狭隘之地的道德，并且说服你在太阳的眼睛面前赤裸裸地站立着。

我用被人们称为是“精神”的风暴吹袭那你汹涌澎湃的大海；我将你头顶之上的所有云朵都吹走了，我甚至紧紧勒住了被称作是“罪恶”的扼杀者。

啊，我的灵魂啊，我给予你大声说出不可以的权力，就像大风暴一样，并且向开放

away from it; I strangled even the strangler called "sin."

O my soul, I gave you the right to say No like the storm, and to say Yes as the open heaven says Yes: calm as the light remain you, and now walk through denying storms.

O my soul, I restored to you liberty over the created and the uncreated; and who knows, as you know, the voluptuousness of the future?

O my soul, I taught you the contempt which does not come like worm-eating, the great, the loving contempt, which loves most where it contemns most.

O my soul, I taught you so to persuade that you persuade even the grounds themselves to you: like the sun, which persuades even the sea to its height.

O my soul, I have taken from you all obeying and knee-bending and homage-paying; I have myself given you the names, "Change of need" and "Fate."

O my soul, I have given you new names and gay-colored playthings, I have called you "Fate" and "the Circuit of circuits" and "the Navel-string of time" and "the Azure bell."

O my soul, to your domain gave I all wisdom to drink all new wines, and also all immemorially old strong wines of wisdom.

O my soul, every sun shed I upon you, and every night and every silence and every longing:-then grew you up for me as a vine.

O my soul, exuberant and heavy do you now stand forth, a vine with swelling udders and full clusters of brown golden grapes:-

-Filled and weighted by your happiness, waiting from superabundance, and yet ashamed of

的天堂一样说出可以：你还保持着犹如光亮一样的宁静，现在，你走入了予以否定的风暴之中。

啊，我的灵魂啊，我在有创造力和没有创造力当中恢复了你的自由；究竟有谁能够像你所了解的那样，知道什么才是未来的纵欲吗？

啊，我的灵魂啊，我曾经跟你说过一种蔑视，它并不会像吞噬虫子、伟大的、充满爱意的蔑视一样到来，它最喜欢的正是蔑视最猖獗肆意的地方。

啊，我的灵魂啊，我曾经跟你说过说服，你甚至可以说服这片大地来到你的身边：就像太阳一样，它能够说服大海攀升到它所在的高度。

啊，我的灵魂啊，我已经从你的身上拿走了所有的服从、屈膝跪拜以及盲目崇拜；我自己已经给你起了名字，“需求的改变”以及“命运”。

啊，我的灵魂啊，我已经给予了你新的名字以及五彩斑斓的玩物，我称你“命运”、“循环之循环”、“时间的脐带”以及“蔚蓝色的钟”。

啊，我的灵魂啊，我已经将我全部的智慧都给予了你，以此来畅饮所有新的酒水以及所有无法追忆的、古老的智慧之烈酒。

啊，我的灵魂啊，我将所有的太阳以及所有的夜晚、所有的宁静和所有的渴望之光亮全都照射在了你的身上：——然后，我就会让你像一个藤蔓一样为我成长。

啊，我的灵魂啊，现在，枝繁叶茂的你生气勃勃的、庄重地站在前面，一个拥有膨胀的乳房以及满满的棕金色的葡萄丛藤蔓：

——被你的幸福充满并且加重负担，等待着富足之多余，但是却对你的等待感到羞愧。

啊，我的灵魂啊，在这里根本就不存在更加受人爱戴、更加综合全面、更加广阔深

your waiting.

O my soul, there is nowhere a soul which could be more loving and more comprehensive and more extensive! Where could future and past be closer together than with you?

O my soul, I have given you everything, and all my hands have become empty by you:- and now! Now say you to me, smiling and full of melancholy: "Which of us owes thanks?-

-Do the giver not owe thanks because the receiver received? Is giving not a necessity? Is receiving not- pitying?"

O my soul, I understand the smiling of your melancholy: your over-abundance itself now stretches out longing hands!

Your fulness looks forth over raging seas, and seeks and waits: the longing of over-fulness looks forth from the smiling heaven of your eyes!

And verily, O my soul! Who could see your smiling and not melt into tears? The angels themselves melt into tears through the over-graciousness of your smiling.

Your graciousness and over-graciousness, is it which will not complain and weep: and yet, O my soul, longs your smiling for tears, and your trembling mouth for sobs.

"Is not all weeping complaining? And all complaining, accusing?" Thus speak you to yourself; and therefore, O my soul, will you rather smile than pour forth your grief-

-Than in gushing tears pour forth all your grief concerning your fulness, and concerning the craving of the vine for the vintager and vintage-knife!

But will you not weep, will you not weep forth your purple melancholy, then will you have

远的灵魂！未来和过去要在哪里才能比跟你在一起的时候，彼此距离的更近呢？

啊，我的灵魂啊，我已经把世间万物全都给你了，因为你的缘故，我的双手已经变得空无一物：——现在！现在你面带微笑、一脸忧郁地跟我说道：“在我们两个人当中，谁更应该亏欠感谢呢？

——难道给予者不亏欠感谢是因为接受者接受了来自给予者的馈赠吗？难道给予不是一种必不可少的东西吗？难道接受不是一种——慈悲吗？”

啊，我的灵魂啊，我非常能够理解你那面带忧郁的微笑：现在，你那过度富足的自我开始向外伸展充满渴望的双手了！

你那注视着前方汹涌澎湃的大海，寻找着、等待着：过度的渴望注视着你的眼睛之微笑的天堂！

啊，我的灵魂啊，说真的，有谁能够看到你的微笑，而不会融化成泪水？那些天使们就通过你的微笑之过度亲切而融化成了泪水。

啊，我的灵魂啊，你的亲切以及你的过度的亲切，是不会抱怨也不会低声啜泣的：但是，它渴望你那流泪的微笑，渴望你那因为啜泣而颤抖的嘴唇。

“是不是所有悲伤的哭泣都会抱怨？是不是所有的抱怨都会控诉？”你会对自己如是说道；啊，我的灵魂啊，所以，你宁愿微笑也不愿意倾吐你的悲痛。

——也不愿意在痛哭流涕的情况之下，倾吐所有有关于你的悲痛以及对葡萄酿酒和古董刀的渴求！

但是，你并不愿意悲伤地哭泣，你并不愿意悲伤地哭泣，倾吐你那紫色的忧郁，然后，你会开始放声高歌，啊，我的灵魂啊，快看啊！我在对自己微笑，那个对你提前预

to sing, O my soul!- Behold, I smile myself, who foretell you this:

-You will have to sing with passionate song, until all seas turn calm to hearken to your longing,-

-Until over calm longing seas the bark glides, the golden marvel, around the gold of which all good, bad, and marvellous things frisk:-

-Also many large and small animals, and everything that has light marvellous feet, so that it can run on violet-blue paths,-

-Towards the golden marvel, the spontaneous bark, and its master: he, however, is the vintager who waits with the diamond vintage-knife,-

-Your great deliverer, O my soul, the nameless one- for whom future songs only will find names! And verily, already has your breath the fragrance of future songs,-

-Already glow you and dream, already drink you thirstily at all deep echoing wells of consolation, already reposes your melancholy in the bliss of future songs!- -

O my soul, now have I given you all, and even my last possession, and all my hands have become empty by you:- that I bade you sing, behold, that was my last thing to give!

That I bade you sing,- say now, say: which of us now- owes thanks?- Better still, however: sing to me, sing, O my soul! And let me thank you!-

Thus spoke Zarathustra.

言了这些的人：

——你会放声高唱充满激情的歌曲，直到所有的大海都会安静下来，仔细地聆听你的渴望，——

——直到渴望在平静的大海之上滑行，那金灿灿的传奇，围绕在所有的善与恶的金子以及欢呼雀跃的令人感到不可思议的事物：——

——同样地，许多体型巨大的以及体型微小的动物们，还有世间万物都拥有轻便的、令人感到不可思议的双脚，正因为这样，它们才可以在紫罗兰色的道路之上纵情的奔跑，——

——接近金灿灿的奇迹、无意识的尖叫以及它的主人：然而，他是那个拿着镶嵌着钻石的葡萄小刀苦苦等待的采葡萄的人，——

——啊，我的灵魂啊，你这伟大的递送者，你这没有名字的人——那些只有未来的歌曲才能找到名字的人！说真的，你已经呼吸到了未来之歌曲的浓烈的芳香，——

你已经开始散发出光芒，并且做起了美梦，无比饥渴的你已经在所有幽深的、安慰之回声泉水里畅饮，你的忧郁已经在未来之歌曲的祝福当中休眠静养了！

啊，我的灵魂啊，现在，我已经把我的全部都给予你了，我甚至把我最后的私有物品也给予了你，所以，因为你的缘故，我的双手已经变得空无一物：——我命令你唱歌，快看啊！这是我最后一件要给予的东西了！

我命令你歌唱：——现在说吧，说吧：现在，我们二人当中——到底是谁亏欠感谢呢？——但是，比这更好的是，你给我唱歌，放声高歌，啊，我的灵魂啊！让我感谢你吧！

查拉图斯特拉如是说。

59. The Second Dance Song

1.

"INTO thy eyes gazed I lately, O Life: gold saw I gleam in your night-eyes,- my heart stood still with delight:

-A golden bark saw I gleam on darkened waters, a sinking, drinking, reblinking, golden swing-bark!

At my dance-frantic foot, do you cast a glance, a laughing, questioning, melting, thrown glance:

Twice only moved you your rattle with your little hands- then did my feet swing with dance-fury.-

My heels reared aloft, my toes they hearkened,- you they would know: has not the dancer his ear- in his toe!

To you did I spring: then fled you back from my bound; and towards me waved your fleeing, flying tresses round!

Away from you did I spring, and from your snaky tresses: then stood you there half-turned, and in your eye caresses.

With crooked glances- do you teach me crooked courses; on crooked courses learn my feet-crafty fancies!

59．另一支舞曲

（1）

最近，我凝视着你的眼睛，啊！生命：我看到金子在你那犹如黑夜一般的眼睛里闪耀着光芒，我的心灵快乐地站立在那里：

——我看到一个金灿灿的树皮在奇黑无比的水里散发着耀眼的光芒，一个下沉的、喝着水的、反复闪光的、金灿灿的摇摆之树皮！

在我无比疯狂的舞步之中，你投来了注视的目光，一种充满笑声的、充满质疑的、温柔的、被投掷过来的目光。

你只是喋喋不休地用你的小手移动了两下——然后，我的双脚开始用狂热的舞步来回摇摆。

我的后脚跟悬在空中，我的脚趾头在聆听着——它们肯定都认识你：在他的脚趾头里面，他的耳朵并不是什么舞蹈家！

我为了你而跳跃：然后我会从我这里快速地跳到你的背后；你那稍纵即逝的、在风中飞舞的女性之长发，在向我这边舞动着！

我跳跃着从你的身边离开，离开你那犹如蛇一般弯曲的长发：然后在你那眼睛的爱抚下，半转着身子站在你的面前。

你利用弯曲的注视教导我不平坦的路线，在这些不平坦的路线之下，我学习我那灵巧、梦幻的舞步！

I fear you near, I love you far; your flight allures me, your seeking secures me:- I suffer, but for you, what would I not gladly bear!

For you, whose coldness inflames, whose hatred misleads, whose flight enchains, whose mockery- pleads:

-Who would not hate you, you great bindress, in-windress, temptress, seekress, findress! Who would not love you, you innocent, impatient, wind-swift, child-eyed sinner!

Where pull you me now, you paragon and tomboy? And now fool you me fleeing; you sweet romp does annoy!

I dance after you, I follow even faint traces lonely. Where are you? Give me your hand! Or your finger only!

Here are caves and thickets: we shall go astray!- Halt! Stand still! See you not owls and bats in fluttering fray?

You bat! you owl! you would play me foul? Where are we? From the dogs have you learned thus to bark and howl.

You gnash on me sweetly with little white teeth; your evil eyes shoot out upon me, your curly little mane from underneath!

This is a dance over stock and stone: I am the hunter,- will you be my hound, or my chamois anon?

Now beside me! And quickly, wickedly springing! Now up! And over!- Alas! I have fallen myself overswinging!

我害怕你靠近我的身边，我喜欢你离我远远的；你的飞行在诱惑着我，你的寻找在保护着我：——我为了你，而忍受那些我并不愿意去承担的苦难！

对于你而言，谁的冷淡会燃起熊熊烈火，谁的仇恨会偏离了方向，谁的飞行会被紧紧地束缚起来，谁的嘲笑会苦苦辩护：

——有谁不会憎恶你，你这伟大的束缚，在微风之中、在诱惑之中、在探索之中以及在寻找之中！有谁会不喜欢你，你这天真无邪的、没有耐心的、迅疾如风的、有着孩子般的眼睛的罪恶之人！

现在，你这是要把我拖拉到哪里去？你这优秀之人和带着男子风范的野丫头？现在，你欺骗了我，然后就突然消失了；你这个可爱的顽皮女孩实在是让人讨厌！

我在你的身后跳舞，我甚至独身一人追随着逐渐消逝的足迹。你到底在哪里？快把你的双手给我吧！或是只给我你的手指！

这里有洞穴和错综复杂的灌木丛：我们一定是偏离了正确的道路！——快停下来吧！安静地站在那里！难道你们没有看到扑闪着翅膀打架的猫头鹰和蝙蝠吗？

你的蝙蝠！你的猫头鹰！你想缠住我吗？我们这是在什么地方？你从那些狗的身上学会了嚎叫和咆哮。

你用洁白的小牙齿温柔地咬着我；你那邪恶的眼睛将目光射向了我，你这个来自地下的、卷曲的小鬃毛！

这就是一种在储备物和石头上的舞蹈：我就是猎人——你就是我的猎犬，或是我的麂皮？

现在来到我的身边！快一点，居心叵测地跳起来吧！现在跳起来！哎！就连我自己

Oh, see me lying, you arrogant one, and imploring grace! Gladly would I walk with you- in some lovelier place!

-In the paths of love, through bushes variegated, quiet, trim! Or there along the lake, where gold-fishes dance and swim!

You are now a-weary? There above are sheep and sun-set stripes: is it not sweet to sleep- the shepherd pipes?

You are so very weary? I carry you there; let just your arm sink! And are you thirsty- I should have something; but your mouth would not like it to drink!-

-Oh, that cursed, nimble, supple serpent and lurking-witch! Where are you gone? But in my face do I feel through your hand, two spots and red blotches itch!

I am verily weary of it, ever your sheepish shepherd to be. You witch, if I have hitherto sung to you, now shall you- cry to me!

To the rhythm of my whip shall you dance and cry! I forget not my whip?- Not I!"-

2.

Then did Life answer me thus, and kept thereby her fine ears closed:

"O Zarathustra! Crack not so terribly with your whip! You know surely that noise kills thought,- and just now there came to me such delicate thoughts.

也一块跟着过度摇摆了！

啊，你看着我躺在这里，你这个傲慢的家伙，恳求慈悲！我很高兴能跟你一起走——一起去一些令人心旷神怡的地方！

——在爱情的道路之上，静悄悄地修剪五颜六色的灌木丛！或是金色的鱼在小湖边跳舞和游泳！

你现在没有感到疲倦吗？在我们头顶之上的是绵羊和日落的条纹：难道这里不是适合睡觉的地方吗——牧羊人的风笛声？

你现在是不是感到非常疲倦？我把你带到这里来；让你把手放下来！你一定是渴坏了——我这里应该有一些东西；但是，你的嘴巴似乎并不愿意喝类似这样的东西！

——啊，那条被诅咒的、灵活的、极其柔软的毒蛇，潜伏的巫师！你到底去哪里了？在我的脸上，我能够感受到你的双手、两个小点点以及皮肤上红色的、发痒的疹斑！

说真的，我已经对你这个无比懦弱的牧羊人感到疲倦了。你这个巫师，倘若我要对你歌唱，现在，你就应该大声地向我哭诉！

你就应该在我的鞭子的韵律之下，尽情地跳舞和哭诉！难道我忘记带我的鞭子了吗？——不，我没有忘记！

（2）

然后，生命如是回答了我，并且她时刻紧闭着自己那精致的耳朵：

“啊，查拉图斯特拉！你的鞭子的鞭打声实在是太刺耳了！毋庸置疑，你知道噪音能够杀死思想——而且，就在现在，一种非常细腻的思想来到了我的脑海里。

We are both of us genuine ne'er-do-wells and ne'er-do-ills. Beyond good and evil found we our island and our green meadow- we two alone! Therefore must we be friendly to each other!

And even should we not love each other from the bottom of our hearts,- must we then have a grudge against each other if we do not love each other perfectly?

And that I am friendly to you, and often too friendly, that know you: and the reason is that I am envious of your Wisdom. Ah, this mad old fool, Wisdom!

If your Wisdom should one day run away from you, ah! then would also my love run away from you quickly."-

Then did Life look thoughtfully behind and around, and said softly: "O Zarathustra, you are not faithful enough to me!

You love me not nearly so much as you say; I know you think of soon leaving me.

There is an old heavy, heavy, booming-clock: it booms by night up to your cave:-

-When you hear this clock strike the hours at midnight, then think you between one and twelve thereon-

-You think thereon, O Zarathustra, I know it- of soon leaving me!"-

"Yes," answered I, hesitatingly, "but you know it also"- And I said something into her ear, in amongst her confused, yellow, foolish tresses.

"You know that, O Zarathustra? That knows no one- -"

And we gazed at each other, and looked at the green meadow o'er which the cool evening

我们二者都是非常诚实正直的人，从来不做好事，也从来都不做坏事。我们发现我们的小岛以及我们的绿意葱葱的牧场已经超越了善与恶——我们二者是多么的孤独寂寞！因此，我们必须非常友好地对待彼此！

甚至于我们都不应该在我们的内心深处爱着彼此——倘若我们不能全身心地爱着彼此，那么，我们必将会对彼此怀恨在心？

我对待你是非常友好的，在通常的情况下，我对待你是过于友好的，我了解你：我这样对待你的理由就是因为我嫉妒你的智慧。啊，这个疯狂的老傻瓜，智慧！

如果有一天，你的智慧从你的脑子里逃掉了，啊！那么，我的爱也会飞快地从你的身体里逃离出去。”

然后生命细致入微地环顾了后面以及四周，并且用非常轻柔的语气说道：“啊，查拉图斯特拉，你并没有对我表现出足够的忠诚！

你对我的爱并不像你嘴里说的那样；我知道，你心里在想能够尽早地从我的身边离开。

这里有一个非常古老、非常沉重的，能够发出轰隆隆声的钟表：到了夜晚，它发出来的轰隆隆声能够直接传到你的洞穴里面去：

当你听到这个钟表到了午夜敲响自己的时候，你就会想现在的时间肯定介于 1 点和 12 点之间。

你就这么想着，啊，查拉图斯特拉，我知道的——你很快就要离开我！”

“一点也没错，”我支吾其词地回答道，“但是，你同样还知道”——并且我在她的耳边、在她那充满疑惑的、黄色的、愚蠢的女性之长发里面说了一些悄悄话。

“你知道的，啊，查拉图斯特拉？没有别人知道。”

紧接着，我们彼此凝视着对方，我们看向了寒冷的夜晚刚刚经过的绿色牧场，我们

was just passing, and we wept together.- Then, however, was Life dearer to me than all my Wisdom had ever been.-

Thus spoke Zarathustra.

3.

One!
O man! Take heed!
Two!
What says deep midnight's voice indeed?
Three!
"I slept my sleep"-
Four!
"From deepest dream I've woke and plead":-
Five!
"The world is deep",
Six!
"And deeper than the day could read".
Seven!
"Deep is its woe"-

在一起低声啜泣，但是，对于我来说，生命要比我以前所拥有的全部智慧都要弥足珍贵。

查拉图斯特拉如是说。

（3）

第一！
一个人！要小心提防！
第二！
那么，幽深的午夜之声音到底都说了些什么？
第三！
我睡过了我的睡眠。
第四！
我从最幽深的梦境之中惊醒，然后开始恳求：——
第五！
这个世界是幽深的，
第六！
它的幽深就连白昼都无法看透。
第七！
幽深就是它的悲痛。

Eight!
"Joy- deeper still than grief can be":
Nine!
"Woe says: Hence! Go!"
Ten!
"But joys all want eternity"-
Eleven!
"Want deep profound eternity!"
Twelve!

60. The Seven Seals

1.

IF I be a diviner and full of the divining spirit which wanders on high mountain-ridges, 'twixt two seas,-

Wanders 'twixt the past and the future as a heavy cloud- hostile to sultry plains, and to all that is weary and can neither die nor live:

Ready for lightning in its dark bosom, and for the redeeming flash of light, charged with lightnings which say Yes! which laugh Yes! ready for divining flashes of lightning:-

第八！
快乐仍旧要比悲痛更加幽深；
第九！
悲痛说道：从现在起，开始奔跑！
第十！
但是快乐想要的全部就是永恒。
第十一！
它想要幽深的、有深度的永恒！
第十二！

60. 七个印记

（1）

如果我是一个预言家，拥有能够在高耸的山峦上游荡的预测精神，在两个大海之间，就像一个沉重的、与闷热的平原为敌的云朵在过去和未来之间尽情地游荡，对于那些感到疲倦的事物来说，它们既不能死亡也不能生存：

准备好在黑暗的内心中接受电闪雷鸣，准备好迎接光亮的补偿之闪光，充满了闪电的它说道：是的！它笑着说道：是的！准备好迎接闪电的神圣之闪光吧：

-Blessed, however, is he who is thus charged! And verily, long must he hang like a heavy tempest on the mountain, who shall one day kindle the light of the future!-

Oh, how could I not be ardent for Eternity and for the marriage-ring of rings- the ring of the return?

Never yet have I found the woman by whom I should like to have children, unless it be this woman whom I love: for I love you, O Eternity!

For I love you, O Eternity!

2.

If ever my wrath has burst graves, shifted landmarks, or rolled old shattered law-tablets into precipitous depths:

If ever my scorn has scattered mouldered words to the winds, and if I have come like a besom to cross-spiders, and as a cleansing wind to old charnel-houses:

If ever I have sat rejoicing where old gods lie buried, world-blessing, world-loving, beside the monuments of old world-maligners:-

-For even churches and gods'-graves do I love, if only heaven looks through their ruined roofs with pure eyes; gladly do I sit like grass and red poppies on ruined churches-

Oh, how could I not be ardent for Eternity, and for the marriage-ring of rings- the ring of the return?

——但是，受到祝福的他已经被闪电充满了！说真的，他一定是长时间悬在了高耸的山峦上，就像一阵沉重的暴风一样，它总有一天会点亮未来的光亮！

啊！我怎么能不对永恒以及回归之环的结婚戒指致以最热情的关注呢？

我从来都没有找到过那个能够让我产生让她给我生孩子的想法的女人出现，除非，这个女人是我喜爱的女人：因为我喜欢你，啊，永恒！

因为，我喜欢你，啊，永恒！

（2）

如果我的愤怒曾经冲破坟墓，改变地面标识，或是将滚动的、老旧并且破碎的榜，卷入到险峻的深谷：

如果我的轻蔑曾经将扩散的、腐朽的话语迎风撕碎，如果我能够像一个长扫帚一样，清扫十字架蜘蛛，像一阵风一样，清扫阴冷古旧的尸屋：

如果我曾经无比欢快地坐在古老的诸神被埋葬的地方，祝福的世界、充满爱的世界，就在古老的愤世嫉俗之人的墓碑的旁边：

——因为我甚至爱那些教堂和诸神位的坟墓，要是天堂用它们纯净的眼睛看向那些破碎的屋顶，我就会像草地和红色的罂粟花一样坐在破碎的教堂之上。

啊！我怎么能不对永恒以及回归之环的结婚戒指致以最热情的关注呢？

我从来都没有找到过那个能够让我产生让她给我生孩子的想法的女人出现，除非，这个女人是我喜爱的女人：因为我喜欢你，啊，永恒！

Never yet have I found the woman by whom I should like to have children, unless it be this woman whom I love: for I love you, O Eternity!

For I love you, O Eternity!

3.

If ever a breath has come to me of the creative breath, and of the heavenly necessity which compels even chances to dance star-dances:

If ever I have laughed with the laughter of the creative lightning, to which the long thunder of the deed follows, grumbling, but obedient:

If ever I have played dice with the gods at the divine table of the earth, so that the earth quaked and ruptured, and snorted forth fire-streams:-

-For a divine table is the earth, and trembling with new active dictums and dice-casts of the gods:

Oh, how could I not be ardent for Eternity, and for the marriage-ring of rings- the ring of the return?

Never yet have I found the woman by whom I should like to have children, unless it be this woman whom I love: for I love you, O Eternity!

For I love you, O Eternity!

因为，我喜欢你，啊，永恒！

（3）

如果一种呼吸曾经来到我那创造性的呼吸之中，来到甚至能够驱散跳星星之舞的机会的神圣的必要性之中：

如果我曾经同充满创造力的闪电之笑声一起谈笑风生，嘲笑那喃喃诉苦但却无比顺从的行动的长久之惊雷：

如果我曾经在大地之神圣的桌子旁同诸神们玩掷骰子的游戏，因此，大地会颤抖、会破裂，并且喷涌出熊熊的烈火之溪流：

——因为一种神圣的桌子就是这片大地，并且因为新的积极的格言以及诸神位的抛掷骰子而颤抖不已：

啊！我怎么能不对永恒以及回归之环的结婚戒指致以最热情的关注呢？

我从来都没有找到过那个能够让我产生让她给我生孩子的想法的女人出现，除非，这个女人是我喜爱的女人：因为我喜欢你，啊，永恒！

因为，我喜欢你，啊，永恒！

4.

If ever I have drunk a full draught of the foaming spice- and confection-bowl in which all things are well mixed:

If ever my hand has mingled the furthest with the nearest, fire with spirit, joy with sorrow, and the harshest with the kindest:

If I myself am a grain of the saving salt which makes everything in the confection-bowl mix well:-

-For there is a salt which unites good with evil; and even the evilest is worthy, as spicing and as final over-foaming:-

Oh, how could I not be ardent for Eternity, and for the marriage-ring of rings- the ring of the return?

Never yet have I found the woman by whom I should like to have children, unless it be this woman whom I love: for I love you, O Eternity!

For I love you, O Eternity!

5.

If I be fond of the sea, and all that is of the sea, and fondest of it when it angrily contradicts me:

If the exploring delight be in me, which impels sails to the undiscovered, if the seafarer's delight be in my delight:

（4）

如果我曾经满满畅饮一樽散发着醇香、百味俱佳的佳酿。

如果我曾经用自己的双手将最远的距离和最近的距离融合在一起、将烈火和精神融合在一起、将快乐和悲伤融合在一起、将最严厉和最善良融合在一起：

如果我自己是拯救之盐的谷物，能够让世间万物在樽里面巧妙地混合：

——因为这里的盐能够将善与恶联合在一起，在这里就连最邪恶的也是有价值的，就好像香料和最后的泡沫一样：

啊！我怎么能不对永恒以及回归之环的结婚戒指致以最热情的关注呢？

我从来都没有找到过那个能够让我产生让她给我生孩子的想法的女人出现，除非，这个女人是我喜爱的女人：因为我喜欢你，啊，永恒！

因为，我喜欢你，啊，永恒！

（5）

如果我喜欢海洋以及海洋里面所有的东西,并且我最喜欢它恼羞成怒的反驳我的样子:

如果我的身上拥有充满探索欲望的快乐，它能够驱使我扬起风帆，在大海之上探索从未被人类发现的新大陆，如果我的快乐当中拥有航海家的快乐：

如果我的欣喜若狂曾经大声喊道：“海岸线已经从我的视线里消失了——现在，最

If ever my rejoicing has called out: "The shore has vanished,- now has fallen from me the last chain-

The boundless roars around me, far away sparkle for me space and time,- well! cheer up! old heart!"-

Oh, how could I not be ardent for Eternity, and for the marriage-ring of rings- the ring of the return?

Never yet have I found the woman by whom I should like to have children, unless it be this woman whom I love: for I love you, O Eternity!

For I love you, O Eternity!

6.

If my virtue be a dancer's virtue, and if I have often sprung with both feet into golden-emerald rapture:

If my wickedness be a laughing wickedness, at home among rose-banks and hedges of lilies:

-or in laughter is all evil present, but it is sanctified and absolved by its own bliss:-

And if it be my Alpha and Omega that everything heavy shall become light, everybody a dancer, and every spirit a bird: and verily, that is my Alpha and Omega!-

Oh, how could I not be ardent for Eternity, and for the marriage-ring of rings- the ring of the return?

Never yet have I found the woman by whom I should like to have children, unless it be this

后一条锁链也从我的身上掉落下去了：

无穷无尽的嘶吼围绕在我的身旁，空间和时间在遥远的地方向我闪耀着耀眼的光芒——好吧！快点振作起来！古老的心灵！”

啊！我怎么能不对永恒以及回归之环的结婚戒指致以最热情的关怀呢？

我从来都没有找到过那个能够让我产生让她给我生孩子的想法的女人出现，除非，这个女人是我喜爱的女人：因为我喜欢你，啊，永恒！

因为，我喜欢你，啊，永恒！

（6）

如果我的道德是一个跳舞之人的道德，倘若我经常用自己的双脚在金灿灿的奢华之狂喜中尽情地跳跃：

倘若我的罪恶是一种欢声笑语的罪恶，畅游在玫瑰之山谷和百合树篱之间：

——或者说，所有的罪恶全都出现在了欢声笑语之中，但是却被自身的祝福净化和赦免：——

倘若我的“阿尔法”与“欧米茄”，是能够让所有的沉重变得轻快，让所有的躯体都变成舞者，让所有的精神都变成鸟儿：说真的，这就是我的“阿尔法”与“欧米茄”！

啊！我怎么能不对永恒以及回归之环的结婚戒指致以最热情的关怀呢？

我从来都没有找到过那个能够让我产生让她给我生孩子的想法的女人出现，除非，

woman whom I love: for I love you, O Eternity!

For I love you, O Eternity!

7.

If ever I have spread out a tranquil heaven above me, and have flown into my own heaven with my own pinions:

If I have swum playfully in profound luminous distances, and if my freedom's avian wisdom has come to me:-

-Thus however speaks avian wisdom:- "Lo, there is no above and no below! Throw yourself about,- outward, backward, you light one! Sing! speak no more!

-Are not all words made for the heavy? Do not all words lie to the light ones? Sing! speak no more!"-

Oh, how could I not be ardent for Eternity, and for the marriage-ring of rings- the ring of the return?

Never yet have I found the woman by whom I should like to have children, unless it be this woman whom I love: for I love you, O Eternity!

For I love you, O Eternity!

这个女人是我喜爱的女人：因为我喜欢你，啊，永恒！

因为，我喜欢你，啊，永恒！

（7）

倘若我曾经是我的头顶之上铺展开来的静谧，并且用我自己的翅膀飞到属于我的天堂之中：

倘若我在深邃的、散发着光芒的遥远夜空中嬉戏玩耍，倘若我拥有了自由的飞鸟的智慧：

——因此，我那自由的飞鸟的智慧如是说：“快看啊！这里既没有上也没有下！自由自在地飞舞吧！向前、向后，你这轻快者！歌唱吧！不要再说话了！

——所有的话语难道不都是为沉重所用吗？对于轻盈者来说，所有的言语难道不都是谎言吗？歌唱吧！不要再说话了！”

啊！我怎么能不对永恒以及回归之环的结婚戒指致以最热情的关怀呢？

我从来都没有找到过那个能够让我产生让她给我生孩子的想法的女人出现，除非，这个女人是我喜爱的女人：因为我喜欢你，啊，永恒！

因为，我喜欢你，啊，永恒！

PART FOUR

61. The Honey Sacrifice

-AND again passed moons and years over Zarathustra's soul, and he heeded it not; his hair, however, became white. One day when he sat on a stone in front of his cave, and gazed calmly into the distance- one there gazes out on the sea, and away beyond sinuous abysses,- then went his animals thoughtfully round about him, and at last set themselves in front of him.

"O Zarathustra," said they, "gaze you out perhaps for your happiness?"- "Of what account is my happiness!" answered he, "I have long ceased to strive any more for happiness, I strive for my work."- "O Zarathustra," said the animals once more, "that say you as one who has overmuch of good things. Lie you not in a sky-blue lake of happiness?"- "You wags," answered Zarathustra, and smiled, "how well did you choose the simile! But you know also that my happiness is heavy, and not like a fluid wave of water: it presses me and will not leave me, and is like molten pitch."-

第四部

61. 蜜之祭品

月亮和岁月再一次经过查拉图斯特拉的灵魂，但是他对此并没有丝毫的察觉，然而，他的头发已经变得苍白。有一天，当查拉图斯特拉坐在他的洞穴前的一块石头上的时候，他内心无比平静地向远方凝视，他凝视着大海，越过蜿蜒曲折的深渊，然后，他那些若有所思的动物们全都会围绕在他的身边，最终，他们全部驻足在查拉图斯特拉的面前。

“啊，查拉图斯特拉，”他们说道，“你向远方凝视，难道是为了寻找你的幸福吗？”——“我的幸福到底是什么呢！”查拉图斯特拉回答道，“我已经很久没有去奋力寻找那些所谓的幸福了，我在为了自己的工作而努力奋斗。”——“啊，查拉图斯特拉，”那些若有所思的动物们再一次说道，“也就是说，你是那个做了太多善意之事的人。难道你没有在犹如蓝天般蔚蓝的幸福之湖水里说谎吗？”——“你们这些喋喋不休之人，”查拉图斯特拉微笑着回答道，“你们是如此出色地选择了暗喻！但是你们同样也知道我的快乐是无比沉重的，它并不像流动的水之波浪。它在按压着我，就像炽热的溪水之急流一样，不愿意让我离去。”

Then went his animals again thoughtfully around him, and placed themselves once more in front of him. "O Zarathustra," said they, "it is consequently for that reason that you yourself always becomes yellower and darker, although your hair looks white and flaxen? Lo, you sit in your pitch!"- "What do you say, my animals?" said Zarathustra, laughing; "verily I reviled when I spoke of pitch. As it happens with me, so is it with all fruits that turn ripe. It is the honey in my veins that makes my blood thicker, and also my soul stiller."- "So will it be, O Zarathustra," answered his animals, and pressed up to him; "but will you not today ascend a high mountain? The air is pure, and today one sees more of the world than ever."- "Yes, my animals," answered he, "you counsel admirably and according to my heart: I will today ascend a high mountain! But see that honey is there ready to hand, yellow, white, good, ice-cool, golden-comb-honey. For know that when aloft I will make the honey-sacrifice."-

When Zarathustra, however, was aloft on the summit, he sent his animals home that had accompanied him, and found that he was now alone:- then he laughed from the bottom of his heart, looked around him, and spoke thus:

That I spoke of sacrifices and honey-sacrifices, it was merely a ruse in talking and verily, a useful folly! Here aloft can I now speak freer than in front of mountain-caves and hermits' domestic animals.

What to sacrifice! I squander what is given me, a squanderer with a thousand hands: how could I call that- sacrificing?

紧接着，他的动物们再一次若有所思地围绕在查拉图斯特拉的周围，然后，他们再一次驻足在了查拉图斯特拉的面前。“啊，查拉图斯特拉，”他们说道，“说到底，那就是让你总是变得更加泛黄，更加黑暗的原因吗？尽管，你的头发看起来既苍白又淡黄。快看啊！你坐在了你的溪水之急流上面！”——“你们都说了些什么，我的动物们？”查拉图斯特拉大笑着说道，“说真的，当我开口说到溪水之急流的时候，我咒骂了起来。因为它发生在了我的身上，那么它也一定会发生在那些熟透了的水果的上面。它就是我的血管里的蜂蜜，它让我的血液变得更加厚重，并且还让我的灵魂变得更加宁静。”——“啊，查拉图斯特拉，但愿如此吧，”他的动物们回答道，并且按压着他：“但是，今天你难道不去攀登一座高耸的山峰吗？今天的空气非常纯净，你今天所看到的世界要比你以往所看到的都要多。”——“你们说得很对，我的动物们，”查拉图斯特拉回答道，“你们的建议非常好地迎合了我的内心的要求：今天我要攀登一座高耸的山峰！但是，我在这里所看到的蜂蜜就是淡黄的、白的、质量上乘的、冰爽的、金色之巢的蜂蜜。因为我知道，当我开始上升的时候，我可以制作出蜜之祭品。”

然而，当查拉图斯特拉站在山顶之上的时候，他让那些陪伴着他的动物们全都回家去了，他发现他现在已经孤身一人：——然后他笑了起来，发自内心深处地笑了起来，他环顾四周，如是说道：

我之前说过了献祭和蜜之祭品，那只不过是一种说话的策略和技巧，说真的，那就是一种非常有用的愚蠢！现在，我站在山峰之上，我能够比在山峰之洞穴以及隐士自养的动物们的面前更加自由自在地畅所欲言了。

什么是牺牲！我将给予我的全都挥霍一空，我就是一个拥有上千只手的挥霍者：我

And when I desired honey I only desired bait, and sweet mucus and mucilage, for which even the mouths of growling bears, and strange, sulky, evil birds, water:

-The best bait, as huntsmen and fishermen require it. For if the world be as a gloomy forest of animals, and a pleasure-ground for all wild huntsmen, it seems to me rather- and preferably- a fathomless, rich sea;

-A sea full of many-hued fishes and crabs, for which even the gods might long, and might be tempted to become fishers in it, and casters of nets,- so rich is the world in wonderful things, great and small!

Especially the human world, the human sea:- towards it do I now throw out my golden angle-rod and say: Open up, you human abyss!

Open up, and throw to me your fish and shining crabs! With my best bait shall I allure to myself today the strangest human fish!

-My happiness itself do I throw out into all places far and wide 'twixt orient, noontide, and occident, to see if many human fish will not learn to hug and tug at my happiness;-

Until, biting at my sharp hidden hooks, they have to come up to my height, the motleyest abyss-groundlings, to the wickedest of all fishers of men.

For this am I from the heart and from the beginning- drawing, here-drawing, upward-drawing, upbringing; a drawer, a trainer, a training-master, who not in vain counselled himself once on a time: "Become what you are!"

Thus may men now come up to me; for as yet do I await the signs that it is time for my

又怎么能够称它为牺牲呢？

当我想要蜂蜜的时候，那仅仅意味着我渴望得到诱饵、甜蜜的黏液以及黏质物，甚至是咆哮的灰熊的嘴巴，古怪、阴沉并且邪恶的鸟儿以及水。

——这些是猎人们以及渔夫们所需要的最好的诱饵。倘若这个世界是一个阴沉的动物森林，是一个为所有荒野的猎手们准备的充满乐趣的场地，然而，在我看来，我宁愿这个世界看上去更像是深不见底的、富饶的海洋。

——一个充满了五颜六色的鱼类和螃蟹的海洋，在那里甚至诸神也会充满渴望，他们或许会成为渔夫，成为撒网者，这个世界真是充满了大大小小的美好的事物。

特别是人类的世界，人类的海洋：——现在，我面朝它，伸出了我的黄金的手杖，然后说道：快快打开吧！你这人类的深渊！

快快打开吧，快点将你的鱼和闪闪发亮的螃蟹全都扔给我吧！今天，我用我最好的诱饵，可以捕捉到最稀奇古怪的人类之鱼！

——我会把我的快乐本身扔向所有遥远并且宽广的介于东方的、正午以及西方的世界，来看一看人类之鱼是否学会了拥抱并且用力拖拽我的幸福。

直到啃咬我那尖锐的、隐秘的钩子，他们已经来到了我的高度，来到了最炽热的深渊之海，来到了所有最邪恶的人类之渔夫的面前。

正因为如此，我开始从我的内心拖曳，从这里拖曳、向上拖曳；一个拖曳者、一个训练者、一个训练大师，他曾经有一次卓有成效地奉劝自己：“要成为你自己！”

因此，人类现在来到了我的身边；我在等待着属于我的向下走的时间的到来；因为我自己不会向下走，我必须这样做，在人类当中。

down-going; as yet do I not myself go down, as I must do, amongst men.

Therefore do I here wait, crafty and scornful upon high mountains, no impatient one, no patient one; rather one who has even unlearnt patience,- because he no longer "suffers."

For my fate gives me time: it has forgotten me perhaps? Or does it sit behind a big stone and catch flies?

And verily, I am well-disposed to my eternal fate, because it does not hound and hurry me, but leaves me time for merriment and mischief; so that I have to-day ascended this high mountain to catch fish.

Did ever any one catch fish upon high mountains? And though it be a folly what I here seek and do, it is better so than that down below I should become solemn with waiting, and green and yellow-

-A posturing wrath-snorter with waiting, a holy howl-storm from the mountains, an impatient one that shouts down into the valleys: "Hearken, else I will scourge you with the scourge of God!"

Not that I would have a grudge against such wrathful ones on that account: they are well enough for laughter to me! Impatient must they now be, those big alarm-drums, which find a voice now or never!

Myself, however, and my fate- we do not talk to the Present, neither do we talk to the Never: for talking we have patience and time and more than time. For one day must it yet come, and may not pass by.

What must one day come and may not pass by? Our great Hazar, that is to say, our great,

因此，我在这里等待，狡猾并且轻蔑之人站在高耸的山峰之上，没有不耐烦之人，也没有充满耐心之人，这里甚至还有已经忘记了耐心的人；因为他已经不再是“遭受苦难之人”了。

我的命运给予了我时间：难道它已经把我遗忘了吗？又或是它坐在一个大石头的后面，抓苍蝇吗？

说真的，我对我的永恒的命运抱有着好感，因为它并不会烦扰和催促我，而是给予我嬉戏玩耍和搞恶作剧的时间；所以，我今天攀登上了这座高耸的山峰来抓鱼。

难道没有人在高耸的山峰之上抓过鱼吗？尽管我在这里寻找和做事愚蠢至极，那也比我下降，并且变得庄严肃穆、变得充满活力、变得淡黄要好得多。

一个装腔作势、怒气冲冲的可笑之人，一个来自山峰的神圣的咆哮之风，一个在山谷里大声喊叫的不耐烦之人：“快听听吧！我会用上帝的咒骂来怒斥你！”

我并不是因为这些缘故而对那些愤怒之人怀恨在心：他们足够好能够嘲笑我！他们现在一定是迫不及待了，那些巨大的找到永恒之音的警示之鼓！

但是，我自己以及我的命运——我们并不会谈论现在，我们也不会谈论永久：因为关于谈论，我们拥有耐心、时间以及比时间多得多的时间。因为总有一天它会来到我们的身边。

有什么是必须在某一天来到我们身边的呢？我们伟大的哈扎尔，也就是说，我们伟大的、遥远的人类王国，拥有一千年历史的伟大的查拉图斯特拉王国。

那个所谓的“遥远”究竟有多么的遥远？究竟是什么让我如此担忧？但是这些并不

remote human-kingdom, the Zarathustra-kingdom of a thousand years- -

How remote may such "remoteness" be? What does it concern me? But on that account it is none the less sure to me-, with both feet stand I secure on this ground;

-On an eternal ground, on hard primary rock, on this highest, hardest, primary mountain-ridge, to which all winds come, as to the storm-parting, asking Where? and Whence? and Where?

Here laugh, laugh, my hearty, healthy wickedness! From high mountains cast down your glittering scorn-laughter! Allure for me with your glittering the finest human fish!

And whatever belongs to me in all seas, my in-and-for-me in all things- fish that out for me, bring that up to me: for that do I wait, the wickedest of all fish-catchers.

Out! out! my fishing-hook! In and down, you bait of my happiness! Drip your sweetest dew, you honey of my heart! Bite, my fishing-hook, into the belly of all black affliction!

Look out, look out, my eye! Oh, how many seas round about me, what dawning human futures! And above me- what rosy red stillness! What unclouded silence!

62. The Cry of Distress

THE next day sat Zarathustra again on the stone in front of his cave, whilst his animals roved about in the world outside to bring home new food,- also new honey: for Zarathustra had spent and wasted the old honey to the very last particle. When he thus sat, however, with a stick in his hand, tracing the shadow of his figure on the earth, and reflecting- verily! not

能让我确定，我用双脚安稳地站在这块大地之上：

——站在这块永恒的大地之上，站在坚硬的原始之岩石之上，站在这个最高耸的、最坚硬的原始之山脊之上，面向所有的微风来到的地方，来到风暴分离的地方，大声问道：在哪里？在哪里？在哪里？

我那真诚的、健全的邪恶在这里微笑！你从高耸的山峰之上投射下了你那闪闪发光的轻蔑之微笑！用你那闪闪发光的精致的人类之鱼诱惑我！

在所有的海洋里，凡是属于我的东西，在万物之中凡是属于我的东西——鱼，快将它带给我：我会在这里等待着，等待所有最邪恶的捕鱼之人的到来。

快出来！快出来！我的鱼钩！我的幸福之诱饵在上下攒动！溢出最甜美的露珠，我的内心之蜂蜜！啃咬沉入所有黑色的苦难的腹部的鱼钩！

注意点！注意点！我的眼睛！啊，究竟有多少海洋围绕在我的身边，泛起曙光的人类之未来！红冉冉的宁静盘旋在我的头顶之上！这是多么无云的寂静啊！

62．苦难的呼声

到了第二天，查拉图斯特拉再一次坐在了他的洞穴前面的一块大石头上，而他的动物们则在外面四处游荡，以便给家里带来新的食物以及新鲜的蜂蜜：因为查拉图斯特拉已经把所有的蜂蜜全都挥霍一空了。但是，当他坐下来的时候，他手里拿着一根棍子，在地上追逐着他的手指的影子，然后开始思考——说真的！不是他自己和他的阴影，突

upon himself and his shadow,- all at once he startled and shrank back: for he saw another shadow beside his own. And when he hastily looked around and stood up, behold, there stood the soothsayer beside him, the same whom he had once given to eat and drink at his table, the proclaimer of the great weariness, who taught: "All is alike, nothing is worth while, the world is without meaning, knowledge strangles." But his face had changed since then; and when Zarathustra looked into his eyes, his heart was startled once more: so much evil announcement and ashy-grey lightnings passed over that countenance.

The soothsayer, who had perceived what went on in Zarathustra's soul, wiped his face with his hand, as if he would wipe out the impression; the same did also Zarathustra. And when both of them had thus silently composed and strengthened themselves, they gave each other the hand, as a token that they wanted once more to recognize each other.

"Welcome here," said Zarathustra, "you soothsayer of the great weariness, not in vain shall you once have been my messmate and guest. Eat and drink also with me to-day, and forgive it that a cheerful old man sits with you at table!"- "A cheerful old man?" answered the soothsayer, shaking his head, "but whoever you are, or would be, O Zarathustra, you have been here aloft the longest time,- in a little while your bark shall no longer rest on dry land!"- "Do I then rest on dry land?"- asked Zarathustra, laughing.- "The waves around your mountain," answered the soothsayer, "rise and rise, the waves of great distress and affliction: they will soon raise your bark also and carry you away."- Then was Zarathustra silent and wondered.- "Do you still hear

然之间，他像受到了惊吓一样，开始退缩了起来：因为他看到了另一个影子就在他自己的影子的旁边。当他匆忙地环顾四周，并且站起来看的时候，他发现一个预言家就站在他的身边，这个预言家和那个被我给予了食物和水并且在我的餐桌旁就食的是同一个人，伟大之疲倦的宣告者，如是教育道：“任何事物都是彼此相像的，没有什么事物是有价值的，整个世界都是毫无意义的，知识让人窒息。”但是自那之后，他的脸色发生了变化；当查拉图斯特拉看向他的眼睛的时候，他的心脏再一次受到了惊吓：许许多多的邪恶的公告和灰色的闪电从他的脸上一闪而过。

那个预言者，他感受到了发生在查拉图斯特拉的灵魂上的事情，他用他的双手擦拭着他的脸庞，就好像他能够把印记擦去；查拉图斯特拉也同样做过这样的事。但他们全都悄悄地镇定了下来，并且给予了自己力量，他们把双手给予了彼此，作为一种记号，他们要再一次认出彼此。

“欢迎你来这里，”查拉图斯特拉说道，“你这个伟大之疲倦的预言家，你曾经是我的同餐之友和贵宾。你今天同样可以跟我一同共进美餐，请原谅一个快乐的老男人陪伴着你坐在餐桌的旁边！”——“一个快乐的老男人？”那个伟大之疲倦的预言家摇晃着脑袋问道，“但是，你到底是谁呢，啊，查拉图斯特拉，你已经来到了最长久的时间的上面——过不了多久，你的吼叫就没法再停留在干燥的大地之上了！”——“那么，我还能停留在干燥的大地之上吗？”查拉图斯特拉微笑着问道。“那些围绕在你的山峰周围的波浪，”预言家回答道：“不停地在上升，伟大的危难和苦痛之波浪：它们很快就会上升到你的吼叫，与此同时它们还会将你带走。”

然后，查拉图斯特拉安静了下来，他开始沉思，“你仍旧什么都没有听到吗？”预言家接着说道，“难道它没有冲刷并且咆哮着离开深度吗？”查拉图斯特拉再一次沉默

nothing?" continued the soothsayer: "does it not rush and roar out of the depth?"- Zarathustra was silent once more and listened: then heard he a long, long cry, which the abysses threw to one another and passed on; for none of them wished to retain it: so evil did it sound.

"You ill announcer," said Zarathustra at last, "that is a cry of distress, and the cry of a man; it may come perhaps out of a black sea. But what does human distress matter to me! My last sin which has been reserved for me,- know you what it is called?"

-"Pity!" answered the soothsayer from an overflowing heart, and raised both his hands aloft- "O Zarathustra, I have come that I may seduce you to your last sin!"-

And hardly had those words been uttered when there sounded the cry once more, and longer and more alarming than before- also much nearer. "Hear you? Hear you, O Zarathustra?" called out the soothsayer, "the cry concerns you, it calls you: Come, come, come; it is time, it is the highest time!"-

Zarathustra was silent then, confused and staggered; at last he asked, like one who hesitates in himself: "And who is it that there calls me?"

"But you know it, certainly," answered the soothsayer warmly, "why do you conceal yourself? It is the higher man that cries for you!"

"The higher man?" cried Zarathustra, horror-stricken: "what wants he? What wants he? The higher man! What wants he here?"- and his skin covered with perspiration.

The soothsayer, however, did not heed Zarathustra's alarm, but listened and listened in the

了起来，开始仔细聆听：然后，他听到一个无比幽深的叫喊，深渊将这一叫喊抛给了另一个深渊，并且开始如此传递下去；因为，没有任何一个深渊想拥有这样的叫喊：因为它听起来是如此的邪恶。

“你这个邪恶的宣告者，”最后，查拉图斯特拉说道，“这是一种不幸的呐喊，这是一种人类的呐喊；它或许来自于一片黑色的海洋。但是人类的危难和不幸跟我又有什么关系呢！我最后的罪恶已经为我保存好了：——你知道它的名字是什么吗？”

“慈悲！”预言家发自肺腑地回答道，并且他把自己的双手高举到空中——“啊，查拉图斯特拉，我将会引诱你，让你去见你最后的罪恶。”

那个预言家刚把这些话说完，这里便再一次响起了呐喊，而这一次的呐喊要比以前的都要长久，并且更加令人感到惊恐——同样也离我们更近。“你听到了吗？你听到了，啊，查拉图斯特拉？”那个预言家大声地呼喊道，“那个呐喊在为你担忧，那个呐喊在呼唤你：快来啊！快来啊！快来啊；是时候了，现在是最合适的时候了！”

然后，查拉图斯特拉开始安静了下来，他一脸的疑惑，步履也蹒跚了起来；最后，他就像一个犹豫不定的人一样问道：“究竟是谁在这里呼唤我？”

“你心里应该非常清楚，”那个预言家亲切地回答道，“你为什么要将你自己隐藏起来呢？这是一个更加高尚的人在呼唤着你啊！”

“更加高尚的人？”被吓坏了的查拉图斯特拉大叫道：“那个更加高尚的人究竟想要什么？他究竟想要什么？更加高尚的人啊！他究竟想要这里的什么？”他全身的皮肤都已被汗水覆盖了。

然而，那个预言家并没有注意到查拉图斯特拉的那种惊慌失措，而是朝下方的方向聆听再聆听。但是，当他在这里沉静了很长一段时间以后，他开始朝后面看去，他看到

downward direction. When, however, it had been still there for a long while, he looked behind, and saw Zarathustra standing trembling.

"O Zarathustra," he began, with sorrowful voice, "you do not stand there like one whose happiness makes him giddy: you will have to dance lest you tumble down!

But although you should dance before me, and leap all your side-leaps, no one may say to me: 'Behold, here dances the last joyous man!'

In vain would any one come to this height who sought him here: caves would he find, indeed, and back-caves, hiding-places for hidden ones; but not lucky mines, nor treasure-chambers, nor new gold-veins of happiness.

Happiness- how indeed could one find happiness among such buried-alive and solitary ones! Must I yet seek the last happiness on the Blessed isles, and far away among forgotten seas?

But all is alike, nothing is worth while, no seeking is of service, there are no longer any Blessed isles!"- -

Thus sighed the soothsayer; with his last sigh, however, Zarasthustra again became serene and assured, like one who has come out of a deep chasm into the light. "No! No! Three times No!" exclaimed he with a strong voice, and stroked his beard- "that do I know better! There are still Blessed isles! Silence then, you sighing sorrow-sack!

Cease to splash, you rain-cloud of the forenoon! Do I not already stand here wet with your misery, and drenched like a dog?

查拉图斯特拉浑身颤抖着站在那里。

“啊，查拉图斯特拉，”他开始用非常悲伤的声音说道，“你并不像那些被自己的幸福弄得眼花缭乱的人一样站在这里：你将会翩翩起舞，以免你摔倒在地！

但是，尽管你应该在我的面前跳舞，并且舞动你那些灵巧的步伐，不过没有人会跟我说：“快看啊，最后的充满快乐的人在这里跳舞呢！”

那些追逐他到这里的人，要想达到这样的高度，但是他们这样做是徒劳无获的：他会发现洞穴，确切地说是背面的洞穴，这是给为了将自己隐藏起来的人准备的隐秘之地；但是这里没有幸运的矿产，没有保存宝藏的房间，也没有新的快乐的金色之血脉。

快乐——人们是如何在这些被活埋之人以及孤独的隐士之中发现幸福的呢！我必须要在远离那些被遗忘的海域、被祝福的岛屿之上寻找最后的幸福吗？

但是，任何事物都是彼此相像的，没有什么事物是有价值可言的，没有什么寻找具有服务的性质，在这个世界上再也没有任何的祝福的岛屿了！”

因此，那个预言家叹息了起来，这是他最后一次叹息了，但是，查拉图斯特拉再一次变得安静，并且自信了起来，他就像一个从幽深的深渊里出来进入到光明之中的人一样。“不！不！三声不！”他敲打着自己的胡子，然后用非常强烈的声音高呼道——“我知道的更准确！在这个世界上仍然存在着祝福的岛屿！你这只知道叹气的悲伤之人给我安静下来吧！

不要再泼洒了，你这午前的阴雨云！我不是已经站在这里，并且被你的悲伤所淋湿，仿佛一条溺水的狗一样吗？

现在，我要抖动我自己，并且逃离你的身边，这样的话，或许我会再一次变得干燥

Now do I shake myself and run away from you, that I may again become dry: thereat may you not wonder! Do I seem to you discourteous? Here however is my court.

But as regards the higher man: well! I shall seek him at once in those forests: from thence came his cry. Perhaps he is there hard beset by an evil beast.

He is in my domain: therein shall he receive no scath! And verily, there are many evil beasts about me."-

With those words Zarathustra turned around to depart. Then said the soothsayer: "O Zarathustra, you are a rogue!

I know it well: you would rather be rid of me! Rather would you run into the forest and lay snares for evil beasts!

But what good will it do you? In the evening will you have me again: in your own cave will I sit, patient and heavy like a block- and wait for you!"

"So be it!" shouted back Zarathustra, as he went away: "and what is my in my cave belongs also to you, my guest!

Should you however find honey therein, well! Just lick it up, you growling bear, and sweeten your soul! For in the evening we want both to be in good spirits;

-In good spirits and joyful, because this day has come to an end! And you yourself shall dance to my lays, as my dancing-bear.

You do not believe this? you shake your head? Well! Cheer up, old bear! But I also- am a soothsayer."

起来：因此，你并不会感到惊奇！难道我在你看来是粗俗无礼之人吗？但是，这里就是我的宫廷。

但是考虑到更加高尚的人：好吧！我应该立刻动身前往那些森林寻找他的踪影：从那时起，他的呐喊来临了。或许他在这里受到了一个邪恶的怪物的攻击。

他现在就在我的领地范围之内：他在我的领地之内不应该受到任何的伤害！说真的，有许许多多的邪恶的怪兽围绕在我的身边。”

在说完了那些话之后，查拉图斯特拉转过身子，离开了这里。然后，那个预言家说道：“啊，查拉图斯特拉，你就是个流氓、无赖！

我心里非常清楚：你宁肯摆脱我！你宁肯跑进森林，然后给那些邪恶的怪物们放置陷阱！

但是，你这样做会给你带来什么好处呢？

到了夜晚，你将不会再一次拥有我：我会坐在属于你自己的洞穴里面，我就会像一个既耐心又沉重的障碍物一样——等待着你！”

“所以就顺其自然吧！”查拉图斯特拉走掉了，然后他转过身大叫道，“我的洞穴里面的所有东西也同样属于你，我的贵宾！

但是，你应该在这里找到蜂蜜，好吧！好好地舔舔吧！你这咆哮的灰熊，快点让你的灵魂变得甜蜜！因为到了夜晚，我们要让它们全都处于精神饱满的状态；

——处于精神饱满，非常开心快乐的状态，因为今天就要画上一个句号了！你应该当作我的跳舞之灰熊，在我躺下的地方跳舞。

你难道不相信我所说的吗？你难道没有摇晃你的头吗？好吧！打起精神来，老灰

Thus spoke Zarathustra.

63. Conversation With the Kings

1.

ERE Zarathustra had been an hour on his way in the mountains and forests, he saw all at once a strange procession. Right on the path which he was about to descend came two kings walking, bedecked with crowns and purple girdles, and variegated like flamingoes: they drove before them a laden ass. "What do these kings want in my domain?" said Zarathustra in astonishment to his heart, and hid himself hastily behind a thicket. When however the kings approached to him, he said half-aloud, like one speaking only to himself: "Strange! Strange! How does this harmonize? Two kings do I see- and only one ass!"

Then the two kings made a halt; they smiled and looked towards the spot whence the voice proceeded, and afterwards looked into each other's faces. "Such things do we also think among ourselves," said the king on the right, "but we do not utter them."

The king on the left, however, shrugged his shoulders and answered: "That may perhaps be a goat-herd. Or an hermit who has lived too long among rocks and trees. For no society at all

熊！但是，我同样也是一名预言家啊！”

查拉图斯特拉如是说。

63．与国王的谈话

（1）

查拉图斯特拉已经在通往山峰和森林的路上走了一个小时的时间了，突然之间，他在路上看到了一个非常奇怪的队列。就在他准备要下来的路上，他看到有两个国王在走路，他们的头上戴着皇冠，腰上还有紫色的腰带，他们的装扮过于华丽，看上去就像是火烈鸟一样：他们驱赶着走在他们前面的一头满载着货物的驴。“这些国王在我的领地之内到底想要些什么呢？”查拉图斯特拉的心里无比震惊地说道，于是，他匆忙地藏在了一处灌木丛中。然而，当这两个国王向查拉图斯特拉的地方靠近的时候，他开始用似大非大的声音说道，听起来就好像是他在跟自己说话一样：“太奇怪了！太奇怪了！我看到了两个国王，但是我只看到了一头驴！这样的情况怎么能够如此和谐？”

这两个国王停了下来，他们微笑着看向那处发出声音的地点，然后，这两位国王又彼此看了看对方的面孔。“我们自己也同样会思考类似这样的事情，”站在右侧的国王说道，“但是，我们并不会把类似这样的问题表达出来。”

然而，站在左侧的国王，耸了耸肩他的肩膀，回答道：“刚才说话的或许就是一个放羊的牧羊人。又或者是一个在岩石和树林里生活了太长时间的隐士而已。因为没有任何一个社会会糟蹋良好的礼貌和品行。”

spoils also good manners."

"Good manners?" replied angrily and bitterly the other king: "what then do we run out of the way of? Is it not 'good manners'? Our 'good society'?

Better, verily, to live among hermits and goat-herds, than with our gilded, false, over-rouged rabble- though it call itself 'good society.'

-Though it call itself 'nobility.' But there all is false and foul, above all the blood- thanks to old evil diseases and worse curers.

The best and dearest to me at present is still a sound peasant, coarse, artful, obstinate and enduring: that is at present the noblest type.

The peasant is at present the best; and the peasant type should be master! But it is the kingdom of the rabble- I no longer allow anything to be imposed upon me. The rabble, however- that means, hodgepodge.

Rabble-hodgepodge: therein is everything mixed with everything, saint and swindler, gentleman and Jew, and every beast out of Noah's ark.

Good manners! Everything is false and foul with us. No one knows any longer how to reverence: it is that precisely that we run away from. They are fulsome obtrusive dogs; they gild palm-leaves.

This loathing chokes me, that we kings ourselves have become false, draped and disguised with the old faded pomp of our ancestors, show-pieces for the stupidest, the craftiest, and

“良好的礼貌和品行？”另一个国王气愤地、怨恨地回答道：“那么，我们疯狂地逃离这里是为了什么？难道这不是良好的礼貌和品行吗？我们所谓的‘伟大的社会’？

说真的，我们宁肯生活在隐士和放羊的牧羊人当中，也不愿意生活在富有的、虚假的、过于浓妆艳抹的乌合之众当中——尽管，它们称自己为‘伟大的社会’。

——尽管它们称自己为‘贵族’。但是，这里所有的事物全都是虚假的、污秽的，尤其是因为古老的邪恶之疾病以及糟糕的治疗者所导致的血腥。

从现在来看，我认为最好的、我最喜爱的仍旧是一个身心健康的农民，他粗俗下等、他诡计多端、他固执倔强，并且具有忍耐力：对于现在来说，这就是最高贵的贵族形式。

从目前来看，农民是最好的贵族，农民的模范应该成为主人！但是，这里是乌合之众的王国——我不会再允许任何能够强加于我之上的事情出现。但是，乌合之众意味着人间的大杂烩。

乌合之众——人间的大杂烩：在这里，所有的事物都是彼此混合在一起的，圣人和江湖骗子、绅士和犹太人，以及所有从诺亚方舟上走下来的怪兽。

良好的礼貌和品行！对于我们来说，所有的事情都是虚假的，污秽的。没有人还能知道应该如何表示尊敬：而这正是我们为什么要疯狂地离开这里的原因。他们都是令人讨厌的、莽撞的狗；他们都是镀金的、棕榈树的叶子。

这种厌恶感让我感到窒息，我们这些国王本身开始变得虚假，并且被我们过去的先人的逝去的浮华所掩盖和伪装，并且将它们展示给那些最愚蠢、最诡计多端以及任何在当前交易权力的人。

我们并不是第一批人——不过我们还是要支持他们：因为这样的欺骗和欺诈，我们

whosoever at present trafficks for power.

We are not the first men- and have nevertheless to stand for them: of this imposture have we at last become weary and disgusted.

From the rabble have we gone out of the way, from all those bawlers and scribe-blowflies, from the trader-stench, the ambition-fidgeting, the bad breath-: fie, to live among the rabble;

-Fie, to stand for the first men among the rabble! Ah, loathing! Loathing! Loathing! What does it now matter about us kings!"-

"Thine old sickness seizes you," said here the king on the left, "thy loathing seizes you, my poor brother. You know, however, that some one hears us."

Immediately then, Zarathustra, who had opened ears and eyes to this talk, rose from his hiding-place, advanced towards the kings, and thus began:

"He who hearkens to you, he who gladly hearkens to you, is called Zarathustra.

I am Zarathustra who once said: 'What does it now matter about kings!' Forgive me; I rejoiced when you said to each other: 'What does it matter about us kings!'

Here, however, is my domain and jurisdiction: what may you be seeking in my domain? Perhaps, however, you have found on your way what I seek: namely, the higher man."

When the kings heard this, they beat upon their breasts and said with one voice: "We are recognized!

最后会变得疲倦和厌恶。

我们在乌合之众当中已经迷失了方向，我们已经从那些哞叫声和绿头苍蝇当中、从商船的恶臭、由野心产生的焦躁不安、糟糕的口臭当中迷失了方向：呸，生活在乌合之众当中；

——呸，支持那些第一批生活在乌合之众当中的人们！啊，真是令人厌恶啊！真是令人厌恶啊！真是令人厌恶啊！现在，这些事对于我们这些国王来说又有什么关系呢！”

“你这古老的疾病抓住了你，”站在左侧的国王说道，“你这令人感到厌恶的憎恶抓住了你，我可怜的兄弟啊！但是，你知道有人听到了我们的谈话。”

于是，查拉图斯特拉马上张开了耳朵和眼睛，开始仔细聆听和注视这两位国王的谈话，他从藏匿的地方站了起来，并且朝着国王的方向走去，查拉图斯特拉开始如是说：

“是他倾听了你们的谈话，是他高兴地倾听了你们的谈话，他的名字就叫作查拉图斯特拉。

我就是查拉图斯特拉，我曾经说过：‘现在，这些事对于我们这些国王来说又有什么关系呢！’请你们原谅我吧；当你们对彼此说道：‘这些事对于我们这些国王来说又有什么关系呢’的时候，我的内心真是无比的高兴。

但是，这里是属于我的领地，我对这片领地拥有管辖权：你们究竟在我的领地之内寻找什么？或许，你们已经发现了通向我一直在寻找的东西的道路：换句话说就是，更加高尚的人。”

当这两位国王听完查拉图斯特拉的讲话之后，他们开始捶胸顿足，并且异口同声

With the sword of your utterance severest you the thickest darkness of our hearts. You have discovered our distress; for behold, we are on our way to find the higher man-

-The man that is higher than we, although we are kings. To him do we convey this ass. For the highest man shall also be the highest lord on earth.

There is no sorer misfortune in all human destiny, than when the mighty of the earth are not also the first men. Then everything becomes false and distorted and monstrous.

And when they are even the last men, and more beast than man, then rises and rises the rabble in honor, and at last says even the rabble-virtue: 'Lo, I alone am virtue!'"-

What have I just heard? answered Zarathustra. What wisdom in kings! I am enchanted, and verily, I have already promptings to make a rhyme thereon:-

-Even if it should happen to be a rhyme not suited for every one's ears. I unlearned long ago to have consideration for long ears. Well then! Well now!

(Here, however, it happened that the ass also found utterance: it said distinctly and with malevolence, Y-E-A.)

'Twas once- methinks year one of our blessed Lord,-
Drunk without wine, the Sybil thus deplored:-
"How ill things go!"
Decline! Decline! Ne'er sank the world so low!
Rome now has turned harlot and harlot-stew,
Rome's Caesar a beast, and God- has turned Jew!

地说道："我们被认出来了！你用你那话语之宝剑刺裂了我们的内心当中最深厚的黑暗。你已经发现了我们的危难与不幸；快看吧！我们正在通往更加高尚的人的道路上前行——这个更加高尚的人比我们还要崇高，尽管我们都是国王。我们用这头驴子将我们送达到更加高尚的人那里，因为最崇高的人同样也应该是地球上地位最高的领主。

在所有人类的命运当中，没有什么要比地球的圣人不再是第一批人还要痛苦的不幸了。没有什么要比所有的事物全都变得虚假、扭曲和丑陋还要痛苦的不幸了。

甚至于当他们成为最后一批人类，他们变得比人类还要具有兽性的时候，那么，那些乌合之众就会因为恐慌而造反，最后，甚至于拥有乌合之众的道德的人们也会说：'快看啊，我是唯一拥有道德的人啊！'"

我刚才都听到了些什么？查拉图斯特拉回答道。在国王的头脑里究竟藏有什么样的智慧！我对此非常的感兴趣，说真的，受到激励的我已经开始为此创造韵律诗了：

——即使这样的韵律诗并不是为每一个人的耳朵量身定做的。我在很久很久以前就已经忘记了要为长耳朵着想。那么好吧！好吧就是现在！

（但是，凑巧的是，那头驴同样也开口说话了：它带着恶意，清楚地说道：是的。）

曾经——我在思考我们受到祝福的领主，
没有喝酒便已如醉，因此，西比尔悲叹道：
邪恶的事物是如此的前行！
快下降！快下降！不要让这个世界沉入到如此低贱的地位！
现在的罗马已经变成了娼妓场，罗马的恺撒就是一头怪兽，上帝已经变成了犹太人！

2.

With those rhymes of Zarathustra the kings were delighted; the king on the right, however, said: "O Zarathustra, how well it was that we set out to see you!

For your enemies showed us your likeness in their mirror: there looked you with the grimace of a devil, and sneeringly: so that we were afraid of you.

But what good did it do! Always did you prick us anew in heart and ear with your sayings. Then did we say at last: What does it matter how he look!

We must hear him; him who teaches: 'You shall love peace as a means to new wars, and the short peace more than the long!'

No one ever spoke such warlike words: 'What is good? To be brave is good. It is the good war that hallows every cause.'

O Zarathustra, our fathers' blood stirred in our veins at such words: it was like the voice of spring to old wine-casks.

When the swords ran among one another like red-spotted serpents, then did our fathers become fond of life; the sun of every peace seemed to them languid and lukewarm, the long peace, however, made them ashamed.

How they sighed, our fathers, when they saw on the wall brightly furbished, dried-up swords! Like those they thirsted for war. For a sword thirsts to drink blood, and sparkles with

（2）

查拉图斯特拉创作的韵律诗让那两个国王欣喜若狂；但是，站在右边的国王开口说道：“啊，查拉图斯特拉，我们动身前去看望你是多么的美好！

因为你的敌人们在他们的镜子里为我们展示出了你的模样：你的脸上露出了恶魔般的鬼脸，并且轻蔑地笑了起来：因此，我们都很惧怕你。

但是，你这样做又有什么好处呢！你总是一而再再而三地戳击我们的心灵，并且用你的话语冲击我们的耳朵。然后，到了最后时刻，我们会说：他长成什么样子又有什么关系呢！

我们必须要聆听他的声音；他如是说教道：‘你应该把和平视作是一种对于新的战争的解决方式去爱戴它，短暂的和平要多于长久的和平！’

没有人曾经说过这样的话：‘什么才是好的？勇敢、无所畏惧就是好的。正义的战争会让所有的原因变得神圣不可侵犯。’

啊，查拉图斯特拉，在这样的话语的挑动下，我们的先父的血液开始在我们的血管里激荡：这就好像是春天的古老之酒桶的声音。

当刀剑像红色斑点的毒蛇一样在彼此之间穿梭的时候，我们的先父们开始变得热爱生活；对于他们来说，所有的平和之太阳都是倦怠的、不够温暖的，然而，长久的和平却又让他们感到无比的羞愧。

当我们的先父看到墙壁上的被擦得熠熠生辉的、干缩的宝剑的时候，他们是如此的叹息！看上去就像是那些无比渴望战争的人们。因为一把宝剑渴望痛饮鲜血，它的渴望散发着耀眼的光芒。”

desire."- -

-When the kings thus discoursed and talked eagerly of the happiness of their fathers, there came upon Zarathustra no little desire to mock at their eagerness: for evidently they were very peaceable kings whom he saw before him, kings with old and refined features. But he restrained himself. "Well!" said he, "there leads the way, there lies the cave of Zarathustra; and this day is to have a long evening! At present, however, a cry of distress calls me hastily away from you.

It will honor my cave if kings want to sit and wait in it: but, to be sure, you will have to wait long!

Well! What of that! Where does one at present learn better to wait than at courts? And the whole virtue of kings that has remained to them- is it not called to-day: Ability to wait?"

Thus spoke Zarathustra.

64. The Leech

AND Zarathustra went thoughtfully on, further and lower down, through forests and past moory bottoms; as it happens, however, to every one who meditates upon hard matters, he trod thereby unawares upon a man. And lo, there spurted into his face all at once a cry of pain, and two curses and twenty bad invectives, so that in his fright he raised his stick and also struck

就在这两个国王热切地谈论着有关于他们的先父的幸福快乐的时候，查拉图斯特拉却丝毫没有任何要嘲笑他们的那种渴望的欲望：因为非常明显，站在查拉图斯特拉的面前的这两位国王都是爱好和平、性情温顺的国王，他们拥有古老并且优雅的特点。但是，他在尽力地克制自己。“好吧！”他说道，“这条路通向你们要去的地方，这里坐落着查拉图斯特拉的洞穴；今天注定会有一个非常漫长的夜晚！但是，现在一种悲痛的叫喊在呼唤我尽快地远离你。

如果国王们要想在我的洞穴里坐一坐，等待片刻的话，那将会是我的莫大的荣幸：但是，你们必须要在此地等上相当长的时间，这一点儿也没错！

好吧！那又有什么关系呢！现在，人们要在哪里才可以比在宫廷里更好地学习该如何等待呢？在他们的内心当中，仍旧拥有国王所具备的道德品质——从今天来看，这种道德品质不就是所谓的等待的能力吗？”

查拉图斯特拉如是说。

64．水蛭

查拉图斯特拉小心翼翼地走着，他朝着更远更低的方向前行着，他穿越了森林，途径了荒凉的沼泽地；但是，他不知不觉地走到了一个人的身上，这对于所有正在思考重要的事情的人来说，都是会经常发生的。快看啊，突然之间，一种痛苦的喊叫，两种诅咒以及二十种恶意的恶言谩骂，喷射到了他的脸上，于是，受到了惊吓的查拉图斯特拉，赶忙拿起了手中的棍子，并且用棍子击打那个行走之人。但是，没过多久，他就恢复了往日的平静，而他的心灵则在嘲笑他刚刚所表现出来的极端愚蠢的行为。

the trodden one. Immediately afterwards, however, he regained his composure, and his heart laughed at the folly he had just committed.

"Pardon me," said he to the trodden one, who had got up enraged, and had seated himself, "pardon me, and hear first of all a parable.

As a wanderer who dreams of remote things on a lonesome highway, runs unawares against a sleeping dog, a dog which lies in the sun:

-As both of them then start up and snap at each other, like deadly enemies, those two beings mortally frightened- so did it happen to us.

And yet! And yet- how little was lacking for them to caress each other, that dog and that lonesome one! Are they not both- lonesome ones!"

-"Whoever you are," said the trodden one, still enraged, "you tread also too nigh me with your parable, and not only with your foot!

Lo! am I then a dog?"- And then the sitting one got up, and pulled his naked arm out of the swamp. For at first he had lain outstretched on the ground, hidden and indiscernible, like those who lie in wait for swamp-game.

"But whatever are you about" called out Zarathustra in alarm, for he saw a deal of blood streaming over the naked arm,- "what has hurt you? has an evil beast bit you, you unfortunate one?"

The bleeding one laughed, still angry, "What matter is it to you!" said he, and was about to go on. "Here am I at home and in my province. Let him question me whoever will: to a dolt,

“请原谅我吧，”查拉图斯特拉对那个愤怒地站起身，并且又坐下来的行走之人说道，“请原谅我吧，我最先听到的是一个寓言。

一个梦想着孤独寂寞的大路上的遥远的事物的漫游者，他在奔跑着，但是一不留神踩到了正在熟睡的狗，一只躺在太阳上的狗：

——那个漫游者和狗全都打起了精神，开始彼此狂咬对方，他们看上去就像是能够置人于死地的敌人，这两者的内心都非常的害怕：——所以类似这样的事情也发生在了我们的身上。

但是！但是——他们显然并不缺乏对彼此的相互爱抚，那条狗以及那个孤独寂寞的人！他们二者都不是孤独寂寞的！”

——“无论你是谁，”那个行走之人说道，很显然他的火气还没有消，“你的踩踏也太过于接近我了，不仅仅是你的脚，还有你的比喻！

“快看呀！难道我是一条狗吗？”——然后，那个坐着的人站了起来，他将自己裸露的胳膊从沼泽中拽了出来。起初，他四肢伸开躺在地面上，这样非常隐蔽，人是很难能够察觉出来的，他就像是那些躺下来准备玩沼泽游戏的人。

“但是你到底是怎么了！”查拉图斯特拉惊慌地叫喊道，因为他看到了鲜血正在从他赤裸的胳膊上流淌出来，“究竟是什么东西伤害了你？难道有什么邪恶的怪兽咬伤了你，你这个倒霉的不幸之人？”

那个胳膊还在淌血的人笑了起来，他仍然在生气，“我受不受伤跟你有什么关系！”他说道。然后他接着说，“我现在在我的家里面，我在我的领地里。谁想问就问我吧：但是，我是不会向傻子回答问题的。”

however, I shall hardly answer."

"You are mistaken," said Zarathustra sympathetically, and held him fast; "you are mistaken. Here you are not at home, but in my domain, and therein shall no one receive any hurt.

Call me however what you wilt- I am who I must be. I call myself Zarathustra.

Well! Up there is the way to Zarathustra's cave: it is not far,- will you not attend to your wounds at my home?

It has gone badly with you, you unfortunate one, in this life: first a beast bit you, and then- a man trod upon you!"- -

When however the trodden one had heard the name of Zarathustra he was transformed. "What happens to me!" he exclaimed, "who preoccupies me so much in this life as this one man, namely Zarathustra, and that one animal that lives on blood, the leech?

For the sake of the leech did I lie here by this swamp, like a fisher, and already had my outstretched arm been bitten ten times, when there bites a still finer leech at my blood, Zarathustra himself!

O happiness! O miracle! Praised be this day which enticed me into the swamp! Praised be the best, the livest cupping-glass, that at present lives; praised be the great conscience-leech Zarathustra!"-

Thus spoke the trodden one, and Zarathustra rejoiced at his words and their refined reverential style. "Who are you?" asked he, and gave him his hand, "there is much to clear up and elucidate between us, but already methinks pure clear day is dawning."

"你一定是搞错了，"查拉图斯特拉富有同情心地说道，然后他加快了语速，"你一定是搞错了。你现在并不在你的家里，而是在我的领地之内，任何人在我的领地之内都不会受到任何伤害。

但是，你可以按照你自己的意愿称呼我。我称呼自己为查拉图斯特拉。

好吧！这条路能够通往查拉图斯特拉的洞穴：那个洞穴离这里并不远——难道你不想来到我的家里好好治疗一下伤口吗?

你的人生已经非常糟糕了，你这倒霉的不幸之人：首先，邪恶的怪兽咬了你，然后——一个人又踩踏了你！"

但是，当那个踩踏之人听到了查拉图斯特拉的名字之后，他发生了改变。"我到底是怎么了！"他大声地喊叫道，"究竟是谁让我对这个人的生活如此的着迷，这个被称为查拉图斯特拉的人，还有那条依靠饮血为生的动物，水蛭?

由于水蛭的缘故，我躺在了沼泽的旁边，就像是一个渔夫一样，我已经准备好伸开我那已经被叮咬了十次的胳膊，查拉图斯特拉本身仍旧被一条巨大的水蛭吸食着鲜血！

啊，快乐！啊，奇迹！这个将我引诱的沼泽的一天是值得被赞美的！在当下的生物当中，最好的水蛭是值得被赞美的；拥有良好的良知之水蛭的查拉图斯特拉是值得被赞美的！"

那个踩踏之人如是说道，而查拉图斯特拉则对他的话语以及他们的优雅的尊敬风格感到非常高兴。"你到底是谁？"他问道，并且他把自己的手递给了他，"在你和我之间有太多的事情需要被清理和阐明，但是依我看来，纯净、晴朗的日子已经到来了。"

"I am the spiritually conscientious one," answered he who was asked, "and in matters of the spirit it is difficult for any one to take it more rigorously, more restrictedly, and more severely than I, except him from whom I learnt it, Zarathustra himself.

Better know nothing than half-know many things! Better be a fool on one's own account, than a sage on other people's approbation! I- go to the basis:

-What matter if it be great or small? If it be called swamp or sky? A handbreadth of basis is enough for me, if it be actually basis and ground!

-A handbreadth of basis: there can one stand. In the true knowing-knowledge there is nothing great and nothing small."

"Then you are perhaps an expert on the leech?" asked Zarathustra; "and you investigate the leech to its ultimate basis, you conscientious one?"

"O Zarathustra," answered the trodden one, "that would be something immense; how could I presume to do so!

That, however, of which I am master and knower, is the brain of the leech:- that is my world!

And it is also a world! Forgive it, however, that my pride here finds expression, for here I have not my equal. Therefore said I: 'here am I at home.'

How long have I investigated this one thing, the brain of the leech, so that here the slippery truth might no longer slip from me! Here is my domain!

-For the sake of this did I cast everything else aside, for the sake of this did everything else

"我是精神上非常有良知的人，"他回答了提问的人，"而且对于任何人来说，用比我更加严苛、更加局限、更加严格的态度对待精神的问题是极其困难的，除了那个我有所了解的人，查拉图斯特拉他自己。

宁肯对所有事情都一无所知，也不愿意对许多事情一知半解！宁肯成为一个傻子，也不愿意成为其他人普遍认可的圣人！说到底就是：

——无论是高大还是渺小，又有什么关系呢？无论是被称作沼泽还是天空，又有什么关系呢？对于我来说，拥有一只手宽度的根基已经足够了，如果它确实是根基的话！

——一只手宽度的根基：一个人可以站在那上面。在真正的已知的知识当中，没有什么知识是伟大的，也没有什么知识是微不足道的。"

"这么说来的话，你或许是一名研究水蛭的专家呢？"查拉图斯特拉问道，"你从最根本的基础之上，研究了水蛭，你这认真尽责之人？"

"啊，查拉图斯特拉，"踩踏之人回答道，"这是一种无穷无尽的事情；我怎么能够假定自己这么做呢！

但是，我就是大师，我就是智者，我就是水蛭的大脑：——这就是我的世界！

而且它也是一个世界！但是，请原谅我的傲慢在这里找到了表现的方式，在这里，我并没有我自己的平等。因此，我说道：'这里就是我的家。'

我调查研究这个东西究竟有多长的时间了，这个水蛭的大脑，不明确的真相或许不会再从我的身上溜出来了！这里是我的领地！

因为这个的缘故，我将所有的事物全都抛到了脑后，因为这个的缘故，我对任何的事情都漠不关心；而我的知识则紧紧地跟我的邪恶的无知靠在一起。

become indifferent to me; and close beside my knowledge lies my black ignorance.

My spiritual conscience requires from me that it should be so- that I should know one thing, and not know all else: they are a loathing to me, all the semi-spiritual, all the hazy, hovering, and visionary.

Where my honesty ceases, there am I blind, and want also to be blind. Where I want to know, however, there want I also to be honest- namely, severe, rigorous, restricted, cruel and inexorable.

Because you once said, O Zarathustra: 'Spirit is life which itself cuts into life';- that led and allured me to your doctrine. And verily, with my own blood have I increased my own knowledge!"

-"As the evidence indicates," broke in Zarathustra; for still was the blood flowing down on the naked arm of the conscientious one. For there had ten leeches bitten into it.

"O you strange fellow, how much does this very evidence teach me- namely, you yourself! And not all, perhaps, might I pour into your rigorous ear!

Well then! We part here! But I would rather find you again. Up there is the way to my cave: to-night shall you there by my welcome guest!

Fain would I also make amends to your body for Zarathustra treading upon you with his feet: I think about that. Just now, however, a cry of distress calls me hastily away from you."

Thus spoke Zarathustra.

我的精神良知需要我应该这样做——我应该知道一件事情，但是却对其他的事情一无所知：他们对于我来说就是一种令人讨厌的厌恶，所有的半神半鬼，所有的朦胧的、在空中盘旋的，并且充满幻象的事物。

但凡是能够让我的诚实、正直停止工作的地方，都将意味着我在这里开始变得盲目，而且我也想要变得盲目。一个我想要去了解的地方，在这里，我同样也想要让自己变得坦诚、诚实——换句话说就是，严格、严苛、局限性、残忍并且不屈不挠。

因为你曾经说过，啊，查拉图斯特拉：‘精神就是一种将自己切入生命的生命。’正是这句话吸引了我，让我对你的教条充满了好奇。说真的，我通过自己的血液提升了自身的知识！”

“正如证据所表明的那样，”查拉图斯特拉打断了他的话；因为，那个有良知的人的裸露的胳膊仍旧在流淌着鲜血。因为他的胳膊上还有十只水蛭在啃咬他。

“啊，你这个奇怪的家伙，这个证据又能教育我多少呢——换句话说，它能够教育你自己多少呢！或许还不如我给你那严苛的耳朵灌输的东西有价值呢！

那么好吧！我们就在此分别吧！但是我宁愿再一次找到你。这条路就是通向我的洞穴的道路：今晚，你在这里就是我的贵宾！

同样地，我也非常愿意为查拉图斯特拉用他的双脚对你的身体进行的踩踏做出弥补和赎罪：但是，就在现在，一阵悲痛的呐喊声在呼唤着我，它让我快点远离你。”

查拉图斯特拉如是说。

65. The Magician

1.

WHEN however Zarathustra had gone round a rock, then saw he on the same path, not far below him, a man who threw his limbs about like a maniac, and at last tumbled to the ground on his belly. "Halt!" said then Zarathustra to his heart, "he there must surely be the higher man, from him came that dreadful cry of distress,- I will see if I can help him." When, however, he ran to the spot where the man lay on the ground, he found a trembling old man with fixed eyes; and in spite of all Zarathustra's efforts to lift him and set him again on his feet, it was all in vain. The unfortunate one, also, did not seem to notice that some one was beside him; on the contrary, he continually looked around with moving gestures, like one forsaken and isolated from all the world. At last, however, after much trembling, and convulsion, and curling-himself-up, he began to lament thus:

Who warm'th me, who lov'th me still?
Give ardent fingers!
Give heartening charcoal-warmers!
Prone, outstretched, trembling,
Like him, half dead and cold, whose feet one warm'th-
And shaken, ah! by unfamiliar fevers,

65. 魔术师

（1）

但是，当查拉图斯特拉绕过一块岩石的时候，他看到在同一条道路上，一个人在离他不远的下方，像个疯子一样疯狂地甩动着他的四肢，最后，他摔倒了，他的肚子撞到了地上。“快停下啊！”查拉图斯特拉用发自内心的声音说道，“毋庸置疑，他在这里是更加高尚的人，那阵令人感到胆寒的悲痛之呐喊就是从他这里传出来的。——让我来看看，我是不是能帮助他。”但是，当查拉图斯特拉来到那个疯子躺着的地方的时候，他发现了一个浑身打战、目光呆滞的老人；尽管查拉图斯特拉拼尽全力打算把那个人抬起来，让他重新站起来，可是，他所做的一切努力都是徒劳无功的。而且，那个非常不幸的人好像也并没有注意到有人正站在他的身边；正好相反，他继续用移动的姿势环顾四周，看上去就像是一个被整个世界所抛弃、所孤立的人。不过，最后在经历了许许多多的颤动、惊厥以及卷曲之后，他开始如是哀叹道：

有谁在温暖我，有谁仍旧在爱着我？
给予我热情似火的手指！
给予我能够振奋人心的木炭之温暖者！
俯卧、向外伸展、战栗，
就像他一样，半死半寒，他的脚是温暖的，

Shivering with sharpened, icy-cold frost-arrows,
By you pursued, my fancy!
Ineffable! Recondite! Sore-frightening!
You huntsman 'hind the cloud-banks! Now lightning-struck by you,
You mocking eye that me in darkness watches:
-Thus do I lie,
Bend myself, twist myself, convulsed
With all eternal torture,
And smitten
By you, cruel huntsman,
You unfamiliar- God...
Smite deeper!
Smite yet once more!
Pierce through and rend my heart!
What mean'th this torture
With dull, indented arrows?
Why look'st you hither,
Of human pain not weary,
With mischief-loving, godly flash-glances?
Not murder will you,

并且在抖动，啊！因为不同寻常的发热所致，
因为尖利的、冰冷的冰霜之箭而颤抖，
在你的追逐下，我的幻想！
无法形容！深奥难懂！令人胆寒的疼痛！
你那捕猎之人就躲在云团的后面！那么现在，受到你的闪电的袭击，
你那轻蔑的眼睛在黑暗之中注视着我：
——因此，我躺了下来，
我将自己弯曲起来，扭曲起来，因为
所有永恒之苦难而痛苦地抽动，
并且被你摧毁，
残忍的捕猎之人，
你这个与众不同的上帝。
再打击得更深一些吧！
再沉重地打击一次吧！
刺穿并且撕碎我的心脏！
拥有钝的、锯齿状的弓箭的苦难
到底意味着什么？
为什么用不详的爱意以及神圣的闪电之注视
着向你的人类之痛苦并没有感到疲倦呢？
你不会去谋杀，

But torture, torture?
For why- me torture,
You mischief-loving, unfamiliar God?-
Ha! Ha!
You stealest nigh
In midnight's gloomy hour?...
What will you?
Speak!
You crowd me, pressest-
Ha! now far too closely!
You hearst me breathing,
You o'erhearst my heart,
You ever jealous one! -Of what, pray, ever jealous?
Off! Off!
For why the ladder?
Would you get in?
To heart in-clamber?
To mine own secretest
Conceptions in-clamber?
Shameless one! you unknown one!- Thief!

但是折磨呢，折磨呢？
为什么我要折磨，
你这不详的爱意，非同寻常的上帝？
哈哈！哈哈！
你会在午夜阴沉的时刻进行偷窃？
难道不是吗？
快说话！
你把我围堵了起来，压迫着我，
哈哈！现在，你离我有点太近了！
你能够听到我的呼吸声，
你能够无意听到我的心跳之声，
你这个永恒的嫉妒之人！——哀求，永远都嫉妒？
快下来！快下来！
为什么要上梯子呢？
你要不要进来呢？
去听一听里面的攀爬之声？
去听一听里面的攀爬中
属于我自己的秘密之设想？
真是不知羞耻的家伙！你这个无名小卒！——小偷！

What seekst you by your stealing?
What seekst you by your hearkening?
What seekst you by your torturing?
You torturer!
You- hangman-God!
Or shall I, as the mastiffs do,
Roll me before you?
And cringing, enraptured, frantical,
My tail friendly- waggle!
In vain!
Goad further!
Cruel goader!
No dog- your game just am I,
Cruel huntsman!
Your proudest of captives,
You robber 'hind the cloud-banks...
Speak finally!
You lightning-veiled one! you unknown one! Speak!
What will you, highway-ambusher, from- me?
What will you, unfamiliar- God?

你想偷的东西，究竟是什么？
你想听到的东西，到底是什么？
你要折磨的东西，又是什么？
你这个折磨之人！
你这个——刽子手——上帝！
又或是，我应该像猛犬一样，在你的面前来回滚动？
然后，阿谀奉承、欣喜若狂，并且疯狂地
摇晃我那友好之尾巴！
一切都是徒劳啊！
继续前进吧！
无比残忍的走路者！
没有狗——我就是你唯一的游戏，
无比残忍的捕猎之人！
你为被俘获的猎物感到骄傲自满，
你这躲藏在云团之后的抢劫者。
最后说说话吧！
你这闪电之隐藏者！你这无名小卒！快说话啊！
你想从道路上埋伏我，究竟是为了什么？
你这个不为人知的上帝？

What?
Ransom-gold?
How much of ransom-gold? Solicit much- that bid'th my pride!
And be concise- that bid'th mine other pride!
Ha! Ha!
Me- wantst you? me?
-Entire?...
Ha! Ha!
And torturest me, fool that you are,
Dead-torturest quite my pride?
Give love to me- who warm'th me still?
Who lov'th me still?-
Give ardent fingers
Give heartening charcoal-warmers,
Give me, the most lonesome,
The ice (ah! seven-fold frozen ice
For very enemies,
For foes, do make one thirst).
Give, yield to me,
Cruel foe,

什么？
赎身之金？
赎身之金究竟有多少价值？恳求更多，我的傲慢如是要求到！
一定要简洁明了——我其他的傲慢如是要求到！
哈哈！哈哈！
我需要你吗？我？
完全需要吗？
哈哈！哈哈！
折磨我，你还真是愚蠢，
我的傲慢就是疯狂的折磨？
快给予我爱——那个仍旧在温暖着我的人，
那个仍旧在爱着我的人？
予我热情似火的手指！
给予我能够振奋人心的木炭之温暖者！
冰（啊！七个折叠的、冻住的冰，
对于敌人来说，
对于反对者来说，会让人感到口渴）。
快给予啊，向我屈服吧！
无比残忍的反对者，
——你们自己！

-Yourself!- -
Away!
There fled he surely,
My final, only comrade,
My greatest foe,
Mine unfamiliar-
My hangman-God!...
-No!
Come you back!
With all of your great tortures! To me the last of lonesome ones,
Oh, come you back!
All my hot tears in streamlets trickle
Their course to you!
And all my final hearty fervor-
Up-glow'th to you!
Oh, come you back,
Mine unfamiliar God! my pain!
My final bliss!

快离开！
他坚定地逃离了这里，
我最后的、唯一的同伴，
我最伟大的反对者，
我那与众不同的，
我的刽子手——上帝！
——不！
你快回来吧！
带着所有属于你的伟大的折磨！
啊，你快回来吧！对于我来说，这最后的孤独之人，
啊，你快回来吧！
我所有的炽热的泪水在小河中细细地流淌
他们通向你的过程！
以及我所有最后的诚挚的热情
正在向你闪耀着光芒！
啊，你快回来吧，
我这非比寻常的上帝！我的痛苦！
我最后的祝福！

2.

-Here, however, Zarathustra could no longer restrain himself; he took his staff and struck the wailer with all his might. "Stop this," cried he to him with wrathful laughter, "stop this, you stage-player! you false coiner! you liar from the very heart! I know you well!

I will soon make warm legs to you, you evil magician: I know well how- to make it hot for such as you!"

-"Leave off," said the old man, and sprang up from the ground, "strike me no more, O Zarathustra! I did it only for amusement!

That kind of thing belongs to my art. You yourself, I wanted to put to the proof when I gave this performance. And verily, you have well detected me!

But you yourself- have given me no small proof of yourself: you are hard, you wise Zarathustra! Hard strike you with your 'truths,' your cudgel forces from me- this truth!"

-"Flatter not," answered Zarathustra, still excited and frowning, "you stage-player from the heart! you are false: why speak you- of truth!

You peacock of peacocks, you sea of vanity; what did you represent before me, you evil magician; whom was I meant to believe in when you wailed in such wise?"

"The penitent in spirit," said the old man, "it was him- I represented; you yourself once created this expression-

-The poet and magician who at last turns his spirit against himself, the transformed one who

（2）

然而，查拉图斯特拉实在无法在这里抑制他自己了；他拿上他的东西，并且用他最大的力气打那个哀叹之人。“快停下来，”查拉图斯特拉用愤怒的笑声说道，“快停下来，你这个舞台剧演员！你这个虚假的伪币制造者！你这个彻头彻尾的大骗子！我实在是太了解你了！

很快，我就会为你制造温暖的双脚，你这邪恶的魔术师：我非常清楚应该如何让类似你这样的人感到无比炽热！”

“快离开我，”那个老人从地上跳了起来，然后说道，“不要再打我了，啊，查拉图斯特拉！我这么做只是因为好玩！

类似这样的事物就是我的艺术。当我进行这样的表演的时候，我想实验一番。说真的，你真是很好地察觉到了我！

但是你——并没有向我证明：你是个强硬的、智慧的查拉图斯特拉！你的‘真理’在冲击着你，而你的棍棒却在强行逼迫我离开这样的真理！”

“不要拍我的马屁了，”查拉图斯特拉回答道，他仍旧非常兴奋，并且皱起了眉头，“你这个彻头彻尾的舞台剧演员！你就是个虚假之人：你为什么不说出真相呢！

你是孔雀之王，你是虚荣之海；你在我的面前到底代表着什么，你这邪恶的魔术师；当你用这样的聪慧苦苦哀号的时候，我到底应该相信谁呢？”

“精神的忏悔者，”那个老人说道，“我代表的就是他；你曾经创造过这样的表达方式——

freezes to death by his bad science and conscience.

And just acknowledge it: it was long, O Zarathustra, before you discovered my trick and lie! you believed in my distress when you held my head with both your hands,-

-I heard you lament 'we have loved him too little, loved him too little!' Because I so far deceived you, my wickedness rejoiced in me."

"You may have deceived subtler ones than I," said Zarathustra sternly. "I am not on my guard against deceivers; I have to be without precaution: so wills my lot.

You, however,- must deceive: so far do I know you! you must ever be equivocal, trivocal, quadrivocal, and quinquivocal! Even what you have now confessed, is not nearly true enough nor false enough for me!

You bad false coiner, how could you do otherwise! your very malady would you whitewash if you showed yourself naked to your physician.

Thus did you whitewash your lie before me when you said: 'I did so only for amusement!' There was also seriousness therein, you are something of a penitent-in-spirit!

I divine you well: you have become the enchanter of all the world; but for yourself you have no lie or artifice left,- you are disenchanted to yourself!

You have reaped disgust as your one truth. No word in you is any longer genuine, but your mouth is so: that is to say, the disgust that cleaves to your mouth."- -

-"Who are you at all!" cried here the old magician with defiant voice, "who dares to speak thus to me, the greatest man now living?"- and a green flash shot from his eye at Zarathustra.

——诗人以及魔术师在最后用他的精神反抗自己以及用他的邪恶的科学以及良知冻结死亡的变形之人。

你就承认了吧：啊，查拉图斯特拉！在你之前的很久以前，我的诡计以及谎言就已经被发现了！当你用你的双手捧住我的脑袋的时候，你就能相信我的悲痛。

我听到了你的悲叹：‘我们并没有给予他足够的爱，并没有给予他足够的爱！’因为我欺骗了你，我的邪恶在我的内心里欣喜若狂。”

“你或许欺骗过比我更加狡猾的人，”查拉图斯特拉无比严厉地说道，“我并没有小心提防那些欺骗者；我不能提高警惕：我的意志要我如是。

但是，你必然会欺骗：到目前为止，我非常了解你！你一定是品行有问题的、可疑的、靠不住的！即便是你现在公开坦白承认的，对于我来说，也不足够真实或是足够虚假！

你这邪恶、虚假的伪币制造者，你怎么可以这样呢！如果你要在你的医生面前展示你的赤身裸体的话，你一定会掩饰你身上的疾病。

因此，当你说‘我这么做只是因为好玩！’的时候，你在我的面前掩饰了你的谎言！同样严肃的还有，你是精神的忏悔者！

我猜测着你：你成为全世界的魔术师；但是对于你自己来说，你并没有留下谎言或是诡计——你已经不再对自己感到着迷了！

你将得到的厌恶当作是你的一个真理。你的话语中的任何一句话，都不再真诚，但是你的嘴巴还保持着诚挚：也就是说，厌恶将你的嘴劈开。”

——“你到底是谁！”那个老魔术师用带有挑衅的腔调大喊道，“你好大的胆子，竟然敢这样跟我说话，竟敢跟我这个活在世上的最伟大的人这样说话？”——他的眼睛

But immediately after he changed, and said sadly:

"O Zarathustra, I am weary of it, I am disgusted with my arts, I am not great, why do I dissemble! But you know it well- I sought for greatness!

A great man I wanted to appear, and persuaded many; but the lie has been beyond my power. On it do I collapse.

O Zarathustra, everything is a lie in me; but that I collapse- this my collapsing is genuine!"-

"It honors you," said Zarathustra gloomily, looking down with sidelong glance, "it honors you that you sought for greatness, but it betrays you also. You are not great.

You bad old magician, that is the best and the honestest thing I honor in you, that you have become weary of yourself, and have expressed it: 'I am not great.'

Therein do I honor you as a penitent-in-spirit, and although only for the twinkling of an eye, in that one moment wast you- genuine.

But tell me, what seek you here in my forests and rocks? And if you have put yourself in my way, what proof of me would you have?-

-Wherein did you put me to the test?"

Thus spoke Zarathustra, and his eyes sparkled. But the old magician kept silence for a while; then said he: "Did I put you to the test? I- seek only.

O Zarathustra, I seek a genuine one, a right one, a simple one, an unequivocal one, a man of perfect honesty, a vessel of wisdom, a saint of knowledge, a great man!

向查拉图斯特拉投射出了一种绿色的闪光。但是，他立刻悲伤地说道：

“啊，查拉图斯特拉，我已经感到厌倦了，我对我的艺术感到恶心，我一点儿也不伟大，为什么我要掩饰呢！但是你心里非常清楚——我在寻找伟大！

我要以一个伟大人物的形象出现，并且说服更多的人；但是谎言已经超越了我的能力所能企及的范畴。我开始在这上面分崩离析。

啊，查拉图斯特拉，对于我来说，任何的事物都是一种谎言，但是，我的分崩离析——这个令我分崩离析的事物是真实的！”

“它很尊重你，”查拉图斯特拉沮丧地说道，他斜着眼睛向下看去，“它尊重你寻找伟大，但是，与此同时，它也背叛了你。你并不伟大。

你这个可恶的老魔术师，这是我所能敬重你的最好、最诚实的事情，你已经对自己感到了厌倦，并且你将这种感觉表达了出来：‘我一点儿也不伟大。’

因此，我尊重你，把你视作是精神的忏悔者，尽管只是一眨眼的时间，但只有在那一刻，你是真实的。

不过，请你告诉我，你究竟在我的森林和岩石里寻找着什么？倘若你挡住了我的去路，你有什么可以让我信服的证据？

——你究竟会在哪里测验我？”

查拉图斯特拉如是说道，他的眼睛闪耀着光芒。但是，那个老魔术师沉默了一会儿，然后他说道：“我有测验过你吗？我只是在寻找。

啊，查拉图斯特拉，我在寻找一个真实的人、一个正义之人、一个单纯之人、一个豁达之人、一个诚实之人、一个聪慧之人，拥有知识的圣人，一个伟大的人！

Know you it not, O Zarathustra? I seek Zarathustra."

-And here there arose a long silence between them: Zarathustra, however, became profoundly absorbed in thought, so that he shut his eyes. But afterwards coming back to the situation, he grasped the hand of the magician, and said, full of politeness and policy:

"Well! Up there leads the way, there is the cave of Zarathustra. In it may you seek him whom you would rather find.

And ask counsel of my animals, my eagle and my serpent: they shall help you to seek. My cave however is large.

I myself, to be sure- I have as yet seen no great man. That which is great, the acutest eye is at present insensible to it. It is the kingdom of the rabble.

Many a one have I found who stretched and inflated himself, and the people cried: 'Behold; a great man!' But what good do all bellows do! The wind comes out at last.

At last bursts the frog which has inflated itself too long: then comes out the wind. To prick a swollen one in the belly, I call good pastime. Hear that, you boys!

Our today is of the popular: who still knows what is great and what is small! Who could there seek successfully for greatness! A fool only: it succeeds with fools.

You seek for great men, you strange fool? Who taught that to you? Is today the time for it? Oh, you bad seeker, why do you- tempt me?"- -

Thus spoke Zarathustra, comforted in his heart, and went laughing on his way.

啊，查拉图斯特拉，难道你不知道吗？我在寻找查拉图斯特拉。”

沉默在他们两个人之间持续了好久，但是，查拉图斯特拉已经深深地陷入了思考当中，以至于他紧紧地闭上了眼睛。但是，他随后恢复了正常的状态，他牢牢地抓住了魔术师的手，然后用彬彬有礼的腔调说道：

“好吧！这里就是通路，这里就是查拉图斯特拉的洞穴。在这个洞穴里面，你能够找到那个你特别想找的人。

询问一下我的动物们，让它们给你提供建议，我的老鹰和我的毒蛇：它们可以帮助你寻找那个人。但是，我的洞穴是巨大的。

我很确定，我自己从来都没有见过一个伟大的人。他非常伟大，无比尖锐的双眼不易被察觉。这就是乌合之众的王国。

我发现很多人都会伸展自己，让自己膨胀起来，然后人们就会叫喊道：‘快看啊，一个伟大之人！’但是所有那些大声地呼喊又有什么好处呢！最终，大风就会出现。

最后，膨胀的太久的青蛙就会发生爆炸：然后，大风就会出现。在肚子上刺戳一个肿胀之人，我管这个叫美好的娱乐消遣。听清楚了，你们这些小孩子们!

我们的今天仍旧是深受人们欢迎的：它仍然知道什么是伟大的，什么是渺小的！究竟有谁能够在这里成功地发现伟大呢！只有一个傻子才能如是：只有用愚蠢的办法才能成功。

你在寻找伟大之人，难道你也是奇怪的傻子吗？到底是谁教给你这些的？难道今天就是施展你的愚蠢的时候吗？啊，你这个邪恶的寻找者，你为什么要诱惑我？”

查拉图斯特拉如是说，他的内心得到了安慰，然后，他就笑着继续上路了。

66. Out of Service

NOT long, however, after Zarathustra had freed himself from the magician, he again saw a person sitting beside the path which he followed, namely a tall, black man, with a haggard, pale countenance: this man grieved him exceedingly. "Alas," said he to his heart, "there sits disguised affliction; methinks he is of the type of the priests: what do they want in my domain?

What! Hardly have I escaped from that magician, and must another necromancer again run across my path,-

-Some sorcerer with laying-on-of-hands, some sombre wonder-worker by the grace of God, some anointed world-maligner, whom, may the devil take!

But the devil is never at the place which would be his right place: he always comes too late, that cursed dwarf and club-foot!"-

Thus cursed Zarathustra impatiently in his heart, and considered how with averted look he might slip past the black man. But behold, it came about otherwise. For at the same moment had the sitting one already perceived him; and not unlike one whom an unexpected happiness overtakes, he sprang to his feet, and went straight towards Zarathustra.

"Whoever you are, you traveller," said he, "help a strayed one, a seeker, an old man, who may here easily come to grief!

The world here is strange to me, and remote; wild beasts also did I hear howling; and he who could have given me protection- he is himself no more.

66．退职的

然而，就在查拉图斯特拉刚刚从那位老魔法师的身边摆脱后不久，他再一次看到一个人坐在他将要经过的道路的旁边，换句话来说，那个人是一个个子高高的、皮肤黝黑的男人，他一脸憔悴，脸色苍白：这个人疯狂地悲痛着。“哎，”那个人发自内心地说道，“伪装起来的苦难就坐在这里；从我的角度来看，他应该是属于牧师一类的人：他们在我的领地里究竟想要什么？

什么！我刚刚从那个魔术师的身边逃走之后，就必须要再一次面对一个从我的道路上偶然遇到的巫师，——

——一些躺在手上的魔术师，一些忧郁的、喜好幻想的工人，一些被涂油的愤世嫉俗之人，他们都会被恶魔带走！

但是，恶魔从来都不会待在一个对于它来说是最合适的地方：它往往会来的非常晚，并且诅咒小矮人以及畸形足！”

查拉图斯特拉迫不及待地从他的内心深处如是诅咒着，并且他在思考着应该如何避免他的神情偷偷跑到皮肤黝黑之人那里去。但是，快看啊，它还是用某种方式跑了出来。与此同时，那位坐在地上的人已经注意到了查拉图斯特拉；而且他跟那些被突如其来的快乐所占据的人不一样，他从地上跳了起来，然后，径直朝查拉图斯特拉的方向走去。

“你究竟是谁，你这个旅行者。”那个人说道，“快快帮助一个迷路的人、一个寻找的人、一个老人，他在这里，很容易就会陷入悲痛之中！

这里的世界对于我来说实在是太陌生了，也太冷淡了；与此同时，我还听到了野外

I was seeking the pious man, a saint and an hermit, who, alone in his forest, had not yet heard of what all the world knows at present."

"What does all the world know at present?" asked Zarathustra. "Perhaps that the old God no longer lives, in whom all the world once believed?"

"You say it," answered the old man sorrowfully. "And I served that old God until his last hour.

Now, however, am I out of service, without master, and yet not free; likewise am I no longer merry even for an hour, except it be in recollections.

Therefore did I ascend into these mountains, that I might finally have a festival for myself once more, as becomes an old pope and church-father: for know it, that I am the last pope!- a festival of pious recollections and divine services.

Now, however, is he himself dead, the most pious of men, the saint in the forest, who praised his God constantly with singing and mumbling.

He himself found I no longer when I found his cot- but two wolves found I therein, which howled on account of his death,- for all animals loved him. Then did I haste away.

Had I thus come in vain into these forests and mountains? Then did my heart determine that I should seek another, the most pious of all those who believe not in God-, my heart determined that I should seek Zarathustra!"

Thus spoke the hoary man, and gazed with keen eyes at him who stood before him. Zarathustra however seized the hand of the old pope and regarded it a long while with

的怪兽们在咆哮；那个能够给予我保护的人——他也不再是原先的那个自己了。

我在寻找虔诚的人，一个圣人，一个独自生活在他的森林里，关于所有的世界对于现在的事情的了解都一无所知的隐士。”

“什么才是所有的世界对于现在的事情的了解？”查拉图斯特拉问道，“或许是，古老的上帝已经不在人世了，离开了那个曾经被人们相信的世界了？”

“你说吧，”那个老男人悲伤地回答道，“我一直都在服侍着这位古老的上帝，知道他生命中的最后一个小时。

但是，现在我已经是退职的人了，没有了主人，没有自由自在、无拘无束；同样地，我将无法再重新快乐起来，即便是一个小时，除非是对美好的过去的回忆的时刻。

因此，我爬上了这些山峰，最后，我将再一次为我自己好好庆祝一番，祝贺我成为一个古老的教皇以及教堂之父：因为你知道的，我就是最后的教皇！——一个虔诚的美好回忆以及神圣的服侍的庆祝活动。

但是现在，他的那个自己已经死了，最虔诚的人，住在森林里面的圣人，用不间断地唱歌和喃喃自语的方式赞美他的上帝。

当我发现他的小床的时候，我在那里看到了两匹狼，很显然它们是为了他的死而咆哮，我了解到他不再是他自己了——因为所有的动物们都喜爱他。因此我赶紧离开了这里。

难道我要因此徒劳无功的进入到这些森林和山峰之中吗？然后，我的内心才会做出决定，让我去寻找其他人，所有最虔诚的不相信有上帝的人们，我的内心已经做出决定，我应该去寻找查拉图斯特拉！”

那个老人如是说道，然后他用敏锐的眼睛注视着那个站在他的面前的人。但是，查

admiration.

"Lo! you venerable one," said he then, "what a fine and long hand! That is the hand of one who has ever dispensed blessings. Now, however, does it hold fast him whom you seek, me, Zarathustra.

It is I, the ungodly Zarathustra, who says: 'Who is ungodlier than I, that I may enjoy his teaching?'"-

Thus spoke Zarathustra, and penetrated with his glances the thoughts and arrear-thoughts of the old pope. At last the latter began:

"He who most loved and possessed him has now also lost him most-:

-Lo, I myself am surely the most godless of us at present? But who could rejoice at that!"-

-"You served him to the last?" asked Zarathustra thoughtfully, after a deep silence, "you know how he died? Is it true what they say, that sympathy choked him;

-That he saw how man hung on the cross, and could not endure it;- that his love to man became his hell, and at last his death?"- -

The old pope however did not answer, but looked aside timidly, with a painful and gloomy expression.

"Let him go," said Zarathustra, after prolonged meditation, still looking the old man straight in the eye.

"Let him go, he is gone. And though it honors you that you speak only in praise of this dead one, yet you know as well as I who he was, and that he went curious ways."

拉图斯特拉紧紧地抓住了那个老教皇的双手,并且在对他致以崇敬的同时,注视了他良久。

“快看啊！你这个备受人们尊敬的人啊，”他随后说道，“这是一双多么漂亮、多么修长的双手啊！这是准许祝福的人的双手啊。但是，它现在牢牢地抓住了那个你要寻找的人，我，查拉图斯特拉。

没有错，我就是那个不敬畏神的查拉图斯特拉，他说道：‘有谁能够比享受他的说教的我更加不虔诚呢？’”

查拉图斯特拉如是说道，并且他用他的凝视穿透了那个老教皇的思想。最后，那个老教皇开始开口说话了：

“那个最热爱他，并且占有他的人，现在也是失去他最多的人：

——看啊，我自己就非常肯定我现在就是最信奉无神论的人吗？但是有谁能够对这样的想法感到高兴呢！”

“你服侍着他，一直到他生命的最后时刻吗？”在经历了一段寂静之后，陷入了沉思之中的查拉图斯特拉问道，“你知道他是怎么死去的吗？他们所说的怜悯让他窒息而死的话是不是真实的：

——他看到了人是如何被悬挂在十字架之上，并且无法忍受——他对于人类的热爱成为他的地狱，并且到了最后，成为他的死亡？”

然而，那个老教皇并没有回答查拉图斯特拉提出的问题，而是面带一种痛苦的、忧郁阴沉的神色，羞怯地看向了旁边。

“让他走吧，”查拉图斯特拉在进行了漫长的思考之后说道，他仍旧直勾勾地看着那个老教皇。

"To speak before three eyes," said the old pope cheerfully (he was blind of one eye), "in divine matters I am more enlightened than Zarathustra himself- and may well be so.

My love served him long years, my will followed all his will. A good servant, however, knows everything, and many a thing even which a master hides from himself.

He was a hidden God, full of secrecy. He did not come by his son otherwise than by secret ways. At the door of his faith stands adultery.

Whoever extolls him as a God of love, does not think highly enough of love itself. Did not that God want also to be judge? But the loving one loves irrespective of reward and requital.

When he was young, that God out of the Orient, then was he harsh and revengeful, and built himself a hell for the delight of his favorites.

At last, however, he became old and soft and mellow and pitiful, more like a grandfather than a father, but most like a tottering old grandmother.

There did he sit shrivelled in his chimney-corner, fretting on account of his weak legs, world-weary, will-weary, and one day he suffocated of his all-too-great pity."- -

"You old pope," said here Zarathustra interposing, "have you seen that with your eyes? It could well have happened in that way: in that way, and also otherwise. When gods die they always die many kinds of death.

Well! At all events, one way or other- he is gone! He was counter to the taste of my ears and

"让他走吧，他已经逝去了。尽管你只用赞美之词夸耀这个死去的神，从而得到他对你的尊重，然而，你心里跟我一样，都十分清楚，他是什么样的人，他走上了古怪的道路。"

"在三只眼睛的面前说话，"那个老教皇愉快地说道（他的一只眼睛瞎了），"在神圣的事情上，我要比查拉图斯特拉本人受到更多的启发——很可能就是这样。

我用我的爱意服侍了他很多年，我从来都是随着他的意愿。但是，一个优秀的仆人是无所不知的，他知道许许多多的事情，甚至于他还知道隐藏在他身后的主人到底是谁。

他是一个隐秘的上帝，全身上下充满了秘密。他并不是依靠他的儿子来到这里，而是通过秘密的通道。通奸之罪就站在他的信仰之门的前面。

任何赞美他是爱意之上帝的人，都不会把爱本身看的特别高尚和重要。难道上帝不也想要受到评判吗？充满爱心的人喜欢不相关的奖励和回报。

当他还年轻的时候，上帝离开了东方世界，然后，严苛、深藏报复之心的他为自己的偏爱之快乐建造了一个地狱。

但是，到了最后，他变得老迈、柔和并且令人同情，他看上去更像是一位祖父而不是一位父亲，但是他看上去最像一位步履蹒跚的老祖母。

他浑身颤抖着坐在烟囱的角落里，并且为他虚弱的双腿感到苦恼，对世界和意志感到厌倦，终于有一天，他被这种太过于沉重的怜悯压迫到喘不过气来。"

"你这个老教皇，"查拉图斯特拉在这里插话道，"难道是你亲眼所见吗？它可以用这样的方式发生：用这样的方式，同样也可以用其他的方式发生。当诸神们死去的时候，他们往往会有许许多多的死法。

好吧！不管怎么样，是这种方式还是其他的什么方式——他已经死了！他跟我的耳

eyes; worse than that I should not like to say against him.

I love everything that looks bright and speaks honestly. But he- you know it, you old priest, there was something of your type in him, the priest-type- he was equivocal.

He was also indistinct. How he raged at us, this wrath-snorter, because we understood him badly! But why did he not speak more clearly?

And if the fault lay in our ears, why did he give us ears that heard him badly? If there was dirt in our ears, well! who put it in them?

Too much miscarried with him, this potter who had not learned thoroughly! That he took revenge on his pots and creations, however, because they turned out badly- that was a sin against good taste.

There is also good taste in piety: this at last said: 'Away with such a God! Better to have no God, better to set up destiny on one's own account, better to be a fool, better to be God oneself!'"

"What do I hear!" said then the old pope, with intent ears; "O Zarathustra, you are more pious than you believe, with such an unbelief! Some god in you has converted you to your ungodliness.

Is it not your piety itself which no longer lets you believe in a God? And your over-great honesty will yet lead you even beyond good and evil!

Behold, what has been reserved for you? you have eyes and hands and mouth, which have been predestined for blessing from eternity. One does not bless with the hand alone.

朵和眼睛的品位恰恰相反；这要比我不说话反驳他更加糟糕。

我喜欢任何看上去轻快，说话诚实的人。但是，他——你知道的，你这古老的牧师，在他的身上有一些你的影子，有着一种牧师的影子——他是不可靠的。

同样地，他也是难以被看透的。他是如何对我们歇斯底里的，这个狂怒的——鼻息粗重的人，因为我们都非常了解他！但是为什么他就不能把话说得更加简单明了呢？

倘若错误就在我们的耳朵里，那么为什么他会给予我们能够听清他说话的耳朵呢？倘若我们的耳朵中有泥土的话，那么好吧！到底是谁把这玩意放在我们的耳朵里的？

他已经失败很多次了，可是这个陶艺工人并没有从中吸取经验教训！然而，他对他的罐以及他的创作实施了报复，因为它们看上去非常的糟糕——这就是一种对抗好的品位的罪恶。

同样地，在虔诚当中同样有好的品位：最后它如是说道：‘快点远离这样的上帝！宁愿这个世界上没有上帝，宁愿依照自己的情况为自己设计命运，宁愿当一个傻子，宁愿成为一个上帝！’”

“我都听到了什么！”随后，那个老教皇竖起耳朵说道：“啊，查拉图斯特拉，你这个无宗教信仰之人，你要比你自己所想象的还要虔诚！隐藏在你的内心当中的某些神已经将你转变成了不虔诚、不信任神灵的人。

难道不是你的怜悯不再让你相信上帝了吗？而你那过度美好的诚实将会引领着你，甚至能够带领你超越善与恶！

快看啊！你的内心到底都保存了些什么？你有眼睛、有手而且有嘴巴，它们命中注定要受到来自永恒的祝福。人不会用一只手去祝福和保佑的。

Near to you, though you profess to be the ungodliest one, I feel a hale and holy odour of long benedictions: I feel glad and grieved thereby.

Let me be your guest, O Zarathustra, for a single night! Nowhere on earth shall I now feel better than with you!"-

"Amen! So shall it be!" said Zarathustra, with great astonishment; "up there leads the way, there lies the cave of Zarathustra.

Gladly would I conduct you there myself, you venerable one; for I love all pious men. But now a cry of distress calls me hastily away from you.

In my domain shall no one come to grief; my cave is a good haven. And best of all would I like to put every sorrowful one again on firm land and firm legs.

Who, however, could take your melancholy off your shoulders? For that I am too weak. Long, verily, should we have to wait until some one re-awoke your God for you.

For that old God lives no more: he is indeed dead."-

Thus spoke Zarathustra.

67. The Ugliest Man

AND again did Zarathustra's feet run through mountains and forests, and his eyes sought and sought, but nowhere was he to be seen whom they wanted to see- the sorely distressed sufferer and crier. On the whole way, however, he rejoiced in his heart and was full of gratitude. "What

尽管你断言自己是最不虔诚的人，但是我在你附近能够感受到一种受到上帝的浓烈的祝福和神圣的香气：我能从这里感受到快乐和悲伤。

让我成为你的贵宾吧，啊，查拉图斯特拉，就在今天晚上！在这个世界上的任何地方都不如现在我跟你在一起的感觉要好！”

“阿门！就这么如是吧！”查拉图斯特拉内心无比惊讶地说道，“这里就是通路，这里坐落着查拉图斯特拉的洞穴。

我很高兴能够在这里引导你，你这受人尊敬的人；因为我热爱所有虔诚的人。但是现在，一阵无比悲痛的叫喊在呼唤我快点从你的身边离开。

在我的领地之内，任何人都不应该悲痛；我的洞穴就是一个安全的避难所。最好的是，我会再一次将所有悲伤的人放在牢固的大地和牢固的腿上。

但是，究竟是谁将你的忧郁和悲伤从你的肩膀上拿掉了呢？我实在是太虚弱了。说真的，我们应该等上相当长的一段时间，直到某些人为你重新唤醒你的上帝。

因为那个古老的上帝已经离开人世了：他确确实实是死了。”

查拉图斯特拉如是说。

67．最丑陋的人

查拉图斯特拉再一次用他的双脚走过了山峰和森林，而他的眼睛在寻找着，寻找着，但是任何地方都没有他要寻找的那个人——那个感到无比悲痛和绝望的苦难者和叫喊者。但是，在这一路上，他的内心当中都充满了快乐和感激之情。他说道：“今天所

good things," said he, "has this day given me, as amends for its bad beginning! What strange interlocutors have I found!

At their words will I now chew a long while as at good corn; small shall my teeth grind and crush them, until they flow like milk into my soul!"-

When, however, the path again curved round a rock, all at once the landscape changed, and Zarathustra entered into a realm of death. Here bristled aloft black and red cliffs, without any grass, tree, or bird's voice. For it was a valley which all animals avoided, even the beasts of prey, except that a species of ugly, thick, green serpent came here to die when they became old. Therefore the shepherds called this valley: "Serpent-death."

Zarathustra, however, became absorbed in dark recollections, for it seemed to him as if he had once before stood in this valley. And much heaviness settled on his mind, so that he walked slowly and always more slowly, and at last stood still. Then, however, when he opened his eyes, he saw something sitting by the wayside shaped like a man, and hardly like a man, something nondescript. And all at once there came over Zarathustra a great shame, because he had gazed on such a thing. Blushing up to the very roots of his white hair, he turned aside his glance, and raised his foot that he might leave this ill-starred place. Then, however, became the dead wilderness vocal: for from the ground a noise welled up, gurgling and rattling, as water gurgles and rattles at night through stopped-up water-pipes; and at last it turned into human voice and human speech:- it sounded thus:

给予我的万物是多么的美好啊！今天的不良之开始已经被清晨所修正了！看看我发现了何等古怪的谈话者啊！

从现在开始我要长时间地咀嚼他们稀奇古怪的语言，就像咀嚼质地良好的谷物一样；我的牙齿将会小心翼翼地将它们磨碎并且压碎，直到它们能够像牛奶一样流淌进我的灵魂之中！”

但是，当查拉图斯特拉途径的道路再一次绕过了一块岩石的时候，周围的景色突然之间就发生了变化，查拉图斯特拉进入到了一个死亡的国度。这里有高耸的黑色和紫色的悬崖峭壁，这里杂草不生，没有树木，甚至连鸟儿叽叽喳喳的叫声都听不到。因为这是一处所有的动物们都在极力避开的山谷，甚至就连捕捉猎物的怪兽也会尽量避开这里，除了一种长相极端丑陋、臃肿的、绿色的毒蛇，当它们变得老迈的时候，它们来到了这里直到死亡。因此，牧羊人们管这个山谷叫：“死亡的毒蛇之山谷。”

但是，查拉图斯特拉开始深深地陷入了黑暗的回忆之中，因为查拉图斯特拉感觉到他在以前似乎曾经站在这个山谷的面前。一种无比沉重的压迫感降临到了他的脑海当中，以至于他的走路变得缓慢，而且他越走越慢，到了最后，他直接站在那里不动了。但是，当他睁开他的眼睛的时候，他看到有什么东西正坐在道路的边上，从表面来看像是一个人，但是看上去又不像是人，总而言之是一种无法用语言来形容的东西。不过，查拉图斯特拉立刻感受到了一种莫大的羞辱，因为他正在用眼睛死死地盯住这个东西。他那银白色的头发的根部都因为恼怒而发红了，他赶忙看向了一边，并且抬起了双脚，打算离开这个能够给人带来厄运的地方。但是，这个一片死寂的蛮荒之地开始发出了声音：一种从地下发出来的声音，幽怨和悲鸣，就像流水在夜晚幽怨和悲鸣地趟进被堵塞的水管一样；最后，这种声音变成了人的声音、人的说话声：——人的声音如是说道：

"Zarathustra! Zarathustra! Read my riddle! Say, say! What is the revenge on the witness?

I entice you back; here is smooth ice! See to it, see to it, that your pride does not here break its legs!

You think yourself wise, you proud Zarathustra! Read then the riddle, you hard nut-cracker,- the riddle that I am! Say then: who am I!"

-When however Zarathustra had heard these words,- what think you then took place in his soul? Pity overcame him; and he sank down all at once, like an oak that has long withstood many tree-fellers,- heavily, suddenly, to the terror even of those who meant to fell it. But immediately he got up again from the ground, and his countenance became stern.

"I know you well," said he, with a brazen voice, "you are the murderer of God! Let me go.

You could not endure him who beheld you,- who ever beheld you through and through, you ugliest man. You took revenge on this witness!"

Thus spoke Zarathustra and was about to go; but the nondescript grasped at a corner of his garment and began anew to gurgle and seek for words. "Stay," said he at last-

-"Stay! Do not pass by! I have divined what axe it was that struck you to the ground: hail to you, O Zarathustra, that you are again upon your feet!

You have divined, I know it well, how the man feels who killed him,- the murderer of God. Stay! Sit down here beside me; it is not to no purpose.

“查拉图斯特拉！查拉图斯特拉！快点解开我的谜题吧！说话啊！说话啊！究竟什么才是对目击者的复仇？

我引诱你转过身来；这就是顺滑的冰啊！你快看看啊！你快看看啊！你的傲慢并不会在这里折断双腿啊！

你认为你自己非常聪明，你这骄傲自大的查拉图斯特拉！那么，你快点帮我解开谜题啊！你这善于解开谜题的人——我就是那个谜题，快点说吧，我到底是谁！”

——然而，当查拉图斯特拉听到这些话语的时候，——在他的内心当中究竟发生了怎样的变化呢？满满的怜悯感占据了他的内心，他立刻跌倒了下来，就像一颗长时间同伐木者进行对抗的橡树一样，无比沉重地、突然地，它甚至要让那些将要推倒它的人们感到震惊。但是，查拉图斯特拉马上就从地上站了起来，并且，他的面部表情开始变得严肃。

“我非常了解你，”他用一种肆无忌惮的口吻说道，“你就是谋杀上帝的那个人！让我走吧！

你这个无比丑陋之人啊！谁能够看见你，清楚地看见你，必定会让你无法忍受，你这个对目击者实施报复的人！”

查拉图斯特拉如是说道，并且他正准备离开这里；但是，这个无法用语言来形容的“四不像”抓住了他的衣服的一角，并且开始幽怨和诉说。“你不能走，”最后，他说道。

——“你不能走！你不能走开！我在猜测究竟是什么样的斧子能够将你砍倒在地：啊，查拉图斯特拉啊，祝贺你啊，恭喜你重新站了起来！

我心里很清楚，你最理解上帝之谋杀者是如何。快停下！坐到我的身边；这一切都不是有目的的。

To whom would I go but to you? Stay, sit down! Do not however look at me! Honor thus-my ugliness!

They persecute me: now are you my last refuge. Not with their hatred, not with their bailiffs;- Oh, such persecution would I mock at, and be proud and cheerful!

Has not all success hitherto been with the well-persecuted ones? And he who persecutes well learns readily to be obsequent- when once he is- put behind! But it is their pity-

-Their pity is it from which I flee away and flee to you. O Zarathustra, protect me, you, my last refuge, you sole one who divined me:

-You have divined how the man feels who killed him. Stay! And if you will go, you impatient one, go not the way that I came. That way is bad.

Are you angry with me because I have already racked language too long? Because I have already counselled you? But know that it is I, the ugliest man,

-Who have also the largest, heaviest feet. Where I have gone, the way is bad. I tread all paths to death and destruction.

But that you passed me by in silence, that you blushed- I saw it well: thereby did I know you as Zarathustra.

Every one else would have thrown to me his alms, his pity, in look and speech. But for that-I am not beggar enough: that did you divine.

For that I am too rich, rich in what is great, frightful, ugliest, most unutterable! your shame, O Zarathustra, honored me!

除了你之外，我还能去寻找谁呢？快留下来！坐下！不要再看着我了！我恳请你尊重我的丑陋！

他们残忍地迫害我：现在，你就是我最后的避难所。不是他们的仇恨，也不是他们的逮捕；——啊，我会嘲弄这样的迫害，我骄傲并且高兴！

从古至今，所有受到最残忍的迫害的人们不是全都获得了成功了吗？而且那些越受到迫害的人，就越懂得顺从于别人，追随着别人——但是，那是他们的慈悲。——

我为了能够逃避他们的慈悲，所以才逃到你这里来。啊，查拉图斯特拉，我请你保护我吧！你，就是我最后的避难所，只有你才能真正地看透我：

——你能够看出上帝之谋杀者是如何。快留下来吧！倘若你真的要走的话，你这毫无耐心的家伙，那就不要走我来的那条路，那条路不是什么好路。

你是不是对我已经恼羞成怒，就因为我喋喋不休说了很久的话？甚至于我已经劝说了你？不过，我就是想要让你明白，那就是真正的我，这个最丑陋的人，

——他拥有最长，同时也是最沉重的脚。但凡是我的所到之处，那里的道路必定是坏的。我踩踏着所有的道路直到死亡和毁灭。

但是，你无比安静地从我的身边经过，你的脸因为害羞而变得通红——我看得非常清楚：因此，我知道你就是查拉图斯特拉。

每一个人都会把他的安慰、言语和态度上的慈悲给予我。但是仅仅因为这些还不足以让我成为一个乞丐：这些你心里都很明白。

我太富足了，富足于伟大的、令人胆战心惊的、最丑陋的，最无法言表的！啊，查拉图斯特拉啊，你的羞耻，让我感到无限光荣！

With difficulty did I get out of the crowd of the pitiful,- that I might find the only one who at present teaches that 'pity is obtrusive'- yourself, O Zarathustra!

-Whether it be the pity of a God, or whether it be human pity, it is offensive to modesty. And unwillingness to help may be nobler than the virtue that rushes to do so.

That however- namely, pity- is called virtue itself at present by all petty people:- they have no reverence for great misfortune, great ugliness, great failure.

Beyond all these do I look, as a dog looks over the backs of thronging flocks of sheep. They are petty, good-wooled, good-willed, grey people.

As the heron looks contemptuously at shallow pools, with backward-bent head, so do I look at the throng of grey little waves and wills and souls.

Too long have we acknowledged them to be right, those petty people: so we have at last given them power as well;- and now do they teach that 'good is only what petty people call good.'

And 'truth' is at present what the preacher spoke who himself sprang from them, that singular saint and advocate of the petty people, who testified of himself: 'I- am the truth.'

That shameless one has long made the petty people greatly puffed up,- he who taught no small error when he taught: 'I- am the truth.'

Has a shameless one ever been answered more courteously?- You, however, O Zarathustra, passed him by, and said: 'No! No! Three times No!'

You warned against his error; you warned- the first to do so- against pity:- not every one, not

我十分艰难地从充满慈悲的人群中逃离了出来——我或许可以寻找到现在唯一教育着‘慈悲就是唐突’的人——就是你自己，啊，查拉图斯特拉！

——无论是一个上帝的慈悲，又或是人类的慈悲，都是对谦卑的无礼攻击。而不愿意去帮助或许要比去实施援助的道德更加高尚。

然而换句话说，慈悲被现在所有的琐碎之人称之为道德，他们丝毫不会对伟大的不幸、伟大的丑陋以及伟大的失败致以崇高的尊敬。

在所有的这一切之上我注视着,就好像一只狗窥探着一群聚集在一起的绵羊的后背。他们全都是些琐碎的、有着良好质地的毛、拥有良好的意志的人民。

如同鹭鸶抬起头来思考，用无比轻蔑的眼神看向浅浅的湖水，我也如是注视着灰色的小浪花以及灵魂和意志的前后相拥。

长久以来，我们一直都承认那些琐碎的人民就是真理的专擅者：所以到了最后，他们也成为拥有力量的专擅者: ——现在他们说教‘只有琐碎之人称为善的才是真正的善。’

而现在，只有从那些专擅者的嘴巴里说出来的说教者所说的话才算是真理，他就是那些琐碎之人的古怪的圣人和拥护者。他自己证实道：‘我——就是真理。’

长久以来，那些厚颜无耻之人在很大程度上助长了琐碎之人民的矜骄——他说教了不少的错误，当他对人们进行说教：‘我——就是真理。’

那些厚颜无耻的人们是否得到更加有礼貌的答复了吗？——啊，查拉图斯特拉啊，你从他的身边经过，并且说道：‘不！不！连续三个不！’

你对人们所犯下的错误提出了警告; 你是第一个小心提防慈悲的人！不是所有的人，不是没有人，而是警告了你本人以及你的同类。

none, but yourself and your type.

You are ashamed of the shame of the great sufferer; and verily when you say: 'From pity there comes a heavy cloud; take heed, you men!'

-When you teach: 'All creators are hard, all great love is beyond their pity:' O Zarathustra, how well versed do you seem to me in weather-signs!

You yourself, however,- warn yourself also against your pity! For many are on their way to you, many suffering, doubting, despairing, drowning, freezing ones-

I warn you also against myself. You have read my best, my worst riddle, myself, and what I have done. I know the axe that fells you.

But he- had to die: he looked with eyes which beheld everything,- he beheld men's depths and dregs, all his hidden ignominy and ugliness.

His pity knew no modesty: he crept into my dirtiest corners. This most prying, over-intrusive, over-pitiful one had to die.

He ever beheld me: on such a witness I would have revenge- or not live myself.

The God who beheld everything, and also man: that God had to die! Man cannot endure it that such a witness should live."

Thus spoke the ugliest man. Zarathustra however got up, and prepared to go on: for he felt frozen to the very bowels.

"You nondescript," said he, "you warned me against your path. As thanks for it I praise my

你以伟大的苦难者的羞辱而感到可耻；说真的，当你说道：‘从慈悲之上降落下来的一片沉重的云朵；可要当心啊，你们这群人！’

当你如是教育人：‘所有的创造者都是无比坚强的，所有伟大的爱意都会超越他们的慈悲。’啊，查拉图斯特拉啊，从我的角度来看，你是如此精准的气象之征兆啊！

但是，你自己——同样也警告着反对你的慈悲啊！因为，很多人正走在寻找你的路上，他们大多都是一些受过苦难的、饱受别人质疑的、无比绝望的、淹溺的并且冰冻的人们。

我警告你，同样也反对你。你已经解开了我最善的、最邪恶的谜题，那就是我自己以及我所做过的。我知道那个将要砍倒你的斧子。

但是他——必须死：他用无所不知的眼睛注视着——他看到了人类的深度，他看到了所有隐匿的羞辱和丑陋。

他的慈悲并不知道谦卑：他悄悄地爬到了我最肮脏的角落。这个最明察秋毫、最深入、最仁慈的人必须死。

他看到了我：我愿意对这样的目击者实施报复——否则的话，我宁肯就这样死掉。

那个熟知万物以及人类的上帝：这样的上帝必须死！这样的见证者仍旧活在这个世上，人类是无法忍受的。”

那个最丑陋的人如是说道。但是，查拉图斯特拉站了起来，并且他已经准备好离开这里了：因为在他的内心深处，他感到无比的寒冷。

“你这个无法用语言来形容的‘四不像’啊！”他说道，“你警告我不要走你来的路。那么，我就用赞美我自己的道路的方式作为对你的答谢吧，快看啊，这里就是查拉

to you. Behold, up there is the cave of Zarathustra.

My cave is large and deep and has many corners; there finds he that is most hidden his hiding-place. And close beside it, there are a hundred lurking-places and by-places for creeping, fluttering, and hopping creatures.

You outcast, who have cast yourself out, you will not live amongst men and men's pity? Well then, do like me! Thus will you learn also from me; only the doer learns.

And talk first and foremost to my animals! The proudest animal and the wisest animal- they might well be the right counsellors for us both!"- -

Thus spoke Zarathustra and went his way, more thoughtfully and slowly even than before: for he asked himself many things, and hardly knew what to answer.

"How poor indeed is man," thought he in his heart, "how ugly, how wheezy, how full of hidden shame!

They tell me that man loves himself. Ah, how great must that self-love be! How much contempt is opposed to it!

Even this man has loved himself, as he has despised himself,- a great lover methinks he is, and a great despiser.

No one have I yet found who more thoroughly despised himself: even that is elevation. Alas, was this perhaps the higher man whose cry I heard?

I love the great despisers. Man is something that has to be overcome."- -

图斯特拉的洞穴。

我的洞穴非常大，并且深邃，里面还有很多不起眼的角落；在这里，隐秘的人发现了他的最隐匿的住所。而紧挨着查拉图斯特拉的洞穴的是有着爬行的、扑闪着翅膀的、跳跃的生物的一百个潜伏地以及旁门小道。

你这个被抛弃的人，你将自己抛了出去，难道你不是在人类和人类的慈悲中生活的吗？那么好吧，就像我一样！因此，你从我这里学习；只有想行动起来的人才能够学习。

先跟我的动物们好好说说话吧！最骄傲自满以及最聪慧的动物们——或许对于我们两个人来说，它们都是最适合的顾问！”

查拉图斯特拉如是说道，然后他继续向前走，比以前更加若有所思，步伐也比以前更加缓慢：因为他问了自己许许多多的事情，但是他却不知道应该如何去回答。

“真的，人类是多么的匮乏啊，”他发自内心地感慨道，“人类是多么的丑陋、多么的哮喘、多么的充满着隐秘的羞愧！

他们告诉我人类非常的自恋。啊，人类的这种自我怜爱是多么的伟大啊！又有多少反对着自我怜爱的轻蔑啊！

但是这个人对自己的喜欢甚至能够等同于他对自己的鄙视——从我的角度来看，他是一个伟大的怜爱者，一个伟大的蔑视者。

我还从来都没有发现过有哪个人可以彻彻底底地蔑视自己：即便彻底的轻蔑甚至意味着高尚。哎，或许，我听到的悲痛的叫喊声就是从这个更加高尚的人的身上传出来的吧？

我喜爱伟大的蔑视者。人类注定是一种必须要被超越的物种。”

68. The Voluntary Beggar

WHEN Zarathustra had left the ugliest man, he was chilled and felt lonesome: for much coldness and lonesomeness came over his spirit, so that even his limbs became colder thereby. When, however, he wandered on and on, uphill and down, at times past green meadows, though also sometimes over wild stony couches where once perhaps an impatient brook had made its bed, then he turned all at once warmer and heartier again.

"What has happened to me?" he asked himself, "something warm and living quickens me; it must be in the neighborhood.

Already am I less alone; unconscious companions and brothers rove around me; their warm breath touches my soul."

When, however, he spied about and sought for the comforters of his lonesomeness, behold, there were kine there standing together on an eminence, whose proximity and smell had warmed his heart. The kine, however, seemed to listen eagerly to a speaker, and took no heed of him who approached. When, however, Zarathustra was quite near to them, then did he hear plainly that a human voice spoke in the midst of the kine, and apparently all of them had turned their heads towards the speaker.

Then ran Zarathustra up speedily and drove the animals aside; for he feared that some one had here met with harm, which the pity of the kine would hardly be able to relieve. But in this he was deceived; for behold, there sat a man on the ground who seemed to be persuading the

68. 自愿的乞丐

当查拉图斯特拉离开了那个无比丑陋的人之后，他开始瑟瑟发抖，并且感到十分孤独：因为寒冷和孤单从他的心底里油然而生，甚至就连他的四肢都开始变得冰凉了。但是，当他不断地行走，上山下山，既有途径绿意葱葱的牧场的时候，同样也有经过流淌着干涸溪流的空旷的沙沟的时候，突然之间，他又再一次变得更加温暖以及更加快乐。

“我的身上到底发生了什么？”他自言自语道，“一些温暖并且富有活力的东西鼓舞了我；想必那种东西就在我的身边。

我已经不再觉得孤单了；无意识的同伴们以及兄弟们全都在我的身边游荡；他们那温暖的气息碰触着我的灵魂。”

但是，当他在四周搜查并且寻找他的孤独寂寞的安慰者的时候，快看啊！在一块高地之上站着好多牝牛，离他们越近，你的内心就越能够感受到温暖。但是，那些牝牛看起来正在专心致志地聆听一个演说者的发言，这些牝牛并没有注意到这个正在向他们靠近的人。但是，当查拉图斯特拉离这些牝牛非常近的时候，他清楚地听到在这些牝牛的中间有一个人类的声音在说话，而且，很明显，这些牝牛全都将他们的头转向了那位正在进行说教的演说者。

紧接着，查拉图斯特拉飞快地跑上前去，将那些牝牛们全都驱散开；因为他非常担心有人会在这里受到伤害，那样的状况可不是牝牛的慈悲就能够救济的了的。

但是，他的思想是错误的，因为，快看啊，地上坐着一个人，看起来那个人在说服那些牝牛不要惧怕查拉图斯特拉，一个平和的人，一个在山上进行说教的人，“你在这

animals to have no fear of him, a peaceable man and Preacher-on-the-Mount, out of whose eyes kindness itself preached. "What do you seek here?" called out Zarathustra in astonishment.

"What do I here seek?" answered he: "the same that you seek, you mischief-maker; that is to say, happiness upon earth.

To that end, however, I would rather learn of these kine. For I tell you that I have already talked half a morning to them, and just now were they about to give me their answer. Why do you disturb them?

Except we be converted and become as kine, we shall in no wise enter into the kingdom of heaven. For we ought to learn from them one thing: ruminating.

And verily, although a man should gain the whole world, and yet not learn one thing, ruminating, what would it profit him! He would not be rid of his affliction,

-His great affliction: that, however, is at present called disgust. Who has not at present his heart, his mouth and his eyes full of disgust? you also! you also! But behold these kine!"-

Thus spoke the Preacher-on-the-Mount, and turned then his own look towards Zarathustra-for hitherto it had rested lovingly on the kine-: then, however, he put on a different expression. "Who is this with whom I talk?" he exclaimed, frightened, and sprang up from the ground.

"This is the man without disgust, this is Zarathustra himself, the overcomer of the great disgust, this is the eye, this is the mouth, this is the heart of Zarathustra himself."

And whilst he thus spoke he kissed with o'erflowing eyes the hands of him with whom he spoke, and behaved altogether like one to whom a precious gift and jewel has fallen unawares

里寻找着什么？”查拉图斯特拉无比惊讶地叫道。

“我在这里寻找着什么？”他问道，“我在这里寻找的东西和你要寻找的一样，你这个扰乱和平的制造者，也就是说，我在寻找大地之上的快乐。

但是，我为了要达成那样的目的，我宁愿从这些牝牛的身上学习。因为我告诉你，我已经跟他们说了大半天的话了，而且他们马上就会给我他们的答案。可是你为什么要打扰他们呢?

除非我们能够改变自己，将自己变成牝牛，我们将没有方法进入到天堂的王国之中。因为我们应该从他们的身上学习一件事情：反刍。

说真的，尽管一个人应该拥有整个世界，但是，他并没有学会一件事，那就是反刍，那样还有什么益处呢！他将不能摆脱自己的苦难，——他的伟大的苦难：但是现在，那被叫做厌恶。现在，有谁的心、谁的嘴巴、谁的眼睛不是充满了厌恶呢？你也是一样！你也是一样！但是，快看看这些牝牛吧！”

那个在山上进行说教的人如是说道，紧接着，他将自己的目光转向了查拉图斯特拉——因为就在以前，他曾经用无比亲切的眼神注视着那些牝牛——：但是就在这个时候，他又一次转变了话题。“我跟他说话的这个人到底是谁啊？”他惊讶地大声叫喊道，并且从地上蹿了起来。

“这就是没有内心没有厌恶的人，这就是查拉图斯特拉，这就是伟大之厌恶的征服者，这就是查拉图斯特拉的眼睛，这就是查拉图斯特拉的嘴巴，这就是查拉图斯特拉的内心。”

他如是说道，同时用灿烂洋溢的目光，亲吻着查拉图斯特拉的双手，表现的就像是

from heaven. The kine, however, gazed at it all and wondered.

"Speak not of me, you strange one; you amiable one!" said Zarathustra, and restrained his affection, "speak to me firstly of yourself! are you not the voluntary beggar who once cast away great riches,-

-Who was ashamed of his riches and of the rich, and fled to the poorest to give upon them his abundance and his heart? But they received him not."

"But they received me not," said the voluntary beggar, "you know it, forsooth. So I went at last to the animals and to those kine."

"Then learned you," interrupted Zarathustra, "how much harder it is to give properly than to take properly, and that giving well is an art- the last, subtlest master-art of kindness.

"Especially nowadays," answered the voluntary beggar: "at present, that is to say, when everything low has become rebellious and exclusive and haughty in its manner- in the manner of the rabble.

For the hour has come, you know it , for the great, evil, long, slow mob-and-slave-insurrection: it extends and extends!

Now does it provoke the lower classes, all benevolence and petty giving; and the overrich may be on their guard!

Whoever at present drip, like bulgy bottles out of all-too-small necks:- of such bottles at present one willingly breaks the necks.

一个突然之间获得了从天堂掉落下来的珍贵的礼物和珠宝的人。但是，这些牝牛们凝视着这里的一切，并且充满了好奇。

“不要说我啊，你这奇怪的人；你这和蔼友善之人！”查拉图斯特拉抑制着自己的感情说道，“那么，首先说说你自己吧！难道你不就是那个曾经抛撒伟大的财富的自愿的乞丐吗？

——他以富有以及自己的富裕为耻辱，然后他逃离到了最贫穷的人那里，并且将他的富足和他的内心给予了他们？但是，他们并没有接受来自他的好意。”

“但是，他们根本就没有接受我的好意，”那个自愿的乞丐说道，“说真的，你是知道的，所以到了最后，我走向了动物们，走向了那些牝牛们。”

“那么，你应该知道恰当地给予要比恰当地接受困难得多，而且，这种恰当的给予是一种艺术——善意之最后的、最精细的、超凡的技艺。”

“特别是在现在，”那个自愿的乞丐回答道，“尤其是在现在，也就是说，当所有的低俗和卑贱都变得反叛，变得不易被别人接近，并且按照自己的傲慢的、残暴的方式生活。

说真的，你知道的，因为伟大的、邪恶的、漫长的、缓慢的、暴徒和奴隶的暴动的时代已经到来了：这样的暴动在不断地扩张！

现在，所有的恩惠以及琐碎的给予已经彻底激怒了社会等级极低的卑微者；并且，所有的大富豪们都在小心翼翼地提防着！

现在，无论是谁，无论是哪个滴落者，就像长脖子、膨胀着肚皮的瓶子一样——这样的瓶子随时随地都有可能被人们拧断脖子。

空虚的贪欲、暴躁的嫉妒心、饱经忧患的复仇、低俗的骄傲：所有的这一切全都

Wanton avidity, bilious envy, careworn revenge, rabble-pride: all these struck my eye. It is no longer true that the poor are blessed. The kingdom of heaven, however, is with the kine."

"And why is it not with the rich?" asked Zarathustra temptingly, while he kept back the kine which sniffed familiarly at the peaceful one.

"Why do you tempt me?" answered the other. "You know it yourself better even than I. What was it drove me to the poorest, O Zarathustra? Was it not my disgust at the richest?

-At the culprits of riches, with cold eyes and rank thoughts, who pick up profit out of all kinds of rubbish- at this rabble that stinks to heaven,

-At this gilded, falsified rabble, whose fathers were pickpockets, or carrion-crows, or rag-pickers, with wives compliant, lewd and forgetful:- for they are all of them not far different from harlots-

Rabble above, rabble below! What are 'poor' and 'rich' at present! That distinction did I unlearn,- then did I flee away further and ever further, until I came to those kine."

Thus spoke the peaceful one, and puffed himself and perspired with his words: so that the kine wondered anew. Zarathustra, however, kept looking into his face with a smile, all the time the man talked so severely- and shook silently his head.

"You do violence to yourself, you Preacher-on-the-Mount, when you use such severe words. For such severity neither your mouth nor your eye have been given you.

Nor, methinks, has your stomach either: to it all such rage and hatred and foaming-over is

跳到了我的眼前。穷苦之人会受到祝福，这已经不再是真实的事情了。但是，天堂之国度是和那些牝牛们同在的。”

“为什么天堂之国度不跟富有之人同在呢？”查拉图斯特拉颇感兴趣地问道，与此同时，他驱散了温顺地闻着这个平和之人的牝牛们。

“你为什么要试探我呢？”那个人问道，“你心里明白你比我还要清楚。啊，查拉图斯特拉，到底是谁驱使我到最贫穷之人那里去的？难道那不是因为我无比厌倦那些最富有的人吗？

——我用非常冷漠的眼神以及憎恶的思想，厌恶着这些犯下罪行的富裕之人，他们从各种各样的污秽、垃圾之中谋取利益——这样的丑恶向天堂散发出恶臭。

——厌恶这些镀金的、虚假的贱民，他们的先父们都是些小偷，又或是食腐肉之乌鸦，捡拾破烂的人，下流懒怠之妻，或是因为他们和娼妓之间没有什么区别。

属于上层社会的是贱民，属于下层社会的同样还是贱民！现在所谓的‘贫穷’以及‘富有’到底代表着什么样的含义！我已经忘记了它们二者之间的区别之分——然后，我逃离到更远、更远，直到我来到了这些牝牛们的身边。”

那个平和之人如是说道，他一边说着，一边因为张嘴喘着气而大汗淋漓：因此，这些牝牛们再一次感到好奇。但是，查拉图斯特拉面带着笑容看向他的脸，虽然这个人无时无刻都用非常严肃的态度说话——并且，查拉图斯特拉安静地摇晃着他的脑袋。

“你这个在山上进行说教的人啊，当你运用类似这样剧烈的言语的时候，你实在是太过于兴奋了。因为类似这样剧烈的言语不是你的嘴巴以及你的眼睛可以做得出来的。

不过，依照我的观点来看，你的胃同样也做不到：任何所谓的狂怒、仇恨以及嗔怒，都是和你的胃格格不入的。你的胃想要一些比较柔软的东西：因为你并不是一个屠夫。

repugnant. Your stomach wants softer things: you are not a butcher.

Rather seem you to me a plant-eater and a root-man. Perhaps you grind corn. Certainly, however, you are averse to fleshly joys, and you love honey."

"You have divined me well," answered the voluntary beggar, with lightened heart. "I love honey, I also grind corn; for I have sought out what tastes sweetly and makes pure breath:

-Also what requires a long time, a day's-work and a mouth's-work for gentle idlers and sluggards.

Furthest, to be sure, have those kine carried it: they have created ruminating and lying in the sun. They also abstain from all heavy thoughts which inflate the heart."

-"Well!" said Zarathustra, "you should also see my animals, my eagle and my serpent,- their like do not at present exist on earth.

Behold, there leads the way to my cave: be tonight its guest. And talk to my animals of the happiness of animals,-

-Until I myself come home. For now a cry of distress calls me hastily away from you. Also, should you find new honey with me, ice-cold, golden-comb-honey, eat it!

Now, however, take leave at once of your kine, you strange one! you amiable one! though it be hard for you. For they are your warmest friends and preceptors!"-

-"One excepted, whom I hold still dearer," answered the voluntary beggar. "You yourself are good, O Zarathustra, and better even than a cow!"

"Away, away with you! you evil flatterer!" cried Zarathustra mischievously, "why do you

对于我来说，你看上去更像是一个食草主义者，一个啃食树根的人。或许，你也会啃咬谷粒。但是，毋庸置疑，你厌恶肉体上的快乐，并且你喜爱蜂蜜。”

“看来，你猜透了我啊，”那个自愿的乞丐回答道，他的内心顿时轻快了起来。“我喜爱蜂蜜，同样地，我也啃咬谷粒；因为我在寻求一些品尝起来比较甘甜的东西，能够产生出纯粹的气息的东西：

——与此同时也是非常需要时间的东西，对于那些不急不慢的虚度光阴者以及游手好闲的懒人们来说，这将意味着一天的工作以及一个月的工作。

说真的，这些牝牛们非常的出色：正是他们创造了反刍并且躺在太阳的下面。他们同样也戒除掉了所有能够让心情变得沉重的想法。”

——“那么好吧！”查拉图斯特拉说道，“同样地，你也应该看看我的动物们，看看我的鹰以及我的毒蛇，——从现在来看，这片大地上并不存在他们的同类。

快看啊，那边的道路能够通向我的洞穴：那么，你今晚就成为我的贵宾吧。并且跟我的动物们好好地谈一谈有关动物们的幸福快乐的话题，

——直到我回到家里。因为现在一阵悲痛的叫喊声在呼唤着我，让我快点从你的身边离开。同样地，你也应该在我的屋子里寻找新的蜂蜜，冰凉的、金灿灿的蜂房之蜂蜜，并且品尝那蜂蜜吧！

但是，你这奇怪之人！你这和蔼可亲之人！现在快点离开那些牝牛群吧！尽管这对于你来说非常的困难。因为他们都是你的最热心的朋友以及教师！”

——“但是有一个是个例外，那匹牝牛一直都是我的最爱，”那个自愿的乞丐回答道，“啊，查拉图斯特拉啊，你自己甚至要比一匹牝牛更加温顺更加可爱！”

spoil me with such praise and flattery-honey?

"Away, away from me!" cried he once more, and heaved his stick at the fond beggar, who, however, ran nimbly away.

69. The Shadow

SCARCELY however was the voluntary beggar gone in haste, and Zarathustra again alone, when he heard behind him a new voice which called out: "Stay! Zarathustra! Do wait! It is myself, O Zarathustra, myself, your shadow!" But Zarathustra did not wait; for a sudden irritation came over him on account of the crowd and the crowding in his mountains. "Where has my lonesomeness gone?" spoke he.

"It is verily becoming too much for me; these mountains swarm; my kingdom is no longer of this world; I require new mountains.

My shadow calls me? What matter about my shadow! Let it run after me! I- run away from it."

Thus spoke Zarathustra to his heart and ran away. But the one behind followed after him, so that immediately there were three runners, one after the other- namely, foremost the voluntary beggar, then Zarathustra, and thirdly, and hindmost, his shadow. But not long had they run thus when Zarathustra became conscious of his folly, and shook off with one jerk all his irritation and detestation.

“快离开吧，你快点离开这里吧！你这个邪恶的阿谀奉承之人！”查拉图斯特拉开玩笑的大喊道，“你为什么要用这样的赞美以及阿谀奉承的蜂蜜来戏弄我？”

“快离开吧，你快点从我的身边离开吧！”他再一次大声叫喊道，并且向着这位自愿的乞丐抬起了他的手杖，但是，他早已灵巧地跑掉了。

69．影子

然而，就在这个无比匆忙的自愿的乞丐刚刚跑掉之后，查拉图斯特拉就再一次孤身一人了，就在这个时候，他听到一个全新的声音从他的背后大声叫喊道：“快停下来！查拉图斯特拉！快点停下来！是我啊，啊，查拉图斯特拉，是我啊，我是你的影子啊！”但是，查拉图斯特拉并没有因此停下他的脚步；由于山上的声音嘈杂的缘故，这让查拉图斯特拉突然之间变得怒火中烧。“我的孤独到底跑到什么地方去了啊？”他说道。

“说真的，那实在是太多太多了；在这座山上的蜂群；我的王国早已不再存在于这个世界之中了；我需要的是全新的山峰。

我的影子在召唤我吗？对于我来说，我的影子算得了什么！就让它在我的身后追赶我吧！——我想要——奔跑并且甩掉它。”

查拉图斯特拉一边如是对他的内心说道，一边奔跑了起来。但是，在他身后的影子一直跟随着他，因此，转瞬之间，这里出现了三个奔跑者，他们一个跟着一个——换句话说就是，跑在最前面的那个是自愿的乞丐，而紧跟在他身后的是查拉图斯特拉，排在第三位的，也就是排在最后一位的是查拉图斯特拉的影子。但是，当他们还没有跑多久，

"What!" said he, "have not the most ludicrous things always happened to us old hermits and saints?

My folly has grown big in the mountains! Now do I hear six old fools' legs rattling behind one another!

But does Zarathustra need to be frightened by his shadow? Also, methinks that after all it has longer legs thin mine."

Thus spoke Zarathustra, and, laughing with eyes and entrails, he stood still and turned round quickly- and behold, he almost thereby threw his shadow and follower to the ground, so closely had the latter followed at his heels, and so weak was he. For when Zarathustra scrutinized him with his glance he was frightened as by a sudden apparition, so slender, swarthy, hollow and worn-out did this follower appear.

"Who are you?" asked Zarathustra vehemently, "what do you here? And why call you yourself my shadow? you are not pleasing to me."

"Forgive me," answered the shadow, "that it is I; and if I please you not- well, O Zarathustra! therein do I admire you and your good taste.

A wanderer am I, who have walked long at your heels; always on the way, but without a goal, also without a home: so that verily, I lack little of being the eternally Wandering Jew, except that I am not eternal and not a Jew.

What? Must I ever be on the way? Whirled by every wind, unsettled, driven about? O earth, you have become too round for me!

查拉图斯特拉就开始觉得他这样做无比的愚蠢，突然之间，他摆脱掉了所有的愤怒和憎恨。

“什么！”他说道，“那些最荒唐可笑的事情不都总是发生在我们这些年老的隐士和圣人的身上吗？

说真的，我的愚蠢以前是在山峰之群当中长大的！而现在我听到了六个老蠢货的腿在彼此拼命追赶！

但是，查拉图斯特拉有必要对他自己的影子感到心惊胆战吗？同样地，从我的角度来看，它毕竟拥有着比我还要修长的腿。”

查拉图斯特拉如是说道，并且心中和眼睛里充满了喜悦，他就这么安静地站在那里，然后迅速地转过身来——快看啊，他差一点就把他自己的影子以及那个跟随者一并掀翻在地，那个影子紧紧地跟随在他的脚跟的背后，他是如此的虚弱啊。当查拉图斯特拉仔仔细细地用他的双眼凝视着这个影子的时候，他看起来像是被一种突如其来的、纤细的、黝黑的、空洞的、凋敝的跟随者出现的模样给吓坏了。

“你到底是谁？”查拉图斯特拉愤怒地问道，“你在这里做什么？而且你为什么要自称是我的影子？你并没有取悦我。”

“请原谅我吧，”查拉图斯特拉的影子回答道，“那就是我，倘若我不能够取悦你的话——那么好吧，啊，查拉图斯特拉！我会赞美你以及你那高雅的品位。

我是一个四处游荡的人，我曾经如影随形地跟随在你的身后；我时时刻刻都在行走，但是，我没有目标，同时也没有归属：所以说真的，我虽然不是永久的，也不是犹太人，但是，我已经跟永恒的畅游的犹太人没有什么区别了。

什么？难道我必须永远都在路上行走吗？难道我必须任凭所有的大风的吹袭、居无定

On every surface have I already sat, like tired dust have I fallen asleep on mirrors and window-panes: everything takes from me, nothing gives; I become thin- I am almost equal to a shadow.

After you, however, O Zarathustra, did I fly and hie longest; and though I hid myself from you, I was nevertheless your best shadow: wherever you have sat, there sat I also.

With you have I wandered about in the remotest, coldest worlds, like a phantom that voluntarily haunts winter roofs and snows.

With you have I pushed into all the forbidden, all the worst and the furthest: and if there be anything of virtue in me, it is that I have had no fear of any prohibition.

With you have I broken up whatever my heart revered; all boundary-stones and statues have I o'erthrown; the most dangerous wishes did I pursue,- verily, beyond every crime did I once go.

With you did I unlearn the belief in words and worths and in great names. When the devil casts his skin, does not his name also fall away? It is also skin. The devil himself is perhaps-skin.

'Nothing is true, all is permitted': so said I to myself. Into the coldest water did I plunge with head and heart. Ah, how oft did I stand there naked on that account, like a red crab!

Ah, where have gone all my goodness and all my shame and all my belief in the good! Ah, where is the lying innocence which I once possessed, the innocence of the good and of their noble lies!

所，并且四处漂泊吗？啊，大地啊，对于我来讲，你变得也太圆了吧！

我曾经坐在所有的地面之上，就像疲惫不堪的尘土，我在镜子和玻璃窗上睡着了：从我的身上拿走了所有，什么也没有给我留下；我渐渐变得消瘦——我几乎已经等同于一个影子了。

啊，查拉图斯特拉啊，我已经在你的身后游历了很久了；尽管我藏身在你的背后，但是，我仍旧是你最好的影子：无论你坐在什么地方，我都会坐在你的身边。

我和你一起畅游在最遥远、最寒冷的世界里，就好像一个幽灵一样，自愿地徘徊在冬天的屋顶以及冰雪之中。

我和你一起深入到所有的被禁之地中，所有最糟糕的以及最遥远的地方，倘若在我的身上拥有任何形式的道德的话，那么我将不会害怕任何性质的禁止。

我和你一起粉碎了我的心中所敬仰的；我推翻了所有的界限的石头以及雕像；我追求了最危险的愿望——说真的，我曾经穿越过所有的罪恶。

我和你一起遗忘了信仰，言语、价值以及伟大的名号，当恶魔将他的皮抛出去的时候，难道他的名字不会一样被剥离掉吗？因为那也是一层皮啊。或许，就连那个恶魔本身也是一层皮吧。

‘任何事物都不是真实的，所有的事物都是合法的’：我如是对自己说道。我将自己的脑袋和心灵深深地沉入到了最冰冷的水当中。哎，我是如此经常赤身裸体地站在这里，就像一个红扑扑的螃蟹一样！

哎，我的所有的善意都跑到哪里去了，我所有的羞耻、所有的对于善意的信仰全都跑到哪里去了！哎，我曾经拥有过的欺诈的纯真都跑到哪里去了！我那善意的纯真以及

Too oft, verily, did I follow close to the heels of truth: then did it kick me on the face. Sometimes I meant to lie, and behold! then only did I hit- the truth.

Too much has become clear to me: now it does not concern me any more. Nothing lives any longer that I love,- how should I still love myself?

'To live as I incline, or not to live at all': so do I wish; so wishes also the holiest. But alas! how have I still- inclination?

Have I- still a goal? A haven towards which my sail is set?

A good wind? Ah, he only who knows where he sails, knows what wind is good, and a fair wind for him.

What still remains to me? A heart weary and flippant; an unstable will; fluttering wings; a broken backbone.

This seeking for my home: O Zarathustra, do you know that this seeking has been my home-sickening; it eats me up.

'Where is- my home?' For it do I ask and seek, and have sought, but have not found it. O eternal everywhere, O eternal nowhere, O eternal- in-vain!"

Thus spoke the shadow, and Zarathustra's countenance lengthened at his words. "You are my shadow!" said he at last sadly.

"Your danger is not small, you free spirit and wanderer! you have had a bad day: see that a still worse evening does not overtake you!

他们的高贵的谎言全都跑到哪里去了！

说真的，我经常紧紧地跟随在真理的脚踝的背后：然后，真理的脚踝就会踢我的面庞。有时候，我想撒谎的时候，但是快看啊！只有在这一时刻，我会打中——真理。

有太多的事情给我带来了启示：而现在，我再也不会去顾虑了。我所热爱的东西早就已经从这个世界上消失了——我是如何仍旧热爱着我自己呢？

‘依照我的所爱而生活，否则那根本就不叫生活’：所以我如是意欲；以至于就连最高尚的人也如是意欲。但是，哎！我是如何仍然拥有着我的所爱的呢？

难道我仍然拥有目标吗？难道还有我的船帆要进发的港口吗？

难道还有恰到好处的风吗？哎，只有那些懂得向何处扬帆的人，才知道什么样的风才叫好风，知道什么是对他最为有利的风。

究竟还给我留下了些什么呢？一颗令人厌恶并且轻率的心脏；一个反复无常的意志；飘忽不定的翅膀以及一个破碎的脊骨。

这些寻找着我的家园：啊，查拉图斯特拉啊，你知不知道这些寻找着我的家园，它把我一口吞了下去。

‘我的家园究竟在什么地方？’我一边提问，一边寻找着，我已经开始寻找了，但是，我并没有找到。啊，永恒的去处啊，啊，永恒的去处啊，啊，永恒的——徒劳的啊！”

查拉图斯特拉的影子如是说道，然后，查拉图斯特拉的面部表情因为他的话语而被拉长了。“你就是我的影子啊！”最终，查拉图斯特拉非常悲伤地说道。

“你这自由的精神以及漫游者啊！你可是个极其危险的家伙啊！你有一个无比糟糕的一天：千万要小心提防不要让更加糟糕的夜晚来拜访你就好了！

To such unsettled ones as you, seems at last even a prisoner blessed. Did you ever see how captured criminals sleep? They sleep quietly, they enjoy their new security.

Beware lest in the end a narrow faith capture you, a hard, rigorous delusion! For now everything that is narrow and fixed seduces and tempts you.

You have lost your goal. Alas, how will you forego and forget that loss? Thereby- have you also lost your way!

You poor rover and rambler, you tired butterfly! will you have a rest and a home this evening? Then go up to my cave!

There leads the way to my cave. And now will I run quickly away from you again. Already lies as it were a shadow upon me.

I will run alone, so that it may again become bright around me. Therefore must I still be a long time merrily upon my legs. In the evening, however, there will be- dancing with me!"- -

Thus spoke Zarathustra.

70. At Noontide

-AND Zarathustra ran and ran, but he found no one else, and was alone and ever found himself again; he enjoyed and quaffed his solitude, and thought of good things- for hours. About the hour of noontide, however, when the sun stood exactly over Zarathustra's head, he

对于类似你这样的无家可归的人，就好像到最后只有成为一名罪犯才会拥有幸福感。你有没有看到过那些被抓起来的犯人们是如何睡觉的呢？他们都是静悄悄地睡觉，他们很是享受他们的全新的安全感。

一定要小心提防啊，以免让一种狭隘的信仰，一种冷血的、残酷的迷惑捕获了你！因为现在，所有的狭隘以及固定的，都在诱惑着你、引诱着你呢。

你已经失去了你的目标。哎，你怎么能够放弃并且遗忘那样的损失呢？因此——你同样也失去了你前进的道路！

你这个可悲的畅游者以及漫步者，你这个疲惫不堪的蝴蝶！就在今晚，你愿不愿意有一个休息的住处以及一个家呢？那么，我请你到我的洞穴里来！

这边的道路直接通向我的洞穴。现在，我会再一次快速地从你的身边离开。已经有一个类似影子的东西依附在我的身体之上了。

我宁肯独自一人奔跑，因为通过这样我可以再一次让我的四周变得光亮。因此，我必须长时间的奔跑并且保持快乐的情绪，但是，到了夜晚，就在那里跟我一起跳舞吧！”

查拉图斯特拉如是说。

70. 正午

就这样，查拉图斯特拉开始奔跑了起来，但是，他在路上一个人都没有见到，他依旧孤独一人，他永远都只能发现他自己；他无比享受并且痛饮了他的孤独寂寞，并且开始思考一些好的事情——时间就这么一分一秒地过去了。但是，时间大约到了正午时分，

passed an old, bent and gnarled tree, which was encircled round by the ardent love of a vine, and hidden from itself; from this there hung yellow grapes in abundance, confronting the wanderer. Then he felt inclined to quench a little thirst, and to break off for himself a cluster of grapes. When, however, he had already his arm out-stretched for that purpose, he felt still more inclined for something else- namely, to lie down beside the tree at the hour of perfect noontide and sleep.

This Zarathustra did; and no sooner had he laid himself on the ground in the stillness and secrecy of the variegated grass, than he had forgotten his little thirst, and fell asleep. For as the aphorism of Zarathustra says: "One thing is more necessary than the other." Only that his eyes remained open:- for they never grew weary of viewing and admiring the tree and the love of the vine. In falling asleep, however, Zarathustra spoke thus to his heart:

"Hush! Hush! has not the world now become perfect? What has happened to me?

As a delicate wind dances invisibly upon parqueted seas, light, feather-light, so- dances sleep upon me.

No eye does it close to me, it leaves my soul awake. Light is it, verily, feather-light.

It persuades me, I know not how, it touches me inwardly with a caressing hand, it constrains me. Yes, it constrains me, so that my soul stretches itself out:-

-How long and weary it becomes, my strange soul! has a seventh-day evening come to it precisely at noontide? has it already wandered too long, blissfully, among good and ripe

当太阳正好矗立在查拉图斯特拉的头顶之上的时候，他途径一颗盘枝错节的参天古树，并且在被一个葡萄藤的喜爱所拥抱的情况之下，将自己隐藏了起来；面对着畅游者的是高高悬挂在空中的熟透了的葡萄。突然之间，查拉图斯特拉感到非常的口渴，他要采摘葡萄吃呢。但是，正当他伸出双手去摘葡萄的时候，他忽然又想起了其他什么事情——换句话说就是，他要在这个完美的正午时分躺在树底下，美美地睡上一觉。

查拉图斯特拉即刻躺了下来；还没等他躺在安静的大地以及五彩缤纷的绿地上的时候，他忘记了口渴，然后进入了梦乡。因为正如查拉图斯特拉的格言所说的那样：“此事要比其他的事情更加重要。”只不过，查拉图斯特拉的眼睛并没有闭上：——它们仍旧不知疲倦地欣赏并且仰慕着这棵参天古树以及这个葡萄藤的爱意。但是，就在睡梦之中，查拉图斯特拉对他的心灵如是说道：

“注意了！！安静一点！难道，现在这个世界不是变得完美了么？我的身上究竟发生了什么？

睡眠在我的身上纵情的舞蹈，就好像一阵柔和的微风一样，在不可见的情况之下，在微漾的大海之上跳舞，轻盈，犹如羽毛一样的轻盈。

它不让我的眼睛闭上，它让我的灵魂保持清醒的状态。说真的，它非常轻盈，就像是羽毛一样的轻盈。

它用话语说服我，我并不知道该怎样做，它用一双爱抚的手亲切地触碰着我，压迫着我。是的，它压迫着我，以至于我的灵魂已经感到厌倦了：

——我这奇怪的灵魂是如何变得怠慢和厌倦！难道第七日的夜晚不是在正午时分准时来到这里吗？现在，它不是已经在善意和成熟的事物之中游荡了太久了吗？

它要更加舒展自己，更大范围地舒展自己！它就这么安安静静地躺在这里，我这奇

things?

It stretches itself out, long- longer! it lies still, my strange soul. Too many good things has it already tasted; this golden sadness oppresses it, it distorts its mouth.

-As a ship that puts into the calmest cove:- it now draws up to the land, weary of long voyages and uncertain seas. Is not the land more faithful?

As such a ship hugs the shore, tugs the shore:- then it suffices for a spider to spin its thread from the ship to the land. No stronger ropes are required there.

As such a weary ship in the calmest cove, so do I also now repose, nigh to the earth, faithful, trusting, waiting, bound to it with the lightest threads.

O happiness! O happiness! Will you perhaps sing, O my soul? you lie in the grass. But this is the secret, solemn hour, when no shepherd plays his pipe.

Take care! Hot noontide sleeps on the fields. Do not sing! Hush! The world is perfect.

Do not sing, you prairie-bird, my soul! Do not even whisper! Lo- hush! The old noontide sleeps, it moves its mouth: does it not just now drink a drop of happiness-

-An old brown drop of golden happiness, golden wine? Something whisks over it, its happiness laughs. Thus- laughs a God. Hush!-

-'For happiness, how little suffices for happiness!' Thus spoke I once and thought myself wise. But it was a blasphemy: that have I now learned. Wise fools speak better.

The least thing precisely, the gentlest thing, the lightest thing, a lizard's rustling, a breath, a

怪的灵魂啊！它已经品尝了太多的美好的事情了；这种金灿灿的悲伤正在压迫着它，它将自己的嘴巴裂了起来。

——就好比一艘船停泊在最风平浪静的海港里——它已经对漫长的海上航行以及飘忽不定的大海感到了厌倦，现在，它开始准备靠岸，难道陆地不是更加忠实可靠吗？

这艘船靠近了海岸，将自己拖拽到岸边：——然后一只蜘蛛从那艘船上来到了陆地上面，它开始织起了丝网。这已经绰绰有余了，我们不再需要更加结实的绳索了。

现在，我如是相信、依托以及等待，就像这艘停泊在最风平浪静的海港里地感到疲惫厌倦的船一样，开始闭目养神，紧紧地靠着大地，用最纤细的蜘蛛丝同陆地连接在一起。

啊，幸福！啊，幸福！或许，你会放声高歌，啊，我的灵魂！你躺在清澈的草地上。但是，这是神秘的、庄重的时刻，没有牧羊人会吹奏他的竖笛。

你要小心提防！炽热的正午时光正在田野上沉睡。不要放声歌唱！你快安静下来！这个世界是完美的。

不要放声歌唱，你这个松树鸟，我的灵魂！甚至于，你不能轻声说话！快点给我安静下来啊！这个古老的正午时分在沉睡，它动了动它的嘴巴：难道它现在没有饮一口快乐之水吗？

——畅饮着金黄色的酒水，金灿灿的幸福之古老的棕色的滴露？他的面部表情出现了一闪而过的变化，他的幸福笑了起来。就好像一个神在笑一样。快安静下来！

——‘为了幸福，微小的幸福是如何被满足的！’我曾经如是说道，并且我认为自己是如此的聪慧。但是，这就是一种亵渎神灵的行为：这一点，我现在已经知道了。愚蠢之人的话语往往更加聪明智慧。

不过，正是细微的事情、微小的事情，一种蜥蜴的沙沙作响，一次呼吸、一次轻弹，

whisk, an eye-glance- little makes up the best happiness. Hush!

-What has befallen me: Hark! has time flown away? Do I not fall? Have I not fallen- hark! into the well of eternity?

-What happens to me? Hush! It stings me- alas- to the heart? To the heart! Oh, break up, break up, my heart, after such happiness, after such a sting!

-What? has not the world just now become perfect? Round and ripe? Oh, for the golden round ring- where does it fly? Let me run after it! Quick!

Hush- -" (and here Zarathustra stretched himself, and felt that he was asleep.)

"Up!" said he to himself, "you sleeper! you noontide sleeper! Well then, up, you old legs! It is time and more than time; many a good stretch of road is still awaiting you-

Now have you slept your fill; for how long a time? A half-eternity! Well then, up now, my old heart! For how long after such a sleep may you- remain awake?"

(But then did he fall asleep anew, and his soul spoke against him and defended itself, and lay down again)- "Leave me alone! Hush! has not the world just now become perfect? Oh, for the golden round ball!-

"Get up," said Zarathustra, "you little thief, you sluggard! What! Still stretching yourself, yawning, sighing, failing into deep wells?

Who are you then, O my soul!" (and here he became frightened, for a sunbeam shot down from heaven upon his face.)

一双眼睛的凝视——这些微不足道的事情造就了最好的幸福。快安静下来！——究竟是什么降临到了我的身上：快听听吧！难道时光已经飞走了吗？难道我没有坠落下来吗？快听听吧！难道我没有坠入到永恒的深井之中吗？

——我的身上到底发生了什么？快听听吧！它正在叮咬着我呢——哎——叮咬到我的心脏里了吗？它叮咬到了我的心脏里了！啊，粉碎掉，粉碎掉，我的心灵，在这样的幸福之后，在这样的叮咬之后！

——什么？难道，现在这个世界不是变得完美了么？并且变得圆润和成熟了吗？啊，金灿灿的黄色之圆环——它到底飞到什么地方去了？让我去追赶它吧！要赶快！

不要出声音——”（查拉图斯特拉开始在这里拉伸自己的身体，并且他感觉到自己已经进入了梦乡。）

“快起来啊！”查拉图斯特拉对自己说道，“你这个贪睡之人！你这个在正午时分的睡觉之人！你快点起来吧！你这老迈的双腿啊！现在是时候了，现在是最合适的时候了；还有许许多多平坦的道路在你的前方等待着你呢！

现在，你正躺在你的满溢之中；你到底沉睡了多久呢！你沉睡了半个永恒的时间！那么好吧，你现在应该起来了，我的老迈的心脏！在经历了这样的沉睡之后，你要到什么时候才能从睡梦中醒来？”

（但是，接下来，查拉图斯特拉再一次进入了梦乡，而且，他的灵魂在用话语反对着他，并且保护着自己，不过，它再一次躺了下来）——“让我一个人静一静！快点安静下来！难道，现在这个世界不是变得完美了么？啊，这个金灿灿的圆润之球！”

“快点起来啊，”查拉图斯特拉说道，“你这个渺小的小偷，你这个懒散之人！什么！你愿意伸着懒腰，打着哈欠，叹着气，然后，掉进幽深的水井之中吗？

"O heaven above me," said he sighing, and sat upright, "you gaze at me? you hearken to my strange soul?

When will you drink this drop of dew that fell down upon all earthly things,- when will you drink this strange soul-

-When, you well of eternity! you joyous, awful, noontide abyss! when will you drink my soul back into you?"

Thus spoke Zarathustra, and rose from his couch beside the tree, as if awakening from a strange drunkenness: and behold! there stood the sun still exactly above his head. One might, however, rightly infer therefrom that Zarathustra had not then slept long.

71. The Greeting

IT WAS late in the afternoon only when Zarathustra, after long useless searching and strolling about, again came home to his cave. When, however, he stood over against it, not more than twenty paces therefrom, the thing happened which he now least of all expected: he heard anew the great cry of distress. And extraordinary! this time the cry came out of his own cave. It was a long, manifold, peculiar cry, and Zarathustra plainly distinguished that it was composed of many voices: although heard at a distance it might sound like the cry out of a single mouth.

那么，你到底是谁啊，啊，我的灵魂啊！”（在这里，他开始变得胆战心惊，因为一道从天堂射下来的光线直接照射到了他的脸上。）

“啊，在我头上的天堂啊，”他叹着气，随后又坐了起来说道，“你是在凝视着我吗？你有没有听到我的奇怪的灵魂呢？

什么时候你会饮下掉落到世间万物之上的甘露呢？——什么时候你会饮下这个奇怪的灵魂？

——你这永恒之水井！你这愉快的、令人畏惧的、正午时分之深渊！什么时候你会把我的灵魂吸走呢？”

查拉图斯特拉如是说道。紧接着，他从树旁边那个供他休息的地方站了起来，就好像他刚刚从一个稀奇古怪的醉酒状态中惊醒了过来：快看啊！那时候的太阳刚好照射在他的头顶之上。但是，这会让人们认为，查拉图斯特拉并没有睡多长时间。

71．致礼

这是在一个天色即将变暗的时分，查拉图斯特拉在毫无用处的搜寻以及游荡之后，打算重新返回到他的洞穴中去。不过，就在他距离自己的洞穴只有二十步之遥的地方，一件超乎查拉图斯特拉想象的事情发生了：他再一次，听到了伟大的悲痛之喊叫。这真是太神奇了！这一次，这个伟大的悲痛之喊叫是从他自己的洞穴之中传出来的。这是一种悠长的、复杂的，并且非常奇怪的叫喊，查拉图斯特拉非常清楚地认识到这种声音是由很多种声音组成的：尽管是在非常遥远的地方听到的，但是，听起来这个叫喊好像是从一个人的嘴巴里传出来的。

Then Zarathustra rushed forward to his cave, and behold! what a spectacle awaited him after that concert! For there did they all sit together whom he had passed during the day: the king on the right and the king on the left, the old magician, the pope, the voluntary beggar, the shadow, the intellectually conscientious one, the sorrowful soothsayer, and the ass; the ugliest man, however, had set a crown on his head, and had put round him two purple girdles,- for he liked, like all ugly ones, to disguise himself and play the handsome person. In the midst, however, of that sorrowful company stood Zarathustra's eagle, ruffled and disquieted, for it had been called upon to answer too much for which its pride had not any answer; the wise serpent however hung round its neck.

All this did Zarathustra behold with great astonishment; then however he scrutinized each individual guest with courteous curiosity, read their souls and wondered anew. In the meantime the assembled ones had risen from their seats, and waited with reverence for Zarathustra to speak. Zarathustra however spoke thus:

"You despairing ones! You strange ones! So it was your cry of distress that I heard? And now do I know also where he is to be sought, whom I have sought for in vain today: the higher man-:

-In my own cave sits he, the higher man! But why do I wonder! Have not I myself allured him to me by honey-offerings and artful lure-calls of my happiness?

But it seems to me that you are badly adapted for company: you make one another's hearts

然后，查拉图斯特拉飞快地向他的洞穴的方向跑去，快看啊！听到了那种前奏曲之后，一种无与伦比的表演还在等待着他呢！因为查拉图斯特拉在白天看到的人，现在全部都坐在了一起：站在左右两边的国王以及那个老魔术师、教皇、自愿的乞讨者、自己的影子、聪明谨慎的人、悲痛的预言家，还有那头驴；然而，最丑陋的人在他的头顶之上放了一顶皇冠，并且，还在他的身上放了两个紫色的花环，——因为他就跟所有的丑陋之人一样，特别喜欢打扮自己，喜欢把自己打扮成英俊潇洒的人。但是，陪伴在查拉图斯特拉身边的忧伤的老鹰站在他们的中间，它浑身竖起了羽毛，并且很不安分，因为他们问了它太多，它的傲慢根本就不屑于回答的问题；而聪明的毒蛇仍旧缠绕在查拉图斯特拉的脖子上。

查拉图斯特拉用无比惊讶的表情注视着眼前所发生的一切；随后，他用彬彬有礼的好奇心，小心仔细地检查了在场的每一位宾客，讨论着他们的灵魂，然后，他再一次产生了好奇。与此同时，那些聚集在一起的人们纷纷从他们的座位上站了起来，他们都怀着无比敬畏的心情等待着查拉图斯特拉再一次跟他们说话。但是，查拉图斯特拉如是说道：

“你们这些感到绝望的人们啊！你们这些奇怪的人们啊！难道我刚才听到的伟大的悲痛之叫喊，是从你们这里传过来的？我现在终于知道可以在什么地方找到他了，那个让我今天苦苦寻找却一无所获的人：那个更加高尚的人：

——他现在就坐在我自己的洞穴之中，那个更加高尚的人！但是，我为什么要为此感到好奇呢！难道我没有用甘甜的蜂蜜以及我的幸福之狡猾的呼唤来诱使他来到我这里吗？

但是，从我的角度来看，你们好像都是无法调和的同伴：你们让其他人们的心灵感到焦躁不安，当你们一同坐在这里的时候，你们开始叫喊求援？必须有一个人是第一个到达这里的。

fretful, you that cry for help, when you sit here together? There is one that must first come,

-One who will make you laugh once more, a good jovial fool, a dancer, a wind, a wild romp, some old fool:- what think ye?

Forgive me, however, you despairing ones, for speaking such trivial words before you, unworthy, verily, of such guests! But you do not divine what makes my heart wanton:-

-You yourselves do it, and your aspect, forgive it me! For every one becomes courageous who beholds a despairing one. To encourage a despairing one- every one thinks himself strong enough to do so.

To myself have you given this power,- a good gift, my honorable guests! An excellent guest's-present! Well, do not then upbraid when I also offer you something of mine.

This is my empire and my dominion: that which is mine, however, shall this evening and tonight be yours. My animals shall serve you: let my cave be your resting-place!

At house and home with me shall no one despair: in my purlieus do I protect every one from his wild beasts. And that is the first thing which I offer you: security!

The second thing, however, is my little finger. And when you have that, then take the whole hand also, yes and the heart with it! Welcome here, welcome to you, my guests!"

Thus spoke Zarathustra, and laughed with love and mischief. After this greeting his guests bowed once more and were reverentially silent; the king on the right, however, answered him in their name.

——那些能够让你们再一次放声大笑的人们，一个善良快乐的小丑、一个舞蹈家、一阵风、一个顽皮的小女孩以及一些老迈的愚蠢之人——但是，你们对此有怎样的想法呢？

但是，我恳请你们能够原谅我，你们这些感到无比绝望的人，请原谅我在你们这些珍贵的宾客们面前说一些毫无价值的、琐碎的话语！但是，你们并不知道究竟是什么让我的心灵如此精神振奋：

那就是你们自己以及你们的特点，我恳请你们原谅我吧！因为任何一个人看见了无比绝望的人之后，都会变得勇敢。去激励一个无比绝望的人——任何一个人都会把自己想象的足够强大。

你们已经把这样的力量给予了我——这是一个非常好的礼物，我的值得尊敬的宾客们啊！这是一个多么卓越的宾客之馈赠啊！那么好吧，当我同样向你们献上我的礼物的时候，请你们不要训斥我啊。

这里就是我的帝国，这里就是我的领地：这里所有的一切都属于我，但是，今天的夜晚是属于你们的。我的动物们也会为你们服务：那么就让我的洞穴成为你们的住处吧！

跟我一同居住在房屋里的人是不会感到无比绝望的：在我的领地之内，我会保护所有人，让他们远离狂野的怪兽的袭击。这个就是我要送给你们的第一件礼物：安全！

不过，我要送给你们的第二件礼物则是我的小小的手指头。当你们拥有了它之后，那么，你们就等于拥有了整个手掌，是啊，同样你们也拥有了内心！欢迎你们来到这里，欢迎你们，我的贵宾们！”

查拉图斯特拉如是说道，并且用爱意以及顽皮微笑了起来。在经历了这次的致礼之后，他的贵宾们再一次鞠起了躬，而且虔诚无声；但是，站在右边的国王以他们的名义回答他：

"O Zarathustra, by the way in which you have given us your hand and your greeting, we recognize you as Zarathustra. You have humbled yourself before us; almost have you hurt our reverence-:

-Who however could have humbled himself as you have done, with such pride? That uplifts us ourselves; a refreshment is it, to our eyes and hearts.

To behold this, merely, gladly would we ascend higher mountains than this. For as eager beholders have we come; we wanted to see what brightens dim eyes.

And lo! now is it all over with our cries of distress. Now are our minds and hearts open and enraptured. Little is lacking for our spirits to become wanton.

There is nothing, O Zarathustra, that grows more pleasingly on earth than a lofty, strong will: it is the finest growth. An entire landscape refreshes itself at one such tree.

To the pine do I compare him, O Zarathustra, which grows up like you- tall, silent, hardy, solitary, of the best, supplest wood, stately,-

-In the end, however, grasping out for its dominion with strong, green branches, asking weighty questions of the wind, the storm, and whatever is at home on high places;

-Answering more weightily, a commander, a victor! Oh! who should not ascend high mountains to behold such growths?

At your tree, O Zarathustra, the gloomy and ill-constituted also refresh themselves; at your look even the wavering become steady and heal their hearts.

And verily, towards your mountain and your tree do many eyes turn to-day; a great longing

“啊，查拉图斯特拉，你用这样的方式给予了我们你的双手以及你的致礼，我们认得出你就是查拉图斯特拉。你在我们大家的面前刻意地贬低自己；你几乎损害到了我们对你的尊敬：

但是，又有谁能够像你一样如此矜高地贬低自己呢，你这样做抬高了我们的地位；这让我们的双眼以及心灵焕然一新。

只要是看到了这些，我们宁肯高高兴兴地攀爬比这还要高耸的山峰。因为我们是更加热忱的追求者；我们都非常想看看到底是什么东西能够让我们如此阴暗的眼睛变得熠熠生辉。

快看啊！现在我们所有的悲痛之叫喊都已经过去了。现在，我们的思想以及我们的内心既开放又喜悦。我们并不缺乏能够让我们的精神变得放肆的勇气。

啊，查拉图斯特拉，在这片大地之上，没有任何东西能够比一个崇高的、强大的意志给人们带来更多的欢声笑语：他就是植物之中最完美的。就是这样的一棵树，能够让整个的景色焕然一新。

啊，查拉图斯特拉，像你一样生长起来的人，我们将他比作是松树——高大、安静、坚强、孤独，它是最好的、最有使用价值的木头。

——但是，在树枝的末端，它用强健的、翠绿的树枝，在自己的地盘内伸展，询问严肃的关于风的问题，暴风雨的问题以及所有在最高处的问题；

——并且用更加严肃的态度回答这些问题，一个指挥官，一个胜利者！啊，有谁不愿意攀爬上高耸的山峰来注视这样的森林呢？

啊，查拉图斯特拉，那些心情忧郁之人，倍感绝望之人，全都因为你的树而焕发了

has arisen, and many have learned to ask: 'Who is Zarathustra?'

And those into whose ears you have at any time dripped your song and your honey: all the hidden ones, the lone-dwellers and the twain-dwellers, have simultaneously said to their hearts:

'Do Zarathustra still live? It is no longer worth while to live, everything is indifferent, everything is useless: or else- we must live with Zarathustra!'

'Why does he not come who has so long announced himself?' thus do many people ask; 'has solitude swallowed him up? Or should we perhaps go to him?'

Now does it come to pass that solitude itself becomes fragile and breaks open, like a grave that breaks open and can no longer hold its dead. Everywhere one sees resurrected ones.

Now do the waves rise and rise around your mountain, O Zarathustra. And however high be your height, many of them must rise up to you: your boat shall not rest much longer on dry ground.

And that we despairing ones have now come into your cave, and already no longer despair:- it is but a prognostic and a presage that better ones are on the way to you,-

-For they themselves are on the way to you, the last remnant of God among men- that is to say, all the men of great longing, of great loathing, of great satiety,

-All who do not want to live unless they learn again to hope- unless they learn from you, O Zarathustra, the great hope!"

Thus spoke the king on the right, and seized the hand of Zarathustra in order to kiss it; but Zarathustra checked his veneration, and stepped back frightened, fleeing as it were, silently

生机；就连反复无常、摇摆不定的人也因为看到了你而变得坚定，并且治愈了他们的心灵。

说真的，现在，无数双眼睛全都把目光投向了你的山峰以及你的树林；一种伟大的渴望就此出现了，许许多多的人学习提问：‘谁是查拉图斯特拉？’

并且，你可以随时随地将自己的歌声以及自己的蜂蜜放在他们的耳朵边：所有隐居的人们、所有独自生活的隐居者们以及偕隐者们，全都异口同声地在内心里说道：

‘查拉图斯特拉现在还活着呢吗？现在还活着已经没有价值可言了，世间万物都是无关紧要的，世间万物都是没有使用价值的：除非，我们必须跟查拉图斯特拉同在！’

‘为什么他已经宣讲了那么久，却还没有来到这里呢？’因此，很多人都问道，‘难道，孤独与寂寞已经将他吞噬掉了吗？又或是，我们应当去寻找他？’

现在，我的孤寂的自身已经因为成熟而变得破碎，就好像一个坟墓一样，它已经破碎地不能再掩埋尸体了。在任何地方都能够看到被复活的人们。

啊，查拉图斯特拉啊，现在，不断喷涌的波浪持续的上升，并且已经将你的山峰包围了起来，而且，无论你是怎样的高耸，他们当中的大部分人必定会上升到跟你相同的高度：你的小船肯定不会长久地停留在干燥的陆地上。

现在，我们这些感到无比绝望的人们来到了你的洞穴，而且，我们已经不再感到绝望了——这是一种更加高尚、更加优秀的人正行进在寻找你的道路上的一种预兆和预示。

——因为他们已经在寻找你的道路上了，那些人类当中，上帝的最后剩余，——换句话说就是，一切拥有伟大的希望、伟大的憎恶以及伟大的满足的人们。

——所有不想再生活下去的人们，除非他们能够再一次学习去渴望——除非他们能够从你，啊，查拉图斯特拉啊，学到了伟大的渴望！”

and suddenly into the far distance. After a little while, however, he was again at home with his guests, looked at them with clear scrutinizing eyes, and said:

"My guests, you higher men, I will speak plain language and plainly with you. It is not for you that I have waited here in these mountains."

("'Plain language and plainly?' Good God!" said here the king on the left to himself; "one sees he does not know the good Occidentals, this sage out of the Orient!

But he means 'blunt language and bluntly'- well! That is not the worst taste in these days!")

"You may, verily, all of you be higher men," continued Zarathustra; "but for me- you are neither high enough, nor strong enough.

For me, that is to say, for the inexorable which is now silent in me, but will not always be silent. And if you appertain to me, still it is not as my right arm.

For he who himself stands, like you, on sickly and tender legs, wishes above all to be treated indulgently, whether he be conscious of it or hide it from himself.

My arms and my legs, however, I do not treat indulgently, I do not treat my warriors indulgently: how then could you be fit for my warfare?

With you I should spoil all my victories. And many of you would tumble over if you but heard the loud beating of my drums.

Moreover, you are not sufficiently beautiful and well-born for me. I require pure, smooth mirrors for my doctrines; on your surface even my own likeness is distorted.

站在右边的国王如是说道，他为了能够亲吻查拉图斯特拉的双手，紧紧地抓住了他的双手；但是，查拉图斯特拉拒绝了他的尊敬，并且，心惊胆战地向后退去，就好像要逃离一样，安静地、突然地离开了。但是，还没过多一会儿，查拉图斯特拉就再一次返回了家里，来到了他的宾客们的身边，他用清澈、洞察的眼神看向了他们，然后说道：

“我的宾客们啊，你们这些高尚的人啊，我会说简单朴实的话语，并且坦率地跟你们讲话。其实，我在这些山群之中，等待着的并不是你们。”

（“说简单朴实的话语，并且坦率地讲话？啊，慈悲的上帝啊！”站在左边的国王对自己如是说道，“很明显，这个从东方而来的圣人，并不知道善良的西方人！

但是他的意思是用‘迟钝、直率的口吻说的’——那么好吧！这些并不是这些天以来最糟糕的品位！”）

“说真的，你们或许可以是更加高尚的人，”查拉图斯特拉继续说道，“但是，从我的角度来看，你们所有人并不足够高尚，也并不足够强大。

换句话来说，为了我以及我心中不可抗拒的精神，现在已经默不作声了，但是，也不是经常保持安静。倘若你们所有人都属于我，那也仍旧比不上我的一只手臂。

因为他就跟你们一样，用虚弱的、纤细的双脚站立，无论他自己是否意识到，他总是要在一切之上能够受到放任、纵容地待遇。

然而，我并没有用放任、纵容的方式来对待我的双手以及我的双脚，我并没有对我的勇士们采取放任、纵容的方式来对待：那么，你们又怎么能够适应我的战争呢？

和你们在一起，我会糟蹋掉我所有能够获得胜利的机会。如果你们能够听到我的战鼓发出嘹亮的击打声的话，那么，你们当中的大多数人一定会因为害怕而瘫倒在地。

而且，对于我来说，你们的美貌并不充分，出生的血统和人种也不是最优秀的。我

On your shoulders presses many a burden, many a recollection; many a mischievous dwarf squats in your corners. There is concealed rabble also in you.

And though you be high and of a higher type, much in you is crooked and misshapen. There is no smith in the world that could hammer you right and straight for me.

You are only bridges: may higher ones pass over upon you! You signify steps: so do not upbraid him who ascends beyond you into his height!

Out of your seed there may one day arise for me a genuine son and perfect heir: but that time is distant. You yourselves are not those to whom my heritage and name belong.

Not for you do I wait here in these mountains; not with you may I descend for the last time. You have come to me only as a presage that higher ones are on the way to me,-

-Not the men of great longing, of great loathing, of great satiety, and that which you call the remnant of God;

-No! No! Three times No! For others do I wait here in these mountains, and will not lift my foot from thence without them;

-For higher ones, stronger ones, triumphanter ones, merrier ones, for such as are built squarely in body and soul: laughing lions must come!

O my guests, you strange ones- have you yet heard nothing of my children? And that they are on the way to me?

Do speak to me of my gardens, of my Blessed isles, of my new beautiful race- why do you

需要的是纯粹的、平滑的镜子，用它来照射出我的教条；在你们的表面上，就连我自己的模样都会发生扭曲。

在你们的肩膀上肩负着许许多多的重担、许许多多的回忆；很多充满恶意的小矮人们隐伏在你们的洞穴的小角落里。在你们的内心当中同样拥有隐秘的暴民。

并且，虽然你们都是非常高尚的人，你们是高尚之人的族类，但是在你们的内心当中很多的事物都是扭曲的、变形的。在这个世界上，没有任何一个铁匠能够为我将你们锤正并且锤直。

你们只不过是桥梁而已：或许更加高尚的人们会从你们的身上经过！你们站着就好像是梯子一样：不要斥责那些在你们身上攀登到他的高度的人！

总有一天，会从你们的子子孙孙中为我诞生出货真价实的儿子以及完美的后代：但是距离这样的时刻还非常的遥远！你们这些人并不是我的遗产以及名义的继承人。

我在这样的山群之中等待的并不是你们；也并不是和你们同在，我才能够作最后一次的下降。对于我来说，你们来到我这里仅仅是意味着更加高尚的人正在前行于寻找我的道路之上的预兆而已。

——不是你们口口声声说的上帝的残余，不是什么伟大的渴望、伟大的憎恶以及伟大的满足的人们；

——不是！不是！第三个不是！我在这样的山群之中等待的是其他人，除了他们，我不愿意轻易挪动我的脚步；

——我期待着更加高尚的人、更加强大的人、更加优胜的人、更加高兴快乐的人，期待着身体以及灵魂健全的人们：欢声笑语的狮子们一定会来到这里的！

啊，我的宾客们啊，你们这些奇怪的人们——难道你们就没有听到过任何关于我的

not speak to me thereof?

This guests'- present do I solicit of your love, that you speak to me of my children. For them am I rich, for them I became poor: what have I not surrendered.

What would I not surrender that I might have one thing these children, this living plantation, these life-trees of my will and of my highest hope!"

Thus spoke Zarathustra, and stopped suddenly: for his longing came over him, and he closed his eyes and his mouth, because of the agitation of his heart. And all his guests also were silent, and stood still and confounded: except only that the old soothsayer made signs with his hands and his gestures.

72. The Last Supper

FOR at this point the soothsayer interrupted the greeting of Zarathustra and his guests: he pressed forward as one who had no time to lose, seized Zarathustra's hand and exclaimed: "But Zarathustra!

One thing is more necessary than the other, so say you yourself: well, one thing is now more necessary to me than all others.

A word at the right time: did you not invite me to table? And here are many who have made long journeys. You do not mean to feed us merely with speeches?

孩子们的消息吗？他们正在前行于寻找我的道路上吗？

跟我谈一谈我的花园、我的祝福之岛屿以及我的全新的漂亮的族类——为什么你们就不能跟我谈一谈这样的话题呢？

我向你们的爱意渴求这样的宾客的赠礼，你们都来跟我说一说我的孩子们吧。我为此而变得富裕，我为此而变得贫困：我还有什么事不能够让与的呢。

为了此事，我还有什么是不能够让予的呢：为了这些孩子们、为了这些活生生的植物、我的意志以及我的最高希望的生命之树！”

查拉图斯特拉如是说道，然后突然之间，他停了下来：因为他的渴望来到了他的身边，紧接着，由于查拉图斯特拉的内心的颤动，他闭上了他的眼睛和嘴巴。

与此同时，他的所有的宾客们全都安静了下来，他们全都安静地站在那里，一脸迷惑的表情。只有那个老迈的预言家在用他的双手和他的脸色做着手势。

72. 最后的晚餐

就在这个时候，那个老迈的预言家打断了查拉图斯特拉以及他的宾客们的致礼：他随即变成了要珍惜时间的人一样，紧紧地抓住了查拉图斯特拉的双手，并且大喊道：“但是，查拉图斯特拉！你曾经不是说过吗，这件事要比其他所有的事情都要重要：那么好吧，现在对于我来说，这件事情要比其他所有的事情都重要。

一句在恰当的时间说的话：难道你没有邀请我们吃晚餐吗？这里有很多经历了漫长的旅行来到这里的人。你该不会是想用你的演说来喂饱我们吧？

况且，你对于那些关于冻死、溺亡、窒息死以及其他给肉体带来伤害的危险都想得

Besides, all of you have thought too much about freezing, drowning, suffocating, and other bodily dangers: none of you, however, have thought of my danger, namely, perishing of hunger-"

(Thus spoke the soothsayer. When Zarathustra's animals, however, heard these words, they ran away in terror. For they saw that all they had brought home during the day would not be enough to fill the one soothsayer.)

"Likewise perishing of thirst," continued the soothsayer. "And although I hear water splashing here like words of wisdom- that is to say, plenteously and unweariedly, I- want wine!

Not every one is a born water-drinker like Zarathustra. Neither does water suit weary and withered ones: we deserve wine- it alone gives immediate vigour and improvised health!"

On this occasion, when the soothsayer was longing for wine, it happened that the king on the left, the silent one, also found expression for once. "We took care," said he, "about wine, I, along with my brother the king on the right: we have enough of wine,- a whole ass-load of it. So there is nothing lacking but bread."

"Bread," replied Zarathustra, laughing when he spoke, "it is precisely bread that hermits have not. But man does not live by bread alone, but also by the flesh of good lambs, of which I have two:

-These shall we slaughter quickly, and cook spicily with sage: it is so that I like them. And there is also no lack of roots and fruits, good enough even for the fastidious and dainty,- nor of

太多了：但是，在你们当中没有一个人会想一想我的危险，也就是说因为饥肠辘辘而死亡的危险。”

（那个老迈的预言家如是说道。但是，当查拉图斯特拉的动物们听到了这些话语之后，他们纷纷因为恐惧而跑掉了。因为他们看到，他们在白天带回家里来的东西并不能够满足那个预言家的胃口。）

“同样地，也因为口渴而死亡，”那个预言家继续说道，“尽管，我听到水流在这里喷洒，听上去就像是智慧的语言——换句话说就是，我十分迫切并且不知疲倦地要痛饮酒水！

并不是所有的人都跟查拉图斯特拉一样生来就是个饮水之人。水并不适合那些疲倦并且老迈的人们：我们需要酒水——只有酒水才能给予我们快速的活力以及亢奋的健康！”

恰好在这个时候，那个预言家渴望得到酒水，而站在左边的国王，那个一言不发的人，同样又一次找到了可以畅所欲言的机会。“关于酒水的事情，”他说道，“我和我的兄弟，右边的国王早已准备妥当：我们拥有足够的酒水——有整整一驴驮的酒水。所以我们这里已经不缺少什么东西了，除了面包。”

“面包，”查拉图斯特拉微笑着回答道，“准确地说，隐士们没有的正是面包。但是人类并不只是依靠面包为生，他们同样还会依靠优良的羊羔肉为生，而我拥有两只山羊羔：

——我们应该快速地屠宰它们，然后谨慎地烹调：我是如此地喜欢它们。这里面也不能够缺少供挑剔者以及美食家享用的树根和水果——也不缺少胡桃以及能够被敲碎的谜题。

因此，没过多一会儿，我们就拥有了一顿丰盛的晚餐，但是，无论是谁要想跟我们

nuts and other riddles for cracking.

Thus will we have a good repast in a little while. But whoever wishes to eat with us must also give a hand to the work, even the kings. For with Zarathustra even a king may be a cook."

This proposal appealed to the hearts of all of them, save that the voluntary beggar objected to the flesh and wine and spices.

"Just hear this glutton Zarathustra!" said he jokingly: "do one go into caves and high mountains to make such repasts?

Now indeed do I understand what he once taught us: Blessed be moderate poverty!' And why he wishes to do away with beggars."

"Be of good cheer," replied Zarathustra, "as I am. Abide by your customs, you excellent one: grind your corn, drink your water, praise your cooking,- if only it make you glad!

I am a law only for my own; I am not a law for all. Yet he who belongs to me must be strong of bone and light of foot,-

-Joyous in fight and feast, no sulker, no John o' Dreams, ready for the hardest task as for the feast, healthy and hale.

The best belongs to mine and me; and if it be not given us, then do we take it:- the best food, the purest sky, the strongest thoughts, the fairest women!"-

Thus spoke Zarathustra; the king on the right however answered and said: "Strange! Did one ever hear such sensible things out of the mouth of a wise man?

And verily, it is the strangest thing in a wise man, if over and above, he be still sensible, and

一同共进晚餐，都必须跟我们一起工作，即便是国王也不能例外。因为，在查拉图斯特拉看来，甚至于一个国王也可以是个厨子。”

在场的所有人全都发自内心地同意这个提议，只有那个自愿的乞讨者在抗议着酒水、肉以及香料。

“大家快来听听这个暴饮暴食的查拉图斯特拉吧！”他滑稽地说道，“难道人们走进洞穴，攀爬高山就是为了能够享受这样的晚宴吗？

现在，我已经知道他曾经教给我们的话：节制的贫穷是能够受到祝福的！以及为什么他要将所有的乞讨者们全都排除在外。”

“尽情地快乐吧，”查拉图斯特拉回答道，“就像我一样。信守你的意愿，你这卓越之人：磨碎你的谷粒、痛饮你的水、高度赞扬你自己的烹饪——只要这样做就能够让你开心高兴！

我是一部只属于我自己的族类的法律；我并不是一部适用于所有的族类的法律。然而，属于我的族类的人，必须拥有坚硬的骨骼以及轻快的双脚，

——为了战斗和宴会而欣喜若狂，没有犹豫、没有朦胧，奔赴宴会就好比是奔赴最艰难的任务一样，必须要保持健康以及强健。

最优秀的事物全都属于我以及我自己；而且如果这些优良的东西不属于我们的话，那么我们就去把它抢过来——最好的事物、最纯净的空气、最强大的思想以及最漂亮的女人！”

查拉图斯特拉如是说道；但是，站在右边的国王回答道：“真是奇怪！在场的所有人当中有没有人听到一个智慧之人的嘴里能够说出类似这样明智的事物？

not an ass."

Thus spoke the king on the right and wondered; the ass however, with ill-will, said you-A to his remark. This however was the beginning of that long repast which is called "The Supper" in the history-books. At this there was nothing else spoken of but the higher man.

73. The Higher Man

1.

WHEN I came to men for the first time, then did I commit the hermit folly, the great folly: I appeared on the market-place.

And when I spoke to all, I spoke to none. In the evening, however, rope-dancers were my companions, and corpses; and I myself almost a corpse.

With the new morning, however, there came to me a new truth: then did I learn to say: "Of what account to me are market-place and rabble and rabble-noise and long rabble-cars!"

You higher men, learn this from me: On the market-place no one believes in higher men. But if you will speak there, very well! The rabble, however, blinks: "We are all equal."

"You higher men,"- so blinks the rabble- "there are no higher men, we are all equal; man is man, before God- we are all equal!"

说真的，这是一个聪慧之人的内心里最奇怪的事物，如果他足够聪明的话，那么他就不是一头驴。”

站在右边的国王如是说道，他感到非常好奇；但是，那头驴用憎恶的口吻回答道：“唏——哈！”不过，这还只是这个漫长的晚宴的开始部分，也就是在历史上所谓的晚餐。在这里除了更加高尚的人之外，再也没有其他的话题被谈及到。

73. 高人们

（1）

当我第一次来到人间的时候，我认为隐士愚蠢，那是一种伟大的愚蠢：我在市场现身了。

当我在那里对所有人说话的时候，我等于在对着虚空说话。然而，到了夜晚，在绳索上跳舞的人以及尸体们就会成为我的伙伴；而就连我本身也几乎是一个丧尸。

但是，在崭新的清晨来临之际，一个全新的真理就会来到我的身边：然后，我学会说：“市场、暴民以及暴民的噪音和暴民的长耳朵，跟我又有什么关系呢！”

你们这些高人们啊，快点从我这里学习这些吧：在市场里，没有人会相信高人们。但是，如果你们在那里面说话，至美尽善！但是，那些暴民会眨巴着眼睛说道：“我们之间都是相互平等的。”

“你们这些高人们啊，”那些暴民们眨巴着眼睛如是说道——“在这里根本就没有什么高人，我们都是平等的；在上帝面前，人类就是人类——我们都是平等的！”

Before God!- Now, however, this God has died. Before the rabble, however, we will not be equal. You higher men, away from the market-place!

2.

Before God!- Now however this God has died! You higher men, this God was your greatest danger.

Only since he lay in the grave have you again arisen. Now only comes the great noontide, now only does the higher man become- master!

Have you understood this word, O my brothers? You are frightened: do your hearts turn giddy? does the abyss here yawn for you? does the hell-hound here yelp at you?

Well! Take heart! you higher men! Now only travails the mountain of the human future. God has died: now do we desire- the Superman to live.

3.

The most careful ask to-day: "How is man to be maintained?" Zarathustra however asks, as the first and only one: "How is man to be overcome?"

The Superman, I have at heart; that is the first and only thing to me- and not man: not the neighbor, not the poorest, not the sorriest, not the best.-

在上帝面前！——但是，现在这个上帝已经死了。然而，在这些暴民的面前，我们是不平等的！你们这些高人们，快点离开市场吧！

（2）

在上帝面前！——但是，现在这个上帝已经死了！你们这些高人们啊，这个上帝就是你们最大的危险。

只有当他躺在坟墓里的时候，你们才能再一次死而复生。现在只有伟大的正午时分来到这里，现在只有高人们会成为——支配者！

啊，我的兄弟们啊！你们听明白这些话的意思了吗？你们的心里感到害怕：你们的内心是否开始变得晕眩？这里的深渊是否向你们张开了嘴巴？地狱之犬是否在向你们吠叫？

那么好吧，你们这些高人们啊！向上面进发吧！现在只有人类未来的高山能够感受到巨大的痛苦，上帝已经死了：现在，我们由衷地希望——超人能够存在。

（3）

现在，最热切的人开始问道："人类究竟是如何维持的呢？"然而，查拉图斯特拉是第一个，也是唯一一个人，他发问道："人类是如何被超越的呢？"

我只会认真留意超人；这就是我第一也是唯一需要注意的事情——不是人类，不是邻居，不是最可怜之人，不是最痛苦之人，不是最优良之人。

O my brothers, what I can love in man is that he is an over-going and a down-going. And also in you there is much that makes me love and hope.

In that you have despised, you higher men, that makes me hope. For the great despisers are the great reverers.

In that you have despaired, there is much to honor. For you have not learned to submit yourselves, you have not learned petty policy.

For to-day have the petty people become master: they all preach submission and humility and policy and diligence and consideration and the long et cetera of petty virtues.

Whatever is of the effeminate type, whatever originates from the servile type, and especially the rabble-mishmash:- that wishes now to be master of all human destiny- O disgust! Disgust! Disgust!

That asks and asks and never tires: "How is man to maintain himself best, longest, most pleasantly?" Thereby- are they the masters of today.

These masters of today- overcome them, O my brothers- these petty people: they are the Superman's greatest danger!

Overcome, you higher men, the petty virtues, the petty policy, the sand-grain considerateness, the ant-hill trumpery, the pitiable comfortableness, the "happiness of the greatest number"-!

And rather despair than submit yourselves. And verily, I love you, because you know not today how to live, you higher men! For thus do you live- best!

啊，我的兄弟们啊，我之所以热爱人类就是因为他能够上升和下降。而且，在你们的心中同样也有能够让我喜爱和让我可以期望的。

你们这些高人们啊！你们感受到了蔑视，这让我有了希望。因为伟大的轻蔑者都是伟大的虔敬者。

你们感受到的绝望是非常光荣的。因为你们并没有学会听天由命，你们并没有学会琐碎的权术。

今天，那些琐碎之人全都变成了支配者：他们都在说教着服从、谦逊、权术、勤奋、顾虑以及琐碎的道德之排成长串，等等。

不管是什么，只要是女人的，只要是奴隶的，尤其是暴民的混种：——现在，这些都将支配人类所有的未来——啊，真厌恶啊！真厌恶啊！真厌恶啊！

这样的问题被问了又问，永远也不觉得疲倦：“人类到底是如何用最好的、最悠长的以及最快乐的方式维持自己的呢？”因此，他们才是今天的支配者。

啊，我的兄弟们啊，超越了今天的这些支配者们，这些琐碎的人们啊：对于超人来说，他们就是最大的危险！

你们这些高人们啊，超越这些琐碎的道德，这些琐碎的权术，这些沙子谷物的深思熟虑、中看不中用的蚂蚁窝、可怜的舒适安逸以及数量众多的幸福吧！

宁肯感到绝望也不要听天由命。说真的，你们这些高人们啊，我喜欢你们，因为你们根本就不知道今天应该如何生存，因此，你们的生活是——最优良的！

4.

Have you courage, O my brothers? Are you stout-hearted? Not the courage before witnesses, but hermit and eagle courage, which not even a God any longer beholds?

Cold souls, mules, the blind and the drunken, I do not call stout-hearted. He has heart who knows fear, but vanquishes it; who sees the abyss, but with pride.

He who sees the abyss, but with eagle's eyes,- he who with eagle's talons grasps the abyss: he has courage.- -

5.

"Man is evil"- so said to me for consolation, all the wisest ones. Ah, if only it be still true today! For the evil is man's best force.

"Man must become better and eviler"- so do I teach. The evilest is necessary for the Superman's best.

It may have been well for the preacher of the petty people to suffer and be burdened by men's sin. I, however, rejoice in great sin as my great consolation.-

Such things, however, are not said for long ears. Every word, also, is not suited for every mouth. These are fine far-away things: at them sheep's claws shall not grasp!

（4）

啊，我的兄弟们啊，你们拥有勇气吗？你们拥有坚定的决心吗？难道在见证者面前的勇敢，不是连上帝都不敢注视太久的隐士和老鹰的勇气吗？

冷淡的灵魂者、执拗者、看不见东西的人以及醉鬼，不是我所谓的拥有坚定的决心的人。用征服的心灵面对恐惧，用骄傲的心灵看待深渊，这才是我所谓的拥有坚定的决心。

用老鹰的双眼去注视深渊，——用老鹰的利爪去牢牢抓住深渊：这才是我所谓的拥有勇气。

（5）

“人类是邪恶的”——所有充满智慧的人为了安慰我，如是说道。啊，那么今天还是真实的吗！因为邪恶是人类最优良的力量。

“人类必须变得更加强大，更加邪恶”——我如是说教道。为了能够达到超人的最优良的境界，人类的最邪恶是必不可少的。

这些对于琐碎的说教者来说是非常适合的：他遭受过苦难，并且肩负着人类的罪恶。但是，我却对用最伟大的邪恶来作为我的最伟大的安慰而感到欣喜若狂。

但是这样的事情并不是为了长耳朵说的。同样地，所有的话语并不适合于一切的嘴巴。这些都是既精美又非常遥远的东西：这些并不是用绵羊的蹄子就能抓得到的！

6.

You higher men, think you that I am here to put right what you have put wrong?

Or that I wished henceforth to make snugger couches for you sufferers? Or show you restless, miswandering, misclimbing ones, new and easier footpaths?

No! No! Three times No! Always more, always better ones of your type shall perish,- for you shall always have it worse and harder. Thus only-

-Thus only grows man aloft to the height where the lightning strikes and shatters him: high enough for the lightning!

Towards the few, the long, the remote go forth my soul and my seeking: of what account to me are your many little, short miseries!

You do not yet suffer enough for me! For you suffer from yourselves, you have not yet suffered from man. You would lie if you spoke otherwise! None of you suffers from what I have suffered.- -

7.

It is not enough for me that the lightning no longer does harm. I do not wish to conduct it away: it shall learn- to work for me.-

My wisdom has accumulated long like a cloud, it becomes stiller and darker. So does all

（6）

你们这些高人们啊，你们以为我今天站在这里是为了纠正你们之前所犯下的过错吗？又或者是，你们认为我会给你们这些苦难者们准备了既温暖又舒适的床榻？或者是为那些心神不宁的、迷失方向的、在登山中偏离路线的人们，指出全新的、更加简单便捷的道路吗？

不是！不是！第三个不是！越是在你们的族群内，优秀的、出色的人就越会过早死亡——因为你们的生活永远都是更加糟糕、更加苦难的。唯有——

——唯有让人攀爬到高处，让闪电击打他、震颤他：让他攀爬到足以触碰到闪电的高度！

我的灵魂以及我的渴望都在向往着悠长并且遥远的事物：你们这些众多的、琐碎的以及短促的悲哀对于我来说又算得了什么呢！

从我的角度来说，你们遭受到的苦难还远远不够！因为你们只是从你们的自身遭受苦难，你们并没有从人类的身上遭受到苦难。倘若你们不赞同的话，那么你们就是在说谎话！你们当中的任何一个人都没有经历过我曾经所遭受过的苦难。

（7）

对于我来说，闪电已经不再具有破坏力，这还远远不能满足我。我并不想将它移开，它应当学习为了我而工作。

wisdom which shall one day bear lightnings.-

To these men of today will I not be light, nor be called light. Them- will I blind: lightning of my wisdom! put out their eyes!

8.

Do not will anything beyond your power: there is a bad falseness in those who will beyond their power.

Especially when they will great things! For they awaken distrust in great things, these subtle false-coiners and stage-players:-

-Until at last they are false towards themselves, squint-eyed, whited cankers, glossed over with strong words, parade virtues and brilliant false deeds.

Take good care there, you higher men! For nothing is more precious to me, and rarer, than honesty.

Is this today not that of the rabble? The rabble however knows not what is great and what is small, what is straight and what is honest: it is innocently crooked, it ever lies.

我的智慧全都凝聚在了一起，看起来就像一团云彩，渐渐地，它开始变得越来越宁静，越来越黑暗。因此，总有一天所有的智慧会产生出火花。

对于今天的人们来说，我既不是光，也不能被人们称为光。我要让他们变得目盲：我的智慧之闪电！将他们的双眼电出来吧！

（8）

不要让任何的事物凌驾于你们的力量之上：在那些凌驾于他们的力量之上的人们的身上都有一种恶劣的虚假。

尤其是当他们意欲着伟大的事情的时候！因为他们会唤醒对于伟大的事物的不信任，这些巧妙的制造伪钱币的人们以及舞台上的表演者们：

——直到最后，他们将他们自己也欺骗了，斜视着眼睛、流脓溃烂，用夸夸其谈的道德、辉煌虚假的行为，扭曲了事情的真相。

你们这些高人们啊，在这里一定要多加小心啊！因为，对于我来说，天底下没有什么要比正直更加宝贵、更加稀有的东西了。

难道今天的时代不是那些暴民的时代吗？但是，这些暴民们并不知道什么是伟大、什么是渺小、什么是坦率、什么是正直：暴民永远都是无知的扭曲，他们从来都是喜好说谎话的人。

9.

Have a good distrust today you, higher men, you enheartened ones! You open-hearted ones! And keep your reasons secret! For this today is that of the rabble.

What the rabble once learned to believe without reasons, who could- refute it to them by means of reasons?

And on the market-place one convinces with gestures. But reasons make the rabble distrustful.

And when truth has once triumphed there, then ask yourselves with good distrust: "What strong error has fought for it?"

Be on your guard also against the learned! They hate you, because they are unproductive! They have cold, withered eyes before which every bird is unplumed.

Such persons vaunt about not lying: but inability to lie is still far from being love to truth. Be on your guard!

Freedom from fever is still far from being knowledge! Refrigerated spirits I do not believe in. He who cannot lie, does not know what truth is.

10.

If you would go up high, then use your own legs! Do not get yourselves carried aloft; do not

（9）

你们这些高人们啊，你们这些内心倍受鼓舞的人们啊，你们这些直率的人们啊，你们不要轻信这个时代啊！并且让你们的理智严格保守秘密！因为今天就是那些暴民们的时代。

那些暴民们曾经学会了没有理智的信仰，有谁能够通过有理有据的方式来反驳他们呢？

在市场上，手势能够说服人们。但是，理智让那些暴民们心生怀疑。

倘若真相在那里获得了胜利，那么你会用很好的怀疑问自己：“究竟是什么强大的谬论在那里取得了胜利呢？”

但是，你们同样也要小心提防那些博学家们！他们憎恶你们，因为他们是不生产的！他们拥有无比冷酷并且凋敝的双眼，那样的目光能够让所有鸟类的翅膀掉落。

类似这样的人大概会因为不说谎话而夸夸其谈：但是，不能说谎跟热爱真相仍旧相去甚远。你们一定要小心提防啊！

脱离了热病的自由跟真正的知识仍旧相去甚远！我并不相信冷冻的心灵中的一切。不能够说谎话的人，也就不会知道什么是真相。

（10）

如果你要向上攀爬的话，那么你就用自己的两条腿吧！不要让别人将自己背到高处

seat yourselves on other people's backs and heads!

You have mounted, however, on horseback? you now ride briskly up to your goal? Well, my friend! But your lame foot is also with you on horseback!

When you reach your goal, when you alight from your horse: precisely on your height, you higher man,- then will you stumble!

11.

You creators, you higher men! One is only pregnant with one's own child.

Do not let yourselves be imposed upon or put upon! Who then is your neighbor? Even if you act "for your neighbor"- you still do not create for him!

Unlearn, I pray you, this "for," you creators: your very virtue wishes you to have naught to do with "for" and "on account of" and "because." Against these false little words shall you stop your ears.

"For one's neighbor," is the virtue only of the petty people: there it is said "like and like," and "hand washes hand":- they have neither the right nor the power for your self-seeking!

In your self-seeking, you creators, there is the foresight and foreseeing of the pregnant! What no one's eye has yet seen, namely, the fruit- this, shelters and saves and nourishes your entire love.

Where your entire love is, namely, with your child, there is also your entire virtue! Your

去，不要让自己坐在其他人的后背上以及脑袋顶上！

但是，你不是已经骑在了马背上了吗？你现在不是飞快地奔向你的目标吗？好吧，我的朋友！但是，你那双虚弱的双腿同样也在马背上！

但你来到了你的目的地，当你从你的马背上下来的时候：啊，你这高人啊，即使你在高处，你仍旧会跌倒！

（11）

你们这些创造者，你们这些高人啊！一个人只能够孕育他自己的孩子。

千万不要让你们自己被欺骗或是被说服！那么，你们的邻居究竟是谁呢？即便是你们为了你们的邻居而工作——你们仍旧不是为了他而创造！

你们这些创造者啊，我恳请你们忘记这个“为”字：你们内心深处的道德希望你们能够同“为”、“以此”以及“因为”等等词语完全脱离关系。你们已经会紧闭耳朵对这些虚假的渺小的言语充耳不闻。

“为了自己的邻居，”这是一种只有琐碎之人才具备的道德：他们在那里说着“同气相求”、“同类相亲”——他们既没有权力也没有力量来谋求你们的自我追求！

你们这些创造者，在你们的自我追求当中，拥有着孕育的预见和预兆！这些是任何人都无法看到的，你们的果实，你们用这个避难所来保护并且滋养了你们全部的爱意。

你们全部的爱意在哪里呢，也就是说你们的孩子究竟在哪里呢，换句话说就是你们的全部道德究竟在哪里呢！千万不要让任何虚假的价值影响了你：你的工作，你的意志

work, your will is your "neighbor": let no false values impose upon you!

12.

You creators, you higher men! Whoever has to give birth is sick; whoever has given birth, however, is unclean.

Ask women: one gives birth, not because it gives pleasure. The pain makes hens and poets cackle.

You creators, in you there is much uncleanliness. That is because you have had to be mothers.

A new child: oh, how much new filth has also come into the world! Go apart! He who has given birth shall wash his soul!

13.

Be not virtuous beyond your powers! And seek nothing from yourselves opposed to probability!

Walk in the footsteps in which your fathers' virtue has already walked! How would you rise high, if your fathers' will should not rise with you?

Yet he who would be a firstling, let him take care lest he also become a lastling! And where

就是你的“邻居”！

（12）

你们这些创造者，你们这些高人们啊！生育后代的人遭受苦难；但是，生育后代的人是不干净的。

问问女人们吧：自己生子，并不是因为生子能够给她带来快乐。能够让老母鸡咯咯叫，能够让诗人们放声高歌的就是痛苦。

你们这些创造者啊，在你们的内心当中充满了不干净。这是因为你们迫不得已要做孩子的母亲。

一个新生儿：啊，又有多少新鲜的污秽来到了这个世界上啊！快走开吧！已经生育后代的人应该清洗她的灵魂！

（13）

不要要求超过你自身的能力范围的道德！不要要求不可能做到的事情！

跟随着你们的祖先的道德已经踩踏过的地方留下来的足印前进吧！如果你们祖先的意志并不能跟你们一同上升，那么你们又怎么能够上升呢？

然而，那个最早出生的孩子，要让他小心提防，以免成为末胎的孩子！但凡是留有你们祖先的罪恶的地方，你们都无法企图成为圣人！

the vices of your fathers are, there should you not set up as saints!

He whose fathers were inclined for women, and for strong wine and flesh of wildboar swine; what would it be if he demanded chastity of himself?

A folly would it be! Much, verily, does it seem to me for such a one, if he should be the husband of one or of two or of three women.

And if he founded monasteries, and inscribed over their portals: "The way to holiness,"- I should still say: What good is it! it is a new folly!

He has founded for himself a penance-house and refuge-house: much good may it do! But I do not believe in it.

In solitude there grows what any one brings into it- also the brute in one's nature. Thus is solitude inadvisable to many.

Has there ever been anything filthier on earth than the saints of the wilderness? Around them was not only the devil loose- but also the swine.

14.

Shy, ashamed, awkward, like the tiger whose spring has failed- thus, you higher men, have I often seen you slink aside. A cast which you made had failed.

But what does it matter, you dice-players! You had not learned to play and mock, as one must play and mock! Do we not ever sit at a great table of mocking and playing?

他的祖先痴迷于女人们，沉迷于烈酒以及野猪肉；如果他要自洁，他应该怎么做？

那真是一种愚蠢啊！说真的，我认为，那真是太过于愚蠢了，倘若他是一个或是两个，又或是三个女人的丈夫。

如果他修建了修道院，并且在大门上铭刻：“通往神圣的道路，”——我仍旧要说：这有什么好的！这不过就是一种新的愚蠢！

并且他为自己修建了一个可供忏悔和避难的地方：这对于他来说是再好不过了吧！但是，我并不相信这些。

在孤寂之中，生长着任何人的内心都拥有的——同样也生长着人类残忍的本性。因此，对于很多人来说，孤寂并不适合于他们。

难道在这个世界上还有什么要比荒郊野外的圣人更加污秽的事物吗？围绕在他们身上的不仅仅有恶魔的束缚——同样还有横行霸道的怪兽。

（14）

你们这些高人们啊，我经常能够看到你们犹如跳跃失败的老虎一般，腼腆地、羞愧地、笨拙地将自己隐藏起来。你们的投掷已经失败了。

但是对于你们这些投掷骰子的人来说，那又有什么关系呢！你们并没有学会玩耍和嘲弄，就如同人们必须要玩耍和嘲弄！难道我们大家不是永远都坐在一张巨大的嘲弄和玩耍的桌子的旁边吗？

倘若你们在伟大的事情当中失败了，那么，你们自己也就因此成为所谓的失败了吗？

And if great things have been a failure with you, have you yourselves therefore- been a failure? And if you yourselves have been a failure, has man therefore- been a failure? If man, however, has been a failure: well then! never mind!

15.

The higher its type, always the seldomer does a thing succeed. You higher men here, have you not all- been failures?

Be of good cheer; what does it matter? How much is still possible! Learn to laugh at yourselves, as you ought to laugh!

What wonder even that you have failed and only half-succeeded, you half-shattered ones! Do not- man's future strive and struggle in you?

Man's furthest, profoundest, star-highest issues, his prodigious powers- do not all these foam through one another in your vessel?

What wonder that many a vessel shatters! Learn to laugh at yourselves, as you ought to laugh! You higher men, Oh, how much is still possible!

And verily, how much has already succeeded! How rich is this earth in small, good, perfect things, in well-constituted things!

Set around you small, good, perfect things, you higher men. Their golden maturity heals the heart. The perfect teaches one to hope.

而且倘若你们自己就是失败的话，难么，人类也就因此成为失败了吗？假设人类就是一种失败的话：那么好吧！不要在意这些了！

（15）

越是崇高的品质，做事情成功的概率就会越低。这里，你们这些高人们啊，难道你们不都是失败者吗？

尽情地欢喜吧，那又有什么关系呢？仍旧有多大的可能性呢！学会对自己微笑，就像人们应该微笑一样！

你们这些接近支离破碎的人们啊，那又有什么可惊奇的呢，你们这些失败或者成功了一半的人们！难道人类的未来不是在你们的内心当中奋斗着、挣扎着前行吗？

人类的最遥远的、最深奥的、最高深莫测的精神，人类最惊人的力量——难道所有的这些不都在你的酒桶里泛着泡沫吗？

许许多多的酒桶都支离破碎了，这有什么可惊奇的呢！学会对自己微笑吧，就像人们应该微笑一样！你们这些高人们啊，啊，仍旧有多大的可能性呢！

说真的，已经成功的有多少呢！在这片大地上的微小的、优良的、完美的、完善的事物是如此的丰富！

你们这些高人们啊，将这些微笑的、优良的、完美的事物全都放在你们的身边吧。它们的金灿灿的成熟能够治愈人类的心灵。完美的事物能够教会人们以希望。

16.

What has hitherto been the greatest sin here on earth? Was it not the word of him who said: "Woe to them that laugh now!"

Did he himself find no cause for laughter on the earth? Then he sought badly. A child even finds cause for it.

He- did not love sufficiently: otherwise would he also have loved us, the laughing ones! But he hated and hooted us; wailing and teeth-gnashing did he promise us.

Must one then curse immediately, when one does not love? That- seems to me bad taste. Thus did he, however, this absolute one. He sprang from the rabble.

And he himself just did not love sufficiently; otherwise would he have raged less because people did not love him. All great love does not seek love:- it seeks more.

Go out of the way of all such absolute ones! They are a poor sickly type, a rabble-type: they look at this life with ill-will, they have an evil eye for this earth.

Go out of the way of all such absolute ones! They have heavy feet and sultry hearts:- they do not know how to dance. How could the earth be light to such ones!

（16）

那么自从来到这片大地的时候，最伟大的罪恶是什么呢？难道那不是他所说过的话吗！他说道：“真是悲哀啊，那些在这片大地上微笑的人们！”

难道他自己没有在这片大地上寻找到能够微笑的理由吗？即使是那样，那也只是因为他并没有好好地寻找。即便是一个小孩子也能够找到微笑的理由。

他的爱意还远远不够：要不然，他也同样会热爱我们，热爱喜欢微笑的人们！但是，他憎恨我们，他大声地怒斥我们；他承诺我们可以哀声、可以咬牙切齿。

倘若一个人不去爱的话，那么他就必须受到诅咒吗？这在我看来确实是一种恶劣的品位。但是，他就这么做了，这个绝对之人。他从暴民群中跳了出来。

说真的，他自身并没有足够的爱意；不然的话，他宁肯不再施暴，因为他并不会得到别人对他的爱。所有伟大的爱意，并不会渴望着爱意——它渴望着更多。

快点远离所有绝对之人所要经过的道路！他们都是贫穷的、虚弱的族类，他们都是一种流氓群体的族类：他们用一种邪恶的意志看待这种人生；他们用一种邪恶的双眼看着这片大地。

快点远离所有绝对之人所要经过的道路！他们全都拥有沉重的双脚以及炽热的内心——他们并不知道应该如何跳舞。这片大地对于这样的人来说又如何会是轻便的呢！

17.

Tortuously do all good things come nigh to their goal. Like cats they curve their backs, they purr inwardly with their approaching happiness,- all good things laugh.

His step betrays whether a person already walks on his own path: just see me walk! Yet he who comes nigh to his goal, dances.

And verily, a statue have I not become, not yet do I stand there stiff, stupid and stony, like a pillar; I love fast racing.

And though there be on earth fens and dense afflictions, he who has light feet runs even across the mud, and dances, as upon well-swept ice.

Lift up your hearts, my brothers, high, higher! And do not forget your legs! Lift up also your legs, you good dancers, and better still, if you stand upon your heads!

18.

This crown of the laughter, this rose-garland crown: I myself have put on this crown, I myself have consecrated my laughter. No one else have I found to-day potent enough for this.

Zarathustra the dancer, Zarathustra the light one, who beckons with his pinions, one ready for flight, beckoning to all birds, ready and prepared, a blissfully light-spirited

（17）

所有充满善意的事物全都曲折地到达了他们的目的地。他们就像小猫一样将自己的后背弯曲了起来，他们因为即将到来的幸福而开心地呜呜叫——所有充满善意的事物都在发笑。

一个人的脚步能够说明他是不是漫步于他自己的道路之上：好好看看我是如何走路的！慢慢接近自己的目标，并且跳着舞步。

说真的，我并没有成为一尊塑像，我也没有僵硬地、愚蠢地、坚硬地犹如一根石柱一样站在那里，我喜欢飞快地奔跑。

尽管在这片大地之上有沼泽和凝重的苦难，但是那些拥有轻便的双脚之人甚至可以跑过泥浆，并且在无比平滑的冰面上翩翩起舞。

我的兄弟们啊，将你们的心灵高高地抬起来吧，高一点，再高一点！还有不要忘记你的双腿！你们这些优秀的舞蹈者们，同样也抬高你们的双腿吧！倘若你们能够倒立于你们的头顶之上，那就再好不过了！

（18）

这个笑声不止的王冠，这个拥有玫瑰——花环的王冠：我要亲自将这顶王冠戴在我的头顶上，我要亲自将我的微笑神圣化。直到现在，我还没有发现有人能够拥有如此充足的魄力。

one:-

Zarathustra the soothsayer, Zarathustra the sooth-laugher, no impatient one, no absolute one, one who loves leaps and side-leaps; I myself have put on this crown!

19.

Lift up your hearts, my brothers, high, higher! And do not forget your legs! Lift up also your legs, you good dancers, and better still if you stand upon your heads!

There are also heavy animals in a state of happiness, there are club-footed ones from the beginning. Curiously do they exert themselves, like an elephant which endeavors to stand upon its head.

Better, however, to be foolish with happiness than foolish with misfortune, better to dance awkwardly than walk lamely. So learn, I pray you, my wisdom, you higher men: even the worst thing has two good reverse sides,-

-Even the worst thing has good dancing-legs: so learn, I pray you, you higher men, to put yourselves on your proper legs!

So unlearn, I pray you, the sorrow-sighing, and all the rabble-sadness! Oh, how sad the fools of the rabble seem to me today! This today, however, is that of the rabble.

查拉图斯特拉这个跳舞之人，查拉图斯特拉这个轻便之人，他震颤着他的翅膀，他已经准备好飞翔了，他在向所有的鸟类们示意，他已经准备就绪随时出发了，一个幸福的、拥有着轻便的灵魂的人：

查拉图斯特拉这个预言家，查拉图斯特拉这个无比真实的大笑者，这个无法忍耐的人，这个非绝对之人，一个喜欢跳跃以及飞跳的人；我要亲自将这顶王冠戴在我的头顶上！

（19）

我的兄弟们啊，请高高地举起你们的心灵吧！高一点，再高一点！还有不要忘记了你们的双腿！你们这些优秀的舞蹈者们啊，同样举起你们的双腿吧！如果你们能够将自己倒立于脑袋之上，那就再好不过了！

即便是在快乐的状态当中，同样会有沉重的动物们，那些畸足的动物们从一开始就已经存在了。他们好奇地推动着自己，就好像一头努力站立在头顶之上的大象一样。

但是，为了幸福而愚蠢要比为了不幸而愚蠢好得多，用笨拙的脚步跳舞要比用笨拙的脚步走路好得多。所以，你们这些高人们啊，我恳请你们学习我的智慧：即便是最糟糕的事情也会有两个良好的反面，

——即便是最糟糕的事情也会有优秀的舞蹈之腿：所以，你们这些高人们啊，我恳请你们跟我学习，站立在你们自己的真正的腿上！

所以，我恳请你们忘记悲哀的叹息以及所有残暴之人的悲伤！啊，在我看来，今日的暴民之蠢材是何等的悲哀啊！但是，今天的时代正是那些暴民们的时代。

20.

Do like to the wind when it rushes forth from its mountain-caves: to its own piping will it dance; the seas tremble and leap under its footsteps.

That which gives wings to asses, that which milks the lionesses:- praised be that good, unruly spirit, which comes like a hurricane to all the present and to all the rabble,-

-Which is hostile to thistle-heads and puzzle-heads, and to all withered leaves and weeds:- praised be this wild, good, free spirit of the storm, which dances upon fens and afflictions, as upon meadows!

Which hates the consumptive rabble-dogs, and all the ill-constituted, sullen brood:- praised be this spirit of all free spirits, the laughing storm, which blows dust into the eyes of all the melanopic and melancholic!

You higher men, the worst thing in you is that you have none of you learned to dance as you ought to dance- to dance beyond yourselves! What does it matter that you have failed!

How many things are still possible! So learn to laugh beyond yourselves! Lift up your hearts, you good dancers, high! higher! And do not forget the good laughter!

This crown of the laughter, this rose-garland crown: to you, my brothers, do I cast this crown! Laughing have I consecrated; you higher men, learn, I pray you- to laugh!

（20）

就好像从山峰的洞穴里突然吹袭而出的风一样：它在自己的旋律中翩翩起舞；大海在它的脚步之下颤抖并且跳跃着。

它给予了驴子们能够飞翔的翅膀，它用母乳哺育了狮子们——用语言赞美那善良的，并且难以驾驭的灵魂，它看起来就像是一阵龙卷风一样，来到了所有的现在，来到了所有的暴民的面前，

——它强烈反对所有的荆棘之头以及谜题之头，强烈反对所有的凋零的树叶以及种子：——用言语赞美这些狂野的、善良的、自由自在的暴风之灵魂吧，它在沼泽和悲痛之上尽情地舞蹈，它在牧场之上尽情地舞蹈！

它憎恶那些患有肺病的贱民之狗，憎恶所有阴沉、郁郁寡欢的族类：——用语言赞美所有这些自由自在的精灵以及这欢声笑语的暴风，它将尘土吹拂进了所有的悲观主义者以及忧郁症患者的眼睛里！

啊，你们这些高人们啊，在你们的心灵当中最恶劣的事情应该是在你们所有人当中，没有一个人学会跳舞，就如同人类必须会跳舞一样——跳舞超越你们能够掌控的范畴之外，你们这些优秀的舞蹈者啊，快快抬升你们的心灵吧，高一点，再高一点！还有也别忘记了尽情地微笑！

这个开怀大笑之王冠啊，这个玫瑰花环之王冠啊：我的兄弟们啊，我会把这个王冠投给你们！我已经将微笑神圣化了：你们这些高人们啊，我恳请你们学习——学习微笑吧！

74. The Song of Melancholy

1.

WHEN Zarathustra spoke these sayings, he stood nigh to the entrance of his cave; with the last words, however, he slipped away from his guests, and fled for a little while into the open air.

"O pure odours around me," cried he, "O blessed stillness around me! But where are my animals? Here, here, my eagle and my serpent!

Tell me, my animals: these higher men, all of them- do they perhaps not smell well? O pure odours around me! Now only do I know and feel how I love you, my animals."

-And Zarathustra said once more: "I love you, my animals!" The eagle, however, and the serpent pressed close to him when he spoke these words, and looked up to him. In this attitude were they all three silent together, and sniffed and sipped the good air with one another. For the air here outside was better than with the higher men.

2.

Hardly, however, had Zarathustra left the cave when the old magician got up, looked cunningly about him, and said: "He is gone!

74．忧郁之歌

（1）

当查拉图斯特拉说完这些话之后，他站在靠近他的洞穴的入口处；但是，就在查拉图斯特拉说完最后一句话之后，他悄悄地从他的宾客们的身边溜掉了，然后他小跑了一阵儿，进入到了空旷的地带。

“啊，围绕在我周围的纯粹的香气啊，”查拉图斯特拉大叫道，“啊，围绕在我周围的受到祝福的宁静啊！但是，我的动物们都在哪里呢？在这里，我的老鹰以及我的毒蛇在这里呢！

我的动物们，快快告诉我：这些高人们，他们所有人——或许他们身上散发着令人作呕的味道？啊，围绕在我周围的纯粹的香气！现在，我只知道并且感受到我是如何的爱你们，我的动物们。”

——然后，查拉图斯特拉再一次说道：“我爱你们，我的动物们！”然而，当查拉图斯特拉说完这些话的时候，老鹰以及毒蛇开始接近他，并且抬起头来看着他。在这样的情形之下，他们三个全都默不作声，然后，他们开始一个接着一个地嗅着并且啜饮着干净的空气。因为外面的空气要比里面那些高人们周围的空气好得多。

（2）

但是，就当查拉图斯特拉刚刚离开他的洞穴的时候，那个老迈的魔法师就站了起来，

And already, you higher men- let me tickle you with this complimentary and flattering name, as he himself does- already does my evil spirit of deceit and magic attack me, my melancholy devil,

-Which is an adversary to this Zarathustra from the very heart: forgive it for this! Now does it wish to beseech before you, it has just its hour; in vain do I struggle with this evil spirit.

To all of you, whatever honors you like to assume in your names, whether you call yourselves 'the free spirits' or 'the conscientious,' or 'the penitents of the spirit,' or 'the unfettered,' or 'the great longers,'-

-To all of you, who like me suffer from the great loathing, to whom the old God has died, and as yet no new God lies in cradles and swaddling clothes- to all of you is my evil spirit and magic-devil favorable.

I know you, you higher men, I know him,- I know also this fiend whom I love in spite of me, this Zarathustra: he himself often seems to me like the beautiful mask of a saint,

-Like a new strange mummery in which my evil spirit, the melancholy devil, delights:- I love Zarathustra, so does it often seem to me, for the sake of my evil spirit.-

But already does it attack me and constrain me, this spirit of melancholy, this evening-twilight devil: and verily, you higher men, it has a longing-

-Open your eyes!- it has a longing to come naked, whether male or female, I do not yet know: but it comes, it constrains me, alas! open your wits!

The day dies out, to all things comes now the evening, also to the best things; hear now, and

他用非常狡猾的眼神看着查拉图斯特拉，然后说道："他已经走了！

你们这些高人们啊，让我用这种赞美的、阿谀奉承的名号来让你们高兴吧，就如同他做的那样——我的邪恶的欺骗之精神以及魔法在攻击我，我那忧郁的恶魔，

——打心底里来说，这是查拉图斯特拉的一个敌人：请原谅他这么做吧！现在，它要在你的面前苦苦地哀求，它只有一个小时；我却徒劳地同这种邪恶的精神奋力的搏斗。

致以你们所有人，给你们的名号带来荣誉的人们，称呼自己为'自由的精神'，或是'小心谨慎的人'、'精神的忏悔者'或是'无拘无束的人'、'伟大的渴求之人'的人们。

致以你们所有人，那些喜欢看我遭受到伟大的憎恶的折磨，古老的上帝已经死了，然而，还没有新的上帝躺在摇篮里，身上裹着婴儿的衣服——你们所有人就是我的邪恶的精神以及魔法——恶魔的最爱。

我了解你们，你们这些高人们，我了解他，我同样了解这个让我坠入爱河的恶魔，这个查拉图斯特拉：对于我来说，他永远都像一个圣人的漂亮的面具，——就好像是我的邪恶的精神、忧郁的恶魔乐此不疲地观看一种全新的、奇怪的哑剧表演：——由于我那邪恶的精神，所以在我看来，我喜爱查拉图斯特拉。

但是，这种忧郁的精神、这种夜晚之曙光的恶魔在攻击我、束缚着我：说真的，你们这些高人们啊，它自身有着渴求。

——快快睁开你们的双眼！——它有一种要赤身裸体的渴求，无论是男人还是女人，我并不太清楚：但是，它来了，它在束缚着我，哎！快快开动你们的智慧！

白天已经悄然消失，现在，所有的事物都会来到这个夜晚，同样还有最好的事物；

see, you higher men, what devil- man or woman- this spirit of evening-melancholy is!"

Thus spoke the old magician, looked cunningly about him, and then seized his harp.

3.

In evening's limpid air,
What time the dew's soothings
To the earth downpour,
Invisibly and unheard-
For tender shoe-gear wear
The soothing dews, like all that's kind-gentle-:
Bethinkst you then, bethinkst you, burning heart,
How once you thirstedest
For heaven's kindly teardrops and dew's down-droppings,
All singed and weary thirstedest,
What time on yellow grass-pathways
Wicked, occidental sunny glances
Through sombre trees about you sported,
Blindingly sunny glow-glances, gladly-hurting?
"Of truth the wooer? You?"- so taunted they-

现在，你们这些高人们好好听听并且观看吧，看看这个恶魔之男人或女人——夜晚之忧郁的精神到底是什么！”

那位老迈的魔法师如是说道，他用无比狡猾的目光看向查拉图斯特拉，然后，他一把抓住了手中的竖琴。

（3）

在夜晚，清澈透敏的空气当中，
露珠安抚人心的时刻，
直到倾盆大雨降落到地面，
不可见也听不到，
因为它穿着柔软的鞋，
抚慰人心的露珠，就像所有温柔善良的事物一样：
那么，从我看来，熊熊燃烧的心脏，
你究竟有多么渴望来自天堂的充满善意的泪滴以及露珠向下的滴落物，
所有已经烧焦以及厌倦的渴望，
究竟何时邪恶的、来自东方的快乐之凝视，
通过黄色的绿草地穿越了忧郁的树林来到
你这盲目的、快乐的闪亮之光芒以及愉快的伤害？
“你？你就是那个追求真理的人？”——他们如是嘲讽道，

"No! Merely poet!"
A brute insidious, plundering, grovelling,
That ayou must lie,
That wittingly, wilfully, ayou must lie:
For booty lusting,
Motley masked,
Self-hidden, shrouded,
Himself his booty-
He- of truth the wooer?
No! Mere fool! Mere poet!
Just motley speaking,
From mask of fool confusedly shouting,
Circumambling on fabricated word-bridges,
On motley rainbow-arches,
'Twixt the spurious heavenly,
And spurious earthly,
Round us roving, round us soaring,-
Mere fool! Mere poet!
He- of truth the wooer?
Not still, stiff, smooth and cold,

不是的！他只是个诗人！
那个残忍的、丑陋的、掠夺的、卑躬屈膝的你，
肯定说了谎话，
那个刻意的、肆意的你，肯定说了谎话：
对战利品的强烈欲望，
混杂的、掩饰的，
半遮半掩的，遮蔽的，
他自己就是战利品——
他就是追求真理的人吗？
不是！他只是个愚蠢之人，他只是个诗人！
只是笼统地说，
愚蠢之人的面具困惑地叫喊，
在凭空捏造的语言之桥上绕行，
在五颜六色的彩虹之拱桥上绕行，
神圣的虚假，
尘世的虚假，
在我们的周围流转，在我们的周围飞升，
他只是个愚蠢之人！他只是个诗人！
他就是追求真理的人吗？
要想成为一个形象，

Become an image,
A godlike statue,
Set up in front of temples,
As a God's own door-guard:
No! hostile to all such truthfulness-statues,
In every desert homelier than at temples,
With cattish wantonness,
Through every window leaping
Quickly into chances,
Every wild forest a-sniffing,
Greedily-longingly, sniffing,
That you, in wild forests,
'Mong the motley-speckled fierce creatures,
Shouldest rove, sinful-sound and fine-colored,
With longing lips smacking,
Blessedly mocking, blessedly hellish, blessedly blood-thirsty,
Robbing, skulking, lying- roving:-
Or to eagles like which fixedly,
Long adown the precipice look,
Adown their precipice:- -

还不够宁静、不够严肃、不够平滑和冷酷，
一个类似神灵的雕像，
建立在寺庙的前面，
就好像是上帝自己的看守者一样：
不是！它反对所有真诚、率真的雕像，
在任何的沙漠里都要比在寺庙里更有家的感觉，
在狡猾的放纵的引领下，
穿过了所有的窗户，
快速跳进了机遇当中，
你，在野外的森林当中，
在所有的野外的森林当中，嗅探着，
无比贪婪地、充满渴望地，嗅探着，
在多种多样——带有斑点的凶猛的动物当中，
漂泊、带有罪恶感的声音以及出众的色彩，
跟充满渴求的嘴唇一起津津有味的咂嘴，
祝福的嘲弄、祝福的穷凶极恶，以及祝福的嗜血如命，
抢劫着、躲藏着、躺下来——漂泊：
或是像老鹰一样，用坚定的目光
向下看向悬崖峭壁，
朝下看向悬崖峭壁：

Oh, how they whirl down now,
Thereunder, therein,
To ever deeper profoundness whirling!-
Then,
Sudden,
With aim aright,
With quivering flight,
On lambkins pouncing,
Headlong down, sore-hungry,
For lambkins longing,
Fierce 'gainst all lamb-spirits,
Furious-fierce all that look
Sheeplike, or lambeyed, or crisp-woolly,
-Grey, with lambsheep kindliness!
Even thus,
Eaglelike, pantherlike,
Are the poet's desires,
Are your own desires 'neath a thousand guises.
You fool! you poet!
You who all mankind viewed-

啊，它们现在是如何地盘旋，
它们向下降，
甚至于在更加幽深的深奥之盘旋！
紧接着，
突然之间，
在准确的瞄准，
在颤动的飞行中，
在小羊的猛扑中，
头朝下急速地下降，疼痛——饥饿，
因为小羊的渴求
在猛烈地反对所有小羊的精神，
所有狂怒的凶猛看起来
那么像绵羊、小羊或是拥有卷曲羊毛的羊，
——灰色的，绵羊之亲切！
即便是这样，
犹如老鹰一般，犹如美洲豹一般，
都是诗人的渴望，
你们自己的渴望隐藏在一千种伪装之下，
你这个愚蠢之人！你这个诗人！
你被所有人视作是

So God, as sheep-:
The God to rend within mankind,
As the sheep in mankind,
And in rending laughing-
That, that is your own blessedness!
Of a panther and eagle- blessedness!
Of a poet and fool- the blessedness!- -
In evening's limpid air,
What time the moon's sickle,
Green, 'twixt the purple-glowings,
And jealous, steal'th forth:
-Of day the foe,
With every step in secret,
The rosy garland-hammocks
Downsickling, till they've sunken
Down nightwards, faded, downsunken:-
Thus had I sunken one day
From mine own truth-insanity,
From mine own fervid day-longings,
Of day aweary, sick of sunshine,

上帝，就好像绵羊一样
被人类撕成碎片的上帝，
就好像在人类中生存的绵羊一样，
并且在笑声中被撕碎，
这，这就是你自己的幸福！
这就是一头美洲豹和老鹰的幸福！
这就是一个诗人以及一个愚蠢之人的祝福！
在夜晚，清澈的空气当中，
月亮的绿色镰刀究竟在何时
闪耀出紫色的光芒，
并且快乐的，悄然前行；
走向白昼的敌人，
每走一步都小心谨慎，
玫瑰花环的吊床，
向下翻倒，直到它们开始沉没，
开始下降，退去色彩，向下沉没：
因此，终有一日我会开始沉没，
从我自身的真理之疯狂，
从我自身的热忱的渴望中沉没，
在白昼的厌倦，日光的虚弱，

-Sunk downwards, evenwards, shadowwards:
By one sole trueness
All scorched and thirsty:
-Bethinkst you still, bethinkst you, burning heart,
How then you thirstedest?-
That I should banned be
From all the trueness!
Mere fool! Mere poet!

75. Science

THUS sang the magician; and all who were present went like birds unawares into the net of his artful and melancholy voluptuousness. Only the spiritually conscientious one had not been caught: he at once snatched the harp from the magician and called out: "Air! Let in good air! Let in Zarathustra! you make this cave sultry and poisonous, you bad old magician!

You seduce, you false one, you subtle one, to unknown desires and deserts. And alas, that such as you should talk and make ado about the truth!

Alas, to all free spirits who are not on their guard against such magicians! It is all over with their freedom: you teach and tempt back into prisons,-

——向下沉没，永恒的沉没，在阴影中沉没：
在唯一的真相当中，
所有的事物都被烧焦并且口渴难耐：
从我来看，你是宁静的，从我来看你这熊熊燃烧的心脏，
那么，你是如何的渴求？
我应该被禁止接近所有的真实！
只是个愚蠢之人！只是个诗人！

75．科学

那个魔法师如是歌唱道；而在场的所有人全都像毫无意识的小鸟一样飞进了他那狡猾的、忧郁的欲望之鸟巢里。只有在精神上保持着良知、正直的人才没有被他抓住：突然之间，他从那个魔法师的手里抢走了竖琴，并且大声地叫喊道："空气！快放点新鲜的空气进来！快让查拉图斯特拉进来！你让这个洞穴变得闷热，并且充满毒性，你这个恶劣的、老迈的魔法师！"

你这个受到怂恿的虚假之人，你这个敏感之人，来到未知的渴望和沙漠中。哎，你应该说话，并且给真相带来忙乱和纷扰！

哎，对于那些所有没有小心提防邪恶的魔法师的自由自在的精神，它们已经覆盖了他们的自由：你说教，并且在诱惑之下进了监狱，

——你这个老迈的、忧郁的恶魔，从你的悲叹之中传出了诱惑之声：你和那些纯洁

-You old melancholy devil, out of your lament sounds a lurement: you resemble those who with their praise of chastity secretly invite to voluptuousness!

Thus spoke the conscientious one; the old magician, however, looked about him, enjoying his triumph, and on that account put up with the annoyance which the conscientious one caused him. "Be still!" said he with modest voice, "good songs want to re-echo well; after good songs one should be long silent.

Thus do all those present, the higher men. You, however, have perhaps understood but little of my song? In you there is little of the magic spirit.

"You praise me," replied the conscientious one, "in that you separate me from yourself; very well! But, you others, what do I see? You still sit there, all of you, with lusting eyes-:

You free spirits, where has your freedom gone! You almost seem to me to resemble those who have long looked at bad girls dancing naked: your souls themselves dance!

In you, you higher men, there must be more of that which the magician calls his evil spirit of magic and deceit:- we must indeed be different.

And verily, we spoke and thought long enough together before. Zarathustra came home to his cave, for me not to be unaware that we are different.

We seek different things even here aloft, you and I. For I seek more security; on that account have I come to Zarathustra. For he is still the most steadfast tower and will-

-Today, when everything totters, when all the earth quakes. You, however, when I see what

的赞美被邀请到肉欲当中的人们很相像！

那个有良心的人如是说道；然而，那个老迈的魔法师看向他，尽情地享受着他的胜利，并且忍受那个有良心之人给他带来的烦恼。“安静下来！”他用一种谦逊的语气说道，“悠扬的歌声要在空中回荡；在悠扬的歌声回荡过后，就会在很长的一段时间之内，陷入安静之中。”

那些在当前的高人们就是如此做的。但是，你或许能够理解我的歌声，可是你又能理解多少呢？在这里，你就是一个小小的魔法之精神。

“你们赞美我，”那个有良知的人回答道，“你们将我从你们的身上分离出来，非常好！但是，你们其他人，我能够看到什么呢？你们仍旧坐在这里，你们所有人，带有充满欲望的眼睛的人——：

你们这些自由自在的精神，你们的自由全都跑到哪里去了呢！从我的角度来看，你们几乎和那些久久地注视着赤身裸体，大跳艳舞的恶劣女孩没什么两样：你们的灵魂在注视着她们跳舞！

在你们这些高人们的身上，肯定拥有很多被那个魔法师称作是他的邪恶的魔法和欺骗之精神的东西：——毋庸置疑，我们必定是与众不同的。

说真的，我们以前在一起已经谈论过以及思考过很久了。查拉图斯特拉返回他的家，回到了他的洞穴里。对于我来说，我们已经意识到了我们是与众不同的。

我们都在寻找与众不同的事情，即便我们在这样高耸的地方，你和我。因为我要寻找更多的安全感；所以，我来到了这里，来找查拉图斯特拉。因为，他仍旧是最坚定的手巾以及意志。

——今天，当所有的事物全都摇摆不定的时候，当整个大地都在震颤的时候。然而，

eyes you make, it almost seems to me that you seek more insecurity,

-More horror, more danger, more earthquake. You long (it almost seems so to me- forgive my presumption, you higher men)-

-You long for the worst and dangerousest life, which frightens me most,- for the life of wild beasts, for forests, caves, steep mountains and labyrinthine gorges.

And it is not those who lead out of danger that please you best, but those who lead you away from all paths, the misleaders. But if such longing in you be actual, it seems to me nevertheless to be impossible.

For fear- that is man's original and fundamental feeling; through fear everything is explained, original sin and original virtue. Through fear there grew also my virtue, that is to say: Science.

For fear of wild animals- that has been longest fostered in man, inclusive of the animal which he conceals and feares in himself:- Zarathustra calls it 'the beast inside.'

Such prolonged ancient fear, at last become subtle, spiritual and intellectual- at present, me thinks, it is called Science."-

Thus spoke the conscientious one; but Zarathustra, who had just come back into his cave and had heard and divined the last conversation, threw a handful of roses to the conscientious one, and laughed on account of his "truths."

"Why!" he exclaimed, "what did I hear just now? it seems to me, you are a fool, or else I

当我看到你们，看到你们的眼神的时候，从我的角度来看，你们几乎是在寻找更多的安全感。

——更多的恐惧、更多的危险以及更多的地震。你们渴望着。（在我看来，你们像是在原谅我的傲慢，你们这些高人们）

——你渴望能够过上最糟糕、最危险的生活，这样的生活是最让我感到心惊胆战的，——因为这是野外的怪兽们的生活，因为这是森林、洞穴、陡峭的山峰以及犹如迷宫般曲折的山谷的生活。

并且，那些能够引导我们从危险之中逃脱出来的人，并不是最能够让你开心的人，而是那些能够带领你远离所有道路的人，那些错误的引导者们。但是，如果类似这样的、在你心中的渴求是真实的话，对于我来说，这些确实是完全不可能的。

因为恐惧——这是人类最原始的、最基础的感受之一；通过恐惧，任何事物都能够得到合理的解释，最初的罪恶以及最初的价值。通过恐惧，我的道德也同样得到了成长，换句话说就是：科学。

对野外动物的恐惧——这种恐惧是在人类当中孕育时间最长的一种，其中包括隐藏在他的心中以及他的恐惧之中的动物：——查拉图斯特拉称这种情况为‘隐藏在内心的怪兽’。

类似这样的延续了很久的古老的恐惧，最终变成了微妙、精神以及聪慧——而在当前，依照我的观点来看，这就是所谓的科学。”

那个有良心的人如是说道；但是，查拉图斯特拉刚刚回到他的洞穴之中，他听到了，并且好好思考了一下最后的谈话，紧接着，他向那个有良知的人扔了一把玫瑰花瓣，并且对他刚才所说的“真理”哈哈大笑了起来。

myself am one: and quietly and quickly will I Put your 'truth' upside down.

For fear- is an exception with us. Courage, however, and adventure, and delight in the uncertain, in the unattempted- courage seems to me the entire primitive history of man.

The wildest and most courageous animals has he envied and robbed of all their virtues: thus only did he become- man.

This courage, at last become subtle, spiritual and intellectual, this human courage, with eagle's pinions and serpent's wisdom: this, it seems to me, is called at present-"

"Zarathustra!" cried all of them there assembled, as if with one voice, and burst out at the same time into a great laughter; there arose, however, from them as it were a heavy cloud. Even the magician laughed, and said wisely: "Well! It is gone, my evil spirit!

And did I not myself warn you against it when I said that it was a deceiver, a lying and deceiving spirit?

Especially when it shows itself naked. But what can I do with regard to its tricks! Have I created it and the world?

Well! Let us be good again, and of good cheer! And although Zarathustra looks with evil eye- just see him! he dislikes me-:

-Ere night comes will he again learn to love and laud me; he cannot live long without committing such follies.

He- loves his enemies: this art knows he better than any one I have seen. But he takes

“什么！”他大叫道，“我刚才到底听见了什么？看来，要么你是个傻子，要么我是个傻子：我会悄悄地，快速地颠覆你所谓的‘真理’。

因为恐惧——是我们的一种特例。但是，在不确定的、未经尝试当中的勇气、冒险以及快乐——对于我来说，勇气就是人类早期所有的历史。

他嫉妒那些最狂野的、最有胆量的动物们，并且，他抢走了他们所有的道德：因为只有这样他才能成为——人类。

这种勇气，到了最后就会成为微妙、精神以及聪慧，这种人类的勇气，拥有老鹰的翅膀以及毒蛇的智慧：对于我来说，这个就是所谓的当下。”

“查拉图斯特拉！”那些聚集在这里的人全都大声叫喊道，就好像是异口同声地叫喊一样，同时迸发了出来，并且变成了哄堂大笑；然而犹如一朵沉重的云彩一样的东西在他们之中升了起来。甚至就连魔法师都笑了起来，然后他聪明地说道：“好吧！它已经走了，我的邪恶之精神！

当我说那就是一个欺骗者，一个爱说谎话、爱欺骗的精灵的时候，我难道没有警告过你要反抗它吗？

特别是当它将自己以赤身裸体的方式展现出来的时候。但是，对于这样的小把戏，我又能做些什么呢！难道是我创造了它以及这个世界吗？

那么好吧！让我们再一次变得善良。再一次变得快乐吧！尽管查拉图斯特拉用充满邪恶的双眼看向他！但是他并不喜欢我：

在夜晚到来之前，他会再一次学习如何去爱以及称赞我；如果不能做出这样愚蠢的事情的话，那么，他就不会活得长久。

revenge for it- on his friends!"

Thus spoke the old magician, and the higher men applauded him; so that Zarathustra went round, and mischievously and lovingly shook hands with his friends,- like one who has to make amends and apologise to every one for something. When however he had thereby come to the door of his cave, lo, then had he again a longing for the good air outside, and for his animals,- and wished to steal out.

76. Among Daughters of the Desert

1.

"GO NOT away!" said then the wanderer who called himself Zarathustra's shadow, "abide with us- otherwise the old gloomy affliction might again fall upon us.

Now has that old magician given us of his worst for our good, and lo! the good, pious pope there has tears in his eyes, and has quite embarked again upon the sea of melancholy.

Those kings may well put on a good air before us still: for that have they learned best of us all at present! Had they however no one to see them, I wager that with them also the bad game would again commence,-

-The bad game of drifting clouds, of damp melancholy, of curtained heavens, of stolen suns, of howling autumn-winds,

他——热爱他的敌人们：他是我所见过的最了解这种艺术的人。但是，他却对他们做出了报复的行为——对他的朋友们！”

那个老迈的魔法师如是说道，然后，那些高人们开始拍手称赞他；因此，查拉图斯特拉开始绕起圈子，用略带恶作剧和仁慈的姿态跟他的朋友们一一握手——就好像一个要做出弥补，并且向所有人致以歉意的人一样。但是，当查拉图斯特拉来到他的洞穴的门前的时候，快看啊，他对外面良好空气以及他的动物们的渴望再一次要悄悄地溜出来。

76. 在荒漠女儿们中间

（1）

“不要离开！”那个自称是查拉图斯特拉的影子的游荡者开始说道，“和我们待在一起吧——要不然的话，古老的、忧郁的苦难有可能会再一次降临在我们的身上。

现在，那个魔法师为了我们的善意，将自己的最糟糕的东西给予了我们，快看啊！这里的善良的、虔诚的教皇的眼角泛起了泪水，并且再一次踏上了忧郁之海。

那些国王们会在我们面前呈现出良好的空气：因为现在他们已经很好地了解了我们！但是，还没有任何人见到过他们，我敢打赌，有了他们，邪恶的游戏会再一次开始，

——漂浮的云朵、潮湿的忧郁、装有窗帘的天堂、被偷走的太阳以及咆哮的秋天之风的邪恶游戏，

——我们寻求帮助的咆哮以及叫喊！和我们住在一起吧，啊，查拉图斯特拉啊！

-The bad game of our howling and crying for help! Abide with us, O Zarathustra! Here there is much concealed misery that wishes to speak, much evening, much cloud, much damp air!

You have nourished us with strong food for men, and powerful aphorisms: do not let the weakly, womanly spirits attack us anew at dessert!

You alone make the air around you strong and clear. Did I ever find anywhere on earth such good air as with you in your cave?

Many lands have I seen, my nose has learned to test and estimate many kinds of air: but with you do my nostrils taste their greatest delight!

Unless it be,- unless it be-, do forgive an old recollection! Forgive me an old after-dinner song, which I once composed amongst daughters of the desert:-

For with them was there equally good, clear, Oriental air; there was I furthest from cloudy, damp, melancholy Old-Europe!

Then did I love such Oriental maidens and other blue kingdoms of heaven, over which hang no clouds and no thoughts.

You would not believe how charmingly they sat there, when they did not dance, profound, but without thoughts, like little secrets, like beribboned riddles, like dessert-nuts-

Many-hued and foreign, forsooth! but without clouds: riddles which can be guessed: to please such maidens I then composed an after-dinner psalm."

Thus spoke the wanderer who called himself Zarathustra's shadow; and before any one answered him, he had seized the harp of the old magician, crossed his legs, and looked calmly

这里有许多隐藏起来的悲痛，它们要说话，还有很多夜晚、很多云朵以及很多潮湿的空气！

你用给人类供养的食物以及振奋人心的人生格言来滋养我们：不要让虚弱的、阴柔的精神再一次在沙漠里攻击我们了！

你让你周围的空气变得强大且干净。难道我在这片大地的其他任何地方还见过比在洞穴里围绕在你周围还要优质的空气吗？

我曾经看到过很多的陆地，我的鼻子曾经检测并且评估过很多不同种类的空气：但是，在你的身上，我的鼻孔能够嗅出他们最伟大的快乐！

除非是，除非是——请原谅一个古老的回忆！请原谅我这一首古老的、晚宴之后的歌曲，这首我曾经在荒漠女儿们中间创作的歌曲：

因为和她们在一起，就等同于这里拥有了美好的、纯净的来自东方的空气，而我从遥远的、多云的、潮湿的、忧郁的古老欧洲而来！

之后，我爱上了来自东方的少女们以及其他来自天堂的蓝色王国的少女们，在那里天上没有云彩和思想。

你或许不会相信，她们坐在这里是多么的有魅力，当她们不跳舞的时候，她们有深度，但却没有思想，就像小秘密一样，像缎带般复杂的谜题一样，像是甜品坚果一样。

她们实在是色彩丰富，并且异常奇特！但是这里没有云朵：能够被猜出来的谜题：为了能够取悦这样美丽动人的少女们，我才创作了一首晚宴过后的圣歌。”

那个自称是查拉图斯特拉的影子的游荡者如是说道；并且在任何人回应他之前，

and sagely around him:- with his nostrils, however, he inhaled the air slowly and questioningly, like one who in new countries tastes new foreign air. Afterward he began to sing with a kind of roaring.

2.

The deserts grow: woe him who does them hide!
-Ha!
Solemnly!
In effect solemnly!
A worthy beginning!
Afric manner, solemnly!
Of a lion worthy,
Or perhaps of a virtuous howl-monkey-
-But it's naught to you,
You friendly damsels dearly loved,
At whose own feet to me,
The first occasion,
To a European under palm-trees,
At seat is now granted. Selah.

他一把抓住了老迈的魔法师的竖琴，然后将自己的腿交叉，用平静并且贤明的目光注视着他：——但是，他用他的鼻子缓慢地、充满质疑地吸了口空气，就像一个置身于全新的国家，品位新鲜的、与众不同的空气的人一样。之后，他开始用一种近似咆哮的声音唱歌。

（2）

沙漠在成长：悲哀啊！将他们隐藏起来的人！
哈！
庄重！
颇具效果的庄重！
一个具有价值的开端！
一只狮子的非洲习惯与风俗，庄重地！
或是一只善良的、咆哮的猴子
——但是，它对于你来说太淘气了，
你这友好的、可爱并且受人喜爱的少女，
站在自己的双脚之上面向我，
第一次，
一个欧洲人在棕榈树下，
现在，他被准许坐下来。瑟拉。

Wonderful, truly!
Here do I sit now,
The desert nigh, and yet I am
So far still from the desert,
Even in naught yet deserted:
That is, I'm swallowed down
By this the small oasis-:
-It opened up just yawning,
Its loveliest mouth agape,
Most sweet-odoured of all mouthlets:
Then fell I right in,
Right down, right through- in 'mong you,
You friendly damsels dearly loved! Selah.
Hail! hail! to that whale, fishlike,
If it thus for its guest's convenience
Made things nice!- (you well know,
Surely, my learned allusion?)
Hail to its belly,
If it had e'er
A such loveliest oasis-belly
As this is: though however I doubt about it,

真是太美妙了，真是太真实了！
现在，我就坐在这里，
沙漠就在附近，然而，我仍旧
在距离沙漠很遥远的地方，
甚至在无价值的虚无中也是荒芜的：
也就是说，我在被吞噬掉，
被这片小的绿洲吞噬掉：
它在打哈欠的时候，张开了嘴，
它那张美丽至极的嘴巴张开了，
许许多多的甜美的香气从它的嘴里飘了出来：
紧接着，我掉了进去，
硬生生地掉了下去，硬生生地穿过你们掉了下去，
你这友好的、可爱并且受人喜爱的少女，瑟拉。
万岁！万岁！致以那条犹如鱼一般的鲸鱼，
倘若它能够给宾客们带来方便的话，
那就把事情做好！（我很确定，你很清楚，
我的博学的暗示？）
让我们向它的肚脐致敬，
如果它拥有犹如

-With this come I out of Old-Europe,
That doubt'th more eagerly than do any
Elderly married woman.
May the Lord improve it!
Amen!
Here do I sit now,
In this the small oasis,
Like a date indeed,
Brown, quite sweet, gold-suppurating,
For rounded mouth of maiden longing,
But yet still more for youthful, maidlike,
Ice-cold and snow-white and incisory
Front teeth: and for such assuredly,
Pine the hearts all of ardent date-fruits. Selah.
To the there-named south-fruits now,
Similar, all-too-similar,
Do I lie here; by little
Flying insects
Round-sniffled and round-played,
And also by yet littler,
Foolisher, and peccabler

这样美丽至极的绿洲之肚脐的话：
尽管，我对此感到很是质疑，
——由于它的缘故，我离开了古老的欧洲，
那样的怀疑要比所有热切的已婚妇女还要热切。
愿真主能够改善它吧！
阿门！
现在，我坐在这里，
坐在这个小的绿洲里，
看起来就像一个约会，
少女圆圆的渴望之嘴唇，
变成了褐色的、甜甜的并且金灿灿的模样，
但是，它仍旧更像是年轻的、跟少女很相像的、
冰冷的、雪白的大门牙：可以确定的是，
为所有热切的约会水果之心灵感到悲哀，瑟拉。
现在在这里，它们被称为西部的水果，
很相似，实在是太相似了，
我躺在这里；那些
小型的、飞行的昆虫
围绕着我抽噎，围绕着我玩耍，

Wishes and phantasies,-
Environed by you,
You silent, presentientest
Maiden-kittens,
Dudu and Suleika,
-Round sphinxed, that into one word
I may crowd much feeling:
(Forgive me, O God,
All such speech-sinning!)
-Sit I here the best of air sniffling,
Paradisal air, truly,
Bright and buoyant air, golden-mottled,
As goodly air as ever
From lunar orb downfell-
Be it by hazard,
Or supervened it by arrogancy?
As the ancient poets relate it.
But doubter, I'm now calling it
In question: with this do I come indeed
Out of Europe,
That doubt'th more eagerly than do any

同样围绕在你身边的还有
更加渺小的、更加愚蠢的、
更加容易犯错误的愿望和幻想，
你这安静的、有预感的，
少女之小猫，
杜杜以及苏莱卡，
——围绕着斯芬克斯，变成了一句话
我的内心挤满了情感：
（请原谅我，啊，上帝啊，
请原谅所有说教的罪恶吧！）
——我坐在这里，呼吸着最清新的空气，
说真的，这是天堂般的空气，
明亮的、轻快的空气，带有金色斑点的，
同从月球上因危险，或是意外发生或是傲慢的缘故而
掉落下来的空气一样清新，
这和古老的诗人们有所关联，
但是，我现在要用质疑的态度
称呼他们为怀疑者：毋庸置疑，我因为这个原因
离开了欧洲，那样的怀疑要比所有热切的已婚妇女还要热切。

Elderly married woman.
May the Lord improve it!
Amen.
This the finest air drinking,
With nostrils out-swelled like goblets,
Lacking future, lacking remembrances,
Thus do I sit here, ye
Friendly damsels dearly loved,
And look at the palm-tree there,
How it, to a dance-girl, like,
Do bow and bend and on its haunches bob,
-One does it too, when one view'th it long!-
To a dance-girl like, who as it seem'th to me,
Too long, and dangerously persistent,
Always, always, just on single leg has stood?
-Then forgot she thereby, as it seem'th to me,
The other leg?
For vainly I, at least,
Did search for the amissing
Fellow-jewel
-Namely, the other leg-

愿真主能够改善它吧！
阿门！
清新的空气同鼻子
一起畅饮，向外膨胀的样子犹如高脚杯一样；
缺少未来，缺少回忆，
因此，我坐在这里，
友好的、可爱并且受人喜爱的少女，
我看向了这里的棕榈树，
它是如何的酷似跳舞的小女孩，
在短发之上鞠躬并且弯腰，
——当你长久注视之后，你也可以做到，
在我看来，就像一个跳舞的小女孩，
太过漫长，在危险中顽强地存在，
总是，总是，只用一条腿站立？
——因此，对于我来说，难道
她忘记了她还有另外一条腿吗？
至少，我寻找了
遗失的珠宝，
换句话说，就是她的另一条腿，

In the sanctified precincts,
Nigh her very dearest, very tenderest,
Flapping and fluttering and flickering skirting.
Yes, if you should, you beauteous friendly ones,
Quite take my word:
She hath, alas! lost it!
Hu! Hu! Hu! Hu! Hu!
It is away!
For ever away!
The other leg!
Oh, pity for that loveliest other leg!
Where may it now tarry, all-forsaken weeping?
The most lonesome leg?
In fear perhaps before a
Furious, yellow, blond and curled
Leonine monster? Or perhaps even
Gnawed away, nibbled badly-
Most wretched, woeful! woeful! nibbled badly! Selah.
Oh, weep you not,
Gentle spirits!

虽然我并没有成功，
在被神圣化的范围之内，
可爱的、脆弱的拍打、
振翅以及闪烁的裙料在悄然接近她。
是的，如果你能够的话，你这美丽、友好的少女，
请听我的话：
她，哎！已经消失了！
呼！呼！呼！呼！呼！
它已经消失了！
永远的消失了！
她的另一只腿！
啊，真是对另外那一条美丽至极的腿感到可惜！
它究竟会在哪里逗留呢？所有被遗弃的哭泣？
最孤独寂寞的腿？
或许它会心惊胆战地站在
一个怒火中烧的、金黄色、卷毛的、
犹如狮子一般的怪兽的面前？又或是它被
咬碎、被猛烈的袭击撕碎了，
真是可怜至极啊，悲哀啊！悲哀啊！它被猛烈的袭击撕碎了！瑟拉。
啊，你不要哭泣啊，

Weep you not, ye
Date-fruit spirits! Milk-bosoms!
You sweetwood-heart
Purselets!
Weep you no more,
Pallid Dudu!
Be a man, Suleika! Bold! Bold!
-Or else should there perhaps
Something strengthening, heart-strengthening,
Here most proper be?
Some inspiring text?
Some solemn exhortation?-
Ha! Up now! honor!
Moral honor! European honor!
Blow again, continue,
Bellows-box of virtue!
Ha!
Once more your roaring,
Your moral roaring!
As a virtuous lion

优雅的小精灵们！
我恳求你们不要哭泣啊，
约会之水果的小精灵们啊！拥有奶汁的乳房啊！
你们这些甜美之心灵啊！
我恳求你们不要再哭泣了，
毫无生气的杜杜！
成为一个男人，苏莱卡！大胆一点！大胆一点！
——又或是这里拥有强健的
最适合强化心灵的事物？
一些能够振奋人心的话语？
一些庄严肃穆的讲道词？
哈！快站起来吧！荣誉！
道德的荣誉！欧洲人的荣誉！
再一次吹拂吧！继续，
道德的盒子之风箱！
哈！
你再一次咆哮了起来，
你的道德的咆哮！
就如同一只有道德的狮子一样，
咆哮着接近了沙漠的女儿们！

Nigh the daughters of deserts roaring!
-For virtue's out-howl,
You very dearest maidens,
Is more than every
European fervor, European hot-hunger!
And now do I stand here,
As European,
I can't be different, God's help to me!
Amen!
The deserts grow: woe him who do them hide!

77. The Awakening

1.

AFTER the song of the wanderer and shadow, the cave became all at once full of noise and laughter: and since the assembled guests all spoke simultaneously, and even the ass, encouraged thereby, no longer remained silent, a little aversion and scorn for his visitors came over Zarathustra, although he rejoiced at their gladness. For it seemed to him a sign of convalescence. So he slipped out into the open air and spoke to his animals.

——道德的怒吼！
你们这些少女们，
要比任何一个热情洋溢的欧洲人、任何一个炽热之饥饿的欧洲人
更加惹人怜爱！
现在，我站在这里，
就像欧洲人一样，
我无法做到与众不同，上帝啊！请你帮助我吧！
阿门！
这个沙漠在成长：悲哀啊！将他们隐藏起来的人！

77．唤醒

（1）

在游荡者以及查拉图斯特拉的影子的歌声逐渐消失之后，查拉图斯特拉的洞穴突然变得噪音以及笑声不断：正当聚集在这里的贵宾们全都异口同声地说道之后，甚至于那头笨驴也受到了鼓舞，它也不再保持沉默无声了，这时，一股对他的宾客们的憎恶感和嘲弄涌上了查拉图斯特拉的心头，尽管，他为他们的快乐感到高兴。因为这些对于他来说，就是一种逐渐开始康复的征兆。于是，他悄悄地溜进了开放的空气中来，然后，他对他的动物们如是说道。

"Where has their distress now gone?" said he, and already did he himself feel relieved of his petty disgust- "with me, it seems that they have unlearned their cries of distress!

-Though, alas! not yet their crying." And Zarathustra stopped his ears, for just then did the you-A of the ass mix strangely with the noisy jubilation of those higher men.

"They are merry," he began again, "and who knows? perhaps at their host's expense; and if they have learned of me to laugh, still it is not my laughter they have learned.

But what matter about that! They are old people: they recover in their own way, they laugh in their own way; my ears have already endured worse and have not become peevish.

This day is a victory: he already yields, he flees, the spirit of gravity, my old arch-enemy! How well this day is about to end, which began so badly and gloomily!

And it is about to end. Already comes the evening: over the sea rides it here, the good rider! How it bobs, the blessed one, the home-returning one, in its purple saddles!

The sky gazes brightly there, the world lies deep. Oh, all you strange ones who have come to me, it is already worth while to have lived with me!"

Thus spoke Zarathustra. And again came the cries and laughter of the higher men out of the cave: then began he anew:

"They bite at it, my bait takes, there departs also from them their enemy, the spirit of gravity. Now do they learn to laugh at themselves: do I hear rightly?

My virile food takes effect, my strong and savory sayings: and verily, I did not nourish them with flatulent vegetables! But with warrior-food, with conqueror-food: new desires did I

“现在，他们的悲痛都跑到哪里去了？”他说道，而且他已经有了摆脱琐碎的厌恶的感受——“看起来，他们已经淡忘了他们的悲痛之叫喊！

哎！尽管他们还没有叫喊。”因为一头驴不可思议的和那些高人们的吵闹的欢呼混合在了一起的缘故，查拉图斯特拉闭上了他的耳朵。

“他们非常快乐，”他再一次开始说道，“谁知道呢？或许，这是以他们的宾客们的代价换来的；倘若他们从我这里学会了该如何微笑，但是他们所习得的仍旧不是我的微笑。

不过，是与不是对于我来说又有什么关系呢！他们都是古老的人们：他们会用自己的方式恢复自己，他们会用自己的方式微笑；我的耳朵已经忍受过了比这还要糟糕的境遇，就算是这样，我也并没有为此而变得脾气暴躁。

今天就是一个胜利：他已经屈服了、他已经逃跑了，重力之精灵，我的古老的拱形之敌人！今天即将结束，它将会恶劣地、忧郁地开始！

现在，就快要到结束的时候了。尽管，夜晚来临了：骑着马跨越海洋来到这里，伟大的骑手！那有着一缕短发的、受到祝福的人，回归家乡的人，是如何在紫色的马鞍里尽情地驰骋的啊！

天空用无比明亮的眼神凝视着这里，整个世界都深深地躺在这里。啊，你们所有来到我这里的稀奇古怪的家伙们，能够和我同住在一个屋檐下，已经是非常值得的了！”

查拉图斯特拉如是说道。紧接着，来自高人们的叫喊以及笑声再一次从查拉图斯特拉的洞穴中传了出来：然后，他重新说道：

“他们在啃咬它，我的诱饵捕获到的东西，那些重力之精灵也从他们的敌人那里分离开来。现在，他们在学习如何对他们自己微笑：我所听到的是正确的吗？

awaken.

New hopes are in their arms and legs, their hearts expand. They find new words, soon will their spirits breathe wantonness.

Such food may sure enough not be proper for children, nor even for longing girls old and young. One persuades their bowels otherwise; I am not their physician and teacher.

The disgust departs from these higher men; well! that is my victory. In my domain they become assured; all stupid shame flees away; they empty themselves.

They empty their hearts, good times return to them, they keep holiday and ruminate,- they become thankful.

That do I take as the best sign: they become thankful. Not long will it be before they create festivals, and put up memorials to their old joys.

They are convalescents!" Thus spoke Zarathustra joyfully to his heart and gazed outward; his animals, however, pressed up to him, and honored his happiness and his silence.

2.

All on a sudden however, Zarathustra's ear was frightened: for the cave which had hitherto been full of noise and laughter, became all at once still as death;- his nose, however, smelt a sweet-scented vapor and incense-odour, as if from burning pine-cones.

我的颇有男子气概的事物产生了作用，我的强有力的、美味的语录：说真的，我并没有用浮夸的蔬菜来滋养他们！而是用勇士的食物、用征服者们的食物：被我唤醒的全新的欲望。

全新的希望就在他们的胳膊、他们的双腿以及他们的心灵中扩展。他们找到了新的词语，很快，他们的精灵就会呼吸到嬉戏玩耍的味道。

毋庸置疑，类似这样的事物并不适合于小孩子们，同样也不适合老迈的、年轻的充满渴望的女孩们。否则就会有人说服她们的内心；我并不是他们的内科医生，我并不是她们的老师。

憎恶离开了这些高人们；好吧！这就是我的胜利。在我的领域之内，他们开始变得自信；所有愚蠢的羞愧全都跑掉了；他们将自己掏空了。

他们将他们的心灵掏空了，美好的时光回到了他们的身边，他们保持假日的传统，并且反复的思考——他们变得懂得感恩和感谢。

因此，我把这看作是一个最好的象征：他们变得懂得感恩和感谢。在他们创造欢庆节日并且为他们过去的快乐建造纪念碑之前，并不需要等待太过漫长的时间。

他们全都是大病初愈的人们！”查拉图斯特拉开心的对他的心灵如是说道，然后他开始凝视着外面；然而，他的动物们正在向他靠近，并且尊敬他的快乐以及他的安静。

（2）

但是，突然之间，查拉图斯特拉的耳朵开始因为害怕而颤抖了起来：因为洞穴充满了噪音和笑声，突然之间，它变得犹如死亡一般宁静：然而，他的鼻子嗅到了一股甜蜜

"What happens? What are they about?" he asked himself, and stole up to the entrance, that he might be able unobserved to see his guests. But wonder upon wonder! what was he then obliged to behold with his own eyes!

"They have all of them become pious again, they pray, they are mad!"- said he, and was astonished beyond measure. And forsooth! all these higher men, the two kings, the pope out of service, the evil magician, the voluntary beggar, the wanderer and shadow, the old soothsayer, the spiritually conscientious one, and the ugliest man- they all lay on their knees like children and credulous old women, and worshipped the ass. And just then began the ugliest man to gurgle and snort, as if something unutterable in him tried to find expression; when, however, he had actually found words, behold! it was a pious, strange litany in praise of the adored and censed ass. And the litany sounded thus:

Amen! And glory and honor and wisdom and thanks and praise and strength be to our God, from everlasting to everlasting!

-The ass, however, here brayed you-A.

He carried our burdens, he has taken upon him the form of a servant, he is patient of heart and never says No; and he who loves his God chastises him.

-The ass, however, here brayed you-A.

He speaks not: except that he ever says Yes to the world which he created: thus does he extol his world. It is his artfulness that speaks not: thus is he rarely found wrong.

味道的气体以及熏香的香味，就像是焚烧松果产生的味道一样。

“究竟发生了什么事？他们怎么了？”他问道，然后他悄悄地来到了洞穴的入口，他这样做可以在不被人察觉的情况下注视着他的宾客们。但是，奇迹之上的奇迹！那么他不得不用自己的双眼去观察什么呢！

“他们所有人再一次变得虔诚，他们祈祷，他们全都疯了！”——他说道，而且他所受到的惊讶已经无法进行估量。千真万确啊！所有这些高人们啊、两个国王、不再履行职务的教皇、邪恶的魔法师、自愿的乞丐、游荡者以及查拉图斯特拉的影子、老迈的预言家、精神上拥有良知的人以及最丑陋的人——他们全都坐在他们的膝盖之上，就好像小孩子们、容易受骗的老妇女以及崇拜的驴一样。就在那个时候，最丑陋的人开始咯咯地笑了起来，并且用鼻子发出了哼哼声，就好像是一些隐藏在他体内的无法说出口的东西试图找到表达的方式；但是，当他真的找到了能够表达出来的方式的时候，快看啊！那是一种虔诚的、奇怪的，赞美崇拜的、散发着熏香味的蠢驴的冗长而枯燥的陈述。冗长而枯燥的陈述如是说道：

阿门！愿我们的上帝充满光辉、荣耀、智慧、感恩、赞美以及力量，从亘古到永远！

——然而，蠢驴在这里冲你叫喊了起来。

他肩负了我们的负担，他将一个仆人的外貌和体型特征安放在了自己的身上，他非常有耐心，永远都不会说不；他喜欢他的上帝惩罚并且责骂他。

——然而，蠢驴在这里冲你叫喊了起来。

他什么话也不说：除了他会对他所创造的世界说出肯定的话语：因此，他赞颂他创造的世界。他选择什么也不说是他机智狡猾的结果：他发现这样做并没有什么错误。

——然而，蠢驴在这里冲你叫喊了起来。

-The ass, however, here brayed you-A.

Uncomely goes he through the world. Grey is the favorite color in which he wraps his virtue. Has he spirit, then does he conceal it; every one, however, believes in his long ears.

-The ass, however, here brayed you-A.

What hidden wisdom it is to wear long ears, and only to say Yes and never No! has he not created the world in his own image, namely, as stupid as possible?

-The ass, however, here brayed you-A.

You go straight and crooked ways; it concerns you little what seems straight or crooked to us men. Beyond good and evil is your domain. It is your innocence not to know what innocence is.

-The ass, however, here brayed you-A.

Lo! how you spurn none from you, neither beggars nor kings. You suffer little children to come to you, and when the bad boys decoy you, then say you simply, you-A.

-The ass, however, here brayed you-A.

You love she-asses and fresh figs, you are no food-despiser. A thistle tickles your heart when you chance to be hungry. There is the wisdom of a God therein.

-The ass, however, here brayed you-A.

他用非常不标致的姿态穿过了他的世界。他最喜欢用灰色的色彩来包裹他的道德。他将自己的精灵藏了起来，但是，所有人都相信了他那长长的耳朵。

——然而，蠢驴在这里冲你叫喊了起来。

究竟有什么隐藏的智慧需要戴上长长的耳朵，而且只能说是，而永远也不能说不！难道他没有用他自己的想象力创造这个世界，也就是说，尽可能的愚笨吗？

——然而，蠢驴在这里冲你叫喊了起来。

你选择了笔直和弯曲的道路；你很少会顾及什么对于我们来说是笔直和弯曲的。超越善与恶就是你的领地。你的天真就是不会去了解什么才是天真无邪。

——然而，蠢驴在这里冲你叫喊了起来。

快看啊！你并没有从你的身上摒弃任何东西，还有乞丐和国王。小孩子们来找你，当坏孩子们欺骗你的时候，你就会大声地叫喊。

——然而，蠢驴在这里冲你叫喊了起来。

你热爱她——驴以及新鲜的无花果，你不是一个蔑视事物的人。当你恰巧感到饥饿的时候，一个荆棘就会抓挠你的心脏。这就是一个上帝的智慧。

——然而，蠢驴在这里冲你叫喊了起来。

78. The Ass Festival

1.

AT THIS place in the litany, however, Zarathustra could no longer control himself; he himself cried out you-A, louder even than the ass, and sprang into the midst of his maddened guests. "Whatever are you about, you grown-up children?" he exclaimed, pulling up the praying ones from the ground. "Alas, if any one else, except Zarathustra, had seen you:

Every one would think you the worst blasphemers, or the very most foolish old women, with your new belief!

And you yourself, you old pope, how is it in accordance with you, to adore an ass in such a manner as God?"-

"O Zarathustra," answered the pope, "forgive me, but in divine matters I am more enlightened even than you. And it is right that it should be so.

Better to adore God so, in this form, than in no form at all! Think over this saying, my exalted friend: you will readily divine that in such a saying there is wisdom.

He who said 'God is a Spirit'- made the greatest stride and slide hitherto made on earth towards unbelief: such a dictum is not easily amended again on earth!

My old heart leaps and bounds because there is still something to adore on earth. Forgive it,

78. 驴子的节日

（1）

但是，在这个地方，在这个冗长而枯燥的陈述中，查拉图斯特拉不能再控制自己了；他对自己大声地叫喊了起来，他的叫喊声要比驴的还响亮，紧接着，他跳进了他的疯狂的宾客们的中间。“你们这些已经成人的孩子们，你们究竟是怎么了？”他大声地呼喊道，然后，他把在地面上做祷告的人拉了起来。“哎，除了查拉图斯特拉，这里还有其他人看到过你：

所有人都会认为你是最糟糕的亵渎者，又或是认为你是拥有新的信仰的、最为愚蠢的老女人！

你自己，你这个老迈的教皇，你是如何跟自己保持一致，用上帝的方式来崇拜一头驴的呢？”

“啊，查拉图斯特拉，”教皇回答道，“请原谅我吧，但是在神圣的事情方面，我要比你更加开明和进步。而且事情本该如此。

用这样的形式来崇拜上帝，要比不用形式的方式好得多！好好地思考一下我所说的话，我的崇高的朋友：你会很轻易就能猜到，在这样的话语中拥有智慧。

那个说‘上帝就是一个精灵’的人——迈着最大的步子，并且开始滑动，在这片大地上朝无信仰的地方走去：类似这样的格言很难在这片大地之上得到修正！

我的老迈的心脏开始来回地跳动，因为在这片大地之上仍旧有很多需要去崇拜的事

O Zarathustra, to an old, pious pontiff-heart!-"

-"And you," said Zarathustra to the wanderer and shadow, "you call and think yourself a free spirit? And you here practice such idolatry and hierolatry?

Worse verily, do you here than with your bad brown girls, you bad, new believer!"

"It is sad enough," answered the wanderer and shadow, "you are right: but how can I help it! The old God lives again, O Zarathustra, you mayst say what you wilt.

The ugliest man is to blame for it all: he has reawakened him. And if he say that he once killed him, with Gods death is always just a prejudice."

-"And you," said Zarathustra, "you bad old magician, what did you do! Who ought to believe any longer in you in this free age, when you believe in such divine donkeyism?

It was a stupid thing that you didst; how could you, a shrewd man, do such a stupid thing!"

"O Zarathustra," answered the shrewd magician, "you are right, it was a stupid thing,- it was also repugnant to me."

-"And you even," said Zarathustra to the spiritually conscientious one, "consider, and put your finger to your nose! does nothing go against your conscience here? Is your spirit not too cleanly for this praying and the fumes of those devotees?"

"There is something therein," said the spiritually conscientious one, and put his finger to his nose, "there is something in this spectacle which even does good to my conscience.

Perhaps I dare not believe in God: certain it is however, that God seems to me most worthy

物。请谅解吧，啊，查拉图斯特拉，请谅解一颗老迈的、虔诚的教皇之心脏吧！”

——“还有你，”查拉图斯特拉对那个游荡者以及自称是查拉图斯特拉的影子的家伙说道，“你称呼自己并且认为自己是自由自在的精灵吗？而且你要在这里锻炼盲目崇拜以及圣物崇拜吗？

说真的，你在这里要比你那邪恶的棕色女孩还要糟糕透顶，你这邪恶的、新的信徒！”

“这可真是太悲哀啊，”那个游荡者以及自称是查拉图斯特拉的影子的家伙回答道，“你是正确的：但是，我又能怎么办呢！那个古老的上帝再一次活了过来，啊，查拉图斯特拉，你可以说你所想。

那个最丑陋的人应该为此而受到责备：正是他唤醒了他。而且倘若他说他曾经杀死了他，对于神灵来说，死亡永远都只是一种偏见。”

——“还有你，”查拉图斯特拉说道，“你这个邪恶的、老迈的魔法师，你都做了些什么！在这样一个自由自在的时代，有谁还应该再相信你呢？你什么时候开始相信这种神圣的蠢驴专制了？

你所做的事情是非常愚蠢的；像你这么精明的人，怎么会做出如此愚蠢的事情来呢！”

“啊，查拉图斯特拉啊，”那个精明的魔法师回答道，“你是正确的，那确实非常愚蠢，——同样地，它还让我感到非常反感。”

——“甚至于还有你，”查拉图斯特拉对那个在精神上有良知的人说道，“好好想一想，然后把你的手指放在你的鼻子上！难道这里没有任何事物反抗你的良知吗？难道你的精灵对于这样的祈祷以及那些信徒们的烟气来说，不是太多于干净了吗？”

of belief in this form.

God is said to be eternal, according to the testimony of the most pious: he who has so much time takes his time. As slow and as stupid as possible: thereby can such a one nevertheless go very far.

And he who has too much spirit might well become infatuated with stupidity and folly. Think of yourself, O Zarathustra!

You yourself- verily! even you could well become an ass through superabundance of wisdom.

Do not the true sage willingly walk on the crookedest paths? The evidence teaches it, O Zarathustra,- your own evidence!"

-"And you yourself, finally," said Zarathustra, and turned towards the ugliest man, who still lay on the ground stretching up his arm to the ass (for he gave it wine to drink). "Say, you nondescript, what have you been about!

You seem to me transformed, your eyes glow, the mantle of the sublime covers your ugliness: what did you do?

Is it then true what they say, that you have again awakened him? And why? Was he not for good reasons killed and made away with?

You yourself seem to me awakened: what did you do? why did you turn round? Why did you get converted? Speak, you nondescript!"

“这里有一些东西，”那个在精神上有良知的人说道，然后他把他的手指放在了鼻子上，“在这样的景象中，有一些东西对我的良知是有益处的。

或许我不敢相信上帝：但是，我很确定，在这样的形式当中，上帝对于我来说是最值得相信的。

依照最虔诚之人的证词，上帝被称作是永恒的：他拥有无限多的时间。尽可能的缓慢并且愚蠢：因此，即便是这样，它仍旧可以走得非常远。

而拥有太多精灵的人或许变得迷恋愚蠢和愚笨。你自己好好想一想吧，啊，查拉图斯特拉！

你自己——说真的！即便是你也可以通过丰富的智慧而成为一头蠢驴。

难道真正的圣人不会心甘情愿地行走在最崎岖的道路之上吗？啊，查拉图斯特拉，证据如是说教到，——你自己的证据！”

——“最后，还有你，”查拉图斯特拉转向那个最丑陋的人说道，他仍旧躺在地面上，朝着那头蠢驴伸展着他的胳膊（因为他给它酒水喝）。“说吧，你这个难以形容的人，你都做了些什么！

从我的角度来看，你好像改变了，你的眼睛散发着光芒，庄严的斗篷掩盖了你的丑陋：你到底都做了些什么？

那么，他们所说的关于你再一次把他唤醒了的话是真实的吗？如果是的话，为什么？难道他不是因为合理的理由而被杀，并且匆匆离开的吗？

从我的角度来看，你自己已经被唤醒了：你究竟都做了些什么？为什么你要转过身来？为什么你要改变信仰？说吧，你这个难以形容的人！”

“啊，查拉图斯特拉啊，”那个最丑陋的人回答道，“你就是个流氓！

"O Zarathustra," answered the ugliest man, "you are a rogue!

Whether he yet lives, or again lives, or is thoroughly dead- which of us both knows that best? I ask you.

One thing however do I know,- from yourself did I learn it once, O Zarathustra: he who wants to kill most thoroughly, laughs.

'Not by wrath but by laughter does one kill'- thus spoke you once, O Zarathustra, you hidden one, you destroyer without wrath, you dangerous saint,- you are a rogue!"

2.

Then, however, did it come to pass that Zarathustra, astonished at such merely roguish answers, jumped back to the door of his cave, and turning towards all his guests, cried out with a strong voice:

"O you wags, all of you, you fools! Why do you dissemble and disguise yourselves before me!

How the hearts of all of you convulsed with delight and wickedness, because you had at last become again like little children- namely, pious,-

-Because you at last did again as children do- namely, prayed, folded your hands and said 'good God'!

But now leave, I pray you, this nursery, my own cave, where today all childishness is carried

无论是他仍旧活着，或是再一次复活，又或是彻底地死了——我问你，我们当中谁对此了解的最清楚？

但是，有一件事情我是知道的——我曾经从你那里学习到的，啊，查拉图斯特拉：想要杀戮的人，多半会疯癫的笑。

‘刺激人去杀戮的不是愤怒，而是笑声’——你曾经如是说道，啊，查拉图斯特拉，你这个隐匿者、你这个没有怒火的破坏者、你这个危险的圣人——你就是个流氓！”

（2）

然而，它从查拉图斯特拉的身边经过，对如此淘气的回答感到无比惊讶，他跳回到了他的洞穴的门口，并且转过身来，面向他所有的宾客们，然后，他用一种强有力的声音大声叫喊道：

“啊，你们所有人，你们这些愚蠢之人！你们为什么要在我的面前掩饰并且伪装自己呢！

你们所有人的内心是如何受到快乐以及邪恶的颤动，因为最终，你们会再一次变得像小孩子一样——也就是说变得虔诚，因为，你最后再一次做了小孩子们做的事情——换句话说就是，祈祷，你将自己的双手折叠在一起，然后说道‘伟大的上帝’！

但是，现在我恳请你离开吧，离开这个温床、离开我的洞穴以及今天所有产生天真幼稚的地方。请冷静下来，在这里、在外面，你这炽热的孩童之淫欲、你这心脏之喧哗！

不可否认：除非你成为小孩子一样的人，否则你是不能够进入到天堂之王国的。”

on. Cool down, here outside, your hot child-wantonness and heart-tumult!

To be sure: except you become as little children you shall not enter into that kingdom of heaven." (And Zarathustra pointed aloft with his hands.)

"But we do not at all want to enter into the kingdom of heaven: we have become men,- so we want the kingdom of earth."

3.

And once more began Zarathustra to speak. "O my new friends," said he,- "you strange ones, you higher men, how well do you now please me,-

-Since you have again become joyful! You have, verily, all blossomed forth: it seems to me that for such flowers as you, new festivals are required.

-A little valiant nonsense, some divine service and ass-festival, some old joyful Zarathustra fool, some blusterer to blow your souls bright. Forget not this night and this ass-festival, you higher men! That did you create when with me, that do I take as a good omen,- such things only the convalescents create!

And should you celebrate it again, this ass-festival, do it from love to yourselves, do it also from love to me! And in remembrance of me!"

Thus spoke Zarathustra.

（然后，查拉图斯特拉将自己的双手高高地举向了天空。）

“但是，并不是我们所有人都要进入到天堂之王国里去：我们成为人类，　所以，我们要地球的王国。”

（3）

然后，查拉图斯特拉再一次如是说道。“啊，我的新的朋友们，”他说道，“你们这些奇怪的人们、你们这些高人们，现在，你觉得能够怎样来取悦我，——说真的，自从你再一次变得开心快乐！你整个人都欣欣向荣了起来：对于我来说，你就像那全新的节日所必备的鲜花。

——这是一种坚定的、荒谬的废话，一些神圣的服侍以及蠢驴的节日、一些古老且快乐的查拉图斯特拉之愚蠢、一些咆哮之人会将你们的灵魂吹拂的熠熠生辉。让我们不要忘记今天的夜晚以及这场蠢驴的节日宴会，你们这些高人们！这就是你们跟我在一起所创造出来的东西，我会把它看作是一个美好的征兆——类似这样的事物只有正处于疾病的恢复期的人才能够创造出来！

为了纪念我，你们应该再庆祝一次，用你们对自己的真心实意来举办这场蠢驴的节日宴会，用你们对我的真心实意来举办这场蠢驴的节日宴会！”

查拉图斯特拉如是说道。

79. The Drunken Song

1.

MEANWHILE one after another had gone out into the open air, and into the cool, thoughtful night; Zarathustra himself, however, led the ugliest man by the hand, that he might show him his night-world, and the great round moon, and the silvery water-falls near his cave. There they at last stood still beside one another; all of them old people, but with comforted, brave hearts, and astonished in themselves that it was so well with them on earth; the mystery of the night, however, came closer and closer to their hearts. And anew Zarathustra thought to himself: "Oh, how well do they now please me, these higher men!"- but he did not say it aloud, for he respected their happiness and their silence.-

Then, however, there happened that which in this astonishing long day was most astonishing: the ugliest man began once more and for the last time to gurgle and snort, and when he had at length found expression, behold! there sprang a question plump and plain out of his mouth, a good, deep, clear question, which moved the hearts of all who listened to him.

"My friends, all of you," said the ugliest man, "what think ye? For the sake of this day- I am for the first time content to have lived my entire life.

And that I testify so much is still not enough for me. It is worth while living on the earth:

79. 醉汉之歌

（1）

与此同时，这些宾客们一个接着一个地走出洞穴来到了开阔的氛围中，来到了冰凉的、沉思的夜晚；但是，查拉图斯特拉却用自己的双手引领着最丑陋的人，查拉图斯特拉或许会向他展示夜晚的世界、壮观的、圆圆的月亮以及靠近他的洞穴的银光闪闪的瀑布。最终，他们站在这里，彼此紧紧地挨着；他们全都是老人，但是，他们拥有安逸并且勇敢的心灵，同这样的心灵如此和谐的生活在这片大地之上，这让他们自己也感到非常震惊；然而，夜晚的谜题距离他们的心灵越来越近。查拉图斯特拉再一次开始自己盘算道：“啊，现在，他们觉得能够怎样来取悦我，这些高人们！”——但是，他并没有大声地说出来，因为他尊重他们的快乐幸福以及他们的安静无声。

但是，在这个令人无比震惊的漫长的一天当中，发生了最令人惊讶的事情：那个最丑陋的人开始再一次，也是最后一次的发出咯咯的笑声，并且开始用鼻子发生哼哼的声音，最后，当他发现了可以表达出来的方式的时候，快看啊！一个饱满、清楚的问题从他的嘴巴里蹦了起来，这是一个良好的、深沉的、清楚的问题，它牵动了所有倾听他的人的心灵。

“我的朋友们，你们所有人，”那个最丑陋的人说道，“你们的意见如何？为了这一天——我头一次用满足的心态去度过我整个的人生。

而且，尽管我证明了这么多次，可这对于我还是远远不够的。在这片大地之上生活

one day, one festival with Zarathustra, has taught me to love the earth.

'Was that- life?' will I say to death. 'Well! Once more!'

My friends, what think ye? Will you not, like me, say to death: 'Was that- life? For the sake of Zarathustra, well! Once more!'"- -

Thus spoke the ugliest man; it was not, however, far from midnight. And what took place then, think ye? As soon as the higher men heard his question, they became all at once conscious of their transformation and convalescence, and of him who was the cause thereof: then did they rush up to Zarathustra, thanking, honoring, caressing him, and kissing his hands, each in his own peculiar way; so that some laughed and some wept. The old soothsayer, however, danced with delight; and though he was then, as some narrators suppose, full of sweet wine, he was certainly still fuller of sweet life, and had renounced all weariness. There are even those who narrate that the ass then danced: for not in vain had the ugliest man previously given it wine to drink. That may be the case, or it may be otherwise; and if in truth the ass did not dance that evening, there nevertheless happened then greater and rarer wonders than the dancing of an ass would have been. In short, as the aphorism of Zarathustra says: "What does it matter!"

2.

When, however, this took place with the ugliest man, Zarathustra stood there like one drunken: his glance dulled, his tongue faltered and his feet staggered. And who could divine

是非常值得的：一天、查拉图斯特拉以及一个节日宴会，教会了我去热爱这片大地。”

“这就是生活吗？”我对死亡如是说道。“好吧！再来一次吧！”

我的朋友们，你们的意见如何呢？难道你们不会像我一样对死亡如是说道：“难道这就是生活吗？为了查拉图斯特拉，好吧！再来一次吧！”

那个最丑陋的人如是说道；但是，它距离午夜并不遥远。到底都发生了些什么呢，你们的意见是如何的呢？就在那些高人们听到他提出的问题之后，他们立刻意识到了他们的改变、他们病后逐渐恢复的状态以及造就了事态的人：紧接着，他们全都匆匆地跑向了查拉图斯特拉，他们每一个人都会用自己独特的方式感谢他、尊敬他、用爱意抚摸他，并且亲吻他的双手；他们有些人喜笑颜开，而有些人则悲伤落泪。然而，那个老迈的预言家，则兴高采烈地跳起了舞；并且，尽管他像某些演说者所猜测的那样，浑身充满了甜蜜的酒水，但是可以肯定的是，他的确拥有更加充实的甜蜜生活，而且丢弃了所有的疲倦。甚至就连那些叙述愚蠢的驴的人们也开始跳起了舞：看起来，那个最丑陋的人在之前给予它的酒水并不是无功而返的。情况或许就是这样的，又或是其他的样子；而且，倘若事情的真相是那头驴并没有在晚上跳舞的话，那么在这里就会发生比一头蠢驴翩翩起舞还要古怪、还要罕见的奇迹。总而言之，正如查拉图斯特拉的格言所说：“这跟我又有什么关系呢！”

（2）

但是，当这样的情况在那个最丑陋的人身上发生之后，查拉图斯特拉就像一个喝醉

what thoughts then passed through Zarathustra's soul? Apparently, however, his spirit retreated and fled in advance and was in remote distances, and as it were "wandering on high mountain-ridges," as it stands written, "'twixt two seas,

-Wandering 'twixt the past and the future as a heavy cloud." Gradually, however, while the higher men held him in their arms, he came back to himself a little, and resisted with his hands the crowd of the honoring and caring ones; but he did not speak. All at once, however, he turned his head quickly, for he seemed to hear something: then laid he his finger on his mouth and said: "Come!"

And immediately it became still and mysterious round about; from the depth however there came up slowly the sound of a clock-bell. Zarathustra listened thereto, like the higher men; then, however, laid he his finger on his mouth the second time, and said again: "Come! Come! It is getting on to midnight!"- and his voice had changed. But still he had not moved from the spot. Then it became yet stiller and more mysterious, and everything hearkened, even the ass, and Zarathustra's noble animals, the eagle and the serpent,- likewise the cave of Zarathustra and the big cool moon, and the night itself. Zarathustra, however, laid his hand upon his mouth for the third time, and said:

Come! Come! Come! Let us now wander! It is the hour: let us wander into the night!

了的酒鬼一样站在这里：他的目光变得呆滞、他的舌头变得不利索了，而他的双脚也开始步履蹒跚。那么，究竟有谁能够猜测出到底是什么穿过了查拉图斯特拉的灵魂？然而，很明显的是，他的精灵撤退了，并且提前逃跑了，它在非常遥远的地方，就像“在高耸的山脊之上漫步、游荡，”就像被人们所描写的那样，“在两个海洋之间，——就像一朵沉重的云彩一样游荡在过去和未来之间。”但是，逐渐地，当那些高人们用双手把他托了起来的时候，他开始渐渐地恢复了意识，然后，他用自己的手反抗着那些尊敬的、关爱的人民群体；不过，他什么话也没有说。然而，突然之间，他快速地转过了他的头，因为，他好像听到了什么东西：紧接着，他把他的手指头放在了他的嘴巴上，然后说道：“快过来！”

几乎是在一瞬间，围绕在他周围的氛围开始变得宁静，并且神秘；但是就在这个时候，一种来自钟表的声音开始缓慢地从深处传了出来。因此，查拉图斯特拉仔细地聆听了起来，就像那些高人们一样；但是，他紧接着第二次把他的手指头放在了他的嘴巴上面，然后他再一次说道：“快过来啊！快过来啊！就快到午夜了！”——接着，他改变了他的语调。但是，他仍旧没有从他的位置上离开。周围的氛围开始变得更加安静、更加神秘，世间万物都在仔细聆听着，甚至包括那头蠢驴以及查拉图斯特拉的高贵的动物们、老鹰和毒蛇，——同样还有查拉图斯特拉的洞穴、巨大且冰冷的月亮以及夜晚本身。但是，查拉图斯特拉却第三次把他的手指头放在了他的嘴巴上，然后如是说道：

快过来啊！快过来啊！快过来啊！现在让我们开始游荡吧！现在就是最合适的时候：让我们游荡到夜晚吧！

3.

You higher men, it is getting on to midnight: then will I say something into your ears, as that old clock-bell says it into my ear,-

-As mysteriously, as frightfully, and as cordially as that midnight clock-bell speaks it to me, which has experienced more than one man:

-Which has already counted the smarting throbbings of your fathers' hearts- ah! ah! how it sighs! how it laughs in its dream! the old, deep, deep midnight!

Hush! Hush! Then is there many a thing heard which may not be heard by day; now however, in the cool air, when even all the tumult of your hearts has become still,-

-Now does it speak, now is it heard, now does it steal into overwakeful, nocturnal souls: ah! ah! how the midnight sighs! how it laughs in its dream!

-Hear you not how it mysteriously, frightfully, and cordially speaks to you, the old deep, deep midnight?

O man, take heed!

4.

Woe to me! Where has time gone? Have I not sunk into deep wells? The world sleeps-

Ah! Ah! The dog howls, the moon shins. Rather will I die, rather will I die, than say to you

（3）

你们这些高人们，现在就快要到午夜了：然后，我会向你们的耳朵里说一些话语，就如同那古老的钟表之声音在我的耳边诉说一样，——犹如午夜的钟表之声对我说话一样神秘、可怕并且诚挚，它经历了不止一个人：——它已经数出了你们的祖先之心脏的伴有剧烈疼痛的悸动——啊！啊！它是如何的叹息！它是如何在梦境之中微笑！这个古老的、幽深的午夜！

安静一点！安静一点！我们在这里听到了许许多多平时在白昼所听不到的事物；但是现在，在冰冷的空气当中，甚至就连你们的心脏的骚动都开始变得宁静，——现在它开口说话了，现在它开始聆听了，现在它开始悄悄潜入到过度清醒的、夜间的灵魂：啊！啊！午夜是如何的叹息啊！它是如何在梦境之中微笑啊！难道你现在没有听到那个神秘的、可怕的，并且非常诚恳的它在跟你说话吗？那个古老的、幽深的午夜吗？

啊，人类啊，请你们多加提防吧！

（4）

我有灾祸了啊！时间都跑到哪里去了呢？难道我没有沉入到幽深的源泉之中吗？这个世界在沉睡！

啊！啊！野狗在咆哮，月亮在闪耀着光芒。我宁愿选择死亡，我宁愿选择死亡，也不会把我这午夜之内心的真实想法告诉给你。

what my midnight-heart now thinks.

Already have I died. It is all over. Spider, why spin you around me? Will you have blood? Ah! Ah! The dew falls, the hour comes- -The hour in which I frost and freeze, which asks and asks and asks: "Who has sufficient courage for it?

-Who is to be master of the world? Who is going to say: Thus shall you flow, you great and small streams!"

-The hour approaches: O man, you higher man, take heed! this talk is for fine ears, for your ears- what says deep midnight's voice indeed?

5.

It carries me away, my soul dances. Day's-work! Day's-work! Who is to be master of the world?

The moon is cool, the wind is still. Ah! Ah! Have you already flown high enough? You have danced: a leg, nevertheless, is not a wing.

You good dancers, now is all delight over: wine has become lees, every cup has become brittle, the sepulchres mutter.

You have not flown high enough: now do the sepulchres mutter: "Free the dead! Why is it so long night? does not the moon make us drunken?"

You higher men, free the sepulchres, awaken the corpses! Ah, why does the worm still

我已经死了，一切都结束了。蜘蛛啊，你为什么要在我的四周结网呢？你拥有鲜血吗？啊！啊！露珠掉落下来了，时刻已经来到了——那个让我结冰、让我感到寒冷的时刻，它在问、它在问、它在问：“究竟有谁对此拥有十足的勇气和胆量？

——究竟是谁能够成为这个世界的统治者？他将会说：你会因此而流动，你这伟大的、渺小的溪流！！！！”

——这个时刻正在逐步逼近：啊，人类啊，你们这些高人们啊！我恳请你们要小心提防啊！这样的话语是专门说给好耳朵听的，是专门说给你们的耳朵听的——那个深沉的、午夜之声音到底都说了些什么？

（5）

它让我失去控制，我的灵魂之舞蹈。一天的工作啊！一天的工作啊！究竟有谁能够成为这个世界的统治者呢？

月亮是凉爽的，风是平静的。啊！啊！难道你们已经飞得足够高了吗？你们已经在翩翩起舞了：然而，一条腿终究不能算是一双翅膀。

你们是优秀的舞蹈者，现在，所有的高兴与快乐全都已经过去了：酒水全都成为避风处，所有的杯子全都变成了易碎。坟墓的喃喃自语。

你们并没有飞到足够高的高度：现在，坟墓喃喃自语道：“快让死去的人获得自由！为什么这夜晚是如此的漫长？难道月亮没有让我们进入酒醉的状态吗？”

你们这些高人们啊，快点让坟墓获得自由，现在，这个时刻正在逐渐向这里逼近，

burrow? There approaches, there approaches, the hour,-

-There booms the clock-bell, there thrills still the heart, there burrows still the wood-worm, the heart-worm. Ah! Ah! The world is deep!

6.

Sweet lyre! Sweet lyre! I love your tone, your drunken, ranunculine tone!- how long, how far has come to me your tone, from the distance, from the ponds of love!

You old clock-bell, you sweet lyre! Every pain has torn your heart, father-pain, fathers'-pain, forefathers'-pain; your speech has become ripe,-

-Ripe like the golden autumn and the afternoon, like my hermit heart- now say you: The world itself has become ripe, the grape turns brown,

-Now does it wish to die, to die of happiness. You higher men, do you not feel it? There wells up mysteriously an odour,

-A perfume and odour of eternity, a rosy-blessed, brown, gold-wine-odour of old happiness.

-Of drunken midnight-death happiness, which sings: the world is deep, and deeper than the day could read!

快点唤醒那些死人们吧！啊，为什么这些虫子仍然在挖洞？现在，这个时刻正在逐渐向这里逼近，这个时刻正在逐渐向这里逼近，——时钟在这里发出轰隆隆的声音，心脏仍然在这里震颤，树虫仍然在这里挖洞，那个心灵之树虫。啊！啊！这个世界是深沉的！

（6）

充满芳香的七弦竖琴！充满芳香的七弦竖琴！我喜欢你的音调，你这醉醺醺的毛茛碱的音调！——你的音调是如何从漫长的、遥远的地方、从爱情的池塘来到我这里的！

你这古老的钟表！你这充满芳香的七弦竖琴！所有的疼痛都在撕扯你的心灵，你这犹如父亲般的疼痛，犹如父亲般的疼痛，祖先的疼痛；你的说教已经变得成熟了，——就像是金色的秋天以及下午，就像是我的隐士之心灵一样成熟——现在，你说道：这个世界本身已经变得成熟，葡萄的颜色变成了棕色，——现在，它要死亡，它要高兴快乐地死亡。你们这些高人们啊，难道你们就感觉不到吗？这些水井神秘的散发出了一种香气，

——一种香水的气味、永恒的香气，受到美好的祝福的、褐色的、古老的快乐的金色之酒的香气。

——醉醺醺的、午夜死亡之幸福，它歌唱道：这个世界是幽深的。它要比白昼能够识别的还要幽深！

7.

Leave me alone! Leave me alone! I am too pure for you. Touch me not! has not my world just now become perfect?

My skin is too pure for your hands. Leave me alone, you dull, doltish, stupid day! Is not the midnight brighter?

The purest are to be masters of the world, the least known, the strongest, the midnight-souls, who are brighter and deeper than any day.

O day, you grope for me? you feel for my happiness? For you am I rich, lonesome, a treasure-pit, a gold chamber?

O world, you want me? Am I worldly for you? Am I spiritual for you? Am I divine for you? But day and world, you are too coarse,-

-Have cleverer hands, grasp after deeper happiness, after deeper unhappiness, grasp after some God; grasp not after me:

-My unhappiness, my happiness is deep, you strange day, but yet am I no God, no God's-hell: deep is its woe.

8.

God's woe is deeper, you strange world! Grasp at God's woe, not at me! What am I! A

（7）

快让我一个人静一静！快让我一个人静一静！我对于你来说，太过于纯粹了。不要触碰我！难道，现在我的世界并没有变的完美吗？

我的肌肤对于你的双手来说实在是太纯净了。快让我一个人静一静吧，你这迟钝的、愚蠢、愚笨的一天！难道午夜不是更加明亮吗？

最纯净的会成为这个世界的统治者，最不为人所知的就是最强壮的、午夜之灵魂要比任何的白昼都要明亮和幽深。

啊，白昼，你在寻找我吗？你能够感受到我的幸福快乐吗？对于你来说，我是不是富有的、孤独的、宝藏之深坑，金色的密室？

啊，这个世界，你想要我吗？难道我对于你来说太世俗了吗？难道我对于你来说太高尚了吗？难道我对于你来说太神圣了吗？

但是，白昼和世界，你太粗俗了，——你拥有更加灵巧的手臂、抓住更加幽深的快乐、抓住更加幽深的不幸、抓住一些神灵；不要抓住我：

——我的不幸、我的幸福快乐是幽深的、你这奇怪的白昼，但是我并不是神灵，我并不是上帝之地狱：幽深就是它的悲痛。

（8）

上帝的悲痛更加幽深，你这奇怪的世界！抓住上帝的悲痛，而不是抓住我！我到底

drunken sweet lyre,-

-A midnight-lyre, a bell-frog, which no one understands, but which must speak before deaf ones, you higher men! For you do not understand me!

Gone! Gone! O youth! O noontide! O afternoon! Now have come evening and night and midnight,- the dog howls, the wind:

-Is the wind not a dog? It whines, it barks, it howls. Ah! Ah! how she sighs! how she laughs, how she wheezes and pants, the midnight!

How she just now speaks soberly, this drunken poetess! has she perhaps overdrunk her drunkenness? has she become overawake? does she ruminate?

-Her woe does she ruminate over, in a dream, the old, deep midnight- and still more her joy. For joy, although woe be deep, joy is deeper still than grief can be.

9.

You grape-vine! Why do you praise me? Have I not cut you! I am cruel, you bleedest-: what means your praise of my drunken cruelty?

"Whatever has become perfect, everything mature- wants to die!" so say you. Blessed, blessed be the vintner's knife! But everything immature wants to live: alas!

Woe says: "Hence! Go! Away, you woe!" But everything that suffers wants to live, that it may become mature and lively and longing,

是什么！一个醉醺醺的、甜美的七弦竖琴，——一个午夜的七弦竖琴，一个钟表之青蛙，没有人能够理解我，但是，我必然会在聋子的面前侃侃而谈，你们这些高人们！因为你们根本就不了解我！

快点离开吧！快点离开吧！啊，青春，啊，正午时分！啊，午后！现在，傍晚、夜晚以及午夜就要到了——狗在咆哮，微风在：——那个哀鸣、咆哮、狂吠的，应该是微风，而不是狗吗？啊！啊！她是如此的叹息啊！她是如此的笑啊，她是如此的喘息，午夜！

现在，她是如此冷静地如是说道，这个醉醺醺的女诗人！或许她饮酒过度？或许是她清醒过度？难道她开始反复思考了吗？

——她开始反复思考她的悲痛，在一个梦境当中，在一个古老的、幽深的午夜当中——她更加快乐。因为快乐，尽管悲痛是幽深的，但是，快乐要比悲痛更加幽深。

（9）

你这葡萄藤！你为什么要赞美我？我还没有把你剪断呢！我是非常粗鲁的，你在流血：你赞美我的醉醺醺的残忍的意义何在？

“无论是什么变得完美，任何成熟的事物——都想要死亡！”你如是说道，受到了祝福，酿造葡萄酒的人的匕首受到了祝福！但是，任何不成熟的事物都想活下去：哎！

悲痛如是说道：“所以，你们走吧！快点离开吧，你这悲痛！”但是，任何遭受过苦难的事物都想要活下来，它们或许会变得成熟、生气勃勃，并且充满了渴望，——充满了对更远、更高、更明亮的渴望。“我想要成为继承人，”任何遭受到苦难的事物如

-Longing for the further, the higher, the brighter. "I want heirs," so says everything that suffers, "I want children, I do not want myself,"-

Joy, however, does not want heirs, it does not want children,- joy wants itself, it wants eternity, it wants recurrence, it wants everything eternally-like-itself.

Woe says: "Break, bleed, you heart! Wander, you leg! you wing, fly! Onward! upward! you pain!" Well! Cheer up! O my old heart: Woe says: "Hence! Go!"

10.

You higher men, what think ye? Am I a soothsayer? Or a dreamer? Or a drunkard? Or a dream-reader? Or a midnight-bell?

Or a drop of dew? Or a fume and fragrance of eternity? Hear you it not? Smell you it not? Just now has my world become perfect, midnight is also mid-day,-

Pain is also a joy, curse is also a blessing, night is also a sun,- go away! or you will learn that a sage is also a fool.

Said you ever Yes to one joy? O my friends, then said you Yes also to all woe. All things are enlinked, enlaced and enamoured,-

-Wanted you ever once to come twice; said you ever: "You please me, happiness! Instant! Moment!" then wanted you all to come back again!

-All anew, all eternal, all enlinked, enlaced and enamoured, Oh, then did you love the

是说道，“我想要孩子，我不想要我自己。”

但是，快乐并不想要继承人，它也并不想要孩子——快乐想要的是它自己，它想要的是永恒，它要的是事情的反复发生，它要的是任何类似于永恒的事物。

悲痛说道：“破碎的、流淌着鲜血的、你的心脏！漫步着，你的双腿！你扑闪着翅膀，飞翔！向外面飞翔！向上飞翔！你的疼痛！”好吧！让我们振作起来！啊，我的古老的心脏：悲痛说道：“所以，快点走吧！”

（10）

你们这些高人们，你们对此有什么想法？难道我是一个预言家吗？或是我是一名梦想家吗？又或是我是一个醉鬼吗？或是我是一个能够读懂梦境的人吗？又或是我是一个午夜的钟表呢？

难道我是一滴露珠吗？或是我是一种香气、散发着永恒的香味？你们听到了吗？你们闻到了吗？就是现在，我的世界变得完美，午夜也成了正午，疼痛也是一种快乐，诅咒也是一种祝福，夜晚也是一种太阳——快点走开吧！否则，你肯定会明白一个圣人也是一个愚蠢之人。

你曾经说过肯定快乐的话语吗？啊，我的朋友们啊，那么，你们同样也对所有的悲痛说过肯定的话语吧。所有的事物之间都是紧密联系在一起的、缠绕在一起的，并且让人迷恋，——你曾经要再到这里来；你曾经说道：“你赞美我，快乐！瞬息间！时刻！”因此，你们全都要再一次来到这里！

world,-

-You eternal ones, you love it eternally and for all time: and also to woe do you say: Hence! Go! but come back! For joys all want- eternity!

11.

All joy wants the eternity of all things, it wants honey, it wants lees, it wants drunken midnight, it wants graves, it wants grave-tears' consolation, it wants gilded evening-red-

-What does not joy want! it is thirstier, heartier, hungrier, more frightful, more mysterious, than all woe: it wants itself, it bites into itself, the ring's will wriths in it,-

-It wants love, it wants hate, it is over-rich, it gives, it throws away, it begs for some one to take from it, it thanks the taker, it would rather be hated,-

-So rich is joy that it thirsts for woe, for hell, for hate, for shame, for the lame, for the world,- for this world, Oh, you know it indeed!

You higher men, for you does it long, this joy, this irrepressible, blessed joy- for your woe, you failures! For failures, longs all eternal joy.

For joys all want themselves, therefore do they also want grief! O happiness, O pain! Oh break, you heart! You higher men, do learn it, that joys want eternity.

-Joys want the eternity of all things, they want deep, profound eternity!

——所有永恒的、所有紧密联系在一起的、所有缠绕在一起的、让人迷恋的事物，啊，你们因此热爱这个世界，——你们这些永恒的人们，你们永恒地、无时无刻地都在热爱着它：同样地，你们对悲痛如是说道：因此！快点走吧！快回去吧！因为，快乐唯一要的就是——永恒！

（11）

所有的快乐要的是永恒的事物，它要的是蜂蜜、它要的是避风港、它要的是迷醉的午夜、它要的是死亡、它要的是死亡之泪水的安慰、它要的是镀金的夜晚之红——还有什么是快乐不想要的！它要比所有的悲痛更加充满渴望、更加沉重、更加饥饿、更加可怕、更加神秘：它要它自己、它在叮咬自己、环的意志植根于它体内，——它想要爱意、它要仇恨、它非常富有、它给予、它抛弃、它恳求其他人来这里索取、它感谢来这里索取的人，它宁愿被痛恨，——快乐非常富有，它渴求悲痛、渴求邪恶、渴求仇恨、渴求羞愧、渴求残疾、渴求世界——啊，毋庸置疑，你了解这个世界！

你们这些高人们啊，你们为了你们的悲痛、为了你们的失败创造了这漫长的快乐，创造了这难以抑制的、受到祝福的快乐！因为失败，渴望所有永恒的快乐。

因为所有的快乐都要它们自己，因此，它们同样还要悲痛！啊，幸福快乐，啊，痛苦！啊，破碎，你的心脏！你们这些高人们啊，你们都知道快乐想要永恒。

——快乐想要所有永恒的事物，它们要的是幽深的、深厚的永恒！

12.

Have you now learned my song? Have you divined what it would say? Well! Cheer up! You higher men, sing now my roundelay!

Sing now yourselves the song, the name of which is "Once more," the signification of which is "To all eternity!"- sing, you higher men, Zarathustra's roundelay!

O man! Take heed!
What says deep midnight's voice indeed?
"I slept my sleep"-,
"From deepest dream I've woke, and plead":-
"The world is deep",
"And deeper than the day could read."
"Deep is its woe"-,
"Joy- deeper still than grief can be":
"Woe says: Hence! Go!"
"But joys all want eternity"-,
"-Want deep, profound eternity!"

（12）

现在，你们学会我的歌曲了吗？你们有没有猜测到歌词是什么？好吧！大家兴奋起来吧！你们这些高人们啊，现在，歌唱我的回旋歌吧！

现在，你们开始歌唱我的回旋歌，这首回旋歌的名字是“再一次，”这首歌曲的含义是“向所有的永恒致敬！”——歌唱吧，你们这些高人们，歌唱查拉图斯特拉的回旋歌吧！

啊，人类啊！你们要小心提防啊！
那个幽深的午夜之声音到底都说了些什么？
我睡着了，
我从最幽深的梦境之中惊醒了，然后我开始恳求：
这个世界是幽深的，
它要比白昼所能够理解的还要幽深，
它的悲痛是幽深的，
快乐仍旧要比悲痛更加幽深：
悲痛如是说道：所以！快走吧！
但是，快乐想要的就是永恒，
它要幽深的、深刻的永恒！”

80. The Sign

IN THE morning, however, after this night, Zarathustra jumped up from his couch, and, having girded his loins, he came out of his cave glowing and strong, like a morning sun coming out of gloomy mountains.

"You great star," spoke he, as he had spoken once before, "you deep eye of happiness, what would be all your happiness if you had not those for whom you shine!

And if they remained in their chambers whilst you are already awake, and come and give and distribute, how would your proud modesty upbraid for it!

Well! they still sleep, these higher men, whilst I am awake: they are not my proper companions! Not for them do I wait here in my mountains.

At my work I want to be, at my day: but they understand not what are the signs of my morning, my step- is not for them the awakening-call.

They still sleep in my cave; their dream still drinks at my drunken songs. The audient ear for me- the obedient ear, is yet lacking in their limbs."

-This had Zarathustra spoken to his heart when the sun arose: then looked he inquiringly aloft, for he heard above him the sharp call of his eagle. "Well!" called he upwards, "thus is it pleasing and proper to me. My animals are awake, for I am awake.

My eagle is awake, and like me honors the sun. With eagle-talons does it grasp at the new

80. 征兆

但是，在经历了这个夜晚之后的清晨，查拉图斯特拉从他的沙发上跳了起来，然后缠绕住了他的腰部，强大并且散发着亮光的他，走出了他的洞穴，就像一个从阴沉的群山之中升起来的清晨之太阳一样。

“你这伟大的行星，”他说道，就像他之前说的那样，“你这幽深的快乐之眼，如果你们并不能照亮你们想要照亮的人，那么，你们的快乐会成为什么呢！

如果当你们已经被唤醒，并且来到这里给予和分发的时候，他们仍旧待在他们的房间里，那么，你们的骄傲的谦逊将会如何训斥他们呢！

好吧！这些高人们，当我已经被唤醒之后，他们仍旧在睡觉：他们对于我来说，并不是合适的同伴！我并不会在这里，在我的群山之中，等候他们。

我要在我的工作当中，在我的白昼当中：但是他们并不能理解我的清晨的征兆是什么，我的脚步——对于他们来说并不是唤醒的呼唤。

他们仍旧在我的洞穴之中睡觉；他们的梦境仍旧在我的醉醺醺的歌声之中畅饮。对于我来说，在他们的四肢当中，仍旧缺乏倾听者的耳朵——顺从的耳朵。”

——当太阳升起的时候，查拉图斯特拉对他的心灵如是说了这样的话：然后，他充满好奇地抬起头看向了空中，因为他听到他的老鹰在头顶发出了刺耳的叫声。“好吧！”他朝着空中叫道，“因为它让我感到愉快，它和我很投合。我的动物们已经被唤醒了，因为我已经被唤醒了。

我的老鹰已经被唤醒了，就如同我尊敬太阳一样。在鹰爪的帮助下，它抓住了新的

light. You are my proper animals; I love you.

But still do I lack my proper men!"-

Thus spoke Zarathustra; then, however, it happened that all on a sudden he became aware that he was flocked around and fluttered around, as if by innumerable birds,- the whizzing of so many wings, however, and the crowding around his head was so great that he shut his eyes. And verily, there came down upon him as it were a cloud, like a cloud of arrows which pours upon a new enemy. But behold, here it was a cloud of love, and showered upon a new friend.

"What happens to me?" thought Zarathustra in his astonished heart, and slowly seated himself on the big stone which lay close to the exit from his cave. But while he grasped about with his hands, around him, above him and below him, and repelled the tender birds, behold, there then happened to him something still stranger: for he grasped thereby unawares into a mass of thick, warm, shaggy hair; at the same time, however, there sounded before him a roar,- a long, soft lion-roar.

"The sign comes," said Zarathustra, and a change came over his heart. And in truth, when it turned clear before him, there lay a yellow, powerful animal at his feet, resting its head on his knee,- unwilling to leave him out of love, and doing like a dog which again finds its old master. The doves, however, were no less eager with their love than the lion; and whenever a dove whisked over its nose, the lion shook its head and wondered and laughed.

When all this went on Zarathustra spoke only a word: "My children are nigh, my children"-,

光芒。对于我来说，你就是合适的动物；我热爱你。

但是，我仍旧缺乏适合我的人类！”

查拉图斯特拉如是说道；但是，突然之间，他开始意识到，他好像被不计其数的鸟儿包围了起来，它们聚集在他的身边，扑闪着翅膀，——然而，许许多多的翅膀的扑扇声以及围绕在他的脑袋周围的紧迫的拥挤感太过于强烈，因此，他闭上了双眼。说真的，它们就像一朵云彩一样来到了他的身边，就像一朵弓箭之云向新的敌人倾泻弓箭一样。但是，请看啊，这是一朵爱意之云，它会将它的爱意倾洒在新的朋友的身上。

“我的身上到底发生了什么事？”内心受到了惊吓的查拉图斯特拉心想，然后，他缓慢地坐在了一块距离他的洞穴的出口非常近的石头上。

但是，当他用自己的双手抓住围绕在他身边的、盘旋在他的头顶的、在他下面的以及抵抗他的脆弱的小鸟的时候，快看啊，紧接着一些非常奇怪的事情发生在了他的身上：因为他无意识地抓住了一大团厚厚的、温暖的、蓬松散乱的头发；然而，与此同时，从他的前方传来了一种咆哮，———种悠长的、温和的狮子的咆哮。

“那个征兆就要来了，”查拉图斯特拉如是说道，而且他的内心也发生了变化。事情的真相是，当这种咆哮在他的前方变得清晰的时候，一只黄色的、强而有力的动物躺[illegible]他的脚下，它将自己的头枕在他的膝盖上休息，——看起来它并不想让他脱离爱意，[illegible]像一条狗一样重新找到它原来的主人。但是，鸽子们对于他们的爱意的渴望丝毫不[illegible]子；而且无论何时，一只鸽子扑闪着翅膀飞过它的鼻子，狮子都会摇晃起脑袋，[illegible]会充满惊奇，并且哈哈大笑。

[illegible]这些事情都发生在查拉图斯特拉的身上之后，他只说了一句话：“我的孩子

then he became quite mute. His heart, however, was loosed, and from his eyes there dropped down tears and fell upon his hands. And he took no further notice of anything, but sat there motionless, without repelling the animals further. Then flew the doves to and fro, and perched on his shoulder, and caressed his white hair, and did not tire of their tenderness and joyousness. The strong lion, however, licked always the tears that fell on Zarathustra's hands, and roared and growled shyly. Thus did these animals do.-

All this went on for a long time, or a short time: for properly speaking, there is no time on earth for such things-. Meanwhile, however, the higher men had awakened in Zarathustra's cave, and marshalled themselves for a procession to go to meet Zarathustra, and give him their morning greeting: for they had found when they awakened that he no longer tarried with them. When, however, they reached the door of the cave and the noise of their steps had preceded them, the lion started violently; it turned away all at once from Zarathustra, and roaring wildly, sprang towards the cave. The higher men, however, when they heard the lion roaring, cried all aloud as with one voice, fled back and vanished in an instant.

Zarathustra himself, however, stunned and strange, rose from his seat, looked around him, stood there astonished, inquired of his heart, bethought himself, and remained alone. "What did I hear?" said he at last, slowly, "what happened to me just now?"

But soon there came to him his recollection, and he took in at a glance all that had taken place between yesterday and to-day. "Here is indeed the stone," said he, and stroked his beard, "on it sat I yester-morn; and here came the soothsayer to me, and here heard I first the cry

们，就在附近，我的孩子们”——紧接着，他开始变得默不作声。

然而，他的心脏是自由的、不受束缚的，眼泪从他的眼睛里面滑落了出来，并且掉落在了他的手上。他并没有进一步的留意任何的事物，而是一动不动的坐在这里，他并没有把这些动物们驱散到远处。紧接着，鸽子在空中来回地飞翔，并且驻足在他的肩膀之上，抚摸着他那头银色的头发，并没有对它们的亲切和快乐感到厌倦。但是，那头强壮的狮子总是舔着掉落在查拉图斯特拉的手臂上的眼泪，并且它开始咆哮，胆怯地咆哮。这些动物们如是做着。

这样的情况一直持续了很长的时间，或是很短的时间：确切地说，在这个地球上，我们没有时间做这样的事情——但是，与此同时，那些在查拉图斯特拉的洞穴里的高人们已经被唤醒了，他们形成一个队列大踏步地朝着查拉图斯特拉的方向行进，并且给了他来自清晨之问候：因为他们发现，当他们被唤醒的时候，查拉图斯特拉已经不再跟他们居住在一起了。但是，当他们来到洞穴的门前的时候，他们走路发出的噪声传到了他们的前方，那头狮子开始变得狂躁；突然之间，它转向了查拉图斯特拉，并且开始狂暴地咆哮，跳向洞穴的门口。然而，那些高人们，当他们听到狮子的咆哮的时候，他们全都大声地叫喊了起来，就如同一个声音落荒而逃，并且在一瞬间消失了一样。

但是，查拉图斯特拉本身受到了惊吓，并且开始局促不安，他从座位上站了起来，环顾四周，无比惊讶地站在这里，询问他的内心，他开始仔细思考，保持着孤零零的状态。“我都听到了什么？”最后他缓慢地说道，“就在刚才，我的身上到底发生了什么事情？”

但是很快，他就想起了他之前的回忆，然后他用目光扫视所有发生在昨天和今天的事情。“不错，这里有一块石头，”他抚摸着自己的胡子说道，“昨天的清晨，我就坐

which I heard just now, the great cry of distress.

O you higher men, your distress was it that the old soothsayer foretold to me yester-morn,-

-To your distress did he want to seduce and tempt me: 'O Zarathustra,' said he to me, 'I come to seduce you to your last sin.'

To my last sin?" cried Zarathustra, and laughed angrily at his own words: "what has been reserved for me as my last sin?"

-And once more Zarathustra became absorbed in himself, and sat down again on the big stone and meditated. Suddenly he sprang up,-

"Fellow-suffering! Fellow-suffering with the higher men!" he cried out, and his countenance changed into brass. "Well! That- has had its time!

My suffering and my fellow-suffering- what matter about them! Do I then strive after happiness? I strive after my work!

Well! The lion has come, my children are nigh, Zarathustra has grown ripe, my hour has come:-

This is my morning, my day begins: arise now, arise, you great noontide!"- -

Thus spoke Zarathustra and left his cave, glowing and strong, like a morning sun coming out of gloomy mountains.

在这块石头上；然后，那个预言家来到了我的身边，并且我第一次听到了刚才听到过的叫喊，那种伟大的悲痛之叫喊。

啊，你们这些高人们啊，有关于你们的悲痛，那个老迈的预言家在昨天的清晨就已经跟我预言了，——为了你们的悲痛，他要引诱和诱惑我：‘啊，查拉图斯特拉，’他对我说道，‘我来到这里诱惑你，将你带入你的最后的罪恶。’

将我带入我的最后的罪恶？”查拉图斯特拉大叫道，并且，他气急败坏地笑着说道：“那个为我保留的，所谓的我的最后的罪恶到底是什么呢？”

——查拉图斯特拉再一次全神贯注于他自己，然后，他又一次坐在那块大石头上，沉思了起来。突然之间，他从石头上跳了起来，“同胞们遭受到了苦难！同胞们连同那些高人们一起遭受到了苦难！”他大声地叫道，然后，他脸上的颜色变成了黄铜色。“好吧！它已经获得了时间！

我遭受到的苦难以及我的同胞们所遭受到的苦难，这跟他们又有什么关系呢！那么，我还要苦苦追寻幸福与快乐吗？我努力工作、辛勤奋斗！

好吧！那头狮子已经来了，我的孩子们就在附近，查拉图斯特拉已经成长得非常成熟了，我的时刻已经到来了：

这就是我的清晨，我的白昼开始了：现在，升起来吧！升起来吧，你这伟大的正午光！”

查拉图斯特拉如是说道，然后他离开了他的洞穴，强壮无比的他散发着光芒，就像阴沉的群山之中升起来的清晨之太阳一样。